Social Work

Processes

The Dorsey Series in Social Welfare

THIRD EDITION

Social Work
Processes

BEULAH ROBERTS COMPTON
University of Alabama

and

BURT GALAWAY
University of Minnesota, Duluth

1 9 8 4

THE DORSEY PRESS
Chicago, Illinois 60604

ISBN 0-256-02866-4

Library of Congress Catalog Card No. 83–72197

Printed in the United States of America

5 6 7 8 9 0 ML 1 0 9 8 7

Dedicated to those from whom we have learned much—our families, the clients with whom we have worked, the students we have known, and our professional colleagues.

Preface
to the Third Edition

As we complete this third edition of our work, it is our hope that it continues the process of clarifying our earlier notions and enriching the ideas presented in the first two editions. Readers of our earlier works will note a significant change in the first chapter. This represents the development of our concept of the elements of social work practice since the earlier editions of the text. It attempts to advance the profession's thinking about what should be explored as generic and what is specific in social work practice. We have altered the structure of the book somewhat in order to more clearly present our thinking that social work practice may be divided into two central tasks: (1) deciding what to do and (2) doing the decided. In revising the book we have eliminated some readings and added others to reflect some recent additions to social work literature related to material in the text. We hope that people who have used previous editions of the book do not miss too many favorite and useful articles from the past. In addition to the above, we have included more case material in this edition, believing that actual cases and examples from practice will both advance understanding of the conceptual material in the chapters and be a stimulus to further class discussion.

As in previous prefaces, we want to express our debt to those individuals who have made comments about the book, especially the teachers whose suggestions came from their use of the text in their classes. Such comments have been invaluable to us in our work on this edition. We wish to give special recognition and credit to Marianne Pennekamp who suggested the reorganization of the text to more closely follow our earlier suggestion that social work practice could be divided into deciding and doing. In addition we need to recognize the contribution of students whose questions and comments about the material have helped to clarify both our thinking and our explanations of that thinking.

And finally, and most importantly, we must thank Indiana University School of Social Work students Marci Flanders, Sue Hornstein, and Marsha King. Especially we want to express our thanks to Marci Flanders for her responsible and careful work on the reference list. We want to thank Shirley

Overby of the secretarial staff of the School of Social Development, University of Minnesota, Duluth, for help in securing an accurate list of contributors and pursuing permissions. Ms. Patsy Branscum, administrative secretary at Indiana University School of Social Work, deserves both special recognition and our heartfelt thanks for typing the manuscript, checking the consistency and accuracy of the references, and taking care of the myriad of details with cheerfulness, calmness, and efficiency. Her efforts truly played a significant part in our ability to get this edition to the publisher on time. We also wish to gratefully acknowledge Francis Yuen, doctoral student in the School of Social Work, University of Alabama, for his assistance with preparing the index.

Finally, all editions of this book have come from the authors' experience and the desire to introduce others to a profession that we have found so challenging and satisfying as a lifework. In spite of the generous help of others, we must accept the sole responsibility for this and all other editions of the text.

Beulah Roberts Compton
Burt Galaway

Preface
to the Revised Edition

As we complete this revision of our work, we have little to add to our earlier preface. While we have attempted to make changes and additions, including two new chapters, that will clarify our earlier notions and enrich the ideas presented, the purpose, structure, and focus of the book remain the same.

Perhaps the most significant change we have made, and one that we feel is important to call to the reader's attention, is our effort to eliminate sexist terms and language from the text. In our attempt to present to the student a consistently nonsexist approach we requested permission of authors of earlier works to edit their articles. All authors, except as specifically noted in the text, generously gave their permission for these desired changes. We recognize that such changes may do some damage to the material in that the authors were working at a particular time in our history and thus the editing of the material may result in some loss of historical value. And we recognize that some articles may seem to carry a less personal message to the reader when singular personal pronouns are changed to the plural. However, we are presenting the material in the text as an aid to students in today's world; thus we thought the historical context was not critical, and, while the use of such phrases as "the worker . . . he . . . ." may seem to focus more directly on the person of the reader, they also may seem to today's feminine readers to exclude them. We do wish to thank the authors of the reprinted material who were willing to let us tamper with their writing in this way.

We do want to express our great debt to those individuals who have made comments about the book, especially the teachers whose suggestions came from their use of the text in their classes. Such comments have been invaluable to us in our work on this revision. In addition we wish to thank the students in our own classes whose questions and comments about the material have helped to clarify both our own thinking and our explanations.

We must express a very significant debt of gratitude to Joan Velasquez who has used the text in her classes at the University of Minnesota School of Social Work in Minneapolis and has been willing to conduct a running dialogue with the authors about her experience. This feedback over the last year has helped us immeasureably in rethinking what we had written three years ago. Joan also reviewed most of our changes and supported them as being worthwhile. Finally, in spite of the generous help of others we must accept the sole responsibility for this text.

Diane Anderson, Maxine Brown, and JoAnne Martz of Minneapolis, and the office staff of the School of Social Development, University of Minnesota, Duluth, deserve special recognition and thanks for their help in typing the manuscript and taking care of many of the details necessary in producing this revision.

B. R. C.
B. G.

Preface
to the First Edition

This book is intended for those who are beginners in the process of learning to be competent social workers. This may include B.A. students, individuals who have entered practice without an undergraduate preparation in college and are now anxious to learn about the work they are doing, or M.S.W. students who are beginning their graduate preparation.

Our purpose in developing this text is to present to the beginning social work student, or to the beginning practitioner, a basic set of concepts and principles from which he or she may be able to develop a foundation of general practice knowledge. It is our belief that what is presented here is both basic enough and realistic enough that, once integrated by the student, it will serve as the foundation for a more elaborate and sophisticated structure of social work competence as the beginner accumulates more experience as both a learner and a practitioner. Our goal is to present a text that describes and analyzes the elements of practice—organized within a problem solving framework—in such a way that the student not only intellectually grasps the nature of social work processes, but also gains some knowledge of the trials and tribulations, joys and satisfactions of social work practice in today's world.

The selection and organization of knowledge in the field of social work is a perennial problem, and probably will continue to plague the profession. We believe that there are at least four large areas of knowledge that the competent social work practitioner will have integrated into his own practice formulations: (1) theories of people and society and their interaction which will help to answer such questions as how individuals and their social systems grow, develop, stabilize, change, function and dysfunction, and what is the effect of each upon the other, (2) knowledge of social work as a profession, and something of its history that takes into consideration the societal context within which it has developed and functioned over time, (3) knowledge of social welfare agencies, institutions, delivery systems, or other organized structures within which social work services have, over time, been lodged; and the effect of the structure and function of these delivery systems upon the way problems have been defined and the way social work practice has been shaped, (4) the nature of social work practice itself which includes some historical perspective of the development of the various practice modalities, general concepts, and principles of the practice processes, and a more sophisticated and specialized practice competence. It was our decision, in keeping with our purpose, that we would focus on the nature of the basic social work processes within this fourth area of knowledge, recognizing that this one volume will not "a social worker make."

The text is organized into 14 chapters. Each begins with the authors' development of the notions and concepts to be dealt with in that particular chapter. This material is followed by two or three reprints of the works of other authors that relate to the issues of that chapter. Each chapter ends with a brief annotated bibliography. The first six chapters of the text deal with the basic concepts of all social work processes. The last seven chapters present a specific model of social work practice and the processes that make the model work.

The readings at the end of each chapter are not presumed to be a representative sample of the literature. They were selected to complement the authors' statement so that the book would stand as a text built upon the authors' approach to social work processes. We attempted to select reprints that would contribute to the richness or the sense of complexity of the issues developed in each particular chapter. From the vast amount of material available, our goal was to select examples that would (in combination with the authors' work) give students a realistic, intellectual grasp of the nature of social work processes and that might serve to raise questions for further work or discussion.

We cannot predict the future of the profession, or the knowledge and skill that the future will demand of those who would practice in the name of social work—so we have developed this text to present what we see as the processes of the profession in today's world. It is precisely because we do not know what problems the future will present to the workers of tomorrow that we believe in the problem solving framework for practice. Such a model recognizes the inherent uniqueness of each problem while recognizing the function of knowledge. It is a relatively open framework which not only allows for use of current knowledge but allows for the integration of new knowledge, and, in fact, encourages seeking after the new. It demands the careful consideration of problem definition and goals in such a way that client system and practitioner become partners, and it demands a continual monitoring of service outcomes and client goal achievement. We have tried to present the material, and have selected and organized the readings and bibliographies, to stimulate the beginning of a journey toward professional competence rather than to present an arrived at destination.

We are indebted to so many people who have helped us in our own professional development, challenged our thinking, and supported us in the development of this book that we cannot possibly mention them all. So we must select only a few. First, we must recognize the contributions of our families, the social work professors we have had, the clients and others with whom we have worked professionally, and the students we have known.

All of these persons, individually and collectively, have served as a source of learning and stimulation for us.

We wish to thank our colleagues of our two schools of social work who offered many insights and ideas and gave generously of their time in reading and commenting on the manuscript. We especially wish to thank professors Helen Yesner and Annalee Stewart who used the manuscript in their classes during this last year, and thus could give us live and objective feedback from both undergraduate and beginning graduate classes as to its utility.

We want to thank our own students of the last three years who have reacted with both criticism and support to the bits and pieces of the manuscript as they have appeared in their assigned readings, and especially the beginning graduate students of this last year who have read and discussed the completed manuscript with us.

We owe special thanks to the reviewers who commented on the manuscript as it was in process and on the finished document: Rhonda Connaway, School of Social Work, Washington University; Sheldon Gelman, School of Social Work, Pennsylvania State University; Gwendolyn C. Gilbert, School of Social Work, The Ohio State University; H. Wayne Johnson, School of Social Work, University of Iowa; Sylvia Krakow, School of Social Work, Boston University; and Louis Lowy, School of Social Work, Boston University. Their willingness to take time to read and share their thinking about the work resulted in strengthening the manuscript. Those who generously gave us permission to reprint their articles or to quote from their writings deserve acknowledgement and gratitude. Their generosity has contributed greatly to the strength of the text. Without their willingness to share, the book would be quite different. In spite of such generous help from others, we must accept the final, sole responsibility for the content of this text.

Wendy Gaskill as the chief typist, Jan Goodno, Sue Nelson, and Sue Newlin who ably assisted her deserve special recognition and our most heartfelt thanks, not only for typing the manuscript, but for taking care of the myriad of details with cheerfulness, calmness, and efficiency. Alice Chen, a social work teaching assistant, was most efficient in locating fugitive materials, supervising reprint reproduction, and in helping in any way she could. We also wish to acknowledge the contribution of Georgia Ann Guevara, Larry Ray, Pamela Jones and Elsie Fairchild, teaching assistants at the School of Social Work, University of Southern Mississippi, who assisted with the indexing.

The book is the result of our collaborative efforts as fellow faculty members at the University of Minnesota Schools of Social Work. We have found both teaching and writing together to be a fruitful venture in cooperation in the fullest sense of the word. The fact that one name precedes the other in the listing of the two authors does not in any way indicate that one member of the team is a senior author and one member a junior. The listing of the names is simply the result of an accident of the alphabet.

Together we have 15 years of practice experience representing the fields of public assistance, child welfare (with emphasis on foster care and protective services), corrections, day care, and private family agencies. We have held positions ranging from beginning B.A. workers to M.S.W. workers to supervisor to associate executive. Between us we have had 25 years of teaching experience in both class and field. The classroom experience includes continuing education courses and numerous institutes and workshops for employed practitioners, undergraduate teaching in the fields of social work practice and social welfare policy, M.S.W. classes in both general practice and specific practice modalities, and Ph.D. seminars. This book has come from this experience and from our desire to introduce others to a profession that we have found so challenging and stimulating.

B. R. C.
B. G.

Contributors

Ashley, A. Ardythe Psychotherapist, Center for Creative Living, New York, New York

Attneave, Carolyn L. Professor, Psychology, University of Washington, Seattle

Auerswald, Edgar H. Chief, Maui Community Mental Health Center, Wailuku, Hawaii

Benavides, Eustolio Coordinator of Social Services to Hispanics, Catholic Charities of the Archdiocese of St. Paul and Minneapolis, Minnesota

Compton, Beulah Roberts Professor, School of Social Work, University of Alabama

Cormican, John D. Associate Professor of English, Utica College, Utica, New York

Cournoyer, Barry Associate Professor, Indiana University School of Social Work, Indianapolis

Donovan, John B. Present affiliation unknown; at time article published was with the Inter American Foundation, New York, New York

Dyal, William M., Jr. President, AFS International/Intercultural Programs, New York, New York

Fordor, Anthony Head of Social Work Department, Liverpool Polytechnic, Liverpool, England

Germain, Carel B. Professor, School of Social Work, University of Connecticut, West Hartford

Gitterman, Alex Associate Dean and Professor, Columbia University School of Social Work, New York, New York

Grosser, Charles F. At time of death was Professor, School of Social Work, Columbia University, New York, New York

Haley, Jay Director, Family Therapy Institute, Washington, D.C.

Halleck, Seymour L. Professor of Psychiatry, University of North Carolina, Chapel Hill

Hardman, Dale G. Professor Emeritus, University of Wisconsin, Oshkosh

Hartman, Ann Professor of Social Work, School of Social Work, University of Michigan, Ann Arbor

Hess, Howard Assistant Professor, Indiana University School of Social Work, Indianapolis

Hess, Peg McCartt Assistant Professor, Indiana University School of Social Work, Indianapolis

Ho, Man Keung Professor of Social Work, University of Oklahoma, Norman

Hooker, Carol E. Emergency Services Social Worker, Park Center Community Counselling Service, Fort Wayne, Indiana

Hooyman, Eugene Director of Training and Development, Providence Medical Center, Seattle, Washington

Hudson, Joe Principal, Office of the Auditor General of Canada, Ottawa

Lewis, Ronald G. Professor, School of Social Work, Arizona State University, Tempe

Mailick, Mildred D. Professor, School of Social Work, Hunter College, New York, New York

Maluccio, Anthony N. Professor of Social Work, School of Social Work, The University of Connecticut, West Hartford

Marlow, Wilma D. At time of death was Assistant Professor, School of Social Work, University of Connecticut, West Hartford

McClure, Marilyn E. Vigil Program Director, People, Inc., Falcon Heights, Minnesota

Morris, Addie Staff Development Supervisor, Arkansas Mental Health Services, Little Rock

Murdach, Allison D. Social Worker, Veterans Administration Medical Center, Palo Alto, California

Pawlak, Edward J. Professor, School of Social Work, Western Michigan University, Kalamazoo

Purcell, Francis P. Professor, Social Work, San Francisco State University, San Francisco, California

Rutman, Leonard Professor, Sociology Department, Carleton University, Ottawa, Ontario, Canada

Seabury, Brett A. Associate Professor, School of Social Work, University of Michigan, Ann Arbor

Specht, Harry Professor and Dean, School of Social Welfare, University of California, Berkeley

Taber, Richard H. Pastor, Congregational Church of Salisbury, Salisbury, Connecticut

Tucker, Samuel Associate Professor, University of Southern Mississippi, Hattiesburg

Velasquez, Joan Research Administrator, Ramsey County Human Services, St. Paul, Minnesota

Walsh, M. Ellen Faculty Lecturer, School of Social Work, University of Washington, Bellevue

Contents

PART ONE
THE CONTEXT FOR DECIDING WHAT TO DO

1. **Nature of Social Work** **3**

Focus of social work intervention. Toward a practice model: *Process for practice. Values for practice. Knowledge for practice. Relationship for practice. Intervention models for practice. Sanctions for practice.* Reducing a divisive dichotomy. Recapitulation. A look forward.

Readings

1–1. The House on Sixth Street, *Francis P. Purcell and Harry Specht,* 15

1–2. Social Work Practice: A Life Model, *Alex Gitterman and Carel B. Germain,* 22

2. **Knowledge for Social Work Practice** **33**

What is a profession? Definition of terms. Development of knowledge and theory in social work. Function of knowledge in social work practice. Is knowledge necessary? Criteria for the selection of theory. Dealing with incomplete knowledge. Recapitulation. A look forward.

Readings

2–1. Learned Helplessness, *Carol E. Hooker,* 50

2–2. Work with Mrs. Manley, 56

3. **Values in Social Work Practice** **67**

What is meant by social work value? Respect for the dignity and uniqueness of the individual. Communications for dignity. Classification and individualization. Using client strength. Expectation of participation. Focus on wants rather than needs. Client self-determination. Legal authority and self-determination. Recapitulation. A look forward.

Readings

3–1. The NASW Code of Ethics, *National Association of Social Workers,* 84

3–2. Not with My Daughter You Don't, *Dale G. Hardman,* 91

4. **Theoretical Perspectives for Social Work Practice** **105**

Criteria for selection. General systems theory as a part of foundation knowledge: *As a conceptual framework. Empirical aspects of systems theory. Boundaries.*

Tension. Feedback and purposive systems. Change and stability. Potential
values of systems theory: *Basic conceptual systems in social work practice.*
Role theory as foundation knowledge. Ego psychology as foundation knowledge:
Psychoanalytic constructs. Ego psychology constructs. Significant contributions
of ego psychology to social work knowledge. Concepts of stress, coping, and
crisis. Concepts of diversity and difference. Recapitulation. A look forward.

Readings

4–1. Social Work and System Theory, *Anthony Fordor*, 144

4–2. Interdisciplinary versus Ecological Approach, *Edgar H. Auerswald*, 158

4–3. Minority Issues in Community Mental Health, *Samuel Tucker*, 167

5. Sanctions for Social Work Practice 177

The interstitial profession. The bureaucratic organization. Conflicts between
the bureaucracy and the professional. Types of bureaucrats. Agency
bureaucracy and the worker. Client, worker, and bureaucracy. Changing
the bureaucracy. The profession as a system. Recapitulation. A look
forward.

Readings

5–1. Organizational Tinkering, *Edward J. Pawlak*, 200

5–2. Four Pennies to My Name: What It's Like on Welfare, *Addie
Morris*, 205

6. Relationship for Social Work Practice 219

A review of the literature. Social work roles and relationship. Purpose as an
element of relationship. Development of relationship. Elements of the
relationship: *Concern for the other. Commitment and obligation. Acceptance
and expectation. Empathy. Authority and power. Genuineness and congruence.
Rational and irrational elements in the helping relationship.* The helping person:
*Maturing people. Creativity. Capacity to observe self. Desire to help. Courage.
Sensitivity.* Race and the social work relationship. Recapitulation. A look
forward.

Readings

6–1. The Impact of Professional Dishonesty on Behavior of Disturbed
Adolescents, *Seymour L. Halleck*, 252

6–2. A Framework for Establishing Social Work Relationships across Racial/
Ethnic Lines, *Joan Velasquez, Marilyn E. Vigil McClure, and Eustolio
Benavides*, 260

PART TWO
TOOLS FOR DECIDING WHAT TO DO

7. Communication and Interviewing for Social Work Practice 271

Communication and interviewing. Barriers to communication. Responsibilities
of the worker. Some ideas about technique. Written communications.
Recapitulation. A look forward.

Readings

7–1. Linguistic Issues in Interviewing, *John D. Cormican,* 288

7–2. Basic Communications Skills for Work with Groups, *Barry R. Cournoyer,* 294

7–3. Point of View, *A. Averchenko,* 302

8. Problem Solving: A Process for Social Work Practice **307**

Problem solving as a life process. Dewey and problem solving. Problem solving in social work. Problem solving and the practitioner's responsibility. The client system and problem solving. Basic assumptions of the model. Presentation of the problem-solving outline. Recapitulation. A look forward. Outline of problem-solving model—Short form: *Contact phase. Contract phase. Action phase.*

Readings

8–1. Identity and Change: Does Development Imply Dependency? *William M. Dyal, Jr. and John B. Donovan,* 325

8–2. A Systems Approach to the Delivery of Mental Health Services in Black Ghettos, *Richard H. Taber,* 330

8–3. A Political Perspective in Problem Solving, *Allison D. Murdach,* 336

9. The Contact Phase: Problem Identification, Initial Goal Setting, Data Collection, and Initial Assessment **345**

Giving and taking help. Getting started. The crossing of system boundaries. Defining the problem. Goal setting. Preliminary contract. Areas of data collection. Sources and methods of data collection. Skills in the contact phase. Recapitulation: *Summary of problem identification activity. Summary of goal-setting activity. Summary of beginning assessment activity.* A look forward.

Readings

9–1. Diagrammatic Assessment of Family Relationships, *Ann Hartman,* 375

9–2. Social Work with Native Americans, *Ronald G. Lewis and Man Keung Ho,* 387

10. The Contract Phase: Joint Assessment, Goal Setting, and Planning **395**

Definition of the service contract. Joint assessment and decision making. Setting goals. Planning for intervention. Worker/client differences of view. Recapitulation. A look forward.

Readings

10–1. The Case for the Contract, *Anthony N. Maluccio and Wilma D. Marlow,* 407

10–2. Negotiating Sound Contracts with Clients, *Brett A. Seabury,* 415

PART THREE
TOOLS FOR DOING THE DECIDED

11. Interventive Roles: Implementation of the Plan **427**

The concept of interventive roles. The role of social broker. The role of enabler. The role of teacher. The role of mediator. The role of advocate. Roles are not functional specializations. Recapitulation. A look forward.

Readings

11–1. Stover Family, 437

11–2. Community Development Programs Serving the Urban Poor, *Charles F. Grosser,* 455

12. Interventive Methods: Implementation of Roles **463**

Encouragement. Enhancing awareness of own behavior. Enhancing the client's awareness of others' behavior. Socialization into effective role performance. Dealing with role transitions or role losses. Supporting role performance. Use of networks as resources. Support and action. The relationship of roles and techniques. Recapitulation. A look forward.

Readings

12–1. An Attempt to Examine the Use of Support in Social Work Practice, *Beulah Roberts Compton,* 477

12–2. Action as a Tool in Casework Practice, *Anthony N. Maluccio,* 486

12–3. Therapy in Tribal Settings and Urban Network Intervention, *Carolyn L. Attneave,* 492

12–4. Rural Social Work Practice: Clinical Quality, *M. Ellen Walsh,* 504

13. Teamwork for Social Work Practice **515**

Observations on teamwork. The problem of competition. The problem of professional and agency culture. The problem-solving approach to teamwork. Methods of planning and sharing. Recapitulation. A look forward.

Readings

13–1. Team Building in the Human Services, *Eugene Hooyman,* 527

13–2. Politics of Interprofessional Collaboration: Challenge to Advocacy, *Mildred D. Mailick and Ardythe A. Ashley,* 541

14. Endings in Social Work Practice **551**

Referral. Transfer. Termination. Recapitulation.

Reading

14–1. Termination in Context, *Howard Hess and Peg McCartt Hess,* 559

15. Evaluation **571**

Balancing sumative and formative evaluations. Continuous client evaluation. Assisting with program evaluation. Recapitulation.

Reading

15–1. Evaluation Research in Human Services, *Leonard Rutman and Joe Hudson,* 580

16. Conclusions **593**

Social work as a problem-solving process. Social work as a client-worker relationship. Social work as a rational process. The beginning.

Reading

16–1. The Art of Being a Failure as a Therapist, *Jay Haley,* 596

INDEX **601**

Part One

The Context for Deciding

What to Do

Chapter 1
Nature of Social Work

Chapter 2
Knowledge for
Social Work Practice

Chapter 3
Values in Social Work Practice

Chapter 4
Theoretical Perspectives for
Social Work Practice

Chapter 1

Nature of Social Work

What do social workers do? Where and how do they intervene? For most of us these are perplexing questions—questions made more perplexing by our lack of contact with social workers and the diffuseness of social work practice. From life experiences most of us have little difficulty identifying the job of the doctor as healing the body—mediating between the physical organism and environmental influences which threaten health. (The doctor's job becomes much less clear and less understood when it moves out of the area of physical illness and into the treatment of mental illness.) Likewise, the lawyer's job as mediator between the individual and the legal institutions which have been developed to insure a reasonably orderly society is usually understood. And few of us, because of our life experiences, have any difficulty identifying the job of the teacher in transmitting the accumulated knowledge of the culture. But what about social workers? What is their job?

William Schwartz (1961, pp. 150–151) takes the viewpoint that "Every profession has a particular function to perform in society: it has received a certain job assignment for which it is held accountable." To Schwartz the social work job assignment is to "mediate the process through which the individual and . . . society reach out for each other through a mutual need for self-fulfillment." The Schwartz mediating model rests on the assumption that the interests of the individual and the interests of society are essentially the same, but that in a complex and changing society the individual's desire to belong as a full and productive member and the society's ability to integrate and enrich its people are sometimes blocked. Social work intervention is directed toward these blockages and toward freeing the "individual's impetus toward health, growth, and belonging; and the organized efforts of society to integrate its parts into a productive and dynamic whole."

What Schwartz calls blockage between the individual's impetus toward growth and the organized efforts of society will be experienced by individuals or groups of individuals as problems. The problems may be varied—finding a job, caring for a child, maintaining communications in a marriage, getting along with others, threats of mugging in the street, boredom because

3

of inactivity, and so on. We speak of social work as a problem-solving process. Problem solving is the way social workers and clients operationalize or put into action the concept of mediation. Thus we think of problem solving as mediation.

In this first chapter we develop further the nature of social work as mediating the person-situation interaction. We will orient you to themes which will be developed through the book such as social work practice consisting of a problem-solving (mediating) process, values, knowledge, relationship, intervention, and sanctions. At this early stage we must emphasize a crucial distinction between practice, process, and intervention which are often confused by social workers themselves. Social work practice is the totality of what social workers do. It encompasses both a process (we call this the problem-solving process) and planned change actions, which can be called methods of intervention. Although methods of intervention are often thought of as social work practice, they are only one piece of practice. We see intervention as one part of the problem-solving process. The focus of this book is on the problem-solving process which we think must be understood and mastered before one turns to ways of intervening to bring about change.

FOCUS OF SOCIAL WORK INTERVENTION

Martin Rein (1970, p. 15) suggests that one of the obstacles to the development of a professional social work creed has been the difficulty in defining the social work profession. Nevertheless, efforts have been made to define both the target and the nature of social work practice. The Commission on Social Work Practice of the National Association of Social Workers (1958, pp. 5–6) published a working definition which defined social work practice as a "constellation of value, purpose, sanction, knowledge, and method." The working definition identified three purposes of social work practice:

1. To assist individuals and groups to identify and resolve or minimize problems arising out of disequilibrium between themselves and the environment.
2. To identify potential areas of disequilibrium between individuals or groups and the environment in order to prevent the occurrence of disequilibrium.
3. In addition to these curative and preventive aims, to seek out, identify, and strengthen the maximum potential in individuals, groups, and communities. (p. 6)

Werner Boehm (1958) has also published a widely used definition of social work:

Social work seeks to enhance the social functioning of individuals, singularly and in groups, by activities focused upon their social relationships which constitute interaction between individuals and their environments. These activities can be grouped into three functions: restoration of impaired capacity, provision of individual and social resources, and prevention of social dysfunction. (p. 18)

More recently the West Virginia Undergraduate Social Work Curriculum Development Project conceptualized social work as

> concerned and involved with the interactions between people and the institutions of society that affect the ability of people to accomplish life tasks, realize aspirations and values, and alleviate distress. These interactions between people and social institutions occur within the context of the larger societal good. Therefore, three major purposes of social work may be identified:
>
> 1. To enhance the problem-solving, coping, and developmental capacities of people;
> 2. To promote the effective and humane operation of the systems that provide people with resources and services;
> 3. To link people with systems that provide them with resources, services, and opportunities. (Baer & Federico, 1978, p. 68)

These definitions clearly place the focus of social work intervention on the interaction or disequilibrium between individuals and their environments. In this sense they are consistent with Schwartz's mediating approach, inasmuch as they consider social work as in some way intervening or mediating between people and their social environments.

Harriett Bartlett (1970, p. 116) writes of a social work focus on social functioning, which she defines as the "relation between the coping activity of people and the demand from the environment." For Bartlett the concept of social functioning does not refer to the functioning of individuals or groups, which she finds characteristic of earlier definitions, but "attention is now directed primarily to what goes on between people and environment through the exchange between them. This dual focus ties them together. Thus person and situation, people and environment, are encompassed in a single concept, which requires that they be constantly reviewed together."

William Gordon (1969, p. 6) with whom Bartlett is in agreement, finds that "the central focus of social work traditionally seems to have been on people in their life situation complex—a simultaneous dual focus on individuals and environment." Gordon further notes that

> Emphasis has been on individualizing the person-situation complex in order to achieve the best match between each person and the environment, in which either person-behavior or environmental situation may deviate widely from the typical or normative. We conclude, therefore, that the central target of technical social work practice is *matching* something in person and situation—that is, intervening by whatever methods and means necessary to help people be in situations where their capabilities are sufficiently matched with the demands of the situations to "make a go of it."

The focus of social work intervention is on the interaction between humans and their environments. In Schwartz's terms social workers mediate; in Gordon's terms social workers match something in environment to something in the individual; and in Bartlett's terms social workers seek to strike a balance between people's coping ability and environmental demands. Social workers may at times (1) direct change strategies toward individuals, (2) direct change strategies toward the environment, and (3) direct change strategies toward the interaction of individual and environment. But in all cases, these strategies are directed toward changing the nature of the person-situation interaction.

But does changing the nature of the interaction mean changing the individual or changing the environment? This is an old issue in social work which was enunciated at an early date by Porter Lee (1929) in his distinction between social work as cause and social work as function. Our contention is that social workers do both and that the debate as to whether the profession should focus primarily on individual change or on environmental change results largely from an incorrect formulation of the focus of social work intervention. The parties to this debate tend to perceive social workers as either focusing on the individual or on the environment and miss the central focus on the interaction of the two. Gisela Konopka (1958, ch. 9) has pointed out the inappropriateness of this dichotomous thinking in social work, and Martin Rein (1970, p. 19) notes that both individual and social change approaches can be used to either support or challenge contemporary standards of behavior. Research by Merlin A. Taber and Anthony J. Vattano (1970) finds no sharp distinction between clinical and social orientations among practicing social workers and suggests that most social workers are able to integrate both functions. Rein's concept of radical casework is particularly well suited to a social work focus on person-situation interaction. For Rein (1970, p. 19), "a radical casework approach would mean not merely obtaining for clients social services to which they are entitled or helping them adjust to the environment, but also trying to deal with the relevant people and institutions in the clients' environment that are contributing to their difficulties."

Alex Gitterman and Carel Germain, in the article included with this chapter, suggest that a gap exists between new knowledge and social work practice; they offer a life model which "integrates the treatment and reform traditions." Social workers focus on problems in living which fall into three areas:

> (1) problems and needs associated with tasks involved in life transitions; (2) problems and needs associated with tasks in using and influencing elements of the environment; and (3) problems and needs associated with interpersonal obstacles which impede the work of a family or a group as it deals with transtitional and/or environmental tasks. (1976, pp. 602–603)

The concept of social functioning and dual focus on both person and situation holds profound implications for social work practice. Traditionally, social workers have considered themselves as caseworkers, group workers, or community organizers. Francis Purcell and Harry Specht in "The House on Sixth Street," a classic social work case study included with this chapter, illustrates the need to move beyond this tripartite division of practice when responding to a housing problem presented by a low-income client. Thinking traditionally as caseworkers, group workers, or community organizers tends to obscure the range of problem definitions and change strategies that might be considered by encouraging a focus on one side or the other of the person-situation interaction.

Martin Rein (1970, p. 19) notes that the association of social change with community organization and of individual change with social casework may oversimplify social work inasmuch as work with individuals can be directed toward change in social standards and work with groups or communities can be directed toward helping people adapt to their current situations. We agree with the Rein formulation, but think that this distinction has been largely missed in social work—the expectation remains that the community organizer works at community change, the caseworker works to produce individual change, and the group worker to do either, depending on the nature of the group. This expectation diverts the focus of social work from the person-situation interaction to either the person or the situation depending on the particular method in which the practitioner has been steeped.

Schwartz (1961, p. 148) notes the inappropriateness of basing a definition of method on the number of persons with whom the worker interacts and suggests that the terms *casework, group work,* and *community organization* refer to the relational system in which the worker implements method. For Schwartz, method is "a systematic process of ordering one's activity in the performance of a function. Method is function in action." The method becomes a systematic way in which social workers carry out their function; that is, the systematic way in which they mediate between the individual and the social environment.

Alex Gittermann and Carel Germain, in the article printed in this chapter, develop a life model of social work practice which ". . . integrates the treatment and reform traditions, by conceptualizing and emphasizing the dysfunctional transactions between people and their social and physical environments."

Our concept of social work practice is consistent with this and the other ecological models which have been developing over the past few years (Baer & Federico, 1978; Germain, 1973; Meyer, 1970; Pincus & Minahan, 1973). These models focus on the transactions of individuals and their environments with both individuals and environments in a constant state of reciprocity, each shaping the other. Social work interventions are directed to the interface of the individual and environment or at problems of living generated from the person-in-situation interaction. We think these models have the potential for bridging the unfortunate social change versus individual change dichotomy which has developed in our profession by removing blinders which limit the vision of some social workers who focus on individuals and other social workers who focus on social conditions. We present here a practice model which will involve you, as a social worker, in activities directed toward resolution of problems which develop in the interactions of individuals and their environments; through your social work education you will develop skills of problem definition and both the commitment and ability to use a range of change strategies.

→ TOWARD A PRACTICE MODEL

Let us now turn to the broad brush strokes of the practice model developed in this book. We are reminded, at this point, of the professor who regularly met her freshman classes by writing

$$\frac{3}{2}$$

in large bold print on the blackboard. She then turned and smiled expectantly at her class. A few braver souls responded 5 to which the professor shook her head negatively, and then a few more would indicate 1 to which there was also a negative head shake. Then in a veritable chorus the class shouted out 6, to which the professor commented, "but, you see, you have given the answer before you knew the problem." Having answers, before we know the problem, is a common temptation to which many inexperienced and, sadly, some experienced social workers succumb.

One way to reduce this risk is to be very clear about the difference between social work process and social work intervention. Intervention, by which we mean a conscious planned effort to produce change, is but one component of social work process. Before intervening one must be clear as to the nature of the problem one is attempting to resolve as well as the goals and purposes of intervention; social work process encompasses all of the elements of practice including intervention and is thus a broader concept. A clear understanding regarding social work process and skills at managing this process are prerequisite to intervention. This book is primarily a book about social work process with intervention treated as one component of social work process. It is not, therefore, a book on models of intervention. We have found it useful to think of social work in terms of process for practice, values for practice, knowledge for practice, relationship for practice, intervention models for practice, and sanctions for practice.

Process for practice

Abraham Kaplan (1964, p. 23) refers to a law of the instrument, "give a small boy a hammer, and he will find that everything that he encounters needs to be pounded. It comes as no particular surprise to discover that scientists formulate problems in ways which require for their solution just those techniques in which they themselves are especially skilled." The same problem has characterized much of social work practice especially when practice is thought about primarily in terms of models of intervention. What is necessary, is the ability to define problems independent of intervention models and then to select the most appropriate model for intervention. Herbert Bisno (1969, p. 9) and John Kidneigh (1969, p. 159) have both suggested ways of thinking about social work activities which may help us avoid the problem of the law of the instrument. They suggest that two sets of skills are necessary for social work—skills in knowing what change strategies to use and skills in actual use of change strategies. Kidneigh believes that social workers must possess both the capability of "deciding what to do" and "of doing the decided." We have found this formulation useful and make use of Kidneigh's terms. The Kidneigh and Bisno division of skills provides a helpful guide to refining the more global Schwartz model of the mediating function of the profession. Operationalizing the mediating function involves arriving at decisions about how to mediate and how to implement these decisions.

You may recall that earlier we suggested that social workers in carrying out their mediating function are engaged in problem solving behavior to assist in the resolution of problems of interaction between persons and their situations. Thus mediation is a problem-solving process. The problem-solving model is overviewed in Chapter 6 and the various components of the model presented in more detail in Parts Two and Three. Problem solving is a rational process including actions to define the problem, actions to collect information on which to base decisions, actions to engage the client in goal setting and decision making, actions to produce change, and actions to evaluate progress. All of these actions, however, take place within a context of values and relationships.

Values for practice

Values guide and direct practice. Values for social work practice are discussed more extensively in Chapter 3, but two aspects of the value orientation should be clarified at the outset.

Social workers have long held a commitment to increasing opportunities for choices available to clients as well as assisting clients in making use of available sources. Note, for example, the work of the social worker in "The House on Sixth Street" to both make use of available resources as well as to increase the availability of housing. Harold Lewis (1972, p. 411) asserts that, "Institutionalized restrictions which limit opportunities, as well as the personal shortcomings of the client which may curtail his options, are legitimate targets for change." We refer to this as increasing client self-determination by increasing opportunities for choice and by assisting clients with decision making. Self-determination is a hollow concept if the environment does not provide opportunities or if the client is unable to use opportunities; thus in carrying out the mediating function you will be working to increase opportunities for choice and, in so doing, increase client self-determination.

Social work is a partnership arrangement. We think the client and social worker function together as partners throughout the problem-solving process. This means the client is fully involved and practicipating in all of the decisions, that we are working with the client, rather than doing things to the client. We frequently see students wishing to come into the social work profession because they want to reform or change people. If this is your interest, we suggest that you carefully rethink your reasons. Unless you can change your point of view, you are likely to find social work a very frustrating experience. Our function as social workers is not to reform or to change people; rather we engage people in a problem-solving process by which they resolve their own problems. Note, for example, how the worker in "The House on Sixth Street" involved the clients in all of the decision making and worked at assisting the clients to strengthen their own ability to deal with city government and public bureaucracies rather than taking over and attempting to solve the problems for this group of tenants. In this sense, social work may well differ from the other professions. We are here to assist clients to participate in a problem-solving process, not to solve problems for others.

Knowledge for practice

Social work is also based on knowledge. Thinking of social work as mediating the person-situation interaction to assist clients in the resolution of problems, suggests the types of knowledge required by the social worker. First, of course, is knowledge about the person—individual behavior and patterns of adaptation and all that impacts upon these. Then, of course, is knowledge about the situation—the community, its institutions, and the various resource structures. Third, we require what Carel Germain (1981, p. 325) calls transactional concepts—concepts to help explain and understand ". . . transactions between people and environments that, on the other hand promote or inhibit growth, development and the release of human potential and, on the other hand, promote or inhibit the capacity of environment to support the diversity of human potential." Fourth, we require knowledge of the process of mediation, which, of course, involves both a problem-solving process as well as knowledge of specific intervention models. To a very large extent our profession borrows knowledge of person and knowledge of situation from supporting social sciences. In Chapters 2 and 4, we discuss some of the types of knowledge and theories useful for social work practice.

Knowledge of mediation and specifically of the problem-solving process is the responsibility of social work. Social work practice, which may be thought of as mediation in action, is clearly the responsibility of our profession. While we may occasionally borrow and integrate practice concepts from other professions, the responsibility for developing, testing, and transmitting knowledge about social work practice—both the process and the models of intervention—must remain a central responsibility of social work. We think that all social workers have a responsibility as researchers to be doing evaluations and studies of their own practice and to be contributing to the profession's knowledge base. This is a theme to which we will return in Chapter 15.

Relationship for practice

One of the powerful forces that supports system change, growth, development, and ability to endure unchangeable pain and loss in social work practice is the emotional and affectional forces that grow and develop between social worker and client system. These forces have been called the social work relationship. Each of us during our lifetime has experienced the connectedness of emotion and intimacy that we call relationship. The professional relationship is a special type of human relationship that is, among other things purposive, focused and time limited. Effective participation in the development and management of appropriate professional relationships for the various practice actions of social workers is a critical part of social work practice skill. In Chapter 7 we discuss in considerable detail this critical element of practice.

Intervention models for practice

Intervention refers to deliberate, planned actions undertaken by the client and worker to resolve a problem. Thus intervention occurs after a problem has been defined and after the desired resolution (we will call this goals) has been identified. An intervention model is an organized set of procedures which, based on research including our practice experience, are thought to be useful to bring about a resolution of the specific problem confronting the client and worker.

We have already noted that intervention is a part, but not the totality, of social work practice. We have also established that the purpose of this book is to present a model for social work practice and is not to present models of intervention—that comes later after the practice model is understood and mastered. We do want to alert you, however, to two errors which we think are commonly made by social workers, especially inexperienced ones. One is to assume that practice is only intervention. A second, equally serious error, is to gobble up, hook, line, and sinker, an intervention model, frequently external to social work, which is then indiscriminantly applied without regard for the definition of the problem or client goals. We have known of social workers, for example, who have indiscriminantly adopted transactional analysis, reality therapy, Adlerian psychology, behavioral modification, or other systems of thought which have then been indiscriminantly applied under the pretext of doing social work. The fish analogy may be appropriate. Grabbing for a tender morsel may be easier than the hard work of developing social work models including a wide range of interventive strategies for use in mediating the person-situation interaction. This may be especially true if the morsel is attractive and the lure faddish.

Sanctions for practice

At the beginning of this chapter we noted that Schwartz (1961, pp. 150–151) emphasizes that every profession has an assigned function in society for which the profession is accountable. Social work is no exception in that the activities of social workers require some type of community sanctions. The community and the client systems need assurance that the interventions of the practitioner with the various systems of practice are within the recognized and approved parameters of society's assignment to the profession. Social work practice is sanctioned through two structures—the profession and the social welfare institutions within which most social workers are employed. Chapter 5 will deal with the meaning of these sanctioning structures to practice actions.

REDUCING A DIVISIVE DICHOTOMY

The focus of social work on the person-situation interaction and conceptualizing the function of social work as using a problem-solving process to mediate or resolve problems in the person-situation interaction will reduce the dichotomy between individual change and social change which has been so divisive through the history of our profession. The model demands that social workers maintain both orientations and possess interventive skills in both areas. The social worker in "The House on Sixth Street" case required skills at organizing the tenants to work toward better housing; in a different circumstance or under a different set of facts, however, the same worker might well have focused the intervention efforts to assist a family to secure more adequate housing, or again with different circumstances and different facts, to assist a family to develop the skills and ability to improve their existing housing. We use the term *client* in a generic way to mean individual, family, group, or community. A client, in this sense, is any individual or group of individuals or community representatives who are experiencing a problem. Communities may experience problems in providing resources for their members as well as individuals' experiencing problems in their person-situation interaction. The problem-solving process is applicable regardless of the client system. What is important is to avoid a focus on either individual or situation to the exclusion of the other; but this dichotomy has been present in social work for years and has detracted from the primary focus on the person-situation interaction.

A closely related dichotomy is the argument between rehabilitation and prevention in social work. Arguments are advanced that social workers may spend too much time with the casualties of our society instead of attacking root problems in efforts at prevention. This is also an unacceptable dichotomy for two reasons. First, to a large extent, it is a renewed manifestation of the issue of work with the community versus work with individuals. Prevention is frequently assumed to require social change with rehabilitation perceived as helping individuals to cope with immediate situations. We consider all social work activity as both preventive and rehabilitative. Helping a mentally ill person is rehabilitative, but also prevents future distress. Efforts to provide deprived children with adequate nutrition, clothing, and, in some cases, substitute living arrangements are both rehabilitative and preventive. A second objection relates to the matter of timing and client readiness. The social worker, as an agent of the client, does not intervene until the client (individual, family, group, or community) perceives a problem and is ready to engage in a process of problem solving; for the social worker to act otherwise increases the danger of doing to or for rather than with. A social worker may at times be called upon to serve as an agent of society (as may occur, for example, in dealing with child abuse or delinquency); in such instances it is highly unlikely that either prevention or rehabilitation will occur until a client and worker discover a mutually acceptable area for a joint problem solving. Rehabilitation is preventive and prevention may be rehabilitative; ideally neither occurs until a client has perceived a problem after which client and worker engage in a mutual problem-solving undertaking.

We have argued that in carrying out a problem-solving approach social work skills can be classified in two broad areas—skills necessary for assessment or for deciding what to do and skills necessary for intervention or doing the decided. Does this imply that all social workers must be able to do all things for all people? We think the model provides a sound basis for thinking of general social work practice and for the development of specialists in relation to highly technical and the more complex models of intervention.

In this approach, a social worker in general practice is a person who is skillful in deciding what to do. These practitioners will not be limited in their vision by any preferred relational system (individual, family, small group, and so on) or prior commitment to any particular change strategy; thus, they will be able to focus attention on the totality of the person-situation interaction. In the process of deciding what to do, the practitioner is free to examine variables in the person, in the situation, and the interaction of the two. Skills for data collection and assessment are essential for such a practitioner in order to both define the problem and arrive at a practical and workable decision as to what needs to be done.

For doing the decided, the profession must be able to provide clients with a wide range of interventive strategies or models. Some of these models may require highly skilled specialists. In some situations the generalist practitioner will possess skills in the necessary interventive strategies and may implement the changed decision, but in other situations the generalist may call in a specialist for assistance. For example, as you read "The House on Sixth Street," note that this social work practitioner relied upon specialists—a city planner and an attorney—to assist in implementing the plan. At least one of these specialists, the attorney, brought knowledge and skill to the situation that were significantly different from those of the social workers. Some plans may well involve the social work generalist in making use of specialists from outside the profession while other plans will involve the social work generalist in the use of specialists from within the profession. In some instances, the specialist may carry most of the responsibility for implementation of the service plans; for others, more of the doing the decided will be the responsibility of the generalist, who will work as a team member with the specialist in meeting the objectives of the service plan. While we find much that has been objectionable with the use of the medical model in social work, we find the relationship between the work of the general practitioner or family doctor and specialists a useful analogy. A specialist is to back up and support the work of the medical practitioner who may retain overall responsibility for the case. In making referrals to a specialist, the generalist is guided by the nature of the problem, the nature of the intervention plan, his or her own skills, and availability of the necessary specialist.

RECAPITULATION

By now you have been introduced to the basic ideas found in this book and themes which will be recurring in subsequent chapters. The focus of social work intervention is on the person-situation interaction, thus a focus solely on the individual or solely on the situation is inappropriate. The long debate in the social work profession about individual services versus social reform detracts from this basic focus of the profession. The function of social workers is to serve as mediators to assist clients to resolve problems in person-situation interactions. Social work involves a partnership arrangement with the client to engage in problem solving. A distinction must be made between social work practice and models of intervention. Social work practice encompasses all components of the problem-solving process which we have subsumed under the rubrics of deciding what to do and doing the decided. Models of intervention, of course, relate to doing the decided and carrying out a plan designed to produce change. The structure of the profession provides for both social work generalists and social work specialists who are available when intervention plans call for particularly complex and technical skills.

A LOOK FORWARD

The two readings reproduced here amplify the themes outlined in this chapter. "The House on Sixth Street" by Purcell and Specht is a classic case study which appeared in the social work literature in the 1960s. It illustrates the potential for the use of social change strategies in relation to an individual request for service. Gitterman and Germain present a summary of their life model of social work practice which integrates the developmental needs of individuals with the social provision structures of the community and which is quite consistent with the focus of social work on the person-situation interaction. Subsequent to publishing this article, Gitterman and Germain have expanded and further developed their ideas, now available in book form. We have also made frequent references to William Schwartz's concept of the mediating function of social work practice; this concept plays a central part in our thinking. Although Schwartz's article is not reprinted here, we recommend it to you and suggest that it would be well worth a trip to your library.

During the balance of this book, we will be sharing with you a model of social work practice which we have found useful. Part One provides a context for deciding what to do and deals with issues regarding the nature of social work, knowledge for social work practice, values for social work practice, theoretical perspectives, sanctions for social work practice, and an introduction to the components of the problem-solving process. In Part Two we will introduce you to the tools and process of deciding what to do including material regarding the social work relationship, communication and interviewing, and discussions of the contact and contract phases of the problem-solving model. Part Three focuses upon intervention on doing the decided and presents material regarding the worker's interventive roles, assisting clients to maintain and develop competence, teamwork and the use of teamwork strategies, termination, and research and evaluation. We have found social work hard, yet rewarding and we hope you will find this book both challenging and rewarding. You may be challenged to further search the literature. We hope you will be rewarded by finding a framework for practice which will be useful in your own career.

Reading 1-1

*The House on Sixth Street**

Francis P. Purcell and Harry Specht

The extent to which social work can affect the course of social problems has not received the full consideration it deserves.[1] For some time the social work profession has taken account of social problems only as they have become manifest in behavioral pathology. Yet it is becoming increasingly apparent that, even allowing for this limitation, it is often necessary for the same agency or worker to intervene by various methods at various points.

In this paper, the case history of a tenement house in New York City is used to illustrate some of the factors that should be considered in selecting intervention methods. Like all first attempts, the approach described can be found wanting in conceptual clarity and systematization. Yet the vital quality of the effort and its implications for social work practice seem clear.

The case of "The House on Sixth Street" is taken from the files of Mobilization For Youth (MYF), an action-research project that has been in operation since 1962 on

New York's Lower East Side. MFY's programs are financed by grants from several public and private sources. The central theoretical contention of MFY is that a major proportion of juvenile delinquency occurs when adolescents from low-income families do not have access to legitimate opportunities by which they can fulfill the aspirations for success they share with all American youth. The action programs of MFY are designed to offer these youths concrete opportunities to offset the debilitating effects of poverty. For example, the employment program helps youngsters obtain jobs; other programs attempt to increase opportunities in public schools. In addition, there are group work and recreation programs. A wide variety of services to individuals and families is offered through Neighborhood Service Centers: a homemaking program, a program for released offenders, and a narcotics information center. Legal services, a housing services unit, a special referral unit, and a community development program are among other services that have been developed or made available. Thus, MFY has an unusually wide range of resources for dealing with social problems.

[1] Social work practitioners sometimes use the term *social problem* to mean "environmental problem." The sense in which it is used here corresponds to the definition developed by the social sciences. That is, a social problem is a disturbance, deviation, or breakdown in social behavior that (1) involves a considerable number of people and (2) is of serious concern to many in the society. It is social in origin and effect, and is a social responsibility. It represents a discrepancy between social standards and social reality. Also, such socially perceived variations must be viewed as corrigible (see Merton & Nisbet, 1961, pp. 6, 701).

THE PROBLEM

"The House on Sixth Street" became a case when Mrs. Smith came to an MFY Neighborhood Service Center to complain that there had been no gas, electricity, heat, or hot water in her apartment house for more than four weeks. She asked the agency for help. Mrs. Smith was 23 years old, black, and the mother of four children, three of whom had been born out of wedlock. At the time she was unmarried and receiving Aid to Families with Dependent Children. She came to the center in desperation because she was unable to run her household without utilities. Her financial resources were exhausted—but not her courage. The Neighborhood Service Center worker decided that in this case the building—the tenants, the landlord, and circumstances affecting their relationships—was of central concern.

A social worker then visited the Sixth Street building with Mrs. Smith and a community worker. Community workers are members of the community organization staff in a program that attempts to encourage residents to take independent social action. Like many members in other MFY programs, community workers are residents of the particular neighborhood. Most of them have little formal education, their special contribution being their ability to relate to and communicate with other residents. Because some of the tenants were Puerto Rican, a Spanish-speaking community worker was chosen to accompany the social worker. His easy manner and knowledge of the neighborhood enabled him and the worker to become involved quickly with the tenants.

Their first visits confirmed Mrs. Smith's charge that the house had been without utilities for more than four weeks. Several months before, the city Rent and Rehabilitation Administration had reduced the rent for each apartment to one dollar a month because the landlord was not providing services. However, this agency was slow to take further action. Eleven families were still living in the building, which had twenty-eight apartments. The landlord owed the electric company several thousand dollars. Therefore, the meters had been removed from the house. Because most of the tenants were welfare clients, the Department of Welfare had "reimbursed" the landlord directly for much of the unpaid electric bill and refused to pay

any more money to the electric company. The Department of Welfare was slow in meeting the emergency needs of the tenants. Most of the children (forty-eight from the eleven families in the building) had not been to school for a month because they were ill or lacked proper clothing.

The mothers were tired and demoralized. Dirt and disorganization were increasing daily. The tenants were afraid to sleep at night because the building was infested with rats. There was danger of fire because the tenants had to use candles for light. The seventeen abandoned apartments had been invaded by homeless men and drug addicts. Petty theivery is common in such situations. However, the mothers did not want to seek protection from the police for fear that they would chase away all men who were not part of the families in the building (some of the unmarried mothers had men living with them—one of the few means of protection from physical danger available to these women—even though mothers on public assistance are threatened with loss of income if they are not legally married). The anxiety created by these conditions was intense and disabling.

The workers noted that the mothers were not only anxious but "fighting mad"; not only did they seek immediate relief from their physical dangers and discomforts but they were eager to express their fury at the landlord and the public agencies, which they felt had let them down.

The circumstances described are by no means uncommon, at least not in New York City. Twenty percent of all housing in the city is still unfit, despite all the public and private residential building completed since World War II. At least 277,500 dwellings in New York City need major repairs if they are to become safe and adequate shelters. This means that approximately 500,000 people in the city live in inferior dwelling units and as many as 825,000 people in buildings that are considered unsafe (Emergency Committee, 1963). In 1962 the New York City Bureau of Sanitary Inspections reported that 530 children were bitten by rats in their homes and 198 children were poisoned (nine of them fatally) by nibbling at peeling lead paint, even though the use of lead paint has been illegal in the city for more than ten years. Given the difficulties involved in lodging formal complaints with city agencies, it is safe to assume that unreported incidents of rat bites and lead poisoning far exceed these figures.

The effect of such hardships on children is obvious. Of even greater significance is the sense of powerlessness generated when families go into these struggles barehanded. It is this sense of helplessness in the face of adversity that induces pathological anxiety, intergenerational alienation, and social retreatism. Actual physical impoverishment alone is not nearly so debilitating as poverty attended by a sense of unrelieved impotence that becomes generalized and internalized. The poor then regard much social learning as irrelevant, since they do not believe it can effect any environmental change (Purcell, 1964, p. 432).

INTERVENTION AND THE SOCIAL SYSTEMS

Selecting a point of intervention in dealing with this problem would have been simpler if the target of change were Mrs. Smith alone, or Mrs. Smith and her co-tenants, the clients in whose behalf intervention was planned. Too often, the client system presenting the problem becomes the major target for intervention, and the intervention method is limited to the one most suitable for that client system. However, Mrs. Smith and the other tenants had a multitude of problems emanating from many sources, any one of which would have warranted the attention of a social agency. The circumstantial fact that an in-

dividual contacts an agency that offers services to individuals and families should not be a major factor in determining the method of intervention. Identification of the client merely helps the agency to define goals; other variables are involved in the selection of method. As Burns and Glasser (1963) have suggested:

It may be helpful to consider the primary target of change as distinct from the persons who may be the primary clients. . . . The primary target of change then becomes the human or physical environment toward which professional efforts via direct intervention are aimed in order to facilitate change. (p. 423)

The three major factors that determined MFY's approach to the problem were (1) knowledge of the various social systems within which the social problem was located (i.e., social systems assessment), (2) knowledge of the various methods (including non-social work methods) appropriate for intervention in these different social systems, and (3) the resources available to the agency (Specht & Reissman, 1963).

The difficulties of the families in the building were intricately connected with other elements of the social system related to the housing problem. For example, seven different public agencies were involved in maintenance of building services. Later other agencies were involved in relocating the tenants. There is no one agency in New York City that handles all housing problems. Therefore, tenants have little hope of getting help on their own. In order to redress a grievance relating to water supply (which was only one of the building's many problems) it is necessary to know precisely which city department to contact. The following is only a partial listing:

No water—Health Department

Not enough water—Department of Water Supply

No hot water—Buildings Department

Water leaks—Buildings Department

Large water leaks—Department of Water Supply

Water overflowing from apartment above—Police Department

Water sewage in the cellar—Sanitation Department

The task of determining which agencies are responsible for code enforcement in various areas is not simple, and in addition one must know that the benefits and services available for tenants and for the community vary with the course of action chosen. For example, if the building were taken over by the Rent and Rehabilitation Administration under the receivership law, it would be several weeks before services would be re-established, and the tenants would have to remain in the building during its rehabilitation. There would be, however, some compensations: tenants could remain in the neighborhood—indeed, in the same building—and their children would not have to change schools. If, on the other hand, the house were condemned by the Buildings Department, the tenants would have to move, but they would be moved quickly and would receive top relocation priorities and maximum relocation benefits. But once the tenants had been relocated—at city expense—the building could be renovated by the landlord as middle-income housing. In the Sixth Street house, it was suspected that this was the motivation behind the landlord's actions. If the building were condemned and renovated, there would be twenty-eight fewer low-income housing units in the neighborhood.

This is the fate of scores of tenements on the Lower East Side because much new middle-income housing is being built there. Basic services are withheld and tenants are forced to move so that buildings may be renovated for middle-income tenants. Still other buildings are allowed to deteriorate with the expectation that they will be bought by urban renewal agencies.

It is obvious, even limiting analysis to the social systems of one tenement, that the problem is enormous. Although the tenants were the clients in this case, Mrs. Smith, the tenant group, and other community groups were all served at one point or another. It is even conceivable that the landlord might have been selected as the most appropriate recipient of service. Rehabilitation of many slum tenements is at present nearly impossible. Many landlords regard such property purely as an investment. With profit the prime motive, needs of low-income tenants are often overlooked. Under present conditions it is financially impossible for many landlords to correct all the violations in their buildings even if they wanted to. If the social worker chose to intervene at this level of the problem, he might apply to the Municipal Loan Fund, make arrangements with unions for the use of non-union labor in limited rehabilitation projects, or provide expert consultants on reconstruction. These tasks would require social workers to have knowledge similar to that of city planners. If the problems of landlords were not selected as a major point of intervention, they would still have to be considered at some time since they are an integral part of the social context within which this problem exists.

A correct definition of interacting social systems or of the social worker's choice of methods and points of intervention is not the prime concern here. What is to be emphasized is what this case so clearly demonstrates: that although the needs of the client system enable the agency to define its goals, the points and methods of intervention cannot be selected properly without an awareness and substantial knowledge of the social systems within which the problem is rooted.

DEALING WITH THE PROBLEM

The social worker remained with the building throughout a four-month period. In order to deal effectively with the problem, he had to make use of all the social work methods as well as the special talents of a community worker, lawyer, city planner, and various civil rights organizations. The social worker and the community worker functioned as generalists with both individuals and families calling on caseworkers as needed for specialized services or at especially trying times, such as during the first week and when the families were relocated. Because of the division of labor in the agency, much of the social work with individuals was done with the help of a caseworker. Group work, administration, and community organization were handled by the social worker, who had been trained in community organization. In many instances he also dealt with the mothers as individuals, as they encountered one stressful situation after another. Agency caseworkers also provided immediate and concrete assistance to individual families, such as small financial grants, medical care, homemaking services, baby-sitting services, and transportation. This reduced the intensity of pressures on these families. Caseworkers were especially helpful in dealing with some of the knotty and highly technical problems connected with public agencies.

With a caseworker and a lawyer experienced in handling tenement cases, the social worker began to help the families organize their demands for the services and utilities to which they were legally entitled but which the public agencies had consistently failed to provide for them.

The ability of the mothers to take concerted group action was evident from the beginning, and Mrs. Smith proved to be a natural and competent leader. With support, encouragement, and assistance from the staff, the mothers became articulate and effective in negotiating with the various agencies involved. In turn, the interest and concern of the agencies increased markedly when the mothers began to visit them, make frequent telephone calls, and send letters and telegrams to them and to politicans demanding action.

With the lawyer and a city planner (an agency consultant), the mothers and staff members explored various possible solutions to the housing problem. For example, the Department of Welfare had offered to move the families to shelters or hotels. Neither alternative was acceptable to the mothers. Shelters were ruled out because they would not consider splitting up their families, and they rejected hotels because they had discovered from previous experience that many of the "hotels" selected were flop-houses or were inhabited by prostitutes.

The following is taken from the social worker's record during the first week:

Met with the remaining tenants, several Negro men from the block, and [the city planner]. . . . Three of the mothers said that they would sooner sleep out on the street than go the Welfare shelter. If nothing else, they felt that this would be a way of protesting their plight . . . One of the mothers said that they couldn't very well do this with most of the children having colds. Mrs. Brown thought that they might do better to ask Reverend Jones if they could move into the cellar of his church temporarily. . . . The other mothers got quite excited about this idea because they thought that the church basement would make excellent living quarters.

After a discussion as to whether the mothers would benefit from embarrassing the public agencies by dramatically exposing their inadequacies, the mothers decided to move into the nearby church. They asked the worker to attempt to have their building condemned. At another meeting, attended by tenants from neighboring buildings and representatives of other local groups, it was concluded that what had happened to the Sixth Street building was a result of discrimination against the tenants as Puerto Ricans and Negroes. The group—which had now become an organization—sent the following telegram to city, state, and federal officials:

We are voters and Puerto Rican and Negro mothers asking for equal rights, for decent housing and enough room. Building has broken windows, no gas or electricity for four weeks, no heat or hot water, holes in floors, loose wiring. Twelve of forty-eight children in building sick. Welfare doctors refuse to walk up dark stairs. Are we human or what? Should innocent children suffer for landlords' brutality and city and state neglect? We are tired of being told to wait with children ill and unable to attend school. Negro and Puerto Rican tenants are forced out while buildings next door are renovated at high rents. We are not being treated as human beings.

For the most part, the lawyer and city planner stayed in the background, acting only as consultants. But as the tenants and worker became more involved with the courts, and as other organizations entered the fight, the lawyer and city planner played a more active and direct role.

RESULTANT SIDE-EFFECTS

During this process, tenants in other buildings on the block became more alert to similar problems in their buildings. With the help of the community development staff and the housing consultant, local groups and organizations such as tenants' councils and the local chapter of the Congress of Racial Equality were enlisted to support and work with the mothers.

Some of the city agencies behaved as though MFY had engineered the entire scheme to embarrass them—steadfastly disregarding the fact that the building had been unlivable for many months. Needless to say, the public agencies are overloaded and have inadequate resources. As has been documented, many such bureaucracies develop an amazing insensitivity to the needs of their clients (Bendix, 1952, pp. 114–134). In this case, the MFY social worker believed that the tenants—and other people in their plight—should make their needs known to the agencies and to the public at large. He knew that when

these expressions of need are backed by power—either in numbers or in political knowledge—they are far more likely to have some effect.

Other movements in the city at this time gave encouragement and direction to the people in the community. The March on Washington and the Harlem rent strike are two such actions.

By the time the families had been relocated, several things had been accomplished. Some of the public agencies had been sufficiently moved by the actions of the families and the local organizations to provide better services for them. When the families refused to relocate in a shelter and moved into a neighborhood church instead, one of the television networks picked up their story. Officials in the housing agencies came to investigate and several local politicans lent the tenants their support. Most important, several weeks after the tenants moved into the church, a bill was passed by the city council designed to prevent some of the abuses that the landlord had practiced with impunity. The councilman who sponsored the new law referred to the house on Sixth Street to support his argument.

Nevertheless, the problems that remain far outweigh the accomplishments. A disappointing epilogue to the story is that in court, two months later, the tenants' case against the landlord was dismissed by the judge on a legal technicality. The judge ruled that because the electric company had removed the meters from the building it was impossible for the landlord to provide services.

Some of the tenants were relocated out of the neighborhood and some in housing almost as poor as that they had left. The organization that began to develop in the neighborhood has continued to grow, but it is a painstaking job. The fact that the poor have the strength to continue to struggle for better living conditions is something to wonder at and admire.

IMPLICATIONS FOR PRACTICE

Social work helping methods as currently classified are so inextricably interwoven in practice that it no longer seems valid to think of a generic practice as consisting of the application of casework, group work, or community organization skills as the nature of the problem demands. Nor does it seem feasible to adapt group methods for traditional casework problems or to use group work skills in community organization or community organization method in casework. Such suggestions—when they appear in the literature—either reflect confusion or, what is worse, suggest that no clearcut method exists apart from the auspices that support it.

In this case it is a manifestation of a social problem—housing—that was the major point around which social services were organized. The social worker's major intellectual task was to select the points at which the agency could intervene in the problem and the appropriate methods to use. It seems abundantly clear that in order to select appropriate points of intervention the social worker need not only understand individual patterns of response, but the nature of the social conditions that are the context in which behavior occurs. As this case makes evident, the social system that might be called the "poverty system" is enduring and persistent. Its parts intermesh with precision and disturbing complementarity. Intentionally or not, a function is thereby maintained that produces severe social and economic deprivation. Certain groups profit enormously from the maintenance of this system, but larger groups suffer. Social welfare—and, in particular, its central profession, social work—must examine the part it plays in either maintaining or undermining this socially pernicious poverty system. It is important that the social work profession no longer regard social conditions as immutable and a social reality to be accommodated as service is provided to deprived persons with an ever increasing refinement of technique. Means should be developed whereby agencies can affect social problems more directly, especially through institutional (organizational) change.

The idea advanced by MFY is that the social worker should fulfill his professional function and agency responsibility by seeking a solution to social problems through institutional change rather than by focusing on individual problems in social functioning. This is not to say that individual expressions of a given social problem should be left unattended. On the contrary, this approach is predicated on the belief that individual problems in social functioning are to varying degrees both cause and effect. It rejects the notion that individuals are afflicted with social pathologies, holding, rather, that the same social environment that generates conformity makes payment by the deviance that emerges. As Nisbet points out ". . . socially prized arrangements and values in society can produce socially condemned results" (Merton & Nisbet, 1961, p. 7). This should direct social work's attention to institutional arrangements and their consequences. This approach does not lose sight of the individual or group, since the social system is composed of various statuses, roles, and classes. It takes cognizance of the systemic relationship of the various parts of the social system, including the client. It recognizes that efforts to deal with one social problem frequently generate others with debilitating results.

Thus it is that such institutional arrangements as public assistance, state prisons, and state mental hospitals, or slum schools are regarded by many as social problems in their own right. The social problems of poverty, criminality, mental illness, and failure to learn that were to be solved or relieved remain, and the proposed solutions pose almost equally egregious problems.

This paper has presented a new approach to social work practice. The knowledge, values, attitudes, and skills were derived from a generalist approach to social work. Agencies that direct their energies to social problems by effecting institutional change will need professional workers whose skills cut across the broad spectrum of social work knowledge.

Reading 1-2

Social Work Practice: A Life Model*

Alex Gitterman and Carel B. Germain

Over the years of its development, social work practice has had difficulty integrating two historical traditions: the emphasis on knowledge and skills to effect change in persons, and the emphasis on knowledge and skills to effect change in environments. Similarly, there has been difficulty in integrating method specializations of casework, group work, and community organization. In the past decade, new social conditions and new knowledge propelled social work to reexamine its formulations of practice and its technical interventions. Most efforts to reconceptualize the profession's practice manifest some common features: a view of human phenomena through a systems perspective, an emphasis on institutional and environmental structures, and the identification of various "target systems" as the loci for professional intervention (Goldberg & Middleman, 1974; Goldstein, 1973; Meyer, 1970; Pincus & Minahan, 1973; Siporin, 1975). Yet, quite naturally, a gap exists between the new knowledge and its use in everyday practice.

The life model integrates the treatment and reform traditions by conceptualizing and emphasizing the dysfunctional transactions between people and their social and physical environments. Through an ecological theoretical perspective and a reciprocal conception of social work function, people and their environments receive simultaneous professional attention. Needs and issues are reconceptualized from "personality states" and "environmental states" to problems in living.

Within the ecological perspective, human beings are conceived as evolving and adapting through transactions with all elements of their environments. In these adaptive processes the human being and the environment reciprocally shape each other. People mold their environments in many ways and, in turn, must then adapt to the changes they create (Germain, 1973).

Increasingly, industrial society has posed complex adaptive tasks to human beings at all stages of the life cycle. The structures and functions of familial, organizational, and other environmental systems have undergone dramatic change.

* Reprinted from *Social Service Review*, vol. 50, no. 4, December 1976, by permission of The University of Chicago Press. © 1976 by the University of Chicago Press. All rights reserved.

The family's capacity for fulfilling its integrative functions has been taxed by its members' divergent opportunities, needs, responsibilities, and interests. At the same time, institutions are experiencing serious problems in managing their intended service functions. These dramatic changes and disjunctions between adaptive demands and the resources available for meeting the demands generate stress. People's styles of coping with stress emerge from their perceptions of environmental demands and resources and of their own response capabilities.

Social work's distinctive functions and tasks arise from its social purpose: to strengthen coping patterns of people and to improve environments so that a better match can be attained between people's adaptive needs and potential and the qualities of their impinging environments (Gordon, 1969; Schwartz, 1971a). Professional action is directed toward helping people and their environments overcome obstacles that inhibit the development of adaptive capacities. Assessment upon which action is based derives from a nonlinear view of causality. Assessment requires an understanding of the functions served by current transactions for the person and for the environment. In helping a person defined by self or others as depressed, for example, professional concern centers on the function of the depression for the person and his primary groups and on how it affects their reciprocal perceptions and transactions. Intervention then takes on the character of natural life processes that alter, use, or support properties of the environment, the coping qualities of the person(s), and the nature of the transactions between them.

Within this transactional focus, problems in living faced by individuals, families, and groups are further specified as: (1) problems and needs associated with tasks involved in life transitions; (2) problems and needs associated with tasks in

using and influencing elements of the environment; and (3) problems and needs associated with interpersonal obstacles which impede the work of a family or a group as it deals with transitional and/ or environmental tasks. Social work processes are directed to client problems and needs within one or more of these areas.

While these problems of living are interelated, each comprises distinctive client tasks and professional interventions. For example, a sixty-five-year-old person may experience interrelated stresses arising out of the transition from employment to retirement, tensions within the immediate family, and unresponsive environmental institutions. The client and worker might contract to focus on the life transitional tasks, or the environmental tasks, or the maladaptive interpersonal processes among the family (or group) members. The focus might be on two or all three areas.[1] While the worker must pay attention to the complex interrelationships among these life forces, both the worker and the client must be clear at any given moment as to the specific problem-in-living receiving attention.

Emerging from the contracting process through which problems or needs are mutually defined, identified, and partialized, a division of labor evolves between client and worker (Gitterman, 1971; Kadushin, 1972; Mallucio & Marlow, 1974; Seabury, 1976). The client focuses on his life tasks; the worker seeks to assure the conditions necessary for the client to achieve the tasks (Studt, 1968). The worker remains continuously in tune with shifts in the client's concern from one area to another, drawing on knowledge and skill in the use

---

[1] In these situations, it is essential that the client and worker work on the same problem in living at any moment in time. Otherwise, one might, for example, focus on an environmental definition while the other might focus on a psychological identity definition.

of communication processes, actions to restructure situations, and environmental processes and resources.

TRANSITIONAL PROBLEMS AND NEEDS

Individual development occurs when internal, age-specific maturational phases transact with phase-specific environmental nutrients (Erikson, 1959). Thus every developmental stage represents mutual tasks for the individual and for the individual's environment. The individual must meet maturational and social demands that may require shifts in self-concept, new ego skills, and the relinquishment of customary coping patterns for novel strategies. At the same time, the environment must provide the required opportunities and resources. Incomplete or thwarted task resolution at one stage tends to create difficulties in task resolution associated with a later stage.

Similarly, there are status-role changes that occur over the life span, such as a new job, migration to a new environment, marriage, and parenthood. Some status changes coincide with developmental stages, as in retirement or entry into junior high school. Some do not necessarily coincide with developmental phases, for example, migration or a new job. These changes, too, pose demands for new ego skills, the replacement of familiar adaptive patterns by new coping mechanisms, and shifts in self-concept.

There are also changes to less valued and to stigmatized statuses when one becomes a foster child, a mental patient, a parolee or probationer, a welfare client, or a physically handicapped person. The tasks associated with these changes, however, are of a different order. In some instances, they are directed toward escaping the status, although the more stigmatized statuses have limited legitimized exits in

our society.[2] In other instances, these changes place heavy coping demands in maintaining a positive self-image, controlling anxiety and depression, and taking effective action to escape the boundaries of these statuses. Moreover, occupants of these statuses are also dealing with the same developmental, status, and crisis tasks as other citizens. Hence, they carry an enormous adaptive burden, but with far less environmental nutriment.

Finally, there are the expectable and the exceptional crisis events of life, the threats and natural losses that come to everyone over time and those catastrophic threats and losses that come too early, or too "unfairly," or too profoundly to be considered expectable in all lives. Such situational crises have an immediacy and enormity of demand that distinguish them, in part, from the developmental and role transitions previously discussed.[3] They often require immediate mobilization of the environment and of the individual in order to prevent collapse.

It is not only the individual, however, who experiences such transitional challenges. Families have a life cycle of their own. They also move through identifiable stages of development, status changes, and crisis events, such as a new marriage, the birth of a child, unemployment, or illness, posing tasks for the collectivity that may not always mesh with the transitional tasks of individual members (O'Connell, 1972, pp. 203–210). Similarly, groups proceed through interactional phases of development (Bennis & Sheppard, 1956, pp. 415–537; Garland, Jones, & Kolodny, 1968,

---

[2] Even though the formal role may be vacated, the person is assigned a similarly stigmatized status such as ex-mental patient or ex-prisoner.

[3] Developmental and social transitions occasionally take on the nature of crisis when the tasks are perceived by the person or the environment as insurmountable.

pp. 12–53), status changes, and crisis events which threaten the life of the group.

In attempts to help individuals, families, and groups with developmental, status-role, and crisis tasks, certain practice principles become particularly relevant. Worker activity is directed toward exploration and mutual clarity of problem definition. People's stresses are legitimized as "normal" life processes appropriate for helping attention. Workers partialize problems into smaller, more manageable elements. At the same time, they search for patterns of behavior and for connections between past and present patterns. At times, it may be difficult for the worker to invite this elaboration. The content may be quite painful (for example, loss), or may touch upon social taboos (for example, sexuality), or may trigger the worker's own unresolved developmental issues (for example, ethnic identity). It becomes essential for the worker to sustain the content, carefully avoiding premature reassurance or interpretations. The worker and client together seek and use information, scan alternatives, and weigh costs and benefits. A central concern is to provide opportunity for resolution of life tasks in the life situation appropriate to the client's sense of time and space, lifestyle and aspirations. (Real life action, or even role play, can be helpful in working on adaptive tasks.)

In families and groups, the worker also helps members to separate out their individual developmental goals and tasks from the expectations exerted by the collectivity and by environmental forces. At the same time, the worker encourages family and group members to be responsive to one another as they seek areas of common developmental expectations and tasks. And people are always encouraged to use family, peer group, and environmental supports in pursuing their transitional tasks.

ENVIRONMENTAL PROBLEMS AND NEEDS

This area of help is concerned with adaptive issues arising from the nature of the social and physical environments. The *social* environment, which man has created and to which individuals must then adapt, includes institutions, organizations, and social networks. The *physical* environment includes both natural and man-made structures and objects, and time and space.

A distinct feature of contemporary urban society is the existence of complex organizations and their impact on people's daily lives. As they become larger and more complex, organizations are more difficult to administer and coordinate. Out of necessity, they become preoccupied with the standardization of policies and procedures. Institutional homeostasis and administrative "peace and quiet" often take precedence over people's individualized service needs.

Within this context, people turn to organizations for essential services (health, education, welfare). At times, their contacts add to their distress instead of mitigating or alleviating it. Their encounters with organizational representatives may lead to a sense of personal inadequacy and stigma. While many organizational representatives are motivated to carry out their specialized functions at least initially, they sometimes build defenses against dehumanizing and frustrating conditions and a sense of failure. They may then become blind to the injustices and social inequities within their own and other organizations, and withdraw affect, zeal, and commitment to their service. Others may become overidentified with organizational need at the expense of client need. Still others may develop and rely on stereotyped characterizations of client behaviors.

Stigmatized by their client status and

unaware of their rights and privileges, people often accept and resign themselves to these conditions. Hence, the social worker has a particularly critical function in helping people to use and to influence elements of their organizational environment. Knowledge and assessment[4] of organizational structures, functions, and processes provide an important basis for professional influence.[5] Interventive strategies of influence[6] include differentially invoking or appealing to the formal organizational objectives, structures, roles, and policies favorable to the client's request but circumvented; the formal organizational and environmental accountability and sanctioning mechanisms; the organizational or individual representative's self-interest and self-esteem; the professional service ethic supportive of individualization; and the informal system in which favors are collected and exchanged (Dalton, 1970; Gouldner, 1960). The effectiveness of these collaborative strategies is dependent on the worker's professional competence, credibility, zeal, and resilience. Within a host setting especially, professional visibility and reputation for competence provide an essential means for organizational involvement and influence. If these collaborative strategies prove ineffective, the worker may turn to more adversarial behaviors, for example, petition, public criticism, and use of mass media.

The concept of *social network* refers to important figures in the environment, including relatives, friends, neighbors, and peers. Such a network often meets the needs of human beings for relatedness; provides recognition, affirmation, and protection from social isolation; and offers the means for identification and for socialization to the norms, values, knowledge, and belief systems of the particular culture. It serves as a mutual aid system essential for adaptation and for coping with stress. Some networks, however, may reinforce deviance, be subject themselves to maladaptive interpersonal processes, or undermine the client's sense of identity and autonomy. Some social networks are too loosely organized and integrated to serve as a source of support. Some clients may be without any social network at all.

Since attachment behavior in the human being has adaptive importance across the life cycle, the social network is an important dimension of the social worker's attention. Client and worker action can be directed toward mobilizing or strengthening real life ties between the client and significant others in the life space, finding new linkages or reestablishing old ones. In the absence of natural networks, worker and client may consider the possibility of relational experiences through the use of other levels of social work personnel, volunteers, and friendly visitors. Together, worker and client may consider the use of organized groups (Parent-Teacher Associations, Parents Without Partners, tenant councils, consumer groups, and so on) to meet relationship (and task) needs, or the construction of mutual aid systems to meet adaptive requirements and to exchange resources. All of these actions are close to life processes and hence are likely to be of more adaptive value than major reliance on the time-limited relationship with the worker.

We are beginning to understand how people organize and use space in the physical environment and how, in turn, spatial variables affect behavior. Ward geography, for example, is an important factor in the social interaction of residents of a geriatric facility or patients in a mental

---

[4] The depth and scope of an organizational assessment are dependent on such factors as client need, whether the worker is employed by the agency being negotiated, and previous contacts with the specific representative.

[5] Brager (1975) makes an important distinction between "helping" and "influencing" an organization.

[6] Prof. Irving Miller has been particularly helpful in identifying various practice strategies.

hospital. Spatial arrangements in class-rooms and treatment cottages may invite or discourage particular behaviors in children. Space, design, color, and decoration in social agencies communicate to users of services their differential statuses (Seabury, 1971). Social work interventions directed to spatial variables or to providing experiences in the natural world are used to enhance relatedness and increase the nutritiveness of the environment.

Whatever interventive strategies are used in helping people to deal with their social and physical environments, workers must take into account the consequences and implications of their actions on clients. At times clients can be hurt by professionals with benign intentions but dysfunctional interventions. Users of service need to be fully involved in the assessment and intervention processes. Through their full participation, users of service become educated to environmental structures, functions, and processes. They develop greater competence in negotiating their environment and in exerting control over achieving their life tasks.[7]

MALADAPTIVE INTERPERSONAL PROBLEMS AND NEEDS IN FAMILIES AND GROUPS

As the family or group works on the tasks associated with life transitions or with using and influencing the environment, it sometimes encounters impediments posed by maladaptive communication processes and relationship patterns. Such impediments may be poorly under-

stood or altogether outside the members' awareness. Behaviorally they are expressed through patterned scapegoating, power struggles, interlocking hostilities, mutual withdrawal, double binds, and other distortions. While these patterned behaviors often serve a latent function in maintaining the family or group equilibrium, the consequences are usually maladaptive for some members. Thus, these interpersonal obstacles to individual and collective growth and adaptation become a third area of help.

Practice interventions, then, include an assessment of the factors which generate the specific transactional obstacles. Our experience suggests that there are several repetitive sources of interpersonal conflict: (1) Discrepancy between an individual's and the collective's life transition tasks: A family may be preoccupied with its survival and maintenance, while its young adult member is striving for separation. Or a group in a late stage of its development may experience serious difficulty incorporating new members. (2) Dysfunctional accommodation to environmental pressures and inadequacies: In response to a hostile environment, some members may develop apathy that then interferes with mutual problem-solving. Others may cope by scapegoating one another. (3) Discrepancy among members' orientations to "power and love": One spouse may seek intimacy while the other requires emotional distance. Or the parents may disagree on matters of authority. (4) Normative conflicts among members, such as differing generational perceptions of right and wrong, attractive and unattractive, good and bad. (5) Compositional problems within the collective: A family or group may experience strain as a member leaves or a new or former member enters. Or a family or group may isolate a member because of deviant descriptive or behavioral characteristics.

When the focus is on helping families

---

[7] Group services have a unique potential for achieving this objective. They possess an inherent advantage in that (1) people can gain strength, security, and relief from being with others in a similar situation; (2) perceptions of personal psychological problems can be transferred into perceptions of collective, social problems; (3) collective action can gain greater institutional responsiveness; and (4) groups can be linked with other groups, thus representing a source for significant political action.

and groups to deal with such transactions as patterned scapegoating (Schulman, 1967; Vogel & Bell, 1968) or double-bind modes of communication (Haley, 1963), the worker invites and encourages the members to view the obstacle through a systemic perspective. The worker encourages mutuality among members by helping them search for common concerns and self-interests. At the same time, the worker reaches for and encourages the elaboration of differential perspectives. Strategically, it is often easier for members with the greater power and personal strength to begin the exploratory process. As work on the obstacle proceeds, the less powerful and more insecure members often require special support and encouragement to risk their perceptions and interpretations. Expression of members' divergent, discrepant perceptions needs to be partialized and the associated affect encouraged. If members attempt to avoid the content, the worker focuses, mediates, and guards the conditions of their agreed-upon contract. Throughout, the worker provides relevant facts, interpretations, and perceptions and lends professional strength, support, and faith in members' capacity to move beyond the painful obstacle.

In a similar way, interpersonal barriers can arise between worker and client(s) manifested in distorted communications and maladaptive relationship processes.

Frequently such barriers are defined as client "resistance" when, in fact, they are transactional in origin. They arise from incongruencies in perceptions and expectations; feelings related to age, sex, race, and ethnic differences; transference and countertransference; and ambivalences, cognitive discrepancies, and ambiguities. The worker has the responsibility for continuous vigilance concerning the possible existence of such barriers and for bringing them into open discussion so that mutual work on them may take place, including assessing their source, nature, and consequences (Gitterman & Schaeffer, 1972).

SUMMARY

The profession's social purpose has always referred to a dual interest in people and situations, but the lack of knowledge about their reciprocity made the practice application of social purpose difficult. This paper has attempted to present an integrated perspective on social work practice based on that reciprocity. The ecological perspective provides a means for capturing the transactional processes between human beings and their environments. The conceptualization of people's needs into three interrelated areas of problems-in-living transcends former methodolgical distinctions among case-work, family therapy, and group work and provides a life model for intervention.

References

Baer, Betty L., & Federico, Ronald C.   *Educating the baccalaureate social worker.* Cambridge, Mass.: Ballinger, 1978.

Bartlett, Harriet M.   *The common base of social work practice.* New York: National Association of Social Workers, 1970.

Bendix, Reinhard. Bureaucracy and the problem of power. In Robert K. Merton, Alisa Gray, Barbara Hockey, & Horan C. Sebrin (Eds.), *Reader in bureaucracy.* New York: Free Press, 1952.

Bennis, Warren, & Sheppard, H. A theory of group development. *Human Relations,* November 1956, *9,* 415–537.

Bisno, Herbert. A theoretical framework for teaching social work methods and skills with particular reference to undergraduate social welfare education. *Journal of Education for Social Work,* Fall 1969, *5,* 5–17.

Boehm, Werner W. The nature of social work. *Social Work,* April 1958, *3,* 10–19.

Brager, George. Helping vs. influencing: Some political elements of organizational change. Paper presented at the National Conference on Social Welfare, San Francisco, 1975.

Burns, Mary E., & Glasser, Paul H. Similarities and differences in casework and group work practice. *Social Service Review,* December 1963, *37,* 416–428.

Commission on Social Work Practice, National Association of Social Workers. Working definition of social work practice. *Social Work,* April 1958, *3,* 5–8.

Dalton, Gene W. Influence and organizational change. In Gene W. Dalton et al. (Eds.), *Organizational change and development.* Homewood, Ill.: Richard D. Irwin, 1970.

Emergency Committee for More Low Income Housing, *Facts about low income housing.* New York, 1963.

Erikson, Erik H. *Identity and the life cycle, psychological issues* (Monograph no. 1). New York: International Universities Press, 1959.

Garland, James A., Jones, Hubert E., & Kolodny, Ralph L. A model for stages of development in social work groups. In Saul Bernstein (Ed.), *Explorations in group work.* Boston: Boston University School of Social Work, 1968.

Germain, Carel B. The ecological perspective in casework practice. *Social Casework,* June 1973, *54,* 223–230.

Germain, Carel B. The ecological approach to people—Environment transactions. *Social Casework,* June 1981, *50,* 323–331.

Germain, Carel B. & Gitterman, Alex. Social work practice: A life model. *Social Service Review,* December 1976, *50,* p. 4.

Gitterman, Alex. Group work in the public schools. In William Schwartz & Serapio Zalba (Eds.), *The practice of group work.* New York: Columbia University Press, 1971.

Gitterman, Alex, & Schaeffer, Alice. The white professional and the black client. *Social Casework,* May 1972, *53,* 280–291.

Goldberg, Gale, & Middleman, Ruth. *Social service delivery: A structural approach to social work practice.* New York: Columbia University Press, 1974.

Goldstein, Howard. *Social work practice: A unitary approach.* Columbia: University of South Carolina Press, 1973.

Gordon, William. Basic constructs for an integrative and generative conception of social work. In Gordon Hearn (Ed.), *The general systems approach: Contributions toward an holistic conception of social work.* New York: Council of Social Work Education, 1969.

Gouldner, Alvin. The norm of reciprocity. *American Sociological Review,* April 1960, *25,* 161–168.

Haley, Jay. *Strategies of psychotherapy.* New York: Grune & Stratton, 1963.

Kadushin, Alfred. *The social work interview.* New York: Columbia University Press, 1972.

Kaplan, Abraham. *The conduct of inquiry: Methodology for behavioral science.* San Francisco: Chandler, 1964.

Kidneigh, John C. A note on organizing knowledge. In *Modes of professional education* (Vol. II). Tulane Studies in Social Welfare. New Orleans: School of Social Work, Tulane University, 1969.

Konopka, Gisela. *Edward C. Lindeman and social work philosophy.* Minneapolis: University of Minnesota Press, 1958.

Lee, Porter R. Social work: Cause or function. *Proceedings of the National Conference of Social Work,* 1929, pp. 3–20.

Lewis, Harold. Morality and the politics of practice. *Social Casework,* July 1972, *53,* 404–417.

Maluccio, Anthony N., & Marlow, Wilma D. The case for the contract. *Social Work,* January 1974, *9,* 28–37.

Merton, Robert K., & Nisbet, Robert A. (Eds.). *Contemporary social problems.* New York: Harcourt Brace Jovanovich, 1961.

Meyer, Carol H. *Social work practice: A response to the urban crisis.* New York: Free Press, 1970.

O'Connell, Patricia. Family developmental tasks. *Smith College Studies in Social Work,* June 1972, *42,* 203–210.

Pincus, Allen, & Minahan, Anne. *Social work practice: Model and method.* Itasca, Ill.: F. E. Peacock Publishers, 1973.

Purcell, Francis P. The helping professions and problems of the brief contact. In Frank Reissman, Jerome Cohen, & Arthur Pearl (Eds.), *Mental health of the poor.* New York: Free Press, 1964.

Purcell, Francis, & Specht, Harry. The house on sixth street. *Social Work,* October 1965, *10,* 69–76.

Rein, Martin. Social work in search of a radical profession. *Social Work,* April 1970, *15*(2), 13–33.

Schulman, Lawrence. Scapegoats, group workers and preemptive intervention. *Social Work,* April 1967, *12,* 37–43.

Schwartz, William. Social worker in the group. In National Conference on Social Welfare, *Social Welfare Forum.* New York: Columbia University Press, 1961.

Schwartz, William. Social group work: The interactionist approach. In Robert Morris (Ed.), *Encyclopedia of social work.* New York: National Association of Social Workers, 1971.

Seabury, Brett. Arrangement of physical space in social work settings. *Social Work,* October 1971, *16,* 43–49.

Seabury, Brett. The contract: Uses, abuses, and limitations. *Social Work,* January 1976, *21,* 16–21.

Siporin, Max. *Introduction to social work practice.* New York: Macmillan, 1975.

Specht, Harry, & Reissman, Frank. Some notes on a model for an integrated social work approach to social problems. New York: Mobilization for Youth, June 1963. (Mimeographed)

Studt, Elliot. Social work therapy and implications for the practice of methods, *Social Work Education Reporter,* June 1968, *16,* 22–24.

Taber, Merlin A., & Vattano, Anthony J.   Clinical and social orientations in social work: An empirical study. *Social Service Review*, March 1970, *44*, 34–43.

Vogel, E., & Bell, N.   The emotionally disturbed child as the family scapegoat. In E. Vogel & N. Bell (Eds.), *A modern introduction to the family*. New York: Free Press, 1968.

Chapter 2

Knowledge for
Social Work Practice

In this chapter we will discuss the attributes of a profession and the importance of knowledge in professional practice. The next task will be to define the various terms that will be found in this chapter. This chapter will also focus on the confusion between different types of knowledge and between knowledge and values that is often found in social work literature. Next, some of the complex problems involved in the selection and organization of knowledge for use as a base for practice actions will be presented. In conclusion, questions concerning the importance of knowledge, criteria for the selection of knowledge, and how to deal with ignorance when one is expected to be an expert will be examined.

WHAT IS A PROFESSION?

Literature on occupations generally lists the following elements as important distinguishing marks of a profession:

1. A high degree of generalized and systemic knowledge.
2. Community sanction.
3. A primary orientation to community interest rather than individual self-interest.
4. A high degree of skill involving responsibility and self-regulation of behavior that are internalized through formal education, work socialization, codes of ethics, and voluntary associations operated by the professionals themselves.
5. A culture including a value system.
6. A system of monetary and honorary rewards that are primarily an acknowledgement of work achievement and thus ends in themselves, not means to promotion of individual self-interest.

In this list of attributes of a profession the first quality on the list is a high degree of knowledge. When we think about a profession we often think first of the use of a superior skill in use of certain intervention techniques involving very complicated operations. Students often think of their education in a professional school as involving primarily training in how to do. Yet, as was developed in Chapter 1, to concentrate on the application of interventive techniques alone is to fail as a professional. To develop a high level of methodological skill, no matter how demanding and complex, and to apply it to all situations regardless of problem, goal, or capacity of the system is to miss the crucial distinction of a profession: that intervention skills are to be used selectively and differentially as determined by a body of theory and a process of deciding. Actually, professional interventive skills flow from the knowledge base of the profession and from the ability of each practitioner to select differentially from the wide range of such knowledge that which is appropriate to the case. The knowledge selected also needs to be that which gives the professional some guide to action. It is this possession of knowledge, together with the capacity to organize and apply it differentially to selection and applications of appropriate intervention actions in individual situations, that distinguishes a profession from other occupations.

Thus the important thing about professional knowledge is not only that it is generalized and systematic but that it must be available for use in unique human situations and congruent with the central values of the profession. This differentiates a profession from an academic pursuit. The acquiring of knowledge may be an end in itself in academic disciplines, but in a profession knowledge and theory is needed as a guide to action. For example, if one is to make some judgment as to what could be helpful to an adolescent with a problem of relationship to parents, one needs to have some knowledge of expected adolescent behavior, of parental responsibilities and feelings, and of the usual problems in the interactions of adolescents and their parents against which to assess this particular adolescent's problems.

In the last two paragraphs the terms *knowledge* and *theory* have been used as though they were interchangeable. And they are often used in this way in the literature. The next section will explore the meaning of these terms and will attempt to differentiate between knowledge and values which, because they both serve as the base of practice actions, are often confused.

DEFINITION OF TERMS

Perhaps a good beginning would be a discussion of what is meant by the term *knowledge* and by the phrase often found in social work literature, "the knowledge base of social work." Alfred Kadushin (1959, p. 39) states that the "knowledge base of social work is a comprehensive topic which encompasses the facts and theories, skills and attitudes, necessary for effective, efficient practice." In discussing the term *knowledge* as used in the working definition of social work practice (formulated by the National Association of Social Workers), William Gordon (1962), a social work educator who has long been interested in the problem of defining the scope of social work knowledge, states:

> Knowledge, in the working definition, designates generalized perceptions of individuals in their world which can be symbolized explicitly enough to be reliably communicated and are susceptible to testing and extension by the procedures of empirical

science. Knowledge differs from value assumptions not only in the degree to which its propositions have already been verified . . . but especially by the intent to verify them by scientific procedures. . . . A revised working definition should include under *knowledge* a wide range of propositions with respect to their degree of verification, but also exclude all assumptive preference rather than scientific necessity.

In this quotation Gordon attempts not only to define knowledge but also to differentiate it from another important base of social work practice which is discussed in Chapter 3—social work values. In a later article Gordon (1965, p. 34) elaborates more completely on this distinction:

Thus knowledge refers to what, in fact, seems to be, established by the highest standards of objectivity and rationality of which people are capable. Value refers to what people prefer or would want to be . . . it becomes clear that the heart of continuity and professional utility lies in what social work wants for people (values) and what it knows about them (knowledge).

Bartlett (1970) also addresses this distinction:

Values . . . refers to what is regarded as good and desirable. These are qualitative judgments; they are not empirically demonstrable. They are invested with emotion and represent a purpose or goal toward which the social worker's action will be directed. Knowledge propositions, on the other hand, refer to verifiable experience and appear in the form of rigorous statements that are made as objective as possible. Value statements refer to what is preferred; knowledge statements to what is confirmable. (p. 63)

Bartlett also points out that the statement "There is interdependence between individuals in this society" has often been included under values in social work literature although it is a demonstrable fact and thus should be classified as knowledge:

At any stage in the development of scientific knowledge there are some propositions that do not appear confirmable and thus must be regarded as value assumptions. In some instances, however, statements that are identical in form can be taken as either part of knowledge or as values. The idea that home is the best place for a child is an example; it can be taken as preferred or as a hypothesis for investigation. Here it is the intention regarding the proposition, rather than the actual substance, that makes the difference. There is also a long-range shift that will take place between a profession's body of knowledge and values. As scientific knowledge increases, some propositions that were at first preferred assumptions will become established as confirmed knowledge.

. . . Knowledge and value play distinctly different roles, both of which are needed. . . . Proper use of knowledge and value rests not only on distinguishing those propositions that belong in different categories but also in recognizing that the user's intent—whether as a preferred or confirmable statement—also makes a difference as to how they should be classified. According to this approach, propositions regarded as verifiable by science and research—and that are intended to be verified—are considered knowledge. (pp. 63–64)

Simply put, values answer the question of whether a proposition is right or wrong while knowledge answers the question as to whether something is true or false. This becomes very important to social work, both from the perspective of the worker and the client. If we believe we have tested evidence that a particular proposition is true and also believe that it is right there will be no desire to change it. In fact, there will be strong opposition to any proposal to change it. Some of our greatest conflicts in social work are found at the point where knowledge conflicts with value. For example, there are significant research findings that children who are treated violently often grow up to be adults who act violently toward others. However, there are people who believe that parents have a right to discipline children in any manner they please in order to control their behavior. A value cannot be challenged with another value, but it can be challenged with knowledge. Thus, one can ask that parents who believe differently about child care look at the evidence. There is significant evidence that living in abject poverty with too little food for adequate nourishment can be severely damaging to children both physically and psychologically, but we often confront a value system that says that people should "stand on their own two feet" and not take help from anyone "no matter what." In a democratic society all individuals have a right to their own value system. These values can only be challenged with empirical evidence that shows them to be damaging to human beings. We cannot demand that people change their values to conform to ours but, if tested knowledge showing a proposition to be true is available, people can be asked to consider this evidence.

Another example of the possible confusion between knowledge and value concerns the social work value of self-determination—the notion that people be allowed as far as possible to determine their own lifestyles (this concept will be discussed further in Chapter 3). If, in working with children, this value is not tempered with the knowledge that children need both freedom to grow and firm, consistent limits, we may be destructive to the child clients and/or to their families that come for help. Another important example of the confusion of value and knowledge is the way in which the knowledge that "clients will change with greater ease and less pain if they are actively involved in the process of deciding about change" is confused with the value that "clients as human beings have the right to make their own decisions about what they will do." In this instance knowledge and value support each other, but it is necessary to be clear in discussing work with the client whether one is acting primarily on the basis of knowledge, of value, or of both in some combination.

In earlier quotations Gordon (1962, 1965) discussed two kinds of knowledge: (1) knowledge that has been confirmed by empirical testing and/or observation and (2) knowledge that is accepted and acted upon as though it were true but has not yet been confirmed, although the intent is to confirm it eventually. This might be called *assumptive knowledge*. The important fact to note is that assumptive knowledge is open to efforts to test whether it is right or wrong. The only concern is that the person who engages in such testing follows the accepted guidelines of research design. If there is resistance to the effort to test a notion, it may be that a value is being dealt with and not a piece of assumptive knowledge. In the human services much knowledge is assumptive knowledge, notions that, given what tested base is available, seem to follow logically. The important thing for us as professional people is not so much the extent of the assumptive knowledge that is presently accepted but our willingness to expose it to exploration and the commitment to active attempts to test what is held as truths.

As pointed out earlier, in the beginning of this chapter, the terms *knowledge* and *theory* are often used interchangeably. What is the difference between these two concepts? Generally, knowledge is considered to be discrete facts while theory is a set of related and logical propositions that orders and relates facts into some sort of meaningful whole. For example, in social work the knowledge of defense mechanisms is often spoken of as psychoanalytic theory. This is because the concept of defense mechanisms is found within psychoanalytic theory.

A *theory* is a coherent group of general propositions or concepts used as principles of explanation for a class of phenomena—a more or less verified or established explanation accounting for known facts or phenomena and their interrelationship. If one thinks of knowledge as discrete bits of truth or discrete facts and observations like a pile of bricks, theory can be likened to a wall of bricks. In a theory the observations of the real world are ordered and put together in a certain way and held together by certain assumptions or hypotheses as bricks in a wall are held together by a material that cements them in place. Thus theory is a coherent group of general propositions, containing both confirmed and assumptive knowledge, held together by connective notions that seek to explain in a rational way the observed facts of phenomena and the relationship of these phenomena to each other.

Thus when the knowledge base of social work is discussed, this may mean tested knowledge, but it is more likely to concern various theories such as theories about people, how they develop, and the genesis of dysfunctioning; theories about people and their institutions and how these grow and change, as well as how they are functional and dysfunctional for people and their society. A list of unrelated facts, no matter how well verified by empirical observations, seldom tells us what they mean. It is theory constructed of known facts and phenomena held together by certain conceptual notions, that speaks to the meaning of facts.

Before leaving these definitions, one other word should also be explained. The term *principle* is often found in social work literature. This term can be used in two ways, and one should be aware of the context of the material to know which is meant. A principle may be an accepted or professed rule of conduct (often built on a value), or it may be a fundamental, primary, or general truth on which other truths depend. Used as an expression of a primary or general truth, a principle may have been empirically tested or it may be an assumption—a proposition taken as given.

To summarize: When one speaks of the knowledge base of social work, one usually is speaking of social work theory which is constructed partially of empirically tested knowledge and partially of assumptive knowledge which has not yet been empirically investigated but which can be subjected to such investigation. All this is in contrast to *values*, which are statements of what is preferred. Principles of action in social work rest upon both its values and its theories.

DEVELOPMENT OF KNOWLEDGE AND THEORY IN SOCIAL WORK

Within a human services profession three levels of theory generally develop: (1) a general theory of humanity which includes growth, development, functioning, and interrelationships; (2) the profession's practice theory, which is a statement of the nature of the principles and processes (general guides to action) of the particular profession and of the responsibilities assumed by the practitioner in the lives of the people with whom one works; and (3) specific operational procedures and skills. In social work, *as in all other professions,* the individual practitioners use knowledge that comes both from their own profession and from other disciplines. In particular, much of social work theory about people and their organizations, about how they grow, change and function, is borrowed. All professions rely on borrowed knowledge generated and tested in the basic disciplines. And all human service professions borrow from each other. This is partly because practicing professionals, social workers included, are more interested in the application of present knowledge than in the creation of new knowledge, and partly because social workers in discussing their practice knowledge in the journals of the profession often write only of unique individual situations without making appropriate attempts to generalize their experiences and to connect them with what is already known and set forth in the literature.

In discussing the problem of the generation of new knowledge vis-à-vis the application of borrowed knowledge, Sidney Berkowitz (1969), a practicing social worker and agency executive, points out that the present-day heroes in the field of medicine are the surgeons who are engaged in organ transplants. Yet, these men are, strictly speaking, technicians who are largely dependent on borrowed knowledge supplied by research biologists, biochemists, geneticists, physiologists, and other scientists. Berkowitz reminds the reader that the majority of professional social work practitioners are largely concerned with practical and emotional motives rather than with intellectual drives; that, although they may have contributed little to theory building in the basic social, behavioral, or biological sciences, they have contributed much to the knowledge of the development and refinement of various social work methods and techniques. In addition they have developed, and passed on to others, a kind of wisdom about human behavior that can come only from skilled clinical practice over time.

It would appear that if social work is to expand its tested knowledge it needs to develop a group of social work researchers interested in the generation and testing of new knowledge; and the practitioner needs to internalize the discipline necessary to keep abreast of the literature so that there may be an orderly accretion of knowledge, a wall built gradually by the appropriate placing of bricks, rather than bricks scattered over the landscape without even a blueprint as to how they might fit together.

In his inquiry into behavioral science, Abraham Kaplan (1964, pp. 304–305), a philosopher of science, points out that "knowledge grows not only by accretion and replacement of dubious elements by more sound ones but also by digestion, by remaking of the old cognitive materials into the substance of a new theory." Although the growth of scientific knowledge is marked by the replacement of poor theories by better ones, if knowledge is to advance, each new theory must take account of the theory it seeks to replace. Each new theory must reshape and integrate the old so that there is a continuity of knowledge development, even in the most revolutionary of times.

Kaplan says that the problem in the behavioral sciences is that this is not done, that individuals do not steep themselves in the theories available before taking off on a charge of their own. He is concerned that the lag in the behavioral sciences comes because researchers or theoreticians are busily drawing their own "new" blueprints. The social and behavioral sciences are replete with low-level empirical findings, but these remain empirical bricks, unusable until someone can find the connection to hold them together. It is frustrating and troubling to read a piece of research in social work that would never have been undertaken if the researcher had done the proper literature search. To use precious time and money to test something that has already been tested because of ignorance of past efforts is almost criminal given the great needs in this field. Thus the first principle of attempting to develop new knowledge is to thoroughly know the old and the work that went into developing it and to build all present efforts on this foundation.

Actually, as pointed out by Kadushin (1959), there is an embarrassingly rich literature that details what the social worker needs to know, do, and feel. But that knowledge is not organized in a manner that allows one to readily specify what one will need to know about what. Thus, nowhere will you find a book on all knowledge necessary for social work practice.

There have been any number of attempts to organize social work knowledge in a manner that would allow it to serve as a base for social work practice. As long ago as 1917 Mary Richmond made the first major attempt to pull together this knowledge in a pioneering work called *Social Diagnosis*. In 1923 the Milford Conference brought together a panel of experts to examine and extract the common elements of social casework practice (American Association of Social Workers, 1929). In his review of the history of social work knowledge Kadushin (1959) points out that between 1929 and 1959 there were two major reviews of social work education throughout the world and five major studies of social work education in the United States. Since then there have been other attempts to specify the knowledge base of social work. Perhaps the most comprehensive and exhaustive attempt yet made is the Curriculum Study of the Council on Social Work Education (Boehm, 1959). This study of 12 volumes can hardly be summarized in the space available in this text, or utilized by students in a discrete course. The most recent example of an attempt to set forth a knowledge base of social work practice is the Undergraduate Social Work Curriculum Development Project (Baer & Federico, 1978). It was undertaken for the purpose of further developing both the educational objectives and the curriculum content essential for the bachelor of social work degree. Kahn (1954) who has studied the knowledge base of social work, gives us some notion of the possible range of data with which social work may be concerned.

> Social work knowledge is, at the present time, in fact, an amalgam of several different things: (1) propositions borrowed from or markedly like those of psychiatry and some branches of psychology; (2) propositions fewer than in (1), borrowed from,

or markedly like those of, sociology, social anthropology, and a scattering from other fields; (3) apparently original propositions about how to do certain things in casework, group work, and community organizations; (4) methods, techniques, and attitudes, clearly derived from the fields of administration, statistics, and social research; (5) propositions about how to do things apparently derived from, or markedly like, those of progressive education. (p. 197)

Bartlett (1970) says:

> These needed concepts and criteria to guide the social worker's use of knowledge come first from the core of the profession. A comprehensive concept concerned with people interacting and coping with their environment gives promise of offering a central focus and a group of related subconcepts adequate to provide the necessary guidance. Here are to be found the ideas relating to life tasks, coping patterns, environmental demands and supports, exchanges, between people and their environment, and new concepts not yet perceived, all of which require disciplined examination and testing by the profession. (p. 152)

Recently the National Association of Social Workers—the professional organization of social workers, devoted two entire issues of *Social Work* (1977, 1981), to a consideration of the conceptual frameworks (theories) underlying social work practice. This gives evidence of the concern of the professional organization with the necessity to examine what social workers need to know in order to practice their profession.

The Council on Social Work Education, a body which speaks with some authority for schools of social work, from time to time issues statements on the council's official curriculum policy as an accrediting body of social work education which, among other issues, outline necessary curriculum for accredited schools. Since the membership of the council consists largely of social work educators, it could be assumed that this statement outlines the knowledge being taught, or seen as essential, by faculties of schools of social work. A recently completed policy statement by the council states that: "Social workers at both the undergraduate and graduate levels must demonstrate, according to their respective levels of entry, proficiency and competency in five professional foundation areas: Human Behavior and Social Environment, Social Welfare Policy and Services, Social Work Practice, Research, and the Field Practicum" *(Social Work Education Reporter,* 1982).

This list may not seem very helpful because it is so general. Yet these areas are the ones mentioned most in lists of social work knowledge. The problem is that these large chunks of knowledge need to be assembled and formed into some kind of meaningful whole in order to be useful. However, these large areas of knowledge have been very differently conceptualized, particularly as to principles that guide action, and there are no conceptual linkages. It is as though the profession had purchased an unfinished foundation in which different types of construction blocks were put together in different ways. This foundation cannot be built on until some way has been found to complete it so that the blocks not only fit together but can bear the weight of the structure being placed on top of it. Social workers are having much difficulty in finding what kind of construction blocks and what kind of construction can bring very diverse foundation walls together in such a way that they can be built on. Or perhaps some of the walls already built need to be torn down and, using the blocks of knowledge from the walls, constructed differently.

FUNCTION OF KNOWLEDGE IN SOCIAL WORK PRACTICE

Perhaps one of the reasons for the great problem in selecting and organizing knowledge has stemmed from the inability to define with any precision what social workers should be expert about in their practice. In the following quotation Meyer (1973, p. 38) speaks to the issue of the function of knowledge in social work practice: "Reliance upon empirical data has not been a hallmark of professional social work practice, partly because of our tools and objectives of research, but also, perhaps, because we have not yet agreed upon the goals and boundaries of social work practice." In the professions, in contrast to the basic sciences, knowledge is sought for use rather than for its own sake. What the social worker is supposed to be about dictates and "defines the boundaries of relevant knowledge as well as stimulating the search for new knowledge. Part of what makes a given profession distinctive is the nature of action or practice evolving from placing knowledge within a particular frame of reference" (Kamerman, Dolgoff, Getzel, and Nelson, 1973, p. 97).

This frame of reference is dictated by the purposes and values of the profession. Thus a profession does not seek to build knowledge outside of or beyond its purposes. However, knowledge and purpose have an interactive relationship in that, as purposes change, new knowledge is sought in order to deal with the new purposes, but also, as knowledge expands within a given purpose, it is sometimes found that the purpose itself is changed by the new knowledge (often more slowly than one would wish). But, remembering the earlier discussion on values, if only one solution is possible, or acceptable, there is no problem for empirical or experimental research. Thus "questions whose answers are dictated by the value system of our society and some questions that depend upon the value system of social work" are not researchable for purposes of knowledge building (Ripple, 1960, p. 28). So, values join purpose in setting a boundary to the knowledge that will be examined and incorporated.

Another problem in utilizing empirical research as a way of knowledge building in social work is the necessity we often face when making immediate choices in crisis situations. Since our society is not very good about planning ahead in relation to human services, problems often seem to arise with such rapidity that planning cannot be delayed while the relative merits of various solutions are investigated or empirical knowledge is acquired about the utilization of solutions. In such situations, social workers must act in the context of the knowledge already possessed, guided by how present knowledge is organized and evaluated in light of the problem.

It is well to remember that social work is a profession concerned with the impact of social problems on the lives of people, and the solutions that it can operationalize must fall within the value system and available resources of the times in which it acts. Thus, from the beginning, each generation of social workers has had to invest most of its energy in helping individuals, families, and institutions deal with the social crisis of the times, using the tools and knowledges available and improvising when these proved inadequate. Yet constantly changing functions of social work, as dictated by our constantly changing and developing society and the constantly expanding knowledge of mankind in interaction with social institutions and the physical world, demand a constantly expanding and reorganized and reformulated knowledge base so that social workers will need to be active learners for their entire professional lives. The demand for a more adequate knowledge base always seems to move ahead as an unachievable goal.

But, before there is too much self-criticism about social work's slowness in developing an adequate tested knowledge base in human services, it might also be considered that we understand mechanical systems better than human systems because we originally developed the parts of mechanical systems and put them together, to form a system after we understood the parts. People have, over the years, developed the wheel, the lever, and the pulley and have learned to know and use them as independent things before they put them together in complex configurations. However, in human societies, by contrast, there existed functioning wholes (individuals, families, groups, organizations, societies, and even nations) long before one became aware of the need to analyze these phenomena in any systematic way. A human family cannot be torn apart to investigate its parts. Observations and collection of data have to be accomplished in the middle of a family's active life, dealing with a living thing that grows, develops, and changes even as it is examined. And even in the physical sciences, the precision of prediction declines rapidly as complexity increases, so that it is not the social sciences alone that suffer from the difficulty of making predictions in relation to complex phenomena (Kuhn, 1974, p. xvii).

However, that may be, as social workers struggle to understand human behavior for the purpose of being helping persons in planned change processes, they very rapidly become aware that in order to acquire such understanding they will need to have some grasp of the goals and purposes of the behavior. Take, for example, a friend who called one day to say that he had quit his job. He had been having a great many disputes with his supervisor and the supervisor had told him that he would not be recommended for the next raise for which he was eligible. In addition, his wife wanted the family to return to the state where they had lived previously and he had been offered a better job with a huge increase in salary in that state. Thus it was no surprise when he resigned. This behavior could have been predicted and, by any commonsense criterion of understanding, it could easily be understood. However, it is necessary to recognize that such prediction and understanding came from one's perception of this man, his circumstances, his preferences, and their interrelationships within him, which are "wholes," rather than from any analysis of specific impulses impinging on his nervous system and of the transformation of such impulses into others leading to the activation of effectors.

To carry this example further and make it more applicable to social work, let us suppose that Mrs. X came to you as a client requesting that you help her make a decision in a situation similar to the friend's described earlier. However, Mrs. X's situation is complicated by the additional fact that her husband is employed and doesn't want to move, their youngest child is both retarded and physically handicapped, and the state in which the new job is located has no resources to continue the treatment and education the child has been receiving. Also, the new job does not provide health insurance under which much of the cost of treatment has been covered in her present employment. Feeling overwhelmed by the problem, Mrs. X really wants you to make the decision. What kinds of knowledge will you need in order to help this woman resolve her problem and come to a decision? And how do you select from and organize these knowledges to bear on this particular problem of this particular woman? Or consider the social worker in a large city high school located in a neighborhood in which there have recently been large population movements involving diverse racial groups. The social worker has been asked for help in handling the conflict between the school's black, Puerto Rican, and white students. What knowledge does the social worker need? Knowledge of the culture and social systems of the groups, knowledge of the problems in the larger community and its organizations, knowledge of the school system as an organization and its resources, and knowledge of community leaders as individuals and as leaders are all necessary. But how are these to be pulled together and utilized? Or consider the social worker employed by a federation of senior citizens' clubs who is asked to help the members obtain free public transportation during certain hours of the day, a privilege enjoyed by the aged in another city. What knowledge does this worker need? This will be further developed in Chapter 4.

IS KNOWLEDGE NECESSARY?

Given all the effort to identify the knowledge base of social work, and given the fact that it keeps eluding our grasp with such persistence, it might be asked whether knowledge and theory are necessary? The authors hold that it is. Although it has proven impossible to come up with a definitive statement of the knowledge base of the profession, all statements issued over the years are in remarkable substantive agreement at a generalized level. Thus there must be more grasp of a common knowledge base by social work practitioners than one might think. In addition the idea that one can operate without theory and knowledge is naive. Briar and Miller (1971) discuss this point:

> The choice for the practitioner is not whether to have a theory but what theoretical assumptions to hold. All persons acquire assumptions or views on the basis of which they construe and interpret events and behavior, including their own. These assumptions frequently are not explicit but are more what has been called "implicit theories of personality." Thus, the appeal for practitioners to be atheoretical amounts simply to an argument that theory ought to be implicit and hidden, not explicit and self-conscious.
>
> It is difficult, however, to defend an argument favoring implicit theory that, by definition, is not susceptible to scrutiny and objective validation and therefore cannot

be distinguished from idiosyncratic bias. The weaknesses of implicit theory are particularly serious for a profession in which a significant portion of the practitioner's activity consists in forming judgments and impressions about persons on the basis of which decisions are made affecting their lives in critical ways. . . .

Whether implicit or explicit, social workers' particular assumptions about human behavior can be expected to influence their professional actions, and therefore, to have important consequences for their clients. (pp. 53–54)

As an example of their point, Briar and Miller (1971, p. 30) indicate that the assumptions social workers hold about the possibilities of change in human nature will probably affect the degree of optimism with which they approach their clients and their problems; and that the premises about what can be changed will largely determine what one attempts to change. Perhaps the important things to keep in mind is that the interventive repertoire (what one does) of social workers grows out of and is dependent on knowledge based theory (what one assumes is the nature of the phenomenon and what one assumes will be of help) and values (what social workers see as desired ends) in interaction with the problems clients bring and the solution sought. The social worker's input into work with any client system depends on social work purposes and values; on how the worker understands the situation through the use of social work knowledge and theory; and on where one thinks "the client is" with the problem presented, based on what the practitioner hears the client say and how that is interpreted.

It is the social worker's responsibility to analyze and understand the situation before taking action. An essential of all professional practice is that it requires the rapid, continuous, expert selection and use of generalizations from the profession's body of knowledge, while remaining open to feedback from the client system that may force the abandonment of the first premise and the selection of another. Social workers put their professional knowledge to its first important use through their ability to "know where the client is," so that client and worker may be actively and appropriately involved in assessing the situation in which they are involved.

To summarize, social workers, particularly educators, are continually trying to identify the knowledge base on which the profession rests. However, the problems in such identification are almost overwhelming in that (1) the primary knowledge of the profession, empirically acquired, is drawn from the immense range of human problems as they are revealed by individuals in their situations and as they emerge in their cumulative aspects; (2) knowledge needed for many of the problem-solving activities of the profession has to be drawn from allied disciplines, with all the problems that this poses for selection, translation, and use; (3) the relevant knowledge is changing constantly and advancing rapidly; and (4) the profession is engaged in multiple functions and is uncertain as to what it should be expert about. For example, as the focus shifts from concern with the internal state of individuals and their adaptive functioning to a broader, and certainly more complex, view of individuals as participants in the interactional field of psychological and social forces, the knowledge base of social work begins to be organized differently than it was in earlier years, and an expanded range of approaches and techniques will have to be used. Helen Perlman

(1957, p. 27) recognizes this point when she says, "Knowledge, no sooner grasped, leaps forward again to excite new pursuit, and this is both the gratification and the frustration of trying to work on problems-in-change."

It is reassuring to realize, however, that all the statements of the Council on Social Work Education, all the minutes of conferences, and all the books and articles on social work knowledge, which if laid end to end might well circle the world several times, are in general agreement on the four broad areas of knowledge important to the social worker: (1) people in interaction with environment, (2) policy and programs, (3) research, and (4) practice actions. However, as already stated, the problem lies not in the task of finding a consensus on the broad areas of knowledge but in the task of selecting the critical concepts for use by the social work practitioner from this immense range of knowledge and in the task of relating these concepts to one another.

CRITERIA FOR THE SELECTION OF THEORY

A number of social work authors have attempted to develop statements of the criteria for the selection and ordering of social work knowledge. Briar and Miller (1971) discussing theories of intervention, develop the following criteria:

> An adequate theory must be explicit about the question of goals. It should be clear what is to be changed. . . . And an adequate theory must deal with the issue of who sets the goals of intervention and how this should be done.
>
> Second, an intervention theory can be evaluated according to its assumptions about what can be changed. . . . The optimistic view has the practical virtue of orienting the practitioner to the potentials for change and to searching for more effective and powerful ways to bring it about.
>
> Third, it should be clear what effective application of the theory would require of the client.
>
> Fourth, an adequate theory should specify, in behavioral terms what the practitioner needs to do in order to bring about the desired changes.
>
> Fifth, . . . an intervention theory should indicate what the practitioner needs to do in order to make sure that changes that occur within the treatment situation are carried over into the client's real life.
>
> Finally, the theory should tell the practitioner how to assess the outcome of . . . intervention efforts. (p. 180)

In a mimeographed paper, Charles Garvin (1972, p. 2) says that in making choices among theories, social workers need to take into account the following issues:

1. Degree of worker responsibility for changes in the situation.
2. Whether society is viewed as a given with social order as a predominant goal or whether society is conceived as composed of conflicting classes with worker choices affected by and having effects upon such conflicts.
3. Degree of control which worker seeks to exert on the client situation, regardless of how much control is potentially possible.
4. Relative importance in ameliorating problematic behavior of cognitive, affective, and motoric elements.

In an article discussing the development of a practice model for working with minority clients, Harriet Trader (1977) suggests the following questions as a criteria for selection of a theory for practice with any group of people, but suggests that they are especially relevant to practice with oppressed minority groups.

1. Pathology-health balance.   Do the basic concepts on which the theory is developed focus either on illness rather than on well-being or on deficits rather than strengths? Are the definitions of pathology and health based solely on the expectations of the dominant group in society? Do standards for health include a range of potentials that allows for minority group differences? Are class differences implied or stated in the models for either normality or abnormality?

2. Practitioner-client control balance.   Does the theory suggest that the worker carries more responsibility than the client in the process of changing the client's situation? Are clients perceived even subtly as being inferior to practitioners? Are practitioners seen as being obliged to use their knowledge and skills to increase clients' coping abilities? Does the theory view human beings as primarily dependent, interdependent, or independent? Can the theory allow for shared control? From what source does the practice derive its legitimacy?

3. Personal-societal impact balance.   In assigning causation for problems, does the theory embody a personal-deficit model rather than a societal model? Does the theory take into account historical as well as current societal conditions? Can the theory account for political-economic influences on behavior? Does the theory assign importance to variations in socialization experiences among oppressed minorities? Does the theory allow for linking of the personal to the social and environmental aspects of behavior?

4. Internal-external change balance.   Does the theory emphasize internal, psychic change in preference to changes that occur in society? Does the theory assume that the nature of society is primarily punitive rather than supportive? Are the definitions for change based essentially on the dominant societal patterns, or do they allow for a variety of patterns? To what extent is the view of change synonymous with adjustment?

5. Rigidity-flexibility balance.   Does the theory allow for the adjustment of concepts to the needs of particular groups? Do the abstract principles lend themselves to creative and differential application in practice? Can the theory accommodate new information about oppressed minorities? Does the theory relate to a view of the class structure of society? Does the theory demand an uncritical adherence to its postulates? Are there built-in criteria for continual assessment of the utility of the theory? (pp. 10–13)

The authors feel the Trader criteria are central to theory selection for practice with any population. In addition they would add the following comments. The knowledge base must encompass concepts (largely borrowed from other fields) of how human systems develop, change, and dysfunction, and how the interrelationships between systems are formed, continue to operate, or dysfunction. Given the goals and purposes of social work in society, it is necessary to select from borrowed knowledge that which helps us determine (1) what in any given situation should be the unit of observation, (2) what events in this unit should be observed, (3) how they should be observed, (4) how they should be related to each other in meaningful ways for the selection of methods of intervention, and (5) how it should be determined whether this intervention produced the kind of change that was sought.

DEALING WITH INCOMPLETE KNOWLEDGE

The practitioner-to-be in the here and now is faced with a great deal of knowledge to master—knowledge that is not very well related or integrated. Some of this knowledge is supported by empirical evidence; and some of it is assumptive and supported, if at all, by only the roughest of evidence. Sometimes knowledge and value are all mixed up, and yet there never seems to be the appropriate interrelationships between bits of knowledge. The fact is that the amount of knowledge needed is so great and some of it is so uncertain that social workers are faced with the uncomfortable fact that they are constantly intervening in people's lives on the basis of incomplete knowledge (as are all other practitioners in the human services). This, however, raises some hard questions. How can we help people to feel some confidence in us as helpers while we remain tentative and often uncertain about what we know? How can we doubt our effectiveness and still be effective? How can we act as experts and yet be so constantly aware of our own ignorance?

The stress of acting on the basis of incomplete knowledge confronts all professionals in the human services, but it may bear heaviest on social workers because of their commitment to individuals and their worth. Some social workers handle it by trying to forget what they do not know, and they become very dogmatic people, certain of their own knowledge but unable to grow because one cannot learn if one already knows. Some social workers try to handle it by emphasizing what they do not know and how helpless they are. They often run around looking for authorities while their client suffers from the lack of a secure helper. Some practitioners try to handle it by blaming the profession for their discomfort. They then find themselves in the bind of representing a profession in which they have no confidence and with which they have no identification. That must be one of the most uncomfortable binds of all. Such workers have neither read nor considered enough literature of other professions to understand that all professions are woefully lacking in knowledge of human beings and their interaction. These workers never come to grips with their need to know.

The demand that we act on uncertain knowledge goes along with being a helping person in complex and everchanging situations. The best way of living with this is to commit ourselves (1) to becoming active learners all the time and (2) to the scientific method as a part of our equipment. We need to pledge to ourselves each and everyday:

> I will try everything I know to help the client with which I am involved. In some aspects I may be too ignorant to truly know what way is best, but I will think carefully about my procedures, and I will be willing to assume the responsibility for my actions. I will neither be blinded by preconceptions nor will I be guilty of impulsively following a fleeting impulse or an easy answer. I will draw thoughtfully and responsibly upon every bit of knowledge that is available, and I will constantly and actively seek for more. I will be an insistent questioner rather than a passive taker, remaining identified with the profession while I vigorously question it. This is my solemn vow to my client. Thus, if my knowledge proves inadequate to the situation and the client's problem, my client and I will know that everything possible, given the present state of knowledge, has been done.

This book will offer some practice knowledge which we believe, from our study, our own questioning, and our own experience as both practitioners and teachers, will be helpful to people who are interested in beginning the challenging journey of becoming a truly competent social worker—a journey that no one ever completes. We believe that any other author, or even two, can offer only partial knowledge. For example, only a little knowledge about either the social services network or the human condition per se will be offered here. We have chosen to offer knowledge about professional social work practice itself, and believe that the other necessary knowledge (at least for now) can be acquired from other sources within the curriculum of the university and the social work major. We also believe that the knowledge given here will be the most valuable and the most immediately needed in fieldwork or on a first job. In some ways we are building the structure and trusting that you will be able to construct the basement from other sources. This may mean that for the time being your building is setting somewhat uncertainly on jacks without the underpinnings that will gradually have to be put in place.

RECAPITULATION

In this chapter we have looked at social work knowledge and the problems involved in the selection and organization of knowledge for professional practice. We have pointed out that the functions of a profession determine the parameters of the knowledge that helps in the delivery of services, the maintenance of organizations, and the effecting of change. We need to know more about the process of human and social change, the design of services responsive to the human systems that seek to utilize our help, and the final evaluation of what we do.

We have attempted to set forth some guidelines for the selection of theory, and have offered some ways of dealing with our feelings when we are aware of the need to act on incomplete knowledge. We would further remind our readers that all knowledge of human systems and their change is now and may be forever incomplete.

A LOOK FORWARD

At the end of this chapter we have included a reading entitled, "Learned Helplessness" by Carol E. Hooker. Read the article carefully. Now turn to the part of the article that is entitled "Loss and Depression." In the beginning paragraphs of this section a number of theories of the cause of depression are briefly set forth. There may be some truth in each of these notions. However, in many situations the authors find the theory of learned helplessness the best explanation of the sense of apathy and of a low-grade pervasive depression that seems to pervade many of the most difficult family situations social workers encounter. Such an approach to certain depressive states fits well with other theories that the authors find compatible with social work purposes, such as White's ego psychology (to be discussed in Chapter 4) which holds that the central push in each of us is to control our own life situation. Thus the belief that we cannot carry out this most central function of our life, the control of our own destiny, would appear very naturally to lead inevitably to depression.

The second piece of material appearing at the end of the chapter is the actual recording of work with a client submitted by a student in a field placement. It is an account of the first interview, the student's assessment of the situation, and the follow-up activities. It would be very helpful in understanding the material in this chapter if readers would make a list of the knowledge they believe the practitioner utilized in the interview and in making an assessment of the situation. What were the assumptions that the worker operated on? Can you think of other pieces of knowledge or theories that might be useful in this situation?

Reading 2-1

Learned Helplessness*

Carol E. Hooker

A guiding principle of social work practice is the disciplined application of professional knowledge and skills to help clients become more functional and adaptive human beings. The author contends that effective, as well as impaired, social and psychological functioning is greatly influenced by one's beliefs—beliefs that are learned through experience with life events. One particular type of impaired social and psychological functioning is learned helplessness—the idea that one's own actions have no influence on or relationship to the outcomes of events and experiences. Learned helplessness is the assumption of no control—the belief that nothing one does makes a difference (Seligman, 1975).

The theoretical concept of learned helplessness is relatively new to the behavioral sciences and its application to mental health practice is even newer. Nevertheless, the learned helplessness model of human dysfunctioning offers a viable framework that social workers and other mental health professionals can use to guide their understanding of reactive depression. In addition, as the author will demonstrate, this model has important implications for crisis theory and intervention. The purpose of this article is to acquaint the reader with the recently developed concept of learned helplessness and to offer suggestions for applying this concept to clinical practice.

Implicit in the concept of learned help-lessness is the assumption that events in life are either controllable or uncontrollable, and that it is a person's experiences with these events which shape the belief in his own adequacy. Controllability or uncontrollability are defined here according to the contingencies that exist between one's behavior when faced with an event and that event's eventual outcome. Thus, if the outcome of an event depends on one's own actions, that event is defined as controllable. As such, there exists a synchrony between one's behavior and the outcome of the event which assumes that what one does makes a difference. In contrast, if the outcome of an event occurs independently of one's actions, this event is considered to be uncontrollable. In uncontrollable events no synchrony exists between action and outcome; rather there is a noncontingent relationship between action and outcome, so that nothing one does will affect the outcome of the event (Seligman, 1975, pp. 9–20).

The way in which one couple faced an uncontrollable event is described in the following case study.

As an early spring rain fell outside, Michael and Linda heard radio newscasts warn that a nearby river was rising to flood level. However, since their home was over two miles from the swelling river, the couple remained unconcerned. What they failed to consider was the possibility that their local drainage system might not be able to absorb the day's steady rainfall. After a relaxed evening Michael and Linda suddenly heard the terrifying sound of water rushing into the lower level of their house. Frantically, they ran downstairs and began their frenzied attempts to halt the water's insistent flow. Baffled by the futility of every alternative, Michael and Linda faced the paralyzing realization

* Copyright 1976, National Association of Social Workers, Inc. Reprinted by permission of the author and publisher from *Social Work*, May 1976, *21:3*, pp. 194–198.

that nothing they could do would stop the rising flood waters.

The flood that Michael and Linda faced was an objectively uncontrollable event whose outcome was not contingent on their actions. Striking parallels exist between their experience and the experimental conditions under which both animal and human subjects have developed the syndrome of motivational, cognitive, and emotional disturbance that characterize learned helplessness.

OBJECTIVE UNCONTROLLABILITY

Using dogs as subjects, Seligman and associates (1967) researched the parameters of learned helplessness by creating experimental conditions that simulated the different action-outcome contingencies of controllable and uncontrollable events. They discovered that subjects who were initially exposed to the contingency of action-outcome independence in an uncontrollable condition made progressively fewer responses of any kind—even under controllable conditions when outcome was dependent on their actions. Instead, after a brief period of "frantic" responding, the subjects apparently gave up and passively endured the trauma (see Maier, Seligman, & Solomon, 1969, pp. 299–342; Overmier & Seligman, 1967, pp. 23–33; Seligman & Maier, 1967, pp. 1–9; Seligman, Maier, & Solomon, 1971, pp. 347–400).

Because their experience with trauma first occurred under uncontrollable conditions and because they had learned from this that their responses were of no avail, these subjects had learned helplessness. Their motivational deficit was manifested by their retarded response initiation even under controllable conditions. In addition, because they learned the independence between action and outcome in the uncontrollable condition, they failed to learn the associative link between action and outcome in the controllable condition.

This cognitive deficit is called the "interference effect" of learned helplessness (Seligman, Maier, & Greer, 1968, pp. 256–262).

In contrast, the subjects whose experience with uncontrollable trauma followed their exposure to controllable trauma did not learn helplessness. Their initial experience with the dependent action-outcome contingency apparently had immunized them against learning helplessness in the subsequent uncontrollable condition. Because they had learned that their behavior controlled outcome, at least under conditions in which this was objectively possible, these subjects suffered neither the motivational nor the cognitive disturbances shown by those who had learned helplessness (Overmier & Seligman, 1967, pp. 23–33; Seligman & Maier, 1967, pp. 1–9).

PERCEIVED UNCONTROLLABILITY

Other studies support the hypothesis that learned helplessness also occurs in humans who are subjected to aversive stimuli over which they have no control. In their studies with human subjects, Thornton and Jacobs (1971, pp. 367–372), as well as Hiroto (1974, pp. 187–193), created experimental conditions similar to those in which Seligman and associates had demonstrated learned helplessness in dogs. Both the motivational and cognitive deficits that had been produced in the helpless dogs were paralleled by the behavior of the helpless humans.

Even more significantly, Hiroto's study (1974, pp. 187–193), revealed that those people who, prior to the experiment, had shown a belief in the independence of behavior and outcome were more likely to learn helplessness under the experimental conditions than were those who entered the experiment with a belief in their own ability to control the outcome of events. This finding suggests that the etiological basis of learned helplessness is not restricted to conditions in which events are objectively uncontrollable. Rather, learned helplessness may also develop when individuals believe they have no control over events—even when those events could actually be affected by their behavior.

The significance of a person's beliefs about his control over life events can be gleaned from the work of Geer, Davison, and Gatchel (1970, pp. 731–738). Their study of the relationship between stress and perceived control revealed that individuals who believed they had control over the aversive stimuli in the experiment found these conditions much less stressful than did those who believed they had no control over them. Geer et al. postulated that the subjects who experienced less stress did so because their belief in their ability to control the aversive stimuli allowed them to label the condition as one in which they were not helpless.

To recapitulate, the experimental evidence indicates that learned helplessness develops when one objectively is or believes oneself to be unable to control the outcome of events. This cognitive disturbance gives rise to the motivational and emotional aspects of learned helplessness. If a person believes himself to be unable to control the outcome of life events and fails to see that his actions make a difference, he is less motivated to try. Based on the observation that helpless subjects quit responding and passively endured trauma—even under controllable conditions—Seligman et al. (Seligman, 1974, pp. 83–107; 1975, pp. 54–55) contended that the emotional manifestation of learned helplessness is reactive depression.

LOSS AND DEPRESSION

The concept of loss as a central etiological component of depression is not new. Freud (1950, pp. 152–172) suggested that the depressed person had suffered the loss of a love object, either real or imagined, which resulted in ego deprivation. According to Klein (1948, pp. 282–310), depression results from a lack of maternal gratification during infancy. Bibring (1961, pp. 13–48) related depression to a loss of self-esteem stemming from early childhood trauma. Learning theorists agree that the depressed person has suffered a loss but they have generally regarded it as a loss of reinforcers (see Lazarus, 1968, pp. 83–89; Lewinsohn & Libet, 1972, pp. 291–295; Lewinsohn, Weinstein, & Shaw, 1969, pp. 231–240; Libet & Lewinsohn, 1973, pp. 304–312).

However, according to the learned helplessness model, the cause of depression is neither the lost love object, nor the loss of maternal gratification, nor the trauma-induced loss of self-esteem, nor even the loss of reinforcers. Instead, at the core of reactive depression is the real or imagined loss of control over life events and the belief in one's helplessness that results (Seligman, 1974, 1975). This is shown by the young woman in the following case study.

Twenty-five-year-old Elizabeth sat listlessly in the visitor's lounge of the Intensive Care Unit at Parklake Hospital, waiting for the hospital staff's report on her middle-aged mother's condition. A few hours earlier, Mrs. G had been stricken by a massive cerebral aneurism. She had shown no previous physical symptoms that might have alerted her or her family to her impending dysfunction. The physician could offer no certainty that she would ever regain consciousness, nor could he predict with confidence that she would survive the necessary corrective surgery or be able to resume normal functioning. And so Elizabeth waited, her hope dissipating rapidly each time the physician reported, "No change." Feeling utterly immobilized and powerless in the face of this trauma, she concluded sadly that there was nothing she could do.

Elizabeth clearly faces a loss of control in this traumatic event. If, on the basis of this or other experiences, she believes herself to be generally helpless and ineffective, she will have developed the cognitive disturbance that typifies depression and learned helplessness.

Beck (1967, 1973) also emphasized the importance of cognitive distortion in the etiology of depression. In contrast to theorists who regard depression as an affective disorder that causes cognitive and behavioral disturbances, Beck postulated that depression is primarily a cognitive disorder. He added that it is the depressed person's negative cognitive set—the negative and helpless way in which he views self, experiences, and the future—that predominates and serves as the referent from which the accompanying affective and behavioral disturbances ensue. As a result, the distorted interpretation of experience precipitates and, in turn, may maintain depression.

Apparent similarities exist between the behavior of helpless subjects and that of depressed individuals—their passivity, negative cognitive set or negative expectations, and tendencies to self-deprecation. These similarities led Miller and Seligman (1973) to test whether depressed subjects tend to perceive reinforcement (or outcome) as response independent or noncontingent on their actions, even in situations in which reinforcement actually is contingent on their actions. The results of their investigation confirmed the hypothesis that depressed subjects were significantly more likely than nondepressed subjects to believe that their actions could not affect outcome. Thus, Miller and Seligman (1973) proposed that reactive depression is "a specific cognitive distortion of the perception of the ability of one's own responses to change the environment" (p. 63). It is this learned cognitive distortion—the belief that action is futile—that results in both the behavioral and affective symptoms of depression.

CRISIS

A review of the literature on crisis theory reveals conspicuous likenesses between the characteristic features of the crisis state and those that are part of the process by which learned helplessness develops. In general, writers on the crisis state seem to agree that crisis occurs when one's normal homeostatic balance is temporarily disrupted by the occurrence of a stressful life event (Parad, 1965).

The occurrence of a stressful event, however, is not in itself a sufficient condition for producing crisis. As Rapoport (1965, pp. 22–31) notes, a stressful or hazardous event creates a problem that one may conceive of as a threat, a loss, or a challenge. Interpreting the event as a loss may precipitate depression, whereas interpreting it as a challenge may motivate appropriate, solution-oriented action. It is the interpretation of the event as a threat, accompanied by a person's inability to respond with adequate coping mechanisms, which, according to Rapoport (1965, pp. 22–31), produces crisis.

A similar conceptualization of crisis is offered by Golan (1969, pp. 389–394). In her view, the "state of active crisis" refers to the stage of disequilibrium in which tension and anxiety have reached a peak and the individual's customary balancing devices no longer operate.

On the other hand, Caplan (1964) describes crisis as a phasic process that begins with a rise in tension as one's habitual problem-solving mechanisms are summoned to reduce the disruptive impact of the precipitating event. If these efforts do not resolve the crisis, tension increases and promotes the use of "emergency" problem-solving mechanisms. As a result, crisis resolution will occur on a continuum ranging from complete solution of the problem to major disorganization of the person's functioning.

Careful scrutiny of these and other definitions of the crisis state underscores the important discrepancies among writers as to which factors actually constitute a crisis. According to Rapoport and Golan, crisis begins when the individual's repertoire of coping devices has been exhausted and the problem at hand remains unsolved. From Caplan's viewpoint, however, the trial and exhaustion of coping mechanisms are actually a part of the crisis state. The learned helplessness model offers a framework within which these discrepancies can be nullified and from which a clearer and more exact delineation of the crisis state can emerge. From this perspective, striking parallels are noticeable between the interacting components of crisis and those by which learned helplessness develops.

Within this framework both the crisis state and the development of learned helplessness can be viewed as processes that are precipitated by the occurrence of a stressful event. Both begin when the affected individual first identifies the stressful event as threatening. The rise of tension accompanied by endeavors to cope during the crisis state are analogous to the fear- or anxiety-elicited "frantic" responding shown by subjects as they developed helplessness. Therefore, from the time when a stressful event is first defined as threatening to the time when coping endeavors or "frantic" responding ceases, the crisis state and the process by which learned helplessness develops show unmistakable similarities.

In the author's opinion, however, it is at this critical point—when coping efforts or frantic responding end—that the two processes diverge. Here either the crisis is resolved or learned helplessness occurs. Thus, this is the crucial point in determining the future functioning or dysfunctioning of the individual involved.

In the learned helplessness model the end of frantic responding marks the point at which the defining symptom—the belief that action and outcome are independent and thus that one has no control over the outcome of events—becomes an actuality. It must be remembered that this belief can be learned whether or not it is based on

an accurate assessment of objective reality. Nevertheless, it is this cognition that is the sine qua non of learned helplessness.

Like learned helplessness, the definition of the crisis state is also contingent on the cognitive operations of the affected individual. Rapoport (1965, p. 25) alludes to the importance of cognition when she states that it is one's interpretation of the stressful event that determines whether or not a crisis will ensue. Likewise in the learned helplessness model, a person's cognitive assessment of the effectiveness or ineffectiveness of coping efforts will logically determine whether or not the problem is, or even can be, resolved. From this perspective the crisis state will not terminate until the affected individual believes either that his coping endeavors have been successful in resolving the problem at hand or that he is unable to resolve the problem. Both these alternative beliefs hinge upon the perceptual, interpretative, and evaluative functions of cognition, as is shown by the following case study.

Frightened and alone, 23-year-old Laura climbed onto her gynecologist's examining table. Three months pregnant with her first child, Laura had moved into town about six months before at the request of her boyfriend who was a student at the local university. She had shared her boyfriend's apartment until, on learning of her pregnancy, he threw her out. During the last few days, Laura had begun to vomit frequently and severely and was bleeding profusely from her vagina. She was worried that these symptoms might indicate an impending miscarriage or some problems of fetal development. Showing neither compassion nor consideration for her inquiries, the gynecologist told her nothing about the meaning of her symptoms. Laura's fearfulness was met by his paternalistic, "Don't worry." Frustrated by her doctor's indifference, frightened by her physical symptoms, Laura angrily left the office.

Following this experience, Laura selected a new gynecologist, one who patiently and helpfully answered her questions and responded to her fears. Unlike the first one, he respected Laura and treated her with dignity. Because Laura continued to take logical, adaptive steps in an attempt to cope with her crisis, and had not given up her belief that she had control over the situation, it is unlikely that she developed the symptoms of learned helplessness. Laura's belief in her ability to find an effective, satisfactory resolution supported her in her efforts to cope with this crisis.

It is possible to conclude that the crisis state is actually a state of "pre-learned helplessness," and vice versa. Similarly, crisis resolution will depend on the affected individual's belief in the contingent relationship between action and outcome—the belief that what he or she does when confronted with a traumatic event makes a difference. On the basis of the experimental evidence previously cited, this belief in one's own effectiveness is learned through experience with situations in which one's actions control the outcome of traumatic events. In contrast, learned helplessness develops when one fails to learn this conjunction between action and outcome. It follows then, that the ineffective functioning or major disorganization that results from the unsatisfactory resolution of a crisis is learned helplessness (Caplan, 1964, pp. 40–41; Rapoport, 1965, p. 25).

IMPLICATIONS

Applying the learned helplessness model to the concept of crisis suggests that prompt, effective intervention in this state is crucial to the prevention of more serious impairment. As a result, the preferred focus in crisis intervention should be on engaging and enhancing the cognitive processes of the affected individual. It is of utmost importance to use therapeutic strategies that help the individual assess accurately the parameters of the prevailing problem, the available alternatives for action, and the probable consequences of these actions (see Aguilera & Messick, 1974). Judicious exposure of the individual in crisis to the contingent relationship between action and outcome should not only help resolve the problem at hand, but should also prevent the development of learned helplessness.

If, however, attempts to resolve the crisis satisfactorily have been abortive, and if the affected individual has come to believe that nothing he or she does makes a difference, learned helplessness and depression may ensue. Again, therapeutic strategies that focus on the individual's cognitive processes are imperative (see Beck, 1970, pp. 184–200; Mahoney, 1974; Meichenbaum & Cameron, 1974, pp. 103–117; Todd, 1973, pp. 91–94). A suggested technique is to start the individual on a program of behavioral change where, following a sequence of incremental steps of action, the affected individual can experience and learn the relationship between behavior and outcome (Alberti & Emmons, 1974; Jakubowski-Spector, 1973, pp. 75–85; Rose, 1975, pp. 33–39).

The learned helplessness model provides a framework through which the concepts of crisis and reactive depression can be understood more clearly. In addition, the model offers a valuable diagnostic tool to help social workers and other mental health professionals assess more accurately whether an individual is in crisis or whether that crisis had ended and the clinical manifestations of learned helplessness or reactive depression have begun. Such an assessment will provide a definitive guide for the planning of appropriate intervention strategies.

Reading 2-2

Work with Mrs. Manley

Mrs. Manley was referred to our outpatient clinic by Dr. S., for evaluation as a candidate for admission to a stress management program conducted by Dr. A. at General Hospital. Her appointment had been made by her husband. Mrs. Manley and I were both aware that this 1½-hour interview was likely to be our only face-to-face contact. (As this was my first interview at the clinic, I was mildly nervous; I soothed myself by viewing the situation as likely to require only a confirmation of already formulated therapeutic plans.) Mrs. Manley presented herself as a poised, well-dressed, attractive 48-year-old, white woman who settled easily into the chair next to my desk. I introduced myself and my position at the agency and continued, "I know you've filled out a data base sheet and I've had a chance to look it over but I think it'll be most helpful if we start from scratch even if we cover some of the same material." (I was focused on my own concerns here: worry that I would not obtain all of the required information.) "Can you give me some idea of what brought you here today?"

Mrs. Manley [*very smoothly*]: I've been under a lot of stress lately—I've never handled stress very well—and Dr. A. and I thought it might be a good idea for me to try the stress management program at General Hospital. If health insurance is to cover the costs, they need a second outside recommendation, so that's why I'm here.

The client has presented me with both a problem, the stress, and a solution, the program, in the same breath and I'm beginning to feel both superfluous and a bit relieved. I make two erroneous assumptions that persist throughout the interview: (1) that Dr. A. is thoroughly familiar with Mrs. Manley and her family and with the program recommended; and (2) that Mrs. Manley and her physician have explored the possibility of other alternatives together and have selected this program as the most suitable for her needs.

Worker: I'm not familiar with that program. Do you know what it involves?

Mrs. Manley: Well, I think it's a group program that teaches relaxation and breathing techniques and that sort of thing.

Worker [*nodding*]: Can you give me some idea of why such a program might be helpful? What kind of stress you've been under?

Mrs. Manley explained that she had accepted a position teaching German in a private junior high school in January 1980 after a 25-year absence from the field. The offer was unexpected; she had little time to prepare and is using a teaching method unfamiliar to her. She has been surprised by the difficulties she has had in coping with the new job. The position is temporary until June; she is not sure she wants to continue after that—coping with seventh and eighth graders all day is really tough—but it's very important to her to uphold the commitment she made to finish out the year. (I am struck by the similarities between Mrs. Manley's position and my own in returning to school after 20 years. I don't mention this because I don't think the "me, too" revelation would have any significance for her at this point and I am reluctant to reveal my own inexperience.)

Case disguised and prepared by Beulah R. Compton from a process recording of a student placed in a comprehensive mental health center.

Worker: Stress is kind of a vague word. I'd like to get a better idea of what it means to you, what kind of problems you're having.

Mrs. Manley explained that she has always had a lot of premenstrual tension, mainly insomnia, but considered the sleeping problem manageable with medication. She has had a prescription for Valium for premenstrual tension since 1977 or 1978 and was accustomed to taking one a night for two or three nights at a time as needed. She dislikes using medication and "wants to find a better way." Lack of sleep gives her "headachy" symptoms. She describes herself as premenopausal; her periods as irregular. Now she feels stress nearly every day: she cries a lot, sometimes loses her appetite and feels nauseous, sometimes feels "paralyzed, falling apart and shaky inside." For the first time, Mrs. Manley seemed ill at ease; she occasionally punctuated her descriptions with a nervous laugh as if to belittle the severity of her symptoms.

Worker: Have you missed any workdays because of your stress?

Mrs. Manley: No, not at all. Mostly I just can't leave the job behind when I get home. I worry about doing a good job—all out of proportion, Jim says. Those parents are paying a lot of money for their kids' education [*laughs*].

Worker: And that makes you feel very responsible?

Mrs. Manley: Of course [*laughs again*].

Worker: Is there any way of making your job easier, less of a strain?

Mrs. Manley: Well, I did have my schedule changed. First I had six classes at four different levels. That was impossible. So, I had it changed to four classes at three levels.

Worker: Did it bother you to ask for that change?

Mrs. Manley: No, not at all. The people at school have been very helpful and supportive.

Worker: What about at home?

Mrs. Manley: Well, we just have one boy at home now, Paul—he's 16—so there isn't that much to do. And my family is pretty understanding about late meals and dust. I don't know. I go to bed a lot right after dinner. Jim says I'm my own worst enemy—I worry that I'm going to either cheat my family or the kids at school.

Worker: Have there been any changes at home since you started to work, any jobs taken over by Jim or Paul?

Mrs. Manley: No, it's really my problem. Jim left the decision to go to work totally up to me. Sometimes he plays devil's advocate but it's my decision really—something I wanted to do for myself. He's really concerned about my being so upset. It isn't good to fall apart. He worries about me and he wants me to learn to handle it. It's my stress, not his.

I think Mrs. Manley is assuming too much responsibility for the situation, but I don't voice my opinion.)

Worker: I believe you when you say Jim is concerned, but has this problem caused any difficulties in your relationship with him?

Mrs. Manley: Well, of course our sex life isn't too great when I go to bed at eight o'clock [*laughs*]. I really have no interest in sex now. And the crying is really upsetting to Jim—he was sympathetic at first but now he doesn't know how to handle it. He thinks I'm making such a big deal out of everything. He tries to reason with me but it doesn't do much good.

Worker: How does that make you feel?

Mrs. Manley: What?

Worker: Is it annoying to be "reasoned with" when you're upset?

Mrs. Manley: Oh, I don't know. When the stress is there I don't listen to anybody about anything anyway.

(I'm interested in Mrs. Manley's relationship with her husband but I don't know quite how to pursue it so I change the topic.)

Worker: Is there anything else in your life besides the job that's worrying you now?

Mrs. Manley: Well, my father-in-law. He's in poor health and will probably die soon or have to go into a nursing home. And he'll fight it. Some decision will have to be made. Jim copes with uncertainty better than I do. He's so busy he doesn't think about it, I guess. I think we should be looking into nursing homes or something.

Worker: Do you feel this is more your responsibility than you would like it to be?

Mrs. Manley: Yes, I think so. I have a better feel for my own parents. I would know better what to do for them. I could accept their death, I think, maybe better than the other alternatives.

(I'm interested in what Mrs. Manley is saying, but I'm very much aware again of having to cover other material.)

Worker: I'd like to talk a little bit more about your own family.

Mrs. Manley described her family of origin history, her own and family medical history. She received a degree in language from State College in 1954 where she taught until her marriage in 1956. In 1956 and 1957 she and her husband studied in Germany as Fulbright scholars. Since that time her husband has done graduate work and held university teaching positions, coming to Central College in 1963. Their first son was born in 1957, the second in 1959, and the third in 1963. She described her early married life as sheltered. "Jim was doing the adjusting; I wasn't." She recalled her husband as not only earning a living, but as sharing parenting responsibilities, being there when the kids needed him.

Worker: You've mentioned several times that you don't handle stress well. Can you think of a time like that?

Mrs. Manley: Well, there was one time with our son, Ted—the middle one. When he was 17 he was hospitalized for what they called a "thinking disorder"—it was drug-related. We just lived through it on a day-to-day basis. But Jim and I handled that together; it brought us closer together. We saw a counselor at Ted's school for a while afterwards.

Worker: Was that helpful?

Mrs. Manley: Well, Ted wouldn't always go, but Jim and I went anyway.

Worker: Do you see any similarities to your problem now?

Mrs. Manley: Well, it was a traumatic time, but there was a valid reason for the stress and it was over pretty quickly.

Worker: Is your present stress "valid"?

Mrs. Manley: Well, *I* think so.

Worker: I think so, too. I think returning to work after 25 years would be very, very difficult. But you *are* here doing something about it.

(Again I think about sharing with her some of my feelings about being in a similar situation, but I don't.) I have some questions now that are a little bit different from the ones I've asked before.

I proceeded with a mental status exam. Mrs. Manley was oriented to person, place, and time. Her remote memory, recent memory, and recall were good. Her immediate memory—ability to repeat a series of digits forward and backward was poor as was her ability to do simple calculations "in the head." She said she felt nervous about this part of the interview and expressed relief when it was over.

(I was feeling anxious now about winding up the interview. I could see no harm in the stress management program for Mrs. Manley, but I had other ideas for treatment that I thought might be more effective. I was just not sure of myself, so I asked.)

Worker: Do you have any objections to my talking to Dr. A. and Dr. S.? I would like to do that—to find out more about the program and how it might be useful for you. I also will be discussing our interview with Dr. K. [the director of our clinic].

Mrs. Manley had no objections, and we agreed that I would call her the following week to let her know our recommendation. I was surprised to learn from Dr. A. that there was no group stress management program at General Hospital at that time. I called Dr. S. and learned that he had only a very sketchy knowledge of the patient, her family, and the problem situation, that the program had been her suggestion (or perhaps her husband's?), and that he had not discussed other alternatives with her. I told Dr. S. we were recommending time-limited marital or family therapy as helpful in coping with some of the issues underlying Mrs. Manley's situational stress. Dr. S. had no objections to this change in service especially as such services were available to Mrs. Manley at the clinic. After discussing our recommendations with me and with Dr. S., Mrs. Manley elected to begin a combination of individual and couple therapy. She was desirous that I make the necessary referral to the clinic and gave me permission to share our interview with the practitioner at the clinic. I called Mrs. J., intake worker, and was able to arrange an appointment for Wednesday at a time convenient for Mrs. Manley.

A.   STUDY DATA

1.   Problem and goal identification

Mrs. Manley perceived the problem as the stress she was experiencing upon returning to work after a 25-year absence—the crying spells, insomnia, the nauseous and shaky feelings, the constant worry that she was not performing her job adequately. She strongly identified precipitating factors contributing to the problem as lying totally within herself and she was reinforced by her husband in defining as a suitable goal—beneficial, not only in the present situation but in the future as well—a change in self: better self-control

of her stressful symptoms. Mrs. Manley sought from the service system instruction in stress management as a means to reach her goal. She sought from our agency a recommendation which would permit her group health plan to cover the cost of this instruction.

As recommending worker, I agreed with Mrs. Manley's identification of her stress as the presenting problem. I believed, however, that there were precipitating factors outside of the client that she was not taking sufficiently into account—most particularly, interactions between herself and others within the family system. I saw the client's goal of symptom control as an acceptable short-term goal, but I also saw as a possibly more challenging long-term goal—elimination, rather than simple management, of much of her stress through changes in perception of self and changes in her interactions with others in the family system. Specifically, our problem-for-work was to agree upon goals and an appropriate service modality.

2.   The client

a.   Motivation. Someone's discomfort with the present situation was high; whether it was Mrs. Manley's, or her husband's, or both was unclear. He had made the appointment for her; she related, "Jim wants me to learn to handle stress better." At the same time, though she made an effort to keep our interview on almost a social level, at times embarrassed to describe her depressive symptoms, her descriptions of an emotional state seriously interfering with her daily functioning were plain. She was determined to finish out her school year commitment, had mobilized herself very quickly—within a month of beginning to experience difficulties—to seek professional help, and had already devised one means of dealing with the problem—the stress management program.

b.   Opportunity.   Although Mrs. Manley repeatedly labeled herself "poor at handling stress," when asked to give specific examples, she identified only a two- or three-year history of premenstrual tension, which had been adequately controlled by minimal use of medication and an episode involving her son which, along with her husband, she had handled quite well. In the present situation she had promptly sought assistance from an outside institution—the health care system, was readily able to identify need for change and use support resources in one interpersonal system—the school environment—but either was reluctant to use or was unable to find these same kind of support resources in the marital or nuclear family system.

c.   Capacity.   Mrs. Manley presented herself as a warm, physically attractive woman who related to the interviewer in a friendly, egalitarian manner. Her energy level was high and, as a former college teacher and Fulbright scholar, she was obviously intelligent. She had fulfilled the demanding social roles of wife to college professor and mother to three boys for many years. Yet the long absence from the teaching field was a tremendous liability to overcome in a matter of weeks—her memory and concentration were not as efficient as she would like and she was finding the work emotionally and physically exhausting. Mrs. Manley was aware of her own tendency to set exceedingly high standards for herself but seemed unable to let up—to her already existing tasks of teaching and homemaking she had now added a third—stress managing.

B.   PSYCHOSOCIAL ASSESSMENT

Social role theory provides one way of conceptualizing Mrs. Manley's problem. Social roles are learned and can reflect personal needs and drives as well as sociocultural and family system expectations. Though Mrs. Manley and her husband had entered their marriage as professional equals, within a very few years she had exchanged her career for the traditional feminine occupation of domestic work and child care and her husband had assumed both the responsibility and the power of being the family's sole economic support. Mrs. Manley's return to work was a significant role change that neither she nor her family seemed quite willing to acknowledge. It is almost impossible to change the role of one family member without changing the role of another, yet the Manley family seemed determined to do just that. Now employed full-time, Mrs. Manley was experiencing a great deal of interpositional role conflict as there had been no reduction of her work load at home. Part of the responsibility may lie with her own anxiety about departing from the familiar patterns of wife and mother or guilt about not fulfilling traditional duties or reluctance to give up some of the power associated with being central in the family. Part of the responsibility may lie with other family members still expecting total availability for their needs. We can only speculate, too, about the significance of her husband's refusal to commit herself about her new work role. Surely he must have some opinion about an extra $10,000+ yearly income or about his wife being out of the home 40 hours a week or about her reentry into their shared professional field. Why the reluctance to reveal his thoughts, to make the decision a shared one?

The idea of resistance to change can be found as well in general systems theory. The Manley family can be viewed as a living unit which, though inherently subject to change and conflict, also has developed unique and stable ways of functioning which are resistant to change.

Individual behavioral deviations—Mrs. Manley's reactions to stress—which seem at first to be wholly dysfunctional, may serve to protect the stability of the system itself. What, for example, would happen to Mr. Manley in his long-standing position as the rational, strong protector if his wife should learn to "handle her stress" as he has directed her to do?

Mrs. Manley's return to work was not prompted by economic concerns. Both she and her husband may have been influenced by a social variable, current "feminist" thinking about the oppressiveness of traditional feminine roles and the desirability of women seeking satisfactions outside the home. Mrs. Manley's depressive symptoms may be attributed less to guilt at indulging in self-fulfillment as to shock at realization that her dual work status is not the fun-filled challenge she envisioned it to be. Mr. Manley in turn may be hesitant to voice objections to her working for fear of denying her right to an enhancing experience.

C. POLICY IMPLICATIONS

1. Working wives

The Manley family is not unique. The employment of the majority of American women has not yet released them from primary responsibility in the home. Wives who work still expect and are expected to be totally responsive to the family's needs. The job itself frequently does not contain the same benefits that it might for a man—respect, high earnings, opportunities to develop personal capabilities. Until this is a reality and until domestic work is shared equally or based on personal preferences and individual talents rather than upon sex-prescribed roles, blanket encouragement of wives to work irrespective of economic needs may be more punitive than rewarding.

2. Family developmental stages

A developmental orientation can be useful in working with families like the Manley family. Families, like individuals, can be viewed as going through stages and facing different developmental tasks over their life spans. A change in work role for a family member is a predictable crisis point for both the individual and the family system. A particularly stressful stage in the life of a marriage is that beginning with the exit of the first child and ending with the exit of the last—a time of marital reassessment of expectations and responsibilities in preparation for the "empty nest." Families can be helped to anticipate such stress points and to maintain adequate functioning.

D. CONTRACT GOALS AND INTERVENTIONS

It was certainly not "by accident" that Mrs. Manley chose to talk about the family's experience in dealing with her son's hospitalization. I think that, regardless of her insistence that the present problem was hers alone, she was feeling quite isolated in her struggles and welcomed the interpretation that this was a suitable problem for the entire family unit to work on. If I had continued working with her, I would have suggested working with the entire family directed toward the achievement of two goals: (1) examination of the meaning to her and the family of her commitment to teach until the end of the school year; and (2) a decision, based on assessment of that experience, of whether or not she should continue working. Some specific directions with the family could include setting less demanding expectations of Mrs. Manley's participation in home tasks, trying out new schedules of household chores which would examine the possibility of assigning some responsibility to father and son, frank exploration of the meaning of Mrs. Manley's return to work for each family member and for the family system as a whole, and attention to related issues involving marital power and responsibility—for example, concerns about the Manley's aging parents' health and ability to live alone.

E.   BARRIERS TO UNDERSTANDING AND APPROPRIATE ACTION

Mrs. Manley was so similar to me in age, education, social class, family composition, and life experience, and her problem situation so closely allied to my own in returning to school after a long absence that, while I could readily understand her problem cognitively and emotionally, I also greatly feared inaccurate projection of thinking and feeling about myself. This prevented me from relating to her as directly and freely as I could have. In addition, during our interview I was consistently under the impression that someone "wiser than I" had already made a therapeutic plan, and I allowed this to inhibit my discussing what I judged to be a better alternative. In effect the client and I were given another opportunity: there was no stress management program available; consultation with Dr. K. gave me the confidence to present the alternatives of marital or family therapy with assurance; and almost in spite of the vagrancies of the health care system, the client ended up with what I believe was a more suitable therapeutic choice.

References

Aguilera, Donna C., & Messick, Janice M.   *Crisis intervention: Theory and methodology.* St. Louis, Mo.: C. V. Mosby, 1974.

Alberti, Robert E., & Emmons, Michael L.   *Your perfect right: A guide to assertive behavior.* San Luis Obispo, Calif.: Impact, 1974.

American Association of Social Workers.   *Social casework—Generic and specific: A report of the Milford Conference, Studies in the Practice of Social Work,* no. 2. New York: AASW, 1929.

Baer, Betty L., & Federico, Ronald C.   *Educating the baccalaureate social worker.* Cambridge, Mass.: Ballinger, 1978.

Bartlett, Harriett M.   *The common base of social work practice.* New York: National Association of Social Workers, 1970.

Beck, Aaron T.   *Depression: Clinical, experimental, and theoretical aspects.* New York: Harper & Row, 1967.

Beck, Aaron T.   Cognitive therapy: Nature and relation to behavioral therapy. *Behavior Therapy,* 1970, *1,* 184–200.

Beck, Aaron T.   *The diagnosis and management of depression.* Philadelphia: University of Pennsylvania Press, 1973.

Berkowitz, Sidney J.   Curriculum models for social work education. In *Modes of Professional Education.* Tulane Studies in Social Welfare. New Orleans: School of Social Work, Tulane University, 1969.

Bibring, E.   The mechanism of depression. In P. Greenacre, (Ed.), *Affective disorders:*

Psychoanalytic contributions to their study. New York: International Universities Press, 1961.

Boehm, Werner W. (Ed.). *Social work curriculum study* (12 vols.). New York: Council on Social Work Education, 1959.

Briar, Scott, & Miller, Henry. *Problems and issues in social casework.* New York: Columbia University Press, 1971.

Caplan, Gerald. *Principles of preventive psychiatry.* New York: Basic Books, 1964.

Freud, Sigmund. Mourning and melancholia. In Ernest Jones (Ed.), *Collected Papers* (Vol. 4). London: Basic Books, 1950.

Garvin, Charles. The selection of theory for social work practice with individuals. Ann Arbor: University of Michigan, 1972. (Mimeograph)

Golan, Naomi. When is a client in crisis? *Social Casework,* July 1969, *50,* 389–394.

Gordon, William E. A critique of the working definition. *Social Work,* October 1962, *7,* 3–13.

Gordon, William E. Knowledge and value: Their distinction and relationship in clarifying social work practice. *Social Work,* July 1965, *10,* 32–39.

Greer, James H., Davison, Gerald C., & Gatchel, Robert I. Reduction of stress in humans through nonveridical perceived control of aversive stimulation. *Journal of Personality and Social Psychology,* 1970, *16,* 731–738.

Hiroto, Donald S. Locus of control and learned helplessness. *Journal of Experimental Psychology,* 1974, *102,* 187–193.

Hooker, Carol E. Learned helplessness. *Social Work,* May 1976, *21,* 194–198.

Houston, Kent B. Control over stress, locus of control, and response to stress. *Journal of Personality and Social Psychology,* 1972, *21,* 249–255.

Jakubowski-Spector, Patricia. Facilitating the growth of women through assertive training. *The Counseling Psychologist,* 1973, *4,* 75–85.

Kadushin, Alfred. The knowledge base of social work. In Alfred J. Kahn (Ed.), *Issues in American social work.* New York: Columbia University Press, 1959.

Kahn, Alfred J. The nature of social work knowledge. In Cora Kasius (Ed.), *New directions in social work.* New York: Harper & Row, 1954.

Kaplan, Abraham. *The conduct of inquiry: Methodology for behavioral science.* San Francisco: Chandler, 1964.

Kamerman, Shelia B., Dolgoff, Ralph, Getzel, George, & Nelson, Judith. Knowledge for Practice: Social Science in Social Work. In Alfred J. Kahn (Ed.), *Shaping the New Social Work,* New York: Columbia University Press, 1973.

Klein, Melanie. A contribution to the psychogenesis of manic-depressive states. In *Contributions to psychoanalysis.* London: Hogarth Press, 1948.

Kuhn, Alfred. *The logic of social systems.* San Francisco: Jossey-Bass, 1974.

Lazarus, Arnold A. Learning theory and treatment of depression. *Behavior Research and Therapy,* 1968, *6,* 83–89.

Lewinsohn, Peter M., Weinstein, Malcolm S., & Shaw, David A. Depression: A clinical-research approach. In Richard D. Rubin & Cyril M. Franks (Eds.), *Advances in behavior therapy: Proceedings, 1968,* New York: Academic Press, 1969.

Lewinsohn, Peter M., & Libet, Julian. "Pleasant events, activity, schedules, and depression. *Journal of Abnormal Psychology,* 1972, *79,* 291–295.

Libet, Julian, & Lewinsohn, Peter M. Concept of social skill with special reference to the behavior of depressed persons. *Journal of Consulting and Clinical Psychology*, 1973, *40*, 304–312.

Mahoney, Michael J.   *Cognition and behavior modification.* Cambridge, Mass.: Ballinger Publishing, 1974.

Maier, Steven F., Seligman, Martin E. P., & Solomon, Richard L.   Pavlovian fear conditioning and learned helplessness. In Byron A. Campbell & Russell M. Church (Eds.), *Punishment and aversive behavior.* New York: Appleton-Century-Crofts, 1969.

Meichenbaum, Donald, & Cameron, Roy.   The clinical potential of modifying what clients say to themselves." *Psychotherapy: Theory Research and Practice*, 1974, *11*, 103–117.

Meyer, Carol H.   Direct services in old and new concepts. In Alfred J. Kahn (Ed.), *Shaping the new social work.* New York: Columbia University Press, 1973.

Miller, William R., & Seligman, Martin E. P.   Depression and the perception of reinforcement. *Journal of Abnormal Psychology*, 1973, *82*, 62–73.

National Association of Social Workers.   Special issue on conceptual frameworks. *Social Work*, September 1977, *22*, 5.

National Association of Social Workers.   Second special issue on frameworks. *Social Work*, January 1981, *26*, 5–69.

Overmier, Bruce, & Seligman, Martin E. P.   Efforts of inescapable shock upon subsequent escape and avoidance learning. *Journal of Comparative and Physiological Psychology*, 1967, *63*, 22–23.

Parad, Howard J.   *Crisis intervention: Selected readings.* New York: Family Service Association of America, 1965.

Perlman, Helen Harris.   *Social casework: A problem-solving process.* Chicago: University of Chicago Press, 1957.

Perlman, Helen Harris.   *Persona.* Chicago: University of Chicago Press, 1968.

Rapoport, Lydia.   The state of crisis: Some theoretical considerations." In Howard Parad, *Crisis intervention: Selected readings.* New York: Family Service Association of America, 1965.

Richmond, Mary.   *Social diagnosis.* New York: Russell Sage Foundation, 1917.

Ripple, Lillian.   Problem identification and formulation. In Norman A. Polansky (Ed.), *Social work research.* Chicago: University of Chicago Press, 1960.

Rose, Sheldon D.   In pursuit of social competence. *Social Work*, January 1975, *20*, 33–39.

Seligman, Martin E. P.   Failure to escape traumatic shock. *Journal of Experimental Psychology*, 1967, *74*, 1–9.

Seligman, Martin E. P.   Depression and learned helplessness. In Raymond J. Friedman & Martin M. Katz (Eds.), *The psychology of depression: Contemporary theory and research.* New York: Halstead Press (1974).

Seligman, Martin E. P.   *Helplessness: On depression, development, and death.* San Francisco: W. H. Freeman, 1975.

Seligman, Martin E. P., & Maier, Steven F.   Failure to escape traumatic shock. *Journal of Experimental Psychology*, 1967, *74*, 1–9.

Seligman, Martin E. P., Maier, Steven F., & Geer, James H.   Alleviation of learned helplessness in the dog, *Journal of Abnormal Psychology*, 1968, *73*, 256–262.

Seligman, Martin E. P., Maier, Steve F., & Solomon, Richard L.   Unpredictable and uncontrollable aversive events. In Robert F. Bush (Ed.), *Aversive conditioning and learning.* New York: Academic Press, 1971.

Social Work Education Reporter, September 1982, *30,* 3.

Thornton, Jerry W., & Jacobs, Paul D.   Learned helplessness in human subjects. *Journal of Experimental Psychology,* 1971, *87,* 367–372.

Todd, Frederick J.   Coverant control of self-evaluative responses in the treatment of depression: A new use for an old principle. *Behavior Therapy,* 3 1973, *3,* 91–94.

Trader, Harriet.   Survival strategies for oppressed minorities. *Social Work,* January 1977, *22,* 10–13.

Chapter 3

Values in Social Work Practice

No issue can be more troublesome for social work than that of values. Efforts to make definitive statements about social work values stir heated controversy. Is there a value base which all social work practitioners must accept? Does social work possess a set of values that are in some way unique in our culture? Are there interventive methodologies that social workers should not use because they may be inconsistent with what the profession believes about the nature of humanity? These questions are commanding the attention of many contemporary social work thinkers. Charles Levy (1973) takes a clear stand: "The social work profession is well advised to tolerate differences in diversity about some things but not about its ideology." Levy goes on to suggest a framework for conceptualization of the profession's ideology along the dimensions of preferred conceptions of people, preferred outcomes for people, and preferred instrumentalities for dealing with people. Henry Miller (1968) notes some of the value dilemmas encountered by contemporary social work practitioners and suggests the withdrawal of social work from settings in which treatment is imposed or coerced. Elizabeth Salomon (1967) suggests the possibility of inherent conflict between the humanistic stance of social work and scientific methodology. Scott Briar and Henry Miller (1971, p. 42) advance the intriguing suggestion that one of the profession's traditional values—client self-determination—might be conceptualized as a treatment technique rather than a basic value. They suggest that clients in one-to-one relational systems make faster progress when extended maximum opportunities for self-determination, and thus self-determination might be viewed as a treatment technique geared toward facilitating client progress rather than as a basic human value which the profession promotes (p. 40).

Rather than offer definitive answers to these questions, we will raise some of the issues for thought and consideration and will present our own positions. The chapter will attempt to accomplish the following three purposes:

1. Arrive at a definition of the concept of social work value.
2. Examine two value premises that are considered essential to social work practice.
3. Note relationships between these value premises and practice.

WHAT IS MEANT BY SOCIAL WORK VALUE?

Webster's defines value as "something . . . intrinsically valuable or desirable." William Gordon (1965) notes that value refers to things which are preferred, whereas knowledge refers to things which are known or knowable. To use Levy's suggestions, values might be further classified as to preferred conceptions of people, preferred outcomes for people, and preferred instrumentalities for dealing with people. Values can be thought of as beliefs which a profession holds about people and about appropriate ways of dealing with people. Paul Halmos (1966), an English sociologist who has devoted considerable attention to the study of helping professions, suggests from an extensive review of their literature that helping professions operate from tenets of faith concerning the nature of people. This faith, Halmos argues, is accepted without proof and provides guidance and direction for the helping professions. Thus values can be considered as unproved (probably unprovable) beliefs which a profession holds about the nature of people. These beliefs are reflected in the day-to-day work of the practitioner and provide direction and guidance to professional practice.

But are a profession's values uniquely its own? Does a profession find its uniqueness and distinctiveness in the value premises underlying its work? We think not. The social work profession exists within a larger cultural context; it identifies and operationalizes value premises already existing in society and not held exclusively by the profession. Schwartz's concept of the sources of limitations on professional social work practice relates to this point. Schwartz identifies three sources of limitations—the norms of the overall society, the function of the agency, and the service contract with the particular client system (Schwartz, 1961, pp. 146–171). The social work profession exists within a culture whose value premises provide a source of limitation to the profession. A complex culture, however, is characterized by diverse value premises—some of which may be in conflict with each other. Like other professions, social work selects from this diversity the premises it will support in practice. The profession may achieve a degree of uniqueness in the particular way in which it operationalizes value premises, but the premises themselves are shared with other components of the culture.

We have tried to establish that values can be construed as unproven beliefs which guide and direct the work of a professional. These beliefs however, are not uniquely the possession of the profession. They are elements of the overall culture and are shared with others in the culture. However, they may achieve a degree of uniqueness in the way they are operationalized by particular groups. What are the value premises with which the social work profession identifies, and how are these premises operationalized? Two essential value premises underlie the practice of social work: (1) belief in the uniqueness and inherent dignity of the individual and (2) belief in client self-determination. Before these premises are examined, a few comments are necessary concerning the levels of abstractness with which values are discussed.

One way of thinking of values is to picture an inverted triangle (see Figure 3–1). The top or wide part of the triangle can represent values in a

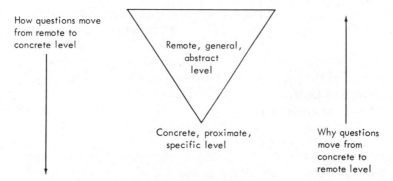

FIGURE 3–1:   Values can be conceptualized at abstract or concrete levels

Principles:
1. Agreement about values increases with remoteness.
2. It is important to know the level of abstraction when values are discussed.
3. The challenge to social work is to apply remote value concepts in concrete situations.

Source: This diagram was suggested by Dr. Philip Heslin, Catholic Charities Bureau, Superior, Wisconsin.

remote, general, or abstract sense. Near the bottom and point of the triangle the values become more proximate, specific, and concrete. The challenge to practitioners is to take abstract value concepts, such as client self-determination or the innate dignity of the individual, and to use these concepts in specific applied situations. When asking *how-to-do-it* questions, movement is from the general to the specific; conversely, in asking a *why* question to seek justification or explanation of actions, movement is from the specific to the remote. In thinking of values at these two levels—remote and concrete—one must recognize that agreement generally increases with abstractness. Agreement, for example, to the abstract principle of client self-determination is readily secured; but at the specific level, say, in working with a 15-year-old who is bent on stealing cars, there may be considerable controversy over how to make this principle concrete. In talking about value premises, we must specify whether the discussion is about an abstract principle or is an attempt to apply an abstract principle in a concrete situation. Our next task is to discuss two abstract principles—client self-determination and the innate dignity of the individual—and to identify ways in which they can be operationalized by the social work practitioner.

RESPECT FOR THE DIGNITY AND UNIQUENESS OF THE INDIVIDUAL

One of the central value premises consistently accepted and supported by the social work profession is that each person is a unique individual with an inherent dignity which is to be respected. People are sufficient ends in themselves and are not to be treated as objects or as means to other ends. Diversity and variety among individuals are to be welcomed and encouraged. Paul Tillich (1962), a theologian who has directed his attention to the philosophy of social work, refers to the uniqueness of every individual and situation as people's existential nature. William Gordon derived his matching concept of the social work function (referred to in Chapter 1) from the same basic notion; Gordon (1969, p. 6) has suggested that the social work profession does not attempt to move either the environment or the person toward some ideal model but rather strives to establish linkages between individuals and their environment allowing for the widest possible diversity of both people and environments.

What are some of the implications of this principle for social work practice? This is the *how* question. How can the premise that every individual is unique and has the right to be treated with respect and dignity be applied in concrete social work situations? We have found five guidelines useful as we struggle to operationalize this value premise.

1. Be sensitive and aware of what we are communicating regarding client dignity by the way we organize and administer our services.
2. Avoid stereotyping clients.
3. Assist clients to discover and make use of their strengths.
4. Expect client participation in problem solving.
5. Focusing on clients' wants is more useful than focusing on clients' needs.

COMMUNICATIONS FOR DIGNITY

Social psychologists have established that people's image of themselves develops largely out of their communication with others (Rose, 1962). People build and incorporate their self-image from the messages they receive from other people about themselves. Further, people who feel good about themselves, see themselves as persons of worth, and have a sense of their own strength and capability, tend to be happier and have the ability to deal constructively and appropriately with their environment.

Social workers and other professionals intervening in the lives of people are well advised to be constantly sensitive to the messages they are extending to others about their worth. Do you, in the little things you do, communicate to other people that they are unique individuals to be highly prized? What, for example, is the message communicated when you safeguard time and provide a client with a specific time to be seen as opposed to a catch-me-on-a-catch-as-catch-can basis? Do appointments in advance communicate to the client a higher sense of respect than unannounced visits or hurriedly arranged telephone appointments? And, speaking of telephoning, how about the all too frequently overlooked return call? What message does the client get when you do not have the courtesy or good sense to return a telephone call promptly? How about the ability to listen to a client, to secure an account of his or her situation, and to avoid prejudgments. And does not privacy, both in terms of how social workers conduct the interview and how they treat the material gained from interviews, communicate something to clients about the esteem in which they are held? When attempting to operationalize the premise of individual uniqueness and dignity, you may find it useful to repeatedly inquire, "What does this action on my part communicate to the client about my perception of the client?"

In Chapter 5 we include an article by Addie Morris describing her experiences as a client of a large public welfare agency. We suggest that you take a few minutes now and read "Four Pennies to My Name: What It's Like on Welfare" (page 205) and think of yourself as a worker in that agency. How might you have responded differently to have shown more respect for the dignity of Addie Morris and her children? Either now or when you read Chapter 5 think about your responsibility as a social worker for what agency procedures and policies communicate to clients. How do agency procedures and their use express values?

CLASSIFICATION AND INDIVIDUALIZATION

A thorny problem which will confront you as you work to operationalize the value of individual uniqueness and dignity is that of striking a balance between classification and the responsibility to respond to persons as individuals. Classification refers to the need to generalize beyond individuals and to organize phenomena on the basis of common characteristics. This process is essential in order to make sense out of a mass of raw data and, as discussed in Chapter 2, is an essential part of the process of knowledge building. When the phenomena being dealt with are people, however, classification may cause social workers to respond to people as objects placed in a particular category rather than as individuals. The pitfalls of this process are being documented in a growing body of literature from sociologists studying deviance from a labeling perspective (Rubington & Weinberg, 1968; Simmons, 1969). Not only does labeling or classification lead to distortion of individual differences, but, as labeling theorists and their supporting research are noting, when a person is labeled deviant, those doing the labeling, and the surrounding audience frequently respond to the deviant on the basis of the label rather than on the basis of individual characteristics. This creates conditions for the development of a self-fulfilling prophecy in which the person becomes what the person has been labeled (Merton, 1957, p. 421–436). Efforts to divert youth out of the juvenile justice system are recognition of the position that the very process of labeling a youngster a delinquent may contribute pressure toward additional delinquencies. Hans Toch (1970, p. 15) states the problem succinctly:

> Playing the classification game in the abstract, as is done in universities, is a joyful, exhilarating experience, harmless and inconsequential. Classifying people in life is a grim business which channelizes destinies and determines fate. A person becomes a category, is processed as a category, plays the assigned role, lives up to the implications. Labeled irrational, the person acts crazy; catalogued dangerous, the person becomes dangerous or stays behind bars.

Karl Menninger (1968, pp. 117–118), a noted psychiatrist, has reacted with strong words to the 1968 publication of a revised set of diagnostic (that is, labeling) categories for psychiatry:

> A committee of our worldly national body has just [1968] published a manual containing a full description of all the bewitchments to which all human flesh is err, with the proper names for each one, the minute suborder and subspecies listed and a code number for the computer. The colleagues who prepared this witch's hammer

manual are worthy fellows—earnest, honest, hard-working, simplistic; they were taught to believe that these horrible things exist, these things with Greek names and Arabic numerals. And if patients show the stigmata, should they not be given the label and the number? To me this is not only the revival of medieval nonsense and superstition; it is a piece of social immorality.

Social workers who are sometimes prone to adopt psychiatric terms and classifications might pay special heed to Menninger's concern.

But is not classification necessary? Or, are we to agree with Salomon's position (1967) that there is an inherent conflict between the needs of science to order and classify and the humanism of social work? Toch (1970, p. 15) suggests that "the point of concern rests in any labels that lead to sorting or disposition." Toch takes the position that the labeling is necessary for thinking or theory building but is not particularly helpful in making dispositional decisions about people; concern should occur when decisions about what is going to happen to people are based on the individual's having previously been placed in a particular category. And yet it is precisely at this point that classification appears to be most useful. Generally classifications come into play when professionals are attempting to assess or diagnose a situation as a guide for selecting appropriate procedures for dealing with the problem. Our point of view on this will be more completely developed in Chapter 10, in which assessment procedures will be discussed in terms of the participation of both the worker and the client. In general, however, we think it possible to develop assessment procedures which maximize individuality and minimize the need for categorization, yet maintain scientific rigor in dealing with valid and reliable data, vigorously pursuing facts, and conscientiously seeking alternative explanations.

USING CLIENT STRENGTH

Our focus on problems and work with disadvantaged populations creates an occupational hazard that you will focus too much on client weakness and problems and fail to identify strengths. Failure to identify strengths is very likely to occur in work with minority groups by a worker unfamiliar with the culture who may fail to recognize the cultural supports and traditions available to a client. Anthony Maluccio's (1979, p. 399) study of social worker and client perceptions of treatment outcome and client functioning find some striking differences of view:

In general, clients presented themselves as *pro-active,* autonomous human beings who are able to enhance their functioning and competence through the use of counseling service along with the resources operant in themselves and their social networks. Workers, on the other hand, tended to view clients as *reactive* organisms with continuing problems, *weakness,* and limited potentialities.

Maluccio (1979, p. 401) concludes that, ". . . there is a need to shift the focus in social work education and practice from problems or pathology to strengths, resources, and potentialities in human beings and their environments. If this shift occurs, practitioners would be more likely to view clients as capable of organizing their own lives." We concur with this suggestion and consider a focus on strengths as in keeping with respect for individual dignity. Think about how differently your reactions are when your strengths rather than weaknesses are mentioned. This is not to deny that there are problems to be addressed and weakness to be considered; but most of us are more willing and able to address weakness when strengths can also be brought into play.

EXPECTATION OF PARTICIPATION

Participation in decision making, planning, and action on one's own behalf is essential to the maintenance of human dignity. Think of the impact on dignity and individualism of entering an institution, such as a hospital, where you have little or no control regarding decisions about what happens to you. We emphasize joint decision making on the part of worker and client and your responsibility to enable client participation because we see this as essential to the maintenance of human dignity. People's dignity is respected and preserved to the extent that they are involved in decisions and actions affecting them.

In this respect we suspect that social work may differ from other professions. In most dealings with professionals in our culture, the decision-making authority of the client is largely overshadowed by the expertise of the professional and, to a large extent, limited to decisions of whether or not to accept the professional's advice. Not so with the social work profession. Expertise of the social worker lies less in the substantive areas of knowing what is best for the client and more in the process area of assisting clients to develop alternatives for themselves, make decisions among the alternatives, and implement decisions. To assume that one knows what is best for the client, both robs the client of dignity and runs the very grave risk of developing what Matthew Dumont (1968, p. 6) refers to as a rescue fantasy:

> The most destructive thing in psychotherapy is a "rescue fantasy" in the therapist— a feeling that the therapist is the divinely sent agent to pull tormented souls from the pit of suffering and adversity and put them back on the road to happiness and glory. A major reason this fantasy is so destructive is that it carries the conviction that the patient will be saved only through and by the therapist. When such a conviction is communicated to patients, verbally or otherwise, they have no choice other than to rebel and leave or become even more helpless, dependent, and sick.

Sometimes the new, or even the experienced, worker feels frustration in coming to grips with the reality that the social worker cannot be the fountainhead of all wisdom who can masterfully assume and resolve the client's problems. A certain humility is necessary to recognize that the client is the chief problem solver. This is not to deny that the worker plays a major part in assisting the client through the process and may at times serve rather forcefully as the client's agent.

Opportunities for client participation will be missed, however, unless you are willing to maintain expectations of clients—expectations for participation, expectations for engagement in problem-solving activities, and expectations that the problem can be solved. Oxley (1966, pp. 432–437) discusses the importance of worker's expectations for client motivation and suggests,

> . . . that the worker should learn to expect a little bit more than the client expects of himself. Social workers are very well versed in beginning where the client is but perhaps too often tend to stay where the client is. If they instead assume the responsibility for leadership and imparting realistic hope, they may more effectively strengthen a client's ego and help him to reach to achieve his full potential and assume social responsibility.

Schwartz (1962, p. 269) refers to this as lending a vision and identifies it as one of the worker's tasks. Lending a vision by expecting, permitting, and encouraging client participation will emphasize and strengthen client dignity.

FOCUS ON WANTS RATHER THAN NEEDS

The social work literature is replete with references to the needs of people. Speaking of needs, however, frequently translates as someone's (perhaps a professional's) view of what is good for someone else. Reid (1978, pp. 25–29) suggests wants as a better concept. A want is a ". . . cognitive affective event consisting of an idea that something is desirable and a feeling of tension associated with not having it." Further, "when a want is experienced without means of satisfaction at hand or in sight, one has the sensation of having a problem." We agree with Reid's analysis that a person's wants provide a more useful frame of reference for social work than needs:

> A want is close to (though not synonymous with) a "need" when the latter is an expression of a person's wishes, as in "I need a job," but not when "need" is used to express an outsider's evaluation of what a person should have, as in "he needs help."
> This distinction is particularly important given the traditional emphasis in social work on the second meaning of "need." Historically, social work programs have been based on professional and agency conceptions of the needs of different classes of people—the poor, mentally ill, delinquents, troubled families, and so on. In the process, not enough attention, in my judgment, has been paid to what people *want*. It is hoped the central position given to wants in the present framework will help to serve as a corrective to one of the primary occupational hazards of social work—acting on the basis of what we think is good for clients.
> A focus on wants rather than needs may give us a different perspective on "unmotivated client." Usually, he is unmotivated to be what social workers or others believe he ought to be. He lacks "motivation" to be a better spouse or parent, or to be more law abiding. To our dismay we see vast numbers of people who do not have motives for self-betterment, as we define it. While many clients lack motivation in these terms, few lack wants. If the client's wants are our concern, then the essential questions become: What does the person want? Can we help him get it? Should we do so? Should we try to create wants he does not have? If so, by what means? These questions are not easily answered, but they may help clarify our position and thinking about the many people who are less than enthusiastic about our efforts to help them.

Placing emphasis on what the client wants should deter zeal to do things for people, ostensibly to meet their needs, which they do not want done to them. Although perhaps well motivated, efforts to meet people's needs have increasingly been coming under attack because many of these efforts may violate the liberty of people (Gaylin et al., 1978). A number of rights movements—children's rights, student's rights, patient's rights, inmate's rights, and so forth—have emerged partially in response to unbridled discretion in the name of doing good. There may indeed be a serious conflict between efforts to meet people's needs and efforts to protect people's rights; certainly the notion that large bureaucracies can be consistently benevolent and act in the best interest of clients or patients is open to a very serious challenge. The concept of wants—needs experienced by people rather than perceived by some external organization—provides a focus for social work which respects individual liberty and dignity of the persons being served. We have identified the premise that the individual is unique and should be treated with respect and dignity as a social work value and have argued that this value premise can be operationalized as you are sensitive and aware of what you are communicating regarding client dignity by the way you organize and administer social services, avoiding classifying clients, discover and assist clients to make use of their strengths, expect client participation in problem solving, and by maintaining a focus on client wants rather than client needs. Let us now turn our attention to a second social work value premise—client self-determination.

CLIENT SELF-DETERMINATION

The principle of client self-determination derives logically from belief in the innate dignity of the person. If people possess an inherent dignity, then it follows that they should be permitted to become what they wish— to determine their own lifestyles insofar as possible. The belief in client self-determination clearly implies that people should be permitted to make decisions for themselves. This carries with it the rather clear assumption that most of the time those decisions will be responsible—responsible in the sense that people in their decision making will, for the most part, make decisions which are consistent with the welfare of the community. The social work stance has generally been to couple the concept of client self-determination with that of responsibility for the total community and to attempt to work out a balance between the two. Barring some clear-cut indication of danger to others, the social worker in day-to-day contacts with clients will generally attempt to maximize opportunities for client self-determination.

Inherent in the concept of client self-determination is the idea of alternatives. Self-determination implies decisions, or the making of choices between one course of action as contrasted with other courses of action. It is fraudulent to think of self-determination without alternatives. If there is only one course of action, how can there be self-determination? The client has no choice and thus no opportunity for self-determining? Much of social work activity with clients consists of a quest for alternatives in order to expand the client's opportunities for self-determination. The quest for alternatives may take various forms—helping the client develop new alternatives and resources within the environment or helping the client find and develop new ways to respond to environmental demands.

In the last chapter you read the article by Carol Hooker (Reading 2–1) on learned helplessness. When people believe there is nothing they can do to control events or there are no decisions they can make which will impact upon their situation, then their self-determination is constrained— if not denied. Self-determination comes as these views can be modified and as people can be helped to exercise choice. In the first chapter you read "The House on Sixth Street" (Reading 1–1). In this case, self-determination was limited by the lack of adequate housing and efforts to permit greater choice regarding housing helped increase self-determination. Self-determination may be increased by activity focused on removing blockages within the environment which are limiting client's opportunities as well as by helping clients remove blockages within themselves which limit their abilities to see and use alternative courses of action. People whose range of response to their environment is limited by their own stereotyped and patterned behavior are as much lacking in opportunity for self-determination as the ghetto client confronted with the lack of environmental opportunities.

Both the value premises of human dignity and self-determination imply respect and support of a wide diversity of client value orientations. But these values also raise many issues for the social worker. For example, if we believe in the self-determination of all people, what do we do when our clients coerce another or interfere seriously with the rights of a vulnerable person? Another issue in self-determination is inherent in the nature of choice itself. What is the meaning of self-determination if alternatives are so seriously limited as to be no choice at all? And, can one really exercise self-determination if one does not understand the consequences of the choice or if one does not have adequate facts upon which to base a decision? Certain laws to protect consumers, or laws relating to warranties and "truth in lending," are examples of society's actions in protecting those who must make certain decisions. If we believe that each person has a right to total self-determination with no limits, then they must support the notion that the race is always for the strong and the uncaring. Some of the most difficult jobs of the social worker are those involving conflicts between those who would exercise self-determination in ways that are destructive to themselves and others and those they damage.

Does the principle of client self-determination require the social worker to support such value orientations among cultural groups in which they are dominant? It is our position that when client behavior results in damages to another individual or another group, damages that our knowledge of the needs of others tells us is severe, workers cannot support the hurtful action. However, this principle—that workers do not support the action—says nothing about what our action should be.

Charles Levy (1972, pp. 488–493) identifies a number of areas in which social workers valuing planned change have value conflicts with potential clients. There may certainly be times in which a social worker's conception of how to operationalize the notion of human dignity and client self-determination may be inconsistent with value orientations held by clients; when this occurs these differences become a matter for discussion and negotiation between the worker and client. The differences must be clarified and a workable resolution achieved before intervention efforts occur. Client values may serve as a barrier to alternatives and a limit to self-determination.

Hardman, in the article included with this chapter, suggests that when the values of a client conflict with the welfare of others or the client's achieving the agreed-upon goals, then the values themselves become an appropriate target for change.

He confronts the question of whether social work is always bound to support the self-determined actions of the client. Hardman's unexamined belief in the client's right to self-determination had left him uneasy but essentially uninvolved with the issue that the values of the client regarding sexual activity were likely to lead to illegal behavior and to damage the dignity and feelings of another. The rights of another only became a real problem for him when he realized that the person being damaged could be his daughter. Suddenly the rights of the other became critical. Thus, Hardman was confronted with an issue not only of his own value system and its difference from the client's but with the issue of the responsibility of a professional person to be concerned with the rights of all people. Another intriguing example is the problem of wife battering which seems to be related to value orientations present in some groups of our society regarding the proper role of women as being subservient to the husband. And what about certain groups in our society that believe that "to spare the rod spoils the child"?

It is our position that social workers are not engaged in the process of forcing people to change behavior. Forced change of behavior is a matter for courts and the legal system. Therefore, any work to change client values or behavior in the interests of increasing life satisfactions of clients, or of others involved with clients, has to come from the engagement of client and worker in an agreed-upon plan. Certainly client values may be such that actions that follow from them may hurt others, and certain values may also serve to limit the adequate choices of the client. However, any effort toward change must involve the client. Thus when the values of a client conflict with the rights of others or get in the way of the client achieving agreed-upon goals then the values themselves become a topic for discussion and for consideration as an appropriate target for change.

The principle of client self-determination will lead the social worker in the direction of engaging the client in three actions: (1) consideration of how these values may restrict progress toward the goals desired by the client, (2) consideration of all possible alternatives and their consequences for goal achievement, and (3) consideration of the rights and needs of others. The principle of client self-determination is misunderstood if it is taken to suggest that the worker does nothing but put the total responsibility for considering choice upon the client with no offer of alternatives or consideration of the outcome of choice.

The client exercising decision making is a key phrase in this formulation. The concept of client self-determination as operationalized in social work calls for maximizing opportunities for clients to make decisions for and about themselves. This is an area in which the social work profession may differ markedly from other professions. Clients generally go to other professionals for expert advice; that is, expecting to be told what in the view of the professional is best for the client. Patients expect the doctor to diagnose an ailment and to recommend a specific course of treatment, and clients expect the lawyer to advise them as to what action should be taken in dealing with a legal problem. In both of these situations there is, of course, an element of self-determination, inasmuch as the patient or client must ultimately decide whether or not to follow the expert's advice.

But the social worker is not an expert in what's best for the client and is not primarily a giver of advice. Rather we manage a process which involves the client in the solution of their own problems including modifying their values if these contribute to the problem.

But does this mean the social worker does not offer an opinion or make a suggestion? Emphatically not. Just as the extreme of taking over and making decisions for the client is to be avoided so is the extreme of never sharing a viewpoint with the client. Such action denies clients the benefit of the worker's judgment and may effectively deny clients alternatives that they may wish to consider in their own decision making. As Charlotte Towle (1965, p. 26) has said: "The social worker's devotion to the idea that every individual has a right to be self-determining does not rule out valid concern with directing people's attention to the most desirable alternative." Workers have the obligations of sharing with clients their own thinking, perhaps their own experiences, not as a way of directing the clients' lives but rather as an additional source of information and input for the clients to consider in their own decision making. It is imperative, however, that the social worker's input be recognized as information to be considered and not as edict to be followed. Schwartz (1961) offers some very helpful suggestions in this regard. He suggests that the worker has a responsibility to contribute data to the client and that the data might include facts, ideas, and value concepts. He goes on to argue that in contributing data the worker should inform the client that the worker is offering only part of the total available social experience and is not the source of all knowledge. Moreover, the data contributed should be clearly related to the purpose of work with the client, and opinions, while important data, should be clearly labeled as opinions and not represented as facts. Client self-determination does not imply worker nonparticipation; the skill, indeed, the mark, of successful practitioners lie in their abilities to share knowledge and thinking without imposing a judgment and leaving the client free to accept or reject their views.

Another aspect of self-determination requires emphasis. Some workers confuse client self-determination with worker self-determination. We are not arguing for the latter. In taking on a professional responsibility, workers agree to limit their own self-determination in the clients' behalf. The National Association of Social Workers Code of Ethics, included with this chapter, clearly limits worker self-determination. When a worker's communication style or dress style arouse the antagonism of clients or others who may influence clients, the worker's professional responsibility may call for the forfeiting of the worker's self-determination in the clients' behalf. This excerpt from an interview with a social worker functioning in a community organization capacity illustrates the frustrations which may be experienced by a worker unwilling to set aside personal self-determination in behalf of the clients.

> I remarked that it certainly must be satisfying to organize and be part of such an event. I was surprised when Alice shook her head slowly and said in a much more somber tone of voice, "No, 99 percent of the time there is very little glamour to organizing." I asked her to explain further, and she went on to say that it is hard, hard work and that one of the most discouraging things for her to realize is that oftentimes the people you are organizing aren't necessarily looking for a change in the system, but rather to become a part of that system. Usually that means playing the same games that those in power play. She talked further about the frustration she deals with constantly. I, too, began to feel that organizing was not the glamorous, romantic job I had pictured it to be.

Does this worker have an obligation to set aside her own goals of "changing the system" and work with clients who want to be successful within the system rather than produce more revolutionary change? We think she does.

In this section on client self-determination we have attempted to establish this concept as one of the value premises underlying social work. Five points have been made: (1) Self-determination commits the social worker and the client to a quest for alternatives. Without alternatives there is no opportunity to make decisions and no opportunity to engage in self-determination. (2) A major responsibility of the social worker is to maximize clients' opportunities for decison making. Social workers are not experts in what is substantively best for clients and thus should avoid making decisions for clients; but social workers are expert in assisting clients in a process of joint decision making. (3) Social workers have the obligation to offer their own viewpoints and suggestions to clients. These are offered as alternatives and input which a client may consider, and not as an edict or a "right" answer for the client. (4) Efforts to modify client's values are not necessarily inconsistent with the concept of self-determination providing the values interfere with the clients' efforts to attain their goals, or with the welfare of others, and clients concur with efforts to produce value change. (5) A differentiation must be made between client self-determination and worker self-determination. In assuming professional responsibility, workers sharply limit their own self-determination and become responsible for conducting themselves in ways which best meet the interests of clients and maximize clients' opportunities.

LEGAL AUTHORITY AND SELF-DETERMINATION

Fields of practice, in which the worker possesses legal authority that may be used to coerce the client, present some special issues in regard to the matter of client self-determination. Coercion is typically mandated for two different types of clients and for different reasons. One group of clients is perceived as being in need of protection because of their dependency status and thus coercion is justified as necessary to protect the client. Dependent children, developmentally disabled persons, and the aged are typically perceived as in need of protection. A second use of coercion is to force rehabilitation for those who have violated the norms of society—persons in this group typically include juvenile and adult offenders, chemically dependent persons, and mentally ill persons. We think the appropriate stance of a profession such as social work with a high commitment to the principal of client self-determination may vary in regard to the use of coercion depending on whether the coercion is used for the protective or the forced rehabilitative purposes.

William Reid and Laura Epstein (1977) make a distinction between the protective and helping functions of the social worker when they suggest that the practitioner must not only recognize these differences but also must make sure the client understands them. We have argued that available knowledge should direct our interventions (see Chapter 2). Our knowledge base confirms that dependent children, developmentally disabled persons, and aged persons may be victimized and harm themselves; responsible action would indicate that some limitations in client self-determination may be warranted in the interest of providing protection to the client. Even within the limits imposed as necessary to protect the client, the worker has responsibility to develop as many practical alternatives as possible for client decision making thus increasing client self-determination. For example, our knowledge may indicate that a physically ill, aged person may no longer be able to live alone at home despite wishes to do so. A need for protection may limit client self-determination in regard to this choice but the astute worker may well be able to engage the client in decision making regarding the type of specific alternative living arrangement to be followed. Likewise, children who must be removed from their homes because of extreme neglect or abuse may be provided considerable involvement in the decision making regarding the alternative living arrangements; indeed, involving the children in this decision making may open up resources such as relatives, neighbors, and others previously unknown to the social worker.

When coercive authority is being used and justified on the basis of protecting the client, we think it is essential that the worker be clear as to the knowledge base which justifies the use of authority as well as the source and extent of the authority; these matters must further be clearly communicated to the client. The source and extent of authority is an example of agency function, Schwartz's (1961) second source of limitation on the worker's activity. Because of possibilities of abusing protective authority we consider it appropriate for clients to have opportunities to request appeal and review of worker's decisions and consider the involvement of courts or guardians independent of the worker as an appropriate check and balance against possible abuses. Social workers in the profession have an obligation to continually reassess whether coercive authority is really necessary to protect the client or is being used unnecessarily to impose a particular standard upon a client. Marvin Silverman (1977, p. 177) addresses this issue in relation to coercion of children:

> If children's rights became a reality, there would clearly be a change in the nature of many social workers' professional relationships. These would become largely voluntary—the kind of relationship most consistent with the traditions of social work. There would also be changes in specific roles. At the present time, there are large and expensive professional and bureaucratic structures which are organized to maintain children in nonvoluntary associations and to work with the problems such associ-

ations generate. They would no longer be needed. If schools were populated by willing students, there would be far less need for school social workers, school psychologists, guidance personnel, and administrators who deal mainly with discipline problems. There are children in residential treatment centers not because of family problems but because of inability to function in school. Police, courts, and probation officers spend a great deal of energy in dealing with truancy, status offences, incorrigibility, and runaways. With increased children's rights, social work roles would flow directly from children's needs rather than being filtered through structures which, to some extent, at least, are organized around social control. Similarly, teachers could concentrate on improving the educational program, and police could concentrate on true crime—juvenile and adult.

The second use of legal authority—to attempt to force rehabilitation upon the client—creates a serious dilemma for the profession. There are at least two distinct directions by which this dilemma might be resolved. One direction is to attempt to integrate the authority and service roles and, within the limitations imposed by the setting, try to expand opportunities for client self-determination. A second alternative is for social work to withdraw from the coercive efforts to rehabilitate.

Typically social workers have attempted to integrate their authority and service functions (Hardman, 1960; Hatcher, 1978; Klockars, 1972; Overton, 1957). While the presence of legal authority may limit areas for client self-determination, it also leaves extensive areas for the exercise of client self-determination. These include determining how the authority will be exercised as well as noting areas in addition to the legal requirements in which self-determination may be emphasized. A probation agency, for example, may enforce the legal requirement that the probationer must report to the probation officer; this is not a matter for client self-determination. But the sensitive probation officer can allow for considerable client self-determination in the frequency of reporting, the length of the interviews, the time of reporting, and the content to be discussed during the interviews. Even in correctional settings clients can be extended considerable self-determination in how they utilize workers including, if they choose, only using them for the minimum mandated by the probation orders. Gerald O'Connor (1972) offers a very insightful position on the question of self-determination in corrections:

> The principle of self-determination, the freedom to choose one's own destiny is based on an assumption of individual dignity. . . . The recognition of people's right to free choice guarantees that they may choose to run their life as they see fit. This choice may run counter to society's welfare and even their own, yet essentially it is their choice and their prerogative. Society may censure, but it cannot take from them the right; nor should society strip them of personal dignity by a censure. The criminal then has a right to say "crime is my choice and I am willing to pay the price. If you send me to prison, I am paying my debt to society and refuse to submit to your attempts to reform me." The principle of self-determination makes it incumbent upon society to honor such a plea.
>
> There are large numbers of inmates in correctional institutions who recognize a need for rehabilitation and are willing to become involved in programs for that end. An inmate's voluntary recognition of a need for assistance does not, in turn, give officals a free reign in outlining the inmate's rehabilitation program. It is reasona-

ble that the offender have input into the definition of the offender's own problem
and have this included in the official assessment. The inmate should have the opportunity to say what type of program would be of assistance and who should provide
the services. Further, it seems appropriate that the inmates have a right, in part, to
determine the conditions under which the services are delivered.

Even in situations involving legal authority, considerable latitude exists
for clients to exercise self-determination. Skillful workers can maximize
these opportunities with the client. At the very least, of course, the clients
have the option of determining whether they are going to do anything more
than the legal minimum as well as the option of ignoring the requirements
of the authority and accepting the consequences.

Another response to the dilemma of self-determination vis-à-vis coercive
services is the withdrawal of social work from these roles (Henry Miller,
1968). The lack of evidence to support the effectiveness of coerced rehabilitation (Lipton, Martinson, & Wilks, 1975; Martinson, 1974) further supports
this notion. Withdrawal of social work from coerced rehabilitative roles
does not, of course, mean that social services should not be provided to
offenders and others who are presently being subjected to forced efforts
of rehabilitation. The services of social workers should certainly be provided
to these populations but structures can be developed which permit the provision of these services on a voluntary basis.

Many offenders would certainly enter into agreements to work jointly
with social workers to resolve problems the offender is experiencing in
their personal situations and interactions. Silverman makes the same asser-
tion for children. While this issue is a complex one and one which will
undoubtedly be debated within the profession for quite some time, our inclination is to begin challenging the appropriateness of social work activity
in coerced rehabilitative settings and to begin development of structures,
policies, and programs to permit a more voluntary association and partnership between client and social worker. Such a process is more consistent
with the principal of client self-determination. This does not, of course, ex-
empt persons who are found guilty of violating laws from being negatively
sanctioned or punished by the society. The authors only suggest that the
role of the social worker should not be to carry out these sanctions but to
provide social services within a partnership arrangement with clients, regardless of their status, who are defining problems in their day-by-day living
and wish to engage in a partnership with the social worker for problem-
solving purposes.

RECAPITULATION

This section has presented our views concerning social work values. Values were defined as things which a profession prefers but which cannot
be proven to be true. Values are not unique to a profession but are adapted
from the overall culture. The uniqueness and innate dignity of the individual
and the principle of client self-determination were analyzed as two value
premises underlying social work practice. The process of operationalizing

these values—especially client self-determination—provides an opportunity for social work to find its distinctiveness among the professions.

Several implicit principles in the preceding discussion should be more explicitly stated: (1) Values are guides to action; they are principles which, whenever possible, are to be maximized. Values, however, are not straitjackets. They are to be used selectively and creatively, although the primary focus will be on maximizing them. (2) In situations where the value premise and knowledge are in conflict, opt for knowledge. In Chapter 2 a potential conflict was noted between self-determination and a child's need for protection and stability in order to meet developmental needs; a lower priority was attached to the value of self-determination because of knowledge of the child's needs. (3) When knowledge is lacking, the value premises should become the prevailing standards. (4) Values limit the uses to which the profession's methodology can be placed. Group processes, for example, might well be used to subvert individualism or to stir up fear and hysteria which threaten diversity and self-determination. This use of group strategies is inappropriate because it is inconsistent with the value premises of the profession. Change strategies and methodology can be used for a variety of ends. Social work practitioners must be sure that their strategies are used to support the uniqueness of the individual and the client's right to self-determination.

A LOOK FORWARD

The Code of Ethics of the National Association of Social Workers and an article by Dale Hardman are reproduced in this chapter. Hardman focuses on an intriguing issue: "Should social workers attempt to change client values?" His answer will provide considerable opportunity for discussion and debate.

The National Association of Social Workers Code of Ethics provides a statement, at an abstract level, of the present values of the profession. But there is not universal agreement that this statement reflects social work values appropriately. We do not necessarily expect agreement with these readings or with the foregoing material. This material is presented to stimulate thought and discussion about some of the difficult value questions confronting the profession.

The pages ahead will present an approach to social work practice which is believed to be both humanistic and scientific. Classification is minimized, clients are involved in a partnership undertaking with workers; and individuality is maximized. Chapter 4 will introduce you to some useful theoretical perspectives for practice and Chapter 5 will introduce the dimension of practice in a bureaucracy. The problem-solving process outlined in Chapter 6 requires a high degree of rationality and discipline on the part of workers. In Chapter 6 the concept of relationship—the medium through which much of the problem-solving work may occur—is introduced. A discussion of communication and interviewing as basic skills is found in Chapter 7. Subsequent chapters provide a detailed description of the phases of the problem-solving model.

Reading 3-1

*The NASW Code of Ethics**

National Association of Social Workers

PREAMBLE

This code is intended to serve as a guide to the everyday conduct of members of the social work profession and as a basis for the adjudication of issues in ethics when the conduct of social workers is alleged to deviate from the standards expressed or implied in this code. It represents standards of ethical behavior for social workers in professional relationships with those served, with colleagues, with employers, with other individuals and professions, and with the community and society as a whole. It also embodies standards of ethical behavior governing individual conduct to the extent that such conduct is associated with an individual's status and identity as a social worker.

This code is based on the fundamental values of the social work profession that include the worth, dignity, and uniqueness of all persons as well as their rights and opportunities. It is also based on the nature of social work, which fosters conditions that promote these values.

In subscribing to and abiding by this code, the social worker is expected to view ethical responsibility in as inclusive a context as each situation demands and within which ethical judgment is required. The social worker is expected to take into consideration all the principles in this code that have a bearing upon any situation in which ethical judgment is to be exercised and professional intervention or conduct is planned. The course of action that the social worker chooses is expected to be consistent with the spirit as well as the letter of this code.

In itself, this code does not represent a set of rules that will prescribe all the behaviors of social workers in all the complexities of professional life. Rather, it offers general principles to guide conduct, and the judicious appraisal of conduct, in situations that have ethical implications. It provides the basis for making judgments about ethical actions before and after they occur. Frequently, the particular situation determines the ethical principles that apply and the manner of their application. In such cases, not only the particular ethical principles are taken into immediate consideration, but also the entire code and its spirit. Specific applications of ethical principles must be judged within the context in which they are being considered. Ethical behavior in a given situation must satisfy not only the judgment of the individual social worker but also the judgment of an unbiased jury of professional peers.

This code should not be used as an instrument to deprive any social worker of the opportunity or freedom to practice with complete professional integrity; nor should any disciplinary action be taken on the basis of this code without maximum provision for safeguarding the rights of the social worker affected.

The ethical behavior of social workers results not from edict, but from a personal commitment of the individual. This code is offered to affirm the will and zeal of all social workers to be ethical and to act ethically in all that they do as social workers.

* Reprinted with permission, from "Code of Ethics of the National Association of Social Workers" as adopted by the 1979 NASW Delegate Assembly, effective July 1, 1980.

The following codified ethical principles should guide social workers in the various roles and relationships and at the various levels of responsibility in which they function professionally. These principles also serve as a basis for the adjudication by the National Association of Social Workers of issues in ethics.

In subscribing to this code, social workers are required to cooperate in its implementation and abide by any disciplinary rulings based on it. They should also take adequate measures to discourage, prevent, expose, and correct the unethical conduct of colleagues. Finally, social workers should be equally ready to defend and assist colleagues unjustly charged with unethical conduct.

I. *The Social Worker's Conduct and Comportment as a Social Worker*

  A. Propriety—The social worker should maintain high standards of personal conduct in the capacity or identity as social worker.

    1. The private conduct of the social worker is a personal matter to the same degree as is any other person's, except when such conduct compromises the fulfillment of professional responsibilities.

    2. The social worker should not participate in, condone, or be associated with dishonesty, fraud, deceit, or misrepresentation.

    3. The social worker should distinguish clearly between statements and actions made as a private individual and as a representative of the social work profession or an organization or group.

  B. Competence and Professional Development—The social worker should strive to become and remain proficient in professional practice and the performance of professional functions.

    1. The social worker should accept responsibility or employment only on the basis of existing competence or the intention to acquire the necessary competence.

    2. The social worker should not misrepresent professional qualifications, education, experience, or affiliations.

  C. Service—The social worker should regard as primary the service obligation of the social work profession.

    1. The social worker should retain ultimate responsibility for the quality and extent of the service that individual assumes, assigns, or performs.

    2. The social worker should act to prevent practices that are inhumane or discriminatory against any person or group of persons.

  D. Integrity—The social worker should act in accordance with the highest standards of professional integrity and impartiality.

    1. The social worker should be alert to and resist the influences and pressures that interfere with the exercise of professional discretion and impartial judgment required for the performance of professional functions.

    2. The social worker should not exploit professional relationships for personal gain.

  E. Scholarship and Research—The social worker engaged in study and research should be guided by the conventions of scholarly inquiry.

1. The social worker engaged in research should consider carefully its possible consequences for human beings.
2. The social worker engaged in research should ascertain that the consent of participants in the research is voluntary and informed, without any implied deprivation or penalty for refusal to participate, and with due regard for participants' privacy and dignity.
3. The social worker engaged in research should protect participants from unwarranted physical or mental discomfort, distress, harm, danger, or deprivation.
4. The social worker who engages in the evaluation of services or cases should discuss them only for professional purposes and only with persons directly and professionally concerned with them.
5. Information obtained about participants in research should be treated as confidential.
6. The social worker should take credit only for work actually done in connection with scholarly and research endeavors and credit contributions made by others.

II. *The Social Worker's Ethical Responsibility to Clients*
   F. Primacy of Clients' Interests— The social worker's primary responsibility is to clients.
   1. The social worker should serve clients with devotion, loyalty, determination, and the maximum application of professional skill and competence.
   2. The social worker should not exploit relationships with clients for personal advantage, or solicit the clients of one's agency for private practice.
   3. The social worker should not practice, condone, facilitate or collaborate with any form of discrimination on the basis of race, color, sex, sexual orientation, age, religion, national origin, marital status, political belief, mental or physical handicap, or any other preference or personal characteristic, condition or status.
   4. The social worker should avoid relationships or commitments that conflict with the interests of clients.
   5. The social worker should under no circumstances engage in sexual activities with clients.
   6. The social worker should provide clients with accurate and complete information regarding the extent and nature of the services available to them.
   7. The social worker should apprise clients of their risks, rights, opportunities, and obligations associated with social service to them.
   8. The social worker should seek advice and counsel of colleagues and supervisors whenever such consultation is in the best interest of clients.

9. The social worker should terminate service to clients, and professional relationships with them, when such service and relationships are no longer required or no longer serve the clients' needs or interests.

10. The social worker should withdraw services precipitously only under unusual circumstances, giving careful consideration to all factors in the situation and taking care to minimize possible adverse effects.

11. The social worker who anticipates the termination or interruption of service to clients should notify clients promptly and seek the transfer, referral, or continuation of service in relation to the clients' needs and preferences.

G. Rights and Prerogatives of Clients—The social worker should make every effort to foster maximum self-determination on the part of clients.

1. When the social worker must act on behalf of a client who has been adjudged legally incompetent, the social worker should safeguard the interests and rights of the client.

2. When another individual has been legally authorized to act in behalf of a client, the social worker should deal with that person always with the client's best interest in mind.

3. The social worker should not engage in any action that violates or diminishes the civil or legal rights of clients.

H. Confidentiality and Privacy—The social worker should respect the privacy of clients and hold in confidence all information obtained in the course of professional service.

1. The social worker should share with others confidences revealed by clients, without their consent, only for compelling professional reasons.

2. The social worker should inform clients fully about the limits of confidentiality in a given situation, the purposes for which information is obtained, and how it may be used.

3. The social worker should afford clients reasonable access to any official social work records concerning them.

4. When providing clients with access to records, the social worker should take due care to protect the confidences of others contained in those records.

5. The social worker should obtain informed consent of clients before taping, recording, or permitting third party observation of their activities.

I. Fees—When setting fees, the social worker should ensure that they are fair, reasonable, considerate and commensurate with the service performed and with due regard for the client's ability to pay.

1. The social worker should not divide a fee or accept

or give anything of value for receiving or making a referral.

III. *The Social Worker's Ethical Responsibility to Colleagues*

J. Respect, Fairness, and Courtesy—The social worker should treat colleagues with respect, courtesy, fairness, and good faith.

1. The social worker should cooperate with colleagues to promote professional interests and concerns.

2. The social worker should respect confidences shared by colleagues in the course of their professional relationships and transactions.

3. The social worker should create and maintain conditions of practice that facilitate ethical and competent professional performance by colleagues.

4. The social worker should treat with respect, and represent accurately and fairly, the qualifications, views, and findings of colleagues and use appropriate channels to express judgments on these matters.

5. The social worker who replaces or is replaced by a colleague in professional practice should act with consideration for the interest, character, and reputation of that colleague.

6. The social worker should not exploit a dispute between a colleague and employers to obtain a position or otherwise advance the social worker's interest.

7. The social worker should seek arbitration or mediation when conflicts with colleagues require resolution for compelling professional reasons.

8. The social worker should extend to colleagues of other professions the same respect and cooperation that is extended to social work colleagues.

9. The social worker who serves as an employer, supervisor, or mentor to colleagues should make orderly and explicit arrangements regarding the conditions of their continuing professional relationship.

10. The social worker who has the responsibility for employing and evaluating the performance of other staff members, should fulfill such responsibility in a fair, considerate, and equitable manner, on the basis of clearly enunciated criteria.

11. The social worker who has the responsibility for evaluating the performance of employees, supervisees, or students should share evaluations with them.

K. Dealing with Colleagues' Clients—The social worker has the responsibility to relate to the clients of colleagues with full professional consideration.

1. The social worker should not solicit the clients of colleagues.

2. The social worker should not assume professional responsibility for the clients of another agency or a colleague without appropriate communication with that agency or colleague.

3. The social worker who serves the clients of col-

leagues, during a temporary absence or emergency, should serve those clients with the same consideration as that afforded any client.

IV. *The Social Worker's Ethical Responsibility to Employers and Employing Organizations*

    L. Commitment to Employing Organization—The social worker should adhere to commitments made to the employing organization.

        1. The social worker should work to improve the employing agency's policies and procedures, and the efficiency and effectiveness of its services.

        2. The social worker should not accept employment or arrange student field placements in an organization which is currently under public sanction by NASW for violating personnel standards or imposing limitations on or penalties for professional actions on behalf of clients.

        3. The social worker should act to prevent and eliminate discrimination in the employing organization's work assignments and in its employment policies and practice.

        4. The social worker should use with scrupulous regard, and only for purpose for which they are intended, the resources of the employing organization.

V. *The Social Worker's Ethical Responsibility to the Social Work Profession*

    M. Maintaining the Integrity of the Profession—The social worker should uphold and advance the values, ethics, knowledge, and mission of the profession.

        1. The social worker should protect and enhance the dignity and integrity of the profession and should be responsible and vigorous in discussion and criticism of the profession.

        2. The social worker should take action through appropriate channels against unethical conduct by any other member of the profession.

        3. The social worker should act to prevent the unauthorized and unqualified practice of social work.

        4. The social worker should make no misrepresentation in advertising as to qualifications, competence, service, or results to be achieved.

    N. Community Service—The social worker should assist the profession in making social services available to the general public.

        1. The social worker should contribute time and professional expertise to activities that promote respect for the utility, the integrity, and the competence of the social work profession.

        2. The social worker should support the formulation, development, enactment and implementation of social policies of concern to the profession.

    O. Development of Knowledge—The social worker should take responsibility for identifying, developing, and fully utilizing knowledge for professional practice.

1. The social worker should base practice upon recognized knowledge relevant to social work.
2. The social worker should critically examine, and keep current with, emerging knowledge relevant to social work.
3. The social worker should contribute to the knowledge base of social work and share research knowledge and practice wisdom with colleagues.

VI. *The Social Worker's Ethical Responsibility to Society*

P. Promoting the General Welfare—The social worker should promote the general welfare of society.

1. The social worker should act to prevent and eliminate discrimination against any person or group on the basis of race, color, sex, sexual orientation, age, religion, national origin, marital status, political belief, mental or physical handicap, or any other preference or personal characteristic, condition, or status.
2. The social worker should act to ensure that all persons have access to the resources, services, and opportunities which they require.
3. The social worker should act to expand choice and opportunity for all persons, with special regard for disadvantaged or oppressed groups and persons.
4. The social worker should promote conditions that encourage respect for the diversity of cultures which constitute American society.
5. The social worker should provide appropriate professional services in public emergencies.
6. The social worker should advocate changes in policy and legislation to improve social conditions and to promote social justice.
7. The social worker should encourage informed participation by the public in shaping social policies and institutions.

Reading 3-2

*Not with My Daughter You Don't**

Dale G. Hardman

It was a balmy spring afternoon at the Blintz County workhouse. The interviewing room was only half separated from the cell corridors. The inmate looked out the dirt-specked window for some time, then returned his gaze to the social worker. "Twelve more days. I could do 12 days on a bed of spikes. You're the reason I got 55 days knocked off my six months. I wouldn'ta got it without you went to bat for me."

Oscar De Curia only nodded, but inwardly he beamed because expressions of gratitude were infrequent among workhouse clients. "I would like," he said, "to get some idea of your plans when you get out. Most guys need some help getting into a job or school or. . . ."

"Nah. I work for my old man, putting up siding. I always got a job waiting."

"Good. What about school?"

"Can't work and go to school too."

"Some guys do." De Curia bit his lip; he knew as soon as he said it. There he was, imposing his middle-class norms on a lower-class client.

"I quit when I was 15. Nine years ago—too late to go back now."

De Curia had an impulse to suggest some Voc-Ed courses, but instead he just nodded and said, "Okay then, what about your social life?"

"That's all I been thinking about since I got my commutation."

De Curia brightened a bit. At least here he didn't have to worry about imposing

his own norms. Here he could relax, be more natural, more human.

"Chicks," said the inmate. He leaned back and clasped his fingers behind his thick black curly hair. "Chicks is my specialty. Take the average guy in here—for him sex is just quick service stuff: roll in the hay, be on your way. No art to it. No class."

"You're most artistic, then."

"That's it. I'm an artist. Most guys in here wouldn't know the difference."

"But you do. How would you go about it that's any different from anybody else?"

"Well see, same as me they've been locked up for six months to a year. Anything would look good to them, and they'll try to make up for the whole year in the first ten minutes they're out. First broad they see. But not me. Like the soup commercial says: 'To make the best you gotta begin with the best. Then prepare it tenderly . . . carefully . . . slowly.' So I begin with the best. Nothing but fresh meat for me—very fresh. A virgin."

"I see. Well, since there's not a lot of those around. . . ."

"Well, ya gotta know where to look. For one thing you gotta start young—maybe 14 or 15—so you find where they hang out."

"Hmm." De Curia opened his mouth to point out that a sex act with an adolescent would constitute a new violation, but he again bit his tongue and admonished himself that he must not be a moralist. And certainly this client was canny enough to know the law on this point.

"They hang out a lot around Whiffy Dip, especially on weekends. Skating rinks and bowling alleys is good hunting grounds. Always full of teeny chicks."

"Hmm." In truth, De Curia felt a bit more uncomfortable with each self-revelation of his client. But he knew that disapproval on his part would only serve to turn off his client's verbal spigot, and certainly the man needed to talk after four months in lock-up.

"There was one little chick I met at the Rollerama just before I got busted. A virgin, I'll bet my shirt. About 14. Real good skater."

"Hmm." De Curia resolved to be nondirective if it killed him, but his discomfort continued to rise.

"I only saw her two, three times before I got sent up. Skated with her each time. I know she likes me. I think she's the one I'll start with."

"I see." De Curia shifted uneasily as his tension mounted.

"Like I say, begin with the best. And she's the best. Long slender legs. Willowy. Little round bazoobs like ripe peaches. Long auburn hair, always in a pony-tail. Her name was Irma Jean something."

Every man has a sort of saftey plug in his boiler; it melts at a lower temperature than the boiler and serves to prevent the boiler from rupturing. And here De Curia blew his plug. Out spewed his professional role, his persona, in a great gust and blast, and he stood before his client a very angry human being. "Hey, wait a minute! That's my daughter you're talking about, you lecherous bastard!"

OSCAR'S CONFLICT

It was several hours later that Oscar De Curia sat in his office, pondering his misdirected interview at the workhouse. In ten years of practice he had held doggedly to the dictum of nondirection: the nonmoralistic listener, eschewing judgments, never imposing his own norms, never playing God, never setting himself up as an ethical model for his clients' emu-

lation. For ten years, he had adhered to these fundamental premises, drilled into his skull in classrooms, in texts and journals, and in interaction with other social workers. He was, he believed, the epitome of Powers and Witmer's delineation (1951): "Modern casework is distinguished . . . by the fact that its practitioners seldom give advice, cite ethical precepts or the consequence of antisocial behavior, or urge particular courses of action." True, he constantly had to remind himself in those pesky situations that clashed against his own middle-class value system. He had come, in fact, to feel a bit apologetic for being middle class or subscribing to its norms. He felt as though he had been called a dirty name when he was referred to as middle class. But now, suddenly, when these norms were violated close to home, his carefully cultivated professional posture had disintegrated and he had blown his cool, the interview, and the case.

Although De Curia was not given to extensive self-contemplation, he was, in those brief and unaccustomed moments of introspection, essentially honest with himself. Perhaps these two facts were related: in introspection he usually came out loser, due to a basic trait of honesty, so he indulged in it rarely.

Oscar had experienced similar interviews in the past, listening with composure to expressions of sexual exploitation, tales of assaults on persons or property, and threats of vengeance or power or violence. He had often felt a rising discomfort and a need to protest, and always, until today, he had successfully repressed such unprofessional impulses. But now, with his treasured, auburn-haired teen-ager as the proposed object. . . .

At this juncture a new thought trekked across Oscar's synapses: suppose the name his client had dropped had not been Irma Jean; suppose instead it had been Sandra or Millie. Wasn't it conceivable that the fathers of other pony-tailed, knobby-kneed damsels might harbor feelings for them as tender as his? De Curia was struck by this thought much as Goliath encountered David's stony projectile: such a thing had never before entered his head. It jolted him in his tracks. A host of balding and paunchy middle-aged fathers arose in his mind's eye, like a legion of Banquo's ghosts, to ask: In how many hundred cases, have you said "Mm hmm" or "I see" and thereby given tacit acquiescence to illegal, immoral, or violent acts? It was well beyond closing time when the janitor found De Curia still at his desk pondering his conflict.

Upon his return home, De Curia was unusually attentive to his daughter, but otherwise his manner was, for him, exceptionally quiet and subdued. His wife reckoned that he had either been fired or out philandering but that in either case he would shortly tell her so. He hadn't and he didn't.

GENERALIZING THE PROBLEM

During the ensuing week, Oscar De Curia resolved that he would, at whatever cost, resolve his newly mounted conflict. One of his first acts was to request that his supervisor transfer the client who had torpedoed his cool. As has been noted, Mr. De Curia was not a profoundly thoughtful man, but an honest one. His supervisor, on the other hand, was not a profoundly honest man, but a thoughtful one, and so he asked the reason for his subordinate's request. And within the next half hour De Curia had upended the whole wretched can of worms.

The supervisor had indeed encountered this knotty question before; he had mulled it over at considerable length and then shelved it. But Oscar would not be shelved. He was a persistent clod, and he insisted on answers. And answered he was. The supervisor said: "Mm hmm."

"Well, it's true, ain't it?" De Curia waxed ungrammatical only when he became emotional. "From the time we enter graduate school we're admonished against imposing our own values on people. So I don't and look what happens! My own daughter is up for grabs!"

"Mm," said the supervisor, thoughtfully.

"Tell me honestly, Jake," (the supervisor encouraged this bit of familiarity) "What would you do? You must have encountered this kind of incongruity before. How did you handle it?"

Jake could not admit that he had resolved the question by shelving it. So he said, "Hmm." Thoughtfully, that is.

"That doesn't exactly answer my question, you know," De Curia persisted.

Jake squirmed considerably, inwardly at least. Outwardly he was all concern and empathy, as a supervisor should be.

"Well, the problem is really much larger than you are recognizing here, Oscar. What you are saying applies to a lot of lower-class values besides sex behavior."

"So?" said Oscar De Curia.

"You have already mentioned one: you tried to get the guy back into school. Walter Miller (1958, 1959) says that dropping out at about age 16 is the norm for lower-class culture. Riessman (1962) calls it anti-intellectualism—actual hostility toward eggheadedness. Yet the poverty experts had a truism: 'In the poverty battle, all roads lead to the schoolhouse.' How are we ever going to get kids—or young adults—back into the schoolhouse without changing their basic values?"

"That doesn't answer my question. Anyway, maybe we middle class do overvalue education. There are still thousands of blue-collar jobs, some with pretty good pay, that don't require literacy, much less a high school diploma."

"Oh, yes. But high school represents something else to an employer. I once went to a foundry to line up a job for a male parolee. The foreman's first question was: 'Has he finished high school?' I asked why a guy needed a high school diploma to tamp sand into a casting mold. His answer was a good one: 'To us, completion of high school means a guy has stick-to-it-iveness, that he'll stick with a job until it's finished, that he's more likely to be here all day every day than a guy who hasn't finished school.' You can't argue with that reasoning."

"Yeah. Now about my question."

"Patience. At least half our welfare bill can be traced directly to family breakdown. Yet it seems pretty clear that the lower class doesn't take family ties as seriously as does the middle class (Goode, 1964; Hollingshead, 1950; Udry, 1966). How are we ever going to crack the poverty cycle without family stability? And how do you get family stability without changing the cultural norms regarding families?"

"You're not giving me answers, you're giving me more questions. I need more questions like Noah needed more rain."

"Let me finish, please." Jake was merely stalling for time, of course. But sometimes if you talk long enough, a problem will go away—or the client will, which is functionally the same. "Sexual exploitation," continued Jake, "is only one corner of lower-class attitudes toward female status (Rainwater, 1960; Reissman, 1962). A general subordination of females is the norm. If you're an advocate of women's rights, or even if you subscribe to the social work Code of Ethics regarding sex discrimination, you're going to run afoul of a major lower-class value."

"There is also an item in the Code of Ethics that says I will subordinate my personal interests to my professional responsibility. Like I have a professional responsibility not to impose middle-class values. Well, I'll be damned if I'm gonna subordinate my daughter's chastity to that or any other code of ethics."

"Of course. But I want you to look at the whole perspective, the whole panorama of lower-class norms."

"To hell with all that. Let's answer the question about my daughter first." Persistent as dysentery.

"But we can't answer for your daughter until we answer some of these broader questions first. They all gotta be answered." Jake immediately cursed himself for this slip. An entire shelf full of unresolved questions, like the contents of Fibber McGee's closet, tumbled down upon him in an avalanche of evaded issues. Damn my big flapping mouth, he thought.

"Okay, then let's answer them," said Oscar De Curia.

"I think we are never going to make a dent in the poverty problem until the anti-intellectual attitudes of the poor are changed. And their male chauvinism too."

"Okay, let's change them."

"But these attitudes are dependent on, related to, and interfunctional with a dozen other lower-class norms—maybe all of them, tied up together like a spider web."

"For instance."

"Masculinity, for instance. The poor emphasize masculinity much more than we do (Walter Miller, 1958). And action—getting things done as opposed to theory and abstraction. Therefore, school is considered sissy-prissy and largely female-dominated."

"You think it would help to hire a few football players and prize fighters for teachers?"

"It would be a step toward the schoolhouse. But it would also reinforce their ideas of masculinity and chauvinism. Further, the poor crave excitement more than do the middle and upper classes (Rainwater, 1960; Reissman, 1962). Schools aren't noteworthy for excitement, you know."

"Judging from the slum schools I've been in, about half the teacher's time and energy is spent in trying to keep a lid on the excitement the kids generate. I think if they took the lid off for a minute the average slum classroom would erupt into bedlam."

"Right. And this leads into teaching methods. Student-centered education is based on the same assumptions as client-centered counseling: the students or clients must carry the ball, must be responsible for their own decisions, must set their own goals and limits, and so on. There is a mountain of research indicating that these student-centered teaching methods produce about the same level of retention of class material as do lecture-recitation methods. But when it comes to measuring such intangible traits as self-confidence, initiative, creativity, and leadership, the student-centered methods will win by ten lengths" (Blair, Jones, & Simpson, 1954; Cronback, 1954).

"Seems like the answer is pretty obvious: use more student-centered teaching in slum schools."

"It would be nice if life were so simple. A guy in California ran off an experimental group project in a boys' club (Maas, 1963). He found that middle-class kids adapted quite readily to group-centered methods. But lower-class kids resisted them to beat hell. They'd stand around with their thumbs in their bums and say: 'Why don't somebody tell us what we're supposed to do?' "

"Mmm," said Oscar De Curia.

"So let me point out, there is nothing the poor need more than self-confidence, creativity, and leadership (Goff, 1954; Keller, 1963). Yet they consistently resist the methods that develop it."

"Hmm."

"And this leads directly to another point. The same guy who did the California study also found that the great majority of correctional workers prefer nondirective methods, even though most of their clients are of the lower class and don't dig them" (Maas, 1954).

"Hmm," said De Curia. "Maybe this is why most counseling agencies have better success with middle-class clients. We've always blamed the lower-class failures on the stratification gap; you know, middle-class social workers can't communicate with lower-class clients."

"Yes. And there's still more to this story. This same guy studied parents bringing kids into guidance clinics (Maas, 1955). He asked specifically about their expectations at the clinic. How long did they think it would take? How much would they, the parents, have to participate? How much would the parents have to change their ways? He found that middle-class parents had much more realistic expectations concerning both time and involvement. The poor usually expected that the treatment would take perhaps a few weeks and that the clinic would straighten the kid out without much parental responsibility."

"So maybe middle-class parents are better risks for therapy regardless of the therapist's socioeconomic background."

"At least you can stop your self-flagellation for being a middle-class caseworker."

"Okay, you have absolved my middle-class guilt. You have also given me a dozen more questions, when all I really wanted was one answer. So how about an answer: Do we or don't we impose middle-class norms on people?"

IMPOSING VALUES

Jake knew when he had talked himself into a corner. He glanced at the desk phone, hoping that perhaps a call might spare him a confrontation with his untenable position. It didn't. He glanced out his window, hoping perhaps to see a tidal wave rolling across the midwestern prairie. There was not so much as a ripple. He glanced out his door, perchance to spot a client in need of his attention. A swatch of blue and a hank of white hair caught his eye. "Hey Dave!" yelled Jake, much as a man might yell when stranded on a sandbar by high tide.

Dave had been retired from the agency for several years now, but occasionally popped in "to see how things were going." These visits by the old warhorse at pasture were usually welcome and especially so today.

"Come in, Dave, and shoot the bull a spell," said Jake with an outward show of camaraderie and an inward sigh of relief. "Oscar and I were just talking about lower-class norms. How they often impede therapy or movement or progress, or whatever you wanna call it, but how we're not supposed to tamper with them."

"So what did you tell him to do?" asked Dave.

"Huh?"

"I imagine he asked you whether he should or shouldn't impose his own value system. What did you tell him?"

I'm stabbed in the back, thought Jake. He was desperate now. "First I'd like to hear your opinion. You must have run into this question in your 20-odd years here?"

"That's the biggest understatement since Genghis Khan was called unneighborly," said Dave. "Not a day went by that that question didn't pop up."

"Ever have a client make a pass at your daughter?" asked Oscar. "Your 13-year-old daughter?"

"That's how we got started," added Jake.

"So what did you tell him?" asked Dave persistently. But Jake was a skilled infighter. He would try a show of honesty to disarm them. When all else fails, a guy should consider being honest. Well, partially. "I really haven't answered it yet," said Jake. "We were just generalizing the problem, sort of."

"That's what I figured," said Dave. "So you want me to get you off the hook."

Jake grinned like a nauseated sailor demonstrating his seaworthiness, but he said nothing. He resolved never again to resort to honesty.

"My friend," said Dave, "there is nothing in social service more frequently encountered than interclass conflict regarding values. Every social worker I know runs into it daily, and most of them, like

you, never really come to grips with the realities of the problem. And every social worker I know, consciously or unconsciously, overtly or covertly, imposes his norms on the poor every day of his working life."

"But you're different," said Jake, with a noticeable edge to his voice.

"Only that I'm honest about it," said Dave. "I do it intentionally. Deliberately. In cold blood. Further, a half dozen studies indicate that the more moralistic, value-imposing workers have better success with their clients" (Parloff, Iflund & Goldstein, 1957; Powers & Witmer, 1951; Rosenthal, 1955).

"Then what about the advice of the experts? You can't pick up a journal today without some author jollyragging us about understanding the poor instead of trying to change them to our nasty middle-class way of life."

"Slop and hogwash," said Dave. "I suggest that the more you understand the poor, the more you will see the need for them to make some basic changes."

Oscar De Curia brightened noticeably. "For instance?" he said.

"For instance, take the time orientation of the Chicanos and Puerto Ricans (Clapp, 1966; Lewis, 1966). Half of them don't own a clock. A street-gang worker I know says a lot of his Chicano teen-agers can't even tell time. You say, 'Let's be ready to go at ten,' and they'll show up maybe at twelve-thirty. While you're at lunch, likely."

"Understandable, though," said Jake. "They come from an agrarian background where you get up when it's morning and go to bed when it's dark. So who needs a clock?"

"General Motors needs one. Bell Telephone and General Electric need one. And there ain't no way that Chicanos are ever going to adapt to an industrial society without getting clock wise. I've never heard of a factory that will let one guy come to work at eight, another at nine-thirty, and another at ten-fifteen. We either impose our middle-class time consciousness or let them remain forever in unemployment."

"Ah, ha!" Jake burst in. "Now you are blaming the victim."

"Ryan's point (1971), I believe. But Alinsky (1946) said it 25 years earlier."

"Well, were they wrong, both of them?"

"Let's pick one—Alinsky, since he had nothing good to say about middle-class values."

"Right."

"Alinsky would have screamed like a ruptured panther if he heard me say this, but I'll say it to you. I suggest that Alinsky made his living precisely by imposing middle-class norms on the poor. A better living, incidentally, than the three of us combined."

"Please go on."

"The poor have always been more comfortable in primary group relations: first names, informal buddy relations, that sort of thing (Barber, 1961; Brager, 1963; Guttentag, 1970; Reissman, 1962). They always shy away from formalized secondary groups, like titled officers, by-laws, committees, *Robert's Rules of Order*. Now, in themselves, a million people are powerless; they are nothing unless they are organized, whether in the military or in power politics. You can't cite an example in history of a primary group wielding any political clout. The major reason that the middle class carries a bigger stick is not their numbers but their organization. And Alinsky made his living teaching the poor to organize for power, to form secondary groups—a middle-class norm."

"Mm hmm," said Jake. Oscar merely said, "Hmm."

FATALISM AND POVERTY

"Let me point up another lower-class norm that, in my mind, constitutes one of the biggest hang-ups the poor have to carry, maybe the biggest."

"What's that?"

"Fatalism. *Que sera sera.* A belief that what happens to you has already been decided by some capricious Fate (Lewis, 1966; Walter Miller, 1958; Reissman, 1962). A conviction that it is not only a waste of time, but actually hazardous to take arms against a perverse and incontrovertible Fate, because she may stomp on you to straighten you out."

"For example?"

"For example, a hundred studies plus common sense confirm that the poor have too many kids. But to date no birth control program among the poor is even moderately successful as compared to middle-class family planning."

"Why?"

"Fatalism. Rainwater found that the number one cause of birth control failures among the poor is a belief that 'you're just gonna have the kids you're s'posed to have and you can't do nothin' to change it'" (Reissman, 1962).

"Seems kinda extreme."

"Not at all. My brother Gus was driving a truck for a mining company in Wyoming. He picked up a couple of hitchhikers and put them in back. 'Now for hell's sake don't you guys smoke,' he told them. 'I've got seven tons of dynamite on here.' They both agreed, but when he stopped for gas an hour later, there they both sat, smoking on top of a box of dynamite. Gus blew his stack and kicked their cans off his truck. As they went stomping off down the highway he heard one mumble, 'Well, the way I figure, if it's gonna blow it's gonna blow.' Now there's extreme."

"But an isolated case."

"Okay, think back. In the years you've been handling offenders, how many times have you heard expressions like 'my luck ran out,' 'my number was up,' 'the dice were loaded against me,' 'it wasn't in the cards for me,' 'the Bear (bad luck) was after me,' 'I was fighting a stacked deck,' 'it wasn't my day,' and so on and on."

"Or, 'I'm a born loser,' " said Oscar. "Or, 'when my ship comes in.' Or 'Dame Fortune smiles on me.' Or 'some guy was born with a silver spoon in his mouth.' Or 'there's no oil on my dipstick.' Or 'I lucked out or crapped out.' "

"Right. Nobody in the hoosegow ever got there by goofing off. Always he fell. Or his foot slipped. Or, he 'landed behind the eight ball.' Or 'the old wheel came up on black.' Some day I'm gonna write a book. There must be a thousand such expressions."

"I think," said Oscar, "that these are defense mechanisms to rationalize getting busted. Like 'if I'm so damn smart, how come I'm locked up? Bad luck, that's why.' "

"Okay, but in no way is this limited to offenders. You find these same expressions among the poor everywhere. And for the same reason: it gets them off the hook for being poor. Fate is to blame."

"Well," said Jake, "without these defenses what do the poor bastards have? Isn't it better to leave them their defenses at least?"

"I suggest that a valid social service is to help them find or develop more realistic defenses—defenses that don't perpetuate the cycle of poverty."

"How do you mean?"

"The culture of poverty is self-perpetuating (Lewis, 1966; D. R. Miller, 1963). It forms a vicious circle that repeats over and over. Like kids believe that school grades are mostly a matter of luck. Incidentally, I think true-false exams reinforce this crap-game concept of grades. So they flunk out or drop out of school. They're unqualified for employment and grow up in poverty. The surrounding culture constantly reinforces their belief in fatalism, which they and the other poor pass on to their kids. And they in turn enter school

expecting Luck or Fate or Chance to determine their outcome. Sure enough, it does, and the cycle repeats. And there are a number of others. McClelland (1961, 1969) says that father dominance—a lower-class norm—has gotta be decreased and that a number of other child-rearing practices of the poor have to be changed too. He also says we gotta push for the good old Protestant ethic and urge more creative and expressive fantasy production. Less traditionalism. All these things, mind you, require changes in lower-class values."

"So you think the place to break this poverty cycle is at the level of norms and values."

"It's all one place. Myrdahl (1948) says that it's not so important where we begin as that we begin somewhere. Consider this one. Mobilization for Youth workers found kids who would say: 'Why go down to the employment office? I'll be here; let the job find me." At first they thought it was the kids' perversity. But it wasn't; the kids were dead serious. Being employed or unemployed, they believed, was a matter of being touched by the fickle finger of Fate. Hustling for a job may only make Fate mad at you. It seems to me this is a good place to make a dent in the poverty cycle."

De Curia pondered this a bit. "It seems to me this is the only place to make a dent."

"I think Hyman (1953) would agree. He says that 'the variable which keeps the poor poor is a system of beliefs and values . . . which reduce the very *voluntary* actions which would ameliorate their low position.' My own view is that this is the best place to make a dent. But there are others: They gotta get back to high school, vocational school, college, on-the-job training. There's delinquency, medical and housing problems, discrimination, exploitation. You name it and it's a good starting place. But working on any one of these will inevitably necessitate some value changes. If not—if no values are changed—we may as well take the poverty funds and dump them in the street for grabs, because volitional behavior doesn't change if attitudes, values, and norms don't change. In fact, I think dumping our funds in the ghetto streets would be at least as effective as some programs I know of."

"Touché!" Oscar De Curia said, but without a smile. "However, you and Jake both mentioned the road to the schoolhouse. Harrison (1972) cites some pretty convincing figures that additional years of school won't affect the ghetto kid's lifetime income as much as dropping school and working a couple of extra years."

"Ah, yes, years of school. But he only gives passing acknowledgment that there may be a difference in quality of lower- and middle-class education. If this goes unrecognized, then the whole area of educational enrichment is meaningless. Yes, a kid can graduate from a ghetto school but be unable to write a purchase order, add up a grocery list, or understand directions on a can of spray paint. About a third of the kids on my caseload couldn't travel across town and find an address because they couldn't read street signs from a bus. Try listening to one of them giving directions to another. They memorize routes, not addresses. Half of them couldn't look up a number in a phone book. They were limited to the numbers they memorized or wrote down because they didn't dig alphabetical listing. And not one in a hundred could write an intelligible letter if the kid's life depended on it, even if they had a high school diploma. They were graduated, not educated. Now who's going to give one of them a job at anything better than tamping sand in a rathole?"

"To me the solution seems obvious— improve slum schools," Oscar said.

"My friend, I suggest that Jesus himself could not teach these kids as long as they retain their self-defeating attitudes. Yes, schools must change, but student attitudes must change also."

SCAPEGOATING

"Dave old boy, you claim to be honest with yourself," Jake put in. "Aren't you really blaming the victim when the real blame lies elsewhere? In social injustice, unequal opportunity, exploitation, discrimination? You've said yourself that the criminal justice system screens out the poor predominantly."

"Right. And all social workers should redouble their efforts to correct all these inequities. But let's say they've all been corrected, no discriminating employers and so on. It's still a competitive job market, and the better trained, the aggressive job hustlers, and the pushers are the ones who'll get the jobs."

"Okay, you will easily find a hundred authors who assert that once these injustices are corrected and people begin to move upward into middle-class society, their cultural norms will change accordingly."

"I think it's true that whenever people are placed in another subculture, whether above or below their own, in time some of that culture will rub off on them. But the preponderance of evidence indicates that the social strivers, the upwardly mobile, change their values *before* they begin their upward mobility. Mobility is much more often a result than a cause of value change" (Berelson & Steiner, 1964; Hyman, 1953; McClelland, 1969).

Jake shook his head. "It still seems to me that by putting the onus on the poor, we lift the blame from the guilty ones."

Dave pondered this one for a few minutes. Finally: "Jake, if there's anything I've learned in 40 years of social work, it's that scapegoating—hunting up someone to blame for a social problem—is not only a gross waste of time, but it actually inhibits the solution of problems." Dave ran his finger across Jake's bookshelf. "Do you have any idea how many tons of pulpwood trees have been butchered in the past decade to make publications that are essentially given over to scapegoating."

He hadn't, and Dave proceeded. "I have never heard of a social problem that was attributable to a single cause. There are always multiple causes if you bother to scratch the surface, so finding a suitable scapegoat merely focuses attention on one factor and ignores the others. As for me, I'm not going to burn up good mental energy either in blaming the poor for being poor or blaming the middle class for being middle class."

But Jake recalled another problem. "Did I misunderstand you when you admitted that you superimpose your own values?"

"That's right, deliberately."

"Then aren't you saying, in effect, that your values are better than those of the lower class?"

"Ah, now comes the stinger. I impose *some* middle-class values. There are quite a number of lower-class values that I prefer to middle-class ones."

"For instance?"

"Comradeship. Closer, more intimate interpersonal relations. More egalitarian views; more emphasis on person than on status. More interpersonal good humor. More freedom of expression. More open expression of affection" (Reissman, 1962).

"Affection?"

"Yes. Take one example: When I was a kid I worked on a string of blue-collar jobs: ranches, mines, factories, railroads, construction. It wasn't uncommon to see two guys who were buddies standing around the fire at night or around the bar or bunkhouse, with an arm slung over the friend's shoulder. No one thought anything of it. Now suppose that on some white-collar job—let's say in an insurance office—you spot two guys at the water cooler with their arms around each other. You'd nudge your neighbor and say, 'Hey, Fred! Lookit!' What a helluva culture when two people can't express honest affection without being considered gay."

"Maybe there are more gays in the lower class."

"Fewer (Kinsey, 1948). I'll tell you another trait of the poor that I'd consider keeping. When a husband and wife are at loggerheads, they are much more likely to have a good old hell-raising, whooping and hollering knock-down-drag-out battle. But in 20 minutes it's over and out of their systems. You and me, when we're on the outs with the old woman, we turn on the deep freeze for about a month. We never speak or look at each other for weeks on end. Now I ask you, honestly, which is better for mental health? And for kids?"

"Hmm."

"And I'll tell you another. I think there's more real honesty in the lower class."

"Aw, come off it, Dave. Nine-tenths of our correctional clients come from the lower class."

"I wasn't thinking of law violations specifically. However, since you've raised the point: a dozen studies of self-reported offenses show no significant class difference in crime and delinquency. Our legal machinery simply screens out more of the poor for processing" (Akers, 1964; Empey & Erickson, 1966; Meyerhoff & Meyerhoff, 1964; Short & Nye, 1957; Voss, 1966).

"Then what do you mean by 'honesty?' "

"Interpersonal honesty. If a lower-class guy doesn't like you, he will say so. Or maybe punch your nose. But we middle class will rationalize it with some kind of mealy-mouthed double-talk. I invite you, for instance, to sit in on a college promotions committee if you want to observe some fancy verbal footwork. Like 'Now understand, I've got nothing personal against old Charlie. But . . .' A blue-collar worker would say, much more honestly, 'I can't stand the damn creep.' "

"Not footwork. Tonguework."

"Okay, I recall one college department of about 25 faculty. There were some faculty cuts coming up, so two sections of the department formed a coalition and voted to abolish the third section in order to save their jobs. I have never heard of this kind of job cannibalism among the blue-collar workers."

FUNCTIONAL NORMS

"Dave, you're not being consistent," Jake said waving his hand. "A minute ago you were the champion of good old middle-class values. Now you've changed sides. You can't play both sides at once. What *do* you want?"

Dave pondered this one briefly: "First, I want social workers to be honest about it when they impose norms, whether middle- or lower-class. Second, I want them to forget the infantile quibble about norms to one class being better than those of another. I want. . . ."

"How do you decide which norms you are going to support, then? You gonna play God?"

"Functionality is how. First we gotta decide on objectives, social workers and clients in dialogue together. And this holds true whether it's one client and one caseworker or a project involving 50 workers and 10,000 clients. We can agree that employment is a goal, or marriage stability or family planning or whatever, but we have to thrash it out and arrive at some consensus regarding our objective. Once the objective is agreed upon, my job is clear. If a certain cultural norm is functional, if it aids in achieving the agreed-upon objective, I will support it. If it's dys-

functional, if it's thwarting our objectives, then it's gotta go, and I'll do my damndest to see that it goes. And I couldn't care less whether the norm comes from the lower, middle, or upper class."

"Meehl and McClosky" (1947), said Jake, "consider that our job definition is to help the client achieve the client's end. Period. That doesn't leave room for negotiation about objectives."

"I'll be damned if I'm gonna help that sonofabitch achieve my daughter's end," said Oscar De Curia hotly.

"And I'll venture no social worker worth his salt would," replied Dave. "In fact, I think they'd draw the line on about half the goals of our correctional clients. Plus a number of others. For instance, I won't help a client toward suicide, if that's his goal. Or to obtain heroin, or to bust out of jail or a hospital. Or to defraud the welfare office or desert his family or go AWOL. Or, in my case, to obtain an abortion. This is why I said we must first agree on objectives."

"And if you and the client can't agree?"

"My personal guideline is this: I will never help clients accomplish something that I consider morally wrong, harmful to them or to me or to others. And I won't help a client to rendezvous with any teenager, not your daughter or anyone else's."

"Okay, let's say we agree on a number of objectives in a certain poverty project," said Jake. "And we find certain lower-class norms that inhibit the achieving of these goals. Dysfunctional, you called them. Now how do you go about changing those norms?"

"That, my friend, is another can of worms. But it can be done and has been done."

"How?"

"Another time, Jake, another time. We've emptied enough worms for today."

References

Akers, Ronald L.   Economic status and delinquent behavior: A retest. *Journal of Research on Crime and Delinquency,* January 1964, *1,* 38–46.

Alinsky, Saul.   *Reveille for radicals.* New York: Random House, 1946.

Barber, Bernard.   Social-class differences in educational life chances. *Teachers College Record,* November 1961, *63,* 102–113.

Berelson, Bernard, & Steiner, Gary A.   *Human behavior: An inventory of scientific findings.* New York: Harcourt Brace Jovanovich 1964.

Blair, Glenn M., Jones, R. Stewart, & Simpson, Ray H.   *Educational psychology.* New York: Macmillan, 1954.

Brager, George.   Organizing the unaffiliated in a low-income area. *Social Work,* 8 April 1963, *8,* 34–40.

Briar, Scott, & Miller, Henry.   *Problems and issues in social casework.* New York: Columbia University Press, 1971.

Clapp, Raymond F.   Spanish Americans of the Southwest. *Welfare in Review,* January 1966, *4,* 1–12.

Cronbach, Lee.   *Educational psychology.* New York: Harcourt Brace Jovanovich, 1954.

Dumont, Matthew.   *The absurd healer.* New York: Viking Press, 1968.

Empey, Lamar, & Erickson, Maynard L.   Hidden delinquency and social status. *Social Forces,* June 1966, *44,* 546–554.

Gaylin, et al.   *Doing good: The limits of benevolence.* New York: Pantheon Books, 1978.

Goff, Regina M.   Some educational implications of rejection on aspiration levels of minority group children. *Journal of Experimental Education,* December 1954, *23,* 179–183.

Goode, W. J.   *The family.* Englewood Cliffs, N.J.: Prentice-Hall, 1964.

Gordon, William E.   Knowledge and value: Their distinction and relationship in clarifying social work practice, *Social Work,* July 1965, *10,* 32–39.

Gordon, William E.   Basic constructs for an integrative and generative conception of social work. In Gordon Hearn (Ed.), *The general systems approach: Contributions toward an holistic conception of social work.* New York: Council of Social Work Education, 1969.

Guttentag, Marcia.   Group cohesiveness, ethnic organization and poverty. *Journal of Social Issues,* Spring 1970, *26,* 105–132.

Halmos, Paul.   *Faith of the counselors.* New York: Schocken, 1966.

Hardman, Dale.   The constructive use of authority. *Crime and Delinquency,* July 1960, *6,* 245–254.

Harrison, Bennett.   Education and underemployment in the urban ghetto. *American Economic Review,* December 1972, *62,* 296–812.

Hatcher, Hayes A.   *Correctional casework and counseling.* Englewood Cliffs, N.J.: Prentice-Hall, 1978.

Hollingshead, August M.   Class differences in family stability. *Annals of the American Academy of Political and Social Science,* November 1950, *272,* 39–46.

Hooker, Carol E.   Learned helplessness. *Social Work,* May 1976, *21,* 194–198.

Hyman, Herbert H.   The value systems of different classes: A social psychological contribution to the analysis of stratification. In Reinhard Bendix & Seymour M. Lipset (Eds.), *Class, status, and power.* New York: Free Press, 1953.

Keller, Suzanne.   The social world of the slum child: Some early findings. *American Journal of Orthopsychology,* October 1963, *33,* 823–831.

Kinsey, Alfred C.   *Sexual behavior in the human male.* Philadelphia: W. B. Saunders, 1948.

Klockars, Carl B.   A theory of probation supervision. *The Journal of Criminal Law, Criminology and Police Science,* 1972, *63,* 550–557.

Levy, Charles S.   Values and planned change. *Social Casework,* October 1972, *54,* 488–493.

Levy, Charles S.   The value base of social work. *Journal of Education for Social Work,* Winter 1973, *9,* 34–42.

Lewis, Oscar.   *La vida: A Puerto Rican family in the culture of poverty.* New York: Random House, 1966.

Lipton, Douglas, Martinson, Robert, & Wilks, Judith.   The effectiveness of correctional treatment—A survey of treatment evaluation studies. New York: Praeger Publishers, 1975.

Maas, Henry S.   The role of numbers in clubs of lower-class and middle-class adolescents. *Child Development,* December 1954, *25,* 241–251.

Maas, Henry S.   Socio-cultural factors in psychiatric services for children. *Smith College Studies in Social Work,* February 1955, *25,* 1–90.

Maas, Henry S.   Group Research Project. Berkeley: School of Social Welfare, University of California, 1963. (Hectograph)

Maluccio, Anthony N.   *Learning from clients: Interpersonal helping as viewed by client and social workers.* New York: Free Press, 1979.

Martinson, Robert.   What works?—Questions and answers about prison reform. *The Public Interest,* 1974, *35,* 22–94.

McClelland, David C.   *The achieving society.* New York: Van Nostrand Rheinhold, 1961.

McClelland David C.   *Motivating economic achievement.* New York: Free Press, 1969.

Meehl, Paul F., & McClosky, Herbert.   Ethical and political aspects of applied psychology. *Journal of Abnormal Social Psychology,* January 1947, *42,* 91–98.

Menninger, Karl.   *The crime of punishment.* New York: Viking Press, 1968.

Merton, Robert K.   *Social theory and social structure.* New York: Free Press, 1957.

Meyerhoff, Howard L., & Meyerhoff, Barbara.   Field observations of middle-class gangs. *Social Forces,* March 1964, *42,* 328–336.

Miller, D. R.   The study of social relationships: Situation identity and social interaction. In S. Koch (Ed.), *Psychology: A study of a science. 1963.*

Miller, Henry.   Value dilemmas in social casework. *Social Work,* January 1968, *13,* 27–33.

Miller, Walter B.   Lower-class culture as a generating milieu of gang delinquency. *Journal of Social Issues,* April 1958, *12,* 5–19.

Miller, Walter B.   Implications of urban lower-class culture for social workers. *Social Service Review,* September 1959, *33,* 219–236.

Myrdal, Gunnar.   *An American dilemma.* New York: Harper & Row, 1948.

O'Connor, Gerald.   Toward a new policy in adult corrections. *Social Service Review,*
December 1972, *46,* 581–596.

Overton, Alice, & Tinker, Katherine.   *Casework notebook.* St. Paul, Minn.: Greater
St. Paul Community Chest and Councils, 1957.

Oxley, Genevieve B.   The caseworker's expectations in client motivation. *Social
Casework,* July 1966, *47,* 432–437.

Parloff, Morris B., Iflund, B., & Goldstein, N.   Communication of "therapy values"
between therapist and schizophrenic patients. Paper presented before American
Psychiatric Association, Chicago, 1957.

Powers, Edwin, & Witmer, Helen.   *An experiment in the prevention of delinquency:
The Cambridge-Sommerville youth study.* New York: Columbia University Press,
1951.

Rainwater, Lee.   *And the poor get children.* Chicago: Quadrangle Books, 1960.

Reid, William J.   *The task-centered system.* New York: Columbia University Press,
1978.

Reid, William J., & Epstein, Laura.   *Task-centered practice.* New York: Columbia
University Press, 1977.

Reissman, Frank.   *The culturally deprived child.* New York: Harper & Row, 1962.

Rose, Arnold M. (Ed.).   *Human behavior and social processes.* Boston: Houghton
Mifflin, 1962.

Rosenthal, David.   Changes in some moral values following psychotherapy. *Journal
of Consulting Psychology,* December 1955, *19,* 431–436.

Rubington, Earl, & Weinberg, Martin S.   *Deviance: The interactionist perspective.*
New York: Macmillan, 1968.

Ryan, William.   *Blaming the victim.* New York: Vintage Press, 1971.

Salomon, Elizabeth L.   Humanistic values and social casework. *Social Casework,*
January 1967, *48,* 26–33.

Schwartz, William.   The social worker in the group. *Social Welfare Forum, 1961.*
New York: Columbia University Press, 1961.

Schwartz, William.   Toward a strategy of group work practice. *Social Science Review,* September 1962, *36,* 268–279.

Short, James S., & Nye, F. Ivan.   Reported behavior as a criterion of deviant behavior.
Social Problems, Winter 1957, *5,* 207–313.

Silverman, Marvin.   Children's rights and social work. *Social Service Review,* March
1977, *51,* 171–178.

Simmons, J. L.   *Deviants.* Berkeley, Calif.: Glendessary Press, 1969.

Tillich, Paul.   The philosophy of social work. *Social Service Review,* March 1962,
36, 13–16.

Toch, Hans.   The care and feeding of typologies and labels. *Federal Probation,*
September 1970, *34,* 15–19.

Towle, Charlotte.   *Common human needs.* New York: National Association of Social Workers, 1965.

Udry, J. Richard.   *The social context of marriage.* Philadelphia: J. B. Lippincott,
1966.

Udry, J. Richard.   *The social context of marriage.* Philadelphia: J. B. Lippincott,
1966.

Voss, Harwin L.   Socio-economic status and reported delinquent behavior. *Social
Problems,* Winter 1966, *13,* 314–324.

Chapter 4

Theoretical Perspectives for Social Work Practice

As discussed in Chapter 2, selected knowledge, skills, and values form the basis of all the social worker does. The knowledge needed by a practitioner can be roughly divided into two large but related classes. The first is practice knowledge dealing with the actual interventive activities of the worker which seeks to answer the questions, "What do I do and how do I do it?" The second large class could be called basic knowledge of the development, growth, functioning, and malfunctioning of human systems of all sizes in interaction. If we look back to the case of "The House on Sixth Street" and "Work with Mrs. Manley" at the end of Chapters 1 and 2, respectively, we will find the worker using such practice knowledge as: knowledge of how to interview, knowledge of agency requirements and services, knowledge of bureaucratic structure, community resources, knowledge of social work roles, and, very importantly, knowledge of own feelings and values as they impacted the practitioner—client interaction. The selection and use of this practice knowledge was guided by certain foundation knowledge such as, in the Manley case, knowledge about the family and the meaning of family interaction, knowledge of what is involved in carrying the various family roles, a knowledge of the changing notions of women's role, the stress of role transition as it affects both the individual members, their interaction and the family as a whole. The practice theory that deals with what social workers do in their professional roles will be the central focus of this book; but this chapter will present very briefly some foundation knowledge that the authors have found useful. It is appropriate to begin this discussion with an examination of criteria for the selection of foundation knowledge for social work.

CRITERIA FOR SELECTION

Given the fact, previously discussed in Chapters 1 and 2, that the assignment for the social work profession is to "mediate the process through which the individual and society reach out for each other in mutual need for self-fulfillment," the first requirement of a foundation theory is that it provide us with a conceptual formulation that takes account of the nature of person-environment relationship. We need a theory that moves us away from the mental image of the person and the environment such as billiard balls, which affect each other by striking one another but in which transaction only the course is changed still leaving the essential nature of each unaffected. In order to carry out society's charge, we must have a theory that helps us to be constantly aware that the structure and culture of society, and transactions with others, is reflected in the self and the life structure of each individual and the way each individual copes with his life affects all the rest of us. Yet, this theory must recognize that a person's life is individual and unique—a reflection of self and choices, that all human beings have their own particular world that presents them with opportunities, meanings, feelings, identities, and myths which each person individually and selectively

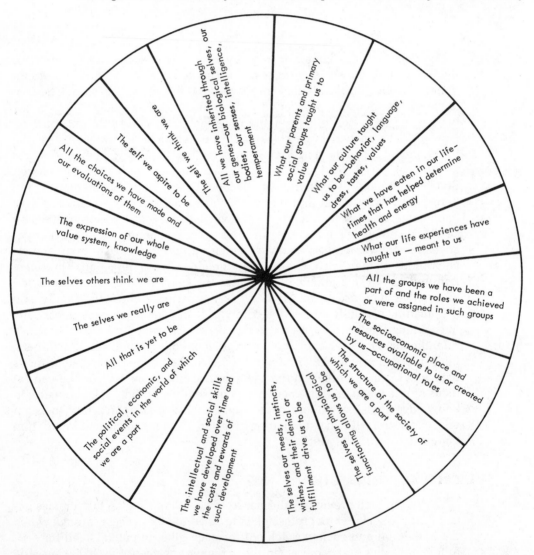

FIGURE 4–1: We, as individuals, are . . .

uses and internalizes (Levinson, 1978, pp. 1–40). See Figures 4–1 and 4–2 for some diagrams showing the complexity of this interpenetration, interaction, and transaction. Studying the diagrams will help the reader to begin to grasp the complexity of understanding the individual in interaction and transaction with the environment. Yet complex as this diagram appears, it deals principally with only a selected aspect of the environment—the social. However, it does deal with several levels of the social environment of people—the individual, the group, the family, the community and class, and the culture. In addition to the social with its various sizes of systems, the environment is divided into another large division—the physical. The physical environment may be further divided into the natural physical environment, such as climate, constructed environment, such as the shelters we build to protect us from the various natural phenomena of environment, and various unforeseen climatic events of nature. The third large division of the environment we have chosen to label temporal, meaning time and

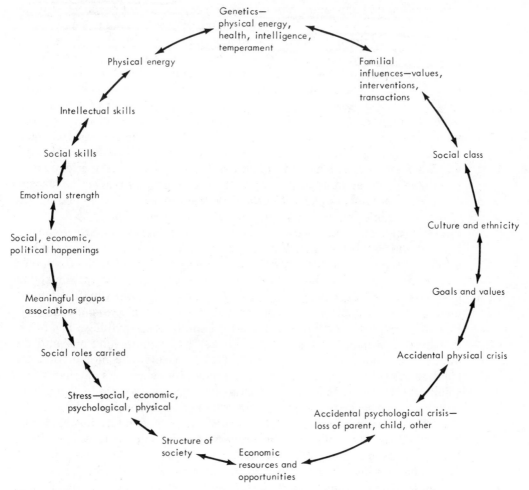

FIGURE 4–2:   Factors that mutually influence each other in the development of the individual

space. Because human life is finite and is lived within certain defined spaces, time and space are critical environmental qualities. Time and space can be further divided into two subclasses: general and personal. Most human beings construct shelters to protect them from the environment but in so doing they also construct a personal and/or family space that gives them a certain privacy from the group. While this construction of shelter and marking of private space may be different from culture to culture, such effort is generally found in all cultures. Most Americans see their shelter in relation to both time and space. The shelter needs to be readily accessible to our place of employment or education. Being our private world it also needs to meet certain other criteria such as having certain electrical appliances, heat, and perhaps air conditioning, as well as a certain attractiveness according to our definition. In evaluation of our private space we are able to create or demand (through money or other resources) that which then interacts with our feelings about ourselves.

Given the above, for social work practice, environment may be defined as a combination of people, their interactions and transactions in a particular geographic, socially defined and constructed space over a particular period of time both in the individual and family's life and in the life of the social and cultural system (Germain, 1979; Pincus & Minahan, 1973; Siporin, 1975).

We cannot regard environment as something outside ourselves—as another billiard ball with which we collide once in a while. Rather environment is of us and we are of it (Figure 4–2). From the moment of our birth it becomes an intimate part of us and presents us with the material from which we construct our lives through the choices we make and the social transactions in which we engage in response to the opportunities and deprivations presented us. John and Richard are both 18-year-old American males who have just graduated in the upper 10 percent of their respective classes. They look very much alike and are both attractive and in very good health. However, John's family is an established professional family with a more than adequate financial base. Since he was born, John has had little exposure to other than a professional life and a university education following high school was a given in his environment. Thus John attended the university his father attended and became, in his turn, a professional man. His choice of this pattern of life was highly approved and came naturally in this environment. To have made another choice would have been extremely difficult. Richard, however, was the oldest son of a family of five siblings. His father had been a farmer, but his terminal illness had been a long one and the family had sold the farm and exhausted its assets. His mother and the children now lived in a small rural community where his mother ran a small grocery store. Money was extremely tight for the family which was without social security support because Richard's father had not been covered. Richard was extremely bright and very interested in farming. He would have liked to have attended the university and majored in agribusiness. However, the university was 100 miles away, and Richard could see no way to finance his education. In addition, his mother needed both his financial and his emotional support. There was a job in a local creamery that was open, and Richard took it. After 10 years he became manager of the creamery. It was a good, steady, and adequately paying job. It meant that Richard had daily contact with the farm life he loved. But it was far short of the contribution he could have made and of the life he had dreamed of. Each of these men constructed their lives from the choices the environment offered them as they saw them. Starting their adult life with very similar internal resources they became very different through the choices they made.

But it is not only our individual lives that are shaped by the choices we make given the environmental opportunities presented us. By our choices and our activities we, in turn, shape the environment. Interested as he was in the land, Richard was concerned with how certain practices of the farmers were destroying the topsoil and depriving birds and small animals of their environmental home. These farmers had forced the land to adapt to their poor practices. Richard organized a group of concerned farmers who were able to arrange for a representative of the local university to come and help them to understand better land usage. The farmers learned to cooperate with the needs of their environment and grew more prosperous for it. So not only did the farmer adapt to the land, but he forced the land to adapt to his practices. Through our interactions and our transactions we shape both our future and the future of our environment. A great deal of social work practice effort is devoted to helping a client system analyze the impact of the environment on the system and making a planned effort to change undesirable conditions. "The House on Sixth Street" is an example of worker helping clients to change some very difficult living conditions.

In considering the transactions between any level of human system and the larger level within which it is embedded, we need to be familiar with the concept of adaptation. In common usage, adaptation is often seen as meaning the way the smaller system capitulates to the power of the larger environment. Thus adaptation is often interpreted as submission and is instinctively rejected as a one-way coercion. However, submission is only one method of adaptation and even so it affects the environment. Adaptation needs to be seen as an active concept meaning the transactional processes by which people shape their environment, physical and social, and in turn are shaped themselves.

In attempting to define the environment of any social system of any size, the work is further complicated because at each level of human organization the environment is the next immediately larger level of social organization. In addition, environment of any system also is the wider system beyond the next immediately larger system. However, the impact and meaning of the wider system is usually mediated through the next immediately larger system. For example, for most of us as individuals the meaning of the community as an environment is mediated through a smaller system (either an intimate social group or the family, or both) of which we are a part.

We also need a theory that supports the importance of difference in the development of human societies, that recognizes that human organizations grow and develop through the expression of individual differences, and that demands respect for diversity. Such foundation theories would mean that our standards of health and/or normality would have to include a range of coping behaviors and value positions that would allow for individual diversity and for minority or ethnic group differences. Such theories are congruent not only with social work functions in society but with the core values of social work practice that demands respect for the individual and the unique ways people deal with their life situations. Figure 4–3 offers a very simple example of human difference. What do you see as you look at it? Do you see a vase or two faces? Both perceptions are correct, but could you imagine an argument between two people who see it differently over which view is "normal" or "correct" and, therefore, evidence of mental health or intelligence?

We believe the theories that serve social workers best as an adequate foundation for the understanding of human growth and human struggle are those theories that see human beings and their organizations as emergent or developing over time and that hold an optimistic view of human potential for growth and change. Their basic concepts should focus on the strengths of people rather than their weaknesses and on the needs and desires of people to cope with the tasks of life and grow from dependence to independence to interdependence. This view of human motivation and growth requires that we build a practice theory in which the worker joins the client system in its struggle toward its goals rather than one in which the practitioner carries the primary responsibility. This type of theory supports the primary social work belief in the right of people to make their own life choices and furthers the deep respect for all human beings and for the growth struggle within each person that is such an important social work value. The theory while recognizing the need of human systems for stability and consistency should give primary weight to the internal push in both individuals and the organizations they create toward growth and change.

Social work practice theory must deal not only with the push toward growth but with the nature of human change in both the individual and

FIGURE 4–3: Do you see a vase? Or is it a picture of two people facing each other?

the human groups created by human interactions and transactions. All basic theories of human and organizational development deal with the need of individuals and groups for stability and the maintenance of some sort of inner integrity and most theories account in some way for the change that inevitably takes place in individuals and groups. Early psychoanalytic theories and many theories of organizational functioning put heavy emphasis on the drive of the unit to maintain a static equilibrium. Understanding certain resistances to change on the part of any human system is necessary, but social workers also need a theoretical stance that gives a place of importance to developmental growth and the human seeking for the new and the different.

All theories of human behavior embody some concepts of motivation. The more useful theories for social work are those that hold that the significant force in motivation is the opportunity provided by the environment to exercise one's powers, a feeling of mastery, of control over one's internal reactions and relevant transactions with one's world, and a belief that one's actions have relevance for the solution of one's problems. Theories that recognize that an individual's or a group's (social group, family, ethnic group, organization, or community) motivation to develop and use coping skills is significantly increased by a feeling of competence and effectiveness in dealing with the tasks of living; and that, when one is the helpless victim of forces beyond one's control, the result is dejection, despair, and demoralization would seem to be central to social work practice.

The importance of this type of theory demands that practitioners make available to their client systems all relevant knowledge and skills that will increase in any way their coping ability. It makes the assumption that the progressive forces in human nature and human groups are stronger than regressive forces. This way of viewing human motivation supports a practice theory that sets forth ways of identifying the progressive forces within any human system and ways of identifying and removing blocks and obstacles that dampen these progressive forces. It means that practitioners no longer are so fearful of "creating dependency" but become primarily concerned with making all resources possible, including worker knowledge and skill, available to people for their use in coping and mastering. It means that theories of organizational behavior must recognize the push toward development as well as the importance of maintenance.

All theories of human functioning make some assumptions as to the cause of human dysfunctioning. Social workers need some concepts about what causes things to go wrong in the human condition. In order to serve social workers well the theories of human dysfunctioning cannot focus totally on the personal-deficit model, seeing problems as lodged entirely within the individual. In order to be useful for social workers in carrying out their functions, theories about the genesis of human troubles must allow for problems of dysfunctioning to be lodged in the transactions and lack of fit between the individual, the environment, and the groups and organizations. This type of foundation theory means that social work practice theory cannot deal exclusively with methods of individual internal change and adaptation but must include ways of dealing with change in individual coping skills, with change in organization and group, and with change in transactions between individuals and their groups (Trader, 1977, pp. 10–13).

GENERAL SYSTEMS THEORY AS A PART OF FOUNDATION KNOWLEDGE

It is the authors' proposal that ecological and general systems theory relating to open human systems may give us a conceptual framework which will allow us to organize our knowledge in ways useful to our professional functions. This is not a new idea. Others have made the same proposal in articles spanning the last 20 years. Therefore, our discussion will be essentially an integration of our understanding of the writings of other authors (Allport, 1964, pp. 39–59; Buckley, 1967, 1968, pp. 31, 304, 330, 354; Chin, 1961, p. 201; Goldstein, 1973, pp. 105–136; Hartman, 1970; Janchill, 1969; Koestler, 1968; Pincus & Minahan, 1973, pp. 530–564; Irma Stein, 1974; Strean, 1971, pp. 123–195; Von Bertalanffy, 1968). An article on systems theory has been reproduced in this chapter to give readers a second view of the use of this theory and to offer them another statement to help them develop further understanding of this complex theory (see Reading 4–1). The Forder article, other authors, and our own experience all serve to highlight the difficulty of grasping this highly abstract theory and its relationship to practice. However, we believe that the struggle to master systems theory is worth the effort. One of the confusions that confronts anyone seeking to understand systems theory is that there are many different theories that are discussed under the common ruberic of "systems theory." This discussion will deal primarily with the notions about open human systems as developed by general systems and ecological systems theorists.

Another problem is the difficulty of understanding systems theory because it uses a vocabulary different from that found in most social work literature. Terms, such as *input, throughput, output, entropy,* and *equifinality,* are strange and unappealing to social workers. These terms come from cybernetics and social science literature and usually seem very mechanical to social workers. This problem with language is of concern to us because we feel that any use of terms that tend to put distance between the client system and the social worker or that tend to introduce a mechanistic feeling—any terms that allow us to feel the client system as object rather than subject— is problematic for social work practice.

As a conceptual framework

A system is usually thought of as a whole consisting of interdependent and interacting parts, or as "a set of units with relationships among them" (Von Bertalanffy, 1968, p. 38). A system may also be described as "a complex of elements or components directly or indirectly related in a causal network, such that each component is related to some others in a more or less stable way within any particular period of time" (Buckley, 1967, p. 41). The interaction of the elements of the system imparts to it aggregate characteristics that are not only different from, but often not found in the components alone. Thus the interrelationships of the components creates a whole that is greater than the sum of its parts. The "sum of the parts" does not refer to the particular parts of the units added together or summed but to the aggregate of the units and the transactions and relationships between them that creates a "whole" with some degree of continuity and boundary. The interrelationship of system parts gives rise to new qualities that are a function of the transactions within the system. Because of the wholeness of the system, a change in any part of the system affects the system as a whole and all of its parts.

In using the system as a model, it is important to specify both a frame of reference and a boundary. An individual may be considered as a psychological, a biological, or a physical system or as an element in a social system (group, organization, or community). Each frame of reference gives us a very different system and presents us with different elements and transactions. Yet, each system includes a human being. We also need to establish a boundary that will limit the field of concern. This conceptual boundary is very different from a recognition of empirical boundaries, such as the boundaries of a school system or the city limits or the boundaries of a family or organization that are established by transactions within the system being studied. Suppose, for example, that we wish to study the interactions of two neighboring cities. A diagram such as the following might be drawn to illustrate the system being studied:

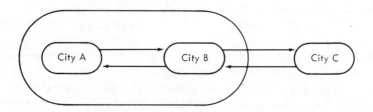

The system elements are the cities, each of which has its own empirical boundary and the relationships are the interstate highways. It is also possible to study other transactions and lines of communication between these cities. But in order to study these two cities as a social system a boundary has been drawn around them and their relationships with other cities have been excluded as beyond our purpose. Such a conceptual model of systems theory requires that the system be defined to take in the elements and transactions of concern. Actually as one looks at this map and thinks about the relationships between the two cities, an infinite number of relationships and transactions can be identified between the two cities beyond the two drawn in.

The systems model shifts attention from characteristics possessed by individual units to interaction and relatedness. Take the example of Maria in the Auerswald article reproduced in this chapter (see Reading 4–2). (The reader may want to read that article at this point.) The staff at the mental health center all regarded Maria as an entity bounded by her skin and used concepts of normality that had little relationship to the totality of this child and the transactions and relationships that were a part of her and her life. To understand her and her uniqueness one has to draw a different picture. Let us compare the differences in the diagrams shown in Figures 4–4 and 4–5.

Figures 4–4 and 4–5 illustrate very clearly the radical difference between ecological systems theory as a knowledge base for social work practice and other approaches. It is far more than a difference in techniques; rather it is a whole different way of thinking that radically changes the basic approach of practitioners. In the first view of Maria various areas of her internal functioning were compared with "normal" functioning and from this view her functioning seemed pathological indeed. However, once the ecological map is drawn, it can be understood that Maria's behavior was a coping response to the transactions affecting her within her life space and was a result of the interactions between Maria and other system elements. What is important about this view is that different data are collected differently, analyzed differently, and lead directly to different interventive actions. There are other ways of viewing the system which would result in different maps and perhaps different points of intervention. Maria's life space could have been diagrammed as shown in Figure 4–6.

This way of viewing Maria's situation comes from the drawing in of some empirical boundaries of certain subsystems within the larger systems picture. The boundaries of the overall map would be a conceptual boundary, but the map would recognize certain empirical subsystem boundaries found in the real world. Working from this map considerable data could be collected about the relationship between Maria's family and the school, or group, or mental health center, rather than Maria herself. In addition the grandfather and the grandmother could be seen as forming a subsystem together that transacts with Maria and her family as a system rather than individuals. Which map one would draw depends upon the notion of the importance of the interactions within the subsystems. It would depend upon whether we defined the central issue as one of Maria's family and its interrelations and its transactions as a unit with other system elements or of Maria and her transactions and interactions. There is still a third way that we could picture the application of ecological systems theory to Maria's life space. It might look something like Figure 4–7. This type of map attempts to picture the different levels of systems, recognizing that there are larger and more encompassing systems and smaller systems that may be seen as subsystems of the larger systems. However, it is almost impossible to draw such a map on paper; one needs a three-dimensional model to picture this. It may be helpful to struggle with such representations if they sensitize us to all the elements in the life space of the human system with which we are working. One of the important elements of Maria's life that is highlighted in this map, but neglected in the others, is that of neighborhood. Maria is Puerto Rican and the family is part of a minority neighborhood which may have considerable significance for the way the social systems from the wider society intervene.

Systems theory is not in itself a body of knowledge, nor does it contain any prescriptions as to actions that a social worker might take. Rather, systems theory presents us with tools of analysis that may accommodate

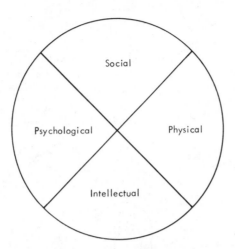

FIGURE 4–4:   View of Maria from the
perspective of the interdisciplinary team

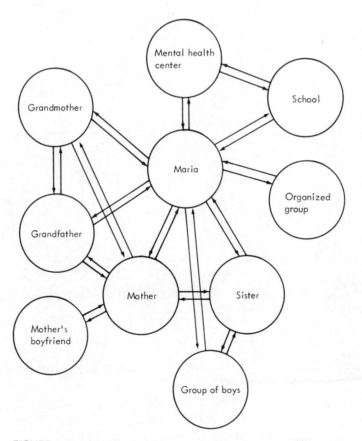

FIGURE 4–5:   Maria's situation as seen from the perspective of the
article

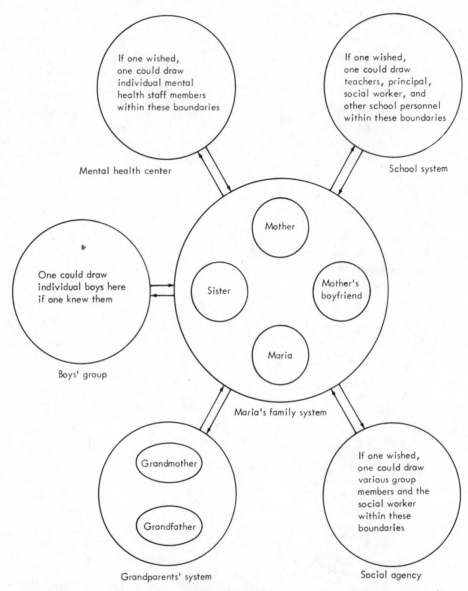

FIGURE 4–6: Maria's situation seen from the perspective of larger systems empirical boundaries

knowledge from many sciences. It is a way of thinking—a way of viewing and organizing data (Janchill, 1969, p. 77). Because it is a way of thinking that requires the abandonment of the linear approach to causation and the substitution of an understanding of the reciprocal relationships among all parts of the field (transactional approach) and an interactive focus, in which the effects of one system on another are dealt with, systems theory requires considerable study for any real understanding.

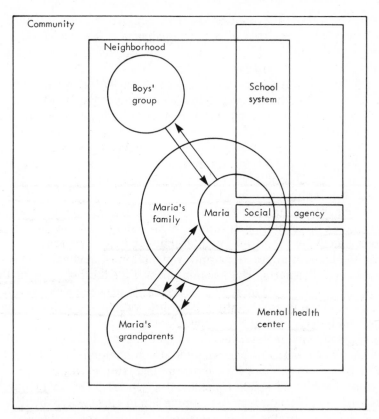

FIGURE 4–7: An attempt to picture Maria's situation from the perspective of different system levels; primary systems (intimate social groups) are drawn as circles, operating on same level. Here the community is seen as the largest social system.

The use of systems theory is proposed as a framework for the organization of data about people and groups, as a way of originating more helpful questions and approaches to problem solving. Used in this way, systems theory helps us avoid the tendency, discussed in Chapter 1, to focus on either the individual or on society as the primary focus of pathology or as the primary target of change. It reminds us that things are not so simple.

Systems theory offers a conceptual framework that shifts attention from discrete units (be those units either individuals or social groups) and their characteristics to the interaction and interrelatedness of units. Noting the success of the physical sciences in building knowledge by splitting "wholes" into pairs of smaller units (variables), establishing causal relationships between those variables, and attempting to understand a total phenomenon by the process of adding such understandings, the social sciences, too have tried to seek direct cause and effect relationships between paired variables. However, this appears to be an inappropriate method for explaining the complex behavior of living things. To demonstrate the inadequacy of this method, see how it would be used to explain the flight of birds. It would have no difficulty explaining the physical and chemical principles of the bird's ability to fly, but it cannot explain why the bird takes off in the first place (Rapoport, 1968).

The "wholes" that are the focus of social work concern are more than the sum of their paired variables. That "more" is found in their purpose (or goal-directed behavior) and in their interactive complexity. The analytic method that breaks a phenomenon into its separate parts only gives us a vast number of items of information and leaves us without the ability either to make sense out of the information or to reassemble the system. The systems approach allows us to replace the older analytic orientation, in which the individual was observed on the one hand and the individual's environment on the other, with a more holistic orientation to the problem of complex organization, in which the individual and the social and physical environment are seen as an interacting whole. We are, thus, concerned with the laws of interactions and transaction rather than with the intrinsic qualities of the parts. The assumption is that the behavior of the parts is seen differently when studied in isolation than when seen within the whole because of the dynamic interactions and organizing patterns that are only observable as a part of the whole.

A system may be described as a set of interrelated elements with a capacity for certain kinds of performance. Each component of the set is related to at least some others in a more or less stable way within a particular period of time and space (Buckley, 1967, p. 41). The assumption is that a system is a complex adaptive organization of parts which, by its very nature, continually generates, elaborates, and restructures patterns of meanings, actions, and interactions. Within a system something is continually going on, including a constant interchange with the environment across its boundary. Although a system is viewed as a constantly changing whole that is always in the process of movement toward a selected purpose, its parts are assumed to interact within a more or less stable structure at any particular point in time.

As a conceptual model the ecological systems model encourages transactional thinking and observations. It allows us to bring order into the massive amounts of data from all different frames of reference that we need to work with in social work practice. It increases our ability to consider the intricate patterns of interactions from many different perspectives. It also helps us to guard against the problem of reductionalism, forcing us to a different method of data collection and thus making it possible to assess the impact of multiple factors that may bear on causation.

Another important point is that viewing reality as systems of related entities not only affects the way we collect and assess data but also presents us with multiple possibilities for intervention (see Figures 4–5, 4–6, and 4–7). When it is understood that affecting one component of a system affects all the other components, the possibilities for intervention are greatly increased. For example, Maria will be profoundly affected by what happens between her mother and the man in her mother's life and her life might conceivably have been altered by a change in the relationship between the grandfather and grandmother as a subsystem. If we operate from an ecological systems perspective, we come to understand that direct therapeutic intervention with Maria might not be the only or the most economical or even the best choice. Intervention with the mother, the grandfather, the family as a whole, or the group social worker might be more helpful. And it certainly would appear that one effective approach might be to the welfare board seeking to assure that assistance for Maria would be continued even if her mother should remarry. Although we have suggested numerous possible avenues of intervention in Maria's situation, a systems view does not necessarily mean that intervention should always be more extensive because the worker uses systems theory. We may be able to make intervention more simple if we consider that a small change in one element of a system may change the total system.

There is one further conceptual formulation that needs to be developed in considering systems theory as a conceptual tool. In working with differing sets of subsystems, or different system levels, the worker must make three important decisions: (1) identify the client system, (2) identify the systems, elements of systems, or subsystems that should be changed, and (3) determine what systems elements or subsystems will be involved in the change efforts. The activities of the practitioner can then be seen as involving a minimum of four types of systems (or subsystems)—the change agent systems, the client systems, the target systems, and the action systems (Pincus & Minahan, 1973, pp. 53–64). These concepts essentially relate to a practice model, but they will be discussed later in this chapter.

Empirical aspects of systems theory

Persons working with systems theory have gone beyond using it as a conceptual framework and have developed various concepts and principles concerned with the functioning of open, living, or human systems that have direct impact on social work practice. Living systems are seen as systems made up of matter and energy that are organized by and function through an exchange of information. They exist in space and time and have boundaries (empirical not conceptual boundaries) which are at least partially permeable, thus permitting transmissions of energy and information to cross them.

The open system.   Perhaps the central concept in the theory of social systems is the view of the system as open, which means that an essential factor of a system's continuity and change is its engagement in interchanges with the environment. The open system receives input from and produces output to its environment. The environment and the transactions with it are basic to the existence of the system. It is because of this quality of openness that human systems grow and evolve toward increased order and complexity (negative entropy).

Closed systems.   These systems do not interact with other systems; they neither accept input from them nor produce output to them. Such systems have a quality called entropy, which means that, over time, they tend toward less differentation of their elements and toward a loss of organization and function. This notion brings us to the concept of boundaries.

Boundaries

A boundary may be defined as a closed circle around selected variables, where there is less interchange of energy or communication across the circle than there is within the circle. Open systems have, by definition, semipermeable boundaries. However, the relative "openness" or "closedness" of those boundaries will vary with the system. All of us are probably familiar with certain communities that are very conscious of themselves, of their entity, and are extremely unwilling to admit strangers or new behavior. Such communities have relatively closed boundaries and in time may well suffer some of the effects of entropy. We all have met families with such boundaries, boundaries well guarded by careful parents, and we may also know other families in which boundaries seem too open and unguarded to preserve the unit, in which social workers are allowed to intrude at will, with no challenge to their business there. In the beginning of the contact between worker and client system it is most helpful for the practitioner to observe the qualities of the boundaries of the systems they contact. All healthy systems have well-defined, semipermeable boundaries and have ways of maintaining these boundaries. If a worker visits a family because a child is in trouble with the school or community and a parent greets you at the door with the statement that they need none of your interference; that they can take care of their own children, thank you, you have two pieces of important data. You know that this parent is probably the person in the family charged with boundary maintenance, and you know that the boundaries on this family appear at first contact to be very closed. Given closed boundaries, you might expect that the system itself will be in trouble, because of lack of input of new information and energy. You also will have questions as to what is involved for you in being admitted inside the boundaries. Are the boundaries just closed to you because of the organization you represent or the mission on which you came? Or is this the family's usual way of functioning? If it's the usual pattern of functioning, is it a desperate attempt to protect the integrity of the system or is it a cultural pattern of the family in relating to outsiders? But, regardless of the cause of the closed boundaries, you know that they need to become more flexible and open for the health of the system. There are other families in which, no matter how serious your message, you are invited in and find yourself sitting in the midst of chaos with no sense that this is any more than a collection of individuals, a collection of people with no meaningful interaction. These families are in serious trouble, and your first clue may be the lack of boundary maintenance. To understand the boundary of a family is simple, but the concept of boundary itself is complex.

The discussion above dealt with the empirical boundaries of an actual social system. But social workers are concerned with a second level of boundaries, conceptual boundaries that social worker and client system establish to limit the range of the systems and phenomena that, given the problem and goals, are within their range of concern. We might call this the boundary of the system of concern. Social workers confronted with a problem involving the functioning of an individual, a family, or a social group will find that the definition of the problem and the definition of the boundaries of the social systems with which they will work are inextricably related. For example, when an individual brings a problem to a social worker, does the worker define the problem and the boundaries of the social system in such a way that the problem is seen as lying within the boundaries of the individual as a complete social system? Or does the worker define the problem in such a way that the system becomes the focus of concern and the individual is seen only as a component of the system? Or does the worker believe that the problem falls within the sphere of another institution? The boundaries of a system of concern are established by the practitioner, and it becomes the worker's task to determine what transactions are central to the solution of the problem (Klenk & Ryan, 1974, p. 21).

A concept that may help in establishing the boundaries of the systems is that of *levels* of systems. Simon (1952, pp. 130–139) has called this notion *layering*, pointing out that the individual, primary groups, organizations, and so on can best be considered as "nests of Chinese blocks" in which any activity taking place in one system at one of these layers will obviously be operating simultaneously in at least one other system (the larger or smaller block) at another level. Another way of conceptualizing this is by use of the system's term *holon*, which means that each level in a system faces both ways, toward the smaller systems of which it is composed and toward the larger system of which it is a part. This concept leads to the principle that any action that a practitioner takes with any piece of the system may affect the whole system and may spread like ripples on the water out into the larger system as well as affect smaller divisions of the system. Thus your action with an individual is going to affect the family or intimate group of which he/she is a part and will spread from there out into the larger social groups and organizations of which the group is a part. In the same way, actions taken with the individual will affect all systems of that individual, physical, psychological, cognitive, and so on.

Tension

Tension in human beings or in their organizations can be viewed as a pathological or disturbing factor that occurs only occasionally or residually. In contrast to this notion, systems theory conceives of tension as characteristic of, and necessary to, complex adaptive systems, though there is recognition that tension may manifest itself in either destructive or constructive ways. Thus systems theory does not attribute a positive or a negative value to tension per se, or even to conflict. Rather, such elements are seen as attributes of all systems simply because they are alive and open to transactions across their boundaries. It is the identification and analysis of how and to what purpose tensions operate within a system and between systems that are of major importance for social work practitioners. Rather than consider "inertia" as a given, or sought for, quality of complex, adaptive systems, with tension occurring as a "disturbing factor, some level of tension must be seen as characteristic of and vital to such systems although it may manifest itself as now destructive, now constructive" (Buckley, 1967, p. 53).

Feedback and purposive systems

A basic characteristic underlying purposive, goal-seeking mechanisms is that of *feedback*. By feedback is meant "a communications network which produces action in response to an input of information and includes the results of its own action in the new information by which it modifies its subsequent behavior" (Deutsch, 1968, p. 390). Feedback-controlled systems (and all human systems are thus controlled) are goal directed "since it is the deviations from the goalstate itself that direct the behavior of the system" (Buckley, 1967, p. 53). The goal-directed feedback loop underlying the self-directing human and social systems involves a receptor that accepts information from the outside, an element that imputes meaning to the information, a selector that establishes priorities of information processed, and a mechanism which measures or compares the feedback input against a goal and passes the information on to a control center which has the capacity of activating appropriate behavior to bring the system in line with its goal (p. 69). The meaning of the feedback is not something in it, or something in the system, but concerns in the interaction between the system and its environment. In the complex adaptive system there are "multistaged mediating processes" (p. 55) between the reception of feedback and the "output."

The question for the social worker is "Under what conditions does the information carried on the feedback loop promote change and under what conditions does it inhibit change?" Two kinds of feedback have been identified. It is generally held that negative feedback carries information that the system is behaving in such a way as to make it difficult to achieve its goal and that such feedback results in behavioral correction in line with goals. Positive feedback is generally held to mean that the system is behaving correctly in relation to its goal and that more behavior of the same quality is called for. Negative feedback is seen as deviation correcting since it results in behavioral change back to the goal, while positive feedback, since it calls for more of the same, is seen as moving toward ever greater deviation from the previous state. The important thing here is the goal of the system. It is critical that social workers understand the system as goal-directed and that they accept the principle that the system will evaluate the usefulness of the social worker's input into the system against the goals of the system. Thus, in order to be optimally helpful, the worker needs to know the goals of the system. This is a critical part of meeting clients where they are and addressing oneself to their central concern. In much of social work practice, goals of the client may be ignored and the helping effort may wander along with no direction or the worker may see it as within the helper's province to set goals. While the goals of work together may be negotiated, it is critical to the understanding of the client system that one understands how that system wants the problem solved and the place of this desired solution in the life goals of the system.

Change and stability

Because of the openness of human systems and the interaction of elements within their boundaries, it is impossible to conceive of such systems as static. They are constantly in the process of change and movement. And such movements in a human system represent the system's attempt to take purposive, goal-directed action. Human systems strive for the enhancement and elaboration of internal order and for the ordering and selection of outside stimuli accepted across the system boundary in such a way that purposive movement toward a selected goal is maintained. At the same time that a system is constantly in a state of change, it must also maintain a dynamic equilibrium. This notion is expressed by the concept of *steady state* or *homeostasis*. This concept deals with the order and structure necessary for any effective movement—without these all is chaos and purposive movement becomes impossible. Thus, although the movement of systems toward some goal is essential to their continued existence, systems also have a need for a certain amount of order and a certain stability. All views of human growth and behavior have some central notion to account for the need for stability and pattern in human life. However, different theories give this notion a more critical place than we do by seeing it as an overwhelming force that needs to be the central concern of the practitioner. Some theories maintain that once a pattern is established it cannot be changed by the system alone. Because of this force, the system cannot change without help. What this position ignores is that a system cannot not change. A system is an emergent entity. This way of viewing social systems means that while one recognizes the forces of stability and their utility, one sees the change forces as inevitable. Such forces are generally used by the system to achieve goals provided that they are not blocked by environmental forces. Thus instead of being concerned with opposing and changing a force within the client system, the worker is concerned with finding ways to ally worker strength with system strength to deal with the obstacles that lie in the way of growth or positive push in the system. If the direction of the movement of the system appears to be destructive, the worker must first examine and perhaps negotiate system goals so that the innate push of the system toward change can be allied with worker strength.

Equifinality and *multifinality* are two concepts relative to the change and stability of systems that are important to social workers. Equifinality is the capacity to achieve identical results from different initial conditions. If a system is open, it can be shown that the final state will not depend on those conditions. Such a system will have a goal of its own, and the end state will depend upon the interactions of the elements of the system and the transactions of the system with other systems in relation to that purpose. The concept of multifinality suggests an opposite principle: similar conditions may lead to dissimilar end states. Thus, similar initial conditions in any living system may or may not be relevant to or causally important in the establishment of the end state.

POTENTIAL VALUES OF SYSTEMS THEORY

Some potential values of systems theory as an organizing framework for social work knowledge are as follows:

1. Systems theory allows one to deal with far more data than does the analytical model, enabling one to bring order into a massive amount of information from all the different disciplines on which social work needs to draw. And it is the collection and ordering of the data that give structure to all else in the social work process, as all else is operational.

2. The concepts relating to systems and their development, function, and structure are equally applicable to the range of clients served by social workers, from the individual to society.

3. Systems theory provides a framework for gaining an appreciation of the entire range of elements that bear on social problems, including the social units involved, their interrelationships, and the implications of change in one as it affects all.

4. Systems theory shifts attention from the characteristics possessed by individuals or their environments to the transactions between systems, changing the vantage point of the data collector and focusing on interfaces and the communication process that takes place there. Social work has long been struggling to see individuals and their environments as complete units.

5. Systems theory sees people as active personality systems capable of self-initiated behavior and thus able to contribute and alter their behavior or even to create new environments. Adaptation of the environment is as much a property of human systems as is the tendency to be affected by or adapt to the environment. These concepts negate the tendency to see disturbances as pathology and move the worker into the present life of the system.

6. The concept of systems as purposive, combined with the concepts of equifinality and multifinality, radically changes the view of both causation and the possibilities for change. It supports the worker's concern with self-determination and with the client's participation in the change process and it emphasizes the necessity of knowing and considering client goals in assessment and planning of intervention.

7. The use of systems theory brings the purpose of the system into the center of the worker's consideration, engendering further concern with self-determination and the necessity of relating professional feedback to client purpose.

8. If a living, open system requires constant transaction with other systems and its environment for its progressive development, it becomes evident that a major function of social workers becomes the provision and maintenance of such interchange opportunities for all populations.

9. Given what systems theory tells us about closed systems, social workers need to be increasingly concerned with populations and systems heading

toward isolation, with the strains in our society that result in isolation, and with our now isolated populations.

10. If change and tension are inherent in open systems, social workers need to direct their attention to why suggested changes may be resisted and why such changes become unbearable for a system. This further emphasizes the principle of meeting clients where they are and with self-determination. It removes the notion that tension or conflict is pathology.

11. The concept of system boundary gives us a new way to observe the systems with which we work. It tells us to expect certain caution and testing from healthy systems and to be concerned with the health of systems that are too open or too closed. It speaks to social workers' concerns with client's rights and recognizes that social workers should be concerned with the ways they and their services move across the boundary of a social system.

12. The recognition that change in one part of a system can often greatly affect the whole means that one must be increasingly aware of the impact of intervention in the broader transactions of clients. In addition it speaks to the fact that it is not necessary to change a whole system to bring meaningful change but that the point of intervention must be chosen with care. It broadens the concept of the points at which a system can be entered, provides one with more ways of entering effectively, and may make the intervention simpler.

13. The systems perspective also places the agency as a social system and the worker and client in the same transactional field. Social workers are a social system and are involved as components of a social system network.

Basic conceptual systems in social work practice

At this point there will be a brief departure from the development of basic knowledge to insert some material related to a conceptual practice framework. We are inserting this material here because it has to do with systems theory and it will be referred to from time to time as the material in the next few chapters is developed. The notions to be discussed were developed originally by Allen Pincus and Anne Minahan (1973, pp. 54–74) as a model for teaching social work practice.

According to the discussion of systems theory, most of the examples used so far have involved what could be called client systems. However, social workers do some of their most important, time consuming, and demanding work with people other than those traditionally viewed as clients. In "The House on Sixth Street," the change efforts were primarily focused on other than the client system, although client skills in problem solving were improved. In the case example of Maria, a social worker using systems theory would probably work with her mother, her sister, her grandparents, the income maintenance and the social service department of the county welfare board, personnel in the clinic, the group worker, and the school system. If the practitioner works in protective services for children, there will also be the necessity to work with court services, medical services, neighbors, police, attorneys, and perhaps the school system and foster parents or other child-care services. As a practitioner in a child-care agency, the worker may be involved with the children and their families, medical resources, the school, foster parents, and perhaps community centers and organized groups outside of the agency boundaries. If the agency has a residential center, the worker will be involved with others who have contact with their clients—the maintenance staff, child-care staff, teachers, and perhaps nurses inside the agency. In addition to the people they see outside of the agency, the workers are always a part of an organized structure in which they do their work. Even in private practice they will usually have a secretary and someone to answer the telephone with whom they interact as a system. Workers usually think first of their clients who they feel are the people they are there to help, but they may want to consider seriously who really benefits from their change efforts. Who is the client in the case of child abuse—the child, the parents, or the community who asked the worker to get involved? Who gives the worker the right to interfere in other people's lives? Who sanctions what the worker does? In daily transactions between themselves and others, workers find that they are working with many different people about different things and for different reasons in order to achieve some overall goal.

Pincus and Minahan (1973, pp. 54–74) suggest that the people with whom the worker interacts in practice actions can be classified into four types of social systems: the client system, the target system, the action system, and the change agent system. To this could be added two more systems: the professional system and the problem-identification system. The decision of the worker as to the purpose and the relationships that should be a part of each encounter will determine the definition of the system. The systems that make up social work practice may be described in the following ways.

The change agent system.   Social workers may be viewed as change agents, who are specifically employed for the purpose of planning and working with the six systems toward the planned change. The agency or organization that employs them or of which they are a part can be thought of as the change agent system. Obviously, the change agent system heavily influences the worker's behavior through various policies and resources that represent sanctions, constraints, and resources. These will be discussed in greater detail in the Chapter 5 section on bureaucracy.

The client system.   People may be considered to be a part of a client system when (1) they have either asked for or sanctioned the worker's services; (2) they are expected to benefit from those services; and (3) they have entered into an explicit or implicit contract with the worker (see the discussion on contracts in Chapter 10). This definition leads to a brief consideration of the nature of the first coming together of client and worker. There are clients who come to the agency voluntarily seeking the help of the worker, but there are large numbers of situations in which the worker approaches the client because the agency function calls for it to assume this type of responsibility in behalf of the community (which should be considered the client at this point); for example, corrections, child welfare, protection for the aged and incompetent, and so on. Also a neighborhood center staff (a change agent system) may identify what they see as a neighborhood need and ask a staff member to attempt to form an organization to deal with it. In all these instances the community or the change agent system itself may more appropriately be considered the client than the people the worker approaches "to help." The people identified as targets of the worker's efforts are more appropriately regarded as *potential clients* until some sort of agreement is reached in which potential clients sanction the worker's intervention in their lives and transactions. This principle will be discussed further in several parts of the text as it is a crucial one that is often not understood. An example of this is found in the Taber article included in Chapter 8. Taber discusses work as a community mental health worker in which the workers went out to offer help to a disorganized neighborhood. Another interesting example is found in Work with Mrs. Stover in Chapter 10 in which the worker attempted for several months to engage Mrs. Stover concerning care of her children, only to have the woman become a client when she needed financial help.

The target system.   The people that the change agents "need to change or influence in order to accomplish their goals" is the target system (Pincus & Minahan, 1973, p. 58). The target system and the client system often overlap when it is the client, or the client's part in an intersystem transaction, that needs to be changed. However, much of social work practice involves the social worker working with the client system toward some desired change in some other system (a target system).

The action system.   The term *action system* is used to describe those with whom the social worker interacts in a cooperative way to accomplish the purposes of the change effort. There are an endless number of different action systems in which the worker may be engaged. Chapter 13 will deal with the skills of teamwork which is essentially a discussion of the ways of working with action systems made up of professional or paraprofessional people. However, action systems may be a neighborhood group, a family group, or others that the worker works with toward bringing about a change helpful to the client. Readers will find two interesting examples in the Taber article of the worker asking an already established client system to serve as an action system for potential clients, helping the worker to influence the potential client to become an actual client and accept some needed services.

The professional system.   This system is made up of the professional association of social workers, the educational system by which workers are prepared, and the values and sanctions of a professional practice. The values and the culture of the professional system strongly influence both the required and the permitted actions of the worker as change agent. In working to change their own agency or in acting as an advocate of social change, practitioners often utilize the professional system.

The problem-identification system.   This system is the system that acts to bring a potential client to the attention of the worker. At the initiation of its contact with the worker, or the change agent system, it might be considered (as Pincus and Minahan discuss) the client system. However, it usually does not consider itself a client, and if, in the course of things, it should appear that it should be the focus of the helping effort, the worker will need to treat it more as a potential client until it makes a role transition.

These systems will be referred to throughout the rest of the text. We believe that the use of these concepts will result in the worker thinking more clearly about their practice decisions and actions.

ROLE THEORY AS FOUNDATION KNOWLEDGE

Another concept that helps us to enrich and expand our understanding and use of systems theory is the concept of role. This concept is a transactional or bridging concept between the environment or larger social system and the individual or microsystem in that it refers to the expected behavior for a person occupying a particular social status or position in a social system. It is a bridging concept in that it gives us a way of seeing a linkage between larger and smaller systems and because both the larger system and the smaller system have socially constructed notions of what the behavior should be and what it means to fulfill the role. The concept of role gives us one of the ties that is important in assessing a systems network in that it is never a notion that is limited to one system but always involves the system that is expected to operate in the role and the system in relation to which the role is performed. It usually involves the larger society and the culture in that the roots of role performance standards and expectations usually lie in this larger system and the larger system often has tremendous investment in the carrying out of certain roles in prescribed ways (Biddle & Thomas, 1966).

Social norms for the position provide guides for the attitudes, feelings, and behavior that are permitted, expected, or prohibited for the individual filling that role. These norms will differ from culture to culture. In other words, the cultural environment in which the system finds itself will set different norms and expectations for role occupants. For example, all cultures have prescribed specific role behavior for a woman filling the role and status of mother within the family system. However, these prescribed attitudes and behavior may differ significantly depending upon the cultural environment of the particular family system. This fact has great importance for the activities of the social worker in problem definition, data collection, assessment, and interventions.

Three related concepts relating to role are the notions of *role set, role complementarity,* and *role conflict.* Important to the notion of role complementarity and reciprocity is the fact that role positions or statuses are usually paired. For every parent there is a child; for every wife there is a husband. If the position of husband is no longer filled in the family system, the role of wife changes to the role of widow, divorced person, or separated or abandoned woman. If a system is to enjoy some stability and integration, there must be some reciprocity of expectations between role partners. If an industrial organization is to be free to pursue its goals, there must be some agreement between those persons occupying management and policy-making roles and those occupying labor roles. If husbands and wives are to create a family system with some stability, there must be some agreement among them as to how their varying roles will be performed.

The patterns of expected role behavior grow from the need of social systems, as discussed earlier, to have a steady state—to have the stability that comes from being able to predict within some acceptable limits the behavior of elements within the system. These patterns of expectation grow from two types of interaction. First, the opportunities, the deprivations, and the needs in the interactions between elements internal to the system will establish role expectations related to system maintenance and growth. For example, children need protection and nurture if they are to grow and make their contribution to life. The system must answer as to what position, or positions, within the system will be given that job and what behavior from that element will assure effective care of the child. The second source of the expectations is found within the transactions the system has with other systems and environments. These come from the same sources as discussed earlier. For example, all individuals need food, clothing, and shelter, and depending on the geographic and climatic environment within which people find themselves, patterns of securing these needs will develop. When individuals group themselves into larger systems, certain differentiation of functions that are essential to the functioning of the system will develop. This differentiation will then result in assigned roles to system elements, and expected role patterns will develop. When other systems and environments change, there will be problems within the system as the various elements of the system continue previously patterned behavior. Thus today one sees conflict between parents and children—the aged and youth—which is largely a conflict between expected role patterns and the changing environment that appears to make certain of these patterns dysfunctional. This will be discussed further under role incongruity.

While there is always room in role expectation for certain individual interpretations and behaviors, when a role is either ascribed or achieved it is often found that certain aspects of the self are developed and brought out and certain aspects are neglected and often very consciously repressed. This is true of all choices of life. However, the more rigid and circumscribed the notion of role behavior, and the more certain characteristics of the person are tied to role position, the more stress individuals may feel in being placed in, or even in self-selecting, that role. At the moment many women in our society are very active in trying to change the woman's role. However, this is most difficult since all members of our society have been conditioned so strongly in sex-role differentiation. Consciousness may be raised, but conditioning is hard to deal with.

The construct of role set or role clusters, which is an array of roles that any one person may be filling at any particular time (Merton, 1957), is an important notion for social workers. Conflict between the various roles in any role set may be particularly painful for the individual or the system involved. For example, employers sometimes defend themselves against charges of discrimination against women by the statement that women are not as interested in advancement as men and will not fulfill certain prescribed behavior for management roles such as accepting night work or travel assignments. For the women involved, this type of demand may conflict in particularly difficult ways with the roles of wife and mother that may also be within their cluster of roles. What happens in this situation is that the woman involved suffers from role conflict. She is involved in two different role sets in two different systems and the expected behavior of the roles involved is defined so that the two roles cannot be simultaneously filled satisfactorily by one person.

The role expectations may conflict in at least three ways. The social system of which the system is a part may provide no acceptable alternative for a different solution. The woman's own internalized notions about acceptable behavior within the role may limit her alternatives. Third, the other occupant of the role pair may hold role expectations that clash (role conflict to be discussed later) with the woman's wishes and generate conflicted interaction between these two primary elements of the system involved.

Role incongruity, another construct in role theory, has been defined as a situation in which one's own perception of one's role is defined differently from the expectations of significant others in the system or the environment. The concept of the behavior expected of women who occupy the role of mother that has been held by our culture over the years has resulted in denying to women the resources of child care that would allow mothers to simultaneously occupy with some comfort the role of employee in occupational systems.

Another example of role incongruity is often found in the differing expectations for the behavior of the client system held by social worker and the client system, or conversely, the difference between the client's notion of the role of the worker and that held by the worker. There have been studies that show that there is often conflict between the client's expectations that the worker will tell them what to do and what actually happens in the interview which is directed by the social worker's notion of what is helpful. In correctional systems the worker may conceive of the role as that of "helper," while the client may conceive of it as one of surveillance and control (Perlman, 1961). There may be unrecognized but very painful and difficult problems when a social worker from one culture attempts to deal with role performances of an individual from another culture unless the worker understands the importance of role incongruity. The two cultures may hold very different and conflicting prescriptions about the attitudes and behavior that are appropriate to the role. For example:

> An Indian social work student was working with an Indian woman who desperately needed medical care but was too frightened to go to the clinic. In an attempt to act as a broker for her troubled client, the student went to talk to the doctor at the clinic. She felt very angry and upset because she felt that the doctor had been rude, suspicious, and rejecting. When she shared her perception with her field instructor, it was revealed that she came to this conclusion because of the fact that the doctor began immediately to question her about the client and continued to ask

many very direct questions. This behavior was incongruent with her norms about the way strangers should behave with each other.

In this example the social worker (change agent), coming from a culturally defined role expectation as to the way strangers should interact, misinterpreted the meaning of the behavior of an element of an action system she was trying to construct for the client system. Incidentally, a very important principle here is that if the worker misinterpreted the doctor's behavior, how do you think the doctor would have related to the client's expectations?

Even the social scientists who originated the concept of role disagree on its definition and some of the basic constructs and propositions that surround it. However, since the authorities from which is is borrowed disagree, and since borrowed knowledge always needs to be reshaped to fit the function of the profession, this discussion on role will be pulled together with some notions of our own (Compton and Galaway) and some notions taken from the work of another social worker, Helen Harris Perlman (1961, 1962).

Social roles are elements of all social systems and are generally assigned or achieved on the basis of the positions within the various social systems in which we all find ourselves. These expectations involve not only our overt behavior but what we are expected to be and feel like in interaction with what the other is expected to be, to act like, and to feel like (1961). In open systems there are two further principles that apply: (1) role prescriptions are very general and allow for certain changes in our behavior, and (2) changes in the way system elements fill their role (acting, feeling, and being) may result in significant system changes (see the discussion in Chapter 5 of the way the change agent may change the change agent system). Thus change in a system may be brought about by some change in the feeling, acting, or being of an element within the system, or by a change in the system's role behavior that affects the transactions of relating systems within larger social systems.

Perlman (1961, p. 375) writes as follows regarding the use of role in social work practice:

> We know it to be true of ourselves that, when we find ourselves in a social situation in which behavioral expectations (role) are not clear, we fumble in trial and error adaptation. When we are clear what the requirements are but find they run counter to our drives and needs, we feel conflicted. When our interpretation of requirements is different from the interpretation made by the person with whom we interact, both conflict and confusion may result. When requirements themselves are ill-defined or inadequately defined, we may feel and act in diffuse and inept ways.

To summarize, the following concepts from role theory are important to social workers:

1. Certain behaviors are prescribed (by us and by other elements of our social system) relative to our position within that system.
2. Every role involves both our own expectations and abilities and one or more others.

3. The notion of role expectation implies that there are certain social norms that set the outside limits for congruent, nonconflicted interactions, and transactions between positions within the system and between systems.
4. There are emotionally charged value judgments to how people carry out their roles both on the part of the person occupying the role position and others.
5. Social functioning may be seen as the sum of the roles performed by a human system (Boehm, 1959, pp. 95–97).
6. The concept of role, role functioning, role expectations, and role transactions may be used to increase the knowledge base used for the assessment of the problem situation. Role failure and/or role conflict will tend to follow:
    a. The loss or absence of resources necessary to a system's ability to perform a role well.
    b. When systems are thrust into new roles without knowing the role expectations.
    c. When there is a conflict in role expectation on the part of interacting systems.
    d. When there is a conflict of role expectations within the cluster of roles carried by one system.
    e. When there is ambiguity on the part of other systems as to role expectations.
    f. When the individual as a system, or as a member of a social system, is deficient or handicapped in physical, intellectual, or social capacities demanded by the role.
    g. When high feeling or crisis situations suddenly and without warning disrupt previous effective role patterns (Perlman, 1962, 17–31).

As an example, the Tucker article (see Reading 4–3) deals with the importance of a change agent understanding the roles of certain social systems in black culture and the effect of these notions on their functioning.

EGO PSYCHOLOGY AS FOUNDATION KNOWLEDGE

The most complete theory of human development is psychoanalytic theory as first developed by Sigmund Freud and further refined and expanded by countless disciples. There are several problems involved in any attempt to treat psychoanalytic theory briefly. First, there is the need to differentiate between the concept of human development found within psychoanalytic theory, the notion of how people get in trouble and how they change that is a part of this theory, and the method of treating human psychological disorders that was developed on the basis of this theory. Because of the complexity and volume of psychoanalytic theory, we will not try to present any coherent summary in this brief chapter. We suggest, instead, that students of social work may want to seek other sources of such understanding. The theory is introduced here only because certain concepts from ego psychology rest on a psychoanalytic base about the development and functioning of the human personality, and thus understanding psychoanalytic theory is important to knowing and using ego psychology.

Psychoanalytic constructs

Psychoanalytic theory conceives of the human being as a dynamic energy system consisting of basic drives and instincts which in interaction with the environment serve to organize and develop the personality through a series of developmental stages. Individuals from birth are pushed by these largely unconscious and irrational drives toward satisfaction of desires which are largely unconscious and irrational. Because of the operation of an unconscious defense system and the structure of the mind, people go through life largely unaware of these irrational forces that have tremendous effect on their behavior and on the way they relate to others. The behavior that others observe, and our own knowledge of our behavior and our purposes, is actually a very incomplete view of what we are as individuals and what drives us. Most of the motivating forces of personality are thus beneath the surface and are available to our conscious and rational understanding and direction only through a careful exploration of these buried regions. Thus an individual's personality is seen primarily as an elaboration of the unconscious, irrational drives with which each of us are born and the early vicissitudes which lay down a foundation of personality in early childhood. The personality system is viewed as primarily a semiclosed energy system which operates primarily to conserve energy by resisting stimulus and change. Because individuals are seen as being driven by these unconscious forces that tend primarily to struggle to maintain a homeostatic balance, real change in behavior after childhood can come only through an experience that is able to reach the deepest levels of one's personality. The environment and happenings in the world around us have an impact on us as individuals and on our behavior only through the meanings we assign such events as a result of our unconscious needs and defenses.

Freud held that the personality was structured into three divisions: "The id comprises the psychic representatives of the drives, the ego consists of those functions which have to do with the individual's relation to his environment, and the superego comprises the moral precepts of our minds as well as our ideal aspirations" (as related in Brenner, 1955, p. 45). The ego is expected to act as the executive officer of the personality dealing with impulses from the id and with moral signals of the superego as well as with the realities of the environment.

Over the years various individuals working with the concepts of psychoanalytic theory and observing human behavior began to focus primarily on the development of the rational, conscious processes in personality. They are given the name of ego psychologists, because, coming from a base in psychoanalytic theory, they have differed in that they have given the central place in human functioning not to the irrational and instinctual forces of the id but to the rational processes of the ego. They hold that the individual comes into this world with rational as well as irrational instincts and that the personality develops and becomes differentiated in relation to the environmental interactions, concerns, goals, and unconscious needs rather than being almost entirely an elaboration of inner instinctual drives.

Ego psychology constructs

Eric Erikson, one of the earliest ego psychologists, held that, although early experience was significant, the personality system all through life was open to meaningful interaction with both the inner and outer life experiences. The notion that throughout life, new tasks and new biopsychosocial demands bring human beings new opportunities for growth and change was an important departure from the older psychoanalytic beliefs. However, the manner in which these opportunities are used will be reflective of the individual's success and failure in dealing with earlier life tasks (Hartman, 1970).

Ego psychologists began to challenge the earlier psychoanalytic view of the conservation of energy and the notion of a semiclosed system. They argued for the construct of an open personality system as they believed there was empirical evidence that human beings were born with an ego need to seek both difference and stimulus from the environment. Thus in ego psychology, personality development is seen as the result of interaction with the environment that is actively sought by the individual. Another earlier concept that was challenged was the notion of the personality's push toward static homeostasis. This concept was replaced by the notion that while the personality needs certain stability, people also seek and must have for appropriate growth and development new experiences and new transactions from the environment. In this notion, systems theory is in agreement with and supported by ego psychology.

Competence and mastery.   Robert White's works (1960, 1963) further developed the notion that individuals are motivated from childhood on to interact actively with the environment not merely as a result of drives such as hunger, thirst or sex but because of a need to explore the world and to import new experiences and stimuli into the system. White has called this motive "effectance" by which he means a kind of general push from the ego to master the environment. When individuals master a new experience in line with their standards and with the approval of the real world (called competence by White), they are innately motivated to try new and more complex tasks. White called this motivational force a push toward mastery. This notion is discussed further by Trader in her article on the theories that form the base of effective work with minorities discussed in Chapter 2.

White holds that as a result of experiences of competency, individuals grow to feel a sense of mastery—a belief that one can change one's environment by obtaining knowledge of how to change it and by the use of effective skills that one has developed. The article dealing with learned helplessness (Reading 2–1) supports this notion by discussing what happens when persons are deprived of ways of controlling their environment. These concepts have tremendous significance for social workers in that they support the notion that, given a relatively benign environment, individuals actively seek control of their lives and welcome new experiences. Resistance toward change and apathy are seen as states resulting from environmental lacks and hurtful interactions and transactions over time. Thus the forces of growth and change are seen as stronger than the resistance to change provided the individual's transactions with the environment and other systems have provided experiences of effectance and mastery leading to a sense of competence.

In ego psychology the ego is seen to be that part of the personality that takes action in life situations—it is the executive officer of the personality. In the process of coping, the ego develops both protective-defensive operations and seeking-discovering-learning operations. "The main categories of ego functions are its clusters of cognitive, affective, motoric, executive, and integrative operations" (Perlman, 1975, p. 214). Cognitive functions are the thought processes that consist of facts, notions, concepts, memories, and beliefs and the way this material is acquired, stored, retrieved, organized, and reorganized. The affective functions of the ego have to do with our feeling processes: anger, guilt, hate, love, caring, and excitement. The executive function of the ego involves decision making and action. Decision making rests on the ability to perceive one's natural and external environment accurately, to think logically and analyze, to integrate thinking, feeling, and a sense of mastery and on the possession of action skills with which to carry through with some satisfaction on the decisions.

All these functions of the ego are interrelated and each affects the other. Feeling affects thought; thought affects feeling. Action can bring significant change in both thinking and feeling. The feedback that a system receives from the environment as to its actions affects both thinking and feeling and future actions. Since this is true, it is equally true that individuals can intervene to change the functioning of any system by approaching any one of the three functions. Thus we may begin work with either thinking, feeling, or action. Where we will begin depends on how we assess the client system, the problem, the goal, and the situation and on what the client wants. It is important to the selection of helping actions to remember that coping skills of the individual can be increased by starting with whichever function seems appropriate and our activity will affect all functions.

Motivation. From these concepts of ego, competence, and mastery, there has developed some important work on motivation. A feeling of mastery, or control over one's internal reactions and relevant external events, appears to be a significant force in motivating human behavior (Liberman, 1978, p. 35). A number of laboratory investigations in the area of the importance of control is summarized by Lefcourt (1966, p. 188) as follows: "When individuals are involved in situations where personal competence can effect . . . outcomes, they tend to perform more actively and adequately than when . . . situations appear less controllable." Thus "insofar as individuals believe that their actions and inactions affect their well-being, the achievement of a sense of mastery becomes a major goal throughout their lives" (Liberman, 1978, p. 36). Liberman further points out that for an individual to acquire a sense of mastery, there must be a framework that links a person's performance to self-esteem. The link between performance and self-esteem is governed, among other things, by the person's background and current situation, task relevance, task difficulty, attribution of performance, and the attitudes of significant others.

The University of Chicago faculty developed a proposition (based on ego psychology and the work of Helen Perlman and Charlotte Towle) that the individual's use of social work services rests on some combination of motivation, capacity and opportunity. Lilian Ripple's attempt (1964) to test this formulation led to a further development of the concept of motivation by the Chicago faculty partly through integrating the work of Thomas French (1952). These notions may be summarized as follows: First, motivation is defined as what one wants and how much it is wanted. In other words, people will not move toward change unless that change is in line with their goals and purposes and there is a significant desire for the goal. Second, the two basic and necessary forces of motivation are the push of discomfort and the pull of hope. People do not have the courage and purposiveness necessary in goal-directed activities without a balance between these factors.

In order to move in a goal-directed way we need a certain amount of discomfort because we have to dislike where we are in order to see a reason for change, and a certain amount of focused discomfort about where we are helps us to withstand certain pressures to scatter our efforts rather than to focus and control them. There are two kinds of discomfort: (1) generalized and (2) focused. In order to move toward change, discomfort must be focused on the thing to be changed. A more generalized discomfort that relates to the whole of our life situation results in disintegration of goal-directed efforts and must be focused before effective planning can be done. This generalized discomfort usually represents a feeling of helplessness, of being out of control.

The pull toward goal-directed effort is provided by hope. Hope increases the amount of pressure that can be withstood before the disintegration of gaol-directed efforts begin. When one is hopeful that one can effectively move toward what one wants, one becomes willing to forego other satisfactions and withstand other pressures from other needs and wants in order to realize the greater goal or want.

Based on the work of Perlman, Towle, French, and White and our own experience, we believe a sense of hope is based on (1) a sense of trust that there is some relationship between one's needs and the intentions of the world around one; (2) a sense that one has meaning for others—one's actions are important; (3) a sense of who one is; (4) a sense of competence built on evaluation of past efforts (past successes as one evaluates them); (5) perception of the opportunities in the environment around one; (6) one's experience with frustration in the past; (7) a generalized sense of mastery; and (8) relationship between one's perception of one's competence and one's perception of the skills needed to reach the goal.

Thus one's capacity to use the want and discomfort of motivation to change in a goal-directed way depends first upon hope and second upon how much one knows of how to achieve a purpose. This includes the ability to see the totality of the situation including the results of choices made in the process, the time factors, and the possible obstacles, reassurance from the real world, experiences with the real world including the pleasure in functional activity, substitute gratifications, and appropriate evaluation of achievement of subgoals or small steps.

In discussing motivation it is important to mention frustration. It is possible to avoid frustration by avoiding a commitment to a goal. Severe and repeated frustration will move an individual in this direction. Frustration is the realization that the goal to which one is committed is unattainable. The intensity of frustration is proportional to the degree of previous commitment to the purpose being thwarted. If goal-directed striving is frustrated after a particular quantum of pressure is committed to it, perhaps it is possible to find substitute goals so that the pressure can be rechanneled. If substitute goals are not found, it is possible that the pressure and desire may be discharged in destructive form and rage. If one has been pursuing a goal with confidence, and then it becomes unattainable, hope is destroyed and an overt rage reaction is produced. The experience of frustration over time is destructive of an individual's sense of competence and mastery. Frustration ends with the disintegration of goal-directed striving. The end phase of loss of hope is apathy and a sense of learned helplessness.

Ripple's research (1964) attempted to assess the importance of the three constructs for the client's effective use of social work services: motivation, capacity, and opportunity. Her findings were that the client's level of hope plus the opportunities available were the critical factors in use of services. In spite of a belief that the personality functioning of the client and the type of problem is important, these factors did not appear to have a critical impact on the use of help. As a result of her research, Ripple recommended that in the initial explorations of the client's problem the worker make a careful assessment of the hope-discomfort balance. Ripple further recommended that workers should be concerned with the impact of their activities on this critical balance during the beginning stages of client-worker interaction.

SIGNIFICANT CONTRIBUTIONS OF EGO PSYCHOLOGY TO SOCIAL WORK KNOWLEDGE

1. The concept of the ego as having its own needs and drives and as being autonomous coupled with the belief in the human personality as emergent and developing over a life cycle gives importance to helping efforts directed to present life experiences.
2. The concept of the personality as an open system gives great weight to the importance of the day-by-day input from transactions with the environment. It joins with systems theory to support the importance of the active involvement of client system with a benign environment.
3. The construct of the individual's need for competence and mastery offers social work an optimistic view of the possibilities of human growth and change while it also demands that social workers be constantly con-

cerned with input from networks of other social systems and environment.

4. Concepts from ego psychology focus on individuals as active, conscious
    participants in their own destiny rather than viewing individuals as reac-
    tors to stimuli or needs beyond their control. This leads to the concept
    of the relationship between the worker and the client system as a partner-
    ship.

5. The constructs of competence and mastery from ego psychology support
    the view of human beings as seeking active experiences and control
    of their own destiny. This gives guidance in assessment and also de-
    mands that client systems be active participants in planning and change
    and supports social work values of self-determination and respect for
    the individual.

6. The notion that motivation is what the client system wants and how
    much it wants it joins with the concept of goal in systems theory to
    remind social workers of the importance of both client system goals
    and the value of self-determination.

7. The importance of hope as a stimulus for active problem solving gives
    social workers a totally new view of the meaning of apathy and chal-
    lenges many of the other concepts of what produces dependency.

CONCEPTS OF STRESS, COPING, AND CRISIS

An understanding of the concepts of stress, coping, and crisis is an important part of the knowledge base of social work practice. Much of social
work practice involves engagement with the client system at some point
between the system's (or some other concerned system's) identification of
a stress situation as threatening and the point at which the individual's
coping devices have been exhausted and the situation remains threatening
(crisis state), or the point at which the system is depressed and apathetic
because of the belief that resolution of troubles is impossible. The notions
of stress, crisis, and coping are important to social work practice in that
they, like role, give us some further linking concepts between the microsystem and the environment. In working for policy and administrative change
in larger social systems, we are essentially working toward making changes
in the larger system that makes the resources of social institutions more
available as a part of the normal coping repertoire of the smaller systems.

There is an extensive literature on stress including considerable work
on the connection between major events in life and physical illness. There
is considerable controversy about how stress should be defined. For our
purposes here we would suggest that stress be defined as the tension that
arises in a system—individual, family, group, and so on—from the perception
of an event as involving uncertainty and risk. For many systems, stress
may precipitate appropriate problem-solving activities leading to effective
choice of alternatives, appropriate choice-directed action, and a satisfying
solution. Thus for many of us the feeling of stress is at least semipleasurable.
We gear ourselves up to meet a challenge, the risk and the uncertainty
imparting an excitement to our efforts to effectively problem solve. Although

we may interpret other life events differently and may perceive them as a loss or a threat. There are other people who interpret all such events as beyond their capacity to influence and therefore as disasters before which they make any attempt to problem solve.

In the literature, stress, and coping are usually linked as related phenomena. Certainly for social workers, the understanding of the coping patterns of the client is critical. We need to understand what are the generalized coping resources of the client and their usual pattern for use. We also need to determine the client's ability or inability to mobilize or successfully use these mechanisms. Generalized coping resources can be divided into several categories that we need to assess in working with client systems. Perhaps the first and most basic category is that of beliefs and attitudes toward life. In keeping with the notion of motivation being composed of hope and discomfort, if we do not believe that our effort will produce results we will not be motivated to marshall our coping resources. And in keeping with the article on learned helplessness at the end of Chapter 2, if we do not see that we have any input into what happens to us or its outcome, we will be apathetic. Antonovsky, a medical sociologist, who has done significant studies on stress and illness throughout the major countries of the world, maintains people who believe that life is an orderly, purposive process in which processes can be understood and outcomes are generally for the best suffer less debilitating illness than their cohorts, no matter how severe the level of stress. While we may often neglect to explore this aspect of our client's lives, it would appear that perhaps the most powerful coping mechanism is a belief in life.

The second large group of coping mechanisms include the range of one's knowledge and successful experiences with life tasks and one's cognitive capacities and ability to reason from cause to effect. The ability to control and use emotional and affective responses to the stress is an important coping ability. The fourth important class is that of the environmental resources available to one. Perhaps one of the most important resources we possess in our society is money. Money aids us in coping both by giving us the means to purchase services or things we may need (a satisfying environment), and its power serves to assure us that we are worthwhile and capable of controlling our own destiny. The second large subgroup of resources is the network of supporting social systems that may be available to us. The last important group of coping mechanisms are the skills in carrying out planned action. Such skills usually come from past successful experiences (Antonovsky, 1980, pp. 98–182).

CONCEPTS OF DIVERSITY AND DIFFERENCE

The last important piece of knowledge to be discussed in this chapter is the importance of social work's understanding of diversity and difference. This notion of equal but different is very difficult for us to understand because of the human tendency to assume that if two objects are different one must be of innately more worth than the other or one must be right and the other wrong. We confuse the concept of same with the concept of equal.

Often in discussing equal rights of men and women, someone will protest that this is impossible as men and women are obviously different thus confusing "sameness" and equality. Yet to offer the "same" education or the same opportunities to two different people with different wants and needs may be an obvious violation of the notion of equality. It appears that no society in the world exists without some oppression of the different by those who, by reason of possession of valued resources, possess oppressive power. Such resources may be money, cattle, physical strength, knowledge, or education. Those who have the power to impose their will on other groups that are different tend to assign the highest value to the qualities they possess and less desirable qualities to the others. For example, in our society, women, blacks, and children tend to be assigned similar qualities. These groups are seen as careless, carefree, emotional, excelling in song and dance, are impulsive and have great difficulty with logical, abstract reasoning. Once certain qualities are assigned members of a group it is assumed all members are alike in the possession of these qualities.

It is often difficult for any one of us to see a person as an individual with individual differences because of the nature of human learning. We learn by categorizing people, objects, experiences, and assuming a certain commonness to whatever falls within the category. We use such categories to communicate with others. For example, when we speak of a tree to another English-speaking person we are understood by the other person to be speaking of a certain group of growing things. However, if the person we addressed was an expert in forestry, he/she would want to know a great deal more about the trees we were describing. As a specialist in trees, he/she must know much more than the broad classification, and each piece of knowledge leads increasingly to the individualization of a particular tree. Thus we, as specialists in human interaction, cannot be satisfied with putting people in broad categories on the basis of certain innate characteristics such as sexual organs or skin color. Neither can we see all people who are of a common ethnic origin or who subscribe to certain common ways of life as alike. We must know enough about each individual to see them as distinctly different from other individuals.

At another level of conceptualization, systems theory and ego psychology point to the importance of diversity in the ongoing development of human systems. Without the stimulation of difference, human systems would not develop. However, the notion of patterned expectations, and the feelings and values attached to them from role theory, the construct of "steady state" from systems theory, and the formulation of homeostasis from psychoanalytic theory all posit a certain resistance to change, diversity, and difference.

Human systems need stability, the security of knowing that, at least in some dimensions of human life, their expectations of the behavior of others and transactions with others will be fulfilled and that the meanings they attach to that behavior will be accurate. This allows systems to shape and control their own actions through being able to predict both (1) the reactions of others to a contemplated action, and (2) what they may expect from others in the ordinary course of their transactions. The question for professionals working with human systems is the question of the balance between diversity and change, stability, and our purpose as a change agent. A strategy for change, particularly when we are concerned with an institution as the target system, is to induce crisis which deprives the elements of the system, and the system itself, of reference points in role behavior and will result in system change. "However, we need to remember that crisis resolution can go either way—toward the development of new adaptive modes or toward regression and defense through the closure of the system and the rigidifying of the structure" (Hartman, 1970).

A part of this need for stability of behaviors and meanings if workers are to make any predictive judgments about behavior and transactions with others results from the intolerance of difference on the part of human systems and their elements and part from the definition of "normal" behavior. As stated earlier, role expectations become internalized as value systems, thus there is a tendency of human systems to view difference in role behaviors as right or wrong rather than considering whether or not they are essential (given social work's present knowledge base from which to make judgments) to the existence and ongoing development of the system. This tends to be particularly true of the family system, so some examples from the operation of that system will be used to illustrate this point. But first, it must be recognized that the importance of the family system stems from the fact that society cannot exist without some form of reproduction of the elements of society (children) and their protection and socialization. There is considerable evidence that children need certain protections which are usually furnished within the family system. However, family systems in different cultures will have different notions as to what member of the family system performs this role and what behaviors are necessary to such safeguarding of children. In white middle-class America this role is usually assigned to the position of mother, but it could be assigned just as effectively to an aunt, grandmother, uncle, father, or even to another system outside the family such as a nursery. The tendency, however, for human systems that assign this behavior to the role of mother is for members of that system to view the assignment of such tasks to any other position in the system, or particularly outside the system, as wrong, or abnormal, and needing change. In fact, in contemporary society, the grandmother, uncle, or another member of the extended family may be considered as properly belonging within another system. It is extremely important for social workers not to mix up their own internalized value exectations of role performance with their knowledge of what are the basic needs of human systems and what systems transactions are truly damaging to humanity.

The definitions of pathology and health seem to have developed solely from the expectations of the dominant groups in society as to role behaviors and the feelings and meanings attached to these behaviors. While it may be necessary to recognize that there is such a thing as health and well-being, definitions are also needed for pathology and health that are based on knowledge of the minimum required needs of individuals and systems and of the maximum allowable transactional behavior. It is also necessary to include a range of behaviors and feelings that allows for difference in the performance of necessary systems roles, particularly when that difference itself may stem from different cultural notions of expected role performance and different interpretations of the meanings of such performance. It is necessary to question the concepts of normality and pathology in relation to knowledge of what constitutes damaging deprivations and transactions and not measure them against the expected role patterns of the dominant society. It is also necessary to recognize that problems in system functioning often stem from a conflict in role expectations, which then leads to failure and conflict in role performance. Thus, social workers must become sensitive to the damage done minority groups, or other groups who live differently, when they are constantly confronted with role expectations through their necessary transactions with systems of the dominant groups in society that conflict with their own notions of expected role performance.

It is important that social workers have a broad knowledge of how cultures develop, of how opportunities and deprivation over time shape the culture of a people, and of how a given culture becomes a part of the human systems that transact with it. The Tucker paper reproduced in this chapter suggests some of the important considerations for workers concerned with the black experience (see Reading 4–3). The notions developed in the paper are important in attempting to assess the experience of any oppressed people.

RECAPITULATION

In this chapter some theoretical constructs have been presented which are identified as being valuable as a base for social work practice. Several selected concepts have also been presented about individual functioning as found in ego psychology. Role theory and concepts of motivation, stress and coping are developed as links between larger and smaller systems. In addition, the systems theory has been proposed as a foundation that gives both theoretical perspective and empirical tools to work within or among all sizes of social systems from the individual to society and its institutions.

However, it is recognized that this is only a very brief look at the knowledge of human beings and their social systems that social workers need if they are to assess the needs of human systems and propose effective actions which will bridge the transactions within, between, and among such systems. The knowledge of the development of the individual, of the human family, of the development of various social groups, of group process, of organizational behavior, and of the sociological and anthropological base for understanding human systems are not included. These subjects should be found in the courses on human growth and social environment and cannot rightly be the subject of a beginning book on social work processes.

A LOOK FORWARD

Readers are urged to spend some time with the articles reproduced in this chapter. Each contributes further to the development of the knowledge outlined in this chapter. Two articles deal with systems theory; the other with knowledge needed to work across boundaries of systems different from that of the majority culture. While the Tucker article relates to black social systems, the basic concepts are applicable to working with any system across barriers of cultural difference.

The next chapter shall leave the knowledge base of social practice and discuss sanctions as an aspect of social work practice.

Reading 4-1

Social Work and System Theory *†

Anthony Fordor

Social workers today are having to understand and use a range of social work methods instead of just one or two. Faced with the task of finding a model that will help them to do this, they are increasingly considering the possible contribution of general system theory. Both Goldstein (1973) and Pincus and Minahan (1973), whose works are recommended by the National Institute for Social Work, make some use of system theory in their exposition of a unitary model. Anne Vickery (1974) has recently suggested ways in which it is relevant to the practice of casework. It is important for social workers to consider whether it is worth their while to master the theory and its jargon themselves, and for social work teachers to decide whether to subject students to it. This is particularly important when the theory is at such a high level of generality.

Faced with the complexity of a new approach like general system theory, there are a number of temptations that afflict writers and teachers in trying to fit their own theories into a new model. The first is to look at the new model quickly, decide that one's own theory is not essentially different or at least not incompatible, and carry on with a few oblique references that make one look more up-to-date. This is what Hollis (1970) appears to be doing when she describes the psychosocial method as a systems approach. She gives no further explanation of this claim although she knows well that the psychosocial approach developed quite independently of system theory.

A second temptation is to absorb the new jargon into one's theoretical presentation by renaming concepts, thus losing intelligibility without gaining precision. This was the impression left on the author by an article by Janchill (1969). This listed characteristics of systems taken from the general theory and related them to social work theory. It failed to put them into the context of the theory itself.

A third temptation is to take an eclectic approach, selecting aspects of the new theory and incorporating them into the old, but without fully relating the two models. This is what Goldstein (1973) appears to have done. Much of the material in his book, particularly in the early chapters, is not related to the system theory used elsewhere. This is more legitimate than the two previous approaches, but it is likely to be confusing to readers, both initially and subsequently as they try to follow it up with further reading.

It is my purpose in this article to give a brief explanation of general system theory and then to discuss its value for social work theory and practice in four areas. The first is its contribution at the philosophical level, the view it presents of humans and of society; the second, its contribution to social work perspective in making social workers aware of the range of systems they should be considering; the third, its contribution to practice in providing a model of the structure of systems which will indicate how to intervene; and the fourth, its contribution to understanding social work process.

* *British Journal of Social Work* 6 (Spring 1976), pp. 13–42.

† This reading retains British spellings.

GENERAL SYSTEM THEORY

General system theory has been developed as a result of the needs of a number of different disciplines from engineering to sociology to find a way of analysing complex situations of interaction, in which, in common terms, "the whole is more than the sum of the parts."[1] The traditional physical sciences deal with "closed systems," which from the point of view of system theory are only one particular class of systems at one end of a continuum. In the typical experiment in the physical sciences, at least until recent years, the aim of the experimenter has been to exclude from the experiment as many variables as possible, and to concentrate on the interaction of a limited number of factors, ideally perhaps two. Subsequently additional variables may be added. The final interaction of these factors is represented by the sum of the individual effects. For example, Newtonian physics begins with a formula for the interaction of two bodies in isolation, and then considers the effect of additional factors, such as the presence of other bodies, atmospheric friction, and so on. The final behavior of the bodies is the result of the combination of all these forces. This approach is called "reductionist," because its essence is the reduction of a situation to its constituent elements before adding them up. It assumes a deterministic causality in which the future and the past condition of an object can be deduced from knowledge of its present condition.

Biologists, psychologists, and social scientists have generally followed this pattern in developing their own theories and assumed that the difficulties presented to them were due only to the complexity of the situations they were considering and their limited tools for analysis. But system theorists regard the model itself as inadequate. The closed system of the physical sciences are seen as one end of a continuum of increasing complexity in which there is still order.[2] Among the higher systems new characteristics emerge of dominating importance.

First, such systems are open, that is to say they maintain themselves by a constant flow of material in and out. A flame is a simple example of an open system. Its continuity is maintained by the input of fuel and oxygen and the output of heat, light, and the oxidized elements of the fuel.

Second, open systems may be goal directed. At its simplest the goal may be merely the maintenance of homeostasis within rigidly defined limits through devices such as thermostats. For more advanced systems homeostasis may be replaced by the concept of "the steady state."[3] In the steady state input and output are related in a way that not only maintains the system and adapts it to changes in the environment but allows work to be done and growth to take place. So as an embryo develops towards adult status, at any one time it is in a steady state that is itself in the process of change.

The steady state is not a condition of equilibrium, but a condition short of equilibrium, in which some degree of tension

---

[1] For further accounts, see Von Bertalanffy (1968) *General System Theory*, and Buckley (1971). Von Bertalanffy, a biologist occupying an intermediate position between the physical and social sciences, has been an important figure in developing the theory.

[2] It is the combination of complexity and order that is significant. Physics is also concerned with systems of "chaotic complexity" like a cloud of gas. For a table giving a summary picture of the systems' continuum and the theories related at each stage see Von Bertalanffy 1968, pp. 26–27.

[3] The term *steady state* is derived from physics where it describes an essentially homeostatic condition which is reached after the initial changes have worked themselves out, for example, a thermostatic system that begins to operate in a steady state after the initial increase in temperature to the minimum limit of the thermostat. My explanation is based on Von Bertalanffy (1968, pp. 132–133). In some ways the term does not seem appropriate to the dynamic picture given by system theory, and Buckley (1967) manages to avoid the term.

is a permanent feature. In an ecological system competing systems stand ready to expand their numbers as environmental conditions make this possible. In some animals given a situation in which all other needs are met, a condition of stress arises from lack of stimulation. In human beings, as one set of goals is reached new goals are specified, so that inner tension is maintained. Hence the continuation beyond childhood of such activities as play, exploration, and creation.

When systems are goal directed, the same goal may be achieved from different initial conditions. This characteristic is known as equifinality. An adult may develop from a single ovum, from a divided ovum as with identical twins, or from two fused ova. The marsupials of the Australian continent have developed a range of forms and ways of life very similar to the mammals of other continents from very different origins. Equally the same final condition may be reached by different routes. Physical maturity in animals and emotional maturity in humans may be achieved through different patterns of experience. Early deprivation, for example, gives no certainty of deformation in the adult. So it is impossible merely from knowledge of the final condition to deduce what happened earlier, nor to forecast the future from knowledge of the present.

Open, goal-directed systems may show a tendency towards increasing elaboration of organization. In the closed system of physical science, the tendency is towards an equilibrium of maximum entropy—entropy being defined as a measure of disorder. But living systems show "negative entropy"—they import into themselves not just enough to maintain themselves, but enough to enable them to grow and develop. The elaboration of the system involves increasing differentiation in its parts. This differentiation is not necessarily based on initial difference in the parts but on the needs of the system. So

cells that are initially undifferentiated in the embryo give rise to cells that form different parts of the body. Similarly the same people will often change their behaviour in quite striking ways when they are given new roles in an organization, for example through promotion, in order to fit in with the expectations of others in the system.

An essential prerequisite of goal-directed behaviour is some means of gaining information about changes in the condition of the system and its environment, and the capacity to modify behaviour in response. So for goal-directed systems, information replaces energy as the stimulus to activity and the link between parts. Information theory is concerned with this.[4] Given a wide range of information being transmitted from a changeable environment, the system needs some method of selecting and mapping the information that can be related to its behaviour. The more variable the environment, the greater the variety of patterns of behaviour that will be required for effective adaptation—that is, there is a need for "a pool of variety" within the system that can be called on as need arises to match the extent of variety in the environment.

In the extreme complexity of modern urban society, there is need for a very large pool of variety in terms of behavioural patterns. Some of these patterns may be defined as illegitimate or deviant and yet have value for the survival of particular groups and potential value for society as a whole in the event of a major change in the environment. For example "terrorist" activity is normally defined as deviant by the dominant groups in a state but may have importance for the survival of a minority group. The same activities

---

[4] *Information* is in this theory interpreted broadly in a way in which it ultimately becomes synonymous with a measure of organization. Buckley (1967, pp. 82–89).

may receive social sanction when a war allows them to be directed against a national enemy. The existence of this pool of variety itself complicates the environment of the subsystems of society and in turn increases the need of these subsystems for flexibility and responsiveness.[5]

A central tenet of general system theory is that all systems but the largest are themselves subsystems of other systems and all systems but the smallest are environments for other systems. Thus to take part of the middle ground of the systems continuum, human beings, who are themselves composed of cells, organs, and members, are subsystems of families, small groups, organizations, communities, and states. Moreover the boundaries of open systems cannot be clearly defined. In considering a candle flame it is an arbitrary decision whether to include or exclude in the definition of the system the wick, the candle, and the surrounding atmosphere which both feeds the flame and receives its output. The same is equally true of human systems, as social workers are well aware. Even individual human beings, whose physical existence is contained within clear bounds, present problems of definition as soon as feelings are taken into account. For example, how can you disentangle what feelings belong to whom, when each child in turn in a family takes on the sick or delinquent role to accommodate the projections of the parents?

PHILOSOPHICAL IMPLICATIONS

System theory, though starting from a mechanical model, is concerned with differences between more complex and simpler systems as well as with similarities between them. As a result it can provide a much less mean picture of people and society than is currently provided by most psychological and sociological theories.

Turning first to psychology, most psychological theorists treat human beings as superior robots, responding to environmental stimuli (Von Bertalanffy, 1968, pp. 217–218). This is most obvious in behavioural theory, which treats humans as though they were rats, not live rats, but ones that have been robbed of all their natural individuality by statistical averaging.[6] The reductionist approach of behaviourism can be seen in the early work of Eysenek (1953, p. 10) who, while recognizing that the personality might be more than the sum of individual traits, believes that the latter is all that can be validly known. Freudian theory is less reductionist in its approach, concentrating attention on the interaction of parts of the personality, and showing awareness of the importance of interpersonal interaction. It is in this sense that Hollis can claim that the psychosocial method of social work, which relies so heavily on Freudian theory, is a systems approach. Yet, for Freud, personality is no more than the product of external pressures on a primitive and devouring id, seeking gratification in a state of equilibrium or homoeostasis. Creativity and other aesthetic and altruistic aims are only sublimations of these basic primitive urges in the interests of psychic comfort.

A few psychologists, such as Rank, Rogers, and Maslow, have given more place to will and purpose, but only Rank has had a direct influence on social work theory through the functional school (Smalley, 1970). Here the concept of choice has been important but has been narrowed by a view of the environment including the social work agency itself, which at times

---

[5] It is worth noting recent concern with maintaining the pool of available variety through both the conservation of endangered biological species and, to a lesser extent perhaps, with the languages and ways of small tribal and national groups.

[6] My colleague John Mayhew has described to me vividly the individuality of rats in the test situation, which one would never guess from the description of experiments.

seems to exclude intervention to change the environment.

In contrast to "robot" psychology, system theory is concerned with behaviour which may be directed towards growth and development and not just the achievement of equilibrium. This does not necessarily require the admission of freewill and conscious purpose within a system. Clearly the development of an ecological system does not imply that the living subsystems that compose it have the ability, either separately or together, to choose the course they will take. Yet, given a self-conscious being like a person, capable of handling symbolic concepts, there is no reason in system theory why the goals should not be conscious and choice should not be a reality. Most system theorists accept that this is the case (Von Bertalanffy, 1968, pp. 45, 230). So Maslow's concept (1954, chap. 11) of the self-actualizing person is consistent with system theory in a way that it is not with Freudian psychology or behaviourism.

In practice, of course, social workers have intuitively rejected the deterministic implications of psychological theories. They have recognized the existence of will, choice, and purpose as important influences on the outcome of behaviour. They have talked of "self-determination" even as they have used a Freudian interpretation of behaviour. Nevertheless the conflict between a determinist psychology and an intuitive belief in free will has often been a real problem for students.

In so far as social workers have in any case rejected a robot view of human nature, system theory adds nothing very new. But it does provide a scientific theory that is compatible with free will and therefore helps to give intellectual respectability to important values in social work.

Turning to sociology, much theory has again been based on an equilibrium model. This has been particularly true of the structural-functional theories associated with Parsons. These have been criticized as providing a spurious justification for the maintenance of the *status quo* (Buckley, 1967, pp. 23–31; Von Bertalanffy, 1968, pp. 207–208).

While sociology has been much less influential than psychology on social work practice, the consensus view of society supported by functional theory has probably given support to the natural bias of a casework approach towards conservatism in social organization. The only real alternative to this model is a conflict theory deriving from Marxism, which is in many ways antipathetic to social work ideals.

System theory by abandoning an equilibrium model leaves open the possibility of a much wider range of developments. It is true that it has sometimes been regarded by sociologists as providing support for the consensus view of society and rejected by them on that account. Some writers on system theory lend support to that view even using Parsonian theory in their examples. However, there is plenty of room within the theory for the inclusion of conflict, and for conflict to be seen as having a positive role. For example, in ecological systems conflict has a most important place, and mathematical formulae have been developed to provide a basis for prediction in this area (Von Bertalanffy, 1968, pp. 63–66). System theory accepts that subsystems within a system may have different objectives from one another and from the system as a whole, which may only partially cohere and thus make conflict possible. Such conflicting objectives have their part to play in the "pool of variety," which is regarded in system theory as one of the conditions for survival in an unpredictably changing environment.

Of theories at a less than societal level both exchange theory and role theory in their different ways present a very limited view of human nature if carried to extremes. Berger (1966), for instance, seeing roles as central to personality, considers that "the self is . . . a process, continuously created and recreated in each social situation that one enters, held together by the slender thread of memory" (Ruddock, 1969, p. 24). Similarly in exchange theory, symbolic goals can be regarded as no more than an extension of personal gratification in a social interaction governed by economic motives (Buckley, 1967, p. 112). System theory can integrate these theoretical approaches while providing some protection against such extreme interpretations. In using role theory to understand the interaction of people within a larger system, it accepts that for the person the adoption of a role may be a way of adapting to the environment within a more consistent pattern of goal-directed behaviour. Turner's concepts of role-making and taking (as discussed in Buckley, 1967, pp. 146–149), which give a more positive role to the person in structuring his situation than Berger does, are more consistent with system theory. Similarly exchange theory provides a useful way of describing interpersonal transactions within systems, but if the transactions are seen as promoting growth rather than merely maintaining equilibrium, ideals can be seen as having a genuine motivating force. They need not be just rationalizations. In this way system theory provides a model that is at once less limited, and, one hopes, more realistic.

THE SYSTEMS PERSPECTIVE

One of the most obvious ways of using system theory in social-work practice is to draw attention to the multiplicity of systems at different levels of complexity that influence any particular situation. This, in turn, makes possible a review of a wider range of possible targets for intervention—referred to as "target systems." Goldstein (1973, pp. 108–119) provides an

example in which an adolescent is involved in drug-taking. The situation is outlined with the aid of a diagram in a way which makes possible a choice of action between individual and family casework, small group action, influencing the school, getting a community group involved, and changing the program of the social worker's own agency—"the change agent system" as it is called.

Diagrams similar to Goldstein's are used by Hunt, Harrison, and Armstrong (1974, pp. 405–424) in an article on group dynamics in social work education. This shows the value of the systems perspective in the analysis of the relationship between social workers and their clients and also of the educational institution within which the social worker is being trained. Anne Vickery (1974, note 22), whose article appears in the same issue of *The British Journal of Social Work,* chooses an example too complex for diagrammatic presentation. Instead she lists more than 16 systems that might be potential targets for intervention.

It is hoped of course that the presentation of a wider range of potential target systems will make it easier for the social worker to select the most appropriate social work method to use in effecting change. However, as Baker (1975, pp. 205–209) points out, little guidance on this point has yet been provided by studies of social work.

In addition to the change agent system and target system, Goldstein also points out that the development of the social worker-client relationship involves the creation of a new system which he calls the "change system" (1973, pp. 120–153). Pincus and Minahan (1973, pp. 61–63) further refine the model by talking about "the action system." This includes all those who are actively working together to create change. This will normally, of course, include the social worker and a member or members of the client system. But it will frequently include members of other systems, too.

In family casework the action system will often be limited to the social worker and one or both parents. In community work it will typically be a committee. In residential work it might be a committee of staff and resident representatives, but it might include all the staff and residents.

THE APPRAISAL OF SYSTEMS

While the contribution of system theory to philosophical/scientific understanding and to social work perspective are useful, the crucial issue is its applicability to the practice situation. Does it provide a model of the working of systems which gives guidance about where and how intervention should take place? Only if it does, will teachers feel justified in giving the time necessary to grasp system theory concepts, and to pass them on.

Anne Vickery (1974, p. 398) puts forward a diagram to illustrate the model (Diagram 1). This diagram has some serious limitations. First, goals, and objectives have no place in it, although Anne Vickery's case analysis brings out the importance of these. Secondly, in the diagram the central feature is the box labelled "transformation." This feature is difficult to locate in either space or time. Is it an activity taking place in the client system alone or in both the client system and the environment simultaneously? While "output" and "feedback" presumably follow input, it is not clear at all how feedback relates to output. There are answers to these questions, but the diagram does not reveal them.

A third problem is much more serious. Neither the diagram nor Anne Vickery's exposition of it allow any place for issues of power. This is a crucial element in community work and important, though often neglected, in other methods of social work. Its neglect is one of the major criticisms of social work, particularly from sociologists.

An alternative diagrammatic presentation is put forward by Buckley (1967, p. 173) in Diagram 2. A control centre or centres (1) determine certain goal parameters (2) and the means to achieve them on the basis of information already gathered about its own internal situation and its environment both of which may be in the process of change. These decisions are translated into an action output (3) which results in certain effects on the system and its environment. Information about these effects (4) is gathered and fed back into the control centre where it is sifted, mapped, and interpreted (5). If the error leaves the system outside the goal param-

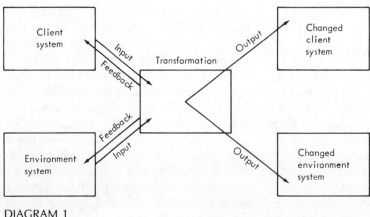

DIAGRAM 1

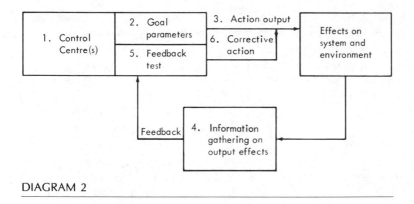

DIAGRAM 2

eters, corrective output action (6) is put into operation by the control system (or the goal parameters revised).

This very simplified model can be applied to any system including of course a social work agency, a client system, or a system created by the interaction of client and social worker. It is a model of a problem-solving process.

However, this diagram has two major

limitations. First, it is confined to the transmission of information and ignores the physical resources that are available to the system internally and externally. Second, while it indicates that there may be more than one control centre, it does not demonstrate any of the implications of this. Diagram 3 is a refinement of Buckley's and is more explicit on both these counts. It shows that one of the effects

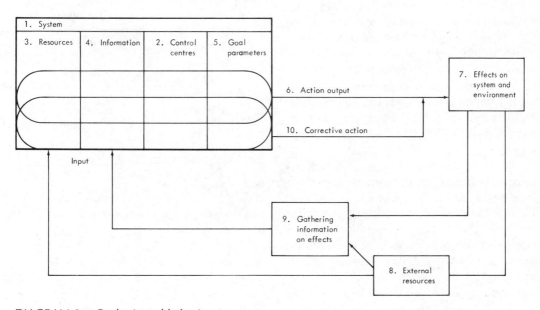

DIAGRAM 3:   Goal-oriented behavior

System (1) with certain control centres (2), on the basis of its current resources (3) and information (4) about its own condition and that of its environment determines certain goal parameters (5), and the means to achieve these goals. The resultant action output (6) has certain effects (7) on the system and its environment. Information is gathered on these effects (8). One of the effects may be a change in the resource input (9) into the system. The system selects and evaluates the information. If the action leaves it outside its goal parameters, it will institute corrective action (10) or revise its goals. Within the system different sizes of the ovals associated with the different decision-making centres is intended to reflect differences in power.

of the action output of the system is to change the resource input into the system and so affect the resources available to it. Internally the two ovals represent subsystems and the overlap indicates that there is only a partial sharing of resources, information, control, and goals of each. The different sizes of the ovals indicate differences of power in the subsystems. Although visually restricted to a dyad to simplify presentation, it is equally relevant to larger systems.

Before carrying on the argument further, it is necessary to say something more about the box labelled "information." Obviously it contains "information" about the system and its environment received through the senses. But this information has to be interpreted within a framework that gives it meaning. A smile for example only has meaning because we can relate the curve of the lips that we see to a sort of dictionary developed from past experience which indicates that this shape according to its context means happiness, or amusement, or disdain, or perhaps "I recognize you and am pleased to see you." This "dictionary," which is usually referred to as a "map," contains a series of propositions. Some of these are concerned with what is right or wrong, others with what is true or false. The former can be regarded as values, the latter as knowledge.[7]

The use of the model for analysing systems with a view to intervention can now be examined. The fact that a problem has been brought to a social worker generally indicates that the action output of a system has left it outside its goal parameters (or sometimes outside the parameters set by others). A steady state could be achieved by either a change in the goals, or a change in the action output. The model suggests that the latter can be

changed either directly, by for instance an improvement in skills, or as a result of changes in the feedback process, in the knowledge map, or in the resource input. But the model also suggests the possible value of changes in the relations between the constituent subsystems. There may be a need for a more effective use of internal resources, possibly by changes in task allocation. Internal communication may need to be improved. The coherence of goals may have to be examined (with an implication that if coherence is not possible it may be in the interests of some that the system should break up). Above all consideration may have to be given to the relative influence of different subsystems on the control of the system, in other words questions of power.

This analysis leads to the following list of areas in a system that may be the subject of intervention:

a. Internal use of resources (including skills) and task allocation.
b. The information "map" (including values and knowledge).
c. Internal communication.
d. The allocation of power.
e. The goal parameters.
f. The action output.
g. The improvement of information gathering with regard to the system itself and its environment.
h. The resource input (including the learning of new skills).

It may be helpful for purposes of comparison to reanalyse a case example presented by Anne Vickery.

The client is a 40-year-old bachelor, Mr. A., living alone in the suburban terrace house where he was born. His parents have been dead for 10 years. He is referred by the local housing department to the social services department. In order to make way for a large housing scheme his house is due for demolition. Mr. A. is refusing to cooperate with plans for his rehousing

---

[7] This is a simplification of a complex issue. See Gordon (1965).

in council property. He will not open the door to housing department officials and has for some time exchanged acrimonious correspondence with the department. The worker offering help to Mr. A. discovers that he has worked for 20 years as a messenger and that he has very little verbal communication with anyone. He was an only child and his elderly parents used him as an almost constant companion. They discouraged him from forming outside relationships even while at school. His house is in ill-repair and very dusty inside. Mr. A. is thin, and he looks tired and undernourished. He is sleeping badly and complains of being miserable and anxious because of threats from the housing department and also because of seemingly sinister things done to him by neighbours' children playing outside his house.

In this example three potential target systems were presented: Mr. A., the housing department, and the potential system created by the interaction between these two. In addition new action systems could be created by the social worker's relationship with one or all of these systems.

In considering Mr. A., Vickery's model focuses on such items as his output of anxiety and depression, and his fear of the output of the housing department (is this an input for him?). The new model, however, begins from his goals and values which Vickery does not mention. What is the meaning of the house for him in terms of his goals? Are his anxiety and depression related to specific external threats to the goals and values enshrined in his way of life, or do they reflect a more general dissatisfaction with that way of life? Is his social isolation due to a lack of social skills, despite a conscious desire for more human contact, or does he prefer a relatively self-contained life? It is as the worker focuses on Mr. A.'s actual and possible goals, that the worker understands the significance of Mr. A.'s lack of skills, resources, and power and his disturbed

perception of the outside world, which create barriers to these goals.

Looking at the housing department, attention is focused on possible inadequate goals (perhaps a policy that ignores the social needs of people like Mr. A.) or inadequate skills in communication and inadequate feedback.

If one takes the system that contains both Mr. A. and the housing department, in addition to the issues that concern each of them separately, one's attention is immediately drawn to the fact that there are two different control centres with conflicting goals. Between these two, there is a considerable imbalance of power. In this situation the worker may feel constrained to accept the inevitability of victory for the housing department, and therefore to help Mr. A. to achieve the best bargain he can in return for his capitulation. But the worker may also think it appropriate to seek to change the balance of power in Mr. A.'s favour.

Finally it is worth looking at the system created by the interrelationship of Mr. A. and the social worker. Again there are two different control centres whose goals are likely to be different, raising issues of power and authority. As the system is created, the contract is developed through agreement about goals and the methods of achieving them. The relative influence of each party on decisions such as these is a crucial philosophical issue for the social work profession and each social worker.

Two further examples may help to illustrate the value of this model for focusing attention on important diagnostic criteria. The first is from casework.

A wife comes to a social worker to complain about her husband's behaviour. They have been married about 18 months and have a baby of 6 months. He goes out almost every evening to his mates in the pub leaving her to stay in with the baby. Before the baby came, they used to go out together and were generally happy. Now she cannot manage on the money he gives her (which seems low to the social worker) so she has got in arrears with the rent. She does not know how much he earns and has not told him about the arrears. When she complains about him going out and leaving her and about the money, he laughs and takes no notice. Last night she got so angry she threw a plate of food at him. He gave her a black eye.

A preliminary assessment of the situation suggests the following hypotheses for exploration with implications for further action:

a. The arrival of the baby has changed a situation which may or may not have been as ideal as the wife pictures it ("spontaneous" change in the family situation).

b. The husband appears unwilling to change his behaviour in response to the new situation and leaves all the adaptation to his wife (corrective action in response to feedback).

c. He does not appear to be committed to the same expectations of family as his wife, obviously in the short run and possibly in the long run (conflicting values and goals).

d. He is using his control over the family income and his wife's commitment to the child to impose his will in the situation. She may be making inadequate use of whatever bargaining counters she has in this situation (power).

e. He does not appear to take his wife's views seriously. This may be because she cannot convey to him the depth of her feelings, or because she conveys them in a way that for whatever reason provokes a negative reaction in him (communication), or because he rightly or wrongly regards them as irrelevant to his goals (power or communication).

f. Financial resources may be inade-

quate as well as apparently being "misused" (resources).

An interview with the husband may of course produce a very different picture of what is happening. For example he may complain that the home is filthy and his wife never cooks him a meal and sits moaning at him all evening when he does stay in—which may of course be a manifestation of her inadequacy or of her attempts to communicate her feelings or use her power. The disparity in the account may be because either or both is deliberately misrepresenting the situation or because if genuinely different perceptions of the situation. But if their stories are in approximate agreement, the analysis gives clear indications of the most profitable lines of exploration with a view to promoting change.

Of course the fact that one is analysing this very personal situation in relatively impersonal terms does not invalidate the use of casework methods in involving clients in the solution of their problems. Nor does it mean that the feelings of clients are neglected in any way. The model does, however, provide the social worker with a guide to certain focal points which are of crucial importance in determining what can or cannot be done to improve the situation.

The second example involves possible community action. A social worker visiting a client on a council estate discovers that the house is in poor condition due to neglect of maintenance. The client says that several of the houses are in a similar condition. When the client and others have told the rent collector, the collector says it will be reported but nothing happens. Some of them have complained to the housing manager in the past. Workers have been sent, but their work has been poor and no permanent improvement has resulted. They have given up trying. There is no tenants' association.

Considering this information in relation to the housing department the following hypotheses emerge:

a. The housing manager may have come to accept inadequate standards of performance either generally or in relation to this estate, because the tenants are not sufficiently influential as compared with other tenants who are making competitive demands on the department (goals and values).

b. The manager may have inadequate means of gathering information (the feedback process).

c. The manager may be deploying the workforce inadequately (internal use of resources).

d. The manager may have inadequate resources, including skilled workers for the work required (resource input).

e. The lack of resources may be due to inadequate communication or inadequate influence on higher levels of the Council system (power and communication).

In relation to the tenants the following hypotheses emerge:

a. As individuals they lack skills in communication and in influencing their environment (skills).

b. Past failures have given them a poor self-image, which may not be justified, and may have given them a misleading impression of the imperviousness of housing department and the council to outside pressure (information gathering about the system and its environment).

c. As a group they lack an organization that could make them into an effective countersystem (power).

Taking the tenants and housing department as a conjoint system the analysis focuses attention on the inadequate communication between them and the inadequate influence of the tenants.

This analysis leaves the social worker with a number of open options:

1. To focus on the housing department by collecting and presenting information on behalf of the informant alone or on behalf of several tenants. If this fails to achieve results, the worker may use personal skills in mobilizing other forms of influence and power.

2. To focus on the tenants, helping them to organize and develop their skills (or possibly to refer them to a community worker for help in this).

3. Some combination of these, for example, helping them to organize while at the same time taking up the individual case as a matter of urgency; or helping them to organize and becoming involved in their actions towards the housing department.

The congruence between the list derived from this model and one produced by Lippitt, Watson, and Westley (1958, chaps. 2 and 3) provides some independent evidence of the relevance of the model.

These authors examined the writings of a range of "change agents" using specialized techniques from psychoanalysts to management consultants and community workers. They did not use system theory, although they did use the term "client system" to provide a common term for the individuals, groups, organizations, and communities with which change agents might be engaged. They appropriately accepted the definitions of their client systems used by each type of specialist. So client systems were seen as having clearly defined boundaries (in contrast to the approach of system theory) and the change agent as only having sanction to operate within those boundaries.

As a result of their study, Lippitt, Watson, and Westley discerned six aspects of a situation on which different change agents focused in their interventions.

These "diagnostic orientations," to use the authors' phrase, were

1. Internal power;
2. Internal mobilization of energy;
3. Internal communication (in which they included the self-image);
4. Correspondence between internal and external reality;
5. Skills and strategies; and
6. Goals and values for action.

Each of these items can be found in one form or another in the list derived from the model. Moreover the model itself provides a basis for ordering these diagnostic orientations which in the original account appear as discrete items.

THE PROCESS OF SOCIAL WORK

Turning to the process of social work, there has long been dissatisfaction with the simplistic casework formula "study, diagnosis and treatment." This dissatisfaction arises mainly because of the authoritative connotations of the medical model. But criticism is also made of the fact that these different stages cannot be readily separated. "Treatment" begins from the first contact, and study and diagnosis never end.

Functional casework rejected the medical model, and particularly the authoritative connotations of "diagnosis." Instead it pointed to the special characteristics of the beginning and ending of a relationship. So casework was seen as having three phases: the beginning, the middle and the end (Smalley, 1970, pp. 77–129).

Lippitt, Watson, and Westley (1958, chap. 6) found in the wider literature of change agents evidence for seven stages.

1. Development of a need for change;
2. Establishment of a change relationship;
3. Clarification or diagnosis of the client system's problem;
4. Examination of alternative routes and goals: establishing goals and intentions of action;
5. Transformation of plans into actual change efforts;
6. Generalization and stabilization of change; and
7. Achievement of a terminal relationship.

This still appears as a linear process but they add an appropriate warning: "Most change processes probably proceed by a kind of cyclic motion, starting over and over again as one set of problems is solved and a new set is encountered: hence the different phases become mixed up and the final objective may be achieved by a process which seems rather muddled to the observer who is looking for a clear-cut developmental sequence (chap. 6).

This account, which is probably readily recognizable to most practising social workers, has a very close relationship to Diagram 3 which offers a cyclical picture of a problem-solving process. Goldstein (1973, pp. 120–153) in fact uses this concept of a cyclical process to develop a model of social work practice involving six stages divided into three phases. The three phases are induction, core, and ending, corresponding to the three phases of functional theory. The induction phase is concerned with the development of the contract with the client-system; the core phase with the problem-solving action. In both these, information is gathered, an activity pursued, and the situation reassessed with a view to planning the next steps. The last phase of course is primarily concerned with reassessment. At every stage the possibility is written into the model that the client may withdraw or there may be a return to an earlier stage in the process, perhaps focusing on a new problem.

Goldstein (1973, pp. 136–137) talks about a contract between client and worker, and this is another way in which the diagram supports current thinking on the process of social work. Increasingly this has been seen as an essential element in the beginning phase (Roberts & Nee, 1970, pp. 45, 155, 196, 237, 244, 291). The diagram gives a clear indication of what this involves. There is first a sharing of information about the situation as the client sees it, about the agency and about the resources available to both. There is a recognition of the power brought to the situation by all the parties concerned and agreement about how the power of the social worker will be used, for example how information given to the social worker will be used, and what conditions may be attached to any help that is given. All this should lead to the establishment of agreement about common goals and a broad indication of how these will be tackled. Thereafter there will be further exploration of means of achieving the goals and the roles to be taken by the different people involved.

Of course the idea of the contract has relevance to other systems with which the social worker is involved as well as the client system. Pincus and Minahan (1973, pp. 164–168) recognize this and discuss the nature of the contract that may be developed by a social worker with his agency, with an action system involving people other than members of the client system and also with target systems which may be different again.

Thus the same model that gives the basis for an assessment of systems also gives guidance on the process of social work in so far as that is concerned with the creation of systems and problem-solving.

CONCLUSIONS

In this article I set out to consider the relevance of general system theory to social work practice and the extent to which social workers would find it worthwhile making themselves familiar with system theory and its jargon. The material presented coupled with the wider reading from which it has been extracted seem to me to justify four conclusions.

First, it is important to recognize one serious limitation of general system theory. As far as human systems are concerned, it provides an "expository model" rather than a "research model," to use Lathrope's terminology (1969). That is to say it is a model that sets out to describe phenomena rather than to explain them. In engineering and biology its status as a research theory is justified because its mathematical formulations can be related to concrete systems and can be used to construct hypotheses and predict results. In the study of human systems the lack of adequate measurement scales for most relevant factors (except perhaps in economics) make the mathematical formulae irrelevant, and the precise formulation of hypotheses that can be proved or disproved very difficult. Nevertheless as an expository model, the approach may be acceptable as "an explanation in principle," as Von Bertalanffy (1971, p. 35) suggests, and give guidance for both research and action.

Second, it is the capacity of system theory to provide a model of goal-directed behaviour which is relevant both to the assessment of human systems and to the process of social work which justifies its study by social workers. The philosophical issues are more relevant to the social science basis of social work than to social work practice itself. The system perspective is largely a matter of common sense, requiring little theoretical backing although it does provide the framework for a wider view of personal and social problems than has commonly been employed by social workers in their practice.

Third, from the point of view of most social workers there is probably no need to spend much time inculcating the elaborate jargon of general system theory which I have largely avoided in this article. Part of the need for the jargon is created by the attempt of the theory to cover such a wide range of systems. Social workers are only concerned with a limited range, and it is sufficient to make use of terms from the social sciences that can easily be applied to most human systems. Simple models can be derived from system theory and provide a framework for analysis, without necessarily having to study general system theory itself. Both Goldstein and Pincus and Minahan demonstrate this.

Fourth, for social work teachers the need for deeper study of the theory will be greater. If these models are to be used in social work courses, teachers will need a grasp of general system theory to give consistency to their teaching, to deal with the confusions that any students may meet, and to assist those students who wish to go deeper into the theory. Some practising social workers may also wish to make deeper study of the theory to extend their thinking.

Reading 4-2

Interdisciplinary versus Ecological Approach*

Edgar H. Auerswald

The explosion of scientific knowledge and technology in the middle third of this century, and the effects of this explosion on the human condition, have posed a number of challenges for the behavioral sciences that most agree are yet to be met. The overriding challenge is, of course, the prevention of nuclear holocaust, but such problems as crime and delinquency, drug addiction, senseless violence, refractive learning problems, destructive prejudice, functional psychosis, and the like follow close behind.

Practically all behavioral scientists agree that none of these problems can be solved within the framework of any single discipline. Most espouse a putting together of heads in the so-called "interdisciplinary approach." The notion is not new, of course. The "interdisciplinary team" has been around for some time. Some new notions have emanated from this head-banging, but there have been few startling revelations in the last decade or so.

However, a relatively small but growing group of behavioral scientists, most of whom have spent time in arenas in which the interdisciplinary approach is being used, have taken the seemingly radical position that the knowledge of the traditional disciplines as they now exist is relatively useless in the effort to find answers for these particular problems. Most of this group advocate a realignment of current knowledge and reexamination of human behavior within a unifying holistic model, that of ecological phenomenology. The implications of this departure are great. Once the model of ecology becomes the latticework upon which such a realignment of knowledge is hung, it is no longer possible to limit oneself to the behavioral sciences alone. The physical sciences, the biological sciences, in fact, all of science, must be included. Since the people who have been most concerned with constructing a model for a unified science and with the ingredients of the human ecological field

* Reprinted by permission of author and publisher from *Family Process* 7 (September 1968), pp. 202–215.

have been the general systems theorists, the approach used by behavioral scientists who follow this trend is rapidly acquiring the label of the "systems approach," although a more appropriate label might be the "ecological systems approach."

These terms are currently being used metaphorically to describe a way of thinking and an operational style. They do not describe a well-formed theoretical framework as does the term "general systems theory." It is with the former, the way of thinking and the operational style, that I am concerned with in this paper.

The two approaches described above differ greatly. Let us examine why the difference is so profound. The ongoing accumulation of knowledge and its application to practice follows a well-known sequence. This might be broken down into steps as follows: the collection of information or data, the ordering of that data within a selected framework, analysis of the data, synthesis of the results of analysis into hypotheses, the formulation of strategies and techniques (methodologies) to test the hypotheses, the construction of a delivery plan for use of these strategies and techniques, the implementation of the plan, and the collection of data from the arena of implementation to test its impact, which, of course, repeats the first step, and so on.

The key step in this sequence is the second one, the ordering of data within a selected framework, because it is this step, and this step alone, that gives structure to the rest, all of which are operational. Not only does the nature and outcome of subsequent steps depend on this structuring framework, but so does the prior step, the collection of data. What data among the infinite variety of available natural data are considered important, and are, therefore, collected in any given arena, will depend on the conceptual framework used. It is here that the difference between the two approaches is to be found.

The "interdisciplinary" approach maintains the vantage point of individual contributors within their own disciplines. While it has expanded the boundaries of the theoretical framework of each discipline to include concepts borrowed from other disciplines, only those concepts which pose no serious challenge or language difficulties are welcomed. More importantly, I think, the interfaces between the conceptual framework of different disciplines are ignored, and, as a result, the interfaces between the various arenas of systematic life operation (for example, biological, psychological, social or individual, family, community) represented by different disciplines are also ignored.

The structural aspects and the clarity of context of the data collected are lost as a result. The precise source, pathway, and integrating functions of messages passing between various operational life arenas in the ecological field cannot be clearly identified. Analysis of such data depends almost entirely on the *content* of these messages, and much distortion can and does take place.

The "systems" approach, on the other hand, changes the vantage point of the data collector. It focuses precisely on the interfaces and communication processes taking place there. It begins with an analysis of the *structure* of the field, using the common structural and operational properties of systems as criteria for identifying the systems and subsystems within it. And by tracing the communications within and between systems, it insists that the structure, sources, pathways, repository sites, and integrative functions of messages become clear in addition to their content. In my opinion, this, plus the holistic nonexclusive nature of the approach, minimizes the dangers of excessive selectivity in the collection of data and allows for much more clarity in the contextual contributions to its analysis. And the steps which follow, including prescription and planning of strategies and techniques, gain in clarity and are more likely to be rooted in concrete realities.

There are some very practical advantages that accrue as a result of the above. At the level of *theory,* for example, the ecological systems model, by clarifying and emphasizing the interfaces between systems, allows for the use of a variety of theoretical models which have to do with interactional processes and information exchange. These models form bridges between the conceptual systems of single disciplines. Information theory, crisis theory, game theory, and general communications theory, for example, represent some of the bodies of research and knowledge which become useable in an integrated way.

Knowledge that has been accumulating from the study of specific ecological systems, such as the family and small groups, the development of which lagged until recently because the systems did not fit neatly into the bailiwick of any one traditional discipline, can also be included without strain. And the developmental model of the life cycle of the individual and of various larger human systems as they move through time in the ecological field of their environment assumes meaning in a larger context.

In addition, the use of this model in planning has demonstrated its many implications for the design and operational implementation of delivery systems, especially for community programs (for example, "comprehensive community health" programs). The ecological systems approach insures that the entire process of planning for a community is rooted in the realities and needs of that community. The organized identification of the ecological systems making up a target community allows for the planned inclusion of information collection stations in each key system and at primary interfaces which provide feedback to the planning arena, thus setting up a servo-system which as-

sures that planning will remain closely related to changing need. Over a period of time, as a picture of a target community emerges from such data, it will emerge as an idiosyncratic template of the structural and operational configurations of that community. It will not, as in the "interdisciplinary" approach, emerge as a predetermined template of the theoretical structure of the dominant discipline.

As a result, program designs constructed in this manner are deeply imbedded in the target community. They will develop as another ecological system among the many, thus greatly clarifying the context in which any program can be integrated into the life of the community as a whole. Furthermore, the delivery organization itself becomes viewed as a system with assigned tasks made up of subsystems performing subtasks including intraorganizational tasks. This allows for more clarity in the selection of staffing patterns, in the definitions of staff role functions, in the construction of communication systems and data collection (recordkeeping) systems, and of the assignment of tasks within the organizational structure to staff members best equipped to handle them. Of special import to community programs is the fact that with the clarification of specific tasks to be performed comes the increased possibility of identifying those tasks that can be carried out by staff members or volunteers who need relatively little training.

At the *operational* level the strategies of evolution and change can be more clearly designed. More important, perhaps, use of the ecological systems approach allows for the development of a whole new technology in the production of change. Many techniques have, as a matter of fact, already appeared on the scene, largely within organized movements aimed at integration in its broadest sense, such as the Civil Rights Movement and the "War on Poverty." Some community organization and community development programs, techniques using economic and political pressure, and techniques which change the rules of the game such as the nonviolence movement, all represent a new technology, and all have their relevance to the broadly defined health needs of socially isolated individuals, families, and groups.

In service programs working with individual people and families, this new technology is also emerging, more slowly perhaps. Many new ways of coping with familiar situations are being developed. Techniques of treating families as systems, for example, represent one advance. In particular, an emphasis which stresses the organization of events in time and traces the movement of the developing infant-child-adolescent-adult-aged individual's degree of participation versus isolation in relation to the family and to the flow of surrounding community life—such an emphasis makes it possible to determine with much more clarity in what life arenas the individual, the family, or a group of individuals needs assistance, and thus to more effectively combat the anomie and dehumanization characteristic of our age. The result is that the targets of therapeutic activity are much clearer and therapeutic work is more clearly focused on forces and situations that are truly etiological in a given problem situation. Techniques of producing therapeutic change can be brought to arenas much larger than the therapy room or even the home. I think that a single story will serve to illustrate more concretely what I mean.

In the story I wish to tell, two therapists, one a "systems" thinker, the other a member of an "interdisciplinary" team, became involved in the case of a runaway girl.

To give you some initial background, I should explain that I have been involved in designing and implementing a "Neighborhood Health Services System" for provision of comprehensive biopsychosocial care to a so-called "disadvantaged" community. The main aim in setting up

this unit was to find ways to avoid the fragmentation of service delivery which occurs when a person's problem is defined as belonging primarily to that person, and the individual is sent to a specialist who is trained to deal primarily with that type of problem. The specialist naturally sees the problem not only as an individual matter but defines it still further according to the professional sector which is inhabited. The specialist is not accustomed to looking at the total set of systems surrounding the individual with the symptom or to noticing the ways in which the symptom, the person, the family, and the community interlock, and the specialist is often in the position of desperately trying to replace a fuse when it is the entire community power line that has broken down. Furthermore, the specialist's efforts to solve the problem are apt to be confined to arbitrarily chosen segments of time called "appointments." And finally, there is that unfortunate invention, the written referral, a process of buck-passing that sends many a person in trouble from agency to agency till the individual finally gives up or breaks down. As a beginning we decided that we would have to pilot some cases in order to gain some experience with the different approach we felt was needed.

At this point, a case providentially dramatizing the points we had in mind fell into our hands. (We have since found that almost every case that falls into our hands providentially dramatizes these points.) One of our psychiatrists was wandering about the neighborhood one day in order to become better acquainted with it and to explore what sort of crises and problems our neighborhood program must be prepared to serve beyond those we already anticipated. I should say here that this psychiatrist,[1] by virtue of several years of pioneering work with families, including the experimental use of game the-

---

[1] I am indebted to Dr. Robert Ravich for the case material reported.

ory and games in diagnosing and treating them, was particularly well qualified to handle the situation I will describe. His explorations that day had brought him to the local police station, and while he was talking to the desk sergeant, a Puerto Rican woman arrived to report that her 12-year-old daughter, Maria, had run away from home. This was apparently not the first time. She described the child to the police, who alerted their patrols to look for her and assigned two men to investigate the neighborhood. Our psychiatrist, whom I will refer to from now on as our "explorer," was intrigued and decided to follow up the situation himself.

He first identified himself to the mother as she left the police station and asked if she would be willing to allow him to help her with her current difficulty. She agreed. He learned that she lived a few blocks away with her now absent daughter and another daughter, aged 14. Her own parents lived nearby, and she had a paramour who also lived in the neighborhood. The father of her two children had long since deserted his family, and she was uncertain as to his whereabouts. The exploring psychiatrist learned also that the runaway girl had been seeing a psychotherapist at the mental health clinic of a local settlement house. In addition, he ascertained the location of her school.

He then decided that his behavior might appear unethical to the child's therapist, so he proceeded to the mental health clinic, a clinic which prided itself on the use of the "interdisciplinary" team approach. The original therapist turned out to be a social worker of considerable accomplishment and experience, who agreed to cooperate with him in his investigation after he explained what he was up to and that he had the mother's permission. He read the child's case record and discussed the girl with the therapist at some length. He learned that at a recent team case conference, the diagnosis which

was originally assigned to the girl, that of childhood schizophrenia, was confirmed. The team also decided that in the light of repeated episodes of running away from home, her behavior was creating sufficient danger to indicate that she be placed in a situation where that danger would be alleviated while her therapy continued. For a 12-year-old Puerto Rican girl in New York City, especially one carrying a label of schizophrenia, this almost always means hospitalization in the children's ward of a state hospital. Accordingly, the arrangement for her admission to the state hospital covering the district had been made and was due to be implemented within a few days.

The next stop for our explorer was the school, where Maria's teacher described her as a slow but steady learner, detached from most other children in the class, vague and strange, but somehow likeable. The guidance counselor reported an incident in which she had been discovered masturbating an older boy under the school auditorium stairs. This behavior had led the school authorities to contemplate suspending her, but since they knew her to be in treatment they decided to hold off, temporarily, at least.

The exploring psychiatrist also learned at the school that Maria was involved in an afterschool group program at the settlement house. He returned there and got from the group worker a much more positive impression of the girl than he had previously encountered. She participated with seeming enthusiasm in the projects of the group and got along very well with the other children. The group worker, by way of providing evidence that Maria had much potential, showed the therapist a lovely and poignant poem she had contributed to a newspaper put out by the group. It was never ascertained whether the girl had written or copied the poem. She had, nevertheless, produced it, and there was general agreement that its theme of isolation was one which was expressive of her.

Back at Maria's home, our explorer talked to Maria's sister, who at first grudgingly, but then with some relish, admitted that she knew where the girl had gone during her previous runaway episodes. She was the sometime mascot of a group of teenage boys with whom she occasionally traveled for two or three days at a time. The sister did not know where she went or what she did during the junkets, but she suspected that sex was somehow involved. She also volunteered the information that neither she or her mother had ever found it easy to communicate with her sister, and that if the therapist really wanted to talk to someone who knew her, he should talk to her grandfather. So off to the grandparents' apartment he went.

The grandmother turned out to be a tight-lipped, highly religious Pentecostalist who was at first unwilling to say much at all about the girl.

The grandfather, however, was a different kettle of fish. Earthy, ebullient, jocular, bright, though uneducated, his love for Maria was immediately apparent. He spoke of her warmly and bemoaned the lack of understanding that existed in her home. Remembering a passing reference in the case record at the mental health clinic to a suspicion that the grandfather may have engaged in seductive play with the girl, if not open sexual activity, our explorer raised the issue of the girl's emerging adolescent sexuality. This brought an outburst from the hitherto silent grandmother that confirmed the mutually seductive quality of the grandfather's relationship with the girl, followed by a return blast from the grandfather who revealed that his wife had refused to sleep with him for several years. He readily admitted his frustrated sexuality and the fact that he was at times aroused by his budding granddaughter.

I have presented only a sparse picture of the rich amount of information collected by our explorer up to this point. In a continuous five-hour effort, without seeing the absent Maria, he was able to construct a picture of her as a child who had grown up in relative isolation in a home where she received little support and guidance. Communication between herself and her mother had become more and more sparse over the years, most likely because of efforts of her older sister to maintain her favored position in the home. She had turned to her grandfather, who, feeling frustrated and himself isolated in his own marriage, brought his sexually-tinged warmth willingly into a relationship of mutual affection with her. Furthermore, it seemed clear that with someone like the group worker who liked her and who, because the group was small, could spend time with her, Maria could respond with warmth and exhibit an intelligence that otherwise remained hidden. But, and this was, of course, speculative, the tools she perceived as useful in her search for a response from others would most likely be limited to infantile techniques of manipulation developed in early years prior to the need for verbal communication or, based on the relationship with the grandfather, some form of seduction where the currency of acceptance was sex. And, at the age of puberty, having been shut out of the female world of her mother and sister, she was using this currency full blast in the world of boys.

The next day our explorer talked again to the mother, who told him that the girl had been found by the police on the street and had been hospitalized at a large city hospital on the adolescent psychiatric ward. Before visiting her, he briefly questioned the mother about her paramour. It turned out that the subject of marriage had come up between the two of them, but because he earned a limited income, both he and the mother had decided against living together or getting married. Either action would result in loss of the support the mother was receiving from the Department of Welfare for herself and her two children.

All that had been predicted the day before was corroborated when our explorer visited the girl in the hospital. Her behavior with him, and, as it turned out with the resident physician on the ward, alternated between childish manipulation and seductive behavior of a degree which appeared bizarre in a 12-year-old. But she was, at the same time, a lithely attractive girl with a lively wit which blossomed once she felt understood. She was ambivalent about the alternatives of going home or of going to a state hospital, mildy resisting both.

Our exploring psychiatrist then returned to the mental health clinic to discuss what he had observed with the child's therapist and the consulting psychiatrist. He suggested a plan of action as an alternative to hospitalization. By targeting on key issues in various systems surrounding this child, it seemed theoretically plausible that the conditions which held her fixed in a pattern of behavior that had been labeled as sick and crazy might be changed, thus freeing her to accept new coping patterns which she could be helped to learn. An effort to reestablish communication between the child and her mother, who had shown with her other daughter that she could raise a child with relative success, would be one step. It might not be feasible to work with the grandparents' unsatisfactory marriage, but an explanation to the grandfather, who had already tentatively understood his contribution to the girl's dilemma, might be useful. If the Department of Welfare were willing, and if the boyfriend's income could be enhanced by a least a little supplementary public assistance, the mother and boyfriend might be induced to marry. Teacher and guidance counselor could be helped to understand the girl's behavior more

fully and might cooperate on a plan for helping the girl learn new ways of relating in school. The group worker's investment in the girl could be used to a good effect in this joint effort to help her grow. And the original therapist, instead of concerning herself with defense systems and repressed conflict could concentrate on helping the family provide the maximum of support and guidance possible, or, if she wished, could still work with the girl herself. With these suggestions, our exploring psychiatrist bowed out.

A month later, a follow-up visit to the mother revealed that the girl had been sent to the state hospital on the recommendation of the resident on the adolescent ward who agreed with the diagnosis and felt that, since she was "a schizophrenic," she should be in a hospital. No one had made any countermove and contact between all of the helping people except the state hospital doctor and the girl's family had been terminated. This outcome had occurred *despite the fact that the mother and her boyfriend had, after a conversation stimulated by our therapist-explorer, presented themselves at the mental health clinic and expressed their willingness to marry if it seemed wise, their wish to have Maria come home, and their hope that someone at the clinic would help them learn what they must now do for her as parents.*

I have, I realize, presented an unusual situation. Reasonable question could be raised, I suppose, as to how often this sequence could occur. And in my own bias is obvious in the manner of my presentation. But I think the case illustrates the radical difference between the two approaches under discussion. The approach of the therapist from the interdisciplinary clinic and that of our exploring psychiatrist are not merely two points on a continuum of techniques. The "ecological systems" approach literally changed the name of the game. By focusing on the nature of the transactions taking place between Maria and the identifiable systems that influenced her growth, it was possible for the "systems" psychiatrist to ascertain what strengths, lacks, and distortions existed at each interface. Two things happened when this was done.

The first was that Maria's behavior began to make sense as a healthy adaptation to a set of circumstances that did not allow her to develop more socially acceptable or better differentiated means of seeking a response to her needs as a developing child. Thus, the aura of pathology was immediately left behind.

The second was that the identification of lacks and distortions in the transactional arena of each interface automatically suggested what needed to be added or changed. Thus the tasks of the helping person were automatically defined. Rigidity of technique in accomplishing these tasks could not, under those circumstances, survive. Flexibility, ingenuity, and innovation were demanded.

The implications of what can happen if this approach is used universally are obvious. If proper data is kept, it seems inevitable that new clusters of data will occur to add to our knowledge, and a new technology of prevention and change develop.

The case of Maria has a certain uniqueness that separates it from most similar cases across our country. The uniqueness is not to be found in the "interdisciplinary" approach used, but rather in the quantity of skilled people who were trying to help her. Despite their dedicated efforts, all they managed to accomplish was Maria's removal from the only system that could be considered generic in terms of her growth and socialization—her family— and her removal from the school and community which should provide the additional experience she needed if she were to become a participant in the life of her society. In addition, they succeeded in stamping a label on the official records

of her existence, a label which is a battleground of controversy among diagnosticians, but which means simply to the lay public that she is a nut.

By chance, Maria wound up in a mental hygiene clinic where her behavior was labeled as sick. She might just as easily have joined the many girls showing similar behavior who wind up in court and are labeled delinquent. Either label puts her in a category over which various members of "interdisciplinary" terms are in continued conflict. The needs of the girl, which are not clearly apparent, in either arena, become hopelessly obscured. Decisions made by those charged with the task of helping her are likely to be made without cognizance of those needs, since they depend for their outcome too often on the institutionalized procedures and momentary exigencies in the caring organization or person.

As a final point, let me explore the nature of the communications breakdown that occurred between the two therapists.

In his explorations, our "systems" psychiatrist collected a good deal of data that was not known to the "interdisciplinary" therapist and team in order to insure that he understood the operations that had been going on at each interface in which he was interested. This additional data only supplemented the data previously collected and agreed with it in content. Thus the two agreed substantially as long as they confined their communications to content and to inferred construction of the internal psychodynamics of the persons involved, Maria and the individual members of her family. And, as it happened, this was all they discussed until the exploring "systems" psychiatrist returned for a final chat. At that time, having ordered his data in such a way as to clarify the transactions which had been taking place at the interfaces between Maria and the various systems contributing to her growth, his suggestions flowed from a plan designed to affect those interfaces. The "interdisciplinary" team, including the original therapist, had not ordered the data in this way. Since the dominant disciplinary framework used in their arena was psychiatric, they had ordered the data around a nosological scheme for labeling illness. The outcome of their plan of action, therefore, was to apply a label signifying the nature of Maria's illness, and to decide, reasonably enough within this framework, that since treatment of her illness on an outpatient basis had not been successful, the next step was hospitalization, a decision backed by the assumption that her runaways were dangerous.

It was literally impossible, at the final meeting, for the suggestions of our "systems" therapist to have meaning to the "interdisciplinary" team. They fell on ears made deaf by a way of thinking which could not perceive them as meaningful. They came across as a dissonance which had to be screened out. Communication between the two approaches thus broke down completely.

This instance of breakdown is characteristic of efforts of communication between people from the two arenas. Conversations I have had with a variety of people who take the ecological systems view, backed by my own experience, seem to add up to the following:

There seems to be no serious problem of communication between the systems thinker who emphasizes structure and the experimental behavioral scientist who does basic research in his laboratory or even the researcher who is attempting to deal with a wide range of natural data. Such researchers have selected and defined the structure of the theoretical framework in which they wish to work and are the first to admit that the outcome of their research carries the label of validity within that framework alone.

Clinical scientists, whose emphasis is more on the content of their data, are for the most part different animals. Most clinical theorists, planners, and practitioners, regardless of discipline, seem caught in the highly specialized sequence of their own training and intradisciplinary experience, upon which they seem to depend for the very definition of their personal identity. Generally speaking, a situation seems to exist in which the integration of the cognitive apparatus of clinicians is such as to exclude as a piece of relevant data the notion that their intradisciplinary "truths," which are carried to the interdisciplinary arena, are relative. They most often will hear and understand the notion when it is expressed. But, again speaking generally, they treat it as unimportant to their operations, as peripheral to the body of knowledge they invest with meaning. Why should this be?

I think it is because clinicans are products of the specialized fragmentation of today's world of science. To them, admission of this fact would mean that they would have to rearrange their cognitive styles, their professional ways of life, and, all too often, their total lifestyles as well, if they were to maintain a sense of their own integrity. Not only would they have to renounce their idols, but they would have to go through a turbulent period of disintegration and reintegration. They would have to be willing and able to tolerate the fragmentation of identity boundaries such a transition entails. They would have to leave the safety of seeming truths, truths they have used to maintain their sense of being in the right, their self-esteem, their sense of values, and their status in the vertical hierarchies of their society. They would have to give up the games they play to maintain their hard-won positions in their disciplines, games such as those which consist of labeling persons from other schools of thought as bright but limited, misguided, or insufficiently analyzed. More often than not, they would rather fight than switch.

I imply, of course, that they should switch. Thus the question must reasonably be asked: "Why should they?" "Why should they attempt such a fundamental change?" After all, they can point with pride to the many accomplishments and successes of their disciplines and their own work within them.

But to rest on their laurels, in my opinion, is to abdicate responsibility. It is like crowing over the 70 percent or so of juvenile delinquents who become law-abiding citizens and ignoring the 30 percent who do not. The major responsibility of today's behavioral scientists is to those who don't or won't make it, not those who do, to Maria, not to Little Hans, whom they already know how to help.

The least they can do is examine their labels and how they are used. In the life-space of Maria's world, there is a serious question as to which system deserves the prefix, *schizo.*

Reading 4-3

*Minority Issues in Community Mental Health**

Samuel Tucker

The purpose of this paper is to build on the emerging knowledge of social structure and cultural differences as the basis of identifying and setting forth knowledge and skills for community mental health practices within minority communities and particularly black communities.

There are several assumptions upon which this practice approach is based; none of which will be elaborated on in this presentation.

1. The term *community* added to mental health is a social structure designation, based on the awareness of the importance of the social structure implications for emotional adjustment.
2. This social structure designation makes possible the expansion of the mental health concept of treatment of individual dysfunctioning to include

intervention into the social structure in which the client lives.
3. This expansion provides the basis upon which "community mental health" is practiced with the primary purpose of social structural intervention, while mental health continues to focus primarily on individual dysfunctioning and treatment.
4. Intervention into the social structure and treatment of individuals and groups are complimentary and reinforce mental health activities.

These assumptions make it possible to discuss community mental health in relation to the peculiar social relationships of black Americans, without arguing the merits of a unique black psyche. Plus, it provides the natural basis of separation to talk about the social community needs of blacks, without arguing with whites about their needs or standards of acceptance, because of a different set of social rela-

---

* An original article prepared for this text.

tionships to the American society. And, it provides a basis of thinking of skills and knowledge in relation to the black community as it exists rather than the required standards established by the societal institutions.

I must constantly remind myself that the peculiar relationship of blacks to American society is constantly in flux, and any statement today could have no relevance under different social circumstances tomorrow. However, I will mention in passing that racism, historically practiced and institutionalized, is the social atmosphere by which majority rule has justified minority status and roles in society. And, it is the black psyche that has suffered this peculiar adjustment.

In popular community language—"to be black and well adjusted under current social circumstances is to be emotionally disturbed."

The basic theoretical frame is social structural conceptalization formulated by the 19th-century French sociologist, Émile Durkheim (1951). The selection of social structure conceptualization emanates from this writer's perception of the black community as an "internal colony." While I recognize the radical characterization Stokely Carmichael and Charles Hamilton gave the concept of *internal colonialism* (Blauner, 1968), in their book *Black Power* (1967), Kenneth Clark in his book, *Dark Ghetto* (1965), demonstrated the colonial nature of Harlem in good acceptable sociological form.

Clark (1965, p. 38) describes the situation as follows:

The community can best be described in terms of the analogy of a powerless colony. Its political leadership is divided, and all but one or two of its political leaders are short-sighted and dependent upon the larger political power structure.

Its social agencies are financially precarious and dependent upon sources of support outside the community. Its churches are isolated or dependent. Its economy is dominated by small busi-

nesses which are largely owned by absentee owners, and its tenements and other real property are also owned by absentee landlords.

Under a system of centralization, Harlem's schools are controlled by forces outside the community. Programs and policies are supervised and determined by individuals who do not live in the community.

While Harlem is not typical of all black communities, the nature of external control differs only slightly. While internal colonialism is not a precise conceptualization, it has sufficient implications to merit serious research and testing as a valid model.

Community mental health practice in minority, and particularly black, communities must be characterized by a different orientation. This orientation requires additional information in problem identification, problem and need assessment, and a social system approach to causation and solution. To implement, such practice would require knowledge and skill in the areas of social structural change, positive assessment of community and cultural life, social structural support, community management, social structural building, and a needs and maintenance approach.

This should not be assumed to indicate a limit on knowledge and skills, but an additional dimension added to existing knowledge and skills. While this presentation will not deal with psychodynamic conceptualization, past personal experiences of individuals, individual support on the ego level, agency service, rehabilitation, problems, and treatment, it should be understood that these are necessary and important treatment activities in mental health. Community mental health is an added interventive arm of the mental health body.

SOCIAL STRUCTURE CHANGE

The notion of social structural change is rooted in the elementary ideas of one of the founders of modern sociology, Émile Durkheim. However, the works of Peter M. Blau (1976), Lewis A. Coser (1956), Ralph Linton (1936), Robert K. Merton (1968), Ernest Nagel (1967), and Talcott Parsons (1951) have legitimized the concept of social structure in theory. The basic idea of social structure change consists of a change in the combination of statuses or roles which make up the structure or change the types of people who occupy that structure. When this concept is applied to the black community, described earlier as having many aspects of an internal colony, it is clear that the social relationship is such that one cannot change the colony without some change in the colonist—or more specifically—"colonial interest." Social work practice must enter such systems, being fully aware that the residual model is not appropriate, if the residual model is practiced, it must be perceived as a means of maintaining "colonial domination" or, to put it more mildly, a means of protecting the status quo.

Under such a social arrangement—internal colonialism—the mental health problems cannot be separated from the economic, political, and social life of the individual in such a relationship. The luxury of such separation is in itself traumatic to the black psyche and lends itself to the sick reality that "a well-adjusted black person in such a social system," is mentally ill.

Consequently, problem identification in a colonial social system requires that we add to community assessment a careful look at external power influences in black communities including:

1. Land ownership;
2. Housing;
3. Business;
4. Employment control;
5. Church affiliation and support;
6. Composition of boards in control of institutional policy that affect local

community conditions. This includes social agencies, schools, city councils, political parties, labor unions, and financial institutions.

All of these forces must be looked at in terms of their influence on the health and well-being of local residents. Their actions must be weighed in direct proportion to their power and be credited with their share of the community climate that creates the atmosphere of emotional chaos—frustration, insecurity, lack of recognition, negative self-image, powerlessness, pessimism, double standard experiences of moral, legal, economic, and political behavior measures.

For example, the worker must be aware of the frustrations and mental agony suffered by minority communities over policy decisions to build roads, expressways, warehouses, halfway houses, drug abuse centers, and junk yards in black areas, rationalized by nonownership or cheap land, while attractive office buildings, universities, and hospitals are by necessity located elsewhere . . . while deliberate or expedient, black communities are constantly devalued. . . . in a social atmosphere that determines the "self-image" on physical appearances.

POSITIVE ASPECTS OF BLACK COMMUNITY LIFE

The assessment process in such a system by necessity should take into account the odds by which the local social structure must function. The functioning of the black institutions, such as the family, church, and community cannot start with identification of the problem but must first begin with an assessment of the strengths.

For example, the black family has managed to fulfill its socializing function to the society even more successfully in many cases than their white counterpart, given the proclaimed societal values (Olson, 1976) of the "work ethic, freedom, local autonomy, equal opportunity, and land ownership." In spite of the circumstances of a colonial system that limits the access of blacks to the fulfillment of those values, blacks unquestioningly hold these in high esteem.

The black family has functioned exceptionally well in spite of the exploitative labor practices committed against black males and the destructive social environment created for black women and children. The black family has functioned in spite of institutionalized dependency of the welfare system (National Advisory Commission on Civil Disorders, 1968) and an educational process that intimidates the black child and the family with opportunities that, in fact, can never exist under racism.

The black church, in spite of its unstable financial base, its often secondhand, converted buildings, its poor attempt at imitating Western rituals has produced from its shabbiness, moral leadership unmatched by the white churches. And, at a time when national morality is in a church, the white church has appeared to "leave the driving to us."

The black community has survived in spite of its segregated character. It has survived in spite of the violation of its privacy by police, bill collectors, "Johns," research surveys, and social workers. The community survives in spite of its unprotected residents who have been left powerless by a majority rule, handcuffed by an economic system based on free enterprise, and demoralized by a social system that teaches democracy and practices colonialism.

But, the black community has survived as a symbol of common goals, language, and experiences that are so nationally profound that "brother and sister" from every social class, geographic region, and age understands and are bound by the common heritage. This again, I suspect, has qualities unparalleled in the majority community.

If the assessment does not begin with strength, a sense of weakness and failure can be fed into the community and solutions on such bases become accommodations to weakness and failure.

SOCIAL STRUCTURAL SUPPORT

In this model of practice, intervention begins at the level of community social structure. The support has to be deliberately designed to support the family structures as they exist; observing functions as a measure of adequacy rather than design. Those aspects of family function that provide biological needs, emotional needs, and support for acceptable values and goals, rather than the process by which they are achieved.

For example, the father role may be played by a grandfather, who enjoys, accepts, and is enhanced by the role. The child loves, accepts guidance, and turns to him for protection and help. The record should reflect this, rather than a long social monolog on illegitimacy, loose morals, absentee father, and weak parental involvement. The state of the family functioning must be reflected and supported.

The role of the black church and its influences must be recognized, accepted, and worked with to broaden its social structural involvement. Its institutional posture has historically evaded overt colonial interference to the degree that it has survived as a perpetuated institution over time. Since the interference with it is more pronounced and reacted to, it stands as a monument in the black community. Community mental health efforts must be tied to the spiritual and moral needs of the black community.

For example, the space available in black churches should be made use of when and on whatever conditions possible. They should be generously reimbursed for lending their community relations, moral sanction, and facilities to mental health services. The role of the minister in the leadership of the local congregation should entail a concentrated financially supported training program for black ministers in mental health leadership and a total congregational participation in a carefully designed, well-delivered membership training in community mental health and counseling knowledge. This is critical to insure the survival of mental health practice when the mental health funds are no longer available.

A deliberate program with local schools, businesses, and absentee vested interest to identify and plan their responsibility in local communitiy mental health is necessary.

For example, the local movie theater owner who builds his business on the showing of "X"-rated movies in local neighborhoods might consider a matinee for the children as well as local residents on a continuous basis of human relations, community development, and black-oriented films on weekend afternoons. This is by no means a limit to local community support structures accessible to the community mental health practitioner.

COMMUNITY MANAGEMENT

Management as a task in intervention into community social structure appears most appropriate. Management is defined by this writer as "the judicious use of means to accomplish an end." Implied in management is activity around the resources of a system. If the system is a community, it means the resources of a community which is expanded beyond a discussion of "social services" or social agencies. However, this does not exclude these as resources to be included in the management effort. Workers must be conscious of their needs to bring all of the resources of a community together to ac-

complish the community's mental health goal. And, in this instance, they are not seeking good mental adjustment in the presence of "unemployment," or self-actualization in the face of rank injustice. They seek these in an environment that is conducive to the nature and development of emotional stability and this currently does not exist for the majority of black Americans—and if I may speculate, this is becoming less and less available to all Americans (Olson, 1976).

For example, a community must look at the security measures used to protect individual property of absentee owners and expand that to protect local residents in the community. It might be better from a management point of view to use five security guards and two dogs to protect the entire community than to use them to protect five private businesses. Such an approach would serve to remove the hostile reminder of many communities that "colonialists prefer the protection of their property over the protection of the natives."

CONSTRUCTION

Construction in social structure intervention demands the ability to build new structures. These new structures are critical in colonial communities, not that they are new in the society but because of the power of external forces such social structures were not permitted to exist in the local community. Social workers now realize from the era of "sanctioned community participation" the attempt to imitate role performance can be chaotic and destructive. The construction of new social systems must be based on the natural behavior of the community. This requires new looks at boards, committees, and groups in terms of structure and operation. One can no longer mindlessly borrow from the standards of boards, committees, and groups that individuals have been socialized into accepting, but they must examine their use and operation in relation to the supportive cultural elements in the community. Every aspect of the decision-making apparatus would need to be explored, examined, and tested against community reality. The professional may have to take the responsibility for integrating these new functional models into the main stream of American thought.

For example, universities might provide "aid-ships" (grants) to outstanding teams of students in the areas of urban planning, social work, nursing, law, journalism, and business to assist local community organization in line with the goals of the community. Maybe they could be called "technical assistants."

EXTERNAL INTERVENTION

While this model of practice is interventive, the focus should be clearly social structural which is external to the individual members who compose the structure. The peculiar character of the colonial structure implies members who are invisible in the structure, but who have power in and over the structure. The reality has made it difficult to understand the black community without understanding the nature of white-vested interest who are invisible to both local residents and the white community, in general. Because of this quality, the worker will, by necessity, need to work with persons outside of the system in instances where those vested interests are moved to employ their system power against the interest of local residents.

For example, a community who approaches a local merchant about expanding the security resources, that is, a security guard and a dog, may find the merchant quite willing. But at the same time, a security company who profits from poor security management may view this move as "bad for business." If the security company refuses to permit the guards to engage in this more practical approach to community security, even though the local shopkeeper has paid for their time, you may find that external force is sufficient to stymie social structural change. These external forces must be worked with. The current social work experience lends itself to a narrow view of work with individuals outside of the "client category." Social work with the "upper class" would be extremely helpful in this model of practice.

NEEDS AND MAINTENANCE

Change in social structure which emanates out of social dysfunctioning often moves to meet the needs in ways that lead to further problems. To this end, the question for social structural change comes from the needs of the social system to function appropriately. The complexity of the black community experience is that the system is composed of alien parts—black needs and interest—white needs and vested interest. Such a system by its very structure is unhealthy in its totality of composition. When a service is moved to correct this hazard, the emotional health of the black community or any community can neither be promoted nor maintained.

The colonial system creates a social atmosphere that is alien to good community mental health. It is impossible to seriously consider community mental health without examining the social structure by which a healthy person is expected to exist—healthy people resist inequities.

Social workers have the opportunity to create new social structures with community mental health practice that can begin to respond to the needs of the black community. The black community can maintain those structures, but it is a task that requires serious resolve. Community mental health practice must meet this challenge if it is to relate itself to the issues of mental health in minority communities and particularly the black community.

References

Allport, Gordon W. *Personality and social encounter.* Boston: Beacon Press, 1964.

Antonovsky, Aaron. *Health stress and coping.* San Francisco: Jossey-Bass, 1980.

Auerswald, Edgar H. Interdisciplinary versus ecological approach. *Family Process,* September 1968, *7,* 202–215.

Baker, Ron. Toward generic social work practice—A review and some innovations. *British Journal of Social Work,* Summer 1975, *5,* 205–209.

Berger, P. *Invitation to sociology.* New York: Doubleday, 1966.

Biddle, Bruce J., & Thomas, Edwin J. *Role theory: Concept and research.* New York: Wiley, 1966.

Blau, Peter M. *Orientations toward clients in a public welfare agency.* New York: Wiley, 1974.

Blauner, Robert. Negro culture: Myth or reality? Paper presented at the Southern Regional Sociological Society Meeting, Atlanta, Georgia, 1968.

Boehm, Werner W. *The social casework method in social work education: The comprehensive report of the curriculum study* (vol X). New York: Council on Social Work Education, 1959.

Brenner, C. *An elementary textbook in psychoanalysis.* New York: Doubleday, 1955.

Buckley, Walter. *Sociology and modern systems theory.* Englewood Cliffs, N.J.: Prentice-Hall, 1967.

Buckley, Walter (Ed.). *Modern systems research for the behavioral scientist.* Hawthorne, N.Y.: Aldine Publishing 1968.

Craine, Lynn. *Widow.* New York: Morrow, 1974.

Carmichael, Stokely, & Hamilton, Charles. *Black Power:* The polities of liberation in America. New York: Random House, 1968.

Chin, Robert. The utility of systems models and developmental models for practitioners. In Warren G. Bennis, Kenneth D. Benne, & Robert Chin (Eds.), *The planning of change.* New York: Holt, Rinehart & Winston, 1961.

Clark, Kenneth B. *The dark ghetto: Dilemmas of social power.* New York: Harper & Row, 1965.

Coser, Lewis. *The functions of social conflict.* New York: Free Press, 1956.

Deutsch, Karl W. Toward a cybernetic model of man and society. In Walter Buckley (Ed.), *Modern systems research for the behavioral scientist.* Hawthorne, N.Y.: Aldine Publishing, 1968.

Durkheim, Émile. *Suicide* (John A. Spaulding & George Simpson, trans.) New York: Free Press, 1951.

Eyseneck, H. J. *The structure of human personality.* London: Methuen, 1953.

French, Thomas M. *The integration of behavior: Basic postulates.* Chicago: University of Chicago Press, 1952.

Germain, Carel B. Ecology and social work. In Carel B. Germain (Ed.), *Social work practice: People and environments,* New York: Columbia University Press, 1979.

Goldstein, Howard. *Social work practice: A unitary approach.* Columbia, S.C.: University of South Carolina Press, 1973.

Gordon, William E. A critique of the working definition. *Social Work,* October 1962, *7,* 3–13.

Gordon, William E.   Knowledge and Value: Their distinction and relationship in clarifying social work practice. *Social Work,* June 1965, *10,* 32–39.

Hartman, Ann.   To think about the unthinkable. *Social Casework* October 1970, *51,* 467–474.

Hollis, Florence.   The psycho-social approach to the practice of casework. In Robert W. Roberts & Robert H. Nee (Eds.), *Theories of social casework.* Chicago: University of Chicago Press, 1970.

Hunt, Linda, Harrison, Kenneth, & Armstrong, Michael.   Integrating group dynamics training and the education and development of social work students. *British Journal of Social Work,* Winter 1974, *4,* 405–424.

Janchill, Sister Mary Paul.   Systems concepts in casework theory and practice. *Social Casework,* February 1969, *50,* 74–82.

Klenk, Robert W., & Ryan, Robert M.   *The practice of social work* (2d ed.). Belmont, Calif.: Wadsworth, 1974.

Koestler, Arthur.   *The ghost in the machine.* New York: Macmillan, 1968.

Lathrope, D. E.   A general systems approach in social work practice. In Gordon Hearn (Ed.), *The general systems approach: Contributions toward an holistic conception of social work.* New York: Council on Social Work Education, 1969.

Lefcourt, H. M.   Belief in personal control: Research and implications. *Journal of Individual Psychology,* 1966, *22,* 185–195.

Levinson, Daniel J.   *The seasons of a man's life.* New York: Alfred A. Knopf, 1978.

Liberman, Bernard.   The role of mastery in psychotherapy: Maintenance of improvement and prescriptive change. In J. Frank et al. (Eds.), *Effective ingredients in successful psychotherapy.* New York: Brunner/Mazel, 1978.

Linton, Ralph.   *The study of man.* New York: Appleton-Century-Crafts, 1936.

Lippitt, Ronald, Watson, Jeanne, & Westley, Bruce.   *The dynamics of planned change,* New York: Harcourt Brace Jovanovich, 1958.

Maslow, A. H.   *Motivation and personality.* New York: Harper & Row, 1954.

Merton, Robert K.   *Social theory and social structure.* New York: Free Press, 1957.

Nagel, Ernest.   *Logic without metaphysics.* New York: Free Press, 1967.

National Advisory Commission of Civil Disorders.   *Report of the National Advisory Commission on Civil Disorders.* New York: Bantam Books, 1968.

Olsen, D. H. L.   Emerging trends in treating relationships. *Journal of Marriage and Family Counseling,* April 1976, 2, 317–329.

Parsons, Talcott.   *The social system.* New York: Free Press, 1951.

Perlman, Helen Harris.   The role concept and social casework: Some explorations. *Social Service Review,* December 1961, *35,* 370–381.

Perlman, Helen Harris.   The role concept and social casework: Some explorations, II. *Social Service Review,* March 1962, *36,* 17–31.

Perlman, Helen Harris.   In quest of coping. *Social Casework, 36,* April 1975, *56,* 213–225.

Pincus, Allen, & Minahan, Anne.   *Social work practice: Model and method.* Itasca, Ill.: F. E. Peacock Publishers, 1973.

Rapoport, Anatol. Foreword.   In Walter Buckley, *Modern systems research for the behavioral scientist.* Chicago: Aldine Publishing Company, 1968.

Rapoport, Lydia.   Creativity in social work. *Smith College Studies in Social Work* (2d ed.). Belmont, Calif.: Wadsworth, 1974.

Ripple, Lilian, Alexander, Ernestina, & Polemis, Bernice.   *Motivation, capacity and opportunity: Studies in casework theory and practice.* Chicago School of Social Service Administration, University of Chicago, 1964.

Roberts, Robert W., & Nee, Robert N. (Eds.). *Theories of social casework.* Chicago: University of Chicago Press, 1970.

Ruddock, Ralph. *Roles and relationships.* Boston: Routledge & Kegan Paul, 1969.

Simon, Herbert. Comments on the theory of organization. *American Political Science Review,* 1952, *46,* 1130–1139.

Siporin, Max. *Introduction to social work practice.* New York: Macmillan, 1975.

Smalley, Ruth E. General characteristics of the functional approach: A brief statement of the origins of this approach." In Robert W. Roberts & Robert H. Nee (Eds.), *Theories of social casework.* Chicago: University of Chicago Press, 1970.

Stein, Herman D. The concept of the social environment of social work practice. *Smith College Studies in Social Work,* 30 (June 1960), pp. 187–210.

Stein, Irma D. *Systems theory, science and social work.* Metuchen, N.J.: Scarecrow Press, 1974.

Strean, Herbert. *Social Casework: Theories in action.* Metuchen, N.J.: Scarecrow Press, 1971.

Trader, Harriet. Survival strategies for oppressed minorities. *Social Work* January, 1977, *22,* 10–13.

Vickery, Anne. A systems approach to social work intervention: Its uses for work with individuals and families. *The British Journal of Social Work,* Winter 1974, *4,* 389–403.

Von Bertalanffy, Ludwig. *General system theory.* New York: Braziller, 1968.

White, Robert W. Motivation reconsidered: The concept of competence. *Psychology Review,* 1960, *66,* 297–334.

White, Robert W. *Ego and reality in psychoanalytic theory.* New York: International Universities Press, 1963.

Chapter 5

Sanctions for
Social Work Practice

As discussed in the first chapter of the text, social work practice is sanctioned through both the accountability of the profession, and the accountability of the agency within which the worker practices, to the community. Historically, social work practice began, grew, and developed to its present stage as a professional practice within a bureaucratic structure. Many social workers over the years have been very unhappy with the notion of working within an agency structure. However, while the private practice of social work is growing (and private practice may not free one from the problems of a bureaucratic structure), practice within an agency is a reality of professional life for most social workers today. Thus, it is important that we understand agency and professional sanctions as an important element of social work practice. In addition to furnishing salaries, office space, utilities, and so on, to workers, it is the agencies of the community that are organized to offer the resources that may be needed to help in the solution of the client's problem. Agencies also specify the policy by which resources are available. And the necessity of meeting the requirements, or conforming to policies by which resources are available, may pose tremendous barriers to client access and use. Thus as social workers we should be aware that our relationship to our client system involves more than just us and the client alone together. The agency, its purposes and policies, is always a vital part of our interaction with our clients. Thus, skill in the effective use of agency resources, an understanding of the network of agencies of the community and their access routes, and a working relationship to the agency of employment are necessary to effective practice.

No practitioner should ever forget that the policies and practices of an agency are communicated to the client through our words and actions with our client system. We would suggest that you might want to turn to the end of the chapter and read the article, "Four Pennies to My Name" and consider how the various agency representatives that came in contact with Mrs. Morgan could have acted to be helpful. How could they have communicated a different climate in the agency without any change in the policy or procedures of the agency? Too often we forget that it is the way we handle ourselves, as concerned professional people, that is critically important to clients when they have to face and deal with less than adequate resources. Workers so often see the agency as a monolithic organization that is a given. We need to recognize that bureaucracies are also systems and as social systems are amenable to change. Workers need to learn the ways of changing agency policy and be alert to using these means. In this chapter we will discuss this point at considerable detail. It is especially important that we recognize that no policy dictates how it is to be used. We are responsible for how we interpret policy, for being creative in the ways we find to make resources available. In addition, all policy, all procedures, all rules have some "slippage," some room for maneuver, and workers need to be alert as to how these may be used to help clients when needed or to expand worker autonomy in decision making. This matter is also discussed further in the chapter.

Perhaps the primary danger in offering service to clients within a bureaucratic structure is the impact of the policy and programs of the agency on the definition of the client's problem. So often it becomes almost second nature to assume that the client's problem falls within the agency's purpose. A worker within a child-placing agency may tend to define all problems concerning children as problems for which placement is a good solution, or to define all problems as problems of placement. We can do great harm to our clients if we define initial problems in terms of known agency resources. This narrow focus severely limits the alternatives we see for solution of the client's problem. It is as we plan alternatives for problem solution that the agency and its resources become critical. This is not to say that one can serve all types of problems within one agency; but if the problem is not one your agency is capable of serving, then you must be willing to make a referral, or at least consider alternative problem solutions. And, finally, we must recognize that it is possible that clients can be a powerful force in changing policy that does not serve them well. Do you think Mrs. Morgan, in "Four Pennies to My Name," might be able to organize and lead an organization of former welfare clients in an effort to humanize the welfare agency? Clients can organize to help in the push toward change, and clients may even have an impact through individual letters or written positions dealing with troublesome policies. Enough individual letters to governor or legislator can sometimes have an important impact. We do not, often enough, think of our clients as our allies in policy change. While we do not want clients to endanger themselves by social action or to relieve us of our responsibility for advocacy, we must recognize that one way clients may act to help themselves is to push for policy changes in areas that affect their lives. Too often we tend to see clients as helpless victims of circumstance and ourselves as knights in shining armour defending them. One of the ways of respecting and helping clients is to recognize their strength, to assume they can also act for themselves in working at life's difficulties. We will now examine some of the realities of sanctions and accountability that impacts social work practitioners and their clients.

THE INTERSTITIAL PROFESSION

In the first chapter of this text we spoke of social workers as concerned with the interactions between the individual and society. We now need to return to a consideration of social work as an interstitial profession which serves both the client in need and society at large. This issue is complex in that the individual social worker's function is defined, and the worker's salary paid, by an agency (public or voluntary, traditional or nontraditional) which receives its sanction from and is accountable to the community or to some community group whose members differ from, although they may include, the members of the client system. This point is of fundamental importance since the parameters of the service any particular professional can offer are determined by the parameters of the agency's societal charge. Social workers utilize two types of tools in their work. The first type are the tools of internalized knowledge and skill, which, while they cannot be used up and, in fact, may be increased and sharpened by practice, are costly in that they are what social workers (or any other professional) sell in order to obtain the money they need to maintain their physical existence in society. Most professionals (lawyers, doctors, and so on) sell their services directly to their clients or patients. In the case of social work, however, services to the client are paid for by the community and may be, at least in theory, available to all members of the community, many of whom cannot afford to pay for them themselves. In addition to knowledge and skill, social workers frequently dispense external resources, such as money. Now, money, whether it is used to pay for the knowledge and skill of the worker or for concrete resources, or is given directly to the client, is usually scarce. And money to support social work efforts is not the social worker's property but belongs to some identified community. The community that allocates its scarce resources to the support of social work services wants to assure itself that these resources are used responsibly.

Clients who go to a lawyer for service, or patients who go to a doctor for treatment, may look elsewhere for help if they think the service they receive is not adequate. Thus they express their evaluation of that professional's competence by depriving the professional of income. If professionals want to support themselves and their dependents, they must practice in a way that satisfies the users of the services by which they support themselves. However, since most client systems do not pay the full cost for social work services, their withdrawal in disappointment and disgust from the inadequate social work practitioner seldom directly penalizes that practitioner. Social workers (and their agencies) are thus well protected from their client's evaluations. However, they are open to the evaluation of their supporting community. The supporting community, however, neither pays nor evaluates workers directly. Rather, it gives its money to an organization, usually called an agency, which hires the professional practitioners. It is usually the agency in interaction with its supporting community through certain representative groups which both sets the parameters of practice within which workers must operate and which evaluates their performance within the parameters.

THE BUREAUCRATIC ORGANIZATION

In the modern world most formal organizations are structured in a particular way. This particular type of administrative organization is known as a bureaucracy and has triumphed in modern society because it is thought to operate with an efficiency superior to that of any other form of secondary group social structure thus far devised. The classical criteria for a bureaucracy were originally set forth by Max Weber (1947, pp. 333–334) as follows:

1. [The employees] are personally free and subject to authority only with respect to their impersonal official [work] obligations.
2. [The employees] are organized in a clearly defined hierarchy of offices.
3. Each office has a clearly defined sphere of competence.
4. The office is filled by a free contractual relationship. (Thus, in principle, each person makes a free selection, or choice, as to whether the person will accept the office and its terms.)
5. Candidates [for offices in the bureaucracy] are selected on the basis of technical qualifications. In the most rational case, this is tested by examination or guaranteed by diplomas certifying technical training, or both. They are appointed, not elected.
6. [The employees] are remunerated by fixed salaries in money, for the most part with a right to pensions . . . The salary scale is primarily graded according to rank in the hierarchy.
7. The [position] is treated as the sole, or at least the primary, occupation of the incumbent.
8. It constitutes a career. There is a system of "promotion" according to seniority or to achievement, or both. Promotion is dependent on the judgment of superiors.
9. The official works entirely separated from ownership of the means of administration and without appropriation of his position.
10. The worker is subject to strict and systematic discipline and control in the conduct of the office.

Weber (p. 334) says that the Roman Catholic Church, the modern army, and large-scale capitalistic enterprise, along with certain "charitable organization, or any number of other types of private enterprises, servicing ideal or material ends are bureaucratic organizations."

Although bureaucracy is usually seen in terms of pragmatic necessity as the most efficient way to organize any large group of people to get any big job done, inherent in its very being are certain dysfunctional characteristics which vitally affect its operations. Social workers are often forced to conclude that the relationship between bureaucracy and efficiency is complex, questionable, and perhaps, at its worst, inverse.

Wilensky and Lebeaux (1958, p. 243) describe the limitations of social work bureaucracy as follows:

Along with its gains, efficiency, reliability, precision, fairness—come what many students have called its pathologies: timidity, delay, officiousness, red tape, exaggeration of routine, limited adaptability. The agency as a means, a mechanism—the agency—for carrying out welfare policy becomes an end in itself. Between the altruist with the desire to help and the client with the need lies the machine, with its own "needs." These needs can result in an emphasis on technique and method, on organizational routines and records, rather than on people and service.

Barbara Lerner (1972, pp. 169–170), a psychologist, is concerned with this last limitation of bureaucracy when she writes:

> Bureaucratic means are intrinsically unsuited to the achievement of ultimate mental health ends because they are standardized means—the whole point of breaking up tasks into component parts and component parts into subcomponents is to standardize procedures—and standardized procedures are rational only if one is striving to produce a standard product. . . .
>
> Each human being is a unique entity and wants to remain so. People who voluntarily seek treatment may do so because they want to achieve an ultimate end, such as the realization of something like their full share of the universal human potential for adequate psychosocial functioning, but people want to achieve their own unique version of that end in their own unique way. . . .
>
> Thus clients who come seeking aid come as unique individuals seeking aid which is individually tailored to the totality of their needs by a person who is in close enough contact with them to apprehend them and who has the freedom and flexibility to respond to them in a unique way.

Lerner (p. 171) goes on to say that the bureaucratically organized agency is organized around "abstract, standard parts: specific programs organized around specific problems that are dealt with by specific procedures," rather than around clients as unique personalities or around the concern of practitioners for their clients. She complains that clients are "then defined in terms of the particular problems around which programs are organized" and are "processed to and through those programs and subjected to the various procedures and techniques which constitute them" rather than seen in terms of their own goals and expectations.

Listening to Lerner, one becomes aware that the problems of professionals in bureaucracies are not restricted to social work. These problems occur in any organization staffed by personnel who spend a considerable number of years in developing a particular expertise. Weissman (1973, p. viii) points out:

> Professionals share a desire for and expect a large degree of autonomy from organizational control; they want maximum discretion in carrying out their professional activities, free from organizational interference or confining procedures. In addition, professionals tend to look to other professionals to gain some measure of self-esteem, are not likely to be devoted to any one organization, and accept a value system that puts great emphasis on the client's interest.
>
> Bureaucrats are different from professionals. They perform specialized and routine activities under the supervision of a hierarchy of officials. Their loyalty and career are tied up with their organization. Therefore, conflict results when professionals are required to perform like bureaucrats.

We would differ with the conclusion of this last quote and might repeat that famous quotation, "We have met the enemy and they is us." Professionals and bureaucrats are not two different sets of people. There are bureaucrats who are not professionals, but, increasingly in our society, given the advancement of group practices in medicine and law, there are few professionals who are not also bureaucrats. With regard to social work, we need to recognize that bureaucratic forms of organization are useful in social services, not because society is unmindful of what is wrong with this form, or because society is basically evil, but because there simply are not at this time any feasible, superior organization models that have properties as well suited to carrying out the very complex functions required of social services involving the cooperative contributions of large numbers of specialized individuals (Pruger, 1978).

For the foreseeable future, individual social workers will find it necessary to relate to a bureaucratic structure as the environment in which they will work. Thus, it will not help either the worker or the client for the worker to see the bureaucracy as something bad that should be condemned at every turn. Rather, it must be understood as a reality—a complex system in which both worker and client are subsystems. Given this important fact of life— we need to learn to work within, to use, and to change bureaucracy rather than to simply make ourselves feel good by holding bureaucracy as bad (Pruger, 1978).

CONFLICTS BETWEEN THE BUREAUCRACY AND THE PROFESSIONAL

Practicing social workers have been confronted with the harsh reality of the conflict between their judgment as to the ideal interventive actions needed to move toward the client's goal and what is possible given the resources and parameters of the agency within which both they and the client are operating. Often the most sensitive and concerned workers find themselves discouraged and angered by the many unavoidable compromises they must make between their client's needs and those of their agency in particular and of society in general. Perhaps some of this frustration could be avoided, and workers could be more effective in bringing about change in agency functioning, if they understood better the bureaucracy within which they of necessity operate. Actually, as we said earlier, social work has been a bureaucratic profession from its very beginning, and social workers employed in agencies are not only professionals but bureaucrats. Thus, while social work has struggled to synthesize bureaucratic and professional norms, it has not always recognized that a profession and a bureaucracy possess a number of norms that are opposed in principle.

Weissman (1973, p. vii) points out that one of the crucial problems of professionals who are working to change the bureaucratic structure is their lack of recognition of the difference between nonprofit and profit-making organizations. "Money serves as an alarm system in private enterprise: Ford sooner or later must respond to the tension caused by lack of Edsel sales." In nonprofit organizations the connection between the product produced and the revenues are indirect. Thus the alarm system that would bring change is severely flawed. Both professionals and agency executives may prefer to be judged by effort expended rather than by the success or failure of the effort. Weissman (p. 3) says that without an effective accountability system social agencies cannot solve their problems and administration has little need to seriously consider the views and ideas of lower level staff since it will not be penalized if it does not. However, today agencies are depending more and more on third-party payments. This causes some very difficult problems as the bureaucracy struggles to find sound measures of accountability. In this struggle, the views of lower level staff are often ignored in favor of outside notions of efficient service.

In an earlier chapter, the importance of evaluation was discussed. This has been a long-standing problem in all professions. Who is to evaluate the professional? Against what standard is the professional's work to be judged? The present struggle of the physician against some kind of publicly supported health care is an example of the problem. Physicians have successfully maintained up until now that only they (or, in some cases, a jury of their peers that they pick) can be allowed to judge their work. Incidentally, this stance probably explains the growing number of malpractice suits, since patients are no longer content, when the results of treatment are negative, to accept the professional's judgment that the process of treatment was correct. So, too, in the social work bureaucracy the question of who shall evaluate the effectiveness of the work is a difficult one. Is it to be the worker, the supervisor, the executive, the board, the general public, or the client? We have said that to achieve contracted goals is the appropriate outcome of service. It would follow that we hold individual goal setting to be a decision of client and worker, not of the agency. Yet the agency has a vital stake both in what the goals are and how they are reached. Agencies may define four or five broad classes of goals appropriate to their function. However, these broad goal classifications usually need to be operationalized and individualized for the individual system. Thus, the agency policy often becomes an important part of goal setting. It often takes a great deal of skill for the worker to negotiate agency policy and client desires so that a realistic, desired goal is set and effective alternative means to goal achievement developed for choice.

Weber (1947, pp. 333–334) held that what is central to bureaucracy is specialization and the standardization of tasks and the rational allocation or assignment of these tasks in accordance with an overall plan. Collective tasks may thus be broken down into component tasks which are means to a collective end. Two assumptions underlie such a concept. The first is that there is something approaching a clear, consistent, complete, and generally agreed-upon definition of the ultimate end toward which the organization is working, and the second is that the end is achievable through standardized means (Lerner, 1972, p. 167). When a social agency defines its function it usually states the ends it intends to pursue in general terms. However, these ends are usually expressed in such general terms (for example, "the support of healthy family life") that the extent to which they have been achieved cannot be measured; or the ends are expressed in programmatic terms, such as *crisis intervention, aftercare program, family therapy program,* or *drug program,* which often result in defining the client's problems in terms of programs rather than of the client's goals. And most of us would agree that we do not have standardized means to apply even if the client could fit within a standardized goal. We are simply not able to say in working with individual human beings, "If this, then that." There are too many variables in the situation of the unique human system. A profession works by applying principles and methods to resolve problems determined by unique client input and professional judgment rather than by employing standardized procedures toward some predetermined goal established by a hierarchical authority. This means that the individual goal of any client system needs to fit within the agency generalized goal but needs to be specific to the client system. In certain public welfare agencies there is a mandatory goal of increased self-care for all clients. This broadly stated, generalized goal applies to all cases, but it really means very little to worker and client. In these agencies, almost without exception, clients come seeking increased ability to care for themselves. However, for each client the specific skills and tasks of self-care will be different. Thus, the client-worker goal needs to be a specific statement as to what must be achieved for this particular client, in this particular situation, to achieve self-care. Self-care becomes the overall general parameters within which individual goals must be developed. Most generalized agency goals easily lend themselves to the development of particular client goals if the worker understands the purpose and function of goals in the helping process. The important point is that any over-all goals of the agency must be individualized for client's use.

Another conflict between the bureaucratic structure and the professional is found in the orientation toward authority. The professional regards authority as residing in professional competence; the bureaucrat sees authority as residing in the office held. An important difference is found in the orientation toward the client, in that professionals orient themselves toward serving the best interests of the client while the bureaucrat seeks to serve the best interests of the organization. Professionals usually identify with their professional colleagues. They should find their identification from their professional association. Bureaucrats identify with their particular social stratum within the bureaucratic hierarchy. And lastly, there is a different orientation toward the method of exercising power. "The professional norm is to influence clients and peers by modes which are oriented toward the pole of free exchange while the bureaucratic norm is oriented toward the pole of coercion" supported by the invoking of sanctions (Morgan, 1962, p. 115).

TYPES OF BUREAUCRATS

In an empirical study of social work performance in large public agencies, Ralph Morgan (1962, pp. 116–125) identified and developed an anchoring description of four ideal types of role conceptions of social workers in a bureaucratic setting. His work is summarized below:

> *Functional bureaucrats* are professionals "who just happen to be working in a social agency." They seek interaction with and recognition from their professional peers both inside and outside the agency. "Such individuals by their skill, good judgment, and technical efficiency often provide a type of service" that is recognized by the agency as being highly effective. As a result the agency overlooks certain violations of agency norms as the price it must pay for having such a competent professional on its staff.
>
> *Service bureaucrats* are social workers who are oriented toward helping their clients but who recognize that they are a part of a bureaucracy. They integrate themselves "into the bureaucratic group while maintaining professional peer group ties." While they are still "ambivalent about their identification with their agency,

they see in it the best means of attaining their goals of practicing" their profession, and as helping resources rather than as antagonists of their clients and themselves.

The *specialist bureaucrat* is a classification that Morgan says encompasses the largest group of social workers. This worker is interested in reconciling the "bureaucracy to humans and humans to the bureaucracy." Specialist bureaucrats use the rules and regulations of the agency to guide their professional judgments. "While they recognize that agency directives are in general necessary, they also recognize the richness of the human situation that can never be fully encompassed by specific rules and regulations." They see the agency as authorizing them to use their professional discretion to protect the interests both of the agency and of its clients. They realize that the agency is a bureaucracy and therefore heir to all the dysfunctional characteristics of this form of human organization. They usually have the professional "courage to sacrifice bureaucratic norms when they interfere with their professional function." They have successfully, through understanding and professional judgment, adapted in practice to norms which in theory are essentially irreconcilable. In fact, they may see this constantly shifting adaptation as the very stuff of professional life.

The *executive bureaucrat* likes "to manage people, money, and materials. While functional bureaucrats are oriented toward their profession, service bureaucrats toward those they serve, specialist bureaucrats toward the profession and the bureaucracy, executive bureaucrats seem oriented primarily toward the exercise of power. While executive bureaucrats are innovators and do not consider themselves bound by a rigid application of rules and regulations [in fact, they may be daring bureaucratic infighters and risk takers], they tend not to appreciate innovations by their own subordinates." They lean toward enforcement of bureaucratic norms for others and run a disciplined agency.

Job bureaucrats are people, professional workers, who "have a substantial career investment in the bureaucracy. At the center of their attention is the security of their own career, and they seek to safeguard and advance it through a meticulous application of regulations and adherence to the norms of the organization." Effective job bureaucrats achieve their greatest success in supervisory or administrative positions. While they hold themselves firmly to official policies of the organization, they realize that the other professionals in their sections have a different orientation, and while they tend to supervise closely, they exercise sufficient "selective nonattention" to the less rigid way in which their subordinate professionals operate, that through the proper amount of "social slippage" the social work job gets done. The ineffective job bureaucrat is characterized by a rigid overcompliance with regulation and norms. Directives that originally were issued to accomplish a mission become ends in themselves, and the mission of social work, or even of the agency itself, become secondary considerations.

AGENCY BUREAUCRACY AND THE WORKER

No one ever meets a pure type in real life, so perhaps it is understandable that the authors are not willing to put themselves in any one of the classes listed. But we suppose that we could probably be located somewhere between the service bureaucrat and the specialist bureaucrat. We do not believe that a worker who accepts a position as a member of an agency staff, who accepts a salary from the agency, and who utilizes agency resources, no matter how unsatisfactory they may be, for helping clients can act as though the worker were a private practitioner or without concern for agency policies and procedures. As a staff member, the worker is bound by the agency policies. If these policies are unacceptable, one must either work to change them, while remaining bound by them, or one must leave the agency and work for change outside it.

The first principle for workers who would give their clients maximum service is to understand the organization for which they work and to know how its structure and function were and are determined. If one is going to be actively involved in change, one needs to know what the possible points of intervention are. Three major factors affect the organization of agencies: their source of support, the source of their sanction or right to operate, and the areas of their concern. Agencies obviously cannot operate without a source of funds. As a rule an agency's funds come either from public tax funds or from private voluntary contributions, although agencies supported primarily by private contributions may utilize tax funds through various contracts and grants. Any agency's policy and structure, procedures, and flexibility will be determined by the source and adequacy of its funding. As a general rule, the funds are never adequate to the demands that workers wish to meet, so that difficult choices among real needs must usually be made.

The public tax-supported agency will usually operate within legislation and will be dependent on some legislative body (for example, county commissioners) for its broad policy and for the appropriation of public funds for its support. In some cases the board or commission of a public service may be appointed by an elected executive officer (that is, governor). Such agencies are usually administered by individuals who may be required to prove their competence by passing various tests. These administrators will determine procedures and more detailed policy issues within the broad legislation that established and maintains the agency.

Private agencies usually operate under the general policy directives of a board of directors. Such a board has three primary functions: it establishes the right of the agency to carry on its program and sanctions the agency's activities; it is responsible for the agency's overall policy; and it is responsible for fund raising. Until very recently almost all boards were composed of an elite group of members with little understanding of the realities of the lives of those for whom they developed programs. Boards almost always operate by consensus. Because the board members of private agencies are volunteers, the members who are constantly on the losing side of an issue soon drop out unless they have a deep commitment. In most situations the board hires the executive of the agency, and it often happens that the executive sees the job as keeping the board happy on the one hand and running the agency the executives' own way on the other. The executive usually controls staff access to the board and the flow of information to the board about the agency's work. So the worker's attempts to represent clients and their interests in policy and program matters are often unheard.

Some social work departments (such as the social service department of a school system, a hospital, a court, and so on) operate as part of a larger host agency. In this situation the financial support and policymaking processes will be determined by those of the host agency, which generally operate under a similar structure.

Agencies have both a function and a program. The program is the ways and means that an agency utilizes to carry out its function as defined by the community. For the practitioner, this distinction has some importance in that although an agency's function may remain constant, its program ought to be responsive to the changing needs of the times. Thus an agency whose function is the care and treatment of children may initially have cared largely for orphaned or dependent children but now may be concerned primarily with disturbed children or with day care.

Each agency has an organizational (bureaucratic) structure by which it delegates its responsibilities and tasks and stabilizes and systematizes its operations. The executive is the primary administrative officer. Officers have direct responsibility for the day-to-day functioning of the agency. Because they are usually responsible for getting the money to run the agency, this responsibility may occupy most of their time and thought. They are responsible for relationships with the board of directors or a public body. They are usually responsible for working with other agencies toward community social work goals and for the public relations functions of the agency.

Below the executive on the organization table of a large agency one may find a bewildering array of division directors, unit supervisors, consultants, and line supervisors. A small agency may have only three levels of hierarchy: the executive, the supervisors, and the workers. Line workers are more conscious of their relationship to their direct supervisor—a professional person who is usually held responsible for two functions that at some times and to some people seem contradictory: (1) helping workers to improve their skills both in the interests of getting the present job done at the best level possible and for the worker's and client's future benefit, and (2) administratively holding workers responsible for doing the job to certain standards and evaluating their performance relative to those standards.

Many articles in social work literature deal with the supervisory process and its problems. Supervisors, like workers, differ, and some may be more interested in their job security and tenure than in the client's needs for service or the worker's need for both support and learning opportunities. All beginning workers can use considerable help in increasing their awareness of themselves and their way of working, and in adding to their fund of knowledge about people, resources, and helping processes. And in a large agency with considerable work pressure and a constant scarcity of resources, all line workers need considerable support of their supervisors in dealing with the constant frustrations of the day-to-day job.

Harry Wasserman (1970) examined the work of professional social workers in a large public agency. He found that structural constraints rather than social work knowledge and skills dictated what the worker was able to offer in the client's life situations. In this instance, 8 of the 12 workers studied had left the agency after two years. Wasserman (p. 99) concluded that "the two principal feelings expressed by the 12 new professional social workers during the two-year period were frustration and fatigue," and that "they were exhausted by having day after day to face critical human situations with insufficient material, intellectual and emotional resources and support." Certainly supervisors cannot wave a magic wand and undo the effects of structural constraints on the worker's capacity to help, but a supervisor who cares about the worker's capacity to help and the worker's mental health can, through support and the offer of intellectual and emotional resources, make a great deal of difference in what the worker is able to do and in how the worker grows on the job.

Because of the constant strains and problems of the supervisor's job there has been some push in certain agencies to do away with supervision. Perhaps social work could develop a better form than the supervisory process, but one cannot do away with the supervisory function. Doing away with authority relationships does not necessarily change either people or structural constraints or result in more effective work. As long as personal needs, attitudes, and differing levels of commitment and skill are brought to a job, there is a need for leadership. As Weissman (1973, p. 131) points out:

> The planning and management of an organization requires specific expertise. . . . there is an ongoing need to reconcile the dilemmas and strains of organizational life. . . . as long as there is concern for the effectiveness of an organization, there will be considerable strain between the needs of the individuals for self-actualization and the needs of organizations for achievement and efficiency.

Somehow these strains need to be reconciled and resolved if clients are to be effectively served. The question concerning the supervisor that is of critical importance for the worker is the supervisor's position on the list of roles that Morgan developed.

Perhaps the primary problem with supervision is not that it is not valuable, or not necessary, but that it has been used in such a way that agencies have avoided consideration of their effectiveness by focusing on the effectiveness of their employees. In most agencies, workers receive yearly evaluations on the anniversary of their joining the staff. Perhaps what is needed are set dates on which both the workers and the agency would be evaluated. In other words the agency needs to look at itself at the same time that it is looking at its workers. As Weissman (1973, p. 58) writes:

> The environment in which the agency operates—physical, social, financial—affects the worker's efforts. To tell workers to refine their skills or work harder in order to be successful is to ignore the impact of environment. The caseload or lack of cooperation from other agencies, not diagnostic or therapeutic skills, may be at fault.
>
> Evaluating individuals at different times during the year solely in terms of their individual therapeutic skills makes it less likely that the agency will have to react as a system to the results of evaluation. The problems of each worker can be viewed idiosyncratically.
>
> . . . Through consultation with experienced workers, agencies should establish the areas of skill needing improvement and the basis upon which to judge improvement—recordings, observations, client queries, and the like. The worker should choose how to get help, whether through conferences with the supervisor, through taking courses, through peer supervision, or through consultation. Letting the worker decide reduces the dependency feelings which develop through forced supervision.

A degree of arbitrariness will always exist unless an agency has some method of appraising success with clients. Without agency standards of success and an evaluation of the worker's record, workers and supervisors are dependent on secondary data. Case presentation becomes more important than the people treated. The way one writes or speaks about a case becomes more important than the results achieved.

Weissman (1973, p. 59) then goes on to discuss the accountability of the agency for evaluation of its job. (This is another side of the earlier argument made by the authors about the need for evaluative research and ways of evaluating services.) He says:

The key to increasing the influence of lower level staff vis-à-vis their superiors lies in a board (or other body) that can hold the agency accountable. Where there is real accountability, the ideas and experience of all levels of staff become valuable, and the incompetence of individuals becomes a matter of serious concern.

If a board discovers that 80 percent of the agency's clients feel they have not been helped by the agency, the incompetent supervisors have something to worry about.

CLIENT, WORKER, AND BUREAUCRACY

The procedures of bureaucracy as well as the limitations of policy may be frustrating to both the client and the worker. It is well to recognize that "red tape" was and is developed to assure what people with equal troubles receive equal help and resources. But often it really operates to reduce the client's access to services or to make an already complex situation more difficult and confusing. It is the worker's responsibility to act as the client's broker and advocate in dealing with the policies and procedures of the bureaucracy. These roles will be discussed later, but we need to introduce the idea here.

If workers are to help the client cope with the problems of access to services in the most helpful way possible, it is critically important that they know with accuracy and understanding the policies and procedures of their agency and the way they operate. Workers are not always as careful and disciplined as they might be in getting a really workable grasp of this knowledge. *Paperwork* can become a very naughty word in the worker's language, but the capacity to handle paperwork efficiently, accurately, and with concern for deadlines and the client's time, is an absolute requirement of the worker who would be a skilled advocate and broker. The authors have worked in agencies where certain chief clerks made more important decisions about who got what than some workers because the clerks had mastered the paper flow and the workers were too impatient to do so. While paperwork can be irritating, the worker needs to understand that it is an attempt to establish procedures by which clients are assured equal service.

One of the authors of this book is old enough to have worked in public welfare before the Social Security Act took effect, when it was the responsibility of the local township to aid people in need of money. At that time paperwork was considerably lighter than it became after the agency was able to secure federal funds if it established certain procedures to assure people equal service and the right of appeal if they felt that they had been capriciously denied. However, at that time people were able to secure aid only if they were able to convince the worker and/or the supervisor that they were "worthy of aid." Sometimes this meant that they had supported the proper political candidate with the proper enthusiasm. This decision could not be challenged—there were no procedures to assure this, no paper on which the basis of the decision was recorded. But back to the present.

The worker needs to thoroughly understand the parameters of the policy of the agency and the authority available for interpretation. A policy is a broad statement. It has to be interpreted by some individual before it can be applied in the interests of another individual. Far too often, a worker will either ask the worker at the next desk what the agency does about such and such or give the supervisor a quick call.

Our position is that the worker starts with what the client and the worker have decided is needed as a resource in the problem solution. Next the worker is responsible for finding out exactly what the written statement of the policy says. Then the worker sits down and thinks long and hard about what that policy actually means and what are all the different possible ways to interpret and apply it. Next the plan made with the client is used to test the various interpretations. The interpretation is selected that will best enable the worker to help the client with what is needed for problem solving. Workers then write down that interpretation of the policy and the way they would apply it to the client situation. If necessary, this statement may be submitted to the supervisor for approval, but in any case it needs to be made a part of the record of service to the client. Our view is that taking the quick and easy route of asking colleagues or supervisors about policy is not the proper way to perform one's role as an independent professional person; and our experience has been that following that course increases the likelihood of receiving a directive that limits what one can do. Others do not always want to do the hard headwork either, and when one is in doubt about a policy the easier thing is to say no. It is out of this way of functioning—the use of the traditional messages about policy that circulate on the office grapevine—that old patterns get stabilized and become harder and harder to change. Far too often workers accept routine word-of-mouth statements about agency resources as givens. They may gripe about them, but they do not question them. By really knowing policy and by utilizing creative interpretations of policy, the worker can help keep the agency active as an everchanging bureaucracy.

Several years ago one of the authors conducted a study to find out (1) whether clients were receiving aid they needed and (2) why or why not. In the agency under study, workers reported great discouragement with the limitations of agency policies and felt that these policies prevented them from really helping their clients. The study revealed that the average client of that agency was receiving less than half of the amount of services and resources to which the client was legally entitled under its policies. In other words, it was not the agency policies that were limiting client access to services, but rather the narrow and traditional way that workers and supervisors were interpreting the policies. In the year following the study, as workers were helped to assume active responsibility for broadly interpreting policy, the aid to their clients more than doubled in cost, yet no one in the agency or on its board reached out to stop this more expensive way of operating. The point being made is that service to the client is not limited to what one does when one sits with the client. Some of the most important work, and sometimes the work that is most difficult and requires the most self-discipline and commitment, is the work involved when the worker takes on the role of broker with the agency's programs and its bureaucracy. Social workers are often the kind of people who prefer to deal with people rather than with paper—yet dealing with paper is a part of everyone's life in today's world. So workers can often fail the client in real and hurtful ways if they do not have expert skills in dealing with paper. Operating contrary to traditional grapevine interpretations of policy may often involve the worker in uncomfortable confrontations with the agency colleagues and the supervisor. And it is not easy for an individual worker as part of a system to move contrary to the patterns and relationships in the system. However, if workers' interpretations conform to written policy they can usually prevail in the client's interests, which is what social work is all about.

But there are times when policy does not permit adequate service to clients. The first rule of policy change is that "griping does not do it"; neither does making eloquent, broad statements of one's feeling. In order to bring about change one must first define the problem concisely, and assume the responsibility to document this definition in some detail. The contention that there needs to be change must be documented by organized and verifying data. This is a beginning in the change effort. We will discuss the other tactics of change in the following section.

CHANGING THE BUREAUCRACY

An article by Edward J. Pawlak on organizational tinkering has been reproduced in this chapter (see Reading 5–1). More important than its title would indicate, it really relates to what is being discussed in this section; the focus is on tactics for "tinkering" with the organizational structures, rules, and policies in order to bring about bureaucratic change. Another author who has written some excellent articles on the social worker's activities within the bureaucratic structure is Robert Pruger (1973). The authors have borrowed some of Pruger's ideas to combine with their own thoughts in putting together this section.

The authors' first suggestion for change would be to be clear about what needs to be changed, about the difficulties that can be anticipated in bringing about the solution, and about the cost of both the problem and its solution (problem definition, goals, and plan). So often people not experienced in the complexity and the balances of the bureaucratic setting will take a drastic step to change the situation and will be completely overwhelmed by the unexpected repercussions that follow. Let us consider, for example, the worker that feels that clients are being poorly served by a policy. Unable to change anything, the worker resigns in anger and frustration. A newspaper reporter hears of the problem and asks the worker about it. Seeing an opportunity to use the power of public opinion and certain of the obvious virtue of the cause, the worker tells the reporter of the problems. However, many people in the community do not see the story as an attempt toward better service. They interpret it as an example of how poorly social workers administer public funds, and a strong community pressure develops to cut the funds of the agency, to set up more stringent rules and regulations for the social workers to follow, and to replace the social work director with a business manager who will see that rules are followed.

The second principle is to determine what factors and forces inside and outside the organization are keeping the problem alive. What the worker did not know in this example was that the executive and the board were as deeply concerned as the staff with certain policies but, given the power position of certain people in the community, they had made a decision that any attempt to change things would result in costly backlash. This is not to say that one does not take on an open fight in spite of the threat of backlash. It is to say that one should know the approximate force of that movement and have decided in advance how it would be met. The "freedom fighters" in the Civil Rights Movement are an example of this. They knew in advance something of the expected response to their activities and they not only seriously considered them, but drilled themselves in advance so they would not be taken unawares by sudden actions of the opposition.

The next point follows logically from the above. One should anticipate the difficulties of the solution. Almost any solution to a social problem brings other problems in its implementation. Be sure that the solution is not worse than the problem and know some ways of dealing with anticipated difficulties of the solution. Find out whether those who have the responsibility of deciding about the problem are simply unaware of it or are strongly invested in present policy or opposed to any movement because a clash of interests and values is involved. And this leads to point four, which is determine where in the organization the responsibility for formal decision making in respect to the problem lies. Who formally makes the decision and who or what can influence this decision?

Timing one's efforts can be crucial. Agencies are more often open to change (as are individuals) when they are in periods of crisis, for example, when budgets are increasing or decreasing, when there are great decreases or increases in the number of clients served, when their performance reports are being questioned, or when new methods of dealing with the problem are being widely acclaimed.

The process by which change takes place must be understood, and it must be recognized that the initiation of change often requires a different approach than does the implementation of change. We have often seen workers fight a hard and bruising battle for the initiation of change only to lose the war because they were unwilling or unable to be an active part of its implementation. It is the changes in the way things are done that are the test of how the client will be served differently.

Consider whether change can be achieved more effectively in this situation by advocacy strategy, by collaborative strategy, or by both. Advocacy strategy employs an impressive array of tools, including the use of citizen groups, unions, and professional organizations to engage with the practitioner in litigation, picketing, bargaining, building pressure alliances, contriving for crises to occur, bringing sanctions to bear through external authorities, and perhaps by encouraging noncompliance with policy by workers and clients. Collaborative strategy may employ some of the techniques outlined by Patti and Resnick (1972). Here the change agent may provide facts about the nature of the problem, present alternative ways of doing things, try to develop an experimental project that involves different ways of doing things and get permission to implement it, seek to establish a committee to study the situation and make recommendations for change, attempt to improve the working climate of the agency so that individuals feel trusted and safe and thus can look beyond securing their own position to the task to be done, attempt to bring professional values and ethics to bear, use a logical argument to persuade, and point out what is really happening under the present policy. This last approach will require documentation of the results of present policy.

Pruger (1973) deals with the strategic concerns of the "good bureaucrat" in some ways similar to the above discussion and adds some additional factors. We have summarized his material as follows:

1. "One important property of a good bureaucrat is staying power." This means a recognition that things happen slowly in complex organizations but that whatever changes workers have in mind cannot be implemented if they do not stay in and with the organization.
2. "The good bureaucrat must somehow maintain a vitality of action and independence of thought." Organizational life tends to suppress vitality of action and independence of thought. Workers must resist such pressure.
3. "There is always room for insights and tactics that help the individuals preserve and enlarge the discretionary aspect of their activity and, by extension, their sense of personal responsibility."

And, these are tactics the good bureaucrat will employ:

1. "Understand legitimate authority and organizational enforcement." The inescapable degree of generality found in the regulatory policies and codes of the organization allows for considerable autonomy of the individuals if they just recognize it and use it. The organization's power to control is less than many realize, but if the limits of legitimate authority are recognized, the individuals may expand their discretionary limits.
2. "Conserve energy." Change agents should not thrash around and feel discouraged and unappreciated because they do not receive in a large organization the kind of support they receive from their friends. Also, as stated earlier, master the paper flow of the organization. This will not only help the client but will also remove from the worker's shoulders the weight of resentment and emotional turmoil one feels as one looks at the uncompleted statistical forms on the desk. Workers should describe what can be changed and work on it rather than spend valuable hours bemoaning what cannot be dealt with.
3. "Acquire a competence needed by the organization."
4. "Don't yield unnecessarily to the requirements of administrative convenience. Keep in mind the difference between that which serves the organizational mission and that which serves the organization." Rules, standards, and directives as to the way things should be done are meant to be means that serve ends. In

organizations means tend to become ends so that a worker may be more concerned about turning in the mileage report than the results of the visit to a
client. Ends and means should be kept clear.

5. Workers should remember that "The good bureaucrat is not necessarily the
    most beloved one."

We would like to stress that these skills in changing the bureaucracy
or acting as an advocate for client groups involve the following knowledge
and abilities. The knowledge of how individual human beings and social
systems develop, grow, exist, change, and cope with problems; the knowledge of how individuals interact within small social systems such as the
family or primary groups (knowledge of family development and interaction,
knowledge of group process); knowledge of transactions within larger social
systems (organizational behavior); knowledge of common human needs and
the way culture affects how these needs are expressed are all critical knowledge bases necessary for effective planning for advocacy and institutional
change. In addition, to carry through such plans, the workers will need
self-awareness, especially in certain areas such as innate pushes toward
the expression of competition and aggression, their own level of anger and
the favorite ways of using it; they will need the capacity to use self in a
disciplined way within the parameters of the plan; they will need a high
level of communication skills and ability to use effectively the various skills
outlined in Chapter 12.

THE PROFESSION AS A SYSTEM

Social work is a profession, as we discussed earlier. All professions can
be viewed as social systems. Because the social work profession is a system
within which every social worker functions, whether it is recognized or
not, every social worker ought to understand something about it. The profession through society's assignment of its functions, sanctions to some extent
the work of all people who call themselves social workers, or who occupy
jobs that are classified as social work positions.

In Chapter 2 we identified the six characteristics of a profession. Throughout the text we have discussed the high degree of generalized and specialized
knowledge needed by the professional. The value systems underlying social
work practice have also been discussed. We certainly have indicated the
need for social workers to have a commitment to community and client
interests instead of being primarily motivated by self-interest. In this chapter
we would like to continue in a more organized way to look at the sixth
system of professional practice—the profession, itself, as a social system.

First, we need to consider the fact that the knowledge and skills possessed
by professionals give them powerful control over persons and things. It is
important to society, which provides the professional the opportunity to
secure this power, that it be used primarily in the community interests and
that is not be used to advance professionals at the costs of the welfare of
those who support their acquisition of such knowledge. Thus, the community
usually has some organized way of sanctioning the persons who may claim
status and who may practice in the name of the profession. Also, the profes-

sion itself, in order to safeguard itself against self-aggrandizement of its members and assure that its function in society is fulfilled, supports the underlying value of community service.

In all professions, the community sanctions the individual's right to practice through some combination of the following elements: (1) completion of a certain prescribed course of education; (2) proving a certain level of competency through an examination process administered by the profession; (3) the licensing and regulation of the practitioner through a license, registration, or certification administered by the state (usually through a board with professionals as members); and (4) employment by an organization authorized by the state to offer certain services. Thus, there exists licensing of teachers and doctors and the registration of nurses. There has been considerable pressure within the social work profession to license social workers. Those who would license social workers usually make the point that such licensing would benefit the client systems by defining standards of service and the competence necessary for practice. It would establish a public accountability that will protect both the client and the practitioner from inconsistent, biased judgment of effectiveness of help offered. It would establish a legal definition of social work and establish levels of social work practice which should operate to protect both the professional and the client. It would give social work status among other professional groups.

Since licensing has come slowly to social work, the National Association of Social Workers (NASW) attempted some time ago to set some standards through the establishment of a restricted title. The title, "Certified Social Worker," has been registered with the federal government and can be used only by persons certified by the professional association, the National Association of Social Workers. In order to use this title, social workers have to possess an M.S.W. degree (a master's degree in social work), have worked two years in practice following the earning of the M.S.W. under supervision of another worker who is an ACSW, must be a member in good standing of the NASW, and must pass a professional examination. People who meet these requirements may call themselves a Certified Social Worker and use the letters ACSW (Academy of Certified Social Workers) after their name. The profession recommends that no one engage in private practice who is not a member of the academy.

All professions are organized into some kind of professional association. These professional organizations serve three purposes: (1) increasing the adequacy of the performance of the individual practitioner; (2) policing the ranks of its membership to insure competent performance of the individual members; and (3) to protect the members' exclusive right to practice their profession. In social work, the professional association is the National Association of Social Workers, a national association operating through regional chapters in each state. It accepts for membership those persons who have a B.A. degree in social welfare or social work.

The admission of the B.A. worker to membership in the professional association was followed by the setting up of professional undergraduate courses in social work in universities and the implementation of an accreditation program of such work by the Council on Social Work Education, the organization that accredits professional social work programs in higher education.

Social work as an emergent profession has never had complete control of who could call themselves a social worker and who could do the job in the field. Generally, the social agencies were the ones who effectively decided who could be social workers in that the persons they hired to fill social work positions were entitled to call themselves social workers. Thus, the education, knowledge, and skill of agency employees filling social work positions, who were known to the public and clients as social workers, has varied widely. In general, the private agencies that have often served the middle class have generally insisted on M.S.W. degrees of employment, while the public services have required only a B.A. (or less) degree. In an effort to deal with this, NASW has developed a statement of levels of social work practice complete with professional qualifications for each level.

Today, the National Association of Social Workers has identified six levels of social work practice. There are two levels—*the social service aide* and *the social service technician* that require less than a college degree in social work. To carry the title *"social worker,"* the person should have a bachelor's degree in social work (B.S.W.).

To be a *graduate social worker,* the person needs a master's degree from an accredited professional school in social work. This usually requires two academic years beyond the B.A. degree, although it may require less time if the person has a B.S.W. degree. To be a *certified social worker,* one must possess a M.S.W., have two years of practice beyond the degree under careful supervision, and must pass an ACSW examination. To be a *social work fellow,* one must possess a Ph.D. or D.S.W. in social work and have either two years' experience in specialization or have passed the ACSW examination plus two further years of specialized practice.

It has long been held that the requisite knowledge to judge professional performance is available only to those who have themselves been trained in applying such knowledge. The professional knowledge and skill of the professional person is so different from general knowledge and skill that no one outside the profession can judge the professional. This is usually discussed under the rubric of professional autonomy. Thus, every profession has some means of the self-regulation of practice.

Generally, these "shoulds" of professional practice are stated in a formal code of ethics. However, as certain professionals may engage in unethical or incompetent behavior, and as the community becomes more and more dependent on professional knowledge, the community is increasingly demanding that the people served by the profession should have the right to judge professionals by the outcome of their service *as the public perceives it.* They are questioning whether it is possible for the operation to be a success if the patient dies. This stance may well mark some unrealistic perceptions of the capacity of professionals on the part of the community, but it also marks a realistic concern with the notion that clients do not have the capacity to know when they have been well served—that only professionals have the ability to judge the outcome of their actions.

Another element in this notion of autonomy is that professionals are supposed to be self-directing in their work. As used here, autonomy refers to the professional's control of the content and terms of the work. However, autonomy is not a simple criterion of who is to be considered professional—at least most people have never been willing to designate those wives and mothers who run their own households as being professional. This introduces the notion that when we speak of professionals, what we are really talking about is some kind of organized autonomy—not the autonomy of the individual practitioner. Thus, the more that a profession as a profession is able to exercise autonomy, the more it represents, and its members are controlled by, a hierarchy of institutionalized expertise (Friedson, 1970, pp. 71–92). The question of the professionalization of social work has been raised by many authors on the basis that social welfare organizations are usually considered bureaucratic, not professional organizations. Thus, there are professionals operating in organizations that are marked by the fact that authority is that of the administrative office held. This conflicts with the notion that in a profession the authority is that of expertise. This has already been discussed under bureaucracy but it should be noted that perhaps one of the problems of all professions is that the rigidity and conservatism in the professions are also enforced by the concept of autonomy.

Each profession has its own culture. The interactions of social and professional roles required by the professional activities and professional groups generate particular ways of thinking and acting, and a particular language, unique to the profession. This may be called a professional culture. The value system of the profession in interaction with the value system of the bureaucracy is an important part of the culture of social work. A critical aspect of all professional education and inservice training is the attempt to socialize the workers to the agency and profession. By this, it is generally meant the internalization of the values and culture of the profession so that the professional person is constrained to work in certain ways and to take certain positions.

One of the problems in the achievement of greater autonomy of the profession is found in the fact that when agencies hire people *who have less than the recognized professional training,* these workers do not have a well-integrated identification with their profession that will allow them to stand outside bureaucratic expectation. Instead, they tend to be socialized to the culture of the agency rather than the culture of the profession. Thus, they may first see themselves as public welfare employees rather than first identifying themselves as social workers. As these workers often cannot easily go elsewhere and find employment as social workers, they are tied to their position in the agency rather than their identification as a professional.

Sound internalization of professional values is critically important as protection to the client system since in the helping process workers must use themselves and their judgments. There is seldom any way that another can interfere in the process of action to protect the client in advance of the worker's action. Therefore, the only assurance people have that a professional person can be trusted with professional tasks is that the person acts on the basis of deeply internalized feelings and judgments that stem from professional values and knowledge. This value system and the feelings and actions that stem from it become a part of the culture of the profession.

The ambiguous position of social work within society in terms of its multiple functions and purposes also contributes greatly to shaping the culture of social work.

Lydia Rapoport (1959) says that "no other profession is as self-examining and critically self-conscious as social work." While she relates some problems of the profession to its youth, she also attributes much stress to the profession's ambiguous position in society and to its multiple purposes and functions. Social work, concerned with the social functioning of people and the adequacy of the social institutions which affect human functioning, "seeks to embrace and implement some principles and values which may be essentially unpopular and uncongenial to the dominant social order." This particular role of the profession, as has been observed, results in its being seen as a minority group that is both tolerated and feared. From this come outright attacks and deprecation by the society that sanctions social work. In addition, the social views of the profession tend to isolate individual workers from other professional groups.

One problem of social work is that the tasks it is expected to perform are unclear and that the responsibilities for which it is held to account are often contradictory. For example, many people expect the social worker to control every expenditure of the welfare client, but at the same time to further independent behavior on the part of welfare recipients. Both expectations cannot be satisfied—one or the other must be chosen. Social work is supposed to be working to produce social change, but the society of which social work is a part is totally unable to reach agreement as to the kinds of social change it will support.

Rapoport (1959) points out other sources of strain for social workers, some of which have been touched on earlier in this text. Among them are the following:

1. Being constantly confronted with the problems of human need, pain, and injustice.
2. The capacity for self-awareness and self-control required for the purposeful use of the social work relationship, and the need "to harmonize personal capacity and inclination with professional behavior and values."
3. The institutional framework within which the social worker practices.
4. The opposing demands for "the maintenance of nearness and distance, of involvement and detachment, of rapport and objectivity."
5. The requirement for the tolerance of uncertainty, given our limited knowledge about human development and our difficulty in attempting to utilize what we do know.

RECAPITULATION

In this chapter we have emphasized what it means for the worker to be a part of the action system of an agency and a profession. It is critically important for workers to understand the situation in which they work. We have tried to contribute to this understanding through a look at the nature of bureaucracy and professionalism; the conflicts between bureaucracy and professionalism; the worker and the client as operating within the parameters of agency policy; ways to bring about change in a bureaucracy; and the worker as a professional.

A LOOK FORWARD

We urge careful reading of the two pieces of material at the end of this chapter. Pawlak's article can be extremely helpful in developing some ways of changing the agency and Morgan's account of experience with a bureaucracy gives much food for thought. In the next chapter we will lay the foundation for the process of practice.

Reading 5-1

*Organizational Tinkering**

Edward J. Pawlak

To tinker means to work at something in an experimental or makeshift way. Although clinicians' positions and roles in many social welfare organizations preclude them from pursuing ambitious organizational change, they still may be able to work at change in modest, makeshift ways. And, despite the fact that clinical social work is usually practiced in an organizational and policy context, many clinicians are uninterested in acquiring the knowledge and skills that might facilitate intraorganizational tinkering on behalf of their practice or their clients. Others are overwhelmed, cynical, or disillusioned by their dealings with bureaucracy (Briar, 1968; Gottlieb, 1974, p. 34; Hanlan, 1971; Piliavin, 1968; Podell & Miller, 1974; Specht, 1968, pp. 42–43). Some front-line practitioners, however, have learned to tinker effectively (Hyman & Schreiber, 1974; Maher, 1974; Senna, 1974).

To help clinicians improve their talent in dealing with organizations, this article identifies tactics they can use to tinker with organizational structure, modes of operation, rules, conventions, policy, and programs. The specific tactics discussed are tinkering with bureaucratic succession and rules, the white paper or position paper, demonstration projects, modification of board composition, bypassing, influencing grant reviews, leaking information, and protest by resignation.

Although the author takes a partisan stand on behalf of clinicians, it does not follow that managers are necessarily the villains. However, some of the tactics identified here are directed toward those administrators who cause clinicians to harbor severe misgivings about the organization.

This article stems not only from the author's observation of and experience with organizational tinkering, but also from the contributions of others who have addressed similar themes (Bennis, 1969; Brager, 1968; Martin, 1971; Patti & Resnick, 1972; Specht, 1968, pp. 42–52; Weissman, 1973, pp. 57–131). It warns clinicians to bear in mind the pitfalls and dilemmas of organizational tinkering—that it takes place in a political climate and in a structure of authority, norms, and sanctions (Epstein, 1968; Green, 1966; Nader, Petkas, & Blackwell, 1972; Patti, 1974; Weisband & Franck, 1975).

BUREAUCRATIC SUCCESSION

Bureaucratic succession usually refers to a change in leadership at the highest levels of an organization. Here, however, the author uses the broader concept that includes changes in leadership at all levels in the hierarchy (Gouldner, 1954, pp. 59–104; Levenson, 1961). Bureaucratic succession must be called to the attention of clinicians because it is an opportunity to influence intraorganizational change. For clinicians to exert influence during this phase of organizational transition, it is essential that they understand certain features of organizational life that frequently accompany succession.

Prior to an administrator's departure, organizations usually go into a period of inaction. Most staff members are aware of the lame-duck character of this phase of organizational life, when any major

* Copyright 1976, National Association of Social Workers, Inc. Reprinted by permission of author and publisher from *Social Work* 21:5 (September 1976), pp. 376–380.

change is avoided until the new administrator takes office. There are, however, ways in which clinicians take advantage of this period. They can, for example, (1) suggest criteria for the selection of a successor, (2) seek membership on the search committee, (3) prepare a position paper for the new administrator, (4) propose a revision in the governance structure to enhance participatory management, (5) organize fellow subordinates to propose changes that had been unacceptable to the outgoing administrator, or (6) propose the formulation of a task force to facilitate transition.

The "first one hundred days" is another critical phase of bureaucratic succession that should be examined for the opportunities it offers. Although new administrators tend to be conservative about implementing changes until they are more familiar with the organization, they still are interested in developing and in making their own mark. This three-month period, therefore, provides opportunities to orient and shape the perceptions of new administrators who, until they acquire their own intelligence about the organization, are both vulnerable and receptive to influence.

The following case illustrates how practitioners can tinker with organizational hierarchy by taking advantage of a resignation.

The resignation of a clinician who had served as director of staff development in a child welfare agency provided the staff with an opportunity to influence the transformation of the position into that of administrative assistant. The agency had recently undergone rapid growth in staff size, resources, and diversity, without an accompanying increase in the administrative staff. Thus, the clinician's resignation became the occasion for examining whether the position should be modified to serve such administrative staff functions as program development and grant management.

Bureaucratic succession, therefore, provides an opportunity for an organization to take pause; to examine its mission, structure, policies, practices, accomplishments, and problems; and to decide what it wants to become. It is incumbent upon practitioners to participate in these processes and to take advantage of the structure of influence during that vulnerable phase.

RULES

Rules are features of organizations that, by their nature, invite tinkering. They act as mechanisms of social control and standardization, provide guidelines for decision-making, limit discretion, and structure relationships between persons and units within the organizational structure and between separate organizations (Perrow, 1972, pp. 23–32). There are two types of rules—formal and informal. Formal rules are derived from law or are determined administratively or collectively. Informal rules—which may be as binding as formal ones—are practices that have been routinized so that they have become organizational conventions or traditions. Rules vary in specificity, in their inherent demand for compliance, in the manner in which compliance is monitored, and in their sanctions for a lack of compliance.

Clinicians can tinker with rules either by the kind of interpretations they apply to them or by using their discretion, as is permitted with an ambiguous or general rule. Rules do not necessarily eliminate discretion, but they may eliminate alternatives that might otherwise be considered (Thompson, 1967, p. 120). Gottlieb (1974, p. 8) describes them as follows:

Rules are not necessarily static. They appear to be a controlling force working impersonally and equally, but they vary both in adherence and enforceability and are used variously by staff in their adaptation to the "welfare bind."

Hanlan (1967, p. 93) suggests that "in public welfare there exists an informal system that operates without invoking the formal administrative machinery of rules." The author overheard the director of a community action program encourage new workers "to err on the side of generosity in determining eligibility for programs." A vocational rehabilitation counselor reported that he had had many teeth fixed by liberally interpreting a rule that provided dental care for only those clients whose appearance and dental problems would otherwise have prevented them from being considered for employment involving public contact. This shows that one can tinker with the manner in which rules are interpreted and enforced.

Another way of tinkering with rules is to avoid what Gottlieb (1974, p. 8) calls "rule interpretations by agents of the system alone." She goes on to report that welfare workers encouraged clients to seek help in interpreting rules enforced by the National Welfare Rights Organization (NWRO). It is generally known that legal-aid clinics have been called on to give a legal interpretation of welfare rules and rules governing commitment to mental hospitals.

A supervisor for public assistance eligibility once reported that a thorough knowledge of all the rules enables the welfare worker to invoke one rule over another in order to help clients get what they need. This observation is supported by Gottlieb (1974, p. 32), who points out that rules allow for exceptions and that many NWRO members know the rules better than the workers and thus can challenge their interpretations. In his study of regulatory agencies, Nader (Nader et al., 1972) suggests that rules not only are opportunities for action but are potential obstacles as well and that major effort is frequently required to persuade the agency to follow its own rules.

Another way of dealing with rules is to avoid asking for an interpretation. One agency administrator has suggested that personnel should not routinely ask for rulings and urges them to use their own discretion. He commented: "If you invoke authority, you put me in a position where I

must exercise it. If I make a decision around here, it becomes a rule."

These ways of tinkering with rules suggest that clinicians should examine the function of rules, discern the latitude they are allowed in interpreting them, and exercise discretion. Although the foregoing examples are primarily taken from welfare settings, the principles outlined can be applied to traditional clinical settings.

INDIRECT INFLUENCE

Too often, clinicians rely on the anecdotal or case approach to influence change in an organization. Such an approach is too easily countered by the rejoinder that exceptional cases do not require a change in policy but should be handled as exceptions. The white paper, or position paper, is a much ignored means of tinkering with organizations.

A white paper is a report on a specific subject that emanates from a recent investigation. A position paper is a statement that sets forth a policy or a perspective. The first is usually more carefully reasoned and documented; the second may be argued instead of reasoned. Both white papers and position papers provide opportunities for social documentation and for formulating a compelling case. Such statements strive for logic and are characterized by their use of both quantitative and qualitative data. As the following example shows, by virtue of their character and quality, both position papers and white papers demand a specific response.

A student social worker wrote a position paper identifying the number of teenage pregnancies, the number of associated medical problems, and the high rate of venereal disease among adolescents. She argued for the redirection of the original planned parenthood proposal from the main office to satellite clinics in public housing developments and schools. The paper was well received and spurred the executive to obtain funding from the housing authority.

Lindblom (1970) has characterized decision-making in organizations as "disjointed incrementalism." Simon (1957) indicates that organizations "satisfice"— that is, they make decisions that are good enough. Uncertainties in the environment, the inability to scan all alternatives, and the unknown utility of a solution or decision all preclude optimal decision-making. If organizations were to try to comprehend all the information and contingencies necessary before making a rational decision, the complexity would be overwhelming. Thus, organizations are reluctant to make changes on a large scale because this could lead to large-scale and unpredictable consequences. Resistance to change, therefore, may often be attributed to structure rather than to a malevolent or unsympathetic administrator. This calls attention to organizational structure and processes, but does not mean that the values and roles of administrators are to be ignored.[1]

Given this perspective of organizational behavior, clinicians may consider approaching innovation incrementally and on a small scale by first gaining authorization for a demonstration project.[2] A demonstration project may be bounded by the duration of time or the proportion of the budget or staff time that is devoted to it. The problem with demonstration projects is that the people for whom the demonstration is being carried out are not always specified, nor are they always kept abreast of developments. Often there is a failure to articulate the ramifications and consequences of a successful or unsuccessful demonstration. Practitioners must develop a strategy of demonstration—a means of diffusing innovation throughout the organization or into other organizations and of obtaining commitments from the administration when the demonstration is complete. The following is an example of the commitment one social worker obtained.

A social worker met with a group of suspended or expelled junior high school students after class to discuss their problems. Realizing that she needed to have a chance to intervene directly in their school behavior, she persuaded the agency supervisor, the principal, and the classroom teacher to develop a pilot project—"the opportunity class"—to be used as a last resort before expulsion. When the project was organized, the social worker remained in the classroom for several periods at least two days each week. She handled the acting-out behavior problems while the teacher continued classroom instruction. Eventually the teacher acquired skill in handling students who were acting out. The class continued without the social worker's presence, and some students returned to a regular classroom while others were expelled.

Agency board committees are typically composed of elected members and the executive director of the agency. In addition, in some agencies, one or two staff members may also serve on the committee or occasionally attend meetings to make reports. One strategy of tinkering with the composition of the committee and the kind of information and influence it receives is to promote the idea that nonboard and nonstaff members with certain expertise be included on the committee. For example, a psychiatrist and a local expert on group treatment with children might be recruited to join a case services committee in order to provide legitimation to innovations that board members were grudgingly resisting.

Bypassing refers to a process whereby practitioners avoid taking proposals for change or grievances to their immediate superiors but seek instead a hearing or decision from a higher level in the hierarchy. In an enlightened organization, this form of bypassing is acceptable and even encouraged; government workers, in fact, are entitled to it as part of "due process." Bypassing is risky, however, in that it can discredit the judgment of the complainants

---

[1] For a useful discussion on organizational resistance to change, *see* Patti (1974).

[2] For a negative view of demonstration grants, *see* Pratt (1974).

if the matter is trivial or if it appears that it could have been resolved at a lower level in the hierarchy. Bypassing also places the administration in a vulnerable situation because if the tactic is justified, it reflects poorly on the judgment of the superior and the administrators who hired them. This may lead to questions of nonretention or spur a desired resignation. A successful instance of bypassing is described in the following example:

When a clinician's complaints concerning the physical plant and security of a youth home went unheeded by the director, he demanded to meet with the executive committee of the board. The director admitted that his own sense of urgency differed from that of his staff, but arranged for the meeting. The executive committee approved some of the recommendations for change and authorized that they be implemented as soon as possible.

Agencies often write grant applications for funds to support their programs. A critical phase of the application process occurs at a public review of the grant application when the funding agency invites comment or a letter of support from the agency or from interested parties. If clinicians are dissatisfied with a particular program, and if it is an important matter, they can provide the agency issuing the grant with dissenting information, testify at the review of the grant application, or respond from the standpoint of an "expert witness." In any event, the grant-review process may be an opportunity to voice concern about an agency's program and to influence the advisory group to give conditional approval or disapproval. As is shown in the following example, clinicians may attempt to influence the review process indirectly—by encouraging an expert third party to raise questions about the grant application—or directly.

A social worker was asked to serve as a technical reviewer for a volunteer program for young offenders in a regional planning advisory group. The pro-

gram was modeled after an existing program in another part of the state. The documents supporting the application contained a manual that described the role of the volunteer. It suggested that a volunteer should report any violations of parole to the corrections authority but should not reveal this action to the offender. In seeming contradiction, it emphasized that the volunteer should be a "friend" of the offender. The social worker informed the advisory group of this provision and of his strenuous objection to it. The director of the program had failed to read the manual thoroughly and was unaware of the statement. The advisory group approved the program on the condition that the volunteer not serve as an informer and demanded that the staff codify the conditions under which it may be morally imperative for the volunteer to reveal the offender's behavior.

Social workers are often asked and frequently do endorse a program or a grant application perfunctorily, without having read the proposal. In other instances, programs and grants are endorsed in spite of strong reservations. Notwithstanding the pressures toward reciprocity that exist among agencies, such exchanges of professional courtesy are questionable.

Social workers should take advantage of requests for endorsement or participation in the grant-review process, particularly if they believe that certain aspects of a proposal or program are questionable. The desire for professional endorsement also underlies agency efforts to recruit clinicians for board membership or as paid consultants. Refusal of such offers is a way of "making a statement" about a program.

RADICAL TACTICS

Leaking information, or the covert release of information about an organization, is a tactic that should be used only in grave matters after all other remedies within the organization have been exhausted. The third party to whom the informant gives the information has to verify it and the credibility of the informant, since this person is not willing to put one's character and job on the line. However, until "blowing the whistle" becomes an accepted institutionalized value, and until protections are legislated, it is likely that members of organizations will continue to act like "guerillas in a bureaucracy" (Nader et al., 1972, pp. 15, 25–33; Needleman & Needleman, 1974).

Clinicians who anticipate the need to leak information would be well advised to seek counsel, for discovery could result in liability damages. They are obliged to have a thorough, accurate, and verifiable account of the objectionable situation. As the ethics of leaking information have not been well formulated, clinicians need to consider carefully the professional, moral, and legal standards that support such action (Nader et al., 1972, pp. vii, 1–8, 29–30, 225–230). One way in which the clinician may choose to attack the problem is shown as follows.

The clinician in a foregoing example who was concerned about the physical plant and security of a youth home notified the state monitor about the condition of the home. At the next site visit, the monitor raised questions about the residents' access to balconies and the roof and about the staff-client ratio on weekends.

Resignation in protest, or public defection, is another tactic that should be used only when a clinician experiences unbearable misgivings and finds it both morally and professionally imperative to reveal them publicly. The major problem is that the organization has the financial and operational resources to counter the protest, but the employee has none. Also, with few exceptions, resignation in protest has a history of aversive consequences for the protester (Weisband & Franck, 1975).

A resignation in protest may also discredit the agency. Therefore, prospective protesters must be prepared to have their observations and conclusions verified and their judgment subjected to public review and scrutiny. In addition, the protester

must realize that future employers will wonder whether such history of protestation will continue. An example follows.

When his concerns went unheeded by the board, a clinician resigned in protest. Moreover, he informed the board and the director that he would discourage any professional worker from accepting employment at the agency. He was effective in discouraging local professionals from accepting employment at the agency unless firm commitments were made to modify policies and practices that were detrimental to clients.

The theory of escalation urges protesters to begin by using conventional and formal means to express grievances and influence change. Only after these have been exhausted, and traditional means have encountered failure and resistance, should they engage in a series of escalations to such unconventional or radical forms of protest as boycotting, "palace revolts," picketing, leaking information, and the like. The essential point of this strategy is that protesters should not begin by engaging in the most radical and abrasive strategy. To document the intransigence of the bureaucracy, change must be approached incrementally. If this is not done, the bureaucracy may point to the failure to follow administrative due process. The protester's etiquette and failure to go through channels then become the bone of contention, and the protester becomes the object of protest (Nader et al., 1972, pp. 16–25; Needleman & Needleman, 1974, pp. 285–289, 335–339; Weisband & Franck, 1975, pp. 55–94).

As a condition of employment and as a professional right and responsibility, clinicians should have the opportunity to bring their insights into the plans and programs of the organization they work for. Such participation requires that clinicians acquire skill in dealing with organizations. It is hoped that the participation of clinicians in organizational activity will promote responsive service delivery systems and satisfactory work climates.

At the risk of appearing to be a "double agent," the author plans to write a second article to advise administrators on how to cope with the tinkering of clinicians. After all, organizational power—whether in the hands of clinicians or administrators—"must be insecure to some degree if it is to be more responsible" (Nader et al., 1972, p. 15).

Reading 5–2

Four Pennies to My Name: What It's Like on Welfare

Addie Morris

I had to get up at 3:30 A.M. and start getting the kids dressed. Sally was five and the oldest, so I started with her. Then I dressed Sam; he was three. I did the baby last. All I had to do was change her diaper and wash her face because I had dressed her before putting her to bed.

It was cool that morning and I didn't have a coat for Sam. He never had a chance to go any place in the winter anyway, so there had been no reason to buy him one. I decided to use Sally's coat that Aunt Jean had given her two years ago. He wouldn't know the difference, and I could care less about what people would say.

I wrapped the baby snugly and the four of us started off for the bus stop. At 4:45 a bus finally came and the four of us boarded. I put forty-five cents in the box and we took a seat in the rear. But I hadn't settled down before the driver called, "Lady, you owe me another fare." I had only forty-five cents left and if I gave that to him, I wouldn't have any money to return home. I approached the front of the bus with the baby in my arms. By this time, I had tears in my eyes. Couldn't this black man understand what was happening to me? Didn't he realize that if I had the money I would have gladly put it in the box?

I stood holding on to the rail beside the driver, unable to say anything. Every time I tried to speak the words choked in my throat. Finally, I got the words out tearfully, "Mister, I am on my way to the social service office. I don't have but forty-five cents to my name. I will need that to return home on."

A lady that was sitting a couple of seats behind the driver said, "Aw, let the woman go. Can't you see what she's going through?"

The driver looked straight ahead and mumbled, "Go on and sit down, lady." That is exactly what I did. I returned to my seat too ashamed to look at anyone.

I sat in my seat silently with tears streaming down my cheeks. Sally put her arms around my neck and asked, "What's wrong, Mama? Do you need my shoulder?" I reached over Sam and gave Sally a big hug.

"No, darling, I don't need your shoulder," I replied.

I heard someone in back of me whisper, "Wasn't that sweet?"

Reprinted with permission of the American Public Welfare Association from *Public Welfare* 37:2 (Spring 1979), pp. 13–22. Copyright 1979 by the American Public Welfare Association.

It was a thirty-minute drive to the social service department. My kids and I went out the side door of the bus. I couldn't bear to face all of the people by walking out the front door. I felt relieved that only one other lady got off at the bus stop. She walked so fast ahead of us I thought she must be going to some place important. I had to take my time walking because I was carrying the baby and Sam couldn't walk too fast.

When we arrived at the social service office, it was 5:05. The door of the office was still locked, and people were standing around waiting for it to open. After standing for a few minutes, I decided it would be better if I sat on the steps for awhile. It was then that I noticed the lady who got off the bus with us. She quickly turned her head when she saw me looking at her. The door finally opened at 5:30. Everyone rushed in and took a number or crowded half in line around the desk. I didn't know what to do so I took a number, too. Then I went to the front desk. I waited in line for at least ten minutes before my turn came to talk to the receptionist.

I came straight to the point, saying, "I'd like to see someone about getting food, clothes, and shelter for me and my children." The receptionist told me I would have to wait and talk to an intake worker but they didn't just hand out money like that. Then she took my name and said someone would call me later. I felt a little sick to my stomach that she thought I was looking for a handout.

Around 9:00 the kids became restless. I kept getting up to give them a drink of water, but the water wasn't relieving their hunger. There was a snack bar next to the information desk and some people were buying things to eat. Naturally this made the kids want food even more. But the only money I had I needed for carfare to get home. Finally, Sam stood up and said, "Mom, can I have one piece of candy?" I was embarrassed and I couldn't think normal. I slapped Sam hard. He be-

gan to cry loudly—maybe because he was hurt but also because he was hungry. I told him he better stop crying right away. And of course, not wanting another slap, he did.

By 11:00 the waiting room was crowded. Some people had to stand. However, when noon came everyone that worked there went out to lunch. By this time, my insides felt like they were melting together. I knew how Sally and Sam must feel. But I wasn't thinking much about them because I was too busy feeling sorry for myself.

All of the employees came back to work at 1:00 o'clock. I approached the receptionist again to find out why I hadn't been called. She told me flatly, "Everyone has to wait their turn; they will call you when they get to your name." I tried to explain that my two older children hadn't had breakfast or lunch and I couldn't afford to purchase them anything from the snack bar. She looked up from her scratch pad and said, "What do you expect me to do? I hear this kind of thing all day long." I quickly took my seat hoping too many people hadn't heard our conversation.

Finally, at 1:15 a lady came out and called, "Mrs. Morgan." My name never sounded so beautiful. I hurried to the front desk. A woman instructed me to follow her to a small room I assumed was her office. She began by saying, "I am Mrs. Jenkins and you are Mrs. Morgan."

"Yes," I replied.

She said, "What can I do for you?"

I began, "My husband left me because he was constantly being laid off. He said we could make it better without him."

"Do you know where your husband is?"

"No, ma'm," I replied.

Giving me an application blank, she said, "Fill this out and bring it in tomorrow by 5:30."

It seemed Mrs. Jenkins had finished, but I continued to sit there. After a few seconds, she said, "You may go now."

"But . . . but Mrs. Jenkins, I don't have any food for my two older children. I do have some milk for my baby. Plus I don't have bus fare to return tomorrow." She went into another room and returned with two bus tickets. I said, "I brought two walking children with me that are sitting in the waiting room." She went out again and returned with two more tickets. Then she told me that she would be unable to provide me with a food order; my application would have to be approved first.

As I left the room I thought to myself, "Anyone who thinks being on welfare is fun has to be mentally unstable." The wait alone is enough to make you go out of your mind. Then after the long wait, what did I get? Four bus tickets. Well, at least the bus driver wouldn't be able to embarrass me.

I walked slowly to where Sally and Sam sat. I was thinking hard. I could tell they were glad to see me—it showed in their eyes. But they were afraid to show me because I had been acting so strange and they thought I might lash out at them again.

Someone was sitting in the chair that I was in earlier, so I asked Sam to stand so I could sit down and compose myself. I decided that since I didn't have to use forty-five cents for bus fare, I could buy a snack. I gave the baby to Sally and went to the snack bar. I bought one pack of potato chips and two candy bars. Now, all I had was four pennies to my name.

When I returned with the candy and potato chips, I could see the joy in Sally and Sam's eyes. I gave them each a candy bar and the three of us shared the potato chips. Afterwards, we filled up with water at the fountain.

As we left the building, I was thinking we might go to Aunt Jean's instead of going home. After all, she didn't live too far away. Maybe she would ask us to spend the night and then it would be easier to return to the social service office the next morning. Besides, we didn't have any food at home and she might offer us a little something to eat.

We took a bus going west toward Aunt Jean's house. I was pleased to have two tickets to put in the box when we boarded the bus. It wasn't long before we had arrived at our stop. We got off and started walking to Aunt Jean's home. Sally and Sam realized where we were going and started skipping instead of walking. I was sure they realized that they would get a meal there. Aunt Jean always gave us food.

Aunt Jean was happy to see us. She was even happier that John had finally decided to leave. I didn't bother to explain how desperate I was. It would have only encouraged her to remind me how bad John was. Right then, I could do without hearing that. I tried to make it appear that I was paying her one of those long awaited visits. She was really pleased and indicated that she knew that John was the reason I could never visit before.

Aunt Jean was full of southern hospitality and offered us food immediately. It wasn't long before Sally, Sam, and I were sitting down to a hot meal. It wasn't the greatest, but it was food: salmon, biscuits, syrup, and grapefruitade to drink. I washed the dishes for Aunt Jean.

Then we sat down to talk and watch television. It wasn't long before Aunt Jean started to encourage me to spend the night. Of course, this was what I had been waiting for, but I didn't want to let on. "I am going to fool you this time," I said. "We are going to spend the night." She was happy with this. The children were pleased, too. And I was glad at the way Sally and Sam had been conducting themselves.

The next morning we were able to get up a little later because we were closer to social services. I didn't have to start dressing the children until 4:30. Either Aunt Jean didn't hear our noise or she didn't want to be bothered. I was hoping she would get up and offer us breakfast. At the last minute, she got up and fixed us coffee with a lot of cream. We enjoyed this because we love coffee with lots of cream.

As I boarded the bus, I thanked the Lord again that I was able to put two tickets in the box. I was also thankful that my insides were not clinging together from hunger.

We arrived just as the door of the social services office was opening. People rushed in to take a number. Others formed lines at the receptionist's desk. I rushed to take a number, too. Then I remembered that I had taken one the day before and hadn't returned it. The next number was fifteen. My number from the day before was six. Naturally, I kept the number six. Then I wondered if that was wise decision. The worker I get with the number fifteen might help me more than the one I would get with the number six.

We waited in the waiting room the same as we did the previous day. People walked back and forth to buy snacks. I know that Sam and Sally were hungry, but neither of them asked for anything. They were probably afraid. In my heart I wanted to be able to buy goodies for my children just like everyone else. I knew this was why I lashed out at them for every little thing. I realized that I wasn't making things any better by doing this, so I promised myself that I would do better.

I was daydreaming about being able to afford things for my children when I heard my name over the paging system, "Mrs. Morgan, front desk." I rushed up to the front desk and identified myself.

A lady said, "This way, please."

She offered me a chair and identified herself as Mrs. Jones. I handed her my application and she began to look it over. She didn't say a word with her mouth, but she said a lot with her facial expressions. I would have felt better if she had spoken. I began perspiring until my hands felt slippery. My knees began to tremble so that it appeared I was shaking my baby. I won-

dered whether Mrs. Jones was enjoying my extreme anxiety. She certainly wasn't trying to alleviate it by breaking the silence.

I suppose it took Mrs. Jones ten minutes to read my application. To me it seemed like ten years. She finally looked up at me and said, "Mrs. Morgan, do you know where your husband is now?" I told her that I didn't have any idea of where he could be. Then she proceeded to tear apart each of my answers on the application. She asked, "Do all three of your children have the same father?" I suppose I was partly to blame on this one. I didn't indicate their last names on the form because I assumed anyone would know their last name was Morgan. Mrs. Jones wanted to know about the length of time I had lived at our address. She threw one question after another at me: "Why don't you have . . . ?" "What have you been doing up to now for . . . ?" "How come you haven't . . . ?" Either Mrs. Jones was asking the questions in a downgrading manner, or I had a complex and was taking all of her questions the wrong way. But I was meek as a lamb answering all of her questions.

My father always said, "Take it easy when you have your head in a lion's mouth." This was certainly true now, and I needed this woman for my survival.

As she continued to question me, I became choked up. When I began to answer her question on what I had been doing for food, I broke down. Here I was a grown woman crying. Mrs. Jones did or said nothing to comfort me. She just sat there. When I managed to control myself, she said, "Maybe I should tell you a little about what we can do for you. We are not intended to be an agency for people to live off. We are designed to help you out with aid until you are able to manage alone. We only take care of things that are essentials or necessities . . ." She rambled on and on but still wasn't saying anything that I wanted to hear. I wanted to know what they were going to give me.

Finally she told me she would work out a budget for me and tell me how much it was when she got back. She left and was gone for thirty minutes. I was relieved because I knew that at least I would be getting some help. I wasn't even angry when I saw her joking and laughing with her friends instead of working on my budget.

She came back with the budget that the department allowed for me. It included the following:

Rent	$100
Lights	15
Gas	20
Food, clothes	120
Total	$255

I was currently paying $130 for rent, but she said the department only allowed $100. She further explained that my checks would arrive on the first and sixteenth of each month. Each check would be for $127.50. She told me about the food stamp program that I was eligible for. The way I understood it I could pay $10 and get enough stamps to buy $15 worth of food.

I was very thankful. In fact, I was so happy I walked right out of her office without asking for bus tickets to get home or a food order to keep us until the following week. I turned around and went back into the office, stumbling over the chair I had been sitting in. "I don't have any food for my two older children," I told her. "I also don't have any money or bus tickets to get home."

"I see your kind every day," she said. "Want everything you can get. Have a seat outside and they will call your name to pick up the tickets and food order."

I was so thrilled. I went back outside, sat down next to my kids, and hummed "Thank You, Jesus." Suddenly, things had begun to look up for me. I could really pray to God now. Before, I was too depressed to pray as I should.

They didn't call my name until 3:00. When I went up to the front desk, Mrs. Jones gave me a $20 food order and $2 worth of bus tickets. I was so hungry and weak, I just thanked her, got the children, and left.

On the way to the bus stop I decided what I was going to do. I would take a bus to the supermarket that was six blocks from my house. We got off the bus and walked proudly to the supermarket. We were going to be able to buy some groceries.

I was careful to add up every item I put into the basket. I knew I couldn't go over $20. I bought potatoes, eggs, milk, bread, sugar, corn flakes, beans, spinach, beef neck bones, chicken livers, and other items that were reasonable and would stretch a long way. After I had finished, I only had a little over $18 worth of groceries. I told Sally and Sam they could go and pick one thing they wanted. I've never seen two happier kids. Sam got a box of six Baby Ruth candy bars; Sally picked a box of vanilla wafer cookies. I was so full of pleasure with their joy that tears rose in my eyes.

When the cashier finished, I had two bags full of groceries. I realized I couldn't carry the groceries and my baby, too. There were drivers by the door calling, "Transportation. Transportation." I sure needed transportation, but I couldn't afford it.

I pushed my groceries outside and decided to give one of the bags to Sally to carry. I carried the other bag and the baby. But I hadn't gone very far when my load became unbearable. I absolutely couldn't go any farther. I managed to get my bag to the ground before it burst.

For about five minutes, I was out of breath. Sally and Sam seemed to sense what was happening to me because they stood there silently with me. I was trying to stuff some of the groceries into Sally's bag when a car pulled to the curb and stopped.

It was one of the men who was at the supermarket calling, "Transportation." He said, "Lady, do you need a ride?" I told him yes but I didn't have any money. "Get in," he said. Sally, Sam, and I crowded in as he held the seat forward. I told him where we lived. To make conversation, I talked about the weather. I offered him some of my groceries for pay but he refused.

The dinner I prepared that evening was a tasty one. I fried the chicken livers with onions and we had rice, spinach, and corn bread. We felt like saying grace before eating for a change. During our meal, I explained my success of the day. "Now we will be able to eat a meal three times a day. And I won't be so worried and upset."

Sam asked, "Is three times a day a lot of times?" I laughed and assured him that it was enough times that he wouldn't be hungry.

We had never been able to afford story books or television in our home. So I decided I must think of something to entertain the kids. As the three of us sat on the floor, I told them stories. I started with "The Three Little Pigs," continued with "Snow White," and ended up with "The Four Little Rabbits." When I finished, Sally said, "Mom, I didn't know you could tell stories."

The following week was beautiful: three meals each day, peace of mind, and most of all giving love and receiving my children's love.

Saturday was the sixteenth of the month and my check was due. My groceries were getting thin. However, I knew I could make it a few more days. I waited for the postman. He finally came around 1 P.M. He left something in my mailbox. I was so excited. I rushed downstairs and found a sample of Ultra Sheen.

I refused to let my disappointment get the best of me and told myself the check was delayed because of the weekend and would definitely be there on Monday. Meanwhile, things would be all right. I must admit that the weekend wasn't a pleasant one. In fact, it was the longest weekend I've known. I wasn't harsh with kids, though. I just wasn't motivated to talk, clean house, or do anything but the necessities.

Finally, Monday came. The postman always came earlier during the week. But today he didn't stop. My heart was beating so hard, I thought it was going to come through my skin. Without thinking, I ran outside after the postman with only my robe and slippers on. He stopped and went through his bag of mail again but didn't find anything for me.

I ran back inside and fumbled through my purse until I found Mrs. Jones' telephone number. I hurried out to the corner telephone booth with my last dime. I dialed the number but every time the line was busy. At twelve noon, I finally got through but no one answered. Then I realized everyone was out to lunch. But I was determined not to hang up until someone answered.

Around 1:00 someone finally answered the phone. I asked to speak to Mrs. Jones. When she came to the phone she asked, "Was that you letting the phone ring for a whole hour?" She hadn't identified herself.

"Yes," I said, "I'd been calling all morning, and the line was busy. I was determined to reach you." I identified myself and told her about my check not coming in the mail. She said that sometimes it takes two to three weeks for checks to get started. She told me to be down at the office at 8 A.M., and she would have a check for me.

Our food was more than thin at this point. We had been eating generously because we thought we'd be getting more food in two weeks. Anyway, I felt at ease because I would be getting a check the next day.

Tuesday morning I was up bright and early. But it suddenly dawned on me that I didn't have any money to take the bus.

I decided I would have to walk. I awakened Sally and told her about feeding the baby and where she could find bread to toast for Sam and herself. I told her to give the baby one bottle in the morning and the other when she wakes from her nap. She agreed to do this faithfully and off I went.

It was a long walk. Although I wasn't wearing a watch, I could tell it was already much later than 8:00. I was so tired I thought my legs would fall from under me. But I couldn't stop. I had to get my check so I could buy food for my children.

Finally, I arrived. I was so exhausted that I had to lean on the receptionist's desk to ask to see Mrs. Jones. She told me to have a seat and Mrs. Jones would call me. There were no vacant seats in the waiting room so I went over to a large ash tray in the corner and sat on it. I was absolutely too tired to stand any longer. As I sat there catching my breath, I looked at the clock on the wall and it said 10:10. Gee whiz, it had taken me more than four hours to walk from home.

Mrs. Jones came out and called different people but not me. Some of the people she called I thought had come in after I had. But I didn't have any proof. And even if I had proof, there was nothing I could do about it.

Just before noon Mrs. Jones came out and called me. As soon as I approached the desk, she handed me a check and two bus tickets. I reached out and tried to shake her hand but she refused. I said, "Thank you so very, very much!" I left humming an old spiritual, "Yes, God Is Real."

What a thrill it was to have a check of my own for $127.50. I had never had a check this large in my whole life. All I could do was sing and pray a thankful prayer all the way to the bus stop.

I got off the bus near the supermarket. Going inside, I asked them to cash my check. Of course, they asked, "Do you have any identification?" All I had was

my marriage certificate that I had forgotten to take out of my purse after I'd taken it to the social service office two weeks before. I gave my marriage license to the clerk and told her that was the only identification I had. She smiled and initialed my check and told me that the cashier would cash it after I had made a purchase. Then she asked me whether I would like an identification card so I could cash all of my checks there. Of course, I was pleased and thanked the clerk. She gave me a wallet-size card.

I was so happy walking around the store picking up my groceries. I began to feel as though I was a princess.

After I finished getting my groceries, I still had $90 left. I felt great. The same men were across from the checkout counter saying, "Transportation. Transportation." I walked across and asked the one that had given the children and me a ride two weeks before.

After he had helped me take my groceries in, I asked him would $1 be enough. He said, "Whatever you want to give." So I gave him a dollar and he thanked me.

Then I noticed something different about my house. My children had attempted to clean the house while I was gone. They jumped up and down with joy when they realized that I was bringing food home. I jumped right along with them for the good job they had done. Then Sam and Sally happily assisted me in putting the groceries away.

After I cooked dinner, we sat down to eat. Everyone was quiet. I thought I would break the silence by asking whether anyone had anything they would like to talk about. Sam spoke up, "Mama, aren't you glad Daddy is gone?"

I quickly replied, "No! Why?"

He began to stammer a bit and continued, "We can eat good food all the time since he's away. I hope he stay gone."

"Oh, don't talk like that," I said. I was sorry I had broken the silence. And I had spoken in such a defensive manner. I knew I wasn't letting my children open up and tell me what was on their minds. Yet, I couldn't seem to help myself.

The rest of the week went fine. I told the children stories and even played games with them—games like guessing who has the penny, or who is knocking at my door. All our games had to be things that didn't require a game set. I decided to do exercises and play running games, too. The house had very little furniture—only the necessities: stove, refrigerator, one bed, a mattress on the floor for Sally and Sam to sleep on, and a cradle. So, there was plenty of space available for running.

On Friday, Mr. Perry came over for the rent. I didn't want to give him all of the money that I had. And, even if I did give him all of the money I had, I would still have a balance due to him. The rent was $130 and I had a little more than $88. I decided to give Mr. Perry $65 of the rent and promised to mail him the balance in two weeks. He wasn't pleased because he'd had trouble with my husband in the past. But he agreed. And I felt more secure with the $23 I kept in case of an emergency.

I kept pretty much to myself the following two weeks and enjoyed my children and having decent food to eat. Before I expected it, my check arrived. It was the first of the month, but somehow I expected it to be late. I now had $150. Happy, I mean I was happy. I only owed a $15 gas bill and a $10 light bill.

I left my children alone, instructing them to keep the door closed and not open it for anyone. First I walked to the grocery store. This way I could get my check cashed. I decided not to get groceries until I was on my way home. After getting my check cashed, I took a bus to the post office and bought three stamped envelopes and three money orders to pay my light, gas, and rent balance.

Then I returned to the supermarket. I

spent $30 for groceries. I also paid the driver $1 to take my groceries home. So I had $29 left—not a lot of money, but some in case of an emergency.

The money I received from social services could pay the rent, utilities, and buy some food. However, the food would have to be mostly second rate such as neck bones, chicken livers, or bacon ends. But I couldn't complain because I could at least live.

The time came for Sally to start school and I began to wonder what we would do for clothes. I started looking for a night job, but I couldn't find work doing anything. I would even have taken a job sweeping the street. I knew there had to be more to life than this. I was barely surviving.

The day before school, I made starch out of flour and ironed Sally's best dress which wasn't much. It was old plus it was up to her butt because she had gotten it two years before. I bought her a pair of gym shoes and socks at the supermarket.

The first day of school I dressed Sally along with Sam, the baby, and myself. Of course, today was Sally's day and the rest of us didn't matter that much. But as we waited in line to register, I noticed the way the other children were dressed.

After being in school for several weeks, Sally began to act strangely. One afternoon she came home and asked, "Mama, why do all of the children laugh at me?" I didn't want to tell her it was because I couldn't afford to buy her nice clothes like the others had. She seemed to sense that I didn't want to talk about it, so she never mentioned it again. But she began to withdraw and talk less and less. That winter she had a mental breakdown and was hospitalized for two weeks. When the doctor told me he thought this had happened because of the way she had been treated by her peers at school, I became even more determined to get a job so I could buy us some clothes.

I soon found the Lord was looking out

for me. The day Sally was discharged from the hospital, her doctor told me about a job at a nursing home working nights as a nurse's aide. He said the man that was the administrator was a friend of his. He told him about me and the administrator had agreed to give me a try. I felt all I needed was a chance like this. I was so elated I had tears in my eyes when I thanked the doctor. He told me to take good care of my children.

I was due to start to work on Sunday night. I knew I couldn't afford to hire anyone to look after the children when I was at work. So I took time and explained to Sally what I was going to do. I told her in order to get money to buy a few toys and clothes like other people, I had to work. I would need her help with Sam and the baby. I assured her they would be asleep most of the time anyway.

I bought a white uniform with my light bill money and used the rest of my emergency savings to catch the bus to and from work.

It was three weeks before my first pay check, but it was well worth the wait. I cleared $120 and had some money to buy clothes. I went to K-Mart and bought Sam a suit, Sally a dress, shoes and socks, and the baby a new dress, socks, and shoes because she had never had any shoes before.

That Sunday when I got home from work, I dressed everyone; and we all went to church. I was sleepy that night at work, but I was pleased we went. The kids enjoyed it and my heart felt all good inside.

From that time forward Sally kept the kids for me while I worked at night. We had better food and clothes—and I even started saving a little. We went to church every Sunday and sometimes during the week. Sally and Sam began to love Sunday school and looked forward to going.

Sometimes I felt a little guilty for accepting money from social services and working, too. But I rationalized to myself that I couldn't survive on either one alone.

So I took the better of two evils and risked going to jail if I got caught.

One night at work an inservice instructor gave a class on "Treating the Patient As a Human Being Through Reality Orientation." I dearly enjoyed the class. Afterwards, I went to the instructor and asked her about continuing my education. She was happy about my interest, especially since I wanted to be a nurse. (I had been thinking about this for some time.) She agreed to bring me literature and an application to a junior college. Of course, I was happy about her promise, but I never expected her to fulfill it. So often people had made promises and never kept them.

The next evening when I arrived at work, I was surprised to find a catalog about a nearby community college and an application. During my lunch break that night I read as much as I could of the catalog and filled out the application.

I wrote a letter to my high school for my transcript. I felt like I was really doing something worthwhile. But in the back of my mind I kept reminding myself that I might not be accepted. Maybe my southern education hadn't been adequate. But I was optimistic. I talked about going back to school with my coworkers and they made fun of me. Even the licensed practical nurse in charge made sarcastic remarks. But this made me keep my head up and try harder.

In less than a month I received a letter from the school to come down for an interview. I became apprehensive, but I decided to go. Surely it couldn't be any worse than my first few visits to social services. Besides, all they can tell me is "yes" or "no."

The interview wasn't as difficult as I expected. The director of nursing was black—although she talked and tried to act like she was white. She was blunt and direct. She informed me that with my academic background I would need one year of liberal arts before entering the nursing program.

I registered early in the summer for the fall semester. I planned to take four courses: English 1, Chemistry 1, Humanities 200, and Speech 200. My classes began at 8:00 A.M. and were over at 11:00. Two were on Monday and Wednesday, and the other two were on Tuesday and Thursday. This meant I would be home by 12:30 every day so Sally could go to school in the afternoon.

Soon summer was over and it was time for Sally and me to start to school. I sat down and explained my plans to Sally. I told her she would be caring for Sam and the baby (now a year and a half old) in the morning while I attended classes. She already knew how to prepare cereal for them. That would be all they would need until I returned home at 11:30. Then I would prepare lunch and dress Sally for school. (Sally was better now and able to return to school.)

This plan worked out well. During that first year, I made two A's in chemistry, four B's in my other courses, and two C's in English. I managed to pay my own way through school in addition to buying our clothing. (I enjoyed dressing Sally each morning after I arrived home from work. I continued to thank the Lord for decent clothes to dress her in.)

In April, I received a letter from the Nursing Evaluation Committee to come for an interview for the nursing program. I was put through the third degree at that interview. I managed to answer their questions and remain calm on the outside. But sometimes two of them would ask a question at the same time. I would answer one. Then, when the opportunity presented itself. I answered the other. At the end of the interview, the director of the program told me that I was accepted to the nursing program and was to begin classes in September. I couldn't have been happier.

The next week I made an appointment to see Mrs. Jones at social services. I told her of my acceptance in the nursing program. She questioned me about my getting

into the program without prior preparation. I told her about attending classes for the past eight months. Then she asked me, "What do you want me to do?" I told her the first thing I would need was money for a babysitter. To this she replied, "You didn't seem to have any trouble getting a babysitter for the past eight months." At this point my hands became sweaty. Couldn't this lady see the sacrifices I had made? I composed myself and told her of the arrangement I had made with Sally.

But Mrs. Jones continued the questioning. She asked how I got the money to attend college. Silently I said, "Lord, forgive me for this lie," before I told her that my boyfriend had paid for my schooling. I added that we had broken up now and I wouldn't be receiving any more help from him. At last, she told me that social services could allow me $30 a week for child care but nothing for tuition. She told me to try the financial aid office at the school.

I did exactly as Mrs. Jones said and went to the financial aid office at the college. I was able to get a loan and a grant to cover my entire tuition. But I decided to continue to work. I planned to save the loan money in case I had to stop working. However, if I didn't use the loan money I could pay the loan back upon completion of the program.

So I continued to work at the nursing home. The jokes and remarks about my going to school became less frequent as I progressed in the nursing program. At the request of the nursing director, I even took charge when the supervisor was unable to come in.

At times, working along with going to school and taking care of my children would get the best of me. Sometimes I would catch myself nodding in class, and once I fell asleep. Everyone was leaving the classroom when I awakened. I was so embarrassed. I immediately went up and explained to my instructor that I was working nights.

Finally I graduated. It was a small graduation, but an extremely happy occasion for me and my children. As I walked across the stage for my associate degree in nursing, my baby Nell stood up in her seat in the rear of the auditorium and said, "That's my mama!" The audience turned to her and cheered and clapped.

I am now off AFDC and I am very thankful to God that he helped me through those years. I am very proud to be a nurse, and it feels great to be able to go to the supermarket and pay for my groceries with cash rather than food stamps. I always felt people were watching me when I paid with food stamps. It doesn't mean that I have that much more money now, but I do have more dignity which seems to make the money go further. Bank tellers and checkout clerks seemed to sneer at me when I cashed my welfare check. With a check I've earned, these people respect me and I feel that I am not a burden to society. I feel good about having earned that money.

I can see now that children act in the same way their parent acts. When I was on welfare and barely able to make ends meet from one month to the next, my kids were sad and struck out at each other. Now that I am more content, they are nice to each other. Another factor that has changed their attitude is that they can do things other children do and have things other children have. Now I am able to buy Sam a truck for his birthday. I can afford to take the kids to the zoo or on a picnic in the park. Sally has pajamas so she can spend the night with a friend. Our life is very different from before.

It's a great feeling to be off welfare.

References

Bennis, Warren. Post-bureaucratic leadership. *Transaction*, July–August 1969, *6*, 44–52.

Brager, George. Advocacy and political behavior. *Social Work*, April 1968, *13*, 3–15.

Briar, Scott. "The Casework Predicament," *Social Work*, January 1968, *13*, 5–12.

Epstein, Irwin. Social workers and social action. *Social Work*, April 1968, *13*, 101–108.

Friedson, Elliot. Dominant professions, bureaucracy and client services. In William R. Rosengran & Mark Lefton (Eds.), *Organizations and clients*. Columbus, Ohio: Charles E. Merrill, 1970.

Gottlieb, Naomi. *The welfare bind*. New York: Columbia University Press, 1974.

Gouldner, Alvin. *Patterns of industrial bureaucracy*. New York. Free Press, 1954.

Green, A. D. The professional worker in the bureaucracy. Social Service Review, March 1966, *40*, 71–83.

Hanlan, Archie. Counteracting problems of bureaucracy in public welfare. *Social Work*, July 1967, *12*, 88–94.

Hanlan, Archie. Casework beyond bureaucracy. *Social Casework*, April 1971, *52*, 195–198.

Hyman, Irwin, & Schreiber, Karen. The school psychologist as child advocate. *Children Today*, March–April 1974, *3*, 21–33, 36.

Lerner, Barbara. *Therapy in the ghetto*. Baltimore: Johns Hopkins Press, 1972.

Levenson, Bernard.   Bureaucratic succession. In Amitai Elzioni (Ed.), *Complex Organizations.* New York: Holt, Rinehart & Winston, 1961.

Lindblom, Charles E.   The science of muddling through. In Fred Cox et al. (Eds), *Strategies of community organization.* Itasca, Ill.: F. E. Peacock Publishers, 1970.

Maher, Thomas F.   Freedom of speech in public agencies. *Social Work,* November 1974, *19,* 698–703.

Martin, Carl.   Beyond bureaucracy. *Child Welfare,* July 1971, *1,* 384–388.

Morgan, Ralph.   Role performance in a bureaucracy. In *Social Work Practice,* 1962. New York: Columbia University Press, 1962.

Nader, Ralph, Petkas, Peter J., & Blackwell, Kate.   *Whistle-blowing.* New York: Grossman Publishers, 1972.

Needleman, Martin L., & Needleman, Carolyn Emerson.   *Guerrillas in the bureaucracy.* New York: Wiley, 1974.

Patti, Rino J.   Organizational resistance and change: The view from below, *Social Service Review,* September 1974, *48,* 367–383.

Patti, Rino J., & Resnick, Herman.   Changing the agency from within. *Social Work,* July 1972, *17,* 48–57.

Perrow, Charles.   *Complex organizations: A critical essay.* Glenview, Ill.: Scott, Foresman, 1972.

Piliavin, Irving.   Restructuring the provision of social services. *Social Work* January 1968, *13,* 34–41.

Podell, Lawrence, & Miller, Ronald.   *Professionalism in public social services,* Vol. 1, No. 2 "Study Series," New York: Human Resources Administration, 1974.

Pratt, George E.   The demonstration grant is probably counterproductive. *Social Work,* July 1974, *19,* 486–489.

Pruger, Robert.   The good bureaucrat. *Social Work,* July 1973, *18,* 26–32.

Pruger, Robert.   Bureaucratic functioning as a social work skill. In Betty L. Baer & Ronald C. Frederico (Eds.), *Educating the baccalaureate social worker.* Cambridge, Mass.: Ballinger, 1978.

Rapoport, Lydia.   In defense of social work. An examination of the stress of the profession. Lecture, June 16, 1959 at School of Social Welfare, University of California at Berkeley.

Senna, Joseph J.   Changes in due process of law. *Social Work,* May 1974, *19,* 319–324.

Simon, Herbert.   *Administrative Behavior* (2d ed.). New York: Macmillan, 1957.

Specht, Harry.   Casework practice and social policy formulation. *Social Work,* January 1968, *13,* 42–52.

Thompson, James D.   *Organizations in action.* New York: McGraw-Hill, 1967.

Wasserman, Harry.   Early careers of professional workers in a public child welfare agency. *Social Work* July 1970, *15,* 98–101.

Wever, Max.   *The theory of social and economic organization.* New York: Free Press, 1947.

Weisband, Edward, & Franck, Thomas M.   *Resignation in protest.* New York: Grossman Publishers, 1975.

Weissman, Harold H.   *Overcoming mismanagement in the human services.* San Francisco: Jossey-Bass, 1973.

Wilensky, Harold L., & Lebeaux, Charles N.   *Industrial society and social welfare.* New York: Russell Sage Foundation, 1958.

Chapter 6

Relationship for
Social Work Practice

This chapter will focus on the social work relationship and will center primarily on the helping relationship that develops between practitioner and the client system. We would remind the reader that in this type of statement, client may be read client system and worker may be read change agent. The terms *client* and *worker* are used because they lend themselves well in communicating the attitudes being discussed by authors. Readers should always be aware that every social work system is either an individual or composed of individuals.

Chapter 4 focused on systems theory and talked of the need of human systems, individuals, and human groups, as open systems, for input from the world around them if they were to grow and develop and to continue to cope with life tasks. As stated earlier, every human system needs input from relationships with others, although not all systems find it easy to accept the thought that they do. During our lifetime each of us has experienced the connectedness of emotion and intimacy with others that is called the "human relationship." When we cannot find these connections with other people, we often name and personalize trees and animals, or perhaps our car. Then we draw comfort from acting as if another human being were present. In fact, though individuals may rarely be conscious of what these relationships mean and what powers they contain (except at certain points in life when people are suddenly bereft of a meaningful relationship or are in the process of becoming involved in a new one), the most critical characteristic of our humanity is that lives are lived within relationships to other people. Thus "relationships" do not originate for any of us within the social work process, or the professional helping effort (and therein may lie the rub, as shall be discussed later). Nor can social work claim to have been the lone discoverer of this attribute of humanity or the only group interested in pursuing its investigation. Psychology and psychiatry, among other professions, have also been very active in attempting to research the helping relationship (Perlman, 1957).

However, social work can take pride in the fact that from its earliest beginnings it recognized the importance of human interaction and attempted to employ the concept of relationship in a conscious and deliberate way for the benefit of the people it served. In the early formulations describing social work activity, the relationship between worker and client was given a special importance—and no concept appears more frequently in the literature of the profession. Although the goals toward which this early activity was directed were those which the worker thought desirable for society and personally redemptive for the client, there was a beginning of the principle of self-help and a very clear conviction of the power of personal influence in the stimulation of this process (Pumphrey & Pumphrey, 1961; Reynolds, 1963; Richmond, 1899).

Perhaps the outstanding author and teacher in the field of social casework at the beginning of the 20th century was Mary Richmond. Her writings contain considerable material about the social work relationship. She asserted that social casework stands for the "intensive study and use of social relationships." Richmond (1917, pp. 211–215) defined the focus of casework activity in terms of "skill in discovering the social relationships by which a given personality has been shaped; an ability to get at the central core of the difficulty in these relationships; power to utilize the direct action of mind upon mind in their adjustment." The importance of the effect of "mind upon mind" was recognized in the development of "friendly visitors" in early social work.

In spite of the early recognition of relationship as a basic concept in social work theory, and in spite of the years of concern with the development and use of relationship in practice, a clearly defined concept of the social work relationship has yet to be articulated. There is great unanimity about the importance of human relationships in the promotion of growth and change, but there is little common understanding about just how these relationships promote such development. In the professional literature authors often merely describe qualities of the relationship that they consider important, or they record very specific instances of their use of relationship in the helping process.

Being convinced that the concept of relationship is central to all of social work practice, we intend in this chapter to consider some attempts of selected social work authors to express the nature of social work relationships and to examine some of the notions, implicit or explicit, in such statements. We shall consider the roles that social workers carry and how these affect and shape social work relationships and the qualities of social workers who would work effectively with others.

A REVIEW OF THE LITERATURE

Felix Biestek (1957, p. 11) has collected a number of excerpts illustrating the attempts of social workers to express the nature of the relationship. He points out that relationship has been compared to an atmosphere, to flesh and blood, to a bridge, and to an open table.

> The essence of the relationship has been called an interplay, a mutual emotional exchange, an attitude, a dynamic interaction, a medium, a connection between two persons, a professional meeting, a mutual process. The concept "interaction"

seems to be the most generic and it was most commonly described as "dynamic."
The purpose of the relationship was described as creating an atmosphere, the development of personality, a better solution of the client's problem, the means for carrying out function, stating and focusing reality and emotional problems, and helping the client make a more acceptable adjustment to a personal problem.

Biestek (p. 4) sees the relationship between caseworker and client as the medium through which the knowledge of human nature and the individual is used. "The relationship is also the channel of the entire casework process; through it flow the skills in intervention, study, diagnosis and treatment." Biestek (1951) defines the casework relationship as

> the dynamic interactions of attitudes and emotions between the caseworker and the client, with the purpose of helping clients achieve better adjustments between themselves and their environments. (p. 12)

In a book on social casework Helen Harris Perlman (1957, pp. 65–66) says of *relationship* that

> It is a condition in which two persons with some common interest between them, long term or temporary, interact with feeling. . . . Relationship leaps from one person to the other at the moment when some kind of emotion moves between them. They may both express or invest the same kind of emotion; they may express or invest different or even opposing emotions or . . . one may express or invest emotion and the other will receive it and be responsive to it. In any case, a charge or current of feeling must be experienced between two persons. Whether this interaction creates a sense of union or of antagonism, the two persons are for the time "connected" or "related" to each other.

Perlman (1957, pp. 64–68) goes on to say that the identifying mark of a professional relationship "is in its conscious purposiveness growing out of the knowledge of what must go into achieving its goal"; that "all growth-producing relationships, of which the casework relationship is one, contain elements of acceptance and expectation, support and stimulation." She also identifies authority as an element of the professional relationship and clearly differentiates between the relationship and other aspects of the helping process. Perlman sees the caseworker as helping people to deal with their problems through (1) the provision of resources, (2) the problem-solving work, and (3) the therapeutic relationship, which she defines in another work (1971, p. 58) as the "climate and the bond" between workers and clients that "acts to sustain and free clients to work on their problems."

Social workers who attempted to help people through the use of groups were also concerned with the development and use of relationships. Grace Coyle (1948, p. 91), who was very influential in the early development of group work, defined relationship as "a discernible process by which people are connected to each other, and around which the group takes its shape and form." Gisela Konopka (1963, pp. 107–118), an international authority in group work theory, does not define the relationship in her writings. She does discuss it as one of the major helping media available to the social group worker and sets forth its elements as purpose, warmth, and understanding.

In her book *Social Work with Groups,* Helen Northen (1969, pp. 53–58) says:

> Relationship has been described as consisting "primarily of emotional responses which ebb and flow from person to person as human behavior evokes different affective reactions." The social worker in a group situation develops a unique relationship with each member, based on an understanding of the individual.

Writing about the giving and taking of help, Alan Keith-Lucas (1972, p. 47) defines the helping relationship as "the medium which is offered to people in trouble through which they are given the opportunity to make choices, both about taking help and the use they will make of it." Keith-Lucas (1972, pp. 47–65) identifies the qualities of the relationships as (1) mutuality, (2) reality, (3) feeling, (4) knowledge, (5) concern for the other person, (6) purpose, (7) takes place in the here and now, (8) offers something new, and (9) is nonjudgmental.

Several years ago Pincus and Minahan (1973, pp. 69–73) wrote that a relationship "can be thought of as an affective bond between workers" and other systems with which they may be involved and that relationships may involve an "atmosphere of collaboration, bargaining or conflict." They classify all social work into three types: collaborative, cooperative, and conflicted. These authors go on to identify the common elements of all social work relationships as (1) purpose, (2) commitment to the needs to the client system, and (3) objectivity and self-awareness on the part of the worker.

SOCIAL WORK ROLES AND RELATIONSHIP

In studying this brief review of relationship, one will readily note that with the exception of Pincus and Minahan the concept of the professional relationship has been most thought about, and most written about, by persons concerned with the one-to-one or one-to-group *helping* relationship. However, as Pincus and Minahan point out, in addition to the direct helping relationship social workers carry many other types of relationships. They may be involved with landlords, teachers, employers, and even boards of directors and executives of other agencies on behalf of their clients. Or workers, noting that a number of the parents with whom they work are concerned about drug problems, may help their agency develop a special seminar for workers on the subject of drug use. Another worker may be helping agency representatives develop plans for increased agency coordination on the assumption that this will be helpful to clients. A third may be lobbying for a law requiring that all group insurance carried by employers for employees must cover the pregnancies of unmarried as well as married employees and the pregnancies of minor daughters of employees. In all of the above situations, the workers would be involved in relationships with others. However, these relationships are neither with clients nor are they helping relationships per se, in that the worker offers no services to the other persons in the relationship and carries no professional responsibility to help them with their personal problems or development.

Social workers engaged in administration, policy, planning, and organization activities often carry a client relationship with the system in which they are involved, but the responsibilities they assume within this relationship are quite different from those of the direct services helping relationship. In these relationships, too, they carry no responsibility to help the other system with personal problems or to provide personal growth experiences for any individual member or the group as a unit. Rather, they are involved in helping the client system to change another (target) system in regard to certain professional policies and programs.

It is our position that all social work relationships carry certain common elements, but that the mix and importance of the elements are different in different types of relationships. Relationships may be classified along two axis: (1) the role of the worker within the change agent system, for example, as helper, administrator, policymaker, and/or researcher and (2) the type of system with which the change agent is involved, for example, the action system, the target system, or the change agent system, as well as different composition and purpose of the client system. However, although relationships may differ with the interaction of elements along these axis, all social work relationships have purposes that have some common aspects because they embody the normative purposes and values of the profession although not necessarily the operational and the unique aspects. All social work relationships involve elements of power and authority, but these elements may be lodged in persons other than the social worker especially in situations involving policymaking or organizational change.

All professional relationships involve self-discipline and self-knowledge paired with the capacity for free, genuine, and congruent use of self. However, different types of relationships may involve different qualities of awareness and the use of different elements of the self. Some relationships particularly those in work in planning, policymaking, and administration, may call for self-awareness in problems dealing with power and status, competitive feelings, and impatience with colleagues; others, particularly those with individual clients or groups, may call for awareness of one's fear of dependency or the need to do for others. One can deal with other persons and systems better if one has some sensitivity to their situation and goals and some empathy for them. However, the content of the empathetic understandings will vary greatly. All social work relationships are emergent and are affected by time and place. In all professional relationships social workers are representing something beyond themselves, either their agency or their profession, and all practitioners share a commitment to client welfare as a base for their professional activities. There are seven essential elements that are a part of social work relationships: (1) concern for others, (2) commitment and obligation, (3) acceptance and expectation, (4) empathy, (5) genuineness, (6) authority and power, and, overriding and shaping all the rest, (7) purpose. In order to carry their professional relationships with professional skill, workers will need to make the following qualities a part of their professional selves: maturing, creativity, the capacity to observe self, the desire to help, courage, sensitivity, and the ability to endure ambiguity.

Although it is our belief that all social workers need to have a grasp of the elements discussed in this chapter, we also believe that these elements of the professional social work relationship are used differentially and that the variables affecting their use may be expressed in the following model (Fraley, 1969, pp. 145–54):

1. The purpose of the relationship.
2. The position of the practitioner in the change agent system.
3. The role of the worker and the role of the other in interaction (remember the earlier description of the differing perceptions of role and their importance).
4. The role and position of the other in the larger social systems of which both worker and other are a part (the community, church, social groups).
5. The goal toward which the social worker is directing change activities.
6. The goal toward which the other systems are directing their activities. Note that in the relationship between client system and change agent system, it is assumed that the goal is to develop a relationship that allows for working together. However, relationships between the change agent and individuals in the target system or the action system may involve relationships of cooperation, negotiation, or conflict.
7. The form of communication. In the direct, helping relationship between an individual client and the practitioner as the change agent, communication is usually verbal. However, in the relationship between practitioners and their own change agent system, or between the change agent and action or target systems, many other forms of communication may be used, such as letters, reports, and so on. It is important that the practitioner be skilled in the use of all methods of communication.
8. The skill of the worker in decision making and the use of appropriate intervention methods.
9. The type of system with which the worker interacts—the practitioner may work toward change in a client system that consists of an individual, group, organization, or community; or workers may work with individuals or groups representing other than client systems.

As an example of these points, Gisela Konopka (1963, pp. 107–116) has written that the relationship between the social worker and the small, helping group differs from that of the social worker involved with an individual in the following ways: (1) members support each other and are not alone with authority, (2) there is greater informality, (3) members are surrounded by others in the same boat and there is a feeling of identification impossible in casework, (4) members are not bound to accept other members, (5) the worker is shared, and (6) there is a lack of confidentiality within the group.

PURPOSE AS AN ELEMENT OF RELATIONSHIP

As was pointed out at the beginning of this chapter, all human beings have experienced connections with other human beings that we call relationships. Most of us are capable of, and most of the time are involved in, many sets of simultaneous relationships. In social intercourse many of us drift into "relationships" with others without being aware of just how or why they developed. However, few of us continue relationships with others without some reason; there is something that brings us into contact with them and some reason why the interaction is continued. When one becomes involved with another person, the nature of one's purpose, goals, or intent, together with one's perception of the other individual's purpose, goals, or intent will determine how one behaves toward that individual and how the relationship will develop.

If purpose is a part of all relationships, why does it need to be discussed as a special part of professional relationships? And how does purpose differ in professional relationships as compared with personal relationships? That the relationship is purposive and goal directed does not give the social work relationship its special mark. What makes the social work relationship special is that its purpose and goal are conscious and deliberate and come within the overall purpose and value system of the profession.

In Chapter 1 the discussion centered on the purpose of social work practice—the changing or altering of something in the interaction of people and their environment so as to improve the capacity of individuals to cope with their life tasks in a way reasonably satisfying to themselves and to others, thus enhancing their ability to realize their aspirations and values. In Chapter 3 the main points dealt with how professional values limit and shape what we do as social workers. These two factors, the overall purpose of the profession and its value system, limit and focus the purpose of the social work relationship so that influence is not used capriciously. This is called the normative limits of purpose in the social work relationship—the normative purpose of all social work relationships is some kind of change in, or development of, a human or social system to the end that the capacity of individuals to cope with their life tasks and to realize their aspirations and values is improved.

In addition to being shaped by the normative purpose, each social work relationship will be deliberately and consciously shaped, in part, by the purpose of the given "type" of encounter. For example, the "helping relationship" is distinguished by a particular type of purpose—an increase in the coping capacity of the client system. However, a social worker may attempt to convince a legislative committee of the necessity for increasing state aid to school systems so that special education classes or open schools for dropouts may be established. The different purpose of this interaction will be critical to the way the relationship develops and is utilized. This aspect of purpose can be termed the *operational purpose* of the relationship. One of the critical differences among types of social work relationships is that they are governed by different operational purposes even though they share a normative purpose. Within the overall limits set by the normative purpose, the operational purpose determines the outer parameters of a relationship.

Besides the normative and operational purpose, each social work relationship will have a unique, individual purpose. And these unique purposes will be affected by time: the immediate, unique purpose of this particular interaction will differ from the long-range purpose of a series of interactions. Thus, Mrs. Jones may have become involved in a helping relationship because she wants to have an enduring and happy marriage (a longtime purpose), but when she comes in today she may want help about the way she responded this morning to her husband's criticism of her housekeeping (an immediate goal which is a step to the long-term goal). The outreach worker at a community center may be involved with a street group in discussions about using the center for its meetings. The worker's immediate purpose is to provide the group with a better meeting place, while the longtime purpose may be to help the group develop less destructive activities.

It is the position of the authors that, while the normative and operational purposes of any social work relationship may be implicit, the social worker needs to be able to clearly formulate the unique, immediate purposes of professional contacts with others and that such purposes should be verbally shared with them. (With some clients who have little acquaintance with the "talking therapies," it might be helpful to discuss the normative and operational purposes as well.) A study by Mayer and Timms (1970) shows that one difficulty in establishing a helping relationship with certain clients is their lack of understanding of the purposes and values of the professional person. Ideally, in the helping relationship, the unique purpose should come out of mutual consideration of what the client wants; but be that as it may, it is the worker's obligation to see that purpose is established. A professional relationship is formed for a purpose consciously recognized by all participants and ends when that purpose has been achieved or is judged to be unachievable. This understanding or perception of purpose sets certain norms for how persons will behave toward one another in the relationship and how the relationship will develop. (Purpose will be considered again in Chapter 8.)

DEVELOPMENT OF RELATIONSHIP

This brings us to a critical point. Relationship in a social work helping process does not emerge spontaneously and whole out of some mysterious chemistry of individuals in interaction but develops out of purposive interaction, out of the business with which the worker and the client (or other system) concern themselves. It cannot be not presumed that the client is looking "for a helping relationship" when entering the social work situation, but rather that the client comes out of concern about a problem in which the professional relationship is instrumental in working toward a solution. This means that we do not speak of the worker's "establishing a relationship" or "offering a relationship"; neither do we speak of needing a good relationship before difficulties can be discussed. The relationship comes out of the communication about difficulties. It grows and develops out of purposive work. The professional relationship as an affective, experimental interaction should develop as necessary to the task. It is not necessarily pleasant or friendly; sometimes the problem is worked out in reaction and anger, in conflict as well as in collaboration or bargaining. A wise social worker writes that "the attempt to keep the relationship on a pleasant level is the greatest source of ineffectual helping known to people (Keith-Lucas, 1972, p. 18). Seek relationship as a goal, "and it will generally elude one." But in a helping situation a relationship will grow wherever people demonstrate to others by their actions and words that they respect the other, that they have concern for them and care what happens to them, and that they are willing both to listen and to act helpfully (Keith-Lucas, 1972, pp. 48–49).

The fact that the relationship develops out of purposive work means that it has motion and direction and emergent characteristics. It grows, develops, and changes; and when the purpose has been achieved, it comes to an end. The time structure is another variable which directly affects the nature and rate of the development of the relationship. Whether time limits are imposed on the process arbitrarily by outside forces or are imposed as necessary for task accomplishment, they have a deep effect on the emergent quality of the relationship. It is generally known that the frequency of meetings and the amount of time the participants spend together affects the climate of the relationship and the speed with which it develops. The authors believe that the imposition of individualized time limits consonant with a shared unique purpose will increase the effectiveness of the joint purposive work. The setting in which the worker and the other system find themselves will also affect relationship, since the setting interacts with time and purpose. In every instance the operational purpose will be affected by the setting and the worker's position within it; and in most instances the limits of the purpose will also be imposed by the setting and the worker's position within it. This is to be expected, since the unique purpose of the relationship must fall within the parameters of the operational purpose.

Relationship is subject to differentiation and differential use. The kind of relationship that develops between social workers and the system with which they are interacting will depend on the particular combination of a number of variables. The overriding variable is purpose, but other variables combine with purpose to form the relationship: the setting in which the worker and the system come together; the time limits of the process; the individuals or groups involved and the interests they represent; the capacities, motivations, expectations, and purposes of those involved; the problem which brings practitioner and system together and the goals each has for its resolution; the qualities of the workers and what they bring of themselves, their knowledge, and their skills; and the actual behaviors of the members of the relational system is transactions over time.

In the helping process the relationship may be used in one of two ways. The worker may use the relationship to sustain the clients as they and the worker work on the problem, or the consideration of the relationship itself may become the task, and the client and worker may focus on the way the client uses this as a prototype of the problems they may have in other meaningful relationships and interactions. Certain problem-focused groups, too, may consist of individuals where the problem-to-be-worked is of their interpersonal transactions with each other, or where the relationship between the worker and the group or the relationships between various members may become the focus of the group's attention. In work with task groups, the relationship between the worker and group, and the relationships between the members, is used to sustain the members as they work on a problem common to all of them but external to their relationships with one another.

It is now time to turn to the workers and what they, as professional helping people, are expected to bring to the helping relationship. Both the worker and the client (or the other system, if this is not a helping relationship) bring to the relationship irrational elements, nonrational elements (emotion, feeling, affect), and rational elements (intellectual and cognitive qualities). In the case of both the worker and the other system these elements come from (1) past experiences that have affected and developed the ability of the individuals to relate to others; (2) the here and now physical and emotional state of those involved; (3) the here and now thoughts or mental images of each individual about him or herself, the process, and the problem; (4) each person's anxiety about the present situation and about the person in it; (5) each person's expectations of how one should behave and what should come out of the interaction; (6) each person's perception of the other, or others, involved; (7) the values and ideals shared in common by the participants in the process; and (8) the influence of other social and environmental factors (Goldstein, 1973, pp. 139–50). However, since workers present themselves as the professional people in the relationship, and because of this are often allowed to share in the most private and sensitive aspects of vulnerable people, they carry special responsibilities for what they bring to the helping process.

If readers will now reexamine the attempts of earlier authors to explain or describe what the worker should bring to the helping relationship, they will find that most of these attempts deal with the communication of certain affective attitudes. While through the years social workers have used different words to express what they saw as the nature of the helping relationship, the notions of what kind of worker behavior is necessary to what particular relationship have changed relatively little. They have simply been better elaborated and differentiated over the years. The literature of other human service professions also discloses that their professional helping persons have developed very similar concepts. Some of these concepts have been broken down into smaller units and have been the object of experimental study, some are very well established because they are based on the clinical observations of many professional helping people over many years with many clients (Truax & Mitchell, 1971). Thus most human service professionals use similar words to describe the emotional quality of the helping relationship. It is generally agreed among professional people in the human service professions that certain qualities are necessary within a human relationship for growth and change to take place.

We believe that all these various qualities can be classified into six groups of essential elements of all professional relationships: (1) concern for the other, (2) commitment and obligation, (3) acceptance and expectation, (4) empathy, (5) authority and power, and (6) genuineness and congruence. These elements will be used according to the purpose and type of relationship (the seventh group).

ELEMENTS OF THE RELATIONSHIP

Concern for the other

To put this as simply as possible, concern for the other means that the worker sincerely cares about what happens to the client and is able to communicate this feeling. In the helping relationship concern for the other involves "the sense of responsibility, care, respect, knowledge of other human beings and the wish to further their lives" (Fromm, 1956, p. 47). It is an *unconditional* affirmation of the client's life and needs—wanting clients to be all they can be, and to do all they want to do, *for their own sake*. Those last four words are critical.

It is obvious that if we want to help others we must become deeply involved with them, and we need to want for them what they would want for themselves as we would want for ourselves what we want for ourselves. However, there is a danger in this, as the closer our emotional relationship with an individual the more likely we are to become overinvolved out of desire to see the trouble removed or the problem solved. When we feel that someone else's problem is our own problem, when we are unable to tolerate the thought of our own pain and need to have the client succeed because that is what we want, rather than to offer what the client wants or needs, then we are too involved.

True concern for another in the helping relationship means that we offer our skills, our knowledge, ourselves, and our caring to the client to be used (or not used, as the case may be) in the client's movement toward desired goals. It means that (within certain limits of purpose, time, and place) we respond as the client needs us rather than as our need to help demands, that we care enough for the other to leave him/her free to fail. For most of us it is so much easier and more satisfying "to do" than to stand and wait (but "he also serves who only stands and waits") that we convince ourselves that concern is expressed through "doing" rather than through "an active waiting." To be truly concerned means that we are willing to be the "agent of a process rather than the creator of it" (Keith-Lucas, 1972, p. 104).

Keith-Lucas (1972, p. 103) gives us an excellent summary of this notion when he writes that concern

> means the willingness to let the helped person decide to what extent and under what conditions he is willing to be helped. It does not mean necessarily agreeing to help under these circumstances, or even refraining from pointing out that help is not possible under them. Nor does it mean refraining from offering what help is available, or even, if the need is desperate, intervening in an attempt to get help started. But it does mean, ever and always, treating the helped person as the subject of the sentence, serving his interest, allowing him all possible freedom to be what he wants to be.

Sometimes workers equate this business of concern for others with "liking." It is the position of the authors that notions of "liking" or "disliking" are misleading, and that to ask workers to "like" everyone often results in the denial or repression of feeling rather than a change in it. What we are speaking of in the use of the concept of concern is a sense of so caring for the other (as the subject of our interactions together) that personal feelings of liking or disliking (which are, after all, related to the person as the object of the response) no longer have any meaning. Again according to Keith-Lucas (1972, p. 106):

> What the helping person develops is a feeling to which liking and disliking are wholly irrelevant. This is what is meant by concern. It means to care what happens

to another person quite apart from whether one finds the person attractive or unattractive.

Under the rubric of the concept of concern we would place many descriptive words used by other authors in discussing the helping relationship, words such as *warmth, liking, support, nonjudgmental respect, expectation,* and *understanding.* Some of these words are descriptive of emotions and attitudes that also fall partially under other concepts; for example, *nonjudgmental respect* is also a part of acceptance and will be discussed in some detail when that concept is taken up.

Understanding may also be a part of other attitudes, but it should be pointed out here that it is an important part of this concept that workers seek understanding out of concern for the other person and out of desire to help in a way that can be used, not out of their own need to know, or understand, for their purposes. It is always disturbing to hear a social worker use the amount and extent of the material that the client "felt free to share with me" as the test of a helping relationship or the "success of an interview." Sharing oneself with a helping person is never an easy or an unmitigatedly positive experience. Knowing this, and being concerned for the privacy and rights of the client, workers seek knowledge about a person, or understanding of the person, only because they are concerned to help. Workers seek only so much understanding as is necessary for the process of helping. To seek knowledge for the sake of knowing, or in order to demonstrate skill at interviewing to others, is, again, to make the client the object rather than the subject of our efforts.

We communicate this attitude of concern and respect in any type of relationship to the people with whom we are working by, among other things, being on time for interviews or conferences; by making appointments before visiting the home or office (which says that the worker respects them and their privacy and wants them to have the opportunity to present themselves as they wish to); by seeing that interviewing or conference space is as attractive as it can be made; by dressing in the way that their culture says is "appropriate to a helping person offering service to a *valued* person"; and by concerned listening.

For the worker, concerned listening is not a passive "hearing." It is an active search for the meaning in, and an active understanding of, the client's communication. One may well disagree with what is being said, but one must value the sharing that is going on. In a helping relationship particularly, the worker values the client's offering of feelings, thoughts, and ideas. The high feeling in a situation heavy with conflict should not obscure the worker's need to hear accurately. In the helping relationship the worker must, in one way or another, convey recognition of the value of the client's communication and the worker's desire to understand it. Responding to the content of the client's communication with relevant questions or comments in the search for understanding is one indication of responsive caring; an expressed desire to understand often conveys concern better than a statement of already achieved understanding.

Concern for the other means that workers view clients as uniquely valuable human beings and in a helping relationship this means that, in addition, workers transcend their own needs and view of the problem and lend themselves to the serving of the clients' interests and purposes of getting together.

Commitment and obligation

Persons cannot enter into interrelationships with others in a meaningful way without assuming the responsibilities that are linked to such interactions. These responsibilities may best be expressed in the concept of *commitment* and in its corollary, *obligation.* In the helping relationship, both client and worker must be bound by commitments and obligations if the purposes of the relationship are to be achieved. A commitment to the conditions and purposes of the relationship and to an interdependent interaction, built upon involvement and investment, allows the client to feel safe and thus to reduce the testing behavior and trial-and-error searching that usually mark the beginning of a relationship. This allows clients to turn their attention and energy to the task at hand rather than to employ this in self-protection. Once a commitment to the relationship has been established, and the limits of time, place, and purpose have been accepted, each participant is able to depend on the predictability of the other's behavior, attitudes, and involvement.

The earlier writings on the helping relationship seldom mention commitment and obligation, but recently there has been more and more social work literature that speaks of the helping contract. Usually, this phrase means that the expectations and terms of the commitments and obligations of both client and worker are explicitly shared. This defining of commitment and obligation, along with the clarification of purpose, time, and setting is an important process and will be discussed in greater detail in Chapters 9 and 10. However, whether or not commitments and obligations are explicitly defined, they are an important, and inescapable, part of every professional relationship involving the giving and taking of help.

Any person asking for help from another is acutely, if unconsciously, aware of the necessity for commitments and the taking on of obligations; and it is often the fear of what may be involved in the expectations and obligations of the commitments that keeps the person from seeking help. The general obligations that clients are usually expected to assume are an open and honest presentation of the problem, of their situation, and of their ways of coping that relate to the problem; an accommodation to the minimum procedural conditions of the helping relationship, such as coming to a certain place at a certain time for an interview and working as they can on the selected problem. Clients are expected to assume these obligations as they can, and their commitments can be renegotiated without penalty.

The worker assumes more binding commitments and obligations and cannot renegotiate the contract without the consent and participation of the client. The worker's obligations include the responsibility to meet the essential procedural conditions of the relationship in the fullest way—being present at prearranged times and places and in certain emergency situations as well; keeping the focus of the work together on the client's problem;

offering a relationship that is conducive to sharing, growth, and change. If these commitments to the contract are violated without adequate reason and adequate explanation to the clients, it is certain that clients will question the worker's desire to help. Perhaps worse, clients may interpret such a violation as a message that we do not consider them important. Being present when we are needed carries a connotation that we think the client important, and being absent or late when we are obligated to be present carries a connotation of rejection.

Thus far the helping relationship has been the focus of discussion. However, in summary, we would broaden our comments to define commitment as an involvement with a client, a client system, or other systems that is unqualified by our idiosyncratic personal needs. It is a freely determined wish to further the purpose of the relationship without the expectation of returns that support a sense of worth, add to our self-esteem, or preserve our status. This commitment is communicated through a resolute consistency, constancy, responsible follow-through, and the preservation of the other's dignity and individuality. This preservation demands more than an awareness of the other's dignity and individuality; it involves actions based on sensitive and thoughtful understanding of the other and the other's position. Commitment requires that the workers assume a simultaneous responsibility and accountability for what they say and do to the client, the client system, or other systems; to the professional system which sanctions their right to offer help; and to themselves (Goldstein, 1973, p. 74).

Acceptance and expectation

In most discussions of acceptance in helping relationships one finds notions to the effect that this means the communication of a nonjudgmental attitude as well as efforts to help workers differentiate between accepting the person and accepting the person's actions. We would prefer that workers regard acceptance as more than a refusal to judge and that they try not to distinguish between a person and the person's actions. We would like them to consider acceptance as an active verb—*to accept*—meaning to receive as adequate or satisfactory, to regard as true, to believe in, to receive what the other offers. To accept others means to receive what they offer of themselves, with respect for their capacity and worth, with belief in their capacity to grow and mature, and with awareness that their behaviors can be understood as attempts at survival and coping. Acceptance means acting in the recognition that the essence of being human is having problems, making choices (good and bad, wise and foolish), and participating in the shaping of one's destiny with the resources at one's command. Therefore, a better meaning than "to refuse to judge" would be "to actively seek to understand."

The basic elements in acceptance are perhaps knowing, individualization, and trust or expectation. *Knowing* relates to one's efforts to take in and understand other people's reality and experience. Their values, needs, and purposes; to acquire some idea of where other people come from, of their life and frame of reference. *Individualization* means the capacity to see the person as a unique human being with distinctive feelings, thoughts, and experiences. The individual must be differentiated from all others, including ourselves. Assumptions must not be made about others based on generalized notions about a group, a class, or a race, although there is a need to appreciate and understand the manner in which race, class, and sex influence client-worker transactions. *Trust* or *expectation* means that workers have a belief and faith in the capacity of individuals for self-determination and self-direction—that they consider it the right and responsibility of each individual to exercise maximum self-determination in the person's own life with due regard for the welfare of others.

Acceptance of the client does not just occur. It grows from the roots of a fundamental belief and faith that the inherent processes of individual development will lead a person toward greater maturity when such processes are fostered and matured, and it develops as one seeks to understand the feelings, thoughts and experiences, resources and lack of resources, opportunities and deprivations that have led the individual to making certain choices. In fact, it is our conviction that one finds it almost impossible to be judgmental when one is fully engaged in a cooperative journey to the understanding of another. One cannot understand if one is observing another through the lenses of what is right or wrong, good or bad. Most human behavior is purposive, and if one can understand the purpose of behavior, then it becomes understandable rather than right or wrong.

Acceptance does not mean that we always agree with the other person. It does not mean that we forego our own values in order to agree with or support the client's values. It does not mean that clients are excused from the world in which they must live. It means rather that workers may present the importance of, and the belief in the importance of, behaving in socially appropriate ways in keeping with established laws and regulations at the same time that they seek to understand the intense anger that drives clients to act impulsively against certain limits and regulations and that workers can empathize with their need to strike out. True acceptance carries with it an assumption that people act as they must in the complexity of their particular human situation and that they are what their nature and their environment, coupled with their vision, permits them to be.

Thus it can be seen that self-determination, nonjudgmental respect, sensitivity, individualization, expectation of growth, and understanding are all part of the general notion of acceptance. One of the most effective ways to communicate acceptance is to try to understand the position and feelings of clients. This can be done by commenting on their communication in ways that indicate a desire to understand or to further understand what they are saying, or by asking questions that are related to the content they are trying to communicate and thus to reveal that you heard and are interested in understanding them.

"A unique characteristic of human beings is that their mental representations of the future powerfully affect their state of well-being in the present" (Frank, 1978, p. 1). Not only does the type of expectations of the future affect the state of well-being in the present, but it also affects behavior in the present which in turn affects present and future sense of well-being and future behavior. Freud wrote: "Expectation colored by hope and faith is an effective force with which we have to reckon . . . in all our attempts at treatment . . ." (Frank, 1978, p. 1). Expectation is a potent force with which social workers have to reckon in all their transactions with other human systems. There are at least three elements of expectation that are important for social workers to consider: (1) how they feel about the system's ability or desire or willingness to change, and their ability to contribute effectively to the change in the situation of the client or target system, (2) the expectation of the social worker held by the system involved, and (3) the system, particularly the client system's expectation of the effect of the helping process.

There has been considerable research in support of the notion that the change agent's expectation that the client system is capable of growth and change, learning and problem solving has a powerful effect on that growth and change. Teachers given a class of students that had a history of learning problems were told that the class was very bright and capable. Not only did the class achieve far beyond what anyone knowing their history would have predicted but at the end of the year IQ tests showed a 20-point improvement. Psychology students, told that a group of experimental rats had been specially bred to run mazes, discovered that indeed this group of rats were unusually able in such behavior. The fact of the matter was that this particular group of rats was randomly selected from the shipment of rats that had arrived at the laboratory that day. The key to the difference in the performance of the rats lay in the students' expectations of their exceptional performance and the way the students' communicated their regard and expectation to these animals by their handling of their subjects.

In medical practice there have been numerous double-blind studies in which patients improve regardless of whether they are given placebos or medication. These improvements are powerful indicators of the importance of the attitude of the attending doctors. Because the physician believed that the placebo was a powerful medication, the physician expected improvement and showed increased interest in the patient's progress in treatment. Both these attitudes had tremendous impact on the patient's improvement. In social work, Ripple found that when the worker was strongly encouraging and optimistic as to outcome the client tended to continue with the worker; while a bland, or neutral attitude of the worker was associated with discontinuance (Ripple, Alexander, & Polemis, 1964, pp. 199–203).

This evidence would support the principle in our relationships to all social systems, to all human beings encountered in the professional life, that social workers need to be very aware of their inner feelings about the system with which they work. The social workers who are most effective in the helping process (or other change) will be those who expect that their clients (or other systems) can and will change in their own way given appropriate help and support. To go back to the concepts from ego psychology: social workers must be convinced of the power of the push toward growth in all of us if they are to be effective change agents.

The second element of expectation with which we must be concerned is the client's (or other system with which we are working) expectation of what we will do to help. Over and over again studies of the effectiveness

of social work help point to the importance of the client's expectation of
social workers' behavior. To quote a cogent example from Mayer and Timms
(1969, p. 1):

> My husband's gambling was driving me around the bend and I thought maybe the
> Welfare could help me do something about it. But all the lady wanted to do was
> talk—what was he like when he gambled, did we quarrel and silly things like that.
> She was trying to help and it made me feel good knowing someone cared. But
> you can't solve a problem by *talking* about it. Something's got to be done.

While this woman received some help by her contacts with the social worker,
she was "dismayed and perplexed by the worker's approach and . . . failed
to return after several sessions" as she could not see that anything was
being accomplished. Clients will probably not be helped from social work
unless their expectations are in accord with what actually happens in their
transactions with the practitioner. This principle can be stated another way
by drawing from our earlier development of role theory: The more congruent
the notions of client and worker are as to what will be going on between
them in their work together, the more effective that work will be. If the
expectations of the worker's behavior are highly discrepant with what actually occurs, the client will rapidly withdraw from involvement in the relationship.

This discussion points out the importance of exploring with the client
in the initial contact what it is that the client (or any other system) expects.
Is this expectation congruent with what can be done in the given situation?
If it is not, what can be done, what is the worker prepared to do, or what
is seen as what ought to be done? At this point it becomes critically important
to both the helping process and the helping relationship that the matter
be discussed. Through this discussion either the other system's or the workers' behavior must be altered and changed in such a way that they are
congruent if workers are to be helpful.

The third important element in expectation is the client's (or other system's) belief that good results will follow from their interaction with the
social worker. Expectations of the future that are critical to the change
process are found in client attitudes of trust and faith. In trusting social
workers the clients (or other systems) not only must perceive them as competent and helpful at the present moment, but they must also perceive the
workers as competent and helpful over time. For example, in a group of
clients seen for approximately six weeks in a mental health clinic, hope
scores before treatment showed a positive correlation with improvement
after their case was closed. (Gottschalk, 1973). There are many examples
of this from medicine such as the finding that patients' scores on an acceptance scale before open heart surgery were considerably better predictors
of poor postoperative recovery or death than the actual severity of their
disease (Frank, 1978, pp. 3–5).

Empathy

All the authors cited in the first section of this chapter agree that empathy
is a necessary quality of the helping relationship. *Empathy* is the capacity

to enter into the feelings and experiences of another—knowing what the other feels and experiences—without losing oneself in the process. The helping person makes an active effort to enter into the perceptual frame of the other person without losing personal perspective, but, rather, using that understanding in order to help the other person. In an article on "Being Understanding and Understood: Or How to Find a Wandered Horse," Wendell Johnson (1951) tells of how experienced western cowboys demonstrated an uncanny ability to find a lost horse:

> The experienced western cowboy was able to find a lost horse with uncanny ability. I understand that he did this by working at the job of trying to feel like a horse. He asked himself, "Now what kind of reason would I have for wandering away if I were a horse? With such a reason where would I go?" Apparently, it is possible to empathize with a horse a good deal—to feel like a horse to a suprising degree.
>
> At any rate, the cowboy would imagine that he was a horse, that he had the horse's reason for going, and then he would go to the place he would go if he were a horse—and usually he would find the horse.[1]

The cowboy found the horse because he was able to feel as if he were the horse—to feel and think as the horse might feel and think. However, since he was not a horse, having found the horse he brought it back.

Carl Rogers (1966, p. 409) defines empathy as "the perceiving of the internal frame of reference of another with accuracy, and with the emotional components which pertain thereto, as if one were the other person but without ever losing the 'as if' condition." Keith-Lucas (1972, pp. 80–81) points out that empathy is the worker's understanding of the feelings the other has about the situation, knowing inside oneself how uncomfortable and desperate these feelings may be for the client, but never claiming these feelings for oneself as the helping person. He goes on to differentiate between pity, sympathy, and empathy with a very cogent illustration:

> Consider three reactions to someone who has told us that he strongly dislikes his wife. The *sympathetic man* would say, "Oh, I know exactly how you feel. I can't bear mine, either." The two of them would comfort each other but nothing would come of it. The *pitying man* would commiserate but add that he himself was most happily married. Why didn't the other come to dinner sometime and see what married life could be like? This, in most cases, would only increase the frustration of the unhappy husband and help him to put his problem further outside himself, on to his wife or his lack of good fortune. The *empathetic person* might say something like, "That must be terribly difficult for you. What do you think might possibly help?" And only the empathetic person, of the three, would have said anything that would lead to some change in the situation.

Empathy requires what may seem to many beginning workers to be antithetical qualities—the capacity to feel an emotion deeply and yet to remain separate enough from it to be able to utilize knowledge. Methods of reasoning are necessary if one is to make an objective analysis of the problem and the possibilities of solution. Even as workers let the full awareness of clients' emotions wash over them, they are aware that they are feeling, not as clients

---

[1] Reprinted from *ETC.*, vol. VIII, no. 3 by permission of The International Society for General Semantics.

feel, but *as if* they were the clients. They must remember that the clients came to them, not to have someone share their feelings (although this is relieving) but to enlist aid in coping with a situation that feeling alone cannot resolve. If it could, clients would not need help, for they have feeling enough invested, and undoubtedly they have hard thinking and trying invested, too. They need a worker who, in standing apart, can bring some difference in feeling and thinking, and who is able, with a clear head, to manipulate or secure resources that were unavailable to the clients' influence, were unknown to clients or were not thought of by them.

In learning to be empathetic, workers have to develop the capacity for imaginative consideration of others and to give up any fixed mental image that may lead one to change reality to fit any preconceived expectation. In this workers are handicapped by two factors: (1) the set of stereotypes carried with them, which are useful in enabling them to quickly grasp the meaning of encounters in daily life but which block greater discernment; and (2) the limited symbols—words, gestures, and reports—available to them to convey another's reality. Thus the accuracy of interpretation is dependent on sensitivity and intuition; the ability to put this together in a dynamic way with all that is known about the clients (their experiences, behavior, problems, and associations), the conception of their potential and what is known about what they want and hope for; all the theoretical knowledge and helping experiences; and all the other experiences with similar kinds of people and situations—real or fantasied. Then, when workers have this mental representation of the other, they must hold it lightly, recognizing that there is always something unknown and unfelt about the other that makes any mental representation tentative, no matter how hard they have struggled to attain it, and no matter how much understanding is brought to it.

In speaking of work with handicapped children, Johnson (1951, pp. 178–179) continues:

> You simply ask yourself, "Now what are the possible reasons for behaving as this child does? If I were the child, what would be my reason for doing what I do? Just what would I be trying to achieve? What would I be trying to avoid?"
>
> You can go from there to a lot of questions, such as "How could I achieve my purposes differently? What other motives could I have? What other effects could I try to achieve, and by what other means? What changes would I have to achieve before I would be able to use other procedures, or work toward other goals?" And so forth.
>
> . . . you never see the child as a whole. You see only what you are prepared to see. You can understand only what you are prepared to understand. It does not matter what books you have read, either—at least, it does not matter as much as we think it does. You had a childhood in which conditions determined and limited what you are now going to do with the books you have read. The child will look different to you from the way he will look to any other worker. The net result is that the child somehow feels that he or she is being understood or evaluated only by one individual, and that he or she is not being evaluated in anything like a complete sense.
>
> There is another reason why we do not understand these children better than we do, a very obvious reason. It is that we do not have their handicaps . . . I

wonder, however, whether it is possible for an individual who has never had a problem—if there are any individuals like that—to have any significant insight into the difficulties of individuals who do have serious problems. The point is that if you have not had a handicap, then all you can ever have in the way of knowledge of the individual that you are attempting to help is the kind of knowledge that is verbal.[2]

Full knowledge of another being is something forever beyond attainment by anyone; it can only be approached, never achieved. It is questionable whether any client wants to be fully and totally known. There is something very frightening about someone's knowing everything about us as an individual for in knowledge lies control; so in the ordinary course of living people reveal their intimate selves only to those they trust. Without the pain of the problem and the hope that the worker can offer some help toward coping with it, few clients would be willing to share themselves with an unknown other person.

The fact that workers can never fully know another except in a limited way, and that if workers felt like the client, workers would be unable to introduce the differences in thinking and feeling that bring change, all require that workers be able to maintain a certain detachment. This demand is often more difficult for the beginning worker than the demand to feel. Each worker maintains this balance differently. This is an area in which supervision can be of great help. By comments and questions the effective supervisor helps practitioners observe themselves and be aware of their contribution to the relationships they form with others. Thus self-awareness—an essential quality of all social work relationships—grows.

While some degree of empathy is needed at the very beginning of a relationship (and without this quality a relationship cannot be formed), it is a quality of the relationship and thus is not something which workers construct by themselves. It comes, grows, and develops from the process of interaction of client and worker in which the client can be encouraged to express personal feelings more and more specifically, fully, and precisely, and the worker grows in capacity to feel with the client and in understanding of what is expressed. What clients seek, especially at the beginning of the relationship, is not full understanding, but rather to enter a relationship with a helping person in which they sense that their feelings and thoughts are acceptable and that what they express is understandable as a possible human response to their situation.

Johnson (1951) shares his notion on how workers better understand a client:

> And how can we do that? Well, I think we do it mainly in two ways. One is by never being dogmatic when it comes to how the other individual feels. We do not know for sure how another feels, and I think we ought frankly to face that. The other thing we tend to do, I think, if we have this point of view, is to be more ready to ask the child what she/he thinks about the problem and about our approaches to it.

---

[2] Reprinted from *ETC.*, vol. VIII, no. 3 by permission of The International Society for General Semantics.

Those who have attempted to help me have always wanted to ask me a good deal about how I felt about my speech problem, and about my mother and father, and so on, but seldom, if ever, have clinical workers asked me how I felt about them, how I felt about what they were doing, how I felt about their ideas. There was always a feeling that the expert was attempting somehow to force on me a point of view, an interpretation, a kind of understanding. And almost always when I would ask questions, or say perhaps, "No, no you don't quite understand . . . ," there was a tendency on the part of the clinical worker to take that to be evidence of what the psychoanalysts call "resistance." It is a rare clinician who listens really effectively to what "the case" tries to share. It could be that as clinicians we are wrong and that "the case" has something to tell us, that they are not resisting at all. They may be trying to teach us something. Some of our methods, for example, sound very good to us and they are backed up by great authorities, but when applied to a particular individual, they do not work. Some of the children and adults on the other side of the desk might be trying to tell us why they do not work.

I had a very strong feeling, most of the time, when I was on the other side of the desk, that the clinician working with me was *interested in the work*. I hardly ever had the feeling that the interest was directed exclusively at me, and I think I have noticed that sort of thing in other cases. In my own clinical work I feel quite sure that I, too, have a tendency to get interested in the theory and the techniques and somehow to lose sight of the child. It is actually hard to stay interested in (the person).[3]

Acceptance and empathy are seldom discussed in social work literature dealing with the social worker's relationship with other than client systems. However, it would seem that such elements could be of help in either cooperative or conflicted relationships that involve purposive change in nonclient target systems. Resistance to change, and conflict will be prevented to the degree that the practitioner is able to help the target system develop its own understanding of the need for change as well as an awareness of how members of the target system feel about change and what change will mean to the target system. If conflict is the chosen method of bringing change, the practitioner's ability to empathize with the feelings of the other will facilitate choosing the most effective way to become engaged in the conflict. The practitioner who is able to accept the members of a client, or a target, system as individuals with both rational and nonrational positions and who can empathize with those positions will, other things being equal, be more productive than the practitioner who does not possess these skills. The way the worker uses these skills will differ in different situations. In the helping relationship the worker may communicate empathy directly. In other types of relationship workers may use it to shape other communications.

Authority and power

The two remaining elements of a helping relationship to be discussed are (1) authority and power and (2) genuineness and congruency. Not only are these perhaps the most difficult concepts to understand, but it is the misunderstanding of the element of authority and power in helping relation-

---

[3] Reprinted from *ETC.*, vol. VIII, no. 3 by permission of The International Society for General Semantics.

ships that often affects a worker's genuineness with clients. Among other things, authority may be defined as a power delegated to the practitioner by client and agency in which the practitioner is seen as having the power to influence or persuade resulting from possession of certain knowledge and experience and from occupying a certain position. Thus there are two aspects of authority in the helping relationship. The first might be called the institutional aspect in that it comes from the social workers' position and function within the agency's purpose and program. The second aspect is psychological in that clients give workers the power to influence or persuade because they accept them as sources of information and advice—as experts in their field. A person in need of help seeks someone who has the authority of knowledge and skill to be of help. If workers accept the clients' assumptions that they carry this authority, the relationship may become infused with a sense of safety and security when the client's own powers of self-dependence fail them.

The primary characteristic of the concepts of power and authority in the helping relationship is that they are neither good nor bad in themselves. Some aspects of these elements are always present, and the attempt of social workers to abdicate their role and pretend that they carry no authority only leaves clients troubled by suspicions and doubts about why workers are unwilling to admit what they, the clients, are so aware of. This incongruence between what the client feels and what the worker says makes an authentic relationship impossible. The crucial significance of power and authority lies in how they are utilized for help.

Social workers have had a hard time with the concepts of authority and power. There has been too little examination of authority and power as factors that enter into all human relationships—all human relationships develop laws about acceptable behavior of the people involved within those relationships (Haley, 1963, pp. 1–68). This is one of the problems that workers often face in using professional relationships for other purposes than the direct helping process. The clients of the community organization worker, the research worker, and the consultant are in a different power relationship to the worker than are the clients in the helping relationship. If what this factor means for the workers and those with whom they work is unexamined (or, worse, even denied), they lack the needed knowledge to guide them. Social workers need to be able to deal with power and authority both when they exercise it and when others exercise it in relation to them.

In his discussion of authority in social work relationships, Goldstein (1973, pp. 84–86) points out that when persons require what another has to offer "that cannot be obtained elsewhere—whether one is seeking the adoption of a child, financial assistance, help with a personal problem, or professional services to assist in a social action enterprise—the relationship cannot be equalized." As the social worker's needs have no relevance to the task, "the seeker cannot reciprocate or supply the provider with any reward that can restore the balance. The fact that the seeker has limited alternatives to meet personal needs, is further heightened by the fact that workers are seen as having competence and knowledge." When social workers say, "We will meet once a week on a Monday, if that is convenient to you," or when they decide to include another family member in treatment, they are setting the conditions of the relationship. Or they may refer clients elsewhere. These are all examples of power and authority.

Genuineness and congruence

In the research that has been done on helping relationships (Truax & Carkhuff, 1967, pp. 1–2; Truax & Mitchell, 1971), it has been found that in an effective helping relationship the helping person needs to communicate four things: empathy, acceptance, unconditional positive regard (we have called this quality "concern for the other," as we find this phrase more expressive of the essential notion), and congruence. Congruence means that workers bring to the relationship a consistent and honest openness and realness and that behavior and the content of communications with, and in regard to, the client must at all times match each other (be congruent) and must match the underlying value system and the essential self as a professional person. (The qualities needed as helping people will be discussed later in this chapter.)

In order to be congruent and genuine, we must seek three things: (1) an honest knowledge of ourselves, of who and what we really are; (2) a clear knowledge of agency procedures and policies and of the professional role, both in their meaning to the worker and in their meaning to the clients; and (3) an internalization of the first two and our concern for the other, acceptance of clients, commitment to their welfare and to the authority aspects of the workers' role and position, so that these qualities are so much a part of us that we no longer need to be consciously aware of them and can turn our full attention to clients and their situation.

People who are real, genuine, and congruent in a helping relationship are ones who know themselves and are unafraid of what they see in themselves or what they are. They can enter a helping relationship without anything of themselves to prove or protect, so they are unafraid of the emotions of others. For example, unwillingness to be honest with clients about authority in a relationship, or about what will be done with the information they share (see Reading 6–1), may be a consequence of negative experiences with authority in one's own life. Therefore, we try to deny (to lie about) what the client sees so clearly is really there. To be congruent we need to have faced and examined our own feelings about many central life experiences that clients share with us, so that we know which feelings are ours and which are the client's. What are our feelings about the lies we encounter? We are angry about them and so we must be different? We want the client to see we are different and that we understand better than anyone else? Do we really? Can we free ourselves of certain behaviors and feelings we dislike? Will our being free of them help our client? Or is it better to admit that they are there so that the two of us can examine what they mean for the client? What are we afraid of, or what do we want, in denying to clients the facts about certain agency restrictions on service and about our capacity to skew these so that they do not bear so heavily on them?

This brings up the second half of the worker's awareness—the meaning of the agency role and position to the worker and to the client. Not how workers want the client to see them, but how the client does see them— as representatives of a particular agency or service. Workers and clients come together, as a rule, within some kind of bureaucratic structure. The client usually does not pay for the costs of service, or at least does not pay the full costs. So the worker is paid by someone other than the client. What do the structure of the agency, its position in the community, and the source of the funds to support its services mean to the client? Workers who have not honestly examined these questions and who have not faced what they mean both to themselves and their clients will often appear to the client to be somewhat divorced from the reality of the client's life. So being honest and real means that workers have examined their roles and tasks in relation to agency, client, and target systems and that they can assume them fully and honestly with an openness about all their parts and of their impact on the client.

Our popular culture tends to place emphasis on irrationality in caring relationships with others, to hold that true caring ought to be something impulsive and instinctive, from the heart as it may be as of this moment, uninhibited and "natural." There is a belief that to think about a feeling distorts it and makes it less an expression of what people are—as though the head were not a genuine part of the body; or as though only the heart were good, and the head must perforce be evil. This stance neglects the common theme of much of the literature of human emotion, in which the heart is held to be fickle and inconsistent, unwilling to be committed to another. Actually, congruent people need a warm and nurturing heart, an objective, open, aware, and disciplined mind, and an open channel of communication between head and heart so that they appear all of one piece to others.

There is a tendency to view *professionalism* and *objectivity* as though these qualities mean "coldness," "cautiousness," and an impersonal, re-stricted reaction to the expressed feeling of others. Actually, these ways of presenting oneself in a relationship are totally unprofessional and are related to one's own need to be self-protective, to be afraid of oneself and thus of others. Both this impersonal way of operating with others and the undisciplined, personal expression of one's impulses of the moment are self-serving modes of behavior that are destructive of the capacity to communicate congruence and genuineness in the helping relationship, which requires that the client be kept squarely in the center of concern.

Perhaps an example will illustrate this point. When a really competent woman figure skater performs a "free skating" program, the viewers do not feel that she is incongruent, or unreal, or dishonest. Instead they feel the spontaneity and creative force with which she puts her whole self into the performance. But the performance required years of slow and painful learning—it required more than a little of self-discipline and persistence, of hard, slow growth and change in the use of self. The creative, free movements of this skater are quite unnatural to the untrained beginner on ice skates. They are not in any way the "natural" movements of the skater the first time she put on skates and tried the ice. Yet, the skater does not think of each movement or gesture. In fact, if she does, she will not give a free preformance. Her performance has the effect it does because she has so internalized the demands of the task that she can give herself to it entirely and can respond freely and spontaneously to what is in herself and in the here and now situation. And as viewers watch her, they are aware that she gets great satisfaction from the use of her competence in a disciplined yet free way. She knows herself and her capacity, and there is a joy in what she does. Workers, too, should enter all professional relationships with a clear knowledge of what can be and what cannot be done, a sense of competence and a belief in what workers are doing. Satisfaction can be received in helping others. How can workers believe that the creative use of self in helping others demands less time, work, and discipline, and knowledge of self and of the limits of action than does the performance of a figure skater?

Rational and irrational elements in the helping relationship

Obviously there are cognitive elements in the professional relationship. Both workers and those with whom they interact think as well as feel in a helping transaction. Both bring knowledge and values to their association. In all professional relationships social workers need to be actively cognitive—relating what is said and done to their knowledge—and making sense out of the interchange of feelings. Much of the rest of the text will be devoted, as have the first five chapters, to setting forth the values and knowledge that the worker needs to master. It is enough to mention here that cognition is an important element of the relationship.

The irrational elements of the relationship are those elements—feelings and attitudes, inherent patterns of behavior—which are not called forth by the present situation but are brought to it, relatively unchanged by the here and now and by reality, from earlier relational experiences. They are irrational in that they are usually unconscious (and thus not available to present awareness) and in that they are, in the form in which they appear, inappropriate to the present situation.

As an example of the power of the irrational: One of the authors was once involved in a helping relationship with a family which had been referred by the school social worker because a son was emotionally disturbed. Bob was one of two sets of twins. Besides the twins, there was one other child in the family. None of the other children showed any unusual difficulty in school. After some observation of the mother's relationship to her children it became obvious that she treated Bob differently from the others. She indulged him more than his brothers and sisters and was totally unable to limit him. When confronted with examples of the different way in which she reacted to Bob, she burst into tears and said she could not deny him because he was just like her. It seems that she had always felt "picked on" as a child, and she was sure Bob felt the same way. She had been the younger and smaller of a set of twins, as Bob was, and she was sure he felt just as she did, so she was trying to help him feel better. In reality, she had no evidence that Bob felt the way she assumed he did. Nor had she ever faced the fact that she and Bob were two very different persons with two very different childhood situations. Her response to Bob was an irrational one with roots in her own painful childhood.

A further, and also important, example of the effects of the irrational in all our lives is found in the attempt to create a congruent honest working relationship across racial, cultural, or social class barriers. Individuals may master all the knowledge about the history and culture of another race; they may plan rationally how to use themselves in the relationship; but, too often, when they actually come together with a member of another race, they find feelings and thoughts rising inside them that may be quite contrary to what they want to feel and think. They condemn themselves for these forbidden feelings and deny them both to themselves and to others, yet they persist. They persist because they are irrational responses that are learned as a part of culture. All individuals live and grow up in a racist society, so they all absorb, to a greater or a lesser extent, the irrational attitudes of that society in regard to race. These attitudes become a part of all persons and are all the more difficult to understand and eradicate because of the very fact that they are irrational.

It is important that workers recognize that such irrational elements are a part of the helping relationship (indeed, of all relationships) because such realization enhances their capacity to understand and accept the expressions of clients, and because it helps them to accept the importance of their own self-awareness. The presence of irrational elements in the most knowledge-able and thoughtful of individuals makes the demand for self-awareness a constant one. All people need to exercise all the care of which they are capable in order to keep such elements in themselves from intruding inappropriately into the helping relationship.

In the development and use of the professional relationship in the service of another there is the demand that workers know themselves. It is necessary to speak of the conscious use of self that carries within it the demand for self-awareness. As one considers the differences in the development and use of the relationship with different size systems and for different purposes, it would appear that these differences are significant enough to demand a differing self-awareness on the part of the worker.

It would appear that in work with client, target, or action groups, one must be self-aware not only in relation to the group as a whole but also to each individual in the group, who relating differently, may call up different responses. Favoritism, rejection, avoidance, demands for special attention—all present the group worker with special demands in self-awareness. In the one-to-group helping process, because group relationships are concurrent with the worker-to-group relationships, workers must be aware of their push to react in areas of power and status problems, sibling rivalries, competitions, and aggressions. It would appear that considerable self-awareness and self-discipline is necessary to maintain focus and purpose while weaving the many strands of individual needs and competitions into a meaningful process. The ability to keep focused on the needs of others in the face of the group's questioning of the worker's operations or authority is a difficult discipline to achieve. Workers with groups must develop an understanding and a discipline of their own status needs, their needs to preserve face before a group, and their innate responses to open conflict.

In the one-to-one relationship, workers can depend less on immediate feedback from clients in relation to inappropriate operations so there is a greater demand to be aware of feelings and responses that are aroused in the transactions with the client that will affect the helping process. Workers need to be particularly aware of their own dependency needs and how these needs affect their reactions to the dependency needs of others and of their feelings about authority. Workers need to be conscious of any feelings of omnipotence and the need for client approval. They need to be aware of their need to take too much responsibility or assume too little with their clients and of self-expectations and the ways these affect client relationships, both in terms of subtle demands for change, growth, and performance and in terms of the bearing this has on the psychic self-determination of the client. Workers need to be aware of the points at which the client's needs and problems touch off feelings in them that may not be helpful in work with the client and the kinds of self-discipline that are effective to control such feelings.

Because of its great overriding importance in all social work practice we want to introduce once again the problems caused in the effective use of relationship by a lack of self-awareness about feeling, thinking about, and attitudes toward racial/ethnic and sex difference. A study of work with women clients revealed that the theoretical position one espoused had little to do with the social worker's stereotyped reaction to women clients (Davenport & Reims, 1978, p. 306). The theories could be used flexibly. The critical variable that resulted in rigid and stereotyped reactions on the part of social workers came from the individual's biased belief systems. It is absolutely basic to social work practice that workers be aware of their belief systems, the impact of such systems on their use of self, and that they find ways to deal with themselves so that they can work without bias with all people.

THE HELPING PERSON

It is difficult to discuss "the helping person" because there are almost as many kinds of helpers as there are people who need help. There is probably no one person who is equally effective in creating helping relationships with all people. And there is probably no one person who is an ideal helping person, so that each of us will probably lack some of the qualities a helping person should have. There are, however, certain qualities, attitudes, and approaches toward life that are found to an uncommon degree among helping people—and, thus, among social workers. There are six qualities that are seen as central to effective social work functioning. Someone once wrote that "helping relationships are created by helping people, not by helping techniques." From this point of view, this means that social work practitioners bring about system change through their use of self—of what they are— of what they have made a part of themselves including their beings, their thoughts, their feelings, their belief systems, their knowledge. In other words, what they do must be congruent with what they are seeking to become as persons.

There are many people who do not have the capacity to help others— just as there are many people who do not have the capacity to design computers or perform surgery. And neither of these jobs is simply a matter of knowledge. Both require certain kinds of people with certain kinds of talents. Among the kinds of people who are not good helpers are those who are interested in knowing about people rather than in serving them (coldly objective students of humanity); those who are impelled by strong personal needs to control, to feel superior, or to be liked; those who have solved problems similar to the problems of the people in need of help but have forgotten what it cost them to do so; and those who are primarily interested in retributive justice and moralizing (Keith-Lucas, 1972, pp. 89–108).

Maturing people

The most effective helping people usually experience themselves as living, growing, developing people who are deeply involved in the process of becoming. They do not exclude themselves from the "human condition" but view all people, including themselves, as engaged in problem solving. Not only are they unafraid of life, but they frankly enjoy the process of being alive with all the struggle that this may involve. They find change and growth exciting rather than threatening. Their anxiety and tension are at an optimum level, so they are free to take on new experiences. Thus they do not need to be "right" to defend where they are. Perhaps most of the other qualities to be discussed will stem from this quality.

Creativity

Helping people need to be nonconformist in that they need to hold most solutions to the problems of life as tentative. Conformity involves accepting prevailing opinion as fact, and this stymies openness to other solutions. However, it is necessary to distinguish nonconformity from *counterconformity,* a term which has been used to characterize a person who is always "against" authority or accepted ways of doing. Such a person is not truly independent but is motivated by a need to defend personal identity and by hostile and/or aggressive needs. Intellectual openness and receptivity suggest a state of freedom to detach oneself from certain theoretical positions or systems of thought. Creative people can allow themselves to be dominated by the problem with which they are grappling rather than search for a known solution. It is not that creative people are not knowledgeable, that they have not given a great deal of themselves to learning what is known, but that they are able, in spite of the heavy investment they have made, to hold this knowledge tentatively. This seems paradoxical to many people, and it is indeed a heavy demand, for when people invest heavily in things they tend to hold them dearly.

This brings up another paradoxical quality of creative people. Although they are often deeply committed to a problem, they are at the same time detached from it. The creative person likes complexity. They do not seek premature closure but can maintain an openness and joy in the contradictory or obscure and have a tolerance for conflict.

Capacity to observe self

Capacity to observe self is usually discussed in social work literature under the rubric of self-awareness, and it has already been discussed as an element of genuineness and congruence. It is an important capacity for the social worker and is discussed in most material that deals with the helping relationship. Perhaps the two previously discussed qualities are an important part of this capacity, which really means to be sensitive to one's own internal workings, to be involved with oneself and one's needs, thoughts, commitments, and values, yet to stand back enough from oneself to question the meaning of what is going on. This means that the helping person must take a helping attitude toward oneself as well as toward others.

We have chosen not to use the term *self-awareness* for this quality because we think it is more than self-knowledge. There have to be other qualities. Self-love and love of others, self-respect and respect for others, self-confidence and confidence in others, acceptance of self and acceptance of others, faith in self and faith in others develop together or not at all. So the capacity to observe self probably requires the ability to care deeply about oneself and one's goals, to respect and to believe in oneself and yet to be able to stand back and observe oneself as an important piece of the complex activity of helping.

This way of regarding self leads to flexibility, a sense of humor, a readiness to learn, an acceptance of one's limitations, and an openness—all of which are important qualities of the helping person. And most of all, the capacity to observe self demands courage—we need to be unafraid of what we will find. All of us, to some extent, distort in one way or another feelings that we do not want to acknowledge, but the more this is true, the less we can help others. It is the need for self-protection, the fear for self, that gets in the way of sincerity, openness, genuineness, and honesty.

Like all other human beings, social workers cannot make themselves over simply because they wish to do so. Like all other human beings, they are the product of their intellectual and physical attributes, they are shaped by the range, expansiveness, and richness of their life experiences, including their educational experiences, and by how they have used those experiences in developing their basic beliefs, values, and attitudes. However, even if we cannot remake ourselves at will, it is important in observing ourselves that we have the capacity to see ourselves as growing and developing people.

Desire to help

A deep desire to increase the ability of people to choose for themselves and to control their own lives is an absolutely essential quality of a helping person. Effective helping relationships or other social work relationships simply cannot be created and sustained without this desire. Basically, the desire is a commitment to oneself rather than to others because it must be our desire, be related to us and a commitment to ourselves. It is this commitment that gives one the courage to know oneself and the willingness to risk oneself in the service of others.

Courage

It takes great courage—not the courage of the unaware and insensitive but the courage of the person who is thoroughly aware yet does what one knows needs to be done—to take the risks with oneself and others that social work relationships inevitably demand. Workers must be willing to assume the risks of failing to help, of becoming involved in difficult, emotionally charged situations that they do not know how to handle, of having their comfortable world and ways of operating upset, of being blamed and abused, of being constantly involved in the unpredictable, and perhaps of being physically threatened. "It is only the person who can be afraid and not be afraid of this fear who is in a position to help" (Keith-Lucas, 1972, p. 100).

It takes great courage to be able to think about ourselves and others as we are. And, even more, it takes great courage and strength to directly face clients with the reality of their problems when this reality appears threatening and hurtful. And it takes courage to engage in honest thinking about others and yet to be basically for people—to be skeptical and inquiring in one's thinking, yet trusting in one's attitude toward others.

Sensitivity

Our methods of sharing ourself completely with others are awkward and imperfect even when we are committed to that sharing. For troubled people the ability to share themselves and their situation is incredibly more difficult because of all their feelings about their problems and about themselves as people with problems, and because of the threat of the unknown in the helping process. Therefore, the worker who would help needs a capacity for feeling and sensing—for knowing in internal ways—the inner state of others without specific clues. This quality probably depends on one's ability to observe even small movements and changes in others and to make almost instantaneous inferences from them, to put oneself into the feeling and thinking of others, and to avoid stereotypes. It is probably closely related to one's capacity to be open to the new and to one's readiness for change.

RACE AND THE SOCIAL WORK RELATIONSHIP

We cannot leave a discussion of the professional relationship without some mention of the impact of racial or cultural difference on the development and use of the professional transaction. It is particularly fitting that this discussion should follow the sections on rational and irrational elements in the helping relationship and on the helping person. Racist attitudes and actions are so deeply embedded in American society that it is impossible for any individual to have escaped their impact on one's conscious and unconscious selves and on the ways one relates across racial lines. It is easy to underestimate the extent of the impact of racist attitudes on individuals of all races because of the multivarious sources which subject all individuals to both explicit and implicit negative stereotypes. Implicit negative messages are more insidious, hence more devastating and difficult to deal with, yet they affect every one and all relationships.

Shirley Cooper (1978, p. 78) expresses it well when she says: "Clearly racism bites deeply into the psyche. It marks all its victims—blacks and whites—with deep hurt, anger, fear, confusion, and guilt."

Cooper urges that workers examine their thinking with special care as "efforts to acknowledge and deal with racial factors are affected by highly emotional attitudes." She points out that white people "influenced by a culture rampant with racism and unfamiliar with the intricacies and nuances of the lives of ethnic people may, even with the best of intentions, fail to recognize when social and cultural factors predominate" in their professional attitudes. Cooper (1978, p. 78) notes that "ethnic therapists are vulnerable to the opposite form of clinical error. Because they are so centrally involved, they may exaggerate the importance or impact of ethnic factors." She goes on to say that in color blindness individuals tend to lose their particular richness and complexity; and that there is a danger of no longer relating to individuals as they are but rather of relating to individuals as though they were "only culture carriers" (1978, p. 78).

Cooper (1978, p. 78) discusses the unavoidable guilt experienced by white practitioners who live in a privileged and segregated society and says that in their struggle with this guilt they may deal with it through "unrealistic rescue fantasies and activities—a form of paternalism."

> When white guilt remains unconscious, it can lead to overcompensation, denial, reaction formation, an intense drive to identify with the oppressed, and a need to offer the victim special privileges and relaxed standards of behavior no more acceptable to minorities than to the general population.

In the black practitioner, oppression produces its own personality and distortion. It may lead to costly overachievement at the expense of more normal development. Whether one achieves or does not achieve, there is the anxiety that hard-won gains, or battles lost, are not, in fact, the consequence of one's performance but rather the result of considerations based on race. With the actuality of one's own productivity in doubt, there are anxieties about self-worth and competence and there is no real way to measure one's own behavior (Cooper, 1978, p. 78).

In speaking of the white-black encounter within the professional relationship, Gitterman and Schaeffer (1972, pp. 280–291) say:

> One direct consequence of the institutionalized racial positions of blacks and whites is social distance. . . . As a result of these conditions, there emerge two separate and distinct experiences, each somewhat unknown and alien to the other. It is this very quality of mutual strangeness which characterizes the initial black-white encounter. It may be camouflaged, denied, or rationalized. The void may be filled by stereotyped "knowledge" and preconceptions, but the essential unknownness

remains. Not only are the two different, but, not having lived or known each other's differences, they can only speculate about them. They see each other and the world, and are in turn viewed . . . by the world, in different ways. . . .

Thus separated . . . white . . . and . . . black . . . come together . . . face each other and are confronted with the necessity of doing something together. . . . First, there is suspiciousness and fear between them. . . .

There is also anger between them. Once again, much has been written, especially in recent years, of the rage that is felt by black people. White workers also feel anger of which they may or may not be aware. They may be angry at the black client for being so troubled, or helpless, or dependent, or hard to reach. They may be angry at themselves for their inability to do very much to really help their clients, or they may be angry at the clients for being angry at them. The anger is there on some level. It is most likely that the client perceives it even if workers do not.

There is also pain between them. This pain is one of the most complex dynamics because it stems from so many different sources . . . pain and suffering connected with whatever presenting problems caused the client to seek service . . . pain at being black in America . . . pain felt by the worker in response to the client's pains . . . pain from the guilt felt by each party. . . . Most profoundly, there is guilt caused by repressed anger and other negative feelings experienced by both.

Gitterman and Schaeffer (p. 281) recommend some ways of dealing with the racial gap between worker and client. Essentially, their recommendations reflect the factors in the relationship that was discussed earlier in this chapter. They point out that the helping process is a mutual endeavor between active participants, that it takes both participants to do the job, and that they must listen to each other. They emphasize that the white worker cannot ignore or minimize the social factors that contribute to the plight of the racially different client.

Perhaps the best way to end this too brief discussion of race is to quote from the preface of the volume in which Gitterman and Schaeffer's contribution appears. Here the editor (Goodman, 1974, p. xiii) says:

The profession of social work cannot afford to sustain practices that would diminish the humanity of any group. It must deny that only blacks can treat blacks, or only whites can treat blacks, or only people of the same culture can understand each other well enough to provide help.

Social work must teach that different is not "better," nor is it "worse," it is different. And its technology must be developed, in every sense, to propagate a multiracial set of identities that will continue and extend the search for a common basis in humanity.

RECAPITULATION

In this chapter the professional relationship has been discussed. The chapter has been long and complex, but even so it does not fully express the richness and complexity of the professional relationship as it is known by workers and the other systems with which they interact in the daily struggle with human problems. We have attempted to summarize the development in social work literature of the concept of relationship, to identify the various components of relationship, to deal briefly with some of the differences in the use of these components in various types of relationships, to discuss workers themselves and their capacities, and to deal with the issue of racism in professional relationships.

A LOOK FORWARD

In this chapter are two articles that deal with special problems in professional relationships. These articles deal with the problem of dishonesty and considerations in establishing a relationship across racial/ethnic lines. They are presented to you as a means of increasing the richness of the chapter, but with no pretense that they are an adequate sampling of the rich, diverse literature on relationship. The next chapter will consider the skills of communication in social work practice.

Reading 6-1

The Impact of Professional Dishonesty on Behavior of Disturbed Adolescents*

Seymour L. Halleck

The role of dishonesty on the part of those who treat the emotionally disturbed has been inadequately examined. Thomas Szasz (1961), a provocative psychiatric theoretician, has made a beginning effort in this direction by examining the issue of lying, both conscious and unconscious, as it relates to communication of the patient to the worker. There has been no attention paid, however, to the problem of dishonesty in the other direction; namely, for the professional worker to the client or patient. Szasz touched on this issue when he discussed the need of persons in our society to maintain traditional cultural patterns by lying to their children. He postulates that much of adolescent rebellion may be related to the fact that it is during this time of life that adolescents first become intellectually mature enough to perceive that significant adults in their lives have lied to them repeatedly.

These concepts raise intriguing issues for those who are entrusted with the professional management of disturbed adolescents. Is it possible that they communicate information, values, and morals to adolescent clients that they themselves do not believe fully? Do professional workers contribute to the perpetuation of rebellious behavior or do they perhaps even precipitate it by a failure to present themselves and their world in an honest, straightforward manner? The answer to

these questions may unfortunately be a qualified "yes."

Most adults, including child-care workers, do fail at times to communicate an honest picture of the adult and adolescent world to their patients. They are often less than straightforward in presenting themselves as helping persons. In subtle ways they communicate a wish for the adolescent to develop values and moral codes that many adults would themselves have difficulty in accepting. The dishonesty described in this paper is frequently perpetuated by parents and other adults who come into contact with adolescents. While such behavior is obviously deleterious when nonprofessionals are involved, it is especially harmful when employed by a professional youth worker.

In approaching an issue as emotion-laden as lying, the author is tempted to be provocative, cynical, or pessimistic. It is not his intention to communicate these attitudes. He contends, however, that adult workers in all the clinical behavioral sciences tend to lie to their adolescent patients. The lying may at times be on a fully conscious basis; at other times it may be more or less beyond awareness. The net effect of this behavior is to confuse and at times infuriate the adolescent, which in itself may produce greater rebellion, more symptoms, and more pain—or exactly the opposite of the original goals. As is true for most dynamic situations, whether one is dealing with individuals or with groups, positive growth must often follow a painful appraisal of less acceptable behavior and motivations. A realistic examination of dishonest behavior on the part of professional workers can then be considered a painful but necessary procedure that may encourage freedom to develop new and more effective techniques.

This discussion is focused primarily on the interaction of professionals with adolescents who are either institutionalized or who are involved with community agencies. This group certainly constitutes a great majority of adolescents who come into contact with psychiatrists, psychologists, sociologists, and social workers. In some instances, particularly in private practice, when the worker may function only as the patient's—or at most the family's—agent, some of the aspects of dishonest behavior may not apply, and these exceptions will be noted. There are at least seven areas in which adolescent clients are deceived either through conscious fabrication or through subtle and unconscious communication of attitudes to which professional workers do not adhere.

THE LIE OF ADULT MORALITY

In confronting the chaotic sexuality and poorly controlled aggressiveness of the adolescent, most professional workers tend to communicate the possibility of a world in which such impulses are resolved easily. They imply that adults control their impulses and that success in the world is dependent upon such restraint. To a limited extent this is certainly true. Too often, however, they present a picture of the world that is far removed from reality and that does not take cognizance of the social usefulness of certain kinds of aggressive and sexual behavior. The adolescent boy knows that aggressiveness, and sometime unscrupulous aggressiveness, may be a prerequisite for success. He knows that the interviewer sitting behind the desk has probably struggled aggressively to gain the status of a professional position. The sexually promiscuous adolescent girl

knows (even if she has not read the Kinsey report) that on a statistical basis the professional people with whom she interacts have probably at some time in their lives been guilty of the same behavior for which she is being punished.

It may be unrealistic to communicate readily the worker's own deficiencies and therefore provide the adolescent rationalizations for disturbed behavior. There is a frequent tendency, however, to err in the other direction. Professionals communicate a picture of themselves and their world as one in which only the highest type of values and moral standards prevail. Adolescents cannot understand this. Their personal experiences, their observational powers, and their intuitiveness tell them that something is wrong. They want to like and to identify with adults, but they are painfully aware of the inconsistency or basic dishonesty in the adult's approach. They may come to believe that adults are incapable of being anything but "phony" and react by rebellious behavior or isolation from the adult world.

This type of dishonesty is seen with considerably less frequency in private psychotherapeutic interactions, especially with adults. Here the worker tries to produce a climate in which the universality of antisocial impulses is accepted and usually discussed freely. An unwillingness to extend this same honesty to a large portion of adolescent patients is a serious error. Adolescents are struggling to understand the adult world. They will learn the truth about it whether they are told or not.

THE LIE OF PROFESSIONAL HELPFULNESS

The professional worker who confronts adolescents in the courtroom, the community clinic, or the state institution serves a dual role, as an agent of the community and as a helping person. The community wants the worker to control, attenuate, or in some way modify the behavior of an individual who is causing it some distress. Workers are also interested in their clients; they feel some wish to make the disturbed adolescent a more comfortable and effective person. It is important to understand, however, that in the majority of these situations (there are exceptions in private practice) the worker does not function as an agent of the adolescent patient. The worker's salary is paid by the community. When the community's needs conflict with the adolescent's needs, it is the community that will be obeyed, and decisions are not always made entirely in the patient's interest. It is still possible within the limitations of this role for the worker to maintain an honest identification as someone who wants to help the adolescent. If workers do not communicate, however, that one of their most basic roles is other than help oriented, they are being dishonest.

Most adolescents do not seek help; they are sent. For example, take the case of an adolescent boy who has been a behavior problem in school and has been referred to the school psychologist. The boy is told that he must see a professional person and that the psychologist will try to help him. He knows, however, that the school is somewhat provoked with him and that its officials are going to act to prevent him from being an annoyance. He does not know what will be done. He does know that the school psychologist, functioning as the agent of the community, may exert a tremendous amount of power over him. As a result of his interaction with this professional worker he may be removed from school, forced to attend special classes, or even removed from his home and sent to an institution. No matter how benign a person the school psychologist then turns out to be, it is very difficult for the adolescent to perceive the psychologist as a helping person.

As long as the worker and the adolescent are aware of the fact that the professional may be participating in mutually antagonistic roles, effective communication is possible. The situation is complicated, however, when workers pretend that their only motivation in seeing the adolescent is to help. The adolescent realizes that this is obviously untrue. The adult worker is then perceived as dishonest, which only makes the adolescent want to be dishonest in return. Experienced workers have learned that the word "help" rarely evinces a positive response from adolescents. They experience it as a kind of "Kafka"-like double talk. In many settings, then, the word *help* is perceived by the adolescent as an unreliable and perhaps dangerous word.

THE LIE OF CONFIDENTIALITY

The issue of confidentiality is closely related to the problem of helpfulness. Most caseworkers, psychologists, and psychiatrists have been taught that the model for a professional helping relationship is derived from the psychotherapeutic situation. In traditional forms of psychotherapy the communications of the patient or client to the worker are considered private material to be shared with no one outside the treatment situation. Many of the techniques professional workers use in interviewing, evaluating, diagnosing, or counseling the adolescent are derived from what they were taught about psychotherapy. Often the worker behaves as though the adolescent is entitled to expect confidentiality and as though it were going to be provided. It is extremely rare for the adolescent to be told directly who is going to see the report the worker writes, who is going to read it, and with whom the case is going to be discussed.

The issue here, as with helpfulness, is that workers cannot guarantee confidentiality to the patient since they are not agents of the patient. The worker has obligations to the child's family, the clinic, the agency, or the institution. Even if after submitting an initial diagnostic report the worker begins to see the adolescent in a more traditional psychotherapeutic relationship, complete confidentiality can rarely be promised. While it is true that useful communication can take place between the worker and the adolescent without the guarantee of confidentiality, it is also true that to imply that this guarantee is extended, or to extend it with the full knowledge that it is not meant to be kept, can result in development of situations that inhibit communication. It does not take a very clever adolescent to understand that the worker has primary responsibilities to the agency and to the community. Adolescents may fully understand that whatever information they give will be shared with others and can be used in making important decisions about them. If professionals do not let adolescents know this, they will perceive their behavior as dishonest, and their communications to the adult world will be effectively diminished.

THE LIE OF REWARDS FOR CONFORMITY

The necessity of conforming to adult standards is most often communicated to adolescents whose behavior deviates from the norms of the community. To this sizable proportion of disturbed adolescents, professional workers seem to be saying, "Your behavior is unacceptable, it produces more difficulty and leads you to experience more pain. It is to your own infinite advantage to be passive, to conform, to obey." There is ample evidence, however, that in attacking the behavioral defenses of the adolescent, workers remove character armor, leaving the adolescent more susceptible to anxiety. There is really little in the way of pleasure that

can be promised to adolescents if they risk giving up characterological defenses. This has been discussed previously in terms of the problems imposed on criminals when they are viewed as "patients."

Society and the psychiatrist in particular may be imposing an almost intolerable burden on delinquents in asking them to exchange the "bad" role for the sick role. It is not surprising that the criminal looks upon the usual rehabilitation program with cynicism and distrust. Only when those in charge of treatment searchingly ask themselves what they are trying to do to delinquents when they try to make them into conforming citizens and are able to appreciate what they are giving up in accepting the sick role, can therapy be successful (Halleck, 1960).

It is always a moving, sometimes an overwhelming, experience to see an adolescent abandon behavioral expressions of conflict for a more introspective way of life. This is never accomplished without considerable pain and sometimes despair. If adolescents are told that the simple expedient of conforming to adult standards produces pleasure, they are told a lie. Conformity on the part of the adolescent certainly meets the immediate needs of the community; whether it meets the needs of the individual adolescent is questionable. When workers pretend to adolescents that it does, they encounter only confusion and anger, especially when they experience the inevitable anxieties that come when they attempt to control their behavior.

DENIAL OF LIMITATIONS

The majority of adolescents who come to the attention of community agencies are from troubled homes and lower socioeconomic groups. Many of them have been subjected to severe psychological and economic deprivations. Their educational experiences have been limited. Psychiatric studies have produced data which indicate that the effects of early emotional deprivation are to a certain extent unmodifiable (Bowlby, 1960; Engel, Reichsman, & Segal, 1956; Harlow, 1958). Deficiencies in early educational experiences may also seriously limit potentialities for achievement in the world.

The average professional worker comes from a middle-class background, which in our culture implies a far greater potentiality than that seen in most adolescent clients. (Here, of course, must be excluded selected disturbed adolescents of superior intelligence, of middle-class background, or from reasonably well-integrated homes.) Many workers fail to see that with a few exceptions they are dealing with people of limited potential who will never be like them. Failing to realize this fact, the worker may then encourage identifications, ambitions, and achievements that are not possible for the client and which leave the adolescent with a feeling of frustration.

Few workers are guilty of consciously pushing their clients to achieve beyond their limits. Many of them, however, repeatedly deny the impressive limitations of some of their patients and assure them that the development of certain identifications and goals is entirely possible. This is a type of unconscious dishonesty that may produce considerable harm. Adolescents may righteously say to themselves. Who are these people kidding? Are they trying to reassure us or reassure themselves? Maybe they are trying to humiliate us by throwing our inadequacies in our faces. They'll never understand us."

"OPEN UP; TRUST ME; ALL WILL GO WELL"

A close relationship is a foundation of any successful therapeutic interaction. Experiencing closeness to another person leads to the possibility of examining one's behavior in such a way that unfavorable personality defenses can be modified or exchanged for more useful ones. Most professional workers leave school with the feeling that they will be successful with clients if they can persuade them to be open and close. Adolescents, however, especially disturbed adolescents, frequently are struggling with some of the negative aspects of closeness that they experience as stultifying or smothering. They have begun to find certain types of relationships among their peers that provide them with a feeling of considerably more safety. To abandon movement in this direction and again attempt to develop a close relationship with an adult involves grave risk-taking for them. They are well aware that the little freedom they have gained may have to be surrendered if too much closeness develops.

If workers realize this, they can gently, tactfully, and with some humility gradually allow a meaningful, nonsymbiotic relationship to develop between them and the child. In a healthy close relationship between adolescent and adult, adolescents are allowed certain kinds of independence, dignity, and, of course, distance when they want it. The social structure in which most professional workers function makes it extremely difficult to provide this kind of relationship. They usually begin in settings in which they have tremendous power over the adolescent, who is thrown into a forced dependency. Adolescents are often forced into a relationship that they, at least on a conscious level, have not sought. The possibility of prolonged relationships is often limited by the fact that both professionals and their clients are extremely mobile, frequently changing responsibilities, jobs, and geographical locations. A sustained, intensive relationship is not a common occurrence in most situations developed in community agencies.

Professional workers are guilty, nevertheless, of continuously exhorting the adolescent to "open up; trust me; if you rely on me and share things with me, all will go well." But disturbed adolescents know that this is not true! They know that the person who is pleading with them to expose themselves may be a person with whom they will have only limited future contacts and whom they can see few reasons for trusting. They are further aware of the possibility that they can lose much in such a relationship and that the worker may not really be offering a true intimacy between equals. To adolescents it seems like a poor bargain. They feel that the worker is dishonest in offering this type of bargain and they react with fear, distrust, and cynicism.

"WE LIKE YOU BUT NOT YOUR BEHAVIOR"

Anyone who has spent much time with adolescents knows that their behavior can be provocative, frustrating, and at times infuriating. It is distressing to see how few professional workers are willing to admit honestly how angry they get with their adolescent clients. This anger frequently is rationalized with statements to the effect that "I like you but not your behavior." Sometimes the worker's anger is totally denied but comes out only through the behavior toward the adolescent. In these types of situations workers sometimes tell adolescents that they are not really angry with them but they feel that they must be disciplined for their own good, and that by depriving them of privileges or changing their situation, workers are really trying to help them. Frequently this anger is displaced onto the parents or onto other professional workers. Anyone who works with adolescents in a community or institutional setting is painfully aware of the extreme rivalry and sometimes open animosity between individual professionals and their groups. The fact is that it is almost impossible to work with adolescents

for any period of time without becoming periodically angered.

It is dishonest and unfair both to the worker and to the adolescent to deny, rationalize, or displace this anger. It belongs in the therapeutic situation and should be communicated with as much restraint, tact, and honesty as the worker is capable of providing. To do less than this establishes a basically dishonest pattern of interaction and precludes the possibility of the adolescent experiencing positive emotional growth. Adolescents know that adults at times find them intolerable and cannot be expected to cooperate or communicate with people who are unwilling to admit this fact.

PREREQUISITES TO AN HONEST APPROACH

By the time professional workers come to their first meeting with adolescents, they are encountering children who have probably been lied to repeatedly by parents and relatives. If adolescents have also had experiences with welfare agencies, this situation may have been compounded through dishonest behavior on the part of professional workers. They may by this time have learned a variety of techniques of resistance to cope with what is perceived to be the "phoniness" of adults. This situation is one of the most important contributing factors to the sullen inertia and negativism so often found with adolescent clients. A good portion of the malignant effects of this factor can be ameliorated through a change in techniques and attitudes on the part of the worker directed toward a more honest interaction. When efforts are made toward more scrupulous honesty with adolescent patients it is almost invariably gratifying to discover a child who is more open, talkative, and willing to discuss areas of life that are not ordinarily communicated. The child seems almost delightfully surprised to discover that adults can be talked to in a free and easy manner.

The methods of developing an honest approach to an adolescent patient or client are uncomplicated and straightforward. They are based on a conviction on the part of workers that they are going to be scrupulously honest with themselves and the child when the seven areas considered earlier are discussed. It is only necessary for the worker to be aware of any tendency to convey untrue attitudes and ideas and to make a constant effort to avoid doing so. A useful illustration can be obtained through outlining the behavior and attitudes of a professional who is trying to avoid the pitfalls previously discussed. The techniques and attitudes employed by this hypothetical male worker in his interactions with adolescent patients will be described. These techniques, whether utilized by youth workers, teachers, or parents, can effectively increase communication between adults and adolescents.

With respect to the "lie of adult morality" no effort is ever made by the worker to criticize, disparage, or in any way condemn the adolescent's antisocial behavior. Rather, it is considered as something the community (rightly or wrongly) will not tolerate if done openly and, most important, as something that *has not served the social or personal needs* of the adolescent. A routine and essential part of an initial interaction with any adolescent consists of a careful assessment of the net gains and losses caused by this behavior. The social usefulness of certain kinds of aggressive behavior is never disparaged. No attempt is made to discuss behavior in terms of right or wrong, neurotic or normal, or good or bad. Workers will attempt at times to communicate their own moral standards, which may or may not be more stringent than those of the patient. These are always clearly labeled as the workers' personal beliefs and it is made clear that

they may not be relevant for the patient.

The lies of professional helpfulness and confidentiality are handled directly by explaining the evaluator's own position as precisely as possible during the initial interview. The child is told who is employing the examiner, what the examiner's responsibilities to the employer are, what kind of report will be written, and exactly who will see and discuss it. Contrary to what might immediately be expected, most adolescents respond favorably to such an approach. When the rules of the "game" of interviewing are wholly apparent to them, there is little need for defensiveness or negativism. The sheer surprising impact of having an adult be so direct with them often in itself produces a favorable effect that encourages them to be more open.

To avoid taking the stand that conformity or adjustment to adult standards breeds comfort and contentment, workers must have deep and thorough understanding of the role of antisocial behavior in maintaining the adolescent's equilibrium. They must be thoroughly able to empathize with the "fun" and at times pleasure associated with behavior that flaunts rules. They must also realize that such behavior may be all that stands between feelings of hopelessness and despair. Adjustment to the adult world is not presented as something that necessarily brings pleasure but rather as a necessary and sometimes unpleasant requisite to survival. At times workers might even openly discuss conformity as a burden and warn the patient as to some of the dangers of such behavior. Such an approach provides leverage when the issue of the adolescent's rigid conformity to the peer group inevitably arises during a prolonged relationship.

Avoiding the communication that most adolescent clients have the same potential as the professional worker involves a careful attention to not confusing the worker's own needs with those of the child. Our hypothetical worker freely discusses with adolescents the problems of moving from one social class to another and makes no effort to pretend that class distinctions do not exist. The barriers to advancement which minority group adolescents profess are more often accepted as realities than interpreted as projections. The adolescent boy who has a long police record and who has missed out on many educational opportunities is not deluded into believing he can "be anything he wants." The girl who may have had one or more illegitimate children is not assured of her potential for making a favorable marriage. The worker's general attitude is that this can be a "tough world" in which only a determined few manage to overcome the deprivations of their early background.

While the worker may firmly believe that a relationship with an understanding and skilled adult promulgates favorable personality change, all efforts are made to let adolescents develop the relationship at their own pace and without extravagant, implied promise of its value. The patient is told exactly when and for how long the worker will be available. Full attention is paid to the risks the client takes in developing a relationship; sometimes these risks are actually spelled out. Strenuous efforts are made to deal with the adolescent fear of being swallowed up in one's dependency needs. "Openness" is encouraged as a necessary prerequisite to gaining understanding but it is not held out as a "cure-all" or as a goal in itself. Exhortations to trust the worker are avoided rigorously. Rather, adolescents are told that they will have to decide about the worker's trustworthiness on the basis of their own experiences.

Perhaps the most outrageous dishonesty perpetrated against adolescents by professionals involves their tendency to cover up their own angry feelings, which invariably develop toward the patient. It is surprisingly easy to tell adolescents when they are annoying and such communications, when presented in a restrained but straightforward manner, rarely have a negative effect upon the relationship. A communication such as "I find your behavior during this interview extremely difficult and I'm having trouble keeping from getting annoyed myself" may in many instances be preferable to "What's bothering you?" or "How can I help?" or even to passive acceptance of provocative behavior. Adolescents appreciate this kind of straightforwardness. It tells them where they stand and enables them to look at their behavior without having to deceive either themselves or the adult.

CONCLUSIONS

Anyone who has reared children knows that occasional dishonesty is essential if the child is to grow up with a reasonable degree of security. The truth to children, if understood, may be unbearable. If an orderly, sane, and relatively nonchaotic way of life is to be maintained, it is essential that children at times be deceived or at the very least kept in the dark as to issues they are not yet ready to master. In the treatment of adults there are clear landmarks for the worker to follow. Adults who enter psychotherapy are greeted with an atmosphere that not only condones but puts a premium on truthfulness on the part of all participants. Exceptions are made only when it is felt that the patient is too seriously ill to comprehend or tolerate the impact of truth. In these cases various deceptive practices may be used for the patient's benefit.

If one could argue convincingly that the great majority of disturbed adolescents were similar to children or to the severely disturbed adult, there would be considerable justification for withholding truth and practicing deception for the adolescent's own gain. Anyone who works with adolescents, even seriously disturbed ones, however, is quickly aware that such a comparison is invalid. Adolescents are extremely open to learning. They are in the process of discovering new aspects of the world around them, and are also increasingly preoccupied with their own inner world. Even the most disturbed adolescent has rarely developed a fixed pattern of rigid personality defenses that preclude being able to look at the truth in a reasonably open way.

The professional worker knows adolescents are capable of serious volatile impulsive behavior and do not have available to themselves the controls that most adults have learned. Perhaps much of the explanation for an unwillingness to be honest with adolescents is related to a fear that they will not be able to tolerate the truth and that it will be used in a destructive, unhelpful way. One can also speculate that dishonest behavior might be related to the frightening impact of aggressive and sexually provocative adolescent behavior

that touches upon areas of one's own problems which have not been completely understood or worked through. When workers present a dishonest picture of the world to their clients, they may really be trying to avoid the despair of facing the frightening world in which they live and thereby to reassure themselves.

To interact honestly with an adolescent, all interested adults must believe that the growth of useful personality traits is more likely to take place in an atmosphere of truth than of dishonesty. This involves a willingness to take the risk of presenting communications that temporarily disturb the adolescent and a tolerance of the possibility that many of these disturbances will be directed against the adult. Any adult who wishes to communicate effectively in this manner must of course come to terms with self-deceptions in one's own life so that they do not interfere with one's ability to face reality with others.

Reading 6-2

A Framework for Establishing Social Work Relationships across Racial/Ethnic Lines*

Joan Velasquez, Marilyn E. Vigil McClure, and Eustolio Benavides

It is well documented that disproportionately large numbers of social work clients, particularly in public agencies, are

* An original article prepared especially for this volume by the authors, two of whom have been instructors, and one a stude t, in a student unit of the University of Minnesota School of Social Work serving Latino clients in Remsey County Mental Health Center, St. Paul, Minnesota.

racial/ethnic minority group members. When we examine the use of social work services by these clients, we find a substantially higher rate of discontinuance than among majority group clients (Miranda, 1976). It is our assumption that many of these clients "drop out" of service because they do not perceive what they are offered as helpful and that the partnership which ideally evolves from engaging a client in a positive, purposeful relationship does not develop.

Our purpose here is to explore the development of the social work relationship across racial/ethnic lines based on a framework of biculturalism. Although this framework has evolved primarily from social work with Latinos, we believe it applies to work with any ethnic or racial minority group.

Defining culture as a relatively unified set of shared values, ideas, beliefs, and standards of action held by an identified people, numerous cultural groups can be identified within this country. The dominant culture integrated the values and norms of European immigrant groups as each was encouraged to drop its language and become assimilated by the majority. Minority groups with recognizable physical characteristics have also been pushed to accept the dominant culture as their own, yet have been responded to as separate and inferior groups and thus not allowed to participate fully in it. Due to this exclusion and to a desire on the part of some to retain their original culture, distinct groups continue to exist. We view the retention of one's culture of origin as desirable and see the perspective of biculturalism as one which encourages acceptance of difference and the capacity to work with it.

Let us diagram a cultural continuum to reflect this perspective.

Relationship

dominant Anglo/ white culture	minority group culture
values, norms, role expectations	values, norms, role expectations

Each group's cultural system is based on a set of values manifested in norms and role expectations which are distinct from those of the majority cultural system. Though a wide range of individual differences exists within each group and parts of one group's system may be similar to that of others, recognizable boundaries exist and must be bridged if relationships are to be developed across them.

At either end of the continuum are located those who function within the boundaries of that cultural system. They identify and interact primarily with other members of the same group, govern their behavior according to its values and norms, and often speak a common language. Movement across the continuum in either direction indicates exposure to another cultural system and generally occurs as one interacts with members of the other group. At least one participant in a relationship which crosses racial/ethnic lines must move toward the other in order to develop common ground for communication. If movement does not occur, interaction remains on a superficial level. As noted earlier, such movement in society has generally been from right to left on this continuum, with differences viewed as negative characteristics in need of alteration. Alfred White's *The Apperceptive Mass of Foreigners as Applied to Americanization* (1971) exemplifies the concerted, largely unquestioned, effort made throughout much of our history to resocialize minority group members to abandon their heritage and become as much like members of the dominant group as possible. Majority group members have traditionally expected others to move toward them to understand their cultural system and modify their behavior accordingly. We maintain that the preferred alternative is for the social worker to develop the capacity to move across the continuum to wherever the client is located on it.

Let us consider the implications of this perspective for social work practice. Movement across the continuum essentially requires that one understand the values and norms of another cultural system, of one's own system, be aware of where differences lie, and accept both as legitimate. The Anglo/white worker, then, must acquire a substantial knowledge base including the values, expected role behaviors, historical experiences, and language of the group to which the client belongs as a basis for their work together. It is essential that the worker accept both self and other before this knowledge can be integrated and applied effectively. Workers, as they offer service to the client, then draw from this understanding and acceptance to assess where the particular individuals involved are located on the continuum.

Social workers who are members of a racial/ethnic minority group have, when working with other members of the same group, the advantage of having learned through life experience what is expected and appropriate within its boundaries. They also have the advantage of being identified by physical characteristics as people with common experiences, more likely to be trusted than Anglo/white workers who must overcome this immediate barrier if service is to be used. Minority workers in addition to understanding their own system, however, must develop the capacity to interact effectively within the Anglo/white system as well since its members predominantly control needed services and resources. When working with members of the other minority groups, the minority worker moves across two continua, developing his/her capacity to interact within both the dominant and other minority cultures.

Worker movement across the bicultural continuum is diagrammed in the examples below. The arrows indicate that workers move from wherever they are located both to where the client is and toward competence in interacting with the Anglo/white system.

Anglo worker/minority (Native American) client

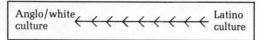

Minority (Latino) worker and client of same minority/Anglo service system

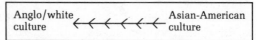

Minority (Asian-American) worker/Anglo client

Anglo/white
culture ← ← ← ← ← ← Asian-American
culture

Minority (black) worker/client of other minority/Anglo service system

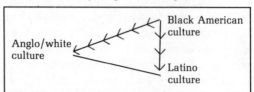

In order to establish helpful, purposeful relationships across racial/ethnic lines, workers of all groups must be able to move along each continuum to interact within the cultural context which has meaning for the client.

The purpose of the social work relationship is to assist clients to become the kind of people they want to become, or to do something they have chosen to do in terms of overcoming barriers in dealing more effectively with the stresses of life. The magnitude of this task for the client will not be understood by the worker if the worker lacks empathy—"the capacity to enter into the feelings and experiences of another—knowing what one feels and experiences—without losing oneself in the process" (Compton & Galaway, 1979, see p. 175).

Unless workers have some knowledge of the values, norms, and expectations of the culture of the client and of this particular client, they will not be able to understand either the client's goals or the barriers impeding progress toward these goals. The worker will thus be unable to fulfill the purpose of the social work relationship. It is easier for each of us as workers to work with clients who share the same cultural values, norms, expectations and world view since it is easier to be appropriately empathic with such clients. A more conscious effort is required of workers to work effectively with clients of another culture who have a different frame of reference, particularly in regard to perceptions of the importance of activity, the nature of relationships, and human nature.

Empathy, which requires openness to the reality of another person's feelings, experiences, and perceptions, facilitates the conscious efforts of workers in establishing relationships with clients of a different culture. Work with clients of a culture different from that of the workers requires, in addition, an openness on the part of workers to values, norms, and world views that their own culture may not share. This requires of the workers the capacity to understand and respect their own culture and the role it has played in their development, and to feel free to respect the culture of the other. It demands from workers a belief that no culture is inherently better than or superior to another, but that each is merely different. Such an attitude will allow workers to attempt to perceive situations from the point of view of the minority client.

We have chosen three dimensions of the Latino culture in order to illustrate factors that must be taken into account in the development of the social work relationship across racial/ethnic lines. The Latino culture is selected for illustration because it is the one with which we are most familiar. The dimensions of language, locus of control, and world view are not the only, or perhaps even the most important, dimensions of the Latino culture. How-

ever, they provide examples of how the bicultural framework can be applied in client-worker situations and illustrate points of possible incongruities between the perceptions of the worker and those of a Latino client.

Although these incongruities may not exist if either the Latino client or the worker has ease of movement on a bicultural continuum, nevertheless the onus of movement on the bicultural continuum is on the worker if he/she is to meet the client wherever the client is and if there is going to be any possibility of establishing a working relationship. This fact again emphasizes the necessity for empathy on the part of the worker.

Verbal and nonverbal communications express a person's feelings, ideas, and world view developed in a particular cultural context. The meanings assigned to verbal and nonverbal communication can result in incongruities between worker and client.

A nonverbal gesture, such as lowering of the eyes or not looking at someone directly, is interpreted by some persons as a sign of respect and deference to authorities and elders, while it is interpreted by other groups as a sign of the lack of veracity in a person. Nonverbal communication is much more open to misinterpretation than is verbal communication. However, verbal communication can also be misinterpreted when one language does not allow for the full expression of the nuances and concepts behind another language. This is especially true in regard to Spanish and English.

In Spanish there are two means of addressing another person depending on their status in terms of both age and social role. *Tu* is the personal pronoun used for addressing peers or persons who are younger, whereas *Usted* is used to address elders and persons in positions of authority. To address an authority or an elder by using *tu,* the familiar form, is not seen as a misuse of language but rather as a lack of respect due to that individual. This is not a cause for embarrassment, for there is no such term in Spanish. Rather it is a cause for shame, since disrespect is never seen as a matter to be taken lightly.

The use of *you,* the familiar pronoun in English, is appropriate at all times, since English usage does not distinguish its salutation either according to function or age. The general trend in the usage of English in this country is to do away with distinctions and to become acquainted with another on a first-name basis. To do the opposite in English is sometimes viewed as an attempt to create an artificial distance between the two parties.

In dealing with persons who are of Spanish heritage, the emphasis is not on creating an artificial distance but rather in acknowledging that which is already so, namely that some people have more power by virtue of position and some have more experience by virtue of age. To address another who is older or in authority on a first name basis is not viewed as an attempt to get closer to the other but rather as an attempt to challenge authority or to discount experience. A person who would do this would be viewed as being ill-bred or, at a minimum, ill-mannered and disrespectful.

Respect, then, becomes the key for dealing with authority. Respect, however, is not the same as *respeto.* In English one can respect another while violently opposing the opinions that that person holds. In English *respect* does not contain the element of acceptance of another's view as one's own. *Respeto,* on the other hand, means that one must not challenge the opinions of others. It means that if one chooses not to adopt the opinions of another as one's own, one must at least pay deference to the other person's views by not saying anything. Thus, the locus of control for Hispanic people tends to be

much more external than internal, whether the locus is God, fate, nature, authority, or age, and this condition is constantly reinforced by means of language.

Because the respect for authority is essential to the highly structured and hierarchical world view of Hispanic people, relationships do not occur as often between equals as they do in the dominant culture. Relationships are perceived as occurring between one who is in authority and one who is not. A social worker is seen as a person who is an authority. The purpose of the social work relationship—the conscious and deliberate use of self for the benefit of the client—remains the same. The way that the purpose is viewed by Hispanic clients may be different from the way it is viewed by the majority clients.

As the Latino client enters into a social work relationship, he/she views the relationship as unequal. The worker is assigned a sense of authority and *respecto.* The client may disagree with the worker but remain silent rather than appear disrespectful. A worker, unaware of this culturally determined approach, may view the silence as resistance. Errors in assessment resulting from culture-based misinterpretations lead to antagonistic relationships and selection of inappropriate methods of intervention. Consider the discordant perceptions which may result from differences on the dimensions of locus of control and world view. Latinos tend to see many aspects of their lives in which the control is external. Anglos consider more aspects of their lives to be under internal control. The fostering of independence and self-reliance, if taken at face value, can be viewed by the Latinos as a lack of concern for others and as a pompous and unrealistic attitude on the part of the proponent. This logically follows from a Latino world view in which there is a balance of pain and pleasure and where the natural order is controlled by God. The white/Anglo world view is one in which the individual is the powerful force. Individuals are in charge of themselves and can change what they want to change about themselves or their world. Latinos view themselves as much more interdependent and not as solely in charge of themselves. What they as individuals can do is more dependent on others and the external environment.

Such contrasting views impede working toward common goals if not recognized and addressed. In working with adolescents, for example, the worker may decide to deal with that adolescent on a one-to-one basis. However, the Latino mother may view this as inappropriate since she sees herself as in control of her child. Failure to recognize and acknowledge the mother's position is likely to result in discontinuance from service. The reason might never be shared with the worker because of the authority element in the relationship.

In empathizing with a Latino client, a worker may want to move too quickly from recognizing the difficulty the client is experiencing to what could be done to help. For the client, it may be more helpful to dwell on the difficulty longer to the point where the worker might interpret this as resistance or that the client does not have the capacity to use the service. From the Latino client's point of view, the dwelling on the difficulty could be viewed as helpful since he/she knows that pain is balanced by pleasure. The worker could acknowledge that cultural element and use it with the client to prepare for the more pleasant phase of life, thus resulting in a more useful service for the client.

We have presented a framework for viewing transracial/ethnic social work relationships as developing across a bicultural continuum. The dimensions of language, locus of control, and world view illustrate points of possible incongruities between the perceptions of an Anglo worker and a Latino client which, in turn, create difficulties in establishing effective working (social work) relationships. Empathy is required if workers of one culture are to move on a bicultural continuum toward clients of a different culture. We believe that recognizing the necessity of, and developing the capacity for, such movement will increase the likelihood of engaging clients of a different culture in positive, purposeful, and effective relationships. From this perspective the worker's capacity to both move across the continuum and to assess where the client is located on it are considered essential elements in the delivery of social services to minority clients.

References

Biestek, Feliz. *The casework relationship.* Chicago: Loyola University Press, 1957.

Bowlby, John. *Grief and mourning in infancy and early childhood.* New York: International Universities Press, 1960.

Compton, Beulah R., & Galaway, Burt. *Social Work Processes.* Homewood: Dorsey Press, 1979.

Cooper, Shirley. A look at the effect of racism on clinical work. *Social Casework,* February 1978, *54,* 78.

Coyle, Grace L.   *Group work with American youth.* New York: Harper & Row, 1948.

Davenport, Judith, & Reims, Nancy.   Theoretical orientation and attitudes toward women. *Social Work,* July 1978, *23,* 306–311.

Engel, G., Reichsman, F., & Segal, H.   A study of an infant with gastric fistula in behavior and the rate of total hydrochloric acid secretion. *Psychosomatic Medicine,* October 1956, *18,* 374–398.

Fraley, Yvonne L.   A role model for practice, *Social Service Review,* June 1969, *43,* 145–154.

Frank, Jerome D.   Expectation and therapeutic outcome—The placebo effect and the role induction interview. In Jerome D. Frank (Ed.), *Effective ingredients of successful psychotherapy.* New York: Brunner/Mazel, 1978.

Fromm, Erich.   *The art of loving.* New York: Harper & Row, 1956.

Gitterman, Alex, & Schaeffer, Alice.   The white professional and the black client. *Social Casework,* May 1972, *53,* 280–291.

Goldstein, Howard.   *Social work practice: A unitary approach.* Columbia: University of South Carolina Press, 1973.

Goodman, James A.   Preface. In James A. Goodman (Ed.), *Dynamics of racism.* Washington, D.C.: National Association of Social Workers, 1974.

Gottschalk, Leonard. A study of prediction and outcome in a mental health crisis clinic. *American Journal of Psychiatry,* 1973, *130,* 1107–1111.

Haley, Jay.   *Strategies of psychotherapy.* New York. Grune & Stratton, 1963.

Halleck, Seymour L.   The criminal's problem with psychiatry. *Psychiatry,* November 1960, *23,* 346–399.

Harlow, H.   The nature of love. *The American Psychologist,* 1958, *13,* 673–685.

Johnson, Wendell.   Being understanding and understood: Or how to find a wandered horse. *ETC,* Spring 1951, *8* 171–179.

Keith-Lucas, Alan.   *The giving and taking of help.* Chapel Hill: University of North Carolina Press, 1972.

Konopka, Gisela.   *Social group work: A helping process.* Englewood Cliffs, N.J.: Prentice-Hall, 1963.

Mayer, John E., & Timms, Noel.   Clash in perspective between worker and client. *Social Casework,* January 1969, *50,* 32–40.

Mayer, John E., & Timms, Noel.   *The client speaks: Working class impressions of casework.* New York: Atherton Press, 1970.

Miranda, Manuel R.   *Psychotherapy with the Spanish-speaking: Issues in research and service delivery.* Spanish-Speaking Mental Health Center, Los Angeles, Calif., 1976.

Northern, Helen.   *Social work with groups.* New York: Columbia University Press, 1969.

Perlman, Helen Harris.   *Social casework: A problem-solving process.* Chicago: University of Chicago Press, 1957.

Perlman, Helen Harris.   *Perspectives on social casework.* Philadelphia: Temple University Press, 1971.

Pincus, Allen, & Minahan, Anne.   *Social work practice: Model and method.* Itasca, Ill.: F. E. Peacock Publishers, 1973.

Pumphrey, Ralph, & Pumphrey, Muriel.   *The heritage of American social work.* New York: Columbia University, 1961.

Reynolds, Bertha C.   *Unchartered journey.* New York: Citadel Press, 1963.

Richmond, Mary E. *Friendly visiting among the poor: A handbook for charity workers.* New York: Macmillan, 1899.

Richmond, Mary E. *Social diagnosis.* New York: Russell Sage Foundation, 1917.

Ripple, Lillian, Alexander, Ernestina, & Polemis, Bernice. *Motivation, capacity and opportunity: Studies in casework theory and practice.* Chicago, School of Social Service Administration, University of Chicago, 1964.

Rogers, Carl. Client-centered therapy. In C. H. Patterson (Ed.), *Theories of counseling and psychotherapy.* New York: Harper & Row, 1966.

Szasz, Thomas S. *The myth of mental illness: Foundations of a theory of personal conduct.* New York: Harper & Row, 1961.

Truax, Charles B., & Carkhuff, Robert. *Toward effective counseling and psychotherapy: Training and practice.* Hawthorne, N.Y.: Aldine Publishing, 1967.

Truax, Charles B., & Mitchell, Kevin M. Research on certain interpersonal skills in relation to process and outcome. In Allen E. Bergin & Sol L. Garfield (Eds.), *Handbook for psychotherapy and behavior.* New York: Wiley, 1971.

White, Alfred. *The apperceptive mass of foreigners as applied to Americanization, The Mexican group, 1923.* Berkeley: University of California, 1971.

Part Two

Tools for Deciding
What to Do

Chapter 7
Communication and Interviewing
for Social Work Practice

Chapter 8
Problem Solving:
A Process for Social Work Practice

Chapter 9
The Contact Phase: Problem
Identification, Initial Goal Setting,
Data Collection, and
Initial Assessment

Chapter 10
The Contract Phase:
Joint Assessment, Goal Setting,
and Planning

Communication and Interviewing
for Social Work Practice

Interviewing is a basic social work skill. The interview is the major tool utilized by the social worker to collect data from which to make intervention decisions. While other data collection tools are available to the worker (these will be discussed further in Chapter 9), the interview remains the primary tool and the client the primary source of data. Many social work interventive strategies are also dependent on interviewing, with the interview used as the modality through which strategies directed toward change are applied. Because of the ubiquitousness of interviewing in social work practice, some brief consideration of interviewing and communication is essential in any book purporting to develop a practice model. A number of excellent books have appeared on the social work interview (De Schweinitz & De Schweinitz, 1962; Garrett, 1972; Kadushin, 1972; Rich, 1968; Schubert, 1982), and social work educational programs usually devote considerable time to the development of interviewing skills. We do not intend either to provide a comprehensive treatment of interviewing or to give the student a bag of tricks. Rather, this chapter will introduce the use of social work interviewing as a central tool of social work practice, identify some of the barriers to communication, offer some ideas concerning the role of the social work interviewer, and, present briefly some techniques we have found useful in the data collection interview. Interviewing skills will continue to be refined and developed throughout your social work career.

COMMUNICATION AND INTERVIEWING

Communication can be defined as an interactional process which gives, receives, and checks out meaning (Satir, 1964, chaps. 8 and 9) and occurs when people interact with each other. The checkout phase of the communication process is essential and is discussed as an interviewing technique by Robert Brown (1973). A, for example, sends a message to B, which B receives. But how does B know that B has received the message A intended to send? Perhaps B's receptors were faulty, perhaps A's transmitter was faulty, or perhaps there was noise or interference between A and B which distorted

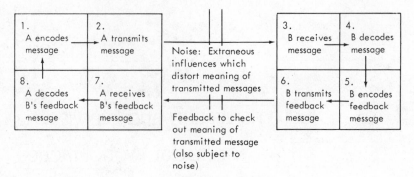

FIGURE 7–1:   The communication process

the message. B checks out the message with A by indicating what has been received in order to confirm that the message B received was the message A intended to send (see Figure 7–1). Communication difficulties result when this checkout process is omitted.

The communication theory concepts of encoding, transmitting, receiving, decoding, and noise provide a useful framework for understanding problems which may arise in the social work interview. Encoding refers to the process of putting the message to be sent into symbol form in preparation for transmission. Transmitting refers to the process of sending the encoded message; receiving to the process of interpreting the stimuli received; noise to extraneous influences that may have distorted the message when it was on its way from the transmitter to the receiver. Checkout or feedback provides a way of overcoming problems created by noise as well as by inadequate encoding or decoding or faulty transmission or reception.

John Cormican, in the article reprinted with this chapter (Reading 7–1), identifies several potential communication problems in social work practice. When he speaks of language differences and communication problems resulting from the use of various dialects, he is making reference to communication problems with the use of symbols—the symbol encoded and transmitted by one party may be received by the other party, but is not decodable. Or the message may be decoded in such a manner that the message sent is not correctly interpreted. An example of this may be found in Chapter 3 in the author's discussion of the Indian student's interpretation of the doctor's questions. Lewis and Ho, in the article included with Chapter 9 (Reading 9–2), give another example of this problem in nonverbal communication between social workers and American Indian clients:

> In an effort to communicate more fully, the social worker is likely to seat himself facing the client, look him straight in the eye, and insist that the client do likewise. A native American considers such behavior covert or overt—to be rude and intimidating; contrary to the white man, he shows respect by not staring directly at others.

Cormican asserts that labels such as borderline state, depressive, behavior disorder, actor outer, and personality disorder create barriers to communication. These labels, when held by the worker, may distort the decoding process because the message sent by a client may be interpreted in relation to the worker's understanding of the meaning of these labels rather than in relation to what the client intended. Feedback is used to check out whether or not the receiver received the message the sender intended. Cournoyer, in the article reproduced in this chapter (Reading 7–2), identifies empathetic communication skills which are reflective on the part of the worker; empathetic communications derive from the worker's conception of a client's frame of reference and reflect content, feeling, thinking, and meaning. Cournoyer discusses reflective skills for work with groups but these skills can be used with any size client system to check out the messages received. Checkout or feedback is also a form of communication and subject to the same potential communication problems as the original message-sending process. Allan Bloom (1980, p. 333) offers a useful illustration of this problem:

> The client in treatment struggles to express a feeling or thought that troubles her. She finally manages to say something that perhaps approximates what is on her mind. The social worker's response is, "I really appreciate where you are coming from." What does the social worker's response mean? What does it reveal and what does it conceal? What contribution, positive and negative, does this remark make toward furthering the treatment of the client and fostering a therapeutic relationship?
>
> This praise is a duplicitous expression of confusion, concealment, and lack of understanding and empathy. If one were to ask the therapist what he intended to convey to the client by using the phrase, he would presumably say something like, "I mean that I understand what the client° is feeling." But his every word proves otherwise. First, nobody can truly understand what another person is feeling. One can come close, and such approximations of empathy are surely what social workers strive toward in their work, but understanding inevitably remains an approximation. The therapist's use of the word really reveals an underlying uncertainty about what the client feels.

Total communication in the sense that one can completely understand what another is saying, thinking, and feeling, is undoubtedly impossible. We can only work to approximate clarity and understanding in our communications. We must strive, of course, to understand the client; but, we also must strive to be sure our own communications to clients are as clear as possible. We agree with Bloom's (1980, p. 337) advice that "communications to clients ought to be simple, clear, accurate, and direct. Social workers should choose words that are precise and cannot be misunderstood, words that are not evasive and vague."

Communications occur simultaneously on many levels. We can speak of verbal and nonverbal communications or overt and covert communications. Virginia Satir (1964, p. 76) speaks of denotative and metacommunication levels of messages. By the denotative level, she means the literal content of the symbols (usually words). She defines metacommunications as messages about the message; a metacommunication refers to such things as a voice inflection, gestures, manner of speaking, and so on, all of which provide additional clues about the meaning of the denotative level of communication. The ability to communicate several messages simultaneously provides opportunity for the famous double bind—the simultaneous transmission of contradictory messages leaving the receiver in a "be damned if I do, be damned if I don't" position (Bateson, Jackson, Haley, & Weakland, 1963).

But what is the meaning of all of this to interviewing in social work? Interviewing can be looked upon as a particular kind of communication. Robert Kahn and Charles Connell (1957, p. 16) define an interview as a

> specialized pattern of verbal interaction—initiated for a specific purpose, focused on some specific content area, with consequent elimination of extraneous material. Moreover, the interview is a pattern of interaction in which the role relationship of interviewer and respondent is highly specialized, its specific characteristics depending somewhat on the purpose and character of the interview.

The social work interview is a set of communications with four special characteristics: (1) it has a context or setting; (2) it is purposeful and directed; (3) it is limited and contractual; and (4) it involves specialized role relationships. The context or setting for the interview will usually be that of a particular agency offering defined services to clients bringing specified problems to the agency. The context, of course, provides a limit to the communications and becomes a basis for the "elimination of extraneous material"— that is, material not related to the particular context. Social work interviews are purposeful and directed in the sense that they are conducted to accomplish specific goals (a legitimate purpose may certainly be the definition of the goals or furthering worker-client communications). Conversely, interviews are not casual exchanges of information or informal conversations. The purposes of interviews provide a basis for limiting communications and eliminating extraneous material. Interviews are limited and contractual in the sense that the interviewer and the interviewee come together in a specific context for defined purposes; their communications are limited to meeting those purposes. And, finally, interviewer and interviewee occupy specialized roles and interact with each other on the basis of those roles. This, again, is a limiting factor inasmuch as client-worker interactions will usually be confined to the expected behaviors of the specialized roles.

To summarize, communication can be viewed as an interactional process involving the giving, receiving, and checking out of meaning; communication occurs on many levels and may not always be congruent. Interviewing is a specialized form of communication which is contextual, purposeful, limited and which involves specialized role relationships. This chapter focuses on interviewing to secure information which client and worker will use jointly in decision making about the nature of the problem and of intervention. The primary source of data is the client; interviewing techniques are used to encourage the client to share data for joint client-worker use.

Since the data is to be used in decision making about intervention, the social worker must be concerned about the reliability and validity of data collection procedures. The concepts of reliability and validity are defined for social work as they are defined in other scientific and research activity. Reliability refers to the extent to which data collection tools (in this case, the interview) produce consistent information. If different messages are received from the client at different times, the social worker wants to be reasonably certain that the differences reflect actual changes in the client and are not a consequence of the worker's interviewing style; otherwise a reliability problem exists. Validity refers to the extent to which the information being obtained reflects the actual perceptions, thoughts, feelings, and behaviors of the client. If the client is not sharing the client's actual perceptions, thoughts, feelings, and behaviors, a validity problem exists; the worker will need to adjust the interviewing techniques in order to secure more accurate information. One responsibility of the social worker is to create a climate in which the client is comfortable in sharing valid and reliable information.

The next section considers some potential barriers to communication—barriers which will affect the validity and reliability of data. In subsequent sections the role of the interviewer will be analyzed and suggestions offered which will assist you to increase the probability of securing valid and reliable data.

BARRIERS TO COMMUNICATION

Barriers to communication may occur at any phase in the communication process—encoding, transmitting, receiving, decoding, and checkout. Many of these barriers are obvious—inability to conceptualize and use symbols (encoding problems), speech impediments, hearing or receptor impediments, failure to understand the concepts received (decoding problems), and environmental influences (noise which interferes with the messages or prevents them from traveling clearly from the transmitter to the receiver). While these barriers are real and are of concern to the worker desirous of reliable and valid data on which to base decisions, they are also reasonably obvious sources of error in communications. In this section we will consider a series of subtler, less obvious, but equally serious barriers to communication which will affect the validity and reliability of the data on which intervention decisions are based. Six worker barriers in addition to the barrier of client resistance will be considered. Approaches on the part of the worker which may serve as barriers to the collection of valid and reliable data include anticipation of the other, the assumption of meaning, stereotyping, confusion of purpose, the urge to change, and inattentiveness.

The first worker barrier to communication—anticipation of the other—is alluded to by Carl Rogers (n.d.) as follows:

> But what I really dislike in myself is when I can't hear the other person because I'm so sure in advance what the other is going to say that I don't listen because it is afterwards that I realize I have only heard what I have already decided the other is saying. I have failed really to listen at those times when I can't hear because what the other is saying is too threatening, because it might make me change my ideas and my behavior.

Cormican (Reading 7–1) is referring to the same problem when he speaks of diagnostic labels or categories interfering with communication. These labels may result in preconceived connotations of what a client is like; preconceived connotations may result in anticipating the client rather than listening and observing carefully. Anticipation of the other occurs when one permits an existing stereotype to shape and distort the current communication. And these are not just the stereotypes we all carry into our practices.

We develop stereotypes from our own practice experience or that of our agencies. Consider, for example, that you have recently begun work with an agency and have been asked to provide service to the Shasta family; the agency record contains this summary:

> Known to the agency for the past 15 years on the basis of 13 applications, mainly result of nonsupport of husband or his jailing. Family consists of Mr. Shasta—age 32, Mrs. Shasta—age 27 and six children. Mr. Shasta in and out of court since young boy due to delinquent and antisocial behavior. Dishonorable discharge from army. In last few years drinking increased to near alcoholism. Mrs. Shasta came from family also long known to department. She married Mr. Shasta, age 17, "to escape an alcoholic father." Recurring pregnancies, health trouble, and abuse by her husband, had left her in poor shape to cope with him, let alone child rearing and running the home. Case looked on by staff as one of the most unpleasant in the department. Several incidents of fraud, continued misuse of funds, and Mr. Shasta's refusal to seek and keep work. Mr. Shasta avoided by workers as much as possible due to his violent temper and drinking. Returning him to employment seen as hopeless; he has quit or been fired from at least 20 jobs. Mr. Shasta's behavior after drinking seems to affect his disposition toward looking for work and toward his wife and children. Question of adequacy of child care frequently in picture. It is reported mother neglects children. Neighbors have reported the father beating children when drunk. Mrs. Shasta tries to protect them from father. Health problems of mother and children are an ongoing issue. Family indifferent to need for medical care.

This summary, presented to a new worker, creates powerful images which may affect any communication you receive from the Shasta family. The fact that background information may affect your perception does not mean that you should not consider background information or receive transfer summaries within an agency. We are encouraging you, however, to be aware that this information may influence your perception and to overcompensate a bit by consciously listening to the client and to work at avoiding anticipation of what he or she might be saying. In addition, you need to recognize that the above summary is only a description of certain discrete behavior of Mr. and Mrs. Shasta and to understand that without much more data you do not know enough about the situation to make sound inferences as to the meaning of such behavior for the Shastas.

The assumption of meaning, a second worker barrier to communication, occurs when a worker receives an ambiguous message, fails to check out its meaning with the client, and proceeds on the basis of a meaning which the worker has read into the client's message. The words themselves may be ambiguous, the way in which they are uttered may convey unclear feelings or thoughts, or the client's behavior may be communicating messages inconsistent with the words. In all of these situations checkout of meaning with the client may prevent erroneous assumptions and proceeding on the basis of invalid and unreliable data. An example of assumption of meaning occurs in this brief excerpt from an interview with a 16-year-old boy on parole:

> I asked how things had gone this past week. He looked at me with a grin and said, "Fine." He added that he had not done anything. During this time he kept leafing through the magazine and pointed out someone's picture to me. At this

point I told him that we were here to talk and that he should put the magazine away. It is very obvious that this boy knows very little or at least practices few of the common courtesies of everyday living.

This worker assumed from the boy's grin and his leafing through the magazine that he was trying to avoid entering into conversation. The worker, however, erroneously acted on the basis of this assumption without first checking it out with the youngster. A few minutes taken to ask the boy what it was about the magazine that interested him or to make a more direct checkout—"I get the message that you are not too interested in talking with me now"—might have clarified the situation and produced a more reliable and valid basis on which to act.

Worker stereotypes of clients are a third barrier to communication. This barrier relates directly to the problems of classification and categorization discussed in Chapter 3. It exists when clients are seen as members of groups—low income, delinquent, schizophrenic, black, and so on—and action is taken without permitting the client's individuality to transcend the stereotype of the client's group. Stereotyping leads to the two previous problems—anticipating the other and assumptions of meaning occur because of stereotypes held by workers. Stereotyping can be very subtle; after experience with several similar clients, workers may note similarities on the basis of which they begin to develop a stereotype of that particular kind of client. The stereotype then interferes with the worker's perception of new clients and may well serve to block out communications inconsistent with it.

Failure on the part of the worker to make explicit the purpose of an interview may lead to a condition in which the worker and client hold differing, perhaps contradictory, purposes. Given such confusion of purpose, both client and worker will then interpret their own and each other's communications in light of their particular understanding of the objective of the interview. As these subtle distortions continue, the client and the worker will be going in two entirely different directions. As an example of what happens when purpose is not clarified and dealt with, we offer the following interview. Had the practitioner started with purpose—to determine how the hospital bill would be met and then moved to the resource most people have—health insurance—the interview could have proceeded without the many uncomfortable feelings that were raised by the indirect questions.

Mr. Johnson approached my desk with a worried expression on his face and told me the nurse had said that I wanted to see him. I asked him his name and to be seated. A quick glance at my list of admissions helped me determine that this was Mr. Johnson's first experience of being interviewed at our hospital. He was very worried about his wife's illness and his apprehensiveness of the interview was apparent in his remark that he was "on the stand." I tried to put him at ease and had no difficulty with simple matters such as names, address, and occupation. The interview was frequently interrupted by numerous phone calls. It was apparent Mr. Johnson was becoming restless. He began to fidget uncomfortably and asked for permission to smoke which unfortunately I had to deny because the office is in a posted area. This incident was unluckily timed with one of the main purposes of the interview, which was to secure financial information to aid in classifying the patient. From a previous question about the patient's address, I had learned that Mr. Johnson was a farmer.

I had a regular form to follow in taking the necessary information, but because of Mr. Johnson's previous attitude toward the interview, I decided to change the order of the questions and try to keep him in a better mood. I asked Mr. Johnson how many acres he was farming. He answered 420, but he only owned 160 and rented the rest. I told Mr. Johnson that this was about the size of the farm on which I had spent my youth. Mr. Johnson seemed to become a little more friendly after this. Instead of asking him what he thought his net income for one year usually averaged, I asked him what he usually raised on his farm. He replied, "corn, usual small grain, beans, some pigs and sheep and quite a few milk cows." I asked if he sold much cream, he answered, "It depends. If the cows are dry, I don't make anything, but when they come in I usually get several hundred a month from cream." We were beginning to become more accustomed to each other so I asked if he kept a checking account. "Yes," he replied, "at the State Bank at home." I asked if he also kept a savings account at the same bank. He replied, "No." I then asked if he could tell me approximately how much he kept in his checking account. He answered, "Several hundred."

I was not succeeding in getting a direct figure so I found it necessary to ask what he thought his net income for one year averaged. He replied, "Between six and seven thousand." I asked if he had a mortgage on the farm. He replied, "No, it's clear." The discrepancy in figures confused me so I asked if he was saving money in another form other than using a savings account. He said he did not believe in banking money except for the convenience of paying bills. He had lost some money when the banks closed during the Depression and now he was putting his money in bonds and had bought some houses in town. It was becoming clear that Mr. Johnson would not need any help in financing his wife's hospital bill. For the matter of records, I completed the financial interview. Mr. Johnson was not too pleased with answering the question as to what kind of car he drove. After some hesitation he finally said, "A new Buick." I asked if he carried any life insurance. "Enough to bury me," he replied. "How about bills," I asked, "you have any?" Mr. Johnson beamed and he proudly answered, "Not a one, I pay cash." I asked what his additional income other than the farm averaged. "A couple hundred a month from rent of the houses in town. Guess that's about it." He brightened as he suddenly remembered something and proudly announced that he had taken out hospital insurance through the Farm Bureau and was glad that they had to pay him for a change, but that it was too bad that somebody had to get sick before you could use it. I explained the advantages of the insurance to him and told him that because of it we would not require a deposit against his wife's hospital bill. Instead, we wanted him to sign over the insurance to the hospital and when they had paid us after his wife's discharge, we would bill him for the remaining bill, if there was any. He thought this was very fair and signed the necessary papers.

The financial interview was over and I asked Mr. Johnson if he was going home or staying in town until his wife was discharged. He replied he wanted to stay, but he didn't know a thing about the city. I asked if he would let me help him and succeeded in finding him a room with board close to the hospital. Mr. Johnson was very appreciative of this last gesture and thanked me a great deal. I asked if he had any further questions that I might be able to help him with. He answered, "No, but I don't think I can find my way back to my wife's station." I directed him to the station, but in case he should forget again, I typed a small card with his wife's station number, hospital telephone number, his rooming house's address and telephone number. He thanked me again and left to visit his wife.

As a further example of this problem, we offer another excerpt from an interview in which the client says clearly that he came to pay his taxes but the practitioner is concerned about his health. It takes several questions before the worker understands the importance of responding to the client's concerns.

> Miss C., the Medical Welfare Consultant from State Office, was here studying records for material to use in teaching a class of medical students at the university medical school. She saw Mr. Allen waiting in the reception room and asked worker about the growth on his head. I was surprised, having seen Mr. Allen a few months ago and there was nothing wrong with his head at that time.
>
> When Mr. Allen came into the office, worker was completely surprised at the growth. Actually, Mr. Allen gave the appearance of having two heads, one on top of the other. I asked about it and Mr. Allen said that it had just started, but that wasn't what he had come to see worker about. He came because he wanted to pay his taxes. He said he had saved some money out of his grant, and with the extra $5.00 this month, he had "settled" with the tax offices. He declared Mrs. Allen still wouldn't pay taxes, but he was going to. Worker told him we would budget the entire tax bill in his grant, and that he would receive a $4.00 raise or a total of $37.
>
> Worker again asked about his head. He has been told that when he was a baby he had fallen off the bed, and has had a small knot since. He said he wanted to keep his taxes current, and would never again be talked out of paying them. Worker assured him his taxes would be included in the future in his grant alone because I knew of Mrs. Allen's attitude. Worker wanted to know when this knot had started growing. Mr. Allen said it suddenly started getting bigger about two months ago. Before getting a breath he started talking about taxes again. He must have had a hard time saving enough money to pay up. He said they "settled" for $18.00, and he had a "clean slate." He told of how he had done without his newspaper, hadn't been running his fans much nor watering his flowers as he should. I remarked I wished he had come to us sooner, but now that the taxes were paid, and the future ones budgeted, suppose we talk about his head. What had he done for it? He replied he had not done anything, and again changed the subject to taxes.
>
> I told him I noticed each time I mentioned his head, he changed the subject to taxes. It made me wonder if he didn't want to talk about his head, or if there was some connection with his head and taxes. He looked surprised, and then slowly, as if explaining to a child, said, "Long ago the doctors told me if this ever started growing in a hurry I would have to have it cut off. I am 77 years old and may or may not get out of that operating room. If I die, my wife can live on her old age pension if she has a home, if not, she can't. So, I have to get those taxes paid before I go to a hospital or even see a doctor."[1]

One of the more serious barriers to communication arises from prematurely engaging clients in change activities. This is a very easy pitfall for the social worker. *Change* is a common word in the profession; by and large, we are committed to being change agents, both to improve the conditions of the community and to assist individuals to utilize the resources of the community more effectively. Difficulties occur, however, when change efforts are attempted without sufficient data on which to base an assessment of the problem. Although change may occur through any human interaction,

---

[1] Reprinted with permission from the Council on Social Work Education teaching record.

effecting change is not the primary purpose of the data collection interview; change efforts should be based on valid and reliable data and on a considered decision of the client and worker to engage in such efforts. The purpose of the data collection interview is to gather the information on which decisions about intervention can be based. To urge change at this early stage may create a barrier to communication—a barrier which limits the availability of important information that could influence decision making. A secondary problem is that change efforts in these early contacts frequently take the form of directive approaches—such as persuasion and advising—which are seldom effective until a high degree of trust has been developed and which, used prematurely, create barriers to continuing communication. And it is the process of continuing communication which provides opportunities for the development of increased trust.

A very potent worker barrier to communication is inattentiveness. A worker whose mind wanders during an interview, who is thinking about other clients or planning future activities, creates barriers for continued client-worker communication. Clients can reasonably expect the workers to give undivided attention to their present communications, and workers have the responsibility for establishing a time frame that will enable them to attend to other matters that require attention without diverting attention from the interview of the moment. But even the most experienced workers will have moments when thoughts wander and attentiveness wanes. Walsh, in the article on rural social work practice included with Chapter 12, recommends owning up to these lapses:

> Should a client's storytelling send a therapist into a couple of minutes of personal reflection, it is recommended that he or she admit this interruption to the client. For example, "Excuse me, Frank. What you were saying made me think of something else that's going on, and I haven't been paying close attention for a minute, here. Can you go over that again? I was with you up to the point where you said Jan had no business interfering with the kids."
>
> Despite most therapists' fears of revealing such incidents, rural clients are probably aware of these lapses anyhow, and the admission wins respect for its honesty and may relieve the client to some degree ("Hmm. Everyone's attention flags from time to time. But *this* person is actually going to let me know when that happens! They don't want to miss anything. They are genuinely interested in me.")

As workers learn to avoid anticipating what the client will say, to check out the meanings of the communications received, to avoid stereotyping, to clarify purposes, to avoid attempts at change until the necessary data is available and change decisions can be made jointly, and to give all clients opportunities for undivided attention, the likelihood of securing reasonably valid and reliable information will be considerably enhanced. But clients may also create barriers to communication. These barriers may be thought of as forms of resistance on their part against entering into a problem-solving process. Resistance may be considered as a specialized kind of defense utilized by the client to ward off the worker and to protect the client from any discomfort involved in participating in a problem-solving process.

Three sources of resistance can be distinguished. (1) Resistance may stem from the usual discomfort of dealing with a strange person and situation.

Essentially this is a "normal" anxiety and discomfort with which many of us approach new situations. (2) Resistance may stem from cultural and subcultural norms regarding involvement with service agencies and asking for help. Norman Johnston (1956), for example, identifies a number of variables in the prison milieu which contribute to distortion and deception in the communications between inmates and prison counselors. Because of cultural norms, some persons may find it particularly difficult, to admit the existence of a problem and to seek a solution. Agencies may exacerbate such cultural differences by establishing procedures which intensify the discomfort of persons of certain cultural backgrounds. An agency emphasis on scheduled appointments and office visits, for example, may aggravate the resistance of clients from lower socioeconomic groups and hamper their ability to utilize more traditional social service agencies. Renate Frankenstein (1982) notes that what is often recorded as resistance on the part of families should also be examined in terms of agency practices and worker expectations which may inhibit establishing communication with troubled families. (3) Some clients may be securing a degree of gratification from their problems. This type of pathological involvement with a problem is a serious source of resistance, which interferes with the client's ability to communicate and makes seeking a solution more difficult.

What is the worker's responsibility in relation to client resistance? To facilitate communication, the worker may need to help the client identify and deal with any of these obstacles to communication. Dealing with obstacles to communication will become a necessary preliminary goal before the client and worker can move into any other problem-solving work. Dealing with resistances is one manifestation of the worker's second task as conceptualized by Schwartz "the task of detecting and challenging the obstacles which obscure the common ground" (Schwartz, 1961, p. 157).

RESPONSIBILITIES OF THE WORKER

What are the social worker's responsibilities in the data collection interview? They can be conceptualized in three interrelated areas. First, social workers are responsible for creating a productive climate in which the client can comfortably participate and in which the client—the primary source of data—will share the thoughts, feelings, and perceptions necessary for intervention decisions. The climate should help secure valid and reliable data. To a large extent, the creation of such a climate involves the worker's skill in avoiding the worker barriers to communication noted earlier and in helping clients to deal with the obstacles to communication presented by their own resistances. The creation of a productive climate for participation might be construed as the development of a helping relationship. In Chapter 6 we referred to relationship as a climate or an atmosphere and suggested strongly that relationship is not the end of service but a stepping-stone toward the provision of problem-solving service for the client. One way to operationalize the concept of relationship is to define it as a climate or milieu which is characterized by open and verbal communications. Thus the presence of relationship might be inferred from the extent to which communications are open and verbal. Creating this kind of climate is a responsibility of the worker, a responsibility which is met primarily by the nature of communications and interactions with clients.

A second responsibility of the worker is to provide a focus for the interview. This occurs by establishing a purpose for the interview very early and focusing the interactions in relation to the purpose. Tangents should be avoided; questions that lead into extraneous areas are not helpful. The worker, when pursuing what the client has said, should pick up on areas related to the interview's central focus. Focusing the interview does not mean dictating the purpose, nor does it mean cutting off the client; it does mean, however, jointly establishing with the client a particular purpose for an interview and fulfilling the responsibility of maintaining that focus. Material brought out in a particular interview may suggest a purpose and focus for subsequent interviews; the worker may deliberately not respond to this material initially but may bring it up later. Aaron Rosen and Dina Lieberman (1972, p. 398) report on an experimental study of the extent to which workers' responses are content relevant—"the extent to which the content of an interactive response is perceived by a participant to be relevant to, and in agreement with, the participant's own definition and expectations of the content to be dealt with in the treatment relationship." With complaint clients, workers with more training did significantly better at maintaining content relevance. Workers with less training had more content-relevant response with aggressive clients; however, many of the responses were harsh and retaliatory and thus ineffective in promoting communications. Rosen and Lieberman (pp. 410–411) suggest that their findings point to the need for clear worker and client orientation as to the purpose of the interview.

A third responsibility of the worker is to separate and identify the client's levels of response. Responses are typically on one of four levels—perceptual, cognitive, affective, and behavioral. The perceptual level of response refers to interactions and communications around what the client perceives or has perceived—what was seen and heard. The cognitive level refers to interactions and communications around what the client thinks—what meaning the client ascribed to what was seen and heard. The feeling, or affective, level refers to interactions and communications around the feelings that were generated in clients by either their perceptions or their cognitions— how the client feels about what was thought or about what was seen and heard. And the behavioral level refers to interactions and communications around either the client's past or anticipated behavior—how the client behaved and how the client might behave in relation to what was and will be seen and heard. You may interact with clients at all these levels. For data collection, however, a thorough exploration of the perceptual and cognitive levels is necessary before moving into the feeling and behavioral levels.

Perhaps an example will clarify this responsibility. Put yourself in the position of the worker whose client is a 16-year-old boy who has frequent arguments with his father and who angrily left the house following an argument and drove off in a neighbor's car. In discussing the situation, the youth will probably initiate the conversation on the cognitive level—with some comment to the effect that he and his dad do not get along, that his dad does not understand him, or that his dad is unfair. These are all cognitive statements: they reflect a meaning or interpretation which the youth has placed on perceived events. A frequent interviewing error is to simply accept the meaning which the client has reported and to move immediately into the areas of feelings and behavior. A careful exploration with the client of his perceptions of the events which led to this interpretation that his father and he do not get along will be very useful. What took place? What did the boy see and hear? What did his father say? What did the boy say? What happened then? After exploring the incident in detail, the boy and worker are both prepared to consider alternative interpretations of the events. After moving back to the perceptual level (What did you see and hear?) and reconsidering the cognitive level (What meanings do you ascribe to what you saw and heard?), the client and worker may move legitimately to the question of feelings (What did you feel when this was occurring? Do I still detect a note of anger in your voice? As you look back on it now, what kinds of reactions are you having?). And from the feeling level the next logical step is to behavior (What did you do when this happened? As you look back, what might have been other ways of handling yourself? In view of such experiences, if you and your father have future arguments, what are ways in which you think you might behave?). Before moving into a consideration of the client's feelings and behavior, considerable effort is expended to collect an account of the incidents that occurred and the interpretation of those incidents. Failure to explore the perceptual and cognitive levels in detail may lead to very incomplete data with which to engage the client in problem-solving plans.

To sum up, the worker has three primary responsibilities in the interview—creating a productive climate, focusing the interview, and separating and clarifying levels of response. While the purpose of this chapter is not to offer a bag of tricks or to deal at any length with interviewing techniques, a few suggestions may help you to make a start in building a repertoire of interviewing methods for creating a productive climate, focusing the interview, and separating levels of response.

SOME IDEAS ABOUT TECHNIQUE

Open-ended questions are useful, especially in early phases of an interview or a subpart of an interview (Payne, 1951, chap. 3). An open-ended question is one that cannot be answered yes or no—rather it is one that requires an essay-type answer. Questions such as "Tell me a little about yourself" or "What would you like us to do?" are extremely open-ended. Open-ended questions are good questions to start with because they allow clients considerable leeway in beginning where they wish. If clients fumble, you can come back with a more focused question. Figure 7–2 illustrates several open-ended responses that permit the interviewer to focus the interview and invite additional participation from clients. An interview can be thought of as a funnel—starting with very broad, open-ended questions that become much more specific and focused as worker and client narrow in on specific areas of concern.

The hypothetical situation I will use is one you will meet many times as a counselor. A client will say, "I don't get along with my parents." Here are numerous responses which can be used to fulfill the two important requirements of interviewing: (1) allowing the client to express feelings, and (2) helping you to direct the interview.

—You don't get along with your parents.

—Your parents?

—What do you mean when you say . . .

—I don't understand what you mean when you say . . .

—Help me understand what you mean . . .

—Give me an example of how you . . .

—Tell me more about this.

—Uh-huh.   —and   —For instance?   —Go on.

—Oh?   —but   —I see.

—When did you first notice that . . .

—How do you feel about this? (Perhaps the most important question one could ask.)

—What are some of the things you and your parents disagree about?

—What are some problems kids like you have—not just you but all kids in general?

—What are your parents like? What is your dad like? What is your mom like? (General questions.)

—You seem to be very upset about this.

—You look worried (or you look unhappy).

—(Avoid asking a question which calls for a yes or no answer.)

—(Just be silent. A word about silence: In patients and particularly in adolescents, silence tends to provoke anxiety. Silence generally loses its effect if too prolonged.)

—You say you have trouble getting along with your parents. What are some of your troubles?

—Perhaps you could share some of your ideas about what has caused these problems.

—(It probably never helps to ask the question why. If they knew why they were having trouble with their parents, they wouldn't be seeing you.)

—Maybe it would help to talk about this.

—Compared to you, what type of people are your parents?

—If your parents were here, what would they say about this problem?

FIGURE 7–2:   Interviewing responses

Source: Dr. Richard J. Bealka, psychiatrist, Mental Health Institute, Independence, Iowa.

The interviewer attempting to secure data on which to base interventive decisions must become adept at probing for additional information. *Probing* may be an unfortunate word—the intent is not to indicate an abrasiveness or harshness but rather an invitation to pursue a particular area. Questions such as "Can you tell me more about that?" or "I'd like to hear a little more in this area" are both open-ended and probing inasmuch as they are related to something the client has said and are asking for more information. Figure 7–2 illustrates a wide number of probing questions which are nonabrasive and which both invite clients to continue to express themselves and enable the worker to provide direction to the interview.

The data collection interview requires that the worker maintain neutrality and carefully avoid biasing questions. While people may joke about the "You do love your wife, don't you?" kind of question, biases creep in in subtler ways. Cournoyer, in the article included with this chapter (Reading 7–2), cautions that:

> When asking questions, be aware that some questions reflect an implied suggestion or judgment. For example, you might seek expression from a group member by asking, "John, have you told your mother yet?" Such a question may be intended as a simple request for information. However, for John it may represent a suggestion that he should tell his mother and that if he doesn't you will be critical or disappointed.

One must be cautious about both the wording of questions and the way in which they are asked. The tone of voice and nonverbal communications can betray bias as well as a loaded question. The requirement of neutrality does not negate earlier remarks about worker input. The purpose of the data collection interview, however, is to secure reliable and valid information about the client's perceptions and interpretations of experiences; worker input at this stage would have a biasing effect and should be avoided. First the worker learns the client's position and thinking and then may consider offering the worker's own experience to the client. The sharing of worker input comes when various intervention strategies are under consideration.

Throughout this chapter frequent references have been made to checkout. Checkout requires the use of feedback in which the worker consciously and deliberately reflects back to the client what the worker is perceiving in order to determine whether the communication is correct. This is what I hear you saying. Or, I seem to be hearing this. Or, I see you're doing this. Or, am I understanding what you are saying in this? These are all feedback probes and are an effort to refer back to the client what the worker is hearing in order to allow the client to correct any errors in meaning. Feedback is a very useful and necessary technique for clarifying communications. While it may sometimes seem awkward, because this technique is seldom used in everyday activity, reflecting back to the client what is seen and heard can avoid both pitfalls and misunderstandings and also serves the function of encouraging the client to pursue conversation in a particular area. Rosen and Lieberman (1972, p. 398) examined the use of feedback among workers of different levels of training. They used the concept of stimulus-response-congruence—"the extent to which a response by one participant in the relationship provides feedback to the other participant that the message sent was actually received"—and found that trained workers maintained a lower rate of incongruent responses than untrained workers (p. 409). This finding suggests that the use of feedback is a skill acquired by training and helps explain an initial awkwardness with its use.

One final suggestion for enhancing communications is to avoid asking why. *Why* is a frequently used word in our language. But the *why* question is defense producing—it is a question that asks a person to explain one's own behavior. Social workers, by and large, are not interested in asking clients to explain their behavior but are interested in asking them to describe the situation in which they are behaving and to explore alternative ways of interpreting and reacting to that situation. Such questions as: What was happening then? What seemed to be going on? Can you tell me what you were doing? and What seemed to be the nature of the situation? are much more likely to elicit material which can be used constructively with the client in problem solving.

WRITTEN COMMUNICATIONS

This chapter has been focused largely around the use of oral communications in an interview setting for data collection purposes. Social workers make extensive use of this type of communication. But we must not negate the importance of written communication skills. Social workers are called upon to write reports, letters, and other written documents both to secure and to give information on the behalf of clients. Ability to prepare written materials may be a necessary part of the data collection phase of service or may be required later as a part of an intervention plan. The ability to express ideas clearly and accurately in written form is just as essential to social work practice as interviewing.

RECAPITULATION

In this chapter we have tried to establish a number of points. Interviewing for data collection purposes can be regarded as a set of communications which the social worker uses to secure valid and reliable data from the client concerning the client's perceptions, thinking, feelings, and behavior. The process involves giving, receiving, and checking out meanings. The client is the primary source of the data on which decisions concerning problem solving are based; thus social work interviewing techniques must be considered in terms of whether or not they contribute to the climate in which the client can share reliable and valid data. The reliability and validity of data may be impaired by six worker barriers to communication—anticipation of what the other is going to say, assumptions of meaning about communications from the other, stereotyping, inexplicit purposes for the interview, premature efforts to produce change, and inattentiveness. The quality of the data may also be affected by resistances stemming from the client's hesitancy to enter into strange situations, cultural norms affecting the client's ability to enter into problem solving, and the client's pathological involvement with the problem. The social worker collecting data has the primary responsibility for creating a climate in which the client can participate productively, for providing a focus, and for securing data on the perceptual and cognitive levels as well as on the affective and behavioral levels. Open-ended questions, probing, neutrality, extensive use of feedback, and avoiding *why* questions are all useful interviewing approaches to data collection.

One final note. We regard interviewing as a disciplined art. But does discipline interfere with spontaneity? Does learning interviewing techniques make the interviewer mechanical and nonhuman? We think not. Learning interviewing techniques may increase the social worker's spontaneity for two reasons. First, in the process of learning about interviewing, social workers become aware of and able to deal with barriers to communication in their usual responses to people. Second, interviewing techniques expand the repertoire of responses available to the worker. The increased repertoire permits increased spontaneity because the worker is not locked into an earlier, limited set of responses. Alfred Kadushin (1972, p. 2) expresses this point eloquently:

> The interviewer should, of course, be the master of the techniques rather than the obedient servant bound by rules. Technical skill is not antithetical to spontaneity. In fact, it permits a higher form of spontaneity; the skilled interviewer can deliberately violate the techniques as the occasion demands. Technical skill frees the interviewer in responding as a human being to the interviewee. Errors in relation to technique

lie with rigid, and therefore inappropriate, application. A good knowledge of techniques makes the interviewer aware of a greater variety of alternatives. Awareness and command of technical knowledge also has another advantage. To know is to be prepared; to be prepared is to experience reduced anxiety; to reduce anxiety is to increase the interviewer's freedom to be fully responsive to the interviewee.

In Chapter 6 we noted that the graceful figure skater could not become spontaneous and "free" without many hours of disciplined practice. So it is with interviewing. Spontaneity and freedom do not come naturally but with discipline, with practice, and with learning.

A LOOK FORWARD

We have made little explicit mention of problems encountered with communication across cultural or racial barriers. Interracial and intercultural communication places even greater responsibility on you to ensure that messages are being clearly received and transmitted, to be sensitive to cultural differences both in communication patterns and in perceptions of your role, and to become disciplined enough to avoid the worker barriers to communication which have been identified. John Cormican analyzes linguistic issues which may develop in interviewing including language differences, problems associated with the use of labels, and inability to articulate problems.

The second article, by Barry Cournoyer, identifies communication skills for work with groups. When interacting with groups you will be concerned about your communications with group members as well as the communications among group members. Cournoyer identifies two general forms of communication—empathic and expressive. Empathic communications draw from the client's frame of reference and are attempts to communicate your understanding of the client's expressions. Expressive communications draw from the worker's frame of reference and are efforts to share knowledge, experience, ideas, feelings, and so forth. Cournoyer's analysis and examples are from work with groups. We think his ideas are equally useful for communication with individuals.

The last article is a very brief story of how the same incident may be interpreted differently by the people involved. If we wish to communicate clearly we must be aware of the dangers of interpreting behaviors from our point of view which may not be congruent with meaning the client may assign.

In the next chapter we begin a more detailed examination of the problem-solving process which was outlined in Chapter 1. We start with a discussion of the total process.

Reading 7–1

Linguistic Issues in Interviewing*

John D. Cormican

Unlike the medical helping profession which has at its disposal biological and chemical tests to help identify a client's problems and thus suggest an appropriate physiological treatment, social work practice relies almost exclusively on language for both diagnosis and treatment.

The social worker depends on the client's speech in obtaining a history of the problem, in making a differential and social diagnosis, and in assessing levels of development and indications of social dysfunction. Social work treatment of all kinds is conducted primarily by oral means, both on the part of the worker and the client. (Portner, 1977, p. 56)

Berta Fantl (1961, p. 430) observes that *"Communication—verbal and nonverbal*—with an *adequate understanding for the subtle aspects of the situation under which communication takes place* is the vehicle for all treatment." It is in the intake interview, however, that appropriate language is most crucial in social work, because this interview provides the information on which the agency's determination of the case lies and the client, if given the choice, chooses to engage himself or herself with the agency.

LINGUISTIC PROBLEM AREAS

Linguistic problem areas which may develop in interviewing center on three major aspects of language use in social work practice. The first area concerns language differences between the worker and the client. The second is the use of labels, di-

agnostic and otherwise, which may lead the worker to lack of individualization of clients, or the clients to lack of individualization of the worker. The last linguistic problem area in interviewing is the client's lack of ability to articulate certain kinds of problems clearly.

LANGUAGE DIFFERENCES

Two kinds of language problems may interfere with communication between the worker and the client. The first occurs between people who do not speak the same languages (for example, the worker speaks English, the client Spanish), and the second involves the use of different dialects of the same language by the interacting people.

NON-ENGLISH-SPEAKING CLIENT

In the United States, an obvious language difference occurs when the client does not speak English. Alejandro Garcia (1971, p. 276) charges that "Most agencies . . . continue their punitive practice of helping only those clients who can communicate in English." He cites a Chicano client whose dealings with social workers who did not speak Spanish had made her "feel guilty and inferior because she knew no English," and who "feared that she and the worker were not really communicating with each other" through an interpreter (p. 275). Ignacio Aguilar (1972, pp. 66–70) identifies another language difference between social workers and Mexican-American clients. Most social workers do not have the time for lengthy conversations preceding the identification of the client's

* Reprinted by permission from Family Service Association of America, publisher, from *Social Casework* 59:3 (March 1978), pp. 145–152.

problem. Aguilar has shown, however, that interviews with Chicano clients that can begin with a leisurely conversation—lasting an hour or more—that is not even related to the problem are most effective, because it is customary in the Mexican-American culture to have a preliminary informal and personal interchange before approaching any serious business to be handled. Inez M. Tyler and Sophie D. Thompson (1965, pp. 215–220) have shown clearly the effectiveness of having a caseworker who speaks the language and understands the culture in dealing with Navajo clients. Clearly then, any interview with non-English-speaking clients will be more effective if the worker is familiar with the particular client's language.

VARYING DIALECTS

The more common kind of language difference between worker and client, however, is that they speak different dialects of English. These dialect differences may be the result of the worker's use of professional jargon when speaking to clients, the difference in social classes of the worker and the client, the difference in geographic areas of origin of the worker and the client, the different ethnic backgrounds of the worker and the client, or the age difference between the worker and the client.

Professional dialects. Alfred Kadushin (1972, p. 29) observes that " 'Eligibility' sounds one way and has one meaning to the worker; it sounds quite different to and evokes a different set of responses in the client. [Workers] say 'home study' and 'court record' and 'therapy' without knowing how these unfamiliar words sound to the client." Florence Hollis (1965, p. 469) notes, "intellectualization and the use of technical language is helpful with neither lower-class nor middle-class [clients]." Social workers who "use simple, everyday

English" are the most effective in conducting interviews.

Social dialects. When social workers who are middle class and whose previous work has been with middle-class clients are employed in lower-class neighborhoods, they sometimes feel that they and their lower-class clients are "conversing in different languages" (Fantl, 1961, p. 429). It is in this circumstance that the difference in social dialects may be most detrimental in an interview. Lower-class clients often "feel self-conscious about their speech . . . and uncertain how to act in initial contacts" with social service agencies (p. 427). A client who speaks a low-class dialect when talking to a middle-class worker may feel uncomfortable because of the social distance betrayed by their different dialects, and particularly so if the worker appears to be condescending toward the client either by emphasizing the differences in their speech or by attempting to speak the lower-class dialect when he or she is clearly uncomfortable doing so (Cormican & Cormican, 1977, p. 19). Hollis (1965, p. 470) points out, however, that lower-class clients are able to communicate effectively with a worker if the worker "uses words that are simple and expressive."

Regional dialects. There may be situations in which the worker and the client speak different regional dialects, because the worker has accepted a position distant from one's native geographic area, or because the client has migrated to another geographic area. In the first case, it is encumbent upon the worker to familiarize him or herself with the vocabulary differences between his or her native geographic area and the new area—for example, Northern "sweet corn" or "corn-on-the-cob" versus Midland and Southern "roasting ears" (Falk, 1973, p. 214), Northern and Midland "take" or "escort" versus

Southern "carry" (Francis, 1958, p. 522). "Turnpikes" in Pennsylvania, Ohio, Indiana, New Hampshire, Massachusetts, and Maine, versus "parkways" in Rhode Island and Connecticut, versus "thruways" in New York, versus "expressways" in Michigan versus "freeways" in California (Marckwardt, 1969, p. 151). The worker must also be aware of his or her own stereotypical attitudes toward the speakers of the regional dialect where the worker is and the attitudes of the people in that particular region toward persons who speak the worker's regional dialect, for example, the attitudes that Northerners and Southerners may have about each other. In some cases, the worker might be expected to become familiar with the regional vocabulary of any large section of the client population in the area that has immigrated from another section of the country and to be aware of the attitudes both he or she and the clients are likely to have about speakers of the different regional dialects in the area.

Ethnic dialects. If the worker and the client come from different ethnic backgrounds, the varieties of English they speak may also differ and interfere with communication in an interview. Kadushin (1972, p. 34) indicates that, "The word 'ghetto' evokes different images in the mind of a black militant in Chicago, a white matron in Greenwich, and a Hasidic Jew in Brooklyn." Thus, individual words may mean different things to the worker and the client when the words are used in an interview. Probably more important, however, are the attitudes held by the worker and the client about the dialects of English spoken by various ethnic groups. Much has been written about how black English differs from white English (Falk, 1973, pp. 224–225) and about "foreignized" English spoken by other ethnic groups (Francis, 1958, p. 517). What is important in interviewing, however, is not

the particular ethnic dialect features that the worker or client uses, but the attitude the other person has about such features (sometimes labeled "nonstandard") and toward persons who use them. There is usually no problem understanding what a person speaking an ethnic social dialect is saying; what the worker needs to be aware of is his or her own and the client's prejudices toward people who speak or do not speak a particular ethnic social dialect. Of course, the worker who speaks a particular ethnic dialect of English would do well to avoid using it whenever possible while interviewing a client who does not speak it, but the worker who is interviewing a client who does speak a different ethnic social dialect must not indicate (or, it is hoped, even feel) any rejection of the client because of his or her speech.

Age difference dialects. The final way that language differences between the worker and the client may cause communication problems in an interview centers on language differences based on age differences. The vocabulary of older persons may differ from that of the professionals dealing with them (J. Cormican, 1975, pp. 104–105), and the vocabulary level of a child client may be lower than that of the worker (J. Cormican, 1976, p. 591). In the first case, the interviewing worker would do well to avoid using contemporary slang or new words with the client. In the second case, the worker might consciously choose Germanic, that is native English, words over Latinate synonyms during the interview. What is really required in both cases is that the worker must have a broad enough and flexible enough vocabulary to communicate clearly with a wide range of clients.

USE OF LABELS

The second major area in which language may present problems within an interview is in the use of labels. Although it is a normal human process to categorize people, a situation in which a social worker mentally categorizes a client during an interview may result in the worker's failure to individualize the client's problem and to hear what the client is actually saying. Much of the social work literature deals with casework with lower-class or low-income clients. Hollis (1965, pp. 470–471) warns that "We must . . . guard against depriving [low-income] clients of the opportunity of receiving adequate casework help by our holding stereotyped and erroneous preconceptions about their limitations." Nevertheless, Carol H. Meyer (1976, p. 598) concludes that "One may wonder whether a poor person any longer has an individual identity" to many social workers.

DIAGNOSTIC LABELS

Carolyn Dillon (1969, p. 337) writes of "the hapless client whose fate is sealed by the terms *anal character* or *pseudoneurotic schizophrenic, borderline state* or *depressive case,* flesh melted from bone and reduced to a record-fattening conundrum on syndrome and synthesis." Dillon argues that diagnostic labels can erect barriers between workers and clients by setting up two distinct classes of people, with the result "that the clients have subtly become simply 'them.' " One cause of the social worker's desire to label may be the traditional medical model for social work practice. Peggy C. Giordano (1977, p. 34) reports that there has been a "deliberate attempt on the part of medical professionals to mystify the client and, by creating language barriers, to keep the client in place." Dillon (1969, p. 337) suggests that diagnostic labels which have "blurred [the worker's] ability to see clients as human beings" may actually be attractive to the worker, because of the "painful similarity"

between the worker's problems and the clients' problems.

Another problem with the diagnostic labels placed by social workers on their clients is that the labels are arbitrary and often not defined. For example, "a variety of terms—*personality disorder, neurotic character, character neurosis, behavior disorder, actor-outer*—are used synonymously with *character disorder*" (Jackel, 1976, pp. 200–201). As another example, "the term *depression* has been used to describe reactions as varied as mild emotional malaise to severe forms of psychotic melancholia" (Deykin, Weissman & Klerman, 1966, p. 288). Because "mental health and psychosis represent the two extremes on a continuum" (Jackel, 1976, p. 204), the diagnostic terms applied to clients between the two poles of the continuum could logically divide that continuum into 30 or 300 parts or into only 2 parts, such as character disorder or neurosis. Because of the problems inherent in these diagnostic labels and because no label sums up the essence of a person, Fantl (1961, p. 430) states, "We have become cautious about the terms we are using to diagnose and describe clients' difficulties." Such caution is always appropriate, but particularly so in the intake interview setting.

CATEGORY LABELS

The more general use of category labels by social workers and their clients is another way that linguistic labels present barriers to communication in interviews. The Sapir-Whorf hypothesis shows that the language one learns as a child contains the language categories that make up one's reality (Chase, 1969, p. 100). Of course, an English-speaking person then learns racial labels such as black and white as part of his reality. Clearly, a person who was actually black or white would be a real novelty because people's skin colors are actually all shades of brown, but that is beside the point. If workers and clients think people are black or white, they are. It is true that other cultures such as the Union of South Africa and Guyana use three categories—*black, white,* and *colored*—to categorize people who would be either black or white in the United States, but that only confirms the arbitrariness of the labels. Nevertheless, category labels may determine the perceptions by the worker of the client and vice versa in an interview situation.

Andrew E. Curry (1964, pp. 163–164) has pointed out that "Difficulties arise when the worker's and the client's subtle responses to *Negro* and *white* begin to spill over into the contractual relationship between them. . . . In the social context, the designations *Negro* and *white* are emotionally laden signs and symbols that have important sociopsychological stimulus value." This is so because ethnic labels as well as labels such as blind man or cripple, which indicate some major incapacity, are what Gordon Allport (1974, pp. 108–109) calls "labels of primary potency," that is, they overshadow all other labels an individual might properly have, such as teacher, father, bald, Democrat, and so on, and carry with them a great many features which the individual so labeled might not actually possess. Shirley Cooper (1978, p. 78) concludes that:

In clinical work with minority patients, an over-balanced stress on difference, on ethnicity, and on its concomitant psychological meaning can distort the helping process. It may lead a therapist to focus so centrally on ethnic factors that individual problems and individual solutions become obscured.

According to Cooper, "There is a danger of no longer treating people—only culture carriers." Similarly, Amy Iwasaki Mass (1976, p. 164) writes that "The social worker who acts on the stereotype of the model Japanese [successful and not in need of help] and expects Japanese clients

to live up to this ideal will be doing the clients a great disservice."

Specific examples of how this use of linguistic category symbols may interfere with interviewing include a recent study of white job interviewers interviewing black applicants which showed "that although the whites felt they had done a credible job with black applicants, the blacks felt there had been scarcely any communication at all" (DeLo & Green, 1977, p. 295). Similarly, caseworkers working with black and white clients in interracial situations conclude "that each case had its unique configuration of factors from both [sociological and psychological] sources, and that the caseworker's interpretation might in itself be a stereotype of psychoanalytical, sociological, or personal derivation" (Fibush & Turnquest, 1970, pp. 459–460). Perhaps Aguilar was right when he wrote, "prejudice in its purest and ugliest manifestations becomes one of the most common problems the minorities face in their encounters with helping professionals" (1972, p. 69).

INABILITY TO ARTICULATE PROBLEMS

The third broad area of language problems in interviewing is the client's real or alleged inability to articulate certain kinds of problems clearly. The phrase "real or alleged" was used in the previous sentence because the author is not convinced that clients who fall within the normal range of intelligence are ever incapable of communication because of a language deficit; they may, however, be incapable of communicating because of the circumstances of the interview. One reads that the poor family "cannot even articulate its concerns well enough to communicate with a social agency" (Meyer, 1976, p. 515), that lower-class mothers are "so inarticulate that they literally did not have the words for their emotions" (Hollis, 1965, p. 463), and that workers interviewing lower-class clients have learned not to "expect verbalization of 'inner conflict,'" (Fantl, 1961, p. 431). Hollis (1965, p. 469) reports, however, that most workers have little difficulty getting clients to discuss feelings if they themselves use appropriate language in the interview. She cautions that "simplicity of language and slowness of thought should not be mistaken for incapacity" and that "once the low-income client's confidence has been established, he is likely to speak freely, particularly of feelings of anger and frustration (p. 469).

There are clients who, because of the particular nature of their problem, may verbalize one thing and mean something entirely different. "The attitude and expression of 'Who cares?' often actually are a cover for 'I care very much but I don't dare show it'" (Leader, 1976, p. 639). Because of "the ambivalence associated with suicide," the worker talking with a potential suicide "may hear: 'Leave me alone; I don't want your help,' from a person crying out loudly for help" (Klugman, Litman, & Wold, 1965, p. 45). Similarly, the alibi system used by an alcoholic may include:

Minimizing retrospectively the harmful consequences of drinking . . . attributing alcoholism to factors no longer present, thus implying that the illness may have waned . . . suggesting that a beverage with a lower alcoholic content will be safe . . . showing self-pity . . . clinging to resentments or blaming others . . . disparaging or avoiding the AA group. (Weinberg, 1973, p. 87)

Even the drug addicts who come voluntarily to drug treatment centers and say they want to get off drugs for good "invariably . . . have a mental reservation that they would use drugs if they felt the need, but with 'proper management'" (St. Pierre, 1971, pp. 84–89). Bok-Lim C. Kim (1972, p. 278) points out that Japanese and Korean wives and their American husbands will often cite "difficulty in communication . . . [as] . . . an excuse for avoiding the inadequacies of both wives and husbands."

SUBCULTURAL DIFFERENCES

One real reason a client may not articulate his or her problem in an interview with a worker is subcultural difference. Herbert H. Locklear (1972, p. 77) notes that American Indians "tend to be reticent about speaking up and demanding their rights" when talking with a worker, and that workers are likely to interpret this reticence as indicating an unwillingness to cooperate. Jimm G. Good Tracks (1973, pp. 30–34) has suggested that the worker who adopts "a coercive tone and intervenes in an American Indian client's personal problems without being asked may very well fail completely in the interview because "any kind of intervention is contrary to the Indian's strict adherence to the principle of self-determination." Kim (1972, p. 279) cautions that "the reluctance of Oriental women to express their needs, feelings, opinions, and thoughts should not be equated with an absence of such emotions."

WORKER ATTITUDES

Of course, another reason that the client may not articulate a particular problem in an interview is the attitude of the worker. If the client fails to feel a rapport with the worker because of any of the language differences between worker and client identified earlier, or because he or she feels that the worker has treated him or her as a category rather than a person, one can hardly expect the client to be willing to discuss personal problems openly in the interview. Also, Alfred Benjamin (1974, p. 93) demonstrates clearly that a worker can tell clients either directly or indirectly that the worker does not want to hear about certain problems because of a personal value system.

CONCLUSION

There are actions, then, which the worker may take to minimize linguistic problems in interviewing. Problems based upon language differences between the worker and client can be ameliorated if the worker becomes familiar enough with the language or dialect of clients to allow clients to use their regular speech patterns in the interview and if the worker uses language that the clients can understand and accept. Problems because of the language labels used can be lessened if the worker can avoid thinking in terms of those categories and certainly if the worker can convey to a client that he or she is being considered as an individual rather than as one of "them." Finally, interviewing problems due to the real or alleged inability of the client to articulate problems can be minimized by creating an atmosphere conducive to the client's willingness to express him or herself, listening to what the client means rather than what is said, and, above all, being patient and tolerant of individual differences.

Reading 7–2

Basic Communications Skills for Work with Groups*

Barry R. Cournoyer

A well-developed competence in communications skills is essential for all social work practice. When you work directly with client systems of a size larger than one person, proficiency in communications skills is indispensable. Communication with a dyad, a family, or a small group for the purpose of problem solving is an enormously more complex interactional process than communication with an individual client alone. In the group setting, you must not only attend to the communications between you and each group member, but must also pay close attention to the communications between each member and every other member, and to those communications that transpire between you and the group as a whole.

As Schwartz (Shulman, 1979, p. 118) and others have so significantly suggested, the group worker has two clients, the individual and the group. You will be continuously shifting focus and redirecting communications back and forth from the group to the individual and back again to the group. Accurate reception of so many messages conveyed from so many sources requires an intense observational and listening effort. Similarly, the transmission of messages to the several potential recipients requires that you have well-developed skill in direct and clear communication.

There are two general forms of communications which have relevance for social work with dyads, families, and small groups. The first form of communication includes those skills which may be called empathic. The second form includes skills which we may term expressive. The major distinction between the two forms of communications and it is a distinction of remarkable significance for both the sender and receiver of messages, is that empathic

* An original article prepared for this text.

communications from the worker to a client (be it individual or group) derive from the client's frame of reference rather than from the worker's. You attempt to communicate to the client an understanding of the client's expressions. You do not introduce your own thoughts or feelings but rather paraphrase as accurately as possible the client's own communication. Expressive communications are significantly different. They derive from the worker's frame of reference and only indirectly, if at all, from the client's. Expressive skills enable you to share knowledge, ideas, experience, feelings, and expectations for the purpose of helping clients "go beyond" where they are likely to progress on their own.

EMPATHIC COMMUNICATION SKILLS

The social work profession has, from the time of its inception, recognized the importance of empathy. The frequently used phrase, "starting where the client is," and the concept of client self-determination reflect an emphasis upon understanding, appreciating, and respecting clients' feelings, thoughts, and experiences from their own point of view. As Hammond, Hepworth, and Smith (1977, p. 3) have suggested, ". . . empathy is an understanding *with* the client, rather than a diagnostic or evaluative understanding *of* the client." It is probably the single most important quality which you must regularly demonstrate in your work with clients.

Empathic communication skills are responsive or reflective. The content of empathic responses may originate with the nonverbal as well as the verbal expressions of the client. The use of these skills leads clients to feel understood and respected. They tend to encourage clients to explore and express further thoughts, feelings, and experiences which are meaningful to them. They also support the development of the interpersonal rapport so essential to the social work relationship.

Consistent with the group work notion of having two clients, the individual and the group, empathic communications may be directed toward an individual member, toward one or more subgroups, or the group as a whole. For example, when you observe or hear an individual group member's nonverbal or verbal expression of sadness and say, "Bill, you look (or sound) pretty down today," you are utilizing an empathic skill in response to an individual's expression. Of course, even though the empathic communication was directed toward one person, it has an effect upon others in the group and upon the group as a whole.

You can also empathically communicate understanding of the expressions of subgroups or the whole group. You may observe for example, that when Joan begins to talk virtually every other member crosses their arms or legs, changes facial expressions, or tilts their heads and eyes downward. You may utilize an empathic communication with the group by saying, "The group seems to be impatient with Joan just now."

Empathic communication occurs through several different specific skills but each require that the worker: (1) nonverbally attend, observe, listen, and remember, and (2) communicate accurately what the client expressed.

Nonverbal attending involves assumption of a comfortable open body position which usually does not include tightly closed hands or crossed arms but does include regular eye contact with the client. In group settings you will periodically make regular eye contact with each member, whether or not they are talking at that moment. Head nods and facial expressions which are congruent with the other's expressions represent further aspects of nonverbal attending. A pleasant accepting tone of voice which is not too loud or soft is also important. In meetings with groups or families be very aware that disproportionate nonverbal attending to one or more persons is likely to be experienced by the others as taking sides or having favorites. Attending will also involve you in observing the nonverbal behavior of each member as well as listening closely and remembering the verbal expressions of the clients. Observing, listening, and remembering are essential if you are to engage in accurate reflections of what the client has expressed. Accurate communication of understanding of the client's expression may occur through the use of these empathic communication skills:

Reflection of content.
Reflection of feelings.
Reflection of thinking/meaning.
Combined reflection.
Summarization.

Reflection of content. Reflection of content involves communicating your understanding of the client's expressions about the problem, the situation, or other aspects of their life (Carkhuff & Anthony, 1979, pp. 69–72). Frequently, you begin by inviting the individual or group to talk about their problems and situations. After the client makes a few statements, you may reflect your understanding of the content of the client's expressions. A typical reflection of content might begin with "You're saying . . ." followed by a paraphrase of the client's message. For example, a group member might share a problem by saying:

I didn't see it coming. She just packed her bags and left without a word. Two weeks ago I received a notification that she is filing for divorce.

Your reflection of the content of the message could be:

You're saying that she left suddenly without telling you and now she wants to end the marriage.

You may also reflect content expressed by subgroups or the group as a whole.

Such a response might begin with "So the group is saying" followed by an expression which demonstrates your understanding of a group problem or situation. For example, several members of a group might express their difficulties in meeting at the time and on the days scheduled. You might reflect the content by saying, "The group seems to be saying that meeting at this time or this day of the week presents a real problem for many of you."

Reflection of feeling. Reflection of feeling skill (Carkhuff & Anthony, 1979, pp. 74–78) involves communicating understanding of the client's verbal and nonverbal expressions of feelings about the problem or situation, other group members, or the worker. A typical reflection of feeling might begin by saying, "You feel . . ." followed by a restatement of the feelings expressed by the client. If the reflection is directed toward a particular subgroup or the group as a whole, you might begin by saying, "Johnny and Sue feel . . ." or "The group seems to feel . . ." For example, a particular group member might express,

I hate it when she talks to me like that. I feel so unimportant to her.

You could reflect the feelings by saying:

You become angry when she treats you that way. You end up feeling like you're a nobody in her eyes.

Should you observe downcast eyes, slouched body positions, and an occasional yawn on the part of a large number of the group members, you might reflect their probable feelings by stating, "The group seems to be tired and perhaps a little bored just now." Frequently feelings expressed by an individual or the group relate to you as a worker. When you reflect these feelings accurately, you enhance the possibility of more complete expression by the group members and a greater level of cohesion and intimacy. When a worker rightly excused a member of a teenage group from a meeting because the youth was obviously intoxicated, the remaining members became silent. They furtively looked at one another and at the worker. The worker reflected the group's feelings by suggesting "the group seems to be feeling kind of stunned right now. Are you surprised that I would ask one of you to leave?"

Reflection of thinking/meaning. Reflection of thinking or meaning (Carkhuff & Anthony, 1979, pp. 72–73) commonly involves communicating an understanding of the thoughts or the meaning that an experience has for a client. A client might share a beginning description of the problem and situation and perhaps express some of the associated feelings. You may encourage the client to proceed and to explore the thoughts about these experiences by saying, "You think . . ." and then reflect the message as implicitly or explicitly sent by the client. In a group context, such reflection may begin with, "The group seems to be thinking . . ." or "The group seems to mean . . ."

For example, a group member might describe concerns and share feelings such as:

I am really mad at my folks. They want me to get all As in school, to help out at home, and to work part-time too.

This thinking and meaning can be reflected by suggesting:

You think that your parents expect too much of you, that their demands are unreasonable.

In one group, after several group sessions in which one person has taken up a disproportionate share of the group's time, the remaining group members began to nonverbally and verbally express their disapproval. This worker might reflect their probable thinking by asking, "I wonder whether the group might be thinking that here in the group each member should have an equal opportunity to speak and when one person takes up a lot of the time not everybody has a chance?"

Combined reflections. Combined reflection involves responding to the client's direct or indirect expression of a mixture of content, feelings, thought, and meaning. Such expressions may reflect the client's view that two or more experiences seem to relate to one another, to occur together, but not necessarily in a causal relationship. At other times the client may see one experience as, in fact, the result of, or caused by, another. When the relationship is associational rather than causal you may connect the two or more empathic reflections with the words *and, but,* or *yet.* When the relationship is seen by the client as causal the connecting word changes to *because.* You might for example, respond to a client's expression by utilizing any of the following combined reflections:

You have just lost your job *and* you feel devastated, like the world just caved in.

You feel devastated *because* you lost your job.

You feel devastated *because* right now you think you will never get another decent job.

You just lost your job *and* you think you'll never get another one.

In a group you may, for example, utilize combined reflection by responding to members' expressions in the following ways:

The group feels annoyed with me just now *because* I carried out my promise to report to the judge any of you who fail the drug-screening tests.

Jean you're angry with Judy *because* she told you that you should grow up.

You all feel proud that Julio has progressed so far *but* since it means that he will be leaving the group you also feel sad.

Summarization. Summarization (Bertcher, 1979, pp. 105–114) is a reflection by a worker of a number of expressions communicated by one or more of the group members over a period of time. It may involve a single empathic skill such as reflection of content or feeling, or reflection of thinking/meaning but more often it occurs in the form of a combined reflection. A summarization might begin with a statement such as, "You've shared a number of important things here today, let's see if I can summarize the major ones." You would then go on to outline the major expressions. For example, you might summarize a group meeting in the following way:

We have explored a number of personal experiences and concerns today. Let's see if I have understood the major ones accurately, and maybe I can pull some of them together. Joseph and William are going through divorces and are experiencing feelings of guilt, anger, and loss. Maria's husband has recently died and this has left her feeling uncertain about the future. She wonders whether she'll be able to make it on her own. Wanda has lost her job and thinks she may never find another one. It seems like all of you in this group are trying to cope with some major changes in your lives and it's really a struggle to see any bright spots, any hope.

EXPRESSIVE COMMUNICATION SKILLS

Expressive communication skills differ from empathic skills in that they involve the worker communicating from his or her own rather than from the client's frame of reference. You will introduce new or extend client-initiated material beyond what the client has actually contributed. When you share knowledge, feelings, perceptions, expectations, judgments, or hypotheses you are using expressive skills. Use of expressive skills is guided by professional values, knowledge, and experience. In groups, a worker most often utilizes group theory, communication theory, role theory, and the values and ethics of

the social work profession to guide the use of expressive skills. Expressive skills are worker rather than client generated and as such must be used with sensitivity, care, and respect for the persons for whom they are intended.

The use of expressive communication skills is likely to increase the client's understanding of your view of your role, the purpose of the working relationship, and your expectations of the client. They are likely to encourage the client to become aware of additional resources and to consider new ways of thinking, feeling, and behaving. They are likely to promote and enhance the interaction between group members. And, they tend to equalize the relationship between the client and you as the client experiences you as a genuine human being. Expressive communication skills commonly used in work with groups are:

Explanation and clarification of roles, purpose, and expectations.
Seeking expression by others.
Sharing feelings and experiences.
Sharing information, knowledge, and opinions.
Focusing.
Confrontation.

Exploration and clarification of roles, purpose, and expectations. Perhaps the most fundamentally important of all the expressive skills is the exploration and clarification of roles, purpose, and expectations (Shulman, 1979, pp. 25–38). It is usually the very first communication skill demonstrated by social workers, whether the client be an individual or a group. It represents the initial contract for work. In group settings, members who are beginning for the first time typically experience a great deal of ambivalence and anxiety. Members may be asking themselves questions such as: "What will this be like?" "What will the worker do or think of me?"

"Who are these other people?" "Will they understand my concerns?" "Will they reject me?"

You can alleviate many of these concerns by clearly and directly expressing your view of the general purpose for the group, by clarifying your role in regard to the group's work, and by outlining the expectations you have for the group members. For example, a social worker beginning a group for battered women might initiate the exploration and clarification of roles, purpose and expectations by stating:

Now that we've all gotten seated I'd like to introduce myself and share my view about how we might use these times together. My name is Sue Walker and I'm a social worker here at the counseling center. As I see it, the general purpose of this group is to provide people like yourselves who are dealing with aggression and violence in the home, an opportunity to share your problems and concerns with others who are in the same boat. I don't see myself as an expert who listens to your problems and then tells you what you should do. Rather, I see my role as helping you help each other. I'll kind of get things started each time we meet and try to make sure that everybody gets a chance to be heard and maybe I'll identify some topics or share some of the information that I have about family violence. What I'd like each of you to do in the group is to share your own concerns and experiences with the other members, listen to others express theirs, and then we'll all try to help each other resolve problems that are presented. How does that sound to you?

Of course, the use of the exploration and clarification skills varies due to the particular purpose for each group, the role that the social worker assumes in regard to the group, and the characteristics of group members. Typically clarification of role, purpose, and expectations needs to be more lengthy with groups than with individuals because these comments may help lessen the relatively greater levels of anxiety and ambivalence that occur in groups. With clients who are more or less forced to participate, the clarification of roles and expectations should be extensive and detailed.

Seeking expression of thoughts, feelings, and experiences. The communication skill of seeking expression (Bertcher, 1979, pp. 43–53; Shulman, 1979, p. 50) typically occurs through the worker asking questions or making comments which are, in effect, questions. The regular use of the empathic skills, however, tends to reduce the need to ask questions. After a group has been together for awhile it will usually be possible for you to reduce the number of your questions as group members begin to seek expression from one another. Questions may be open- or closed-end. Open-end questions lead clients to express themselves in a more lengthy fashion. Examples of such questions are: "How did that occur?" "What were your thoughts?" "How do you feel?" "What did that mean to you?" "How do you explain that?" Closed-end questions lead to short, sometimes even yes or no responses and are likely to yield a great deal of information in a short period of time. Some examples are: "How many children do you have?" "Are you married?" "When did you move there?" "Have you ever received counseling services before?"

When asking questions, be aware that some questions reflect an implied suggestion or a judgment. For example, you might seek expression from a group member by asking, "John, have you told your mother yet?" Such a question may be intended as a simple request for information. However, for John it may represent a suggestion that he should tell his mother and that if he doesn't you will be critical or disappointed in him.

The seeking expression skill is often routinely used after social workers have used other expressive skills, such as exploring and clarifying roles and sharing information. You may seek feedback through such questions as: "How does that sound?" "Does that make sense?" "I'm wondering what you think and feel about what I've just said?"

In problem-solving groups, the seeking expression skill is utilized extensively not only to encourage members to share personal experiences but also as a means for facilitating group interaction. For example, one group member, Diane, might have been talking about her disappointing experience with men. You might then seek expression from another member by asking, "Bill, I wonder if you'd care to share with Diane some of your experiences with women." Other examples of the worker using the seeking expression still include, "Mary, I'd be interested in your reaction to that. "Jack, would you like feedback from the group as to how we see you?"

As the group proceeds, you can sometimes become even more directive in promoting interaction. For example, "Jack, would you move over next to Mary and speak directly with her about this?" You can also facilitate interaction by seeking expression from the group as a whole. For example, "I'd like to hear how the group feels toward Jan just now." Usually, as the group develops, you need to facilitate interaction less and less as the members begin to seek and share expressions directly with one another.

Sharing feelings and experiences. When you as a social worker appropriately share your own feelings and experiences (Hammond, Hepworth, & Smith, 1977, pp. 204–227; Shulman, 1979, pp. 58–65) you are more likely to be perceived by clients as a genuine, nonmechanical human being. You contribute to interpersonal rapport and mutual understanding when you share your feelings and experiences in nonblaming ways. In so doing, you also model effective interpersonal communication. You should be careful however, not to share so many feelings and experiences that meetings become

contexts to work on your own problems. It is difficult for clients to deal with their concerns when they feel a need to take care of you. As a guideline for the sharing of feelings and experiences, you should ask yourself, "Will my expression support the group's work in relation to its purpose and goals?" If the answer is yes, then you may disclose personal feelings and experiences. However, even when it is determined that the nature of the shared feelings or experiences is professionally advised, you should express yourself in such a way as to maintain responsibility for your own feelings. Other persons and particularly clients should not be suggested to be the cause of your feelings. For example, if you were to say to a group member, "You make me feel sad (or angry or protective, and so on)," then you are indicating that the client is responsible for or the cause of your feelings. You would be blaming the client for your own feelings. Such a communication is neither personally nor professionally wise. A better expression would be, "When I listen to your feelings of loss and sadness, I feel like crying right along with you."

Here are some examples of shared social worker feelings and experiences:

Jim, your feelings about your Vietnam experience really hit home with me. I too was in Nam and when I came back, I felt more like a foreigner than an American.

I'm feeling uneasy about what's happening in the group just now. We seemed to skip over Judy's feelings of disappointment in us as a support group. I guess, when you expressed your feelings, Judy, I kind of felt a bit defensive, you know, like the group isn't meeting your needs and maybe I felt guilty, like it's my fault that you don't find the group helpful.

Jack, when your voice becomes loud, and you point your finger at me, I begin to think that you're angry at me and then I get mad too.

Yes, I do feel a bit annoyed when you arrive late for the group meetings and I'd like it better if you were here on time. However, I'd be much more disappointed if you didn't come at all.

Sharing information, knowledge, and opinions. The skill of sharing information (Shulman, 1979, pp. 79–84) is a vital one in social work practice. Social workers frequently share information about community programs and services that may represent resources for clients. Social workers provide details about the time and location of meetings, fees, and other information needed by clients. When conducting in-service training or leading educationally oriented groups, social workers regularly share large amounts of information which relate to their teaching function. However, social workers leading problem-solving groups sometimes feel that members must discover certain information on their own. While it is desirable that the group members share information with and learn from one another, often they do not have relevant, accurate, or complete information. If (Shulman, 1979, p. 79) the information is relevant to the purpose for the group and the current work of the group, then you may appropriately provide such data. If you have relevant data you have a responsibility to provide it to clients seeking or needing such information.

In sharing information, however, you should clearly distinguish between fact and opinion, and should convey the data in such a way that it freely allows the client to accept or reject the information. When sharing opinions you should qualify your expressions through the use of such phrases as: "in my opinion . . ." or "it's my view . . ." You should clearly communicate that the client has every freedom to use or not use, to agree or disagree, with the shared information. Here are some examples:

You folks are talking about something here that I know about. The fees for that program are based on a family's ability to pay. The more income a family has, the more services cost, up to a highest fee of $35.00 per visit.

It's my view that parents ought to gradually loosen the rules that they have and their ways of disciplining as their children grow. I think that the adolescent of 13 should be treated differently by parents than the young adult of 17. What do you think?

Focusing. Focusing (Bertcher, 1979, pp. 95–103) is an expressive communication skill through which social workers highlight or call attention to something that is, or could be, of importance to the group's work. Frequently, groups in their discussions, wander away from their agreed-upon purpose and you may need to redirect the discussion back toward the work to be done. Often there are interpersonal dynamics or processes which you may wish to highlight for the group. For example, a social worker leading a group for persons with personal problems might focus in the following way:

I noticed that when Sheila said she sometimes thinks of doing away with herself, the rest of us suddenly got quiet and then went on to some other topic. I'd like to back up a little and really respond to what Sheila was saying.

Following is another example of a worker using focusing skill with a group member who has expressed a desire to improve interpersonal relationships.

Sue, you've said that all the men in your life have been irresponsible and undependable. Since, I'm a man and there are other men in the group, I wonder if you'd tell us what we might do or have already done that would mean to you that we are irresponsible or undependable?

Confronting. The use of confrontation skill (Hammond, Hepworth, & Smith, 1977, pp. 268–332) involves directly pointing out to a client a discrepancy or an inconsistency between statements and actions. The social worker, in effect, requests that the client examine an apparent contradiction inconsistency in the client's thoughts, feelings, and behavior. You may even suggest that the client consider making a change toward greater congruence between words and deeds. This skill should be used with considerable caution since clients can experience intense emotional reactions when confronted. Typically, confrontation is used infrequently in groups and when used is communicated with warmth, understanding, and concern for the client. It is good practice to utilize empathic communications before and after confrontations.

Confrontations should be delivered in such a way that you assume responsibility for the accuracy of the confrontation and recognized that others may see things differently. Here are examples of confrontations communicated by social workers working with groups:

Julie, you say that you want to get good grades but you also tell us that you don't do a whole lot of studying. Are you able to get good grades without putting in time with the books?

George, you've identified a number of goals that you want to work on in the group but I wonder whether some of them are truly achievable. Are you setting up goals that are impossible to reach?

Everybody here is in this group because the judge gave you a choice between coming here to work on the drinking problem, or going to jail. You've all been coming each time but it seems to me that you're not really interested in trying to get a handle on the drinking problem. I think you're just going through the motions. How about it?

SUMMARY

Successful work with groups, requires that you maintain a dual focus at all times. Attention must be equally given to the individuals and the group as a whole. Empathic communication skills reflect the client's frame of reference and are the relationship building tools for work with groups. Their sensitive and consistent use leads to the development of a cohesive, interactive group where thoughts, feelings, and experiences are freely shared. Expressive communication skills reflect your social work frame of reference and build upon an empathic foundation by assisting clients as they proceed into uncharted territory, exploring and experimenting with new information, new experiences, and new perspectives.

Reading 7–3

Point of View

A. Averchenko

"Men are comic," she said, smiling dreamily. Not knowing whether this indicated praise or blame, I answered noncommittally: "Quite true."

"Really, my husband's a regular Othello. Sometimes I'm sorry I married him."

I looked helplessly at her. "Until you explain—" I began.

"Oh, I forgot that you haven't heard.

About three weeks ago, I was walking home with my husband through the square. I had a large black hat on, which suits me awfully well, and my cheeks were quite pink from walking. As we passed under a streetlight, a pale, dark-haired fellow standing nearby glanced at me and suddenly took my husband by his sleeve.

"Would you oblige me with a light," he says. Alexander pulled his arm away, stooped down, and quicker than lightening, banged him on the head with a brick. He fell like a log. Awful!"

"Why, what on earth made your husband get jealous all of a sudden?" She shrugged her shoulders. "I told you men are very comic."

Bidding her farewell, I went out, and at the corner came across her husband.

"Hello, old chap," I said. "They tell me you've been breaking people's heads."

He burst out laughing. "So you've been talking to my wife. It was jolly lucky that brick came to pat into my hand. Otherwise, just think: I had about fifteen hundred rubles in my pocket, and my wife was wearing her diamond earrings."

"Do you think he wanted to rob you?"

"A man accosts you in a deserted spot, asks for a light, and gets hold of your arm. What more do you want?"

Perplexed, I left him and walked on.

"There's no catching you today," I heard a voice say from behind.

I looked around and saw a friend I hadn't set eyes upon for three weeks.

"Lord!" I exclaimed. "What on earth has happened to you?"

He smiled faintly and asked in turn: "Do you know whether any lunatics have been at large lately? I was attacked by one three weeks ago. I left the hospital only today."

With sudden interest, I asked: "Three weeks ago? Were you sitting in the square?"

"Yes, I was. The most absurd thing. I was sitting in the square, dying for a smoke. No matches! After ten minutes or so, a gentleman passed with some old hag. He was smoking. I go up to him, touch him on the sleeve and ask in my most polite manner: "Can you oblige me with a light?" And what do you think? The madman stoops down, picks something up, and the next moment I am lying on the ground with a broken head, unconscious. You probably read about it in the newspapers."

I looked at him and asked earnestly: "Do you really believe you met up with a lunatic?"

"I am sure of it."

Anyhow, afterwards I was eagerly digging in old back numbers of the local paper. At last I found what I was looking for: A short note in the accident column.

UNDER THE INFLUENCE OF DRINK

Yesterday morning, the keepers of the square found on a bench a young man whose papers show him to be of good family. He had evidently fallen to the ground while in a state of extreme intoxication, and had broken his head on a nearby brick. The distress of the prodigal's parents is indescribable.

References

Aguilar, Ignacio. Initial contracts with Mexican-American/American families. *Social Work*, 17:3 (May, 1972), pp. 66–70.

Allport, Gordon W. Linguistic factors in prejudice. In Paul A. Escholz, Alfred F. Rosa, & Virginia P. Clark (Eds.), *Language awareness*. New York: St. Martin's Press, 1974.

Bateson, Gregory, Jackson, Don D., Haley, Jay, & Weakland, John N. A note on the double bind—1962. *Family Process*, 1963, 2, 154–161.

Benjamin, Alfred. *The helping interview*. Boston: Houghton Mifflin, 1974.

Bertcher, Harvey J. *Group participation: Techniques for leaders and members*. Beverly Hills, Calif.: Sale Publications, 1979.

Bloom, Allen.   Social work and the English language. *Social Casework,* June 1980, *61,* 332–338.

Brown, Robert A.   Feedback in family interviewing. *Social Work,* September 1973, *18,* 52–59.

Carkhuff, Robert R., & Anthony, William A.   *The skills of helping.* Amherst, Mass.: Human Resource Development Press, 1979.

Chase, Stuart.   How language shapes our thoughts. In J. Burl Hogins & Robert E. Yarker (Eds.), *Language: An introductory reader.* New York: Harper & Row, 1969.

Cooper, Shirley.   A look at the effect of racism on clinical work. *Social Casework,* February 1978, *54,* 78.

Cormican, Elin J., & Cormican, John D.   The necessity of linguistic sophistication for social workers. *Journal of Education for Social Work,* Spring 1977, *13,* 18–22.

Cormican, John D.   Breaking language barriers between the patient and his doctor. *Geriatrics,* December 1975, *30,* 104–110.

Cormican, John D.   Linguistic subculture and social work practice. *Social Casework,* November 1976, *57,* 59.

Curry, Andrew E.   The Negro worker and the white client: A commentary on the treatment relationship. *Social Casework,* March 1964, *45,* 131–136.

De Schweinitz, Karl, & de Schweinitz, Elizabeth.   *Interviewing in the social services.* London: National Institute for Social Work Training, 1962.

De Lo, James S., & Green, William A.   Cognitive transactional approach to communication. *Social Caseworker,* May 1977, *58,* 294–300.

Deykin, Eva Y., Weissman, Myrna M., & Klerman, Gerald L.   Treatment of depressed women. *British Journal of Social Work,* Fall 1971, *1,* 277–291.

Dillon, Carolyn.   The professional name game. *Social Casework,* June 1969, *50,* 337–340.

Falk, Julia S.   *Linguistics and language.* Lexington, Mass.: Xerox College Publishing, 1973.

Fantl, Berta.   Casework in lower class districts. *Mental Hygiene,* July 1961, *45,* 425–438.

Fibush, Esther, & Turnquest, BeAlva.   A black and white approach to the problem of racism. *Social Casework,* October 1970, *51,* 459–466.

Francis, W. Nelson.   *The structure of American English.* New York: Ronald Press, 1958.

Frankenstein, Renate.   Agency and client resistance. *Social Casework,* 1982, *63,* 24–28.

Garcia, Alejandro.   The Chicano and social work. *Social Casework,* May 1971, *52,* 274–278.

Garrett, Annette.   *Interviewing: Its principles and methods* (2d ed.). New York: Family Service Assn. of America, 1972.

Giordano, Peggy C.   The client's perspective in agency evaluation. *Social Work,* January 1977, *22,* 34–39.

Good Tracks, Jimm G.   Native American non-interference. *Social Work,* November 1973, *8,* 30–34.

Hammond, D. Corydon, Hepworth, Dean H., & Smith, Veon G.   *Improving therapeutic communication.* San Francisco: Jossey-Bass, 1977.

Hollis, Florence. Casework and social class. *Social Casework*, October 1965, *46*, 463–471.

Jackel, Merl M. Clients with character disorders. In Francis J. Turner (Ed.), *Differential diagnosis and treatment*. New York: Free Press, 1976.

Johnston, Norman. Sources of distortion and deception in prison interviewing. *Federal Probation*, January 1956, *20*, 43–48.

Kadushin, Alfred. *The social work interview*. New York: Columbia University Press, 1972.

Kahn, Robert, & Connell, Charles. *The dynamics of interviewing*. New York: Wiley, 1957.

Kim, Bok-Lim C. Casework with Japanese and Korean wives of Americans. *Social Casework*, May 1972, *53*, 273–279.

Klugman, David J., Litman, Robert E., & Wold, Carl L. Suicide: Answering the Cry for Help. *Social Work*, October 1965, 43–50.

Leader, Arthur. Denied dependency in family therapy. *Social Casework*, December 1976, *57*, 634–643.

Locklear, Herbert H. American Indian myths. *Social Work*, May 1972, *17*, 72–80.

Marckwardt, Albert H. Regional variations. In J. Burl Hogins & Robert E. Yeager (Eds.), *Language: An introductory reader*. New York: Harper & Row, 1969.

Mass, Amy Iwasaki. Asians as individuals: The Japanese community. *Social Casework*, March 1976, *57*, 160–164.

Meyer, Carol H. Individualizing the multi-problem family. In Francis J. Turner (Ed.), *Differential diagnosis and treatment*. New York: Free Press, 1976.

Payne, Stanley. *The art of asking questions*. Princeton, N.J.: Princeton University Press, 1951.

Portner, Doreen Lindsay. Personality development in deaf children. *Social Work*, January 1977, *22*, 54–57.

Rich, John. *Interviewing children and adolescents*. New York: St. Martin's Press, 1968.

Rogers, Carl. Some personal learnings about interpersonal relationships. Filmed lecture provided by Academic Communications Facility, University of California at Los Angeles, n.d.

Rosen, Aaron, & Lieberman, Dina. The experimental evaluation of interview performance of social workers. *Social Science Review*, September 1972, *46*, 395–412.

Satir, Virginia. *Conjoint family therapy: A guide to therapy and technique*. Palo Alto, Calif.: Science and Behavior Books, 1964.

Schubert, Margaret. *Interviewing in social work practice*. New York: Council on Social Work Education, 1982. (Originally published, 1971.)

Schwartz, William. The social worker and the group. In *The social welfare forum*. New York: Columbia University Press 1961.

Shulman, Lawrence. *The skills of helping individuals and groups*. Itasca, Ill.: F. E. Peacock Publishers, 1979.

St. Pierre, C. Andre. Motivating the drug addict in treatment. *Social Work*, January 1971, *16*, 50–88.

Tyler, Inez M., & Thompson, Sophie D. Cultural factors in casework treatment of a Navajo mental patient. *Social Casework*, April 1965, *46*, 215–220.

Weinberg, Jon. Counseling recovering alcoholics. *Social Work*, July 1973, *18*, 84–93.

Chapter 8

Problem Solving:
A Process for Social Work Practice

In the first chapter of this book we briefly discussed six elements which we identified as components of social work practice. In this chapter we will focus on the most critical element of the six—process—and we will begin a detailed discussion of the problem-solving model of process. Considered in this way, process may be understood as a series of interactions between the client system and the practitioner, involving the integration of feeling, thinking, and doing, directed toward achieving an agreed-upon goal. It is the work of process that brings about the solution of the problem, although for process to be effective it must involve an interaction supported and guided by an appropriate knowledge; it must be conducted within the values and sanctions of the profession and a relationship appropriate to working together must develop.

As we stated in the earlier chapters, relationship and understanding do not develop just because two bodies, one called the worker and the other, the client, find themselves in a common enclosed space. Relationship, understanding, and a freedom of communication develop as practitioner and client system work together toward some purpose. Thus, considered in relation to the practitioner's interaction with the client system, social work process can be considered in terms of cooperation—resting on the ability of each to relate and communicate with the other—between the clients (or client system) who has available information about what (1) brings them in contact with the social work practitioner and (2) what they expect of this contact, and the social worker who has at hand *(a)* a body of information about a variety of problems, *(b)* available resources that may be available to bring to bear on the problem, *(c)* certain methods and skills of helping, and *(d)* an orderly way of proceeding (a pattern of thinking if you will) that move client and worker toward a problem solution. This orderly way of proceeding increases the probability of appropriate selection and utilization of (1) what the client brings to the situation and (2) the practitioner's knowledge and information toward the end of improving the client's ability to realize aspirations and values.

Our notion of process as a problem-solving activity rests on the belief that for anyone, or for any social system, effective movement toward purposive change, or altering something that one wishes to alter, rests on the ability of the system, or of the professional helper, to engage in rational goal-directed thinking and to divide this cognitive activity into sequential stages. Each stage involves a particular kind of work aimed at the particular goal of that stage. The way the work on this phase is done will determine the effectiveness with which work on the next stage can go forward. Since this is the process by which each person attempts to solve the inevitable problems of life or reach the necessary decisions as to alternative solutions to be selected, the worker who follows this model is following a life model of human growth and development. This means that the worker is not involved in treating an illness, or in bringing about a cure for client troubles, but rather is joining the forward motion of the client system and is, along with helping the client, strengthening the client's capacity to cope more effectively with life.

PROBLEM SOLVING AS A LIFE PROCESS

There are some particularly pervasive misunderstandings and assumptions that always seem to surround the introduction of the process of social work practice as a problem-solving effort. One assumption seems to relate to a common culturally supported notion that competent people do not have problems or that there is something wrong or bad or weak implied when one speaks of problem solving. These assumptions do violence to our notion of the place of problem solving in the life process of all people. Life itself is a problem-solving process. Reid (1978, p. 26) says it well when he says that "a want . . . experienced without satisfaction becomes a problem." Since human wants are endless, and when one is satisfied another immediately takes its place, we all are constantly involved in problem solving; although some of us, because we do not understand how one problem solves effectively, make a great mess of it. Everything we do in our daily life represents a response to a problem of living, even though few of us are conscious of it in this way. Perhaps that is why we find it so hard to effectively help others problem solve—so difficult to follow the steps of the process. Those of us who are good problem solvers do it so automatically that we do not understand the process, concentrating only on the result. For example, when we awake in the morning we are immediately confronted with a problem: Do we get up, and, if so, when? We quickly and, sometimes quite unconsciously, collect data about this problem. What do we anticipate accomplishing today? How important is it to us? (Goals?) What will be the reaction of meaningful people to our decision? Will those around us impose certain sanctions on us because we have not done this? As we perceive and integrate the data, we come to a decision and (hopefully) take action. We will have further difficulties and a growing set of problems developing around this simple problem if we incorrectly perceive the implications of the problem for what we want to accomplish. For example, we may try to get up when physically we cannot or should not. Or we may decide to remain in bed when getting up and taking certain actions is critically important to our well-being. It is not that those of us who are successful in life are without problems. It is that we solve problems well.

In order to solve problems in living competently there are certain steps we all must take, and these steps are the same as those that social workers use in order to help the client. First, one must perceive a want and then identify the problem that must be solved to satisfy this want. Wants often generate out of our goals for ourselves, and the solution to be satisfactory must relate to these goals. Given our goals, we start to gather data related to the situation. It is impossible at this point to list in detail all the data one would want to collect in any one situation but the data collected, in general, would involve the internal, emotional response, the feelings one has; the feeling of others who are important to one, their wishes; the possible responses, sanctions, and opportunities of the environment; one's abilities and skills to carry through on the action proposed. One then generates a number of alternative responses. The greater number of alternative responses or solutions one is able to consider, the more satisfactory the final action will be, provided that one is able to take action to achieve the solution. It can be devastating if one constantly gets tangled in so many alternatives that one cannot act, or if one selects a solution totally beyond one's ability to achieve. As we consider solutions, we need to consider again the data we have acquired. Action is then taken to carry out one's decision and to evaluate the results of the action so one can learn from the process. This evaluation is an attempt to assess whether the action taken moved one toward the goals one held. If our evaluation of a step taken is negative we often go back and try to assess what step in the problem-solving process was not well done. We say, "if only we had known . . ." When we say this we are usually saying that we either perceived or defined the problem incorrectly, or we did not have the knowledge (data) necessary to an appropriate decision. Sometimes it may mean that our method of action was not effective. There are those of us who may suffer a great deal at this point in the problem-solving process, because we hold ourselves totally responsible for a negative outcome. Actually the only 20/20 vision in life is hindsight. We all approach all problems in living with incomplete knowledge. We can never be sure of the solution. Our only security is the process.

The process of working toward the solution of problems in living always contains emotions or feelings, always involves the knowledge base that we have available to us, always involves our perception of the world around us as well as our internal state, a way of organizing data, skills in action, our values and basic philosophies and attitudes (which often determine our goals) and a way of thinking that involves an orderly approach. These elements interact in a most complex way, and it is with this tangled interaction that most social workers are asked to help. Certainly, if one has a problem that one recognizes that one cannot solve by oneself, or that is perceived as representing a serious threat to the goals one holds, or seriously threatens the needs and wants of those close to us, one may find oneself in a very painful situation. This pain, the high feeling generated by the problem, and one's judgment of self as one recognizes one's inability to solve it, usually obscures parts of the problem, interferes with data collection, and consideration of alternative solutions as well as blocking the effective actions toward solution. In many situations, the client system is quite able to solve the problem, given the help of the social worker to deal with and dissipate the feeling. Thus, if the client has the appropriate knowledge, skills, and resources, it may be that the problem-solving activities concentrate primarily around the dissipation of feeling or understanding and acceptance of self. However, for most of our clients dissipation of feeling is not enough. They may need additional knowledge either about the problem, what data is needed, or appropriate solutions, and, most important, they may need the appropriate resources to enable them to take the necessary action. An example of the interaction of emotion, knowledge, and relationship is well illustrated by the following statement made by the mother of a retarded child when she was asked to evaluate the service given her by the social worker. This mother had gone from physician to physician seeking someone to tell her that her son would eventually be "normal" in intelligence, she had endured the comments of neighbors and her own in-laws that implied that she had done something wrong during the pregnancy, she had become exhausted and near collapse from trying to care for her retarded baby and her family with no knowledge of how to care for him or what the course of his development might be. She came to the social worker at very low ebb indeed, seeking help with the problem of understanding and caring for her son. As you read the case example you see how dealing with feeling, supplying knowledge, and the use of a supportive relationship helped this mother.

> Miss B. helped immeasurably at this point. She gave us a place to start. We were actually relieved to hear, for the first time in Tony's life, our suspicions confirmed, and to find that there were still many things that Tony could do; and that with our understanding and help Tony had a chance to find a fairly satisfactory life. This did not come overnight. It took many meetings, going over and over the subject before it began to take hold. It is a shock to find out that your child isn't as bright as normal, and that his retardation will probably be more apparent as the years go by. At first you feel hopeless, but after many conferences, you begin to realize that there are still many accomplishments of your child that you have a right to be proud of. You also realize that it really isn't too important what your relatives and neighbors think. You realize that it is your problem to work out, and most important you can be happy doing it. You are helped to see the retarded child's rightful place in the home, that he needn't be the hub around which the entire family revolves.
>
> When I started working with Miss B. I was at a very low ebb. I did not think that I would ever be able to handle Tony, and my lack of confidence with him was beginning to tell on the other children. She made me feel that I had done a fine job under very difficult circumstances, and even if it developed that we could not keep Tony at home, that it would not be a particular failure on my part. She helped me sort out my ideas and feelings so that I could see the total picture more clearly. She helped me get over the feelings of guilt I had. I realize now that one of her most important functions was not telling me what to do, but asking a pertinent question at just the right moment. Sometimes when a parent is trying to solve these things alone, I believe, they begin thinking in a circle that they can't escape without aid from someone who understands but who is not emotionally bound up in the

problem. Many times I have come home from the clinic with a perfectly obvious answer that occurred to me only after a question from the social worker stimulated my thinking.

All effective clinical processes involve feeling, on the part of both practitioner and client. These feelings become a part of the content of problem solving—a necessary and vital part—as well as providing a climate in which helping takes place. Because the steps in problem solving in clinical practice resemble the steps of the research process, it is possible for those inexperienced in its use to see it as essentially a cognitive process engaging only the intellectual capacities of the client. Actually the best of research is, in the last analysis, an orderly process of problem solving. Thus we may say that the process of research and social work practice are similar. The difference between the two efforts lies in their purpose and in their content. The purpose of research is to build knowledge, the purpose of problem solving with clients is to help them in their forward progress in living. The content of problem solving in research efforts depends upon the questions asked or the hypotheses developed. The content of problem solving in clinical practice depends upon what the client brings and what the client wants.

DEWEY AND PROBLEM SOLVING

The ancestor to problem solving is typically identified to be *How We Think*, a volume written by John Dewey in 1933, in which he attempted to describe the thought processes of a human being when confronted with a problem. In doing so, Dewey was interested in clarifying reflective or rational thinking, goal-directed thinking, or problem solving. According to Dewey, problem-solving behavior is based on reflective thought that begins with a feeling of perplexity, doubt, or confusion. The person wants to eliminate the difficulty or solve the puzzle, but in order to do this effectively one must follow a rational procedure. If one fails to do so, one can act uncritically or impulsively, leaping to inappropriate conclusions, mistaking the nature of the problem, becoming involved in searching for the answer to the wrong problem, or making a number of other errors. Any one of these behaviors may very well compromise the capacity to cope with the situation and undoubtedly makes it likely that the problem will remain unsolved.

Dewey held that effective problem solving demands the active pursuit of a set of procedural steps in a well-defined and orderly sequence. Dewey referred to these steps as the "five phases of reflective thinking," and they include recognizing the difficulty; defining or specifying the difficulty; raising suggestions for possible solutions and rationally exploring the suggestions, which includes data collection; selecting an optimal solution from among many proposals; and carrying out the solution. Since Dewey, many persons, working in various areas of endeavor, have come to recognize that when one engages in investigation and problem solving, there is a preferred model for orderly thought and action that can be laid out in progressive steps and pointed toward the reaching of a solution, and that the conscientious implementation of such a model materially increases the likelihood that one's objectives can be achieved.

It has been recognized that Dewey's list of five successive phases can be broken down into finer incremental steps and that orderly precision follows when this is done. Further, it has been recognized that Dewey's list failed to include the terminal aspects of problem solving—the evaluation of the effectiveness of the attempted solution, and the use of feedback loops (see Chapter 4) into the process, by which modifications can be made in the procedures employed even as one is engaged in employing them. In social work literature one will find a number of models which divide the activities of a social worker into sequential phases, each phase characterized by some broad goal of its own which must be accomplished before the worker moves on to complete the next phase.

In the early 1940s a mathematics professor, George Polya (1957), developed a model to help mathematics instructors to teach mathematical problem solving, but his aim really went beyond that. He intended that the book should be used as a guide by all problem solvers. He presented a four-phase model: (1) understanding the problem including understanding the problem situation, the goal of the problem solver, and the conditions for solving the problem; (2) devising a plan by which the goal could be attained; (3) carrying out the plan; and (4) evaluation of the plan, its implementation, and the results.

The scientific method itself may also be considered a model of problem solving, and other frameworks have been developed by other authors in the behavioral sciences. Notable among these efforts is the work of Bennis, Benne, and Chin (1969) in their development of strategies of effecting change in human systems. These authors, however, see the problem-solving process as a normative reeducative approach to change. It is the authors' position that the formulation is broader than that.

PROBLEM SOLVING IN SOCIAL WORK

We are neither the first nor only people in social work to have conceptualized social work practice within this type of framework. In social work Helen Harris Perlman must be considered the originator of the "problem-solving framework." Her principal work, *Social Casework: A Problem-Solving Process,* was published in 1957 and has had tremendous impact on social work thinking. She has written extensively, and readers will remember our use of some of her formulations on role in earlier chapters. Both Perlman and the present authors have based their formulations on constructs from ego psychology and on Dewey's work on principles of problem solving. One of the principal differences in the knowledge base utilized by Perlman from that used by the present authors is the use of systems theory as a foundation in the present text. This results in our extending of problem-solving methods of groups, organizations, and communities and in our broadening our model to include more emphasis than one finds in Perlman's work on transactions with and change in other social systems. Further Perlman puts particular emphasis on the professional practitioner's primary responsibility for thinking about the facts and for the other activities of diagnosis and planning. While we believe with Perlman that the worker carries responsibility to do this hard responsible "head work," and to see that the process moves forward, we also believe that the worker must test out such thinking with the client and that there is a shared responsibility between worker and client for every phase of problem-solving work, including especially the assessment/decision-making phase. Perlman basically sees problem solving as both a process and a method of helping. We see it as a process which may lead to use of a number of helping methods. We see the worker engaging in broader array of helper roles than does Perlman. She primarily emphasizes the enabler role of the worker and does not distinguish as sharply as we do between the various stages of the process. She says that treatment begins with the first glance between worker and client, although she puts considerable emphasis on the fact that the work between worker and client cannot proceed until the client has moved from role of the applicant to that of client and thus our notions coincide with hers.

In social work literature one will find a number of other authors writing about problem solving who divide the activities of a social worker into sequential phases, each phase characterized by some broad goal of its own and requiring specific social work skills, which must be accomplished before moving on to complete the next phase. In general such models demand that the worker be successively involved with (1) recognition or definition of the problem and engagement with the client system, (2) goal setting, (3) data collection, (4) assessment of the situation and the planning of action, (5) intervention, or the carrying out of action, (6) evaluation, and (7) termination.

PROBLEM SOLVING AND THE PRACTITIONER'S RESPONSIBILITY

While we believe that the problem-solving process is orderly, that it is sequential, and that any one phase depends on the successful completion of the preceding phase, we also feel that any linear sequencing of tasks is an oversimplification of the process. In any given situation the worker may be operating in more than one phase at a time. In spite of the fact that the phases follow each other in some rough order, one phase does not wait upon the completion of another before it begins. Problem solving in social work probably proceeds, not linearly, but by a kind of spiral process in which action does not always wait upon the completion of assessment, and assessment often begins before data collection is complete. In fact, one often becomes aware that one has not collected enough facts, or the proper facts, only after one begins the process of trying to put all one knows together in some sort of summing-up process. Also, when the worker and the client system begin to take action toward some solution of the problem, it might well be discovered that they have selected an unworkable alternative or they are proceeding on the wrong problem and must start all over again. However, in this case, one begins again with the distinct advantage of having some knowledge and some observations and some working relationships that one did not have before.

We can well understand Perlman's statement about treatment beginning with the first glance between client and worker. However, it might be phrased somewhat differently. We would say that the beginning of the relationship comes with that first glance and that this beginning climate has meaning for the problem identification, analysis and solution. As the problem-solving work progresses through the various phases, this beginning relationship will also change, perhaps, in a progressive developmental way and perhaps radically and abruptly. At the moment of meeting the beginning of work together on an identified problem still is to come, but it will be inevitably affected by that first glance. Thus it is important as we move through the sequence of the phases of the model to remember that it is not a simple linear process.

The fact that the problem-solving process is a squirming, wriggling, alive business which may be grasped as an intellectual concept that concerns what goes on in the worker's head but also vitally concerns the social reality between the worker, the client, and all the interrelated systems of which the worker and the client are a part, makes it a difficult model to carry out in practice. All parts of the model may be present at any one time in a way that may obscure for the ordinary viewer, and often for the worker as well, the fact that there is "rhyme and reason" in what is being done. But it is the worker's business to know, in general, what phase is the primary focus of coming together with the client, and it is the worker's business to check out constantly to see that all phases are dealt with. Failures in helping stem as often from the worker's impulsive leap to some action from what is seen at the moment as the problem, with no pause for thought and consultation in between as from the worker's inability to engage in a helping relationship. In fact, these two parts of the helping process (the capacity to relate to and communicate with others and problem-solving efforts) are so firmly interwoven that we often do not pause to see them as separate things.

The problem-solving process itself, in and of itself, is the process by which worker and client decide (1) what the problem or question is that they wish to work on; (2) what the desired outcome of this work is; (3) how to conceptualize what it is that results in the persistence of the problem in spite of the fact that the client wants something changed or altered; (4) what procedures should be undertaken to change the situation; (5) what specific actions are to be undertaken to implement the procedures; and (6) how the actions have worked out.

For the worker, the use of the process involves considerable skill and the cultivated capacity to keep a clear head as well as an understanding heart. However, the problem-solving framework gives the worker no specific guides to specific procedures. It does not promise that if one does this type of thinking and exploring one will come out with *the* (or with *this*) answer. It promises rather that one must do this type of thinking and exploring, consciously and knowingly, in about this order if one wants to increase the probability of coming out with *an effective answer* that is in the direction of the client's goals. What the answer is, specifically, will depend on (1) what the question is, specifically, (2) what the client wants, specifically, and (3) what the worker and the client can bring to the process in terms of knowledge, understanding, resources, and capacity for joint action.

Thus there are some very significant requirements that relate to workers' use of the model and of workers' approach to clients. There may be a tendency to think that since the model requires a lot of rational headwork on the part of the worker that it is appropriate only for clients who come with a well-developed ability to weigh and measure alternative courses of action. Nothing could be further from the truth. This burden for rational headwork lies with the practitioner, not the client. In fact, this way of working has been used successfully by the authors with families who had been judged by other community helping facilities—schools, mental health clinics, and social agencies to be totally unreachable and beyond help by any professional. It is so helpful to these clients because one of the reasons for their difficulties is that they do not possess these skills to the extent demanded by their living situation.

The key to the use of this treatment model with clients who appear to have no coping skills, or no ability to trust others, is to begin, just as the model indicates, with the problem *as seen by the client* at whatever level the client may present it. Workers run into great difficulty when they are so focused on their own definition of the problem, or their concern with client capacity, or with the real problem or cause of the problem, that they cannot hear the client. Also, workers often appear totally unaware on how they differ with the client as to the understanding of the problem. Not only can there be no use of this model at all, there can be no helpful use of any model, without the active engagement of the client, and that engagement must be around concerns congruent with clients' expectations and problem definition (see the discussion on basic role theory in Chapter 4). Also workers often find it difficult to accept the pace of the clients' early movement and the problems that often are involved in human change.

People who have little ability to weigh and measure alternative courses of action, and who have no reason to trust the help that the worker offers, will neither express their problems in the worker's terms nor will they express their goals in terms of learning to live a more productive life. Rather they express their problems in terms of basic survival needs. What is more important? The worker who understands the problem-solving process in terms of the model will see such expression of concrete needs as the place to begin. Such workers can then join with the client in setting the goals at this level—to secure necessary repairs on the refrigerator or to find a way to get a new stove. These are worthy goals in that *they do help to make the client's life more satisfying, or at least less hard,* and they are the clients' goals. Such problems and goals are the stuff of the beginning engagement. But for the worker there may also be the concern of using this problem and its solution as a way of building some trust and sense of success that can be used to move on to other problems and other goals, if there are others. The problem many people have in using the model is that they assume that the problem has to be a *basic problem in living from their perspective* rather than something that the client identifies as an important want.

Wendell Johnson's article (1951, pp. 176–177) discusses these symptoms and basic causes. Perhaps if the reader could substitute "presenting problem" meaning "the problem the client brings" for Johnson's word "symptom," it would be possible to understand why workers often have difficulty with the problem-solving model that says in essence that they *must start* with where the client is—which is usually not with "cause" but with relief of the symptom.

> Let us make this very absurd. What I am trying to say is that one of the things we do which tends to keep us from understanding handicapped children and adults better is that we do not spend enough time trying to appreciate the symptoms, as we call them. To them, they are not symptoms so much as they are causes of frustration and misery. They want to have everything possible done to alleviate or remove the symptoms. They want to work on the so-called causes, too, of course. But in the meantime, they are in pain or distress.
>
> Now, as I suggested, let us make the situation very absurd. Suppose that we were out in the woods and we came upon a man who had accidentally got his foot caught in a bear trap. There he is, howling and carrying on frightfully, weeping and straining in a most profane fashion. Then two psychologists come by and one of them wants to give the man the Rorschach test and an intelligence test and take a case history. The other psychologist, however, has undergone a different kind of training; and he says, "No let's start intensive psychoanalysis right now." So, they talk it over. They have their differences, of course, but they agree eventually that what this man in the bear trap needs is obviously psychotherapy. If he would just be trained to be a more mature individual; if he could have the release therapy he needs; if he would undergo the needed catharsis, achieve the necessary insight, and work through the essential abreaction, he would develop more maturity, he would understand the difficulty he is having, and he would then be able to solve his problem himself. Obviously, the psychologists agree, that is the only sound way to deal with the poor fellow. Suddenly, however, a farmer comes by and lets the man out of the bear trap. To the utter amazement of the psychologists, the man's behavior changes greatly and quickly. Besides, he seems to take a great liking to the farmer, and goes off with him, evidently to have a cup of coffee.
>
> The basic principle illustrated by this absurd example is that psychotherapy is more beneficial when it is carried on under optimal conditions. And one way to prepare optimal conditions for psychotherapy, or for classroom teaching, for that matter, or for any kind of special instruction, is to do everything possible first—or as you go along—to relieve any distressing symptoms that may be distracting the individual you are trying to help. If the symptoms make a difference to the individual, if they are producing impaired social relationships, impaired self-evaluations, impaired parent-child relationships, or tantrums, or anxiety—then clearly anything that can be done directly, by means of literal or figurative aspirin, to relieve the symptoms will be all to the good in helping to bring about favorable conditions for therapy.

In the problem-solving process, any symptoms or needs or wants become problems to be solved. In problem solving, practitioner and client may work on a whole array of these problems, one at a time. We would like the reader to look at an actual situation of a woman who was seen as unable to use any type of social work help and at her reactions to the problem-solving approach. This case is reproduced in its entirety at the end of Chapter 11. Please read it before you proceed (Reading 11–1).

Now that you have completed reading the case you will note that after the case was accepted, the assigned worker attempted to reach Mrs. Stover. Whenever she found Mrs. Stover home, she was denied admittance to the house for many reasons such as her husband was asleep, and so on. The worker did not press to come in as she did not believe in entering a home for an interview without an appointment. The worker had gone to the house to try to make an appointment because the family did not have a telephone and had not answered letters. Repeated appointments for either office or home visits were broken when Mrs. Stover did not come to the office or was not home. Finally, in July, Mrs. Stover came to the office asking for help with an immediate crisis, which is so often the only time the Mrs. Stovers of the world are seen. Her AFDC grant had been cut off because she had broken so many appointments with the worker and had refused to tell the agency where she was living. She was eight months pregnant and worried about the pain she was having. She had had no medical attention, her husband had left her, and she had returned to live with her mother after having been evicted from the apartment. Her mother was threatening to make her get out if she did not contribute some money to the household. In recounting her problems she threw in the fact that the school had raised questions about accepting her oldest daughter back at the opening of the school year without some kind of psychiatric help which had been refused earlier.

The worker began with Mrs. Stover's most pressing problems: the need of the reestablishment of AFDC and the securing of medical care. The goals were to get economic support reestablished and secure medical care. Whether it would have been possible for the worker to have maintained contact with Mrs. Stover long enough to have established some agreement to work together on problems she had identified in her first approach to the worker, such as a place to live, the children's behavior, and her problems with the welfare board, if childbirth and complications had not kept her in the hospital for a considerable period of time, is not known. The worker used this time to consider with Mrs. Stover her problems, what she wanted from life (initially Mrs. Stover said nothing but to be left alone), and how she thought the worker could help. The worker also acted as an advocate for Mrs. Stover with the welfare board and helped to find her a rather small, cramped apartment. Later chapters will discuss the role and, methods utilized by the worker which followed the model presented in this text, the worker acting as enabler, broker, advocate, and teacher for the client in relation to problems identified by Mrs. Stover. However, we discuss Mrs. Stover here in order to give students an overview of problem solving with resistant, inadequately functioning clients. Although the worker brought significant support and resources to the situation, probably Mrs. Stover's learning how to more effectively carry out the problem-solving process accounted for much of the gains in her functioning. In this sense, in working with many clients, the careful use of the process is in itself a treatment activity.

Two articles that relate to problem solving with larger social systems have been reproduced in this chapter—one dealing with neighborhood and community groups and one with a whole social system. Certainly the reader would not have seen either the "C" street network or the Nobleteens as composed of what might be called well "integrated" and "rationally oriented" people. Yet, these groups responded with growth and strength to the offer of help from social workers who saw themselves as advisers to a neighborhood and a group on self-help projects—in other words, on *problems defined by the members of the systems* that the workers approached. The other article on identity and change puts the same emphasis on helping a society define its problems and its goals as a way of preventing dependency and as a way of assuring the integrity of the culture of the people one wants to help. These two articles are good examples of the considerations that go into the use of the problem-solving model with social systems larger than the individual or the family.

Generally, in carrying out the action plan with client systems, the worker will be involved in four primary activities: (1) provision of needed resources which may involve roles of broker and advocate (among others) and will undoubtedly require work with a target system that is different from the client system and a broad action system; (2) change in transactions between client system and other systems, which, in addition to the roles and systems mentioned earlier, may involve the worker in the role of enabler and teacher with the client system; (3) the problem-solving work which will involve the worker primarily in teaching and enabling a client system to work in this way; and (4) the use of the therapeutic relationship for change in the internal interaction of the client system which calls for roles of enabler, teacher, and therapist.

Although there are other frameworks for social work practice, the authors like the problem-solving framework for a number of reasons:

1. No assumptions as to the cause, nature, location, or meaning of the problem are built into the model itself. Thus the framework allows the problem to be defined as lying within the client system, as lying within the other systems with which the client system has transactions, as lying in some lack in social resources that should be supplied by the environment, or as lying in transactions among these factors. The problem, itself, carries no implication of impaired functioning or personality malfunctioning.

2. The framework is based on a belief in the growth potential for all human systems and thus fits both social work's belief in human struggles toward growth and rests on the knowledge borrowed from systems theory and ego psychology.

3. At the level of foundation knowledge, the framework is based on selected constructs from ego psychology, systems theory, role theory, communication theory, and group dynamics—all of which depart from the personal deficit theory and put emphasis on social transaction. At the level of practice theory, the model is not based on any one theoretical orientation and thus allows the worker and client to agree on any method of help appropriate to the problem, the problem location, the goals, the client system, and the worker's competence and resources.

4. The framework gives a prominent spot to consideration of client goals, or goals of other social systems, with which one is working. This is congruent with social work values of the importance of the individual, of individuals' differences, and of self-determination and with systems theory, role theory, and ego psychology.

5. The way the problem is defined and the goal is established determines which data are relevant and where the emphasis and direction of inquiry will lie. This allows for data collection that is relevant, salient, and individualized. It further requires that intervention in the client's life be kept at a minimum.

6.   The framework is congruent with the function and purpose of the social work profession in that it supports the client's right to personal definition of the problem and, in case the worker has a different view, demands that some negotiation be undertaken in defining the problem-to-be-worked (which simply means that worker and client must agree on what they are going to undertake together). The framework also recognizes the importance of the purposes of the client system.

7.   In addition to supplying a method applicable to a wide variety of situations and settings in which social work is practiced, and to different sizes and types of systems, the problem-solving framework demands that the tasks and activities of the social worker be stated at a very specific level and related to client goals. This seems to the authors to be a distinct advantage over frameworks that allow for a more abstract treatment plan.

THE CLIENT SYSTEM AND PROBLEM SOLVING

It is difficult to speak of what is required of the client apart from the workers' activities. As in any system, including the helping system of worker and client, the behavior of one element has tremendous impact on the actions of other elements. Thus we must start our discussion of what is required of the client by pointing out that we begin with what is required of the worker. To speak of the clients' requirements without recognizing that these requirements rest on the assumption that the worker is concerned and caring, able to communicate a desire to understand, and willing to start with the clients' presenting the problem has little meaning.

In our experience, individuals, families, or groups who were often held by earlier helping systems to be unreachable and beyond help could participate as partners in the problem-solving process once they understood that we (once we learned to listen) really wanted to know them as people and were willing to help them pursue their own goals. They could tell us something about goals they had for themselves that were impossible to achieve because changes were needed that they alone could not effect. And it was here that the problem-solving process began. In other words, this process demands the following of clients (1) that they be able to share with the worker information about something that they would like to have changed, (2) in order to achieve something that is of value to them, and that (3) as the worker is able to demonstrate concern and competence to help with the exploration of this problem, clients are able to trust this concern enough, and (4) to allow the worker to continue to meet with them around this purpose. That is all that is demanded of the client system.

BASIC ASSUMPTIONS OF THE MODEL

This model does not in any way deny people's irrational and instinctive characteristics, but it accepts the findings of social scientists who have studied the social milieu of the mental hospital that even the most regressed psychotic patients are at least as responsive to changes in external reality as to their internal fantasies, that altering their external reality alters their ways of coping, and that "given a chance to participate in making decisions that affected their lives, inmates generally did so in a responsible manner and with constructive results for all concerned—professionals as well as themselves" (Lerner, 1972, p. 161). This model further accepts the view that social work processes are not a set of techniques by which experts who understand what "is really wrong," seek in their wisdom to improve, enlighten, plan for, or manipulate the client system. Rather, it sees social work processes as an attempt "by one human being with specialized knowledge, training, and a way of working to establish a genuinely meaningful, democratic, and collaborative relationship with another person or persons in order to put one's special knowledge and skills at the second person's (or group's) disposal for such use as can be made of it" (Lerner, 1972, p. 11). It recognizes that decisions about what individuals and groups of individuals should be, have, want, and do are cognitive decisions that involve rational and nonrational processes, perceptions of the describer, the possible, and values, an area in which "every person is a legitimate expert for oneself and no person is a legitimate expert for others" (Lerner, 1972, p. 161). The model rests on the assumption that the given in each human being is a desire to be active in one's life—to exercise meaningful control of oneself for one's own purposes. Systems theory states that living systems are purposive, and we believe that practitioners are more effective when they start with the client's purposes and the obstacles to their achievement. This does not mean that one is naive about unconscious and irrational factors. It simply means that one starts with the rational with consciously expressed problems and goals. Such goals may appear to the practitioner as totally irrational and impossible, but the model demands that they be respected and seen as a valuable statement of client wants.

PRESENTATION OF THE PROBLEM-SOLVING OUTLINE

At the end of this chapter you will find a short outline of the steps of the problem-solving process—just the bare bones of the model. It is included here so that the reader can grasp the essentials of the model before being confronted with all the details.

The phases of the problem-solving process and the skills demanded of the worker will be developed further in succeeding chapters. However, the process and skills may be briefly outlined as follows:

I. Contact (or engagement) phase
   A. Activities
      1. Engagement and problem definition.
      2. Definition of the problem for work.
      3. Goal identification.
      4. Negotiation of preliminary contract.
      5. Exploration, investigation, data collection.
   B. Skills needed
      1. Ability to use self in the interests of the client system or potential client system based on self-awareness and understanding of change agent system, resources, and possible target and action systems.

2. Listening, which includes not only listening with ears to words and with eyes to body language, but a total kind of perceptiveness which is best described as "listening with the third ear," attending carefully both physically and psychologically to client.
3. Communication of empathy, genuineness, trustworthiness, respect, and support.
4. Use of such techniques as paraphrasing, clarifying, perception checking, focusing, questioning, reflecting, informing, summarizing, confronting, interpreting, assuring, and reassuring.
5. Skill in use of a range of data collection methods, including not only interviewing skills listed earlier but also the use of records, test data, other written materials, and interviews or conferences with other than the client, observations, and documentary evidence.
6. Skill in using a theoretical knowledge base to guide the collection of salient and relevant information.

II. Contract phase
  A. Activities
    1. Assessment and evaluation.
    2. Formulation of an action plan.
    3. Prognosis.
  B. Skills needed
    1. All of skills listed in contact phase.
    2. Ability to use a basic theory of the growth, development, functioning, malfunctioning, interactions, and transactions of human systems to assign meaning and to analyze the data collected.
    3. Ability based on above, plus knowledge of problems, goals, and resources available, to prioritize and organize data in such a way as to suggest useful action.
    4. Ability to generate a range of alternative plans with associated predictions as to probable success and cost.
    5. Ability to use own judgment and client participation to select among alternatives.
    6. Ability to put all the above together in a statement of actions to be taken, when and by, or with, what systems, within what time frame.

III. Action phase
  A. Activities
    1. Carrying out plan.
    2. Termination.
    3. Evaluation.
  B. Skills needed
    1. All skills listed in contact and contract phrases.
    2. Skills in use of a range of social work methods as appropriate to roles necessary to carrying out the plan (see Chapters 5, 12–16).
    3. Skills in a range of evaluative skills (see Chapter 14).
    4. Skills in ending and disengagement (see Chapter 13).

RECAPITULATION

In this chapter we have introduced the problem-solving model of social work practice as we have developed it. This model is based on five selected theories of human development, growth, and transactions between and among human systems: systems theory, communications theory, role theory, ego psychology, and notions of human diversity and difference. From these theories we have developed the following basic assumptions that are the base of our approach to problem solving: (1) people want to control their own lives and to feel competent to master the tasks they see as important; (2) motivation for change rests on some integration between a system's goals and its hope-discomfort balance; (3) the social worker is always engaged in attempting to change some interactions or transactions within or among systems; (4) systems are open and the input across their boundaries is critical for their growth and change; (5) while a system must have a steady state for its functioning, it is constantly in flux; and (6) all human systems are purposive and goal seeking.

This model is constructed on the notion that the change process has three basic phases, each of which has its own stages and own list of activities. Each stage demands some different skills as well as requiring some similar ones. These phases are so wound together that they are hard to disentangle for study, but it is important that the worker is aware of the primary phase of the work in which they are engaged. We take the position that this model demands three primary things of the worker—(1) is the headwork involved in trying to understand the situation and make an orderly approach to the process; (2) is the ability to engage the client and other systems in order to understand and negotiate the problem and the goals; and (3) the ability to develop and sustain a working partnership. It further requires that the worker be aware of the six systems with which they may be involved and to have the skills necessary to use any system or attempt to change any system. The initial demand on the clients is that they be able to share their view of their trouble with the worker and that they allow the worker to maintain some contact with them long enough to demonstrate the worker's intentions toward them.

One final caution! The following problem-solving outline has been developed to be used selectively by the worker. In Chapter 9 we will develop examples of its use.

A LOOK FORWARD

We would suggest that if the readers have not already read the three articles included with this chapter that they do so now, and that they keep in mind during the reading that the articles are about work within different sizes and types of client systems. Also it should be noted that all articles speak of the worker's activity with other social systems that may be either target systems (need to be changed if the client system is to achieve its goal) or are part of the action system (worker uses them to supply resources needed by client system). We find the third reading particularly interesting in that it develops in different language the same notions of problem solving that we have developed during our first two editions of this text and are further explicating in this text. We agree with the author's observation that empirical studies demonstrate that often client and worker have no consensus on problem and goal. In spite of all we may write and teach about the importance of this principle of effective helping, in spite of empirical work that supports the view, it does not seem to have become a part of daily practice. Perhaps we should now ask "why?" Has Murdach, in this article, begun this process by pointing out the struggles of people in the organizational environment to fulfill their implicit objectives? Is it here we should look for explanations of social worker's lack of use of the problem-solving process in practice? We will discuss this further in the next chapter.

We are not, at this time, going to deal further with the details of the use of the problem-solving model. These details will be presented in later chapters. To conclude this chapter an outline for use of the problem-solving model is presented below.

OUTLINE OF PROBLEM-SOLVING MODEL—SHORT FORM

Contact phase

I. Problem identification and definition
   A. Problem as client system sees it.
   B. Problem as defined by significant systems with which client system is in interaction (family, school, community, others).
   C. Problem as worker sees it.
   D. Problem for work (place of beginning together).
II. Goal identification
   A. How does client see (or want) the problem to be worked out?
      1. Short-term goals.
      2. Long-term goals.
   B. What does client system think is needed for a solution of the problem?
   C. What does client system seek and/or expect from the agency as a means to a solution?
   D. What are worker's goals as to problem outcome?
   E. What does worker believe the service system can or should offer the client to reach these goals?
III. Preliminary contract
   A. Clarification of the realities and boundaries of service.
   B. Disclosure of the nature of further work together.
   C. Emergence of commitment or contract to proceed further in exploration and assessment in a manner that confirms the rights, expectations, and autonomy of the client system and grants the practitioner the right to intervene.
IV. Exploration and investigation
   A. Motivation
      1. Discomfort.
      2. Hope.

    B.   Opportunity

    C.   Capacity of the client system

Contract phase

   V.   Assessment and evaluation

      A.   If and how identified problems are related to needs of client system.

      B.   Analysis of the situation to identify the major factors operating in it.

      C.   Consideration of significant factors that contribute to the continuity of the need, lack, or difficulty.

      D.   Identification of the factors that appear most critical, definition of their interrelationships, and selection of those that can be worked with.

      E.   Identification of available resources, strengths, and motivations.

      F.   Selection and use of appropriate generalizations, principles, and concepts from the social work profession's body of knowledge.

      G.   Facts organized by ideas—ideas springing from knowledge and experience and subject to the governing aim of resolving the problem—professional judgment.

  VI.   Formulation of a plan of action—a mutual guide to intervention

      A.   Consideration and setting of a feasible goal.

      B.   Consideration of alternatives—likely costs—possible outcomes.

      C.   Determination of appropriate *service* modality.

      D.   Focus of change efforts.

      E.   Role of the worker.

      F.   Consideration of forces either within or outside the client system that may impede the plan.

      G.   Consideration of the worker's knowledge and skill and of the time needed to implement the plan.

  VII.   Prognosis—what confidence does the worker have in the success of the plan?

Action phase

  VIII.   Carrying out of the plan—specific as to point of intervention and assignment of tasks; resources and services to be utilized; methods by which they are to be used; who is to do what and when.

  IX.   Termination

      A.   Evaluation with client system of task accomplishment and meaning of process.

      B.   Coping with ending and disengagement.

      C.   Maintenance of gains.

   X.   Evaluation

      A.   Continuous process.

      B.   Was purpose accomplished?

      C.   Were methods used appropriate?

Reading 8-1

Identity and Change: Does Development Imply Dependency?*

William M. Dyal, Jr. and John B. Donovan

From the "new Soviet man" to psychologist David McClelland's man with "high need achievement" the bias of many modern thinkers in social and economic development has been toward changing traditional mentalities into modern ones. The theory assumes, dubiously, that the victory of progress will be a foregone conclusion if subsistence farmers and villagers can be transformed into technocrats, or at least develop the same attitudes as technocrats.

The obverse of this coin has been the approach to development that fails to take cultural traditions and attitudes into account at all. Advanced technology has been perceived as a multiplier of production whose benefits will eventually "trickle down" to those without the capital to take advantage of it immediately. A more advanced version of this notion is the idea that the secret of development is for governments to make massive infusions of technology in some manner whereby the rural poor can get their hands on it.

The notion that traditional small farmers should be modernized, and the notion of revolutionaries that they should be "radicalized," insults their intelligence and value systems while disregarding their creativity and pride. Also, the imposition of labor-saving, energy-eating machinery has imparted many of the superficial values that accompany a devotion to

gadgetry, and in some cases has tragically distorted entire investment systems in favor of consumer luxuries. A contemporary advocate of simpler technology, Edward Schumacher, has expressed it this way:

If the nature of change is such that nothing is left for the fathers to teach their sons, or for the sons to accept from their fathers, family life collapses. The life, work, and happiness of all societies depend on certain "psychological structures" which are infinitely precious and highly vulnerable. Social cohesion, cooperation, mutual respect, and above all, self-respect, courage in the face of adversity, and the ability to bear hardship—all this and much else disintegrates and disappears when these "psychological structures" are greatly damaged.

An important difference exists, in other words, between the kind of change that bears an organic relationship to a person's way of life and attitudes, and one that touches things irresponsibly. If initiatives from elites, for example, intrude on what psychologist William James called the "core" of the personality—"the truest, strongest, deepest self"—out of which role learning and identification emerges, the unfortunate results to economic structures may eventually equal the results of psychological structures.

The point we are making here relates directly to the key notion in the entire North-South dialogue—dependency (and its opposite, self-reliance). As Indian economist Samuel L. Parmar has pointed out, the term "self-reliance" can be seen in the shallow sense—"a mere balancing of accounts in the foreign trade sector of the economy"—or in the deeper sense, in which it refers to the process of structural

* Reprinted from *Américas*, bimonthly magazine published by the General Secretariat of the Organization of American States in English and Spanish; *Americas* 29:4 (April 1977), pp. 13–18.

change *within* the economy. He says, "Thus where growth fails to promote social justice, to utilize the economy's most abundant resources, to engender public participation in the development process, to reduce the concentration of economic power, or to assist in the establishment of more egalitarian patterns of international economic relationships, there may be self-reliance in the narrow sense, but not in the deeper, structural sense."

Thus the solutions to underdevelopment and dependency must relate, as Mahatma Gandhi suggested, directly to the impoverished rural majorities, but without their being capitulated into the modern world by technology.

Traditional development assistance policies have been slow and largely inept in grappling with the two horns of this dilemma. Only very recently has there been any serious recognition of the necessity of relating directly to the rural majorities (and to the slum-dwellers who have recently escaped from the farms). And a full awareness is still lacking that machinery and new seed varieties can accomplish very little without thoroughgoing social change. Foreign investment has often served merely to widen the gap between rich and poor by installing the kind of industry that redounds greatly to the prosperity of the capital-owning class but little to the well-being of the unemployed. The illusion still prevails that this strengthening of the capital-owning class increases stability and discourages radical solutions, but the potentially explosive frustration of those unable to participate in the economy has rarely been calculated.

Only quite recently have those in charge of forming development assistance policy begun to realize that the situation will worsen unless mechanisms are found by which low-income farmers and slum-dwellers can control the direction of their own lives. The poor do not basically need an alteration of their cultural values, and the insistence that they do has chiefly had the effect of diverting attention from the necessity of altering social structures. They *have* the ideas and initiative that can move them forward, and if there is anything that elites and foreigners can do for them it is to collaborate with these initiatives on a small scale and in a nonmanipulated manner. Solutions consistent with local values can be defined and carried out best by those who have grown up struggling with the problems.

Strong evidence for this is seen in the five-year experience of the Inter-American Foundation, a U.S. Government corporation founded to support independent social change groups in Latin America and the Caribbean. Groups under local control are springing up in every part of the Hemisphere. When they seek assistance, it is on their own terms, and almost never on a scale that permits such assistance to become a prevailing factor. Many of their projects have demonstrated for us beyond doubt that when social change proceeds on a locally managed basis it can release a natural creativity and adaptiveness that is little short of astonishing.

The self-reliant psychology engendered by social change is overwhelmingly evident in many projects, and its possibilities for releasing individual potential frequently seem limitless. On one worker-managed farm in the Caribbean, for example, cane pickers devised a way of building a bamboo pipeline to irrigate one of their fields. Furnishing them a metal pipe would have solved the short-run problem equally well. But the finest pipe in the world could never have equalled the long-range impact of the creativity released and the self-concept bolstered. These gains are a direct result of workers assuming responsibility for their own farm, rather than leaving all important decisions to owners. No program of deliberately changing attitudes is involved. The kind of collaboration that can be helpful is usually along the lines of enabling workers to seek technical assistance in the principles of accounting and cooperative management.

A similar project involves sugar workers in Jamaica, where small farmers have 6 percent of the sugar production, with the rest going to large plantation owners. In 1973, with the encouragement of a church-related group, 350 workers came together to form a Sugar Workers Cooperative Council, which petitioned the Government for recently acquired lands. These cooperatives are now surviving successfully with the aid of small worker-education programs.

A different, and innovative, kind of project focuses on the imperatives of self-affirmation without immediate economic objectives. The goal is not merely to affirm the participants' traditions and values, but to enhance their legitimacy in the minds of members of the dominant society.

In one Colombian project, for example, participants have been gathering material for theater presentations from the rich body of traditional folklore to be found throughout the country while recruiting local people to serve as actors. The leaders of the project, called the Theater of Identity, have tried to reconcile two points of view about development. The first point of view is that traditional cultures modernize only when the modern sector penetrates them with material and cultural advances. The second is that forceful confrontation of the dominant society must be encouraged. They feel that the paternalistic model ignores the energy of indigenous values and practices, and that the class struggle model calls for needless polarization.

What the theater has tried to do is provide an alternative to the gallery-and-concert-hall mode of culture forced on the country by the elite as the only legitimate one. The Theater of Identity now stages outdoor performances throughout the country using actors recruited in the areas represented by the particular style of folk life being shown. The directors are also in the process of studying the impact of these performances on both the modern and the traditional sector. Meanwhile, their performances are richly colorful proof of their own first principle, namely, that all men are creators.

The National Dance Theatre in Jamaica was founded along similar principles. According to its artistic director, Rex Nettleford, the meaning of the company's performances relates directly to what he calls the "syndrome of dependency." The relationship between master and servant throughout colonialism, he says, persists now with "our dependence on foreign markets, foreign price mechanism, foreign technology. It's time we worked in the interest of ourselves rather than in the interest of somebody else. . . . We don't have to borrow sound, or dance, or movement; we don't have to borrow anyone else's."

The company is composed mainly of low-income Jamaicans, most of whom are working simultaneously at other jobs. The widely acclaimed originality and power of their performances reveal their dedication. It is difficult to assign an exact socioeconomic meaning to these rhythms, which range from the ethereal and choirlike to the exuberant and explosive. Jamaican arts critic Edna Manley says: "The load of responsibility that he (the artist) carries to society, whether a growing or a dying one, is the validity of his own being." To which Rex Nettleford adds: "Isn't the validity of one's own being the measure of one's own liberation?"

Ethnic obstacles also exist in many areas of Latin America to block productive access to society. The unique fusion of Indian and non-Indian traits in the Paraguayan elite, for example, has determined the social values of the nation. The mestizo elite systematically relegates the pure Indians to a subhuman position, which is well reflected in the Indians' own self-esteem.

Recognizing the paradox of a situation in which Indian culture is officially idealized but in which Indians are neglected, some distinguished anthropologists embarked on an information and communication project to encourage Indians to express themselves to the dominant society in a practical, nonidealized manner. The conferences begun by the project provided the first significant forum for some groups that have been brutally abused by members of the dominant society.

Most local groups, however, have been involved with the kind of cooperative community development and organization that could, town by town and region by region, rise into a force of enormous impact throughout the Third World. Networks and service institutions are already broadening the horizons of many a subsistence farmer, and a few are finding any lack of ideas at the local level.

This is not to say that the traditional mentality of the farmer is compatible with social change in every respect. Some psychological attitudes and social customs do seem to stand in the way of the modernity that many sincerely desire.

One pattern that prevails throughout much of the developing world has been called "familism," or the tendency to narrow one's spirit of cooperation to the immediate family, thus blocking larger enterprises. Edward Banfield of the Massachusetts Institute of Technology, for example, has furnished persuasive evidence that familism is the overwhelming tendency among impoverished peasants in Southern Italy. One cannot conclude from this, however, that the answer would somehow lie in engineering a new set of attitudes among these peasants. In fact, it would seem fairly plausible that the cohesion of the peasant family contributes enormously to psychic stability compared to their modern counterparts struggling with problems of crime and drug abuse. Even if this kind of imposition could be justified ethnically, "progress" might not be a satisfactory label for the results.

Another such pattern is fatalism—the tendency to feel powerless in the face of one's future. No one who has spent much time with villagers and small farmers in the Third World is likely to doubt the prevalence of deep-seated leanings toward submission and resignation. But even this very often has a realistic foundation in an area like the Northeast of Brazil, where people entirely dependent on the whims of nature are often greeted by floods during one part of the year and a scorching drought during another part of the year. Nor should one discount the value of a stoic resignation in dealing with such circumstances. Nevertheless, some modification of these attitudes invariably accompanies any alteration of social structures.

If outsiders are to relate to these attitudes at all, we submit that it should be on a basis of response to local promotion rather than on a basis of imposition. It has been shown that social workers, reformers, and revolutionaries can display the same paternalism as large landlords, enabling identical attitudes of dependency to reappear in another form. In contrast to this, many social promoters throughout the Hemisphere are discovering methodologies whereby, through dialogue, they can help instill in farmers and slum-dwellers an appreciation of themselves, an openness to others, and an understanding of the potential inherent in group action. Such participatory forms of problem-solving are rapidly becoming recognized as the most suitable type of collaboration by local development professionals. The formation of local groups also tends to keep control of the change process in the hands of the poor, and not allow it to pass into the portentially lethal control of elites. As stated by Thomas George, a community promoter in Trinidad: "I blame the governments—and the so-called radicals—for imposing their own ideas on the people, often without consulting them and usually without reference to their feelings. . . . We must light fires of confidence in people's ability to run things for themselves."

Individuals grow in self-concept during the community building process, probably because of the way people tend to mirror each other, so to speak. We develop what U.S. social psychologist C. H. Cooley (1902) called a "looking-glass self" or a later colleague D. R. Miller (1963) called our "subjective public identity"—our perception of how others feel about us, a perception that determines much of our self-concept out of which role learning and identification emerges. Just as children in their self-concept tend to mirror the attitudes of their parents, self-concepts of the poor often seem to mirror the attitudes of those who make the important decisions regarding their lives. Thus when the poor acquire roles as producers and entrepreneurs during the cooperative process, they often seem to experience a gain in self-concept that cannot be matched by a mere windfall profit. Their familism is broadened to include the notion that the welfare of the community in general relates directly to their own; their fatalism is reduced when they realize that their fortunes need not rise and fall with vicissitudes of the upper class.

If this autonomy, this freedom from manipulation, is recognized as the most important end result, it is obvious that aid which creates dependency is a direct contradiction. A commonsense strategy for collaborating with the social change process in the Third World would aim to enter the process *after* solutions have been defined and set in motion. Successful assistance, in our view, relies on bolstering existing community mechanisms and community spirit. Recipients should not be made to feel inferior in some way by virtue of their acceptance of assistance.

Noninterference should be studiously preserved. At the Inter-American Foundation, for example, personnel reviewing prospective projects do not reside in the receiving countries for fear of fostering an "advisor" or "evaluator" relationship with grantees.

In an era when energy-eating technology is losing its luster, these Third-World experiments in cooperative effort should prove valuable to us all. If human development is actually the achievement of a *convivencia,* or art of living together, as Mexican thinker Agustín Basave-Fernández says it is, the growing pains of the poor may yet result in the social enrichment of all mankind.

Reading 8-2

A Systems Approach to the Delivery of Mental Health Services in Black Ghettos*

Richard H. Taber

In our attempt to develop new and more effective models for the delivery of mental health services to children in a black lower socioeconomic community, we have found the concept of the ecological systems approach extremely useful. Using this model, we have explored the ecology of our community in order to define naturally occurring systems of support within the community—systems which, when utilized as a target for special types of intervention, could maximize the impact of our work.

This paper will focus on the rationale for our selection of two small natural groups: a partial social network composed primarily of mothers of highly disorganized families with young children, and a peer subsystem of 14–17-year-old boys. The ecological framework provided significant direction to our attempts to approach and work with these indigenous systems in such a way that members of the natural groups were given mental health services without being required to perceive themselves as patients.

The Rebound Children and Youth Project is jointly sponsored by the Children's Hospital of Philadelphia and the Philadelphia Child Guidance Clinic. It is charged with providing comprehensive health, dental, mental health, and social services to children in the area adjacent to these two institutions.

The community is a black ghetto in which 47 percent of the families have in-

comes below $3,000 and "only 38 percent of the 1,131 children covered in our survey are growing up within an intact family unit" (Leopold, 1968). The project enjoys a positive image in the neighborhood because of the involvement of the community in ongoing planning and the sensitive work of indigenous community workers as well as the provision of much needed pediatric services on a family basis.

We began this project with the view that many children in the black ghetto live with several pervasive mental health problems, primarily poor self-image and the concomitant sense of powerlessness. There are three ways of conceptualizing this problem. One is the individual psychological approach, which would identify early maternal deprivation as a primary cause. This factor can be identified in numerous cases we see clinically. Many children in this population have experienced early separation, abandonment, or maternal depression.

A second is the sociopolitical point of view, which directs attention to the systematic oppression and exploitation of this population by a predominantly white power structure. It also identifies historical and current influences which have undermined the family structure in the black ghetto and points to white racism as the source of black feelings of inferiority.

The ecological systems approach, the third way, directs our attention to the transactions and communications which take place between individual members of the poor black population and the systems within and outside of their neighborhood—that is, what actually goes on between the individual and the family, the individual and the extended family, the individual and the school, the individual and work, the individual and the welfare agency, and so on. Our exploration of these transactions, or "interfaces between systems," shows that most of the transactions which take place are degrading and demoralizing and are experienced by the ghetto resident as "put downs."

When the problems of poor self-image and sense of powerlessness are approached from the concept of ecological systems, pathology is seen as the outcome of transactions between the individual and surrounding social systems. Because no one element of these systems can be moved or amplified without affecting other elements, the ecological approach to the delivery of services requires exploration of the ways in which "the symptom, the person, family and community interlock" (Auerswald, 1968).

As an example, to plan effective services for a 15-year-old boy we must explore not only the boy as an individual but also what takes place at the interfaces between the boy, his family, the school, and other formal institutions and at the interface with peers, adults, and other representatives of the larger society. Chances are that his family expects little of him that is positive except that he stay out of trouble. He may often hear that he is expected to turn out to be a no-good bum like his father. At the interface with adults in the neighborhood he meets with open distrust and hostility. If he should wander out of the ghetto into a white area, his blackness, speech, and dress quickly cause him to be labeled as a hoodlum and treated with suspicion. He sees the police or "man" as a source of harassment and abuse rather than protection. If he is still in school, he has become used to not being expected to learn (Clark, 1965). He may not know that the curriculum was de-

signed with someone else in mind, but he is certainly aware that his style of life and the style of learning and behavior expected in school do not mesh (Minuchin, 1969). If he is in contact with a social or recreational agency, chances are that its program is designed to "keep him off the streets" and control his behavior. Competence is not expected from him and cannot be demonstrated by him. However, his peer system, usually a gang, does give him an opportunity to demonstrate competence. He is needed by the gang in its struggle to maintain "rep" and fighting strength. Gang membership offers him structure, a clear set of behavioral norms, a role and opportunity for status—all essential elements in the struggle toward identity. He is, however, then caught up in a system of gang wars and alliances which he has little or no control over, and which limits the availability of role models.

Adults in the ghetto neighborhood have similarly limited opportunities for self-definition as persons of worth and competence. For reasons which have been dealt with elsewhere (Malone, 1966), a mother may not perceive herself as able to control her children's behavior outside of her immediate presence; yet she is expected to do so by a whole series of people representing systems within her neighborhood—her neighbors and relatives, the school, and so on—and outside her neighborhood—the attendance officer, the police, and so on. Her transactions with people representing formal social agencies and other social systems are usually experienced as destructive. In the interface with welfare, legal, medical, and other services, she receives attitudinal messages which are critical or punitive or, at best, patronizing. If she goes for therapy or counseling in a traditional psychiatric setting, she must accept another dependency role—that of patient. One of the conditions of receiving such help is usually that she admit to a problem within herself. She may also perceive the therapist's interpretations of her behavior as robbing her of any expertise about herself. What may hurt her most are the verbal and nonverbal attacks she receives from moralistic neighbors.

One source to which she can turn for acceptance and support in dealing with personal and interfamilial crises is her social network of friends, relatives, and neighbors. An important function of the network is to offer her guidance in her contacts with external systems. A friend or relative may accompany her to an appointment. Often after an unsuccessful encounter at an interface, the group will offer sympathy from collective experience and suggestions for avoiding or coping with the system the next time the need arises.

Having identified the existence of these two social groups in our community (the social network and the gang), we began to wonder how to utilize our knowledge so as to intervene in these systems in a way that would maximize their natural mental health functions. Unlike members of an artificial group, members of a natural group have day-to-day contacts and ongoing significance in each others' lives. The effects of therapeutic intervention in them should be able to transcend a one-hour-a-week interview and reverberate through the ongoing system. Also, intervention with natural community groups fits with our point of view that the answer to the problems of ghetto residents must come from the emergence of self-help groups within the community. Sources outside the community will never be willing or able to pour enough resources into the ghetto to solve the problems there. And our recognition of the value of local self-help organization brings us to a point of substantial agreement at the interface between our project and emerging black awareness and black nationalism.

We sought to work with natural systems without requiring that the people perceive themselves as patients. The intervenors sought to define their roles as that of advisors rather than leaders or therapists. We felt that this model would prove most effective for the promotion of indigenous leadership and help establish the self-help system on a permanent basis. Through successful task completion, people would have concrete reason to see themselves as worthwhile and competent.

In order to avoid making people patients, we chose to focus attention on transaction and communications at strategic interfaces rather than on individual problems. We find that this focus is more syntonic with the point of view of our target population, because members of the disorganized lower socioeconomic population tend to see behavior as predominantly influenced by external events and circumstances rather than intrapsychic phenomena (Leopold, 1968; Minuchin, 1969).

One advantage of an approach which does not require that people perceive themselves as patients is that the natural group and the intervenor's involvement are visible. This increases the potential of the group for having an impact on other individuals and systems in the community. And individuals far from being shamed because they are patients, feel the pride of being publicly identified as members of a group which enjoys a positive image in and outside the community.

THE "C" STREET NETWORK

The social network we chose to work with was one of highly disorganized family units which had been observed in the course of an anthropological study of families in the neighborhood (Leopold, 1969). The families which formed the core of this network lived on "C" Street, a street which has a reputation in the neighborhood as a center of wild drinking, promiscuous sexual and homosexual behavior, the numbers racket, and gambling.

The approach to the "C" Street network was planned by a project team which included a pediatrician and two indigenous community workers. Our plan was to seek to improve child-rearing practices and parent-child communication by raising the self-esteem and effectiveness of the parents. The indigenous community workers played a key role in introducing the mental health intervenor to members of the network and have played important ongoing roles as linking persons in the interface between network members and the white middle-class social worker.

Our approach to the system was through one couple in the network who in response to a survey question had indicated interest in participating in a discussion group on neighborhood problems. The worker introduced himself as a person interested in working with neighborhood discussion groups. It was agreed that such a group might be most effective if it were limited to people who knew each other well or who were related. Despite the expressions of interest by the network members, it was several weeks before the group began meeting formally. Before the members could trust the intervenor and before they could feel that meeting together might really accomplish something, it was necessary for the social worker to have many contacts with the members in their homes or on the street. In addition to discussions of members' ideas of what could be accomplished by meeting together, these contacts were social in nature, since it was necessary for the members to see the intervenor as a person who was sincerely interested and was not turned off by clutter, roaches, and so on.

Initially we wanted to let the network define itself, but we were also committed to including the men of the community in our intervention program. Because of the sex role separation in this group, however,

we had limited success in including men in formal group meetings, although the intervenor did have other contacts with the men in the network.

One critical step in the development of this program was that the network members, assisted by the community workers, needed to help the intervenor unlearn some of the antiorganizational principles of group therapy and to recognize the importance of ordered, structured communications. In other words, the group itself had to push "to stop running our mouths and get down to business." Once officers had been elected and rules had been developed for conducting meetings and a dues structure set up, the group became task-oriented. The format was that of an evening meeting in the home of one of the members, the formal business meeting followed by a social time during which refreshments including punch and beer are served. The first main areas of concern were more adequate and safer recreation for the children and improvements in housing. Through group and individual activity, houses were fixed up and the street beautified. Recreation for the children included children's parties and bus trips, planned and executed by the mothers, and the sponsorship of a play-street program.

One of the community workers is now working more closely with the group as the social worker begins to step back. The group plans to run its own play-street program this summer, as they are convinced that they can do a better job than the community house that ran it last year.

THE NOBLETEENS

The other natural group which we began to intervene with was a subsystem of the local gang. The boys initially contacted were still in school although far behind; they did not have major police records. The intervenor discussed with them the idea of getting together with other boys to discuss what it's like to grow up black in a ghetto community. They were asked to bring their friends.

Letters and personal reminders were used for the first several weeks. The intervenor was frequently out on the street, available for informal encounters. Unlike the adult network, where almost all our contacts have continued to be in the group's neighborhood, the boys have had their meetings in the clinic from the outset. They still stop by almost daily to see their advisor.

The initial ten-meeting program was focused on current relationships with school, police, and community, on vocation and the development of black pride and awareness, on sex and parenthood. Use was made of movies such as the "Lonely One" and "Nothing But a Man" and dramatizations of written material such as *Manchild in the Promised Land.*

At an early meeting of the group one of the more articulate members referred to the tape recorder and asked if this was to be like a study of ghetto youth. The intervenor said that that was not the purpose but that one project that the boys might be interested in would be to make tape recordings about life in the ghetto to educate "dumb white people." The group picked this up enthusiastically as an opportunity of showing people outside the neighborhood some of the positive things about themselves, since they thought that the papers usually talked about the bad things. The passive process of having discussions that were tape recorded turned into the active process of making tape recordings. From his position as a learner from a white middle-class background, the intervenor could ask questions and promote reflections. It became possible to highlight and underline examples of positive coping. The group became for the boys a place in which they could express the most positive aspects of themselves.

After the initial period, the group decided to become a club, and the intervenor's role was then defined as that of advisor. (One of the club president's functions is to be a "go-between" between members and advisor.) The group structured itself and took a more active task focus—throwing dances, starting a basketball team, starting an odd-job service (which has since involved contracts to move furniture), writing articles for the Rebound Newsletters. Carrying on their "thing" about educating people outside their system, the boys made presentations to the staff and agency board of directors, spoke on a "soul" radio station, and wrote articles about themselves. Maximum use of these experiences was made by the intervenor in promoting recognition and development of individual assets and skills.

As a result, new opportunities for role experimentation and contact with role models have been made available to the boys. Through successful completion of tasks the group has won a "rep" in the neighborhood and gets positive reinforcement from adults. One development is that the Nobleteens have "quit the corner." As they became involved in the Nobleteens and began to see themselves as valuable people with futures, the boys spent less time hanging out with the gang and reduced their delinquent activities. This affected the fighting strength of the gang in the balance of power with other gangs and so it challenged the Nobleteens' existence, beating up several members. The next day, a member of the gang happened to be stabbed, but when a runner came to enlist the Nobleteens for revenge, they refused to fight.

A black male community worker is now co-advisor to the Nobleteens. His focus with the group will be to further promote positive black identity through involvement in activities such as a Black Holiday marking the date of the assassination of Malcolm X. He will also be helping the boys take on a business venture of benefit to the community. The present intervenor hopes to develop a program in which a subgroup of the club will be hired as big brothers to younger boys who have been clinically identified as needing a relationship with an older black male.

THE ROLE OF THE INTERVENOR

Because the intervenor or advisor is in frequent contact with group members, often on a social basis, he enters into and can influence the social context on their behalf. He also stands in a unique position in the group in that he is conversant with external systems. He can therefore provide a linking function by bringing the systems together, promoting what is hopefully a growth-producing transaction for the group member and an educational one for the representative of the external systems. In terms of communication he can act as a translator for both sides. Because accommodation has taken place between him and the group members, he is better able to use their language, and they, his.

Several examples here may illuminate the therapeutic possibilities of the intervenor's role in the interface between the natural group and the external system.

Example 1. In the first several months of the Nobleteens, Rick, a 14-year-old boy, visited as a guest, a cousin of a member. He was known by the nickname "Crazy" because of his impulsivity and lack of judgment. He impressed the worker as a depressed, nonverbal youngster. He then stopped coming.

During the summer the advisor was approached by Rick's mother to act as a character witness. Rick had been arrested for breaking into a parking meter and she was panicky because he had already been sent away once. The advisor talked with Rick while they cleaned paint brushes. Rick convinced the advisor that he really didn't want to be sent away again, and the advisor convinced Rick that it wasn't going to be as easy to stay out of trouble as Rick pretended it would be.

They finally agreed that the advisor would recommend Rick's inclusion in the club and would report his impressions to the court.

Rick was known to the boys in the Nobleteens but usually hung out with a more delinquent subgroup. When the advisor recommended his inclusion in the club, one of the members (who happened to be retarded) questioned why Rick should have preference over the boys who were waiting to get in. He then recalled seeing the advisor coming down in the elevator with Rick's mother, realized that it was about the trouble Rick was in, and quickly withdrew his objection.

Beyond this there was no discussion of Rick's problem, but the message was clear. The club members included him in their leisure activities and protected him when trouble was brewing. Eventually the charge was dropped, and he has not been picked up for delinquent behavior since that time. He has responded positively to the feeling of group inclusion, appears noticeably less depressed, and is more verbal. The payoff came for Rick when he was unanimously elected captain of the basketball team.

Example 2. A well-known child psychiatrist was brought to a Nobleteen meeting to consult with the boys in writing a speech for influential people in the health and welfare field. His goal was to argue for more flexibility on the part of youth-serving agencies. The intervenor's only role was to bring the two together. The psychiatrist was familiar with the boys' language, and they were experienced in discussing topics which focused on their relationships with external systems. Tape-recorded material from the meeting was included in the speech, and the boys gained a great sense of competence in verbalizing their concerns and points of view.

Example 3. At one meeting of the "C" Street network club, two members informed the advisor that Mrs. White, the club president, was having an extremely severe asthma attack. The group discussed this informally and came to the conclusion that it was really her "nerves" and that she should go into the hospital. Mrs. White had been hospitalized several times previously and was diagnosed as a borderline schizophrenic. Mrs. White's main supports, her sister and her closest friend, were extremely anxious, their own fear of death and separation coming to the surface. This placed them in a real approach-avoidance bind. The advisor agreed to visit Mrs. White after the meeting.

Mrs. White was lying on the couch coughing in uncontrollable bursts. The advisor soon labeled the coughing (which was panicking her and the other two women) as a "good thing" and encouraged it. He sympathetically listened to Mrs. White recount her dramatic collapse on the hospital's emergency room floor and her subsequent hallucinations. While she talked, the two network members busied themselves cleaning up the house and attending to the children. Once the advisor had listened, he began exploring areas of stress with her. The most recent crisis was that she was being threatened with eviction for nonpayment of rent. She had contacted her relief worker, who had promised to contact the landlord. The advisor promised to talk to the relief worker. He also learned that in desperation she had gone to a different hospital. She had confidence in the treatment she received there, but did not see how she could go back for an early morning clinic. The advisor agreed that Rebound could provide her with a cab voucher.

Then the three women and the advisor sat and discussed the events of the club meeting. Mrs. White's coughing subsided, and she became calmer as she related to outside reality. The friend's and the sister's anxiety was also reduced. They could then respond in ways which reduced rather than heightened Mrs. White's anxiety.

The significance of this intervention lies not so much in the availability of the professional to meet the immediate dependency needs and to manipulate external systems on the woman's behalf as in his being in a position to repair her system of significant supports. A member of her own system would thenceforth be able to remind her that her rent was due when she got her check and remind her about the attendance officer if she became lax in getting her children off to school. The program continued to meet her dependency needs and support her medical care through the cab vouchers. Initially the vouchers were obtained for her by the professional; later she took responsibility for reminding him about getting them; eventually she went to the clinic's business office to get them herself. She has not suffered a severe attack or psychotic episode since the intervention.

Our commitment was to develop models for the delivery of services which multiply our therapeutic impact by bringing about change in existing systems. By focusing on competence and mutual support rather than on pathology, we have experimented with a model for the delivery of services to people who do not wish to perceive themselves as patients.

Reading 8-3

*A Political Perspective in Problem Solving**

Allison D. Murdach

During the past twenty-five years, problem solving has developed as a major method in social work practice. The problem-solving process has been elaborated in numerous publications, and guidelines

* Copyright 1982, National Association of Social Workers, Inc. Reprinted with permission, from Social Work 27:5 (September 1982), pp. 417–21.

have been developed for its use in daily work with clients (Siporin, 1975, pp. 147–148). However, these efforts have suffered from two limitations: (1) they do not sufficiently address the issue of how the practitioner manages conflict in the helping relationship, and (2) they tend to ignore the influence of the organizational context on problem solving.

This article proposes to avoid such difficulties by adopting a political approach to problem solving—an approach that takes into consideration the processes by which participants in problem solving (the helper as well as the helped) try to order and manage their relationships in dealing with client-oriented problems. The article emphasizes such processes as negotiation, conflict resolution, and the building of support.

The article consists of four parts. First, it reviews some deficiencies in current problem-solving theory. Second, it discusses a conceptual framework for a political approach. Third, it develops some general problem-solving strategies based on this framework and illustrates them with case vignettes drawn from the author's personal observations as a psychiatric social worker in a large public hospital. Fourth, the article discusses advantages of this approach for social work practitioners.

CURRENT DEFICIENCIES

The problem-solving method, as presently formulated in social work, is based on several questionable assumptions about practitioner-client relationships. The first is the assumption that for problem solving to begin, the relationship between helpers and clients must be free of basic conflict. This idea was often expressed in formulations that emphasized the necessity for a "positive relationship" to exist between helpers and clients if genuine problem solving was to take place (Perlman, 1957, pp. 66–67). Along the same lines, recent authors have advocated that helper and client develop a contract embodying agreed-on objectives and shared goals before beginning the problem-solving process (Croxton, 1947).

Recent empirical studies, however, have demonstrated that despite the best efforts of workers and clients, there is often little basic consensus between them on such important matters as the definition of the problem, what interventions are needed, the goals of treatment, and the outcome of the treatment. The studies have also shown that these can remain areas of contention throughout the relationship (Maluccio, 1979; Zuft, Smith & Kace, 1978, pp. 505–511). In other words, work with clients often has to be carried out through helping relationships that are characterized by conflict (Barghi, 1968, pp. 460–473; Davis, 1971; Freidson, 1961; Freud, 1963, pp. 63–75; Lazare et al., 1976, pp. 119–139).

Another flaw in current social work approaches to problem solving is that they tend to ignore the impact of the organizational environment in which problem solving takes place. This is evident in the social work literature on the subject (Perlman, 1972, pp. 129–179). This deficiency is remarkable because most social workers, despite the rise in private practice, still offer their services as employees of complex organizations, such as hospitals, clinics, and agencies. Encounters between practitioners and clients are strongly influenced by the organizational milieus in which they occur. This has been demonstrated in other fields (Bask, 1979; Cicourel, 1968; Goffman, 1961; Strauss et al., 1964). It is important that this factor also be taken into account in discussing problem-solving interactions between social workers and their clients.

What seems to be needed, then, is an approach that recognizes the limitations of problem-solving theory and that generates practice guidelines based on a broader interpretation of the problem-solving process, one that can take a fuller account of social conflict and the organizational milieu. For centuries politics has been the discipline most concerned with such issues, and it is a source of insight into how best to handle them in clinical problem solving.

A POLITICAL FRAMEWORK

Viewing problem solving as a political process implies that it is generated less by the needs of the client than by the joint need of client and practitioner to establish acceptable agreements so that they can work together—a *modus vivendi,* in political terminology. These agreements, although unstable and subject to continual renegotiation, maintain a "negotiated order" within which social work services can be distributed (Strauss, 1978; Strauss et al., 1963, 1964, pp. 147–169). The organizational environment becomes, in this view, not merely a backdrop for the interaction of practitioner and client, but a powerful influence on that interaction because it is peopled by individuals who are vitally involved in and directly or indirectly affected by the outcome of the intervention. Such individuals include (besides service consumers and their families) staff, agency administrators, community representatives—anyone who has a stake in solving a particular clinical problem.

The situation that develops among these participants does not resemble an orderly exercise in rational decision making but often resembles an arena in which each individual struggles to obtain important benefits either for himself or herself or for those he or she represents. In hospitals, for example, patients seek the benefits of proper care and treatment. Their families, relatives, and friends may be equally insistent on gaining such psychic benefits as support, reassurance, and respite. Staff members want professional satisfaction and appropriate deference from their clients. Hospital administrators desire an efficient working operation and lowered costs. This list could also include many other individuals who make demands on the health setting—for example, community health advocates who seek justice in the delivery of benefits and agents of regulatory agencies who strive

to achieve conformity to legal and administrative standards of care.

In such a milieu, the main objective in problem solving becomes less the nurturing of the client's coping efforts than the development and monitoring of joint agreements that will structure the relationships among all the various interested parties so that conflict is minimized. Thus clinical problem solving at times becomes a political act by which the participants seek to accomplish a more satisfactory redistribution of power and control. This can be a messy process, one in which helping becomes not the imposition of a rational scheme, but the satisfying of the diversely expressed interests of each participant, including the helper. To work in such a manner, the social work practitioner needs to develop and use the requisite political skills. What are some of the skills with which the practitioner should be familiar?

PROBLEM-SOLVING SKILLS

Generally, a political approach to problem solving requires the practitioner to use the following skills:

1. Knowledge of the political "setup" of each problem-solving situation.
2. Ability to discover the common interests—the problem—of the participants.
3. Assistance in negotiating a solution.
4. Support for a plan of action.

It will be useful to examine briefly each of these skills, or steps, and to illustrate them with case examples drawn from social work practice in a hospital.

Knowing the setup. It is important for the social worker to be familiar with the cast of characters involved in each problem-solving situation—who the key participants are, how they define their vital interests, what capacities they have to reward or punish, what claims they will invoke, what demands they will tolerate, and so on. Such data help the practitioner to determine not only who should be included in problem solving, but also how and when they should be involved. A thorough knowledge of such factors is often crucial, as the following case history illustrates:

The hospital staff asked the social worker to initiate discharge planning for a 35-year-old psychiatric patient, despite his wish to remain in the hospital. The patient's mother promptly contacted the ward physician and told him she strongly objected to this plan because, in her opinion, her son's treatment was not yet completed. She reiterated similar views to the ward social worker and added that if the hospital staff pursued this plan, she would sue the hospital. Because this was perceived by staff, especially the doctor, as merely an idle threat, discharge planning proceeded accordingly. However, plans changed abruptly when staff members discovered that the patient's mother had retained a lawyer, received the backing of the hospital parents' group, and gained the support of a local congressman. Discharge planning was halted and the social worker was asked to make every attempt to involve the patient's mother as much as possible in any future decision making about discharge planning.

Thus, the patient's mother forced the hospital staff, including the social worker, into a showdown that she easily won because of her alliance with community groups and representatives, all of whom had sufficient capacity to hurt the hospital in various ways—by lodging official protests, by going to the newspapers with their complaints, by initiating legal action, and so on. Such a win-lose situation might have been avoided if there had been a better initial assessment of the mother's abilities, commitments, and investments.

How is one to gather such information? Two methods are particularly useful. First, the practitioner can use data provided by informants in the work setting. These are generally fellow employees—professional colleagues, the secretary, the janitor, anyone who can be helpful in spotting the key actors in problem-solving situations. Second, it is important for the practitioner to observe the key participants in action and thus gather interactional clues to help determine what is going on. Such occurrences as a sudden silence, a slip of the tongue, an embarrassed glance, or a purposely ignored request can provide valuable information about power relationships or capabilities that may need to be considered in problem solving.

Discovering a common interest. From a political perspective, it quickly becomes apparent that each participant in problem solving perceives a different problem. For problem solving to proceed, therefore, it must be focused. Thus, it is essential to determine the principal concerns of the parties involved. Put another way, it is essential to develop a shared definition of the problem situation. Among the many difficulties and dilemmas that abound in each case, usually only a few are really of interest to each party. These constitute the "problem to be worked." Such concerns can best be discovered by a careful assessment of which difficulty calls forth the highest commitment of energy and resources—as opposed to mere interest or concern—by the parties involved. Such an assessment often reveals a common interest in problems that initially might seem trivial or insignificant but on further investigation prove to be highly important:

A 45-year-old depressed single male was involuntarily admitted to an acute, locked psychiatric ward after attempting suicide with a pistol. Almost immediately his condition seemed to improve and he demanded to be discharged, complaining that hospitalization was not helping him and that he needed to return to work. Community authorities and family members expressed concern about his early release, fearing he might attempt suicide again. Further involuntary treatment of the patient seemed impossible because of his rapid recovery. Therefore, the hospital staff asked the social worker to focus all her efforts, not on convincing the patient to stay in the hospital, but on making sure the patient no longer had access to his gun. When it was finally determined that the weapon was safely in the hands of the police, the patient was readied for discharge.

In this example, the problem was not immediately apparent. Was it the demand of the patient for discharge? His refusal to accept further treatment? His occasional suicidal impulses? Although significant, none of these facts engendered much shared concern by the hospital staff, community representatives, or family members. The problem—the difficulty on which all parties were really willing to work—instead turned out to be a relatively simple, but important, practical matter—proper disposition of the patient's weapon. The need for successfully resolving the issue was dramatized by the agreement of all parties involved—family members, community authorities, and hospital staff—that this was an essential step, since its accomplishment would reassure each party, at least symbolically, that the patient was being discharged to safe conditions in the community.

Negotiating solutions.   The process of arriving at solutions tends to be presented in the problem-solving literature as the result of the practitioner's helping clients to develop successful alternatives to their current troubles. However, in the political perspective used here, solutions are seen more as common understandings that develop out of a step-by-step negotiation among the parties involved in the problem solving. In other words, as problem solving proceeds, each decision maker puts forward a number of tentative solutions for consideration. These are then shaped and molded by a process of bargaining and discussion until an agreement is reached about what is to be done:

A 53-year-old female patient suffering from alcoholism frequently escaped from the hospital while on ground privileges. After each escape, she would usually return to the hospital intoxicated. Her guardian (a family member) lodged official complaints with the hospital administration about these incidents and demanded stricter staff supervision of the patient while she was on the grounds. Ward staff, being short of personnel, then tried to restrict the patient to the ward. This plan resulted in steadily escalating misbehavior by the patient, who violently objected to being so confined. After weeks of steady negotiation by the ward staff, a solution to this problem was devised. This involved an agreement among the patient, the guardian, and the hospital staff that the patient's guardian would supervise her on outings on the grounds in return for her "good behavior" elsewhere in the hospital.

The negotiation process in this example involved an elaborate series of trade-offs among the hospital staff, the patient, and the patient's guardian. This exchange enabled them to develop a solution from which each party could gain some benefit and which, therefore, they would be willing to promote and help succeed. In this case, for example, hospital staff gained additional supervision of the patient at no cost to themselves. The patient endorsed the solution because it allowed her to have ground privileges. Finally, the patient's guardian approved the plan because it allowed him to "keep an eye" on the patient by directly assisting in her care.

Building support.   Clarifying one's objectives is often seen as an important goal in problem solving. A political approach to problem solving implies that clearly defining one's objectives, although important, may in the final analysis be less essential than the ability to mobilize the support necessary to their fulfillment. Therefore, it is important that practitioners become skilled in engineering support. Some readers might object to the verb "engineering," seeing in it something sinister. However, it is used here to emphasize that support has to be carefully constructed and that it is not automatically granted to any proposed solution, no matter how brilliant.

Practitioners often forget the important role that support by clients and others plays in the problem-solving process. Thus, they tend to ignore the fact that individuals are more likely to support decisions from which they get something in return. It is the payoff that each participant expects to receive from the proposed solution that builds active support. Therefore, it is necessary for the practitioner to assess carefully what gains each party, including the practitioner, hopes to achieve by offering support to the proposed solution. With these data, the worker can design interventions that each party involved in the problem solving will be able to accept:

A 45-year-old male patient requested social work assistance in improving his hostile relationship with his mother, with whom he had been living for many years. He reported that his main difficulties with his mother were financial. She controlled his benefit checks (his sole income) and would not give him sufficient funds for his needs. The worker then interviewed his mother, who complained that the patient not only "harassed" her constantly with demands for funds, but consistently misused them when they were provided. The worker then urged the patient to seek control of his own funds, assuming this would promote his strivings for independence, lessen tensions at home, and help him to learn more responsibility for money management. However, this plan aroused stiff opposition from both the patient and his mother. They both accused the worker of being "pushy" and unresponsive to their needs.

The hospital staff also became alarmed and urged the worker to adopt a different approach. The worker thus changed direction and approached the problem more indirectly, this time focusing on the development of a budgeting plan that could be used by both the patient and his mother.

The practitioner in this case could have saved much effort by initially assessing what gains existed for each party in the proposed solution to the problem. Such an assessment would have revealed that the patient's becoming financially independent, if achieved, would have caused serious losses for all parties concerned. The patient would have had to forfeit a powerful means of securing his mother's attention, and his mother would have lost a considerable measure of control over the patient. The hospital staff would have had to give up considerable freedom of action because without the mother's help, they would have been required to assume more responsibility for monitoring the patient's irresponsible spending habits. Therefore, this was an approach that realistically could not be supported by any of the parties involved. It proved essential to develop a more modest and acceptable solution—budgeting—that each party could accept. Thus, the patient's support for a solution was finally achieved by offering him some degree of autonomy, while offering at least moderate gains to each of the other parties involved.

DISCUSSION

A political perspective helps to emphasize some aspects of clinical problem solving that are often neglected. First, by recognizing the omnipresence of conflict in social relationships (including helping relationships), this perspective underscores the importance of adopting strategies to maintain balance in such relationships and to control the effects of troublesome power discrepancies. Such an emphasis guards against the tendency to see problem solving as mainly the client's task— instead of an effort involving client, worker, and any other individuals who have an interest in resolving a particular problem. By thus sensitizing practitioners to issues of conflict and struggle in the helping relationship, a political perspective encourages them to see the negotiation of mutually beneficial settlements as a foundation on which further intervention can be based (Haley, 1959, pp. 321–332; Sullivan, 1954, pp. 9–17).

Second, by stressing the impact of the social and organizational context on problem solving, a political approach alerts the practitioner to the importance of factors not ordinarily considered relevant for clinical work—for example, the structure and needs of organizational life, the demands of the administration, bureaucratic requirements in the work environment, and so on. These areas, although recognized, are not usually legitimated in the clinical literature, which tends to focus almost exclusively on developing ways to meet the needs of clients or which, at best, views problem solving as a process governed principally by the requirements of therapeutic or decision-making interactions (Golan, 1969, pp. 286–296; Kane, 1975, pp. 19–32; Keith-Lucas, 1957).

The overall advantage of these concepts, however, is their emphasis on the exchange aspects of the problem-solving interaction. Use of this concept, which stresses that problem solving is an effort in which parties participate to gain certain benefits, including power, status, and recognition, as well as tangible rewards, reminds the practitioner that the genuine interests of the parties have to be honored if problem solving is to be effective (Balint, 1957; Bloom & Wilson, 1979, pp. 275–296; Lazare et al., 1976, pp. 119–139).

The foregoing suggestions are intended to remind practitioners that a third dimension—the political—should be added to the psychological and social dimensions usually considered in problem solving. This third dimension promotes a broader and more comprehensive approach to problem solving and encourages practitioners to re-examine the assumptions on which they base this important work.

References

Auerswald, Edger H.   Interdisciplinary versus ecological approach. *Family Process,* September 1968, *7* 202–215.

Barghi, John H.   Premature termination of psychotherapy and patient-therapist expectations. *American Journal of Orthopsychiatry,* 1968, 22.

Bask, Charles L.   *Forgive and remember.* Chicago: University of Chicago Press, 1979.

Balint, Michael.   *The doctor, his patient, and the illness.* New York: International Universities Press, 1957.

Bennis, Warren.   Post-bureaucratic leadership. *Transaction,* July–August 1969, *6,* 44–52.

Bennis, Warren; Benne, Kenneth D.; and Chin, Robert (Eds.).   *The planning of change,* New York: Holt, Rinehart & Winston, 1969.

Bloom, Samuel W., & Wilson, Robert W.   Patient-practitioner relationships. In Howard Freeman, Sol Levine, & Lev G. Ruder (Eds.), *Handbook of medical sociology* (3d ed.). Englewood Cliffs, N.J.: Prentice-Hall, 1979.

Cicourel, Aaron V.   *The social organization of juvenile justice.*   New York: Wiley, 1968.

Clark, Kenneth B.   *The dark ghetto: Dilemmas of social power.* New York: Harper & Row, 1965.

Cooley, C. H.   *Human nature and the social order.* New York: Scribner's Sons, 1902.

Croxton, Tom A. The therapeutic contract in social treatment." In Paul Glasser, Rosemary Sari, & Robert Vinter (Eds.), *Individual change through small groups*. New York: Free Press, 1947.

Davis, John D. *The interview as arena*. Stanford, Calif.: Stanford University Press, 1971.

Dewey, John. *How we think* (rev. ed.). New York: Heath, 1933.

Freidson, Elliott. *Patient views of medical practice*. New York: Russell Sage Foundation, 1961.

Freud, Sigmund. On psychotherapy. In Philip Rieff (Ed.), *Collected Papers*. New York: Collier Books, 1963.

Goffman, Erving. The medical model and mental hospitalization," *Asylums*. Garden City, N.Y.: Anchor Books, 1961.

Golan, Naomi. How caseworkers decide. *Social Service Review*, September 1969, pp. 286–296.

Haley, Jay. An interactional description of schizophrenia. *Psychiatry* (November 1959), *22*, 321–332.

Johnson, Wendell. Being understanding and understood: Or how to find a wandered horse. *ETC*, Spring 1951, *8*, 171–179.

Kane, Rosalie. The interprofessional team as a small group. *Social Work in Health Care*, Fall 1975, *1*, 19–32.

Keith-Lucas, Alan. *Decisions about people in need*. Chapel Hill: University of North Carolina Press, 1957.

Lazare, Aaron et al. Studies on a negotiated approach to patienthood. *The doctor-patient relationship in the changing health scene*. Washington, D.C.: U.S. Department of Health, Education and Welfare, 1976.

Leopold, Edward. Rebound children and their families: A community survey conducted by the rebound children and youth project. New York: Rebound Children and Youth Project, 1968. (mimeographed)

Leopold, Edward. Hidden strengths in the disorganized family: Discovery through extended home observations. Paper presented at meeting of American Orthopsychiatry Association, 1969.

Lerner, Barbara. *Therapy in the ghetto*. Baltimore, Md.: Johns Hopkins Press, 1972.

Malone, Charles. Safety first: Comments on the influence of external danger in the lives of children of disorganized families. *American Journal Orthopsychiatry*, 1966, *36*, 3–12.

Maluccio, Anthony N. *Learning from clients: Interpersonal helping as viewed by clients and social workers*. New York: Free Press, 1979.

Miller, David R. The study of social relationships: Situation identity and social interaction. In S. Koch (Ed.), *Psychology: A Study of a Science*, 1963.

Minuchin, Salvador et al. Family therapy: Technique or theory. In J. Masserman (Ed.), *Science and psychoanalysis* (vol. 14). New York: Grune & Stratton, 1969.

Perlman, Helen Harris. *Social casework: A problem-solving process*. Chicago: University of Chicago Press, 1957.

Perlman, Helen Harris. The problem solving model in social casework. In Roberts W. Roberts & Robert H. Nee (Eds.), *Theories of social casework*. Chicago: University of Chicago Press, 1972.

Polya, George. *How to solve it*. Princeton, N.J.: Princeton University Press, 1957.

Reid, William J. The task-centered system. New York: Columbia University Press, 1978.

Siporin, Max. *Introduction to social work practice.* New York: Macmillan, 1975. and accompanying bibliography.

Strauss, Anslem. *Negotiations.* San Francisco: Jossey-Bass, 1978.

Strauss, Anslem et al. *Psychiatric ideologies and institutions.* New York: Free Press, 1964.

Strauss, Anslem, et al. The hospital and its negotiated order. In Eliot Friedson (Ed.), *The hospital in modern society.* New York: Free Press, 1963.

Sullivan, Harry Stack. *The psychiatric interview.* New York: Norton, 1954.

Zuft, Lorrain, Smith, Kevin, & Kace, Morris. Therapists', patients' and inpatients', staffs' views of treatment modes and outcomes. *Hospital and Community Psychiatry,* August 1978, *29,* 505–511.

Chapter 9

The Contact Phase: Problem Identification, Initial Goal Setting, Data Collection, and Initial Assessment

As discussed in Chapter 8, the problem-solving process may be divided into three major phases, each with its own tasks. This chapter will deal with the contact phase in which the client and the worker come together and begin the initial exploration that will result in a decision as to whether they will go on together and, if so, how.

The social worker and the client may come together in several different ways; the individual, family, or group may reach out for help with a problem they have identified as being beyond their means of solution, or an individual or group may identify another individual or group as having a problem and request that the social work agency or the social worker become involved. In this situation we could well consider the system that recognizes the problem and asks the social worker to intervene as the client system, in that it is this system that has requested the services of the social worker as change agent to alter the situation. Earlier, the person or the group who makes this initial contact with the change agent was labeled "the problem recognition system."

In social work we sometimes do not give enough thought to the impact of the problem recognition system on the way we approach the potential client system. One of the most common problems occurs when we accept the problem definition or the outcome goals of the problem recognition system as our own without participating with the clients in an examination of the meaning of the referral for them. It is always the responsibility of the social worker who accepts a referral from a client recognition system to determine with the referred system what is involved in the situation. To accept someone else's view without making our own professional assessment and without understanding the meaning of the referral to the client is to court disaster. On the other hand we do not ignore the meaning a referral may have for us or for our potential client. It is important to know if the client had any part in the identification of the problems or the plan for referral. It is also critical to understand the apparent impact on the client of the process of referral.

Two very important principles stem from these concepts. The first one is that the potential client system be approached as just that, a potential client system that has been identified by someone else as needing help, and that we keep an open mind as to whether this is an accurate assessment. Second, recognizing that, at this point the problem recognition system is really the client system, we need to go through a brief problem-solving process with this system. We identify what such systems see as the problem, how they identify it as a problem, what are the facts that bear on the problem, how they see it being changed, and what outcome is sought from the referral. Above all, we need to complete this process by evaluation and termination by reporting back to the problem recognition system whether or not the identified problem-bearer and we have agreed to work together. Further, we need to exercise caution as to giving the problem recognition system any assurance that we will work toward any goals that they may have in mind when clients ask for intervention.

If we feel that we cannot help, or that there is no problem, or the potential client is unwilling to become a client, we need to consider with the problem recognition system how this will be dealt with. It may be that in this process the client recognition system will become the client system in the full sense of the term. As an example of this: there are parents who come to the agency to report a child's problem. Quite often they become the clients and the child may, or may not, be seen. Or another example: a neighborhood group may be incensed and upset over the behavior of a new family in the neighborhood. A visit by the social worker reveals that the new family is functioning quite well, but very differently from the neighborhood. Perhaps the neighborhood needs to become the client for purposes of examining the meaning of their problem in being unable to accept this different behavior. Or a further example: upon contacting the potential client system it is found that it really does need and want some help with some difficulties, but the help to be given does not fall within the defined parameters of sanctioned service. We may then want to suggest to the problem recognition system that they seek help elsewhere. Above all else, we should never ignore the client recognition system's position in the situation. We must engage in a problem-solving process with it and we must bring our contact with it to an orderly termination. This is critical, even though this whole process just described may take place in one telephone call. These notions will be discussed in more detail in the paragraphs on referral found in Chapter 14.

GIVING AND TAKING HELP

What is meant by the term *giving help* to someone? Help needs to be understood as far more than something that one person gives to another. What someone else does on our behalf only becomes help when we can make use of it. Keith-Lucas (1972, p. 15) defines help as something tangible or intangible offered by one person or group to another person or group *in such a way that the helped person or group can use it* to achieve some solution of the issue at hand. Help thus has two important elements: (1) *what* is given and (2) *how* it is given and used. To be helpful, what is given must be something of value and of use to the recipients, and it must be given in such a way as to leave the recipients free to use it in their own way without paying the penalty of loss of self-esteem or a loss of control of their own lives. Potential clients, whether self-initiated applicants or other identified clients, move from being a potential client to being an actual client when they decide that it is possible to accept the help offered.

In our culture, asking for or taking help (at least from others beyond one's intimate circle of associates) is often a severe blow to one's sense of adequacy. The person who accepts help has to face the fact that (1) there is something in one's situation that one wants changed but that one cannot change by oneself; (2) one must be willing to discuss the problem with another person; (3) one must accord to that other person at least a limited right to tell one what to do or to do things for one; and (4) one must be willing to change oneself or one's situation or, at the very least, to go along with changes that others make in one's situation (Keith-Lucas, 1972, p. 20). How difficult these steps are depends on several things. The difficulty in asking for help is greatly increased if the problem is one that is generally seen in our culture as being a fault in the person who has it. When we assume that problems in living are signs of personality malfunction or devalued personal qualities, we erect some very difficult barriers between our client and work on problem solution. If people have usually been taken advantage of or if their confidence has been abused when, in the past, they revealed their situation to another, or if their previous attempts to live in a supposedly better way have always resulted in defeat, the business of asking for help may be excruciatingly painful and difficult. On the other hand, for parents who support a group work agency financially so that their children can have positive developmental group associations, the enrollment of their children in various helping programs, while it is a recognition that they as parents need help in offering their children growth experiences, is usually seen as a positive and normal thing to do. Or the neighborhood group which seeks the worker's help as an advocate to change another system, such as the school or the housing project, may also see this quest for help as a positive step to control its own situation. However, since the social problems of poverty and unemployment are often viewed as the result of individual pathology, the family faced with them may feel totally inadequate and fearful of asking for help.

Anyone who has driven through miles of confused streets before stopping to ask someone for directions might well ask why one had to waste time, gas, and energy before admitting that one did not know where one was going. And how many persons have said to themselves that there was little point in asking because very few "natives" are ever able to give adequate directions? This attitude is a way of preserving a sense of adequacy, if not superiority, while asking for help.

If something that one gives to another only becomes helpful when the other can use it, then it follows that social workers can only be helpful to their clients when they understand what problems the client would like to be able to cope with or to change. Thus, in the beginning phase of their work together practitioner and client have to clarify what the difficulty is that they are going to work on. (Such clarification is the end product of the considerations outlined in Section I of the problem-solving model in Chapter 8.) They have to determine the expectations and goals that the client holds for the outcome of the work together. They have to jointly understand the realities and boundaries of the practitioner's abilities and the service system's resources (see Section III A of the model). The client has to have some realistic understanding of what the work together is going to personally require. As a result of the execution of these tasks, a preliminary contract to proceed with the necessary exploration and data collection is formulated. The mutual decision as to problem, goals, and expectations will determine the focus of the data collection. It is not necessary to know all there is to know about a client, but rather to understand what knowledge is necessary in order to solve the problem and achieve the outcomes sought.

GETTING STARTED

Regardless of the size or type of client system, in the accomplishment of these tasks the practitioner will be involved in two major forms of human association that are typical of social work practice: the interview and the group meeting. The following discussion relates to principles that are important in either instance. (In that discussion the reference will be to the clients rather than to the client system simply because this allows the use of the pronoun they—a human term—rather than the mechanistic *it* which seems to be called for in references to the client system.) The first task the practitioner faces is that of preparation for the initial contact. Because one cannot divide individuals, or groups, or human interactions into discrete and entirely orderly parts, this first meeting will undoubtedly involve some elements that bear on all the tasks outlined in the preceding paragraph. However, the primary focus of the beginning will concern Section 1 A through Section 1 C in the model—the problem as it is seen by the client system, by systems with which the client system is in interaction, and by the worker. Certainly these aspects will need to be clarified before the problem-for-work (Section I D) can be settled, and focused work on data collection (as apart from incidental data collection) cannot begin until this point has been established.

In preparation for the initial contact, workers will want to collect and review any pertinent data they have about the client system and the purposes of the coming encounter. In addition, they may want to discuss with others in the setting the kinds of help that the service system can offer. Because beginnings are important in establishing the pattern of ongoing relationships, and because they wish to demonstrate respect and concern for the client system, the worker will want to do everything possible to reduce unnecessary obstacles to complete and free communication. An understanding about the time and place is essential, as are arrangements to ensure that the meeting will be comfortable, private, and as free from interruptions as possible. The worker may also want to give some thought to contact with other elements of the client system or other systems whose interest and/or participation may impinge on the change endeavor, such as the family of a referred adolescent or the school which suggested that a certain neighborhood group might find a home in a nearby community center. Thought should be given to contact with referral sources—very serious thought, because this action will have many implications for both the practitioner and the client system as they begin work together.

There are no universally applicable rules for information collection which can be set forth before the worker meets with the client system, but some principles of data collection for the practitioner's consideration can be discussed. The key principles of data collection in social work are (1) the client system should be the primary source of information; (2) data is collected for use so that the data collected should be related to the problem at issue; and (3) the practitioner should not acquire information that the worker would be unwilling to share with the client system. In addition the worker should be willing to share the process by which the information was secured with the client system and to explain why it was secured in the way it was. Further, it is our conviction that if a worker has information about a particular aspect of the problem, this information should be shared with the client before asking how the client feels and thinks about that particular point. In this way, the worker scrupulously avoids trapping the client and gives the client the opportunity, before taking a position, to reconcile what the worker knows with what the client thinks and feels. If the worker must seek information in advance of the initial contact with the client system, the worker should limit that data to the situation that brings client and worker together—nothing more. It is possible that amassing large amounts of information unrelated to the problem at hand may well get in the way of the worker's really hearing what the client is saying about the here and now. In general, it is our position that, if information should be sought from other sources than the client system and the files of the worker's agency, this can be done *after* the first meeting when the practitioner and the client have established the need for such information and the purposes it serves. Thus, most data collection will take place after worker and client have agreed to work together and have defined the problem on which they will work and the ends that will be sought.

Perhaps it is time to clarify the earlier discussion in its relationship to two types of clients: (1) the voluntary client who comes to the worker of free will with a problem that has been identified, and (2) the involuntary client who comes to the worker either because someone in a power position has demanded this or because the worker has been asked to see the client and has initiated the transaction. At the first meeting the involuntary client may or may not be willing to share with the practitioner what the client sees as the problem, but usually advance information about the client has been supplied by the individual or agency that took the initiative in forcing client and worker to come together. It is our position that the principles of data collection outlined earlier apply to the worker's contacts with both the volunatry and the involuntary client.

The involuntary client may not (and usually will not) have given permission for information to be shared with the worker or have knowledge of what information was shared. This makes it very important that the worker, at the very beginning, share the advance information and, if possible, the source of that information with the client. Sometimes the worker cannot share the source of information, for example, in cases involving the neglect and abuse of children in which the informant asks not to be identified. In the interest of protecting the children, such requests are granted. With the involuntary client it may also be necessary, in order to protect the rights of others or in the client's own interest, for the worker to collect certain information without the client's permission. This does not relieve the worker of the responsibility to inform the client of the intention to take such action and to report to the client the content of the information collected. In fact, in order to give the client as much control of the involuntary relationship as possible, the sharing of the worker's intent is essential. If one cannot decide the action taken, having knowledge of the action and the reasons for it gives one some sense of being in at least partial control.

As previously mentioned, there are two types of beginnings: in the first, clients have decided that they need to explore what can be done about some want, felt need, lack, or difficulty and have asked for help; in the second, someone other than the client has been concerned about this matter, and the worker has initiated the contact with the client at that other person's request. When someone has asked to see the social worker, the most sensible thing to do is to let one state in one's own terms why the person has come. But the first contact starts on a different note when workers initiate it. Then workers must be prepared to explain why they have taken this action, being careful to allow the client time to respond to the statement of purpose and concern.

When the practitioner initiates contact with the client around a problem identified by someone other than the client, the worker often feels like an intruder. In such instances it is easy to become more worried about oneself than about the client's problem. Following the natural human course of wanting to be liked and accepted by people, we often hope to somehow slip into a pleasant relationship and then to get down to business. This seldom results in a helpful beginning. When a social worker reaches into other people's lives uninvited the worker must be able to define one's reasons so directly, so simply, and so clearly (not with "weaselly" double-talk or words that do not quite portray the situation) that they do not need to worry about what the worker knows or what will be found out—clients do not need to ask themselves why the worker is *really* here. The worker needs to be concerned about the client system and for the stress that one's presence may add to it.

THE CROSSING OF SYSTEM BOUNDARIES

The giving and taking of help requires the crossing of the boundaries of the potential client system. The client system cannot request help without having a member (or if an individual client, the whole system) cross the system boundary to interact with another system, the change agent system and the change agent. Also, the potential client system cannot become a client system without allowing the change agent to cross their boundaries and become a part of their life.

This requires that workers always be sensitive to the meaning of boundaries to the client system, and for the meaning to the client system of the interactions of the system members within its boundaries. This becomes *critically important* when workers are involved with systems that may have different notions about boundaries (where they are located, how one crosses them, and the pattern of transactions necessary to show respect for the boundaries) and different patterns of interaction within the boundaries, as in working with minority groups and families. An article on working with the family behavior of urban American Indians has been reproduced in order to serve as an example of the importance to the worker's actions of an understanding of the system (see Reading 9–2). It does not exactly address the issue of boundary crossing, but workers who have successfully negotiated this with families different from themselves are those who are sensitively aware that there are different culturally determined patterns of appropriate boundary crossing and of the necessity to scrupulously respect the boundaries and the ways of crossing them.

DEFINING THE PROBLEM

So workers begin with a consideration of the problem that is seen by the client as the beginning place. For many individuals and groups, needs and wants come in bulk size. But one cannot do everything at once, so the first job the practitioner has is to engage with the client in the business of deciding where to start. The client's selection of a starting point is where one would ordinarily hope to begin. But if the client's choice is dangerous to self or others, or if it promises more trouble and failure, the worker has the responsibility of pointing out the risks. A social worker cannot be a part to planning that is destructive, but one needs to be very sure of one's ground before rejecting out of hand the client's chosen starting place.

This indicates that the practitioner must utilize the skills of interviewing, communication, and relationship discussed in various chapters to help in arriving at some understanding of the client's perception of the problem. This does not mean that any worker needs to be, or can be, an instant expert on problems. The primary job at this point is to seek to understand what it is that brings the client to ask for help. One of the primary tools of understanding comes from our ability to empathize with the feeling the client brings (see Chapter 6). This means that we must put all other considerations aside for a moment and try to fully hear what the client is saying, the words used, the feeling carried by the words, and the unspoken messages sent by the body languages. While we need to focus an interview and there is certain information we may need, to attempt to rush too quickly to understanding through information collection may be to loose the very thing we seek. If the client is able to share, it is better to listen than to question. It is better to make brief comments, or ask simple questions related to what the client just said, to encourage the client to continue than to proceed forward on our own agenda. Let the clients tell their own story in their own way and time while you seek to understand their pain and the meaning of the way they share it. The critical issue at this point is to understand the clients' view of what brings you together, not to be busy formulating your own judgment or collecting information for your purposes. Not understanding is not necessarily an indication of inadequacy, a cause for despair. One can share with the client one's difficulty in really knowing what they are saying and ask if they can share more. In working with a problem beyond one's understanding or a system very different from one's own it is important that practitioners not burden either themselves or the client with unrealistic expectations of immediate mutual understanding. This is particularly true when practitioners are talking with someone whose life experiences are very different than their own. One can attempt to understand if one can reach into one's self and one's own experience to remember a time when one felt something similar to what the client is feeling. This does not mean the experience was similar, but the emotion one felt may be very similar to the feeling the client expresses. One of the reasons we can understand another human being is the commonness of human emotions and the generality of experience. You may not have lost a husband as the client did; but, surely, you have suffered some loss sometime—a loss that left you in despair. The depth of feeling, the meaning of it, may be different, but the feeling has certain similarities that help you to understand. The other side of this coin is the danger to understanding the client if one has had a similar experience or is at a similar life stage (as the worker and Mrs. Manley). Here it is so tempting to feel you understand because you are alike without remembering that no two people experience the same experience in the same way. The principle to remember is that in order to help, one must start where the client is which means understanding his/her view of what brings you together.

The second piece of knowledge and understanding that goes into problem definition is related to what the client wants from the contact with you. What does the client hope will happen as a result of your coming together. It is through knowing the hopes of the client that one may understand what it is that the client wants changed. Arriving at a notion of the problem is no more an instant process than is arriving at an understanding. It may well take several meetings. The client's perception of the problem and the worker's perception of the problem may not be the same. Frequently, they are not. Then it becomes necessary for the worker and the client to enter into a series of negotiations and discussions directed toward arriving at a definition of the problem on which they are to begin work. An example of this is found in "The House on Sixth Street" which is reproduced at the end of Chapter 1.

"The House on Sixth Street" became a case when Mrs. Smith came to an MFY Neighborhood Service Center to complain that there had been no gas, electricity, heat, or hot water in her apartment house for more than four weeks. She asked the agency for help. Mrs. Smith was 23-years-old, Negro, and the mother of four children, three of whom had been born out of wedlock. At the time she was unmarried and receiving Aid to Families with Dependent Children. She came to the center in desperation because she was unable to run her household without utilities. Her financial resources were exhausted—but not her courage. The Neighborhood Service Center worker decided that in this case the building—the tenants, the landlord, and circumstances affecting their relationships—was of central concern.

Thus the worker who listened to Mrs. Smith's troubles saw the problem as broader than one person. The worker visited the tenament and found conditions were as described and that all families were suffering from lack of adequate facilities in their apartments. The worker then defined the problem as one belonging to all the tenants of the house and secured the tenants' agreement to this definition. The client system became all the tenants of the house, and the problem became to help them to organize their demands for services and utilities in their housing to which they were legally entitled. The target system became the landlord, and an attempt was made to form an action system of the seven different public agencies responsible for housing code enforcement and other agencies responsible for supplying benefits and services to tenants.

One of the greatest difficulties in identifying the problem occurs when workers are so focused on their definition of the problem that they do not hear what their clients are communicating about how they see and feel the difficulty. The workers then continue on their course without being aware of the incongruity between what they are about and what the client requested.

As an example of such a situation the work with Mr. Keene over a 14-month period is summarized below. Mr. Keene had been referred to a private family agency by the court following the hospitalization of his wife for mental illness because the court believed that Mr. Keene would need help in caring for the three children, ages four, two, and one. It appeared that Mrs. Keene had been the family manager and had taken care of Mr. Keene and the children. In this situation both the worker and the court seemed to have defined the problem as securing care for the children, without hearing the pain, guilt, and confusion of Mr. Keene. As a result at the end of the recording the worker is again asking Mr. Keene how he wants to solve the problem she had identified. However, it would appear to us that Mr. Keene probably sees the primary problem as the absence of his wife and, second as his lack of comprehension of mental illness, and third the guilt he carries about what has happened. It could be expected that there will continue to be problems with child care as long as the worker does not recognize Mr. Keene's feelings and begin with Mr. Keene's problem. This case is a good example of how, if we want to be of help, we must start with where the client hurts. If we cannot start there, as in emergency situations involving child care, we can at least recognize with the client what the situation is about and how the views differ. We can at least recognize with clients that we heard them and that their view of the problem is understood.

> Mr. Keene had need of and sought a great deal of help in financial management. He looked to the worker as to a parent to decide on specific expenditures. For several months in weekly contacts the worker had helped him manage through putting money for monthly budget items in envelopes each payday. Gradually he had become able to figure expenditures himself and to regulate some of his erratic spending. His major problems in financial management were an uncontrollable im-

pulse to overspend on useless gifts to his wife and an inability to deny the children toys, sweets, and recreation jaunts. He would agree with the worker when she carefully figured out with him what would be reasonable and appropriate spending on these items, but he would persistently overspend. At times he would laugh at himself for taking his wife something she was not permitted to have and then would justify it by saying someday she could use it. He talked persistently about his wife, about the fact that he had not known she was ill, about not knowing the cause of her illness, about his concern as to when she would come home. The worker did not respond directly to these concerns, but concentrated on the children's needs. In 12 months, however, he was able to assume the expense of the housekeeper.

His relationship to the children was characterized by anxious fretting over them, indulging them, and demanding the utmost in care of them from the housekeepers. Momentary sternness with them would be quickly replaced by petting and indulgence. Any illness or behavior deviations caused extreme worry. Though alarmed at Patrick's temper tantrums he would give in to them. The restlessness, hyperactivity, and food fads of Mary, age two and one half, worried him. Certain comments indicated that he connected the children's symptoms with their mother's behavior. He persisted in taking the children to visit their mother even though the worker advised against this and he himself would agree that the visits meant little to his wife and were exhausting and disturbing to the children. The worker's efforts to help him had been largely that of giving recognition to his desire to be a good parent and using his concern for their welfare to argue for consideration of their health and emotional comfort. Mr. Keene always presented problems to the worker with an earnest request for advice and the worker gave sound child guidance advice freely. However, Mr. Keene had been able to use the advice only fragmentarily.

The worker observed repeatedly in the record that Mr. Keene was very devoted to his wife. He visited regularly and excessively, taking gifts, and writing letters. He talked repeatedly of her eventual return. He would react to slight improvement in her condition with great optimism and with urgent demands for her discharge. Recently he had brought her home against medical advice. She had become disturbed and after she had disrupted a smooth running home, he had been forced to return her to the hospital. It was recorded that he often referred to his wife's competence prior to her illness, adding "And I didn't know she was ill." This statement was not explored.

Mr. Kenne's relationship to the housekeepers had been problematic. The first housekeeper probably was incompetent, but this was not clear because Mr. Keene's nagging and his constant comparisons of her activities to those of his wife. He fired this woman because she was unkind to the children.

The second housekeeper, a competent person who got along fairly well with the children, quit because she could not endure his demands, or his competitive undermining of her efforts with them. Mr. Keene was remorseful about this recognizing too late that she was a good housekeeper and mother substitute. This woman complained to the worker that she was expected to do the man's chores and to coax Mr. Keene to get up every morning. The worker's efforts in helping Mr. Keene with his housekeeper problems had been to try to get him to see their side of the situation and to face the errors of his ways. He readily would admit his wrongdoing and declare his intention to do better next time.

The third housekeeper was a competent, motherly woman who got along smoothly with Mr. Keene through joking with him, mothering him, and bossing him. She mended his clothes and packed his lunches. She allowed the children to play without restraint and they became more quiet and contented. Mr. Keene assumed more responsibility with chores and reported enthusiastically to worker that now his problems were solved and he would not be needing help much longer. Impulsively, without consulting worker or the housekeeper, he brought his wife home from the hospital with grudging medical consent but on the basis of his reports of favorable conditions for her care at home. Later he justified his action through saying that he had been unhappy that his wife was not at home to enjoy everything with them. The housekeeper could not put up with the wife's very disturbed behavior and threatened to leave. Mr. Keene turned to the worker who helped him face the fact that his wife was not ready to live outside a hospital. In returning her, Mr. Keene had to call plain clothes police and win her cooperation through deception. Subsequently, he was very disturbed about this and about his wife's reproachful remarks to him for betraying her.

The present situation

Now, following this episode, Mr. Keene is anxious and undecided as to future plans. He thinks he probably can mend matters with the housekeeper, but she is still angry and fearful and on the verge of leaving. How will he ever bring his wife home if no one will give her a trial? Will she ever get well? He cannot always be changing housekeepers. It is bad for the children. This is a good housekeeper, and perhaps he should urge her to stay. He might never find her equal. Certain comments show some anger with her for not putting up with his wife, even though she was irrational and clearly unable to assume responsibility or to permit anyone else to do so in her home. He cannot endure the thought of separation from the children. Foster home care was discussed but he thought he could not face not seeing his children everyday. The pros and cons of the two plans—foster care and a continuation of the present plan—were reviewed. Mr. Keene left the interview undecided but leaning toward another trial of the housekeeper service.

One of the other problems with a situation such as the one discussed is that the client gradually begins to develop a sense of failure. Mr. Keene must feel that he is not being a "good client." The worker is doing so much for him, but he cannot seem to carry through as she expects him to. In our view, he cannot and will not be able to carry through until the worker understands what is the central issue in the situation for him. Just one further comment on the situation. This is not a chapter on interventive roles, but it would seem to us that the worker should well have involved the hospital and its staff in the action system for Mr. Keene and have utilized roles of broker and advocate for Mr. Keene with the hospital around his understanding of his wife's illness.

We cannot possibly overemphasize the point that *everything else depends upon appropriate problem identification.* The way we define the problem will define what data is collected and will dictate what is seen as appropriate _____ *__t be right or all else fails.* There can be no engagement between client and worker _____ common understanding of what they are about together from the clients' frame of reference. This does not mean that the worker should set aside her definition of the problem. It means that she and Mr. Keene need to spell out both definitions and agree on ordering the problems-for-work.

Another important difficulty often found in problem definition is that workers get the problem and the cause all mixed up. Thus, when presented with a case of a 13-year-old boy, James C., who (1) has just stolen a car, (2) comes from a home in which the father has just died in an automobile accident, and (3) has a mother who says that she may overprotect her son, most students, acting as probation officers and just introduced to the notion of problem definition, will write that the problem is the mother's overprotection and the lack of a father. The *central problem at the moment is that the boy has just been apprehended by the police driving a stolen car.* There may be some relationship between his and his mother's interaction or their situation and the problem. However, consideration of the meaning of the home situation falls under assessment and follows considerable more data collection. The mother recognizes this difference in that she does not say that the problem is her overprotection, but *that the cause of the behavior* stems from this type of relationship with her son.

We need to recognize that if we see the problem as the mother's overprotection, we have shifted the problem from that of the son's behavior to the mother. In addition we may be terribly wrong even in settling on this explanation as cause. For example, if the boy is asked to tell what happened, he may contribute the information that he was a candidate for gang membership and initiation rites required that he steal a car. If this type of explanation is received, assessment would require that these two possible explanations (those of mother and son) be put together in an attempt to plan what can be of help in *preventing a recurrence of the delinquency.* It may be, in the course of the exploration and assessment, that the client system and the worker will redefine the problem-for-work as the mother's overprotection. However, that awaits the problem definition, the goal setting, the data collection, and the assessment of what this all means and what is to be done about it.

Let us return to Mr. Keene. In that case, as in this, the worker has a goal identified by a problem recognition system: Mr. Keene's children have to have care. Obviously that will have to be one problem-for-work between worker and client, but there must be recognition of Mr. Keene's definition of the problem. In the boy's case, there must be recognition of the mother's definition of *cause,* and that may well become the primary problem-for-work. But it is important to recognize that everyone involved saw stealing the car as the primary problem.

Sometimes the development of a common ground for work can be established quickly, sometimes a series of interviews may be necessary, and sometimes a common ground cannot be found. However, without a common place to begin, the worker and the client cannot proceed further. When a common ground cannot be reached, the worker and the client may find it necessary to simply acknowledge this fact and, for the present at least, discontinue their efforts. In an authority-related setting, where the worker has a legal mandate to provide supervision and the client has a legal mandate to report the client's activities, there are two possibilities. Workers may return to the court and acknowledge that there is nothing that can meaningfully be accomplished between the client and the worker and ask that the court decide the next steps. This might be a wise course of action if the situation involves, for example, the court's charge that the practitioner work with a mother who has been abusing her child, and the worker is concerned about the danger of such behavior to the physical well-being of the child. Or the worker might agree with the client that the worker will only attempt to meet the responsibilities mandated by law. In either of these situations, however, the possibility of reaching a common ground at a future date should be kept alive by leaving the door open for future negotiations.

Partialization is an important aspect of problem definition. Partialization refers to the process of separating out from the universe of problems brought by the client and/or identified by the worker the specific problem or problems which are to become the focus of worker-client attention. No one can deal with a whole range of problems at one time, even when they are closely related, and an attempt to do so may lead to floundering, lack of focus, and an overwhelming sense of despair as worker and client recognize the multiplicity of the client's stress experience. These difficulties can be avoided by partializing out from the universe of problems a specifically defined problem (the problem-to-be-worked[1]) as the beginning point. Later other problems may be tackled. Partialization also provides greater opportunities for finding a common ground—client and worker do not have to agree on all problems in order to find a beginning place.

Another word of caution—at this stage in the exploration of the problem, one must be careful not to assume that it lies with the person who first approaches the agency. Although the problem may be very troublesome for this person, it may lie in another system. The target of change may not be the client.

If the client does not have any suggestions as to where to start (as was true for the mother who said to the worker that she did not know which problem was the largest one: "All I know is that we are in a mess for sure"), the worker may introduce suggestions as to a starting place. Sometimes the worker and the client may find that where to begin can very well turn into the immediate problem-to-be-worked. In other words, it is perfectly possible that the problem-for-work is the definition of the problem. And even if this sounds like double-talk, it is not. In order to work on something, one has to decide where one should begin and where one is going. The inability of various interests involved in a situation to perceive the problem in the same way—to define it in a congruent way that allows work to be done on it—may well be a central problem. Consider the following example:

> Miss B, a 29-year-old schoolteacher, was admitted to a rehabilitation service following a massive stroke. She had been diabetic since she was five-years old and, despite constant medical attention and rigid personal self-discipline in diet and medication, the disease was becoming progressively worse. During the last five years she had been losing her sight, and now she is considered legally blind. The stroke, which was also related to the diabetic condition, had resulted in a paralysis of her right side. Miss B had always been a very goal-directed person and, in spite of an ever more handicapping illness, has an advanced degree in the education of handicapped children. She sees her problem as one of getting well quickly so she can return to

---

[1] One of the authors first heard this phrase used by Helen Harris Perlman in a lecture. It seemed so expressive of the concept discussed here that we adopted it. It carries for us at least, the connotation of worker activity with the client toward solution of the problem.

her classroom; and she has a somewhat unrealistic notion of what is involved in such an accomplishment, denying the hard and difficult work of learning to walk with a cane and of learning to read by the use of braille. She is angry with the nurses and often refuses to cooperate with them because she feels that they are trying to keep her dependent. The diagnosis of her doctors (which has been shared over and over again with her) is that she is in the last stages of an irreversible terminal condition and that she can never return to teaching. From their view, the problem is that Miss B is unwilling to accept the diagnosis and behave properly. The staff feel that the problem is that the patient won't accept the massive damage that she has and will not participate with them in the small, painful, and difficult tasks necessary to achieving minimal self-care. A social worker sees the problem as getting Miss B to apply for welfare because her own funds are almost exhausted and to engage Miss B in planning for a move to a nursing home, as the rehabilitation facility cannot keep her much longer.

In this situation, the problem-for-work probably has to be that of attempting to resolve the incongruence among the various views of the problem and of finding a beginning that can permit the client and the various other necessary systems to interact to some productive purpose for the client.

GOAL SETTING

This case situation leads us to another consideration that interacts closely and constantly with the definition of the problem-to-be-worked. That is the question of how the client system or other systems see the problem as working out. Not only did each of the significant participants in this situation have a personal view of the problem, but each view of the problem encompassed an objective or an answer to it. Professional people involved with Miss B wanted her to accept both the inevitability of her physical deterioration and a "realistic" plan for future care—although they differed on the plan. Miss B wanted to return to teaching.

We often find that persons involved in a problem situation present us with the solution rather than with the problem. The client comes to request help in implementing an already decided solution rather than in examining alternatives to action. This makes eminently good sense, in that the search for some desired end is a constant thrust of all of us. Goal seeking is what gives the problem-solving process its thrust and purpose, and the consideration of client goals is an important part of each phase of the problem-solving model. The way workers recognize goals and the way they work with goals will differ in each phase, but client goals must never be ignored. In the beginning contact it is important that the practitioner separate the problem from the goal so that each may be considered separately. Thus when a mother comes to a child welfare agency saying that she needs to place her child, she may well be presenting the worker with her goal in the shape of a problem. This may be her answer to any one of a whole range of problems; but while it is the only answer she can see, it may be an answer that will cause her great pain and despair. The worker will need to become involved in the question to which placing the child is the client's answer. Worker and client may or may not find a better answer, but in any case the worker should not confuse question and answer. However, in the process of defining and exploring the client's problem, the worker must never lose sight of the fact that the client's original goal was placement, and it is essential for the worker to understand the meaning that this goal had for her. We do not dismiss client goals lightly—we simply seek to separate goal and problem for more effective work.

Let us return to Miss B, a real person whom one of the authors knew. How does one reconcile the disparate views of the goals in this situation? Miss B, desperately needing to deny the diagnosis, is determined that she will get well and return to teaching. All she wants is recognition of this goal and help in achieving it. The medical staff are certain that she can never return to teaching, that the illness is progressing rapidly, that her only hope is to stay its progress somewhat by certain attempts at self-care, and they want her to accept these conclusions. A social worker, concerned over the limits of hospital care and Miss B's finances, wants Miss B to plan soon for other care.

There are different types and dimensions of goals that need to be recognized and discussed at this point. One may be concerned with an optimal goal—or an ultimate goal—which is the final desired outcome to which the effort is directed. Or one may be concerned with interim goals—objectives that are significant steps on the journey toward the optimal goal. Before the ultimate objective can be realized, a series of intermediate objectives usually need to be met. Often these intermediate objectives can be a way of testing whether the ultimate goal is sound. There are usually several layers, or levels, of interim goals. The first goal achieved becomes an aid to the achieving of more complex or more advanced interim goals. Just as one needs to determine a problem-for-work with which to begin, one often finds that the initial steps have to do with facilitative or interim goals as a way of collecting data and making decisions on the feasibility of the ultimate goal.

If one examines the different levels of goals stated at the time the social worker entered Miss B's case, one finds that the interim goals are not different for the various systems involved. The struggle is over ultimate goals. All the professional people involved in the situation want Miss B to participate in rehabilitative efforts that will keep her functioning as well as possible for as long as possible. These same efforts are necessary if Miss B is to be able to carry through her ultimate goal of returning to teaching.

The worker's efforts may very appropriately be directed to sharing with Miss B (1) that the medical staff and Miss B see the problem differently, (2) that they are in strong disagreement over the ultimate goals, (3) that the worker questions whether Miss B can return to full-time teaching, but (4) that perhaps the place to start is with the problem of her ability to work on certain interim goals that are necessary to *either* ultimate goal. So they can begin with what is involved for her in trying to walk again, to read braille, to care for herself in certain physical matters, while collecting data about her progress and planning for the future. Eventually there will come a time (and there did) when the worker and Miss B will have to put the results of their efforts together and make an ultimate plan—either she returns to the community as an independently functioning person or she accepts some alternate plan for at least partially sheltered care. The time of assessment and renegotiation of goals and of planning for the longer future will have to come. But for now they can explore the problem and the feasibility of certain long-term goals by starting with interim goals that become the facilitative goals in that all can agree on them and that they allow further data collection before assessment and final decision making.

We believe that both ultimate goals and the means of change are obtained from objective study, evaluation, and planning. These procedures are essential to the effective use of the problem-solving model. But all too often we see cause, truth, and knowledge as absolutes. Sure of ourselves and our understanding, we manipulate our data into firm conclusions, or we use the information to arrive at a psychosocial explanation that seems reasonable to us and set off on a course of action toward our immediate goals—goals that may not be shared with clients or take account of their expectations. Instead, the contact phase of the problem-solving process demands that the practitioner begin with an exploration of the common definition of a problem-to-be-worked and a common understanding of and acceptance of goals which at this stage may only be (and probably should only be) facilitative goals that serve to engage the client systems and the worker in jointly unearthing the ongoing knowledge that will eventually establish (in the contract phase) firmer means and ends around the central issues such assessment will identify. The problem-solving model, as we use it, demands that the client's purposes and expectations in joining the worker in interaction be explored, understood, and kept in the center of concern. It is our firm conviction that lack of initial exploration of expectations and goals and lack of careful selection of the starting place in the contact phase of the worker-client interaction account for a large percentage of the failures of the helping process (Mayer & Timms, 1969).

PRELIMINARY CONTRACT

In arriving at the preliminary contract, which is in essence an agreement between the worker and the client on the problem-to-be-worked and the facilitative goals, there are some other absolutes that must be clarified with the client. The worker must clarify the realities and boundaries of what can be offered and must behave in such a way as to help the client understand the nature of further work together. To make a brief comment on the first point: this requires that the worker be able to convey to the client the limits of the service that can be offered while at the same time conveying to the client the worker's belief in the ability to help within those limits, and interest in helping the client find another resource should the service that can be offered be too limited. In other words, the workers do not want to promise more than they can deliver and so trap the client by false hopes, but neither do they want to operate in such a way as to imply hopelessness to the client. The client may come to the worker out of pain, or despair, or anger but will only become involved in action with the worker when this feeling of discomfort is joined to a hope that something can be done.

One usually finds clients confused about how the helping process will work. As was pointed out in Chapter 1, people find it difficult to grasp the nature of the social work job. There are seldom visible technologies or artifacts that will give others some notion of what the process is all about. The practitioner's actions in the beginning phase can give the client a sample of the social work method. That is one reason the beginning is so important. Another reason is the pattern-setting nature of communication between elements of a system or among systems.

At the end of the beginning phase of problem identification and goal determination, client and worker decide whether they wish to continue together. If they do, the worker is then free to begin to collect the information that will be the data on which assessment and planning will be based. We would caution again that nothing is more sterile than information collecting for the purpose of information collecting. Information is collected for the purpose of taking effective action, and all efforts must be directed to that end. The kind and amount of information collected will be dictated by the defined problem-for-work and the preliminary goal that is established.

AREAS OF DATA COLLECTION

It is difficult to deal with areas of data collection concretely because the specific areas to be explored depend upon the situation. However, there are some principles that should be considered:

1. It is a joint process, and the client should be involved in helping to determine the areas to be explored.
2. The client should be aware of the sources being used for data collection (note: clients are not always asked for their permission).
3. There should be a connection between the problems identified and the data collected. The client should be aware of this connection.
4. It is critical to explore all areas that the clients see as connected as well as helping them to understand the areas the worker seeks to explore.
5. Data collection goes on all the time, but it is critical to the problem identification, goal setting, and assessment stages of work.
6. The primary areas of data collection are all points listed under the contact phase of the model presented in Chapter 8.
7. It is important to note that, under exploration and investigation, the type of client system will determine the areas of data collection to some extent. Please give some attention to these differences.
8. It is crucial that the worker understand the clients' view of all areas of data collection—their thinking about the meaning of the items, their feelings in those areas, and any actions they may have taken.

It is important for the readers to note that there are three areas of data collection that are the same for all systems and all problems. They are the areas of hope, discomfort, and opportunity. Readers may want to go back and read the discussion as to the importance of these areas in human growth, development, and functioning, found in Chapter 4 on foundation knowledge. In our thinking these are the most critical areas in this stage of work—both in terms of the worker's collection of data and in terms of the worker's actions with the client.

What causes people to act? As was stated earlier, for action to take place, discomfort with things as they are must be felt, but this is not enough. If a worker is to act, to discomfort, mild or severe, must be added the hope of being able to reach a goal that is seen as the answer to wants, and in addition there must be some ability to consider what has gone wrong and some opportunity for change in the situation. Productive engagement in the social work process is dependent on the client's "hope-discomfort balance" and on the extent to which the practitioner is able to engage that pressure by the hope and clearly defined opportunity offered. Before work can begin on a problem the client must be uncomfortable about the present state of affairs and hope that something can be done about it, and the worker must be able to communicate understanding (empathy, if you will) of the client's discomfort and, even more important, the worker must engage oneself with the client's hope. As was once said, when hope is weak the practitioners must find a way of "hitching the motor to the client's wagon." For this reason, we would urge that workers always be concerned, with all client systems and in all problem situations, with the level of the client's hope-discomfort balance and with early activity with the client in this area and the way they engage themselves and the client with the opportunities for reaching objectives.

SOURCES AND METHODS OF DATA COLLECTION

Before closing this chapter, we would like to make some general observations about the sources from which worker and client will collect the information that is needed to make an assessment. The first, and most important principle, is that the client system must be aware of the resources the worker is using and why they are being used. If at all possible (as was noted earlier in the chapter), the client's permission should be secured before any particular source of information beyond the client system is used. However, whether or not permission is secured, the client *must know* about the sources used, the information sought, and why the information is believed to be appropriate to the task at hand. If commitment is to the clients' participation in decision making that will lead to action toward their goals, then we must share with them all the information on which decisions may be based. Otherwise, we deprive them of an opportunity for representative participation in the discussion about themselves.

In general, modes of data collection can be divided into five groups: (1) the client's account as they tell it; (2) accounts of others; (3) questions and tests either verbal or written; (4) observation; (5) records of other professional or institutional systems. Perhaps the most widely used tool for data collection is the interview or group meeting with the client system in which questioning and observation are used to gain information. The interview or the meeting requires a knowledge of the principles of relationship and communication that have been discussed in previous chapters. In the use of the face-to-face meeting, the practitioner will need to decide its purpose, the information needed to be obtained from it, and how the worker wants to structure it. At one extreme is the nondirective interview or meeting in which the worker follows the feeling and thinking of the interviewee or allows the group to reveal itself as it will. At the other extreme is the completely structured interview or meeting, in which the worker has a scheduled set of questions from which there will be no departure. However, workers are also giving some structure to the interview and determining what data may be collected when they decide where and when it will be held, when they establish ground rules and norms for content and participation, and even when they arrange the chairs of the persons involved. Careful thought should be given to the place of the first meeting: Is it to be on the "client's turf or the worker's?"

The nondirective interview that allows clients to tell their own story in their own way and at their own pace is an important source of information that usually cannot be gained by direct questions. By listening carefully and observing body language the worker is able to gain an understanding of the stress the problem has brought to the client, and to understand something of the resources the client has tried to use or has found helpful. The worker begins to understand the client's cognitive pattern—the way the client relates cause and effect—the kind of reasoning the client does. The worker can collect knowledge about the coping strategies of the client and the strengths that have served well. In addition the worker can gain considerable knowledge about the client's relationships with others, as well as the client's relationships with others, as well as the client's relationship to the helping person, as much of the client's account may concern interactions with meaningful people. The client's understanding of the world around him/her and of social relationships and their utility can be estimated from his/her account of the problem, the way it came about and what has been done to change it.

Obviously, the interview may be used to collect information from sources other than the client system. In using these other systems, workers will want to consider carefully the kinds of information they think they can provide and the need they have for this information. They will need to give thought to the fact that certain information sources may expect the interview to involve a sharing of information. If workers are to share information, they will need to discuss this with the client system. If they are unwilling to share information, they must make this known to their source when the interview is requested.

Many kinds of written questioning techniques are in use. Clients are often asked to fill out application or information forms when they first approach an agency. There are various questionnaires that may be used with various client systems for various purposes. If a group is trying to decide a focus for future meetings, and members seem reluctant to share their views openly with other members, an anonymous written questionnaire may be helpful. It allows members to express an opinion without penalty. Written exercises are sometimes used in work with families to allow members to express themselves without feeling that they have directly attacked other members of the family. In certain community organization projects, the use of a survey based on a written questionnaire is a very valuable technique. Obviously, one would not want to use a written questionnaire with clients who do not express themselves well in writing, or clients who might see it as a dehumanizing device, or clients to whom it might imply that they were being classified into just one of a similar group of persons.

In speaking of both verbal and written questioning as data collection tools, it should be mentioned the use of other persons to collect information for the worker. In certain situations, someone close to the client system and knowledgeable about the situation may conduct an interview for the worker. An indigenous Spanish-speaking community worker might be asked to talk to a Chicano woman who has just suffered the loss of her husband and who should not be asked to take on the additional burden of speaking in English to a stranger at such a time. Also the worker may have other professionals, such as psychologists, administer tests to gain certain knowledge. These tests may be oral or written. Psychologists often use projective techniques, which allow the respondents to impose their own frame of reference upon some stimulus, such as a picture. Or, in order to have two sources of information, workers may ask a psychiatrist, or perhaps their supervisor, to interview the same client that they are dealing with.

Along with questioning, the worker usually utilizes observation as a way of gathering data. Though we all use observation of others in daily interactions, much will be lost unless we learn to make deliberate, planned use of the technique. As with verbal questions, observation can be structured or unstructured, and the worker can be a totally uninvolved observer, a participant observer, or a leader-and-initiator observer. For example, workers might give a group of children a game to play and then observe and record their actions without being in any way involved in the game. Or they might be a committee member, both involved and observing. Or they might serve as a committee chairperson while trying to observe the interactions of the members. This last possibility will probably cause many to ask how effectively a chairperson can observe the interactions of other committee members. This is an example of questions that are often raised about the use of observations. What about the bias and the selectivity of the observer? No one can possibly observe all the interactions of a group, or even all the facial expressions and changes in posture of one person, in an interview. Observation requires a sensitivity to others and the capacity to see small changes. In addition it requires that workers know themselves and their biases. It requires them to have given thought to what they want to learn through this process and to how they do it. Since they cannot collect all the data on any one transaction, they must recognize that they collect only certain information and are, therefore, selective. Workers must know what framework guides this selectivity.

The last general way one collects information is from the use of existing written material—material not gathered specifically for the present situation. Often workers may find that their agency, or some other place has records of previous contacts with the client system. Usually, it is wise for the worker to know the contents of such records and to discuss them with the client. Otherwise the client may waste valuable time and trouble in worrying over what you may know. If previous written materials are available, they can be a very efficient means of data collection. Their use places little demand on the client system and is within the worker's control. But therein lies a seductive danger—such records can be used so easily without the client's knowledge. There is another danger—when something is read, there is a tendency to feel that it is really known. For these reasons, we would like to especially caution practitioners against the indiscriminate use of such material. They must question written material as they do a human informant. Does it give the facts? Are the facts documented? Or does the material merely reflect another person's judgments? The practitioner must also recognize that such material deals with the past; that it may not bear on the present problem and may even confuse the issue in that it was written or gathered for a purpose unconnected with it; and (to repeat) that it may reflect the biases and selective perceptions and evaluations of the persons who collected it. Often there is a tendency to see written material as holding more of the truth than the practitioner's present experiences. This tendency should be strongly resisted. On the other hand, appropriate written material can be an effective source of data.

One of the problems in data collection is the organizing of the material. An excellent original article by Ann Hartman is reproduced in this chapter that should help workers both to be aware of what data they may need to collect and to organize this data for assessment. The readers may want to compare the model developed by Hartman to Figures 4–4 through 4–7 in Chapter 4 which deals with basic knowledge.

SKILLS IN THE CONTACT PHASE

Most of this chapter has been devoted to answering the *what* question of the activities in the contact phase. We shall now try to answer the *how* question. Once again we must say that it is difficult to be specific and concrete. It is difficult to be sure that our words can communicate to the readers what we think we are saying. This difficulty stems from two factors: words are the symbols of human interaction and they carry meaning only within some context, and the same words often mean different things to different people and a common meaning can be established only by the sender accurately hearing the feedback from the system receiving the communication. Written communication can be put together in such a way that the writer believes that it establishes a context and a meaning, but one can be sure about that only through feedback. Thus we are dreadfully handicapped in communicating with our readers, particularly about some matters such as "self-awareness."

If workers are to carry through effectively on the tasks of the contact phase, they must engage the feelings and the thinking of the client in the process. This is not saying that "a relationship needs to be developed," and especially it is not saying that "a good relationship needs to be developed." What it is saying is that both client and worker must engage with each other (interact with each other in a way *that has meaning to the client system*) as a beginning of what will later become a working relationship.

The first step in this engagement is that the worker needs certain types of knowledge and that the greatest of these is knowledge of self—of the way one feels and thinks about the type of problem and the client, and cognitive knowledge of the resources available in both the change agent system and other usable community systems.

Let us go back for a moment to the Mrs. C's case. There are a constellation of factors that trap people immediately into defining the problem as Mrs. C's overprotection of her son. They are

1. An immediate identification with the son as the "victim" of what has happened.
2. An emotional readiness to blame parents for their childrens' pain and trouble.
3. A belief in the personal-deficit concept of deviant behavior.
4. A belief that childrens' behavior is usually caused by parents' treatment of them.
5. An emotional and intellectual commitment to wanting to find "the real problem" which leads to the mistake of defining "cause" as "problem." (Readers may want to go back and read the quotes from Johnson in Chapter 8 on problem solving.)
6. The fact that the worker is presented with an upper-middle class client who has internalized points 1 through 4 in her own thinking and who is so upset over this crisis situation (following upon another crisis that she may still not have mastered) that she is very ready to fix blame on herself and spare her son. So we define the problem as hers rather than her son's and help her beat herself into a further sense of inadequacy while we give the son a nice way of beginning to blame others for his actions.

Please note that this is not to say that there is no relationship between the mother's treatment of her son and his actions; nor is it to say that that connection and the mother's spontaneously suggesting it is ignored in setting the problem-for-work. One further comment, if we are seeking the "real problem," maybe it lies in the father's death, which is responsible for the mother's feelings and actions, which in turn is responsible for the son's behavior. Should those feelings be the problem-for-work? What would happen to the mother's sense of adequacy and her ability to develop different ways of treating her son if the problem-for-work was defined as her reaction to her husband's death, and that reaction was assessed being a "normal" response to such an overwhelming stress and crisis situation? And what about her son's reaction to his father's death? These questions need to be thought about by the worker and considered thoughtfully with the client system (mother and son). Data will be collected on all these possible life stresses that may have led to the problem behavior. The work of considering their impact and integrating them into some meaningful assessment of the situation and planning the work together is a part of the next several chapters. What we are trying to make very clear here is the importance of not mixing the presenting problem with the cause.

If the readers will go back to the factors listed earlier, they will note that some of these factors are cognitive, some are emotional, and some are both. Perhaps the most critical handicap in problem solving is our tendency to need a consistent frame of reference both intellectually and emotionally. This results in a tendency to define problems within our usual, working notion of the human condition—to view clients' problems, as it were, from within our frame of reference. We may explain our clients' insistence that we look at the problem from their point of view as their resistance to seeing things correctly, and thus in itself proof of the correctness of our formulations.

In order to make this clear, we would like for you to try to solve the following problem.

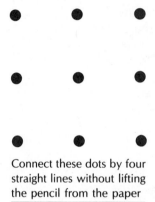

Connect these dots by four
straight lines without lifting
the pencil from the paper

After you have tried to solve the problem we would like for you to turn to the end of the chapter for the solution. Are you surprised? The thing that leads to failure in solving this problem is the fact that the first time people try it, they almost inevitably make an assumption that the dots compose a square and that the problem must be defined as falling within the boundaries of that system. Thus, the failure to solve the problem does not lie within the difficulty of the problem, or the worker's capacity to do the necessary tasks—it lies within the worker's self-imposed assumptions that nowhere are given as a part of the problem. Workers must be aware of their assumptions and make initial contact within the potential client's frame of reference.

Some further cautions before we move on to some specifics in the use of "self" in the contact phase. (1) The questions asked determine the answers given, and it is the worker's responsibility to determine the questions. (2) Any behavior in the presence of another communicates a view of the nature of one's relationship with that person, and this principle applies to the worker as well as to the client. (3) An important part of human communication takes place through silence or lack of communication as well as through what is said and how it is said. Therefore, the worker needs to be aware of what is not being dealt with by the client as well as what is and must recognize that the client will interpret the helper's silence in their own way. (4) Dependency and lack of responsibility for our actions are caused by someone else taking responsibility for our own thinking, feeling and planning and *is not caused by people giving one too much or doing things for us.* The greatest causes of emotional dependency (as distinguished from the "normal" dependency of not being able to deal with concrete tasks because of handicaps of knowledge, skill, or other capacity) is the taking over of feelings, thinking, and decision-making responsibility by an authority. In fact, not doing *appropriate things* for clients may further break down their coping skills and result in further apathy. Readers will want to refer again to the Dyal and Donovan article (see Reading 8–1).

The skills required in this phase require those described in Chapters 6 and 7 on relationship and communication, especially those of the ability to communicate empathy, genuineness, concern, trustworthiness, respect, and the conditions of service. Listening and attending skills are very important, as it is important to attend both physically (in posture and body language) and psychologically to what the client is trying to communicate. It is important to listen both "with ears to the words and with eyes to the body language" and with "the third ear" to some total messages such as how clients feel and think about themselves, the world, significant others, and people in general; how clients perceive others related to them; and what clients' ambitions, goals, and aspirations are.

To be sure that one is interpreting the client's words and feelings accurately, the worker will need from time to time to check this out with the clients. This may be done by restating the basic messages that one thinks one hears in similar but fewer words, in submitting a tentative summary of what one made of the client's discussion, by connecting things that the client leaves unconnected but that one thinks may be connected. One will, of course, need skill in questioning which is discussed in Chapter 7 on communication. There are times when one may use some tentative interpretation ". . . is it possible that what you are telling me means . . . ?" And, often one will be tempted to use reassurance, "I understand . . . ," "that is hard . . . ," "most people would be upset . . ." One should be careful in the use of such phrases. They often serve to cut off the client's further exploration of the difficulty.

Many workers who feel the client's pain and have the impulse to help are greatly tempted to overuse reassurance. They want to remove the pain from the clients. But the purpose for which the clients come to them is not for the removal of the pain but for doing something about it. In order to help others, we must understand what the problem is that brings the client to us, and often this includes great pain for the client. However, help requires empathy, not pity or sympathy, which too early and too often communicates reassurance. Pain is a signal that there is trouble, and understanding the pain will help us to understand and define the problem as the client perceives it.

Emanuel Tropp (1976, p. 223) has developed an important set of statements related to the worker's presentation of self to the group. We see this as not limited to the group but as summing up in a very impressive way the necessary elements of the worker's presentation of self to the potential client system both at the initial contact and during the work together:

1. Compassion—I deeply care about you.
2. Mutuality—We are here on a common human level; let's agree on a plan and then let's walk the path together.
3. Humility—Please help me to understand.
4. Respect—I consider you as having worth. I treat your ideas and feelings with consideration. I do not intrude upon your person.
5. Openness—I offer myself to you as you see me; real, genuine, and authentic.
6. Empathy—I am trying to feel what you are feeling.
7. Involvement—I am trying to share and help in your efforts.
8. Support—I will lend my conviction and back up your progress.
9. Expectation—I have confidence that you can achieve your goals.
10. Limitation—I must remind you of your agreed-upon obligations.
11. Confrontation—I must ask you to look at yourself.
12. Planning—I will always bring proposals, but I would rather have yours.
13. Enabling—I am here to help you become more able, more powerful.
14. Spontaneity and control—I will be as open as possible, yet, I must recognize that, in your behalf, I need to exercise some self-control.
15. Role and person—I am both a human being like you and a representation of an agency, with a special function to perform.
16. Science and art—I hope to bring you a professional skill which must be based on organized knowledge, but I am dealing with people, and my humanity must lend art to grace the science.

RECAPITULATION

In this chapter we have discussed the contact phase of the problem-solving process. We have pointed out that this phase involves eight essential tasks that can be summarized as:

1. The initial contact.
2. The determination of the problem-for-work.
3. Goal clarification.
4. The clarification of service limits.
5. The clarification of what will be asked of the client system.
6. The development of appropriate relationships.
7. The emergence of a commitment to work together.
8. Data collection.

It will be noted that these tasks demand the activity of the worker as well as the client.

This beginning part of the problem-solving process is extremely important because it sets the pattern for the phases of work that follow. We have suggested that, given the limits of any specific situation, we collect information about at least three elements of the client system: the hope-discomfort balance that the client brings to the first encounter; the opportunities that the client sees and that the worker can bring to bear; and factors within the client system and in its relationships to the world around it.

One further caution—it is perhaps a misunderstanding of the level and magnitude of problem definition and goal setting that leads some professionals to view the problem-solving model as only of value to the client capable of highly rational functioning. It is our view that every human being has wants (if only to get rid of the worker) and that these wants can be translated into wishes and wishes into goals. The meaning and value of the goals has nothing to do with the worker's evaluation of their value, rather it relates to the client's wishes. Practitioners often see the only goals worth setting as those that seem to the practitioner to involve a generally better life. However, for many clients the securing of essential survival needs and life supports are the only goals worth setting, at least when they have no reason to trust either the practitioner or life itself. If the problem that the client sees is the lack of certain concrete essentials of life, this can become the problem-to-be-worked, client and worker can agree that the securing of these essentials is the first and most important goal at the moment, and the plan can well be that the worker will find a way to supply this resource. In this situation the worker may have done a good deal of the initial work in defining the problem and the achievement of the goal may have come from the worker's concrete giving. The essential factor here is not the level of goal or who works toward the goal but that the client was involved in the thinking and planning that was done, and that what was given was related to the client's wishes and not something that the worker unilaterally thought was needed. The inability to see small concrete goals as important objectives for work and the assumption that the worker's supplying of concrete needs to apathetic, withdrawn, depressed, or angry people need not involve mutual problem definition and goal setting (no matter how primitive the level) are built upon certain unconscious, or not so unconscious, practitioner assumptions about what is meaningful professional interaction that need to be seriously examined.

As an example of what happens in the contact phase, let us go back to Mr. Keene's situation as outlined earlier in this chapter. Let us assume for a moment that at the point of the last recording the worker left the agency and you were assigned the Keene case. You have an appointment with Mr. Keene for tomorrow and you are planning for your first contact. What is the problem, or problems that will be the focus of the first interview? One problem that must be dealt with at the beginning of the interview is the change in workers. You will want to express your concern that this must come as a shock to Mr. Keene and that you want to do all you can to help him. You will want to do this tentatively and slowly leaving ample time for Mr. Keene to comment as he may wish about the other worker. If he is critical of the other worker, you will want to ask him how he would have preferred things to go. If he says the other worker did not understand how hard it was to care for the children without his wife, you will want to gently ask him if he could tell you about it so you could start with some understanding. In thinking about the interview, you will recognize that Mr. Keene's feelings about the transfer will probably not be taken care of in one interview, but difficult as it is for him, you are going to have to deal with the problem of care of the children. Thus at an appropriate point you will need to summarize where you are with the problem of transfer and move to discussion of the children.

What do you know about care of the children? It appears from the recording that the first worker regarded Mr. Keene as a dependent man who was not a very adequate father. You will want to look at the facts you have about Mr. Keene. What strengths do you find detailed in the record? Although there were signs of Mrs. Keene's growing illness, Mr. Keene seemed unaware of this until the illness reached a crisis stage. Is this unusual behavior, or is it common for family members to be oblivious to changes in other family members? Is it possible that family members ignore changes in other members because they are frightened by the implications of the changes? What have been the demands Mr. Keene has faced since Mrs. Keene's hospitalization? What do you know about the demands of role transitions? What do you know about persons' reactions to grief and loss? Certainly, Mr. Keene has been faced with a multidimensional loss. Did the previous worker deal with the stress that Mr. Keene faced in the loss and role transition? Although there must be a plan for care of the children, would it be important to introduce the question of the stress that Mr. Keene has faced before discussing the children. What would this accomplish? Would it help Mr. Keene to feel understood rather than judged? What facts do you have about any individual support networks that Mr. Keene may have? Are there others with whom he shares the problems he has had and his loneliness for his wife?

What does Mr. Keene understand about his wife's illness and the prognosis. About mental illness in general? How much contact has the hospital staff had with him? Has the only contact been when he has insisted on removing his wife? If so, what has been the tenor of exchange between them? Would Mr. Keene like you to see the hospital staff? Would he like you to visit his wife? Would he want to go with you?

What about the homemaker? Does Mr. Keene want to continue with her? Would he want you to negotiate with her? Would he want to be a part of such a negotiation? What can he share with the homemaker about his actions in bringing his wife home? What can you do to help the homemaker understand Mr. Keene's problems? What progress does Mr. Keene feel that he has made since he began working with the agency? What would he want from the agency now? If you would like to reassess Mr. Keene's problems, how do you help him to understand why you want to do this?

You are now ready to make a tentative plan for the first interview that you will have with Mr. Keene. Your plan might look something like this:

A. Problems that will need to be explored:
   1. Reactions to change in workers.
   2. Problems of grief and loss.
   3. Problem of transition to single parent.
   4. Care of children.
B. Climate of the interview:
   1. An attempt to convey a caring for Mr. Keene and his feelings.
   2. Acceptance and support.
   3. Empathic and responsive. Convey a recognition of value of his statements.
C. Pace of interview:
   1. Relaxed—try to match Mr. Keene's tempo.

    D. Data collection:
1. Be alert to clues. Attempt to expand, amplify, and clarify client's meaning.
2. Ask Mr. Keene to amplify and expand meaning.
3. Within this climate structure, interview to explore support networks and hospital contacts, knowledge of mental illness, and child care.

    E. Plan of interview:
1. Establish a beginning contact with Mr. Keene.
2. Learn more of Mr. Keene's struggles, worries, stresses.
3. Offer help to Mr. Keene in understanding his wife.
4. Offer appropriate support to Mr. Keene.
5. Recognize Mr. Keene's struggles.

    F. Goal of interview:
1. A beginning understanding of the problems to be worked.
2. A beginning engagement with Mr. Keene which allows for working on the problem.

Summary of problem identification activity

1. Define the problem *as the client sees it.*
2. Feed back what you hear; paraphrase; clarify to be sure you really hear correctly.
3. Identify the significance of problem (objectively and subjectively) to the client.
4. What do you see as the problem?
5. Be aware of client feelings about problem and about asking for help. Discuss these or relate to them in other ways as seems helpful, supportive, and clarifying. What are your feelings about problem? Client?
6. Identify the duration, previous occurrences, and precipitating factors contributing to the present problem.
7. Determine how the client has dealt with this or similar problems before.
8. Determine why the client has come for help now.
9. Partialize the problem. Be specific. Maintain focus on one part of the problem at a time.
10. Get an understanding of how other systems relate to the client system and the problem (i.e., with whom does the client interact, share the problem? How does the client think others see the problem?).
11. Determine the nature and location of the problem. Where does client locate it? Where do you locate it? Do *not* assume that the problem lies with the client system.
12. Try to reach a mutually acceptable statement of the problem. (Identify parts of the problem upon which the worker and client system agree that change is possible.)
13. Identify strengths in dealing with situation; ask what the client sees as strengths or successes in dealing with aspects of problem.
14. Summarize your perception of the problem and its impact on the client system.

15. Agree on a problem (or part of a problem) for work. This may be selected on the basis of:
    a. The problem or part of problem that the client system feels is most important or is a good beginning place.
    b. The problem that, to the worker, seems most critical.
    c. Problem or part of the problem the worker believes yields most readily to help.
    d. The problem or part of the problem that falls within the action parameters of the helping system.
16. Summarize the feelings and content of the interview. Check out how the interview has been for the client system.

Summary of goal-setting activity

1. Find out how client would like problem to be solved.
2. What does client think is needed for solution of problem?
3. Find out what the client system wants from you and how this is related to (1). (Are these expectations realistic?)
4. Discuss meaning of goals to client.
5. State the help you and your agency can offer, giving realistic hope for change. Discuss reasons of any limits on help directly, clearly, simply. Check out how the client feels about these limits and reasons for them.
6. From the partialized statement of the problem, partialize goals (long and short term). Be specific. Get feedback.
7. State your commitment to work with client and give hope for change over time.
8. Make a preliminary contract regarding initial goals, problem for work, meetings, times, and length of the contract.
    a. Be clear as to what is realistic.
    b. State that change takes time.
    c. State that the contract can change.
    d. State that together you will evaluate change as you progress.
    e. Consider the advisability of a written contract.
    f. State what you are prepared and able to do.
9. Based on your initial goals, plan with client for the next session as appropriate.

Summary of beginning assessment activity

1. How does client tell story? Is focus maintained on central issues/feelings? What side issues are brought in?
2. Does client seem to relate actions to outcome or other's reactions?
3. Is client consistent in account of feelings?
4. How does client seem to relate to you as worker?
5. From discussions of situation what kind of relationships does client have with others?
6. What account does client give of personal support networks?
7. What account does client give of use of institutional resources?

8. If you pick up on a cue and make a transition, does client follow?
9. If you comment on seeming inconsistencies, how does client respond?
10. How uncomfortable is client? Is this related to problems? Asking for help? Everything in life?
11. Does client seem to have hope of solving problems? Alone? With you? With others? Does client relate to your hope?
12. Observe and begin to assess meaning of patterns of behavior you observe.

A LOOK FORWARD

In the last part of the chapter we discussed some of the modes of information gathering that are available to the practitioner. Thus ends our discussion of the contact phase of the problem-solving process. Articles of two other authors are reproduced in this chapter to extend the development of the points made in it. In the next chapter the contract phase of the transaction will be considered. The contract phase is the core of the work together.

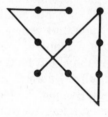

Solution to puzzle

<hr>

Reading 9–1

*Diagrammatic Assessment of Family Relationships**

Ann Hartman

Integrating new knowledge and conceptual frameworks from the many sources that inform and support social work practice is a long and arduous process. General systems theory, which was introduced to social workers over 20 years ago (Lutz, 1956), has been particularly difficult to assimilate because it is so abstract. The distance is great between the lofty principles enunciated by systems theorists and the practical knowledge and skill that guide the practitioner's work with people day by day. The field has made some progress in utilizing systems concepts in developing middle-range theory, in organizing practice models (Hearn, 1969), in extending and clarifying the boundaries of the unit of attention (Germain, 1968), and in prescribing general directions for action (Hartman, 1974). Professionals in the field are now at the point of attempting to translate concepts from this middle-range theory into specific and testable prescriptions for practice.

Particularly interesting is the potential a systems orientation has for altering cognitive styles and enabling practitioners to organize and process increasingly complex systems of variables (Hartman, 1970). The attempt here is to derive from systems framework new conceptual models that can enhance the practitioner's and the client's perceptions of reality, thereby contributing to competence and creative adaptation in therapy.

Social workers, in attempting to understand their traditional unit of attention—

the person in the total life space over time—are faced with an overwhelming amount of data. These data must be ordered, selected, and arranged to reduce confusion and overload. Edward Tolman has likened this mediating process to a map room where intervening cognitive charts shape data, lending meaning and manageability to the influx of information (Bruner, Goodnow, & Austin, 1962). These cognitive patterns have tremendous influence on how reality is perceived but are not readily observed or easily changed. They are an ongoing and familiar part of the self, and, as Frederick Duhl (1969) has pointed out, "that which is constantly experienced is neutral to awareness, being so immersed in the identity, so 'egosyntonic,' that it is rarely open to observation or challenge." As social workers interact with their environment, these mediating cognitive processes so strongly imprint a particular view of reality that they may well be just as crucial as knowledge and values in determining professional decision-making.

In dealing with almost continual information overload, cognitive processes tend to operate analytically: to partialize, to abstract parts from wholes, to reduce, and to simplify. Although this makes data more manageable, it does damage to the complexity inherent in reality. Ways of conceptualizing causation have tended to be particularly reductionist as reality is arranged in chains of simple cause and effect reactions. Such linear views reflect the limitations of thought and language rather than the nature of the real world,

<hr>

* From *Social Casework,* October 1978 (New York: Family Service Association of America).

where human events are the result of transactions among multiple variables.

An emphasis on identifying the roots of problematic conditions in tremendously complex situations has frequently pushed social workers into supporting simplistic explanations and into arguments over what is the cause and hence the cure. Since 19th century scientism found expression in Mary E. Richmond's *Social Diagnosis* (1917), the profession has struggled with the temptation to deal with this "radically untidy universe" through reductionist solutions growing out of reductionist assessments.[1]

If social workers are to avoid reductionism and scientism, if they are to translate a systems orientation into practice, they must learn to "think systems," or to develop within their own cognitive map rooms new and more complex ways of imprinting reality. They must then devise ways of using this view in specific interventive techniques and strategies.

As one learns to "think systems," one tends to move to the use of metaphor and to the use of visual models in order to get beyond the constraints of linear thought and language. Social workers have always been frustrated in writing psychosocial summaries—they find it not unlike the attempt to describe the action in a football game over the radio. In attempting to describe the complex system of transacting variables, the meaning and the nature of the integration of the variables, and the totality of the events and action is lost. The use of metaphor in poetry and of two- and three-dimensional simulations in painting and sculpture demonstrate the integrative power of such approaches. Similar artistry can be used to expand the social worker's understanding of the nature of reality. Of many possibilities, two simple paper-and-pencil simulations have

proved to be particularly useful, not only as assessment tools, but in interviewing, planning, and intervention.

One simulation is the ecological map of "eco-map," which was originally developed three years ago as an assessment tool to help workers in public child welfare practice examine the needs of families.[2] This tool pictures the family or the individual in the life space and has since been tested in a variety of settings with a wide range of clients. The second simulation is the genogram, which has been used by systems-oriented family therapists to chart intergenerational family history.[3] This tool has also been found to be highly adaptable for use with individuals or families in many different settings where it is important to understand the development of the family system through time.

THE ECOLOGICAL METAPHOR

The task of making general systems concepts operational and humane, of giving them flesh and blood meaning, presents a difficult challenge. Although "input," "throughout," "moving steady state," and "deviation amplifying feedback loops" are precise and useful concepts, they mean little to social workers if they are unrelated to a human context. Recently, there has been a growing effort to utilize the science of ecology as a metaphorical way of humanizing and integrating system concepts (Germain, 1973). The

[2] The eco-map was developed in 1975 by the author as a part of the Child Welfare Learning Laboratory, a project of the University of Michigan School of Social Work Program for Continuing Education in the Human Services. The project was supported in part by a grant from Region V, Social and Rehabilitation Service, U.S. Department of Health, Education, and Welfare, Section 426, Title IV, part B of the Social Security Act. The author is grateful to Lynn Nybell, Coordinator of the Family Assessment Module, for her ideas, criticisms, and encouragement.

[3] The genogram has been used extensively by systems-oriented family therapists. For example, see Guerin and Pendagast (1976).

[1] For a discussion of casework's relationship with science ad scientism, see Germain (1971).

science of ecology studies the delicate balance that exists between living things and their environments and the ways in which this mutuality may be enhanced and maintained.

In utilizing the ecological metaphor, it is clear that the salient human environment includes far more than air, water, food, spatial arrangements, and other aspects of the physical environment. Human environments also include networks of intimate human relationships. Further, over the centuries, human beings have erected elaborate social, economic, and political structures that they must sustain and through which their needs are met. People must maintain an adaptive mutuality with these intricate systems which are required for growth and self-realization.

An ecological metaphor can lead social workers to see the client not as an isolated entity for study but as a part of a complex ecological system. Such a view helps them to focus on the sources of nurturance, stimulation, and support that must be available in the intimate and extended environment to make possible growth and survival. It also leads to a consideration of the social, relational, and instrumental skills individuals must have to use possibilities in their environment and to cope with its demands.

THE ECO-MAP

The eco-map is a simple paper-and-pencil simulation that has been developed as an assessment, planning, and interventive tool. It maps in a dynamic way the ecological system, the boundaries of which encompass the person or family in the life space. Included in the map are the major systems that are a part of the family's life and the nature of the family's relationship with the various systems. The eco-map portrays an overview of the family in their situation; it pictures the important nurturant or conflict-laden connections be-

tween the family and the world. It demonstrates the flow of resources, or the lacks and deprivations. This mapping procedure highlights the nature of the interfaces and points to conflicts to be mediated, bridges to be built, and resources to be sought and mobilized. Although all one needs is a piece of paper and a pencil, it saves time to have "empty" maps available. These maps can be worked on by an individual or a family (see Figure 2).

Instructions for drawing an eco-map. First the nuclear family system or household is drawn in a large circle at the map's center. It has been common practice in mapping families to use squares to depict males and circles to depict females. Relationships are indicated as in the traditional family tree or genetic chart. It is useful to put the person's age in the center of the circle or square. Thus, a circle with "80" in the center would represent an elderly woman.

Figure 1 represents a household consisting of a father, a mother, three children, and the wife's mother. The usefulness of this is demonstrated when one considers the number of words it would take to portray the facts thus represented. (The mapping of more complex nuclear family systems will be deomonstrated in the discussion of genograms.)

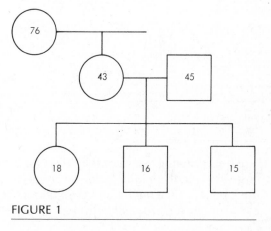

FIGURE 1

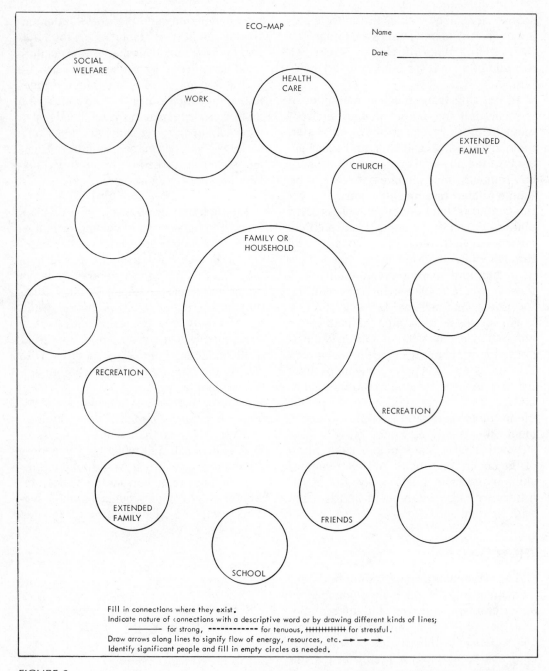

FIGURE 2

After drawing the household in the large circle in the middle, add the connections between the family and the different parts of the environment. In the empty map (see Figure 2), some of the most common systems in the lives of most families have been labeled, such as work, extended family, recreation, health care,

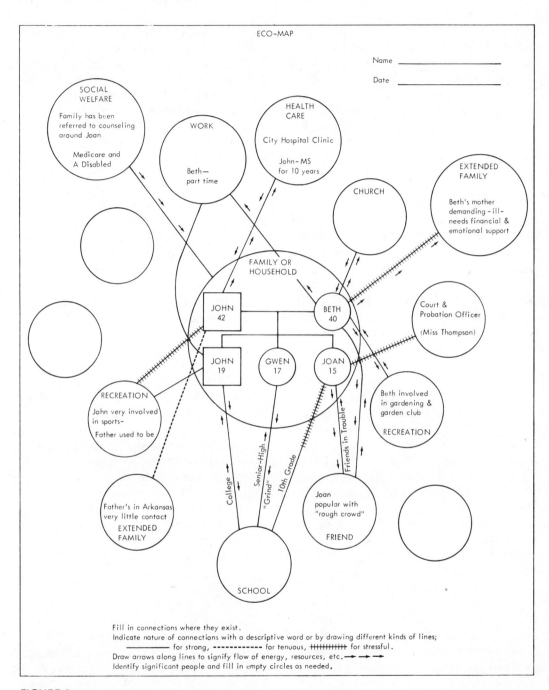

ECO-MAP

Name _____

Date _____

SOCIAL WELFARE

Family has been referred to counseling around Joan

Medicare and A Disabled

WORK

Beth— part time

HEALTH CARE

City Hospital Clinic

John- MS for 10 years

CHURCH

EXTENDED FAMILY

Beth's mother demanding - ill- needs financial & emotional support

FAMILY OR HOUSEHOLD

JOHN 42

BETH 40

Court & Probation Officer

(Miss Thompson)

JOHN 19

GWEN 17

JOAN 15

Beth involved in gardening & garden club

RECREATION

RECREATION

John very involved in sports-

Father used to be

College

Senior-High "Grind"

10th Grade

Friends in Trouble

Father's in Arkansas very little contact

EXTENDED FAMILY

Joan popular with "rough crowd"

FRIEND

SCHOOL

Fill in connections where they exist.

Indicate nature of connections with a descriptive word or by drawing different kinds of lines; —————— for strong, ------------ for tenuous, ++++++++++ for stressful.

Draw arrows along lines to signify flow of energy, resources, etc. —▶ —▶ —▶

Identify significant people and fill in empty circles as needed.

FIGURE 3

school, and so on. Other circles have been left undesignated so that the map can be individualized for different families.

Connections between the family and the various systems are indicated by drawing lines between the family and those systems (see Figure 3). The nature of the connection can be expressed in the type of line drawn: A solid or thick line represents an important or strong connection and a dotted line a tenuous connection; jagged marks across the line represent a stressful or conflicted relationship. It is useful to indicate the direction of the flow of resources, energy, or interest by drawing arrows along the connecting lines:

In testing the eco-map, it has been found that the use of the three kinds of lines for conflicted, strong, and tenuous relationships is an efficient shorthand when the worker uses the eco-mapping procedure, without the family, as an analytic tool. However, when using the map as an interviewing tool, this code has often been felt to be too constraining. Workers have preferred to ask clients to describe the nature of the connection and will then qualify that connection by writing a brief description along the connecting line.

Connections can be drawn to the family as a whole if they are intended to portray the total family systems relationship with some system in the environment. Other connections can be drawn between a particular individual in the family and an outside system when that person is the only one involved or different family members are involved with an outside system in different ways. This enables the map to highlight the contrasts in the way various family members are connected to the world.

It is easy to learn to plot the eco-map, and it is important to become comfortable with the tool before using it with clients. A simple way to learn is to sketch one's own eco-map. It is also useful to practice with friends. By then, one is generally ready to use it with clients.

Uses of the eco-map. No matter how the eco-map is used, its primary value is in its visual impact and its ability to organize and present concurrently not only a great deal of factual information but also the relationships between variables in a situation. Visual examination of the map has considerable impact on the way the worker and the client perceive the situation. The connections, the themes, and the quality of the family's life seem to jump off the page, and this leads to a more holistic and integrative perception. The integrative value of visual experience was aptly expressed by one 12-year-old client when he said, "Gee, I never saw myself like that before!"

Initially, the eco-map was developed as a thinking tool for the worker. It was helpful in organizing material and in making an assessment. Sketching out an eco-map in the early stages of contact brought out salient areas of the family's life space that had not as yet been explored and suggested hypotheses for treatment. Before long, it became apparent that the eco-map would make a useful interviewing tool. Client and worker cooperated in picturing the client's life space. This led to much more active participation on the part of the client in the information-gathering and assessment process. The growing collaborative relationship between worker and client was often expressed in a change in seating arrangements as the two tended to sit shoulder-to-shoulder, working together on the joint project.

Sharing the eco-mapping process also led to increased understanding and acceptance of the self on the part of the client. For example, an almost empty eco-map helps the client objectify and share loneliness and isolation. An eco-map full of stressful relationships showing all of the arrows pointing away from the family may lead a father to say, "No wonder I feel drained, everything is going out and nothing is coming in!" The eco-map has been extensively tested with natural parents working toward the return of their placed children through the Temporary Foster Care Project of the Michigan Department of Social Services (Thomas, 1978). Foster care workers noted that parents who were generally angry and self-protective following placement of their children because of abuse or neglect were almost without exception engaged through the use of the map. Workers were aware of a dramatic decrease in defensiveness. The ecological perspective made it clear to parents that the worker was not searching for their inner defects but rather was interested in finding out what it was like to be in the client's space, to walk in their shoes.

In working with the eco-map, clients have responded in some unanticipated ways. Although it was expected that they would gain a new perception by being able to step outside and look at themselves and their world, the emotional importance of the maps to the clients was a surprise. One mother demonstrated this early in the project by putting the eco-map up on her kitchen wall. In responding to clients' attachments to the maps, workers have regularly arranged to have them photocopied or have used pencil carbon so that clients may have a copy.

Contracting and intervention. The eco-map has also been a useful tool in planning and has had considerable impact on intervention. Because it focuses attention on the client's relationship with the life space, interventions tend to be targeted on the interface, with both worker and client becoming active in initiating changes in the life space. Problematic conditions tend to be characterized as transactional and as a function of the many variables that combine to affect the quality of the individual's or the family's life.

In the Temporary Foster Care Project mentioned earlier, the worker and client moved quite naturally from the eco-map to a task-oriented contract.[4] They talked

together about the changes that would be needed in the eco-map before the family could be reunited. They identified problem areas, resources needed, and potential strengths and planned what actions were needed to bring about change. Further, they established priorities and developed a contract describing the tasks to be undertaken by the worker and by the client.

The uses of the eco-map have multiplied in the hands of creative practitioners. For example, it has been used to portray the past and the future: In a rehabilitation program in a medical setting a social worker used eco-maps with clients to picture their world before their accident or illness; this helped clients to objectify what changes would be made in their lives following hospitalization. It helped them to mourn interests and activities that would have to be relinquished and also to recognize sources of support and gratification that would continue to be available. The mapping encouraged anticipatory planning and preparation for a new life, consideration of appropriate replacements for lost activities, and possible new resources to be tapped, all of which could expand the client's horizons. This technique was not only useful with the patient alone but was very helpful in conjoint work with disabled persons and their families.

Retrospective use of the map tends to highlight changes in a client's life space that could have precipitated current difficulties. When families and individuals seek help, a major question is always "Why has the client sought help now?" A review of the changes that have taken place in the previous months may well bring to light shifts of which the client was quite unaware.

Recordkeeping and measurements of change. A complete eco-map deposited in a case record is a useful tool to present and record a case situation. Not only does

---

[4] The work of William Reid and Laura Epstein (1977) and their collaborators has been useful in this area.

it tend to keep the total situation clear for the worker, it can also serve as a means of communication to others should a staff member have to respond to a client in the absence of the regular worker. A crisis walk-in center where case responsibility is shared by a team to provide extended coverage uses the eco-map this way.

Finally, eco-maps can be used to evaluate outcomes and measure change. For example, a 10-year-old boy on a return visit to a school social worker asked for the map. He had made a new friend and wanted to put him on the map. The mother who had hung the map in the kitchen called her worker after two months of considerable activity on both their parts. She wanted to come into the office to plot another map so that she and the worker could look together at the changes. A comparison of eco-maps done at outset and at termination can help clients and workers measure the changes that have taken place. As such the maps can become an important device in maintaining accountability.

THE GENOGRAM

Families not only exist in space but also through time, and thus a second kind of simulation is needed to picture the development of this powerful relationship system. Not only is each individual immersed in the complex here-and-now life space, but each individual is also a part of a family saga, in an infinitely complicated human system which has developed over many generations and has transmitted powerful commands, role assignments, events, and patterns of living and relating down through the years. Each individual and each family is deeply implicated in this intergenerational family history.

Just as the eco-map can begin to portray and objectify the family in space, so can the genogram picture the family system through time, enabling an individual to step out of the system, examine it, and begin to gain a greater understanding of complex family dynamics as they have developed and as they affect the current situation.

Instructions for drawing a genogram. A genogram is simply a family tree that includes more social data. It is a map of three, four, or more generations of a family which records genealogical relationships, major family events, occupations, losses, family migrations and dispersal, identifications and role assignments, and information about alignments and communication patterns. Again, all that is needed is paper and pencil. For most genograms, a rather large piece of paper is usually required. It is important for the genogram to be uncrowded and clear to make visual examination possible.

The skeleton of the genogram tends to follow the conventions of genetic and genealogical charts. As in the eco-map, a male is indicated by a square, a female by a circle, and if the sex of a person is unknown by a triangle. The latter symbol tends to be used, for example, when the client says, "I think there were seven children in my grandfather's family but I have no idea whether they were males or females." Or, "My mother lost a full-term baby five years before I was born, but I don't know what sex it was."

A marital pair is indicated by a line drawn from a square to a circle; it is useful to add the marital date, on the line. A married couple with offspring is shown as illustrated in Figure 4. Offspring are generally entered according to age, starting with the oldest on the left. The family diagrammed in Figure 4 has an older son followed by a set of twins. A divorce is generally portrayed by a dotted line, and again, it is useful to include dates (see Figure 5). A family member no longer living is generally indicated by drawing an "X" through the figure and giving the year of

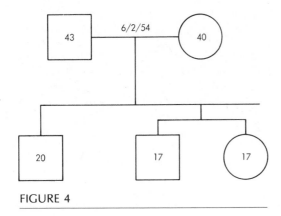

FIGURE 4

death. Thus, a complex, but not untypical, reconstituted family may be drawn as shown in Figure 5.

It is useful to draw a dotted line around the family members who compose the household. Incidentally, such a family chart enables the worker to grasp who is who quickly in complicated reconstituted families.

With these basic building blocks, expanded horizontally to depict the contemporary generation of siblings and cousins and vertically to chart the generations through time, it is possible to chart any family, given sufficient paper, patience, and information (see Figure 6). As one charts the skeletal structure of the family, it is also important to fill this out with the rich and varied data which portray the saga of the particular family being studied.

Many different kinds of information may be gathered. First and middle given names identify family members, indicate naming patterns, and bring identifications to the surface. In understanding where a client may fit into the family and what expectations and displacements may have affected the sense of self, a first step is to discover who, if anyone, the client was named after. Once this person is identified, it is important to discover what he or she was like, what roles he or she carried, and, perhaps most salient, what the nature of the relationship was between the client's parents and this relative.

Sometimes meanings and connections are not obvious and emerge only through careful exploration. For example, in charting a genogram with a young man who was struggling with identity issues and a complex tie with his mother, naming patterns were being discussed. The client's name was Tony; his American soldier father had met his mother abroad and, immediately after their marriage, the couple had moved to the United States. The move and subsequent political events resulted in the wife's being completely cut off from her family. The client, their firstborn child, was born a year after the marriage. When

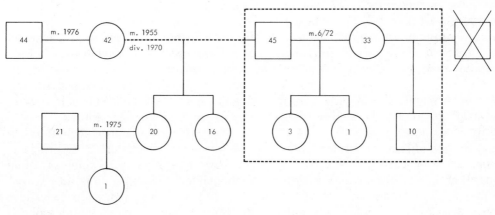

FIGURE 5

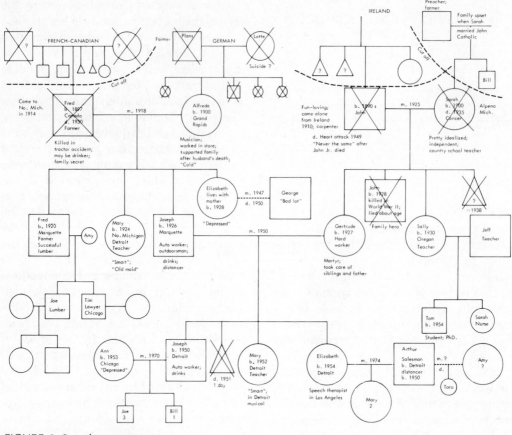

FIGURE 6: Sample genogram

asked whom he was named after, he replied, "I wasn't named after anyone in the family—I was named after St. Anthony—the patron of lost objects." The symbolic meaning of Anthony's name to his mother became dramatically apparent: Tony was named after everyone in his mother's family!

Dates of birth and dates of death record when members joined the family, their longevity, and family losses. Birth dates indicate the age of family members when important events occurred. They indicate how early or late in a marriage a child came and the age of the parents at the birth. In a sense, birth, marriage, and death dates mark the movement of the family

through time. In working with a client's genogram, it is helpful to discover all of the events that took place around the birth. Major losses experienced in the family around that time can be of particular significance. The tendency to use newborn family members as replacements for lost members seems almost universal and has even been institutionalized in some culturally proscribed naming patterns.

Birth dates also identify each individual's place in the sibship. This brings to the surface such potential roles as "older responsible," "firstborn son," or "baby." It is also relevant to discover who else in the family has occupied the same sibling position. Sibling position can be a powerful source of intergenerational identifications.

Place of birth and current place of residence mark the movement of the family through space. Such information charts the family's patterns of dispersal, bringing into focus major immigrations or migrations and periods of loss, change, and upheaval. Such information may also point to the fact that generations of a family have stayed within a fairly small radius except, perhaps, for a particular individual in each generation who moves away. If a client happens to be this generation's "wanderer," that could be a valuable piece of information.

Picturing the family's movement through space may communicate a good deal about family boundaries and norms concerning mobility. Is this a family that holds on or lets go? Further, the impact of world history on families often becomes evident as responses to war, persecution, westward migration, depression, industrialization, and even climatic or ecological changes are often seen in relocations.

Occupations of family members acquaint one with the interests and talents, the successes and failures, and the varied socioeconomic statuses that are found in most families. Occupational patterns may also point to identifications and can often portray family proscriptions and expectations.

Finally, facts about members' health and causes of death provide overall family health history and also may say something about the way clients see their own future. These predictions may well have some power of self-fulfillment.

This demographic data can take a worker a long way toward understanding the family system. However, gathering associations about family members can add to the richness of the portrayal. One can ask, "What word or two or what picture comes to mind when you think about this person?" These associations tend to tap

another level of information about the family as the myths, role assignments, characterizations, or caricatures of family members come into the client's mind. Characterizations such as lazy, bossy, martyr, beautiful, caretaker, are likely to be offered, bringing forth reminiscences or stories that have become a part of the family biography and mythology.

Finally, certain aspects of the family's communication structure can be indicated. Parts of the family that have been cut off become quite obvious because the client generally has very little information about them. Cutoffs can be portrayed by drawing a fence where the cutoff exists whereas tight communication bonds can be demonstrated by drawing a line around portions of the family that form close linkages. It helps to keep things clear if a colored pencil is used to indicate communication linkages and cutoffs so as not to confuse these with the basic genealogical structure. Cutoffs are of particular significance as they are usually indicative of conflict, loss, and family secrets. Cutoffs generally develop to protect family members from pain and conflict, but they are usually indicators of unfinished business and may leave the person out of touch with important aspects of family and perhaps of self.

It is often found that a client doing a genogram will have considerable information about one section of the family, for example, the maternal grandmother's family, and almost none about other relatives. This uneven distribution of knowledge is significant in assessing communication and relationship patterns.

Uses of the genogram. The genogram is a classic tool for gathering and utilizing family data in any family oriented practice. No matter what the setting, if the individual is to be understood in the context of the total family system, the genogram can portray that system and move worker and client toward an understanding of the impact of that system and its relevance to the issues at hand. In counseling regarding marital and parent-child conflict, the routes or prototypes of these conflicts may well emerge. The use of the genogram in conjoint marital counseling can increase empathy between the marital pair and help each to identify the old family issues that have been displaced in the marriage.

In working with the aging, the genogram is an invaluable tool in life review. Elderly people can reminisce and organize memories but also, in working with the genogram, can experience themselves as a central link between the past and the future. This process expresses continuity and the generative process and illustrates that, although the individual's life span may be brief, the family's life reaches back into the past and on into the future. One residence for the aging encourages staff to meet with family members to teach them how to build genograms and help their aged relatives reconnect with their family saga. This sharing of the genogram has been an important experience for both the aged person and the younger family members.

Genograms have also been used in child welfare agencies. As part of an adoptive home study, for example, the genogram may clarify why a couple experiences their family as incomplete and also brings to the surface considerations and plans concerning who an adopted child is intended to be. Charting a genogram with natural parents insures that, should family ties be legally severed, there will be a full family history available to the child in the future. One child-care agency that regularly makes use of the genogram in adoption practice has found that often the experience of doing the genogram has been very meaningful to natural parents who see the process as giving something of themselves to the child. The issue of open adoption has yet to be settled but, in the interim, the genogram can gather and keep available the kind of information adopted children often want.

In a hospital setting, a genogram can be used to gather an expanded health history. Such a history provides information about patterns of illness and health in a family: for instance, a paternal grandmother may have died of heart disease at 38 while the maternal grandmother lived an active life to age 94. Further, patterns of illness as well as attitudes toward illness and ill people may appear.

SUMMARY

The eco-map and the genogram are paper- and pencil-simulations that can organize and objectify a tremendous amount of data about the family system in space and through time. Such objectivity and visual portrayal can lead to new insights and to altered perceptions, of the complexity of human systems. Such altered perceptions may point to new ways of bringing about change, ways that relate to the complexity of human existence.

Reading 9–2

*Social Work with Native Americans**

Ronald G. Lewis and Man Keung Ho

In the past, the social work profession has failed to serve effectively an important segment of the population—the Native Americans. Although social workers are in sympathy with the social problems and injustices long associated with the Native American people, they have been unable to assist them with their problems. This lack of success on the part of social workers can be attributed to a multitude of reasons, but it stems, in general, from the following: (1) lack of understanding of the Native American culture, (2) retention of stereotyped images of Native Americans, (3) use of standard techniques and approaches.

Currently, the majority of social workers attempting to treat Native Americans are whites who have never been exposed to their clients' culture. Even when the social worker is a Native American, if his education and training have been in an environment that has completely neglected the Native American culture, there is still the possibility that he has drifted away from his people's thinking. Social workers with no understanding of the culture may have little or no sympathy for their Native American clients who fail to respond quickly to treatment.

Furthermore, Native Americans continue to be stereotyped by the current news media and often by the educational system. In all likelihood, the social worker will rely on these mistaken stereotypes rather than on facts. As Deloria explained, "People can tell just by looking at us what

we want, what should be done to help us, how we feel, and what a 'real' Indian is like."[1] If a worker wishes to make progress in helping a Native American, he must begin by learning the facts and discarding stereotypes.

The ineffectiveness of social workers in dealing with Native Americans can often be attributed directly to the methods and techniques they use. Naturally, social workers must work with the tools they have acquired, but these may have a detrimental effect on a Native American. For example, the concept of "social work intervention" may be consistent with much of the white man's culture, but it diametrically opposes the Native American's cultural concept of noninterference. There is a great need for social workers to examine carefully those techniques they plan to use in treating their Native American clients. If the worker discovers any that might be in conflict with the cultural concepts of the Native American, he should search carefully for an alternative approach. To do this, of course, the social worker must be aware of common Native American cultural traits.

Although there is no monolithic Native American culture—because each tribe's culture is unique to that individual tribe, and no social worker could be expected to be familiar with the cultures of some two hundred tribes—the worker should familiarize himself with those customs that are generally characteristic of all Native Americans. Only after a worker has gained at least an elementary knowledge of Native American customs and culture can he proceed to evaluate the various ap-

*Copyright 1975, National Association of Social Workers, Inc. Reprinted with permission, from *Social Work*, vol. 20, no. 5 (September 1975), pp. 379–382.

proaches and techniques and choose the most effective ones.

NATIVE AMERICAN TRAITS

The concept of sharing is deeply ingrained among Native Americans, who hold it in greater esteem than the white American ethic of saving. Since one's worth is measured by one's willingness and ability to share, the accumulation of material goods for social status is alien to the Native American. Sharing, therefore, is neither a superimposed nor an artificial value, but a genuine and routine way of life.

In contrast to the general belief that they have no concept of time, Native Americans are indeed time conscious. They deal, however, with natural phenomena—mornings, days, nights, months (in terms of moons), and years (in terms of seasons or winters). If a Native American is on his way to a meeting or appointment and meets a friend, that conversation will naturally take precedence over being punctual for the appointment. In his culture, sharing is more important than punctuality.

Nature is the Native American's school, and he is taught to endure all natural happenings that he will encounter during his life. He learns as well to be an independent individual who respects others. The Native American believes that to attain maturity—which is learning to live with life, its evil as well as its good—one must face genuine suffering. The resilience of the Native American way of life is attested to by the fact that the culture has survived and continues to flourish despite the intense onslaught of the white man.

One of the strongest criticisms of the Native American has been that he is pessimistic; he is presented as downtrodden, low-spirited, unhappy, and without hope for the future. However, as one looks deeper into his personality, another perspective is visible. In the midst of abject poverty comes "the courage to be"—to face life as it is, while maintaining a tremendous sense of humor. There exists a thin line between pathos and humor.

The Native American realizes that the world is made up of both good and bad. There are always some people or things that are bad and deceitful. He believes, however, that in the end good people will triumph just because they are good. This belief is seen repeatedly in Native American folktales about Iktomi the spider. He is the tricky fellow who is out to fool, cheat, and take advantage of good people. But Iktomi usually loses in the end, reflecting the Native American view that the good person succeeds while the bad person loses. Therefore, the pessimism of Native Americans should instead be regarded as "optimistic toughness."

Those who are unfamiliar with the culture might mistakenly interpret the quiet Native American as being stoical, unemotional, and vulnerable. He is alone, not only to others but also to himself. He controls his emotions, allowing himself no passionate outbursts over small matters. His habitual mien is one of poise, self-containment, and aloofness, which may result from a fear and mistrust of non-Native Americans. Another facet of Native American thought is the belief that no matter where any individual stands, he is an integral part of the universe. Because every person is fulfilling a purpose, no one should have the power to impose values. For this reason, each man is to be respected, and he can expect the same respect and reverence from others. Hence, the security of this inner fulfillment provides him with an essential serenity that is often mistaken for stoicism.

Native American patience, however, can easily be mistaken for inactivity. For instance, the Kiowa, like other Native American tribes, teach their young people to be patient. Today, when the young Native American has to go out and compete in another society, this quality is often interpreted as laziness. The white man's world is a competitive, aggressive society that bypasses the patient man who stands back and lets the next person go first.

The foregoing are only a few of the cultural traits that are common to most Native American tribes, but they represent important characteristics about which the effective social worker must be informed. The concepts of sharing, of time, acceptance of suffering, and optimism differ significantly from the white man's concepts. In dealing with a Native American client, the social worker must realize this and proceed accordingly. He must be familiar with the Native American view that good will triumph over evil and must recognize that Native Americans are taught to be patient and respectful. If the worker fails to do this, he is liable to make false assumptions, thus weakening his ability to serve his client effectively.

CLIENT-WORKER RELATIONS

A social worker's ability to establish a working relationship with a Native American will depend on his genuine respect for his client's cultural background and attributes. A worker should never think that the Native American is primitive or that his culture and background are inferior.

In the beginning, the Native American client might distrust the worker who is from a different race and culture. He might even view the worker as a figure of authority, and as such, the representative of a coercive institution. It is unlikely that he will be impressed with the worker's educational degrees or his professional title. However, this uncompromising attitude should not be interpreted as pugnacity. On the contrary, the Native American is gregarious and benevolent. His willingness and capacity to share depend on mutual

consideration, respect, and noncoercion.

Because their culture strongly opposes and precludes interference with another's affairs, Native Americans have tended to regard social work intervention with disfavor. Social workers usually are forced to use culturally biased techniques and skills that are insensitive to the Native American culture and, therefore, are either detrimental to these clients or, at best, ineffective.

In an effort to communicate more fully, a social worker is likely to seat himself facing the client, look him straight in the eye, and insist that the client do likewise. A Native American considers such behavior—covert or overt—to be rude and intimidating; contrary to the white man, he shows respect by not staring directly at others. Similarly, a worker who is excessively concerned with facilitating the display of inner feelings on the part of the client should be aware of another trait. A Native American client will not immediately wish to discuss other members of his family or talk about topics that he finds sensitive or distressing. Before arriving at his immediate concern (the real reason he came to the worker in the first place), the client—particularly the Native American—will test the worker by bringing up peripheral matters. He does this in the hope of getting a better picture of how sincere, interested, and trustworthy the worker actually is. If the worker impatiently confronts the client with accusations, the client will be "turned off."

Techniques of communication that focus on the client—that is, techniques based on restating, clarifying, summarizing, reflecting, and empathizing—may help a worker relate to the client who sometimes needs a new perspective to resolve his problem. It is important that the worker provide him with such information but not coerce him to accept it. The worker's advice should be objective and flexible enough so that its adoption does not become the central issue of a particular interview.

For the Native American, personal matters and emotional breakdown are traditionally handled within the family or extended family system. For this reason, the client will not wish to "burden" the worker with detailed personal information. If the client is estranged from his family and cultural group, he may indirectly share such personal information with the worker. To determine the appropriate techniques for helping a Native American client deal with personal and psychological problems, the worker should carefully observe the client's cultural framework and his degree of defensiveness. The techniques of confrontation traditionally associated with the psychoanalytic approach and the introspective and integrative techniques used by the transactional analysts tend to disregard differences in culture and background between a client and worker.

FAMILY COUNSELING

In view of the close-knit family structure of Native Americans, along with the cultural emphasis to keep family matters inside the family, it is doubtful that many social workers will have the opportunity to render family counseling services. In the event that a Native American family does seek the worker's help, the family worker should be reminded that his traditional role of active and manipulative go-between must be tempered so that family members can deal with their problems at their own pace. Equally important is the worker's awareness of and respect for the resilience of Native American families, bolstered in crisis by the extended family system. The example of the Redthunder family serves as illustration.

The Redthunder family was brought to the school social worker's attention when teachers reported that both children had been tardy and absent frequently in the past weeks. Since the worker lived near Mr. Redthunder's neighborhood, she volunteered to transport the children back and forth to school. Through this regular but informal arrangement, the worker became acquainted with the entire family, especially with Mrs. Redthunder who expressed her gratitude to the worker by sharing her homegrown vegetables.

The worker sensed that there was much family discomfort and that a tumultuous relationship existed between Mr. and Mrs. Redthunder. Instead of probing into their personal and marital affairs, the worker let Mrs. Redthunder know that she was willing to listen should the woman need someone to talk to. After a few gifts of homegrown vegetables and Native American handicrafts, Mrs. Redthunder broke into tears one day and told the worker about her husband's problem of alcoholism and their deteriorating marital relationship.

Realizing Mr. Redthunder's position of respect in the family and his resistance to outside interference, the social worker advised Mrs. Redthunder to take her family to visit the minister, a man whom Mr. Redthunder admired. The Littleaxe family, who were mutual friends of the worker and the Redthunder family, agreed to take the initiative in visiting the Redthunders more often. Through such frequent but informal family visits, Mr. Redthunder finally obtained a job, with the recommendation of Mr. Littleaxe, as recordkeeper in a storeroom. Mr. Redthunder enjoyed his work so much that he drank less and spent more time with his family.

Obviously, treating a family more pathogenic than the Redthunders might necessitate that the social worker go beyond the role of mediator. Nevertheless, since Native Americans traditionally favor noninterference, the social worker will not find it feasible to assume the active manipulative role that he might in working with white middle-class families. The social work profession needs new and innovative approaches to family counseling that take into account social and family networks and are sensitive and responsive to the cultural orientation of Native American families.

GROUP WORK

Groups should be a natural and effective medium for Native Americans who esteem the concept of sharing and apply it in their daily lives. Through the group process, members can share their joy, intimacy, problems, and sorrows, and find a means of improving their lives. Today's society tends to foster alienation, anomie, disenfranchisement, dissociation, loneliness, and schizoid coolness. People wish for intimacy but at the same time fear it. The new humanistic approaches to counseling and psychotherapy have developed a wide variety of powerful techniques for facilitating human growth, self-discovery, and interpersonal relations. The effectiveness of these approaches in cutting through resistance, breaking down defenses, releasing creative forces, and promoting the healing process has been amply demonstrated. However, such approaches are highly insensitive to the cultural orientation of Native Americans. These people consider such group behavior to be false; it looks and sounds real but lacks genuineness, depth, and real commitment.

As the worker uses his skills in forming the group, diagnosing the problems, and facilitating group goals, he may inevitably retain certain elements of manipulation. However, if he is committed to recognizing individual potential and to capitalizing on the group model of mutual assistance, he should come close to meeting the needs of Native Americans who value respect and consideration for oneself as well as for others.

To avoid manipulation and coercion, a group worker needs to utilize indirect and extra-group means of influence that will in turn influence the members. Thus the worker may act upon and through the group as a mediating structure, or through program activities, for the benefit of his clients. This success of the worker's influences and activities is related to his knowledge and acceptance of Native American culture, its formal and informal systems and norms.

Regardless of whether the purpose of the group is for effecting interpersonal change or social action, such Native American virtues as mutual respect and consideration should be the essential components of the group process. Using the group to pressure members who are late or silent will not only jeopardize and shorten the group's existence, but will cause alienation and withdrawal from future group activities.

In view of the vast cultural difference between Native Americans and other ethnic groups, especially whites, it is doubtful that a heterogeneous grouping of members will produce good results. Similarly, group activities that are action oriented may be contradictory to Native Americans who view the compulsion to reduce or ignore suffering as immaturity.

COMMUNITY WORK

Because of the Native Americans' experience of oppression and exploitation —along with their emphasis on noninterference and resolute acceptance of suffering—it is doubtful that a social worker, regardless of his racial identity, could bring about any major change in community policies and programs. The only exception might be the social worker who is accepted and "adopted" by the community and who agrees to confine himself to the existing system and norms. A worker's adoption by the Native American community will depend on his sincerity, respect, and genuine concern for the people. This concern can best be displayed through patience in daily contact with the community as well as through his efforts to find positive solutions to problems.

A worker who uses the strategy of trying to resolve conflict as a means of bringing about social change will undoubtedly encounter native resistance and rejection. On the other hand, a worker who shows respect for the system, values, and norms of the Native American eventually places himself in a position of trust and credibility. Only through mutual respect, and not through his professional title and academic degree, can the worker produce meaningful social change.

Obviously, social work with Native Americans requires a new orientation and focus on attitudes and approaches. The term Native American encompasses many tribes, and within these there are intratribal differences; furthermore, individuals within each subtribe may react differently to problems or crises. Therefore, it is impossible for a social worker always to know precisely how to respond to a Native American client or group. The worker must be willing to admit his limitations, to listen carefully, to be less ready to draw conclusions, and to anticipate that his presuppositions will be corrected by the client. The worker must genuinely want to know what the problem or the situation is and be receptive to being taught. Such an unassuming and unobtrusive humanistic attitude is the key to working with Native American people.

The social worker who can deal most effectively with Native Americans will be genuine, respectful of their culture, and empathic with the welfare of the people. By no means does the Native American social worker have a monopoly on this type of attitude. In fact, the Native American social worker who has assimilated the white man's culture to the extent that he no longer values his own culture could do more harm than good.

Recognizing the distinct cultural differences of the Native American people, those who plan social work curricula and training programs must expand them to include specific preparation for workers who will be dealing with Native American clients. Literature on the subject is almost nonexistent, and researchers and educators would do well to devote more study to how social workers can serve Native Americans. More Native Americans should be recruited as students, faculty, and practitioners in the field of social work. All persons, regardless of race, should be encouraged to develop a sensitivity toward Native Americans whom they may have the opportunity to serve. Social work agencies that deal primarily with Native American clients should intensify and refocus their in-service training programs.

A worker has the responsibility of acquiring knowledge that is relevant to the Native American culture so that he is capable of providing this effective treatment. A joint effort on the part of all those involved is required to give the service to Native Americans that they justly deserve.

References

Bruner, Jerome S., Goodnow, Jacqueline, & Austin, George A.   *A study of thinking* (vol. 7). New York: Wiley, 1962.

Bryde, John F.   *Modern indian psychology.* Vermillion: Institute of Indian Studies, University of South Dakota, 1971, p. 15.

Byler, William.   The destruction of American Indian families. In Steve Unger (Ed.), *The destruction of American Indian families.* New York: Association on American Indian Affairs, 1977.

De Geyndt, Willy.   Health behavior and health needs in urban Indians in Minneapolis. *Health Service Reports,* April 1973, *88,* 360–366.

Deloria, Vine, Jr.   *Custer died for your sins: An indian manifesto.* New York: Macmillan, 1969, p. 45.

Densmore, Frances. *Chippewa customs.* Minneapolis, Minn.: Ross & Haines, 1970.

Dreyfus, Edward A. The search for intimacy. *Adolescence,* March 1967, *2,* pp. 25–40.

Duhl, Frederick. Intervention, therapy, and change. In William Gray, Frederick Duhl, & Nicholas D. Rizzo (Eds.), *General systems theory and psychiatry.* Boston: Little, Brown, 1969.

Germain, Carel. Social study: Past and future. *Social Casework,* July 1968, *49,* 403–409.

Casework and science: An historical encounter. In Robert W. Roberts & Robert Nee (Eds.), *Theories of casework.* Chicago: University of Chicago Press, 1971.

Germain, Carel. The ecological perspective in casework practice. *Social Casework,* June 1973, *54,* 223–230.

Good Tracks, Jimm G. Native american noninterference. *Social Work,* November 1973, *18,* pp. 30–34.

Guerin, Philip J., & Pendagast, Eileen G. Evaluation of family system and genogram. In Philip T. Guerin (Ed.), *Family therapy: Theory and practice.* New York: Halsted Press, 1976.

Gunther, Bernard. *Sense relaxation: Below your mind.* New York: Macmillan, 1968.

Hallowell, A. Irving. Ojibway personality and acculturation. In Paul Bohannon & Fred Plog (Eds.), *Beyond the frontier.* New York: Natural History Press, 1967.

Hartman, Ann. To think about the unthinkable. *Social Casework,* October 1970, *51,* 467–474.

Hartman, Ann. The generic stance in the family agency. *Social Casework,* April 1974, *55,* 199–208.

Hearn, Gordon (Ed.). *The general systems approach: Contributions toward an holistic conception of social work.* New York: Council on Social Work Education, 1969.

Huffaker, Clair. *Nobody loves a drunken indian.* New York: David McKay, 1967.

Keith-Lucas, Alan. Ethics in social work. In *Encyclopedia of Social Work* (vol. 1), New York: National Association of Social Workers, 1971.

Keith-Lucas, Alan. *The giving and taking of help.* Chapel Hill: University of North Carolina Press, 1972.

Krush, Thaddeus P., Bjork, John W., Sindell, Peter S., & Nelle, Joanna. Some thoughts on the formulation of personality disorders: Study of an Indian boarding school population. In *Hearings before the special subcommittee on Indian education of the committee on labor and public welfare, United States Senate. Part 5.* Washington, D.C.: U.S. Government Printing Office, 1969.

Levine, Irving M. Ethnicity and mental health: A social conservation approach. Paper presented at White House Conference on Ethnicity and Mental Health, Washington, D.C., June 1976.

Lewis, Ronald. But we have been helping Indians for a long time. Unpublished research. Milwaukee: University of Wisconsin School of Social Work, 1977.

Lutz, Werner A. *Concepts and principles underlying social casework practice in medical care and rehabilitation settings* (Monograph 3). Washington, D.C.: National Association of Social Workers, Medical Social Work Section, 1956.

Maslow, Abraham. Self-actualization and beyond. In James F. Bugental (Ed.), *Challenges of Humanistic Psychology.* New York: MacGraw-Hill, 1967.

May, Rollo. Love and will. *Psychology Today,* 1969, *3,* pp. 17–24.

Mayer, John E., & Timms, Noel.   Clash in perspective between worker and client. *Social Casework* January 1969, *50,* 32–40.

Native American Research Group.   *Native American families in the city.* San Francisco: Institute for Scientific Analysis, 1975.

Oho, H.   *Explorations in human potentialities.* Springfield, Ill.: Charles C Thomas, 1966.

Red Horse, John G., & Feit, Marvin.   Urban native American preventive health care. Paper presented at the American Public Health Association Meeting, Miami Beach, October 1976.

Reid, William, & Epstein, Laura.   *Task centered practice.* New York: Columbia University Press, 1977.

Richmond, Mary E.   *Social diagnosis.* New York: Russell Sage Foundation, 1917.

Rogers, Carl.   Process of the basic encounter group. In James F. Bugental (Ed.), *Challenges of humanistic psychology.* New York: MacGraw-Hill, 1967.

Schwartz, William.   Toward a strategy of group work practice. *Social Service Review,* September 1962, *36,* pp. 268–279.

Speck, Ross V. & Attneave, Carolyn L.   Social network intervention. In Jay Haley (Ed.), *Changing families,* New York: Grune & Stratton, 1971, pp. 17–34.

Suk, Gerald.   The go-between process in family therapy. *Family Process,* April 1966, *6,* pp. 162–178.

Thomas, Gloria.   Final report of the temporary foster care project. Lansing, Mich.: Department of Social Services, Division of Youth Services, 1978. (Mimeograph)

Tropp, Emanuel.   The group: In life and in social work. *Social Casework,* May 1968, *49,* 267–274.

Tropp, Emanuel.   Theories of Social Work with Groups. NewYork: Columbia University Press, 1976.

Vinter, Robert.   *Readings in group work practice.* Ann Arbor, Mich.: Campus Publishers, 1967, pp. 8–38.

Wax, Rosalie H., & Thomas, Robert K.   Anglo intervention vs. native noninterference. *Phylon 22,* Winter 1961, pp. 53–56.

Chapter 10

The Contract Phase:
Joint Assessment, Goal Setting,
and Planning

This chapter is about participatory decision making—how decisions concerning the nature of the client's problem, desired outcomes (goals) are negotiated, and how the outcomes will be achieved. The chapter will define the contract phase of the problem-solving model, present an outline of the process by which you and your client will jointly arrive at the contract, and enumerate a set of principles to guide your participation in this process.

DEFINITION OF THE SERVICE CONTRACT

In discussing the problem-solving process, identification of the problem, and data collection, we have maintained a consistent emphasis on the partnership nature of the interaction between client and worker. The partnership is working together to define and explore a common task. Mutuality between client and worker needs to be established at the very outset and to continue through all their associations. In the service contract, however, the partnership concept is fully developed and made explicit. Anthony Maluccio and Wilma Marlow, in an article produced in this chapter (see Reading 10–1), say:

> Webster's *Third New International Dictionary* defines contract as a "covenant," a "compact," or "an agreement between two or more persons to do or forbear something." These words suggest mutuality, participation, and action.
>
> For the purposes of social work, the contract may be defined as *the explicit agreement between the worker and the client concerning the target problems, the goals, and the strategies of social work intervention, and the roles and tasks of the participants.* Its major features are mutual agreement, differential participation in the intervention process, reciprocal accountability, and explicitness. In practice these features are closely interrelated.

Research into outcomes of social work practice is accumulating evidence that social work is often not helpful because worker and client are not working toward the same purposes (Lerner, 1972; Mayer & Timms, 1969; Polansky, Borgman, & de Saix, 1972). When clients approach an agency expecting a certain kind of help toward a certain kind of goal, they will be confused and perhaps will feel even more inadequate if you offer something they do not understand and were not aware they wanted. In such situations clients often leave the agency in frustration and disappointment.

When considering the importance of mutuality in the partnership and in the joint understandings and operating principles that are involved in the concept of contract, one should not lose sight of an equally important notion—that of difference. The concept of partnership does not mean that client and worker bring the same knowledge, understanding, feeling, and doing to the business of working together. Partnership and contract also highlight the differences that worker and client can contribute to the process. "The contract is a tool for such delineation, and for both client and worker it is an ongoing reminder of their collaborative relationship and different responsibilities" (Maluccio & Marlow, 1974, p. 30).

The service contract involves input, decision making, planning, and commitment from both the client and the social worker. The process of arriving at a service contract protects the client's individuality and maximizes opportunities for exercise of self-determination. In discussions, negotiations, and choosing among available alternatives, or in making commitments to engage in developing new alternatives, the client's opportunities for meaningful decisions about self and situation are greatly increased.

The next section describes what goes into the process of arriving at a service contract, and a final section will make explicit a number of principles which are implicit in the process. In many respects the process may appear similar to that described in Chapter 9 on the beginning phase of working together. The similarity exists partly because of the "spiral" nature of work with clients (a process which will be made more explicit in Chapter 15 on evaluation) and partly because the concept of contract also appears in the initial contact phase. A preliminary contract is developed to facilitate the process of collecting data—a prerequisite for joint worker and client decision making concerning the problem-to-be-worked, the desired outcomes, and the means or interventive efforts to be utilized in achieving those outcomes.

Arriving at a service contract involves a series of client-worker negotiations directed to answering these questions: Is the problem we want to work on the one that was identified when we began work together? Why has the problem persisted despite earlier client attempts to solve it? What is the desired solution (that is, what outcomes or objectives should the interventive effort be directed toward achieving in relation to the problem)? How will this solution be achieved? (Remember that the client may be an individual, a family, a group, or representatives of a community and that workers may be interacting with clients in a variety of settings.)

JOINT ASSESSMENT AND DECISION MAKING

Joint assessment and decision making is at the very heart of the development of the service contract. In the contact phase, worker and client have arrived at an initial definition of the problem-to-be-worked. They have set initial goals, collected some data, and done some exploration together related to the identified problem and goals. Now they must put this data together to determine what the problem is, what can be done about it (a reworking of the goal), and how they are going to do it. This process involves the ordering and organizing of the information, intuitions, and knowledge that client and worker bring so that the pieces come together into some pattern that makes sense, at least in the here and now, in explaining the problem and in relating this explanation to alternative solutions. There is movement from what is observed, inferred, or deduced, based on knowledge and experience, to some conclusive explanation of what we make of it, and thence to a determination of goals and how they can be implemented. Such assessments evolve not from one person's head, or from the simple addition of one item to another, but rather from a combination of data in relevant ways. They evolve from viewing the relationships of all elements to one another as client and worker appraise the client-in-situation, and from the assessment of their total significance to the client in light of what the client wants to accomplish. Harriett Bartlett (1970, p. 144) refers to these processes as "analysis of a situation to identify the major factors operating within it" and "identification of those factors which appear most critical, definition of their interrelationships, and selection of those to be dealt with." At its best the processes involve both client and worker in assembling and ordering all information and in making judgments as to their meaning for the work together.

Social workers often mistakenly assume that only the worker engages in these tasks. We do not deny that both the worker and the client must do hard and independent thinking (for the worker this is a professional obligation), but the test of the soundness of such thinking is how well their thinking fits together. Sometimes the culmination of this process is erroneously seen as putting the client in a category or affixing a label. That is emphatically not the purpose of the process! The process is not focused on the client alone; it is focused on the client, the problem, and the situation in a systematic interaction. In work with human beings, thinking and action cannot move in a straight line from cause to effect. Systems theory teaches us that problems are the result of complicated interactions among all system variables, and that to seek a single ultimate cause or reason is to doom oneself and, more important, one's client to frustration and failure. So our aim is not to come up with an answer in terms of labels or categories, but to order the understanding of the client-situation-problem for purposes of decision making concerning goals and actions.

Sometimes this process is called *diagnosis*. We dislike this term for several reasons. First, the preferred definition of the term in Webster is "The art or act of identifying a disease from its signs and symptoms." Thus the term carries the implication that there is something wrong with the client. Second, the term implies that the decision about what is wrong is made by the professional person through an examination. There is no inkling of dynamic interaction and joint responsibility in the term. Finally, diagnosis is often seen as a process by which a professional arrives at a label for something. After all, that is what happens when doctors diagnose. They assign labels signifying what is wrong. This is their assessment as the knowing authority, and, at even greater variance with the notions of the contract, doctors usually tell their patients what they have determined to be the most satisfactory form of treatment. We hope that the process of assessment and decision making in social work is understood to be quite different from diagnosis. The phrase *process of assessment* is used because we think that this is the way assessment must be regarded—as an ongoing, joint process, a shared endeavor.

Consistent with the approach outlined in Chapter 1, the problem may be defined as residing with clients, as outside clients but experienced by them, or as the result of the client-situation interaction. The target of change may or may not be the client. After client and worker have jointly defined the problem-for-work (this may or may not be the same as the presenting problem), the next decision is to define goals—what is to be done?

SETTING GOALS

What are the desired outcomes of the joint work? What is perceived as the appropriate solution for the problem? What are the goals of our actions? Essentially the same process is utilized in arriving at an answer to these questions as in developing a definition of the problem-for-work. Your first responsibility is to use interviewing skills to elicit from clients their views of desired outcomes. You may also have developed a view of the desired outcome which is shared with the client. If the two views are not congruent, then this difference must be negotiated, just as incongruent perceptions of the problem were negotiated. Unless you and your client can arrive at mutually agreeable goals, there is no sense in proceeding further because you will be working in opposed directions.

In setting goals, as in defining the problem for work, you will be working with your client to find a common area of agreement. Both Murdach (Reading 8–3) and Seabury in the articles reprinted in this chapter (Reading 10–2) note the likelihood of worker-client conflict in negotiating a contract. This is an issue to which we will return later in this chapter. We suggest, however, that you enter your initial work with clients in a spirit of compromise. Your task, as the worker, is to find a common ground—a common goal to which you and your client can direct your change efforts. This may not be what you consider the most important or even the most urgent goal. But if it is important for the client and a goal which you can appropriately work toward, begin at that point. Opportunities to define other goals will occur as you work together. Consider the case of Mrs. Troy:

> Mrs. Troy was referred to this agency for help in coping with her children. She was referred by a welfare department social worker who is providing brief individual counselling for Margaret, the 16-year-old daughter, regarding plans for her 2-month-old baby. The family consists of Mrs. Troy aged 42, John age 19, Joe age 17, Margaret age 16, Robert age 2 months (Margaret's baby), Marcel age 14, and Raymond age 12.
>
> The social worker who made the referral thought Mrs. Troy needed help in handling the kids, especially the oldest boy, John. Before I saw Mrs. Troy, a second

referral was made by the nurse who is working with Mrs. Troy who is diabetic. The nurse stated that Mrs. Troy would become so upset with the kids, John in particular, that she would forget to take her medication. She thought that Mrs. Troy was at her wits end and was threatening to leave the kids and disappear.

Mrs. Troy was not as desperate when I interviewed her two days later. She did, however, make it clear that she wanted some help to get John out of the house. She also wanted the other kids to do what they were told. Mrs. Troy saw John as the main problem. He deliberately aggravated the other kids, ordered them around, would sit around the house all day and have his friends over, refused to obey her and called her profane names. Mrs. Troy's boyfriend moved out a few months ago because of the frequent arguments he had with John. She also felt that John's bad example was causing her to lose control of the other kids.

Mrs. Troy's primary request was for help in getting John to move out of the house, but she didn't seem to feel there was much hope of doing it. She had tried putting his clothes out, locking him out, and changing the locks. Each time, John persisted in his efforts to get back in by shouting and pounding on the doors and windows. Mrs. Troy, feeling powerless and seeing no alternative, would let him in. On one occasion, when John became belligerent after coming home drunk, she called the police. They simply drove him a few blocks away and released him.

The Troy family presents an example of what Gitterman and Germain (Reading 1–2) refer to as "problems and needs associated with tasks involved in life transitions." This worker may have been interested in other goals—helping Mrs. Troy develop skill at managing her children or assisting Mrs. Troy in managing stress. After some further exploration and negotiation, however, the worker agreed to work with Mrs. Troy toward the goal of getting John out of the house. Working toward this goal, even though it was not the worker's first choice, provided an opportunity for the worker to provide immediate assistance and for Mrs. Troy and worker to negotiate for other goals. The goal also meets two tests for a useful goal—specificity and attainability.

Specifying goals is a crucial element of the service contract. Particular attention must be paid to two characteristics of the goals. First, goals should be sufficiently specific and concrete to be measurable. Only in this way can the client and worker know whether the goals have been accomplished, and only in this way can the profession of social work establish its accountability. Broadly stated goals, such as helping the client feel better, or increasing the client's opportunities for socializing experiences, or improving the parent-child relationship, are meaningless. This topic will be discussed further in Chapter 15 on evaluation. A set of procedures—Goal Attainment Scaling—which requires the setting of specific, measurable goals that will enable the client and worker to determine the extent of goal attainment will be introduced in Chapter 15.

Second, there should be a reasonable chance of attaining the goals set. In establishing goals, you and your clients will consider such variables as the clients' degree of interest in attaining them, the clients' abilities, and the resources available to the clients. Lillian Ripple (Ripple & Alexander, 1956, pp. 38–56) and others have referred to these variables as motivation, capacity, and opportunity. Goals may be established in any of these areas— that is, legitimate objectives of client-worker activity might be to increase the client's motivation, abilities, or opportunities in defined areas. Regardless of the areas in which goals are established, consideration is given to the variables of motivation, capacity, and opportunity with a view toward establishing goals with a reasonable chance of attainment.

In recapitulation, goal setting in social work is a joint client-worker process in which mutually agreeable solutions to the problems are developed. These solutions or goals should be specific enough to be measurable and proximate enough to be attainable.

PLANNING FOR INTERVENTION

Given a mutually determined definition of the problem and its solution, the task of planning a way to move from problem to solution remains. The development of an intervention plan consists of decisions, again jointly made by the client and you, as to the steps which will be taken to solve the problem, that is, reach the goals. The steps taken in making these decisions parallel those taken in defining the problem and arriving at goals. You will first discover from the client what steps the client would like to take to reach the solution and what steps the client expects you to take. You must also establish your expectation of the client as well as what you expect to do to accomplish the goals, and, again, any differences in these expectations are to be negotiated and resolved.

Systems theory suggests to us that there are many routes to any goal. A common temptation (and error) in social work is to offer an intervention plan without considering alternatives with your client. Consider, for example, this excerpt from the Stover case included in the next chapter (Reading 11–1).

> Mrs. Stover brought up a further problem in connection with running the household. She is now getting more interested in housework and cooking. She is realizing how little she knows about cooking. She attempted to cook a goose for the family, but due to improper cleaning of the goose beforehand, spoiled it. She claims the food that she knows how to prepare is plain and unattractive and she feels she is lacking in knowledge of skill in cooking. The children do some complaining about the food; George recently pointing out that other children he knows get more variety than he does. I agreed to bring a recipe file for Mrs. Stover containing a large variety of recipes and some instructions on food preparation and menus.

There appears to be agreement that the problem is Mrs. Stover's lack of knowledge about cooking and the goal is for her to be able to prepare more attractive, and a greater variety of, meals. This worker then rather precipitiously develops the intervention plan of providing Mrs. Stover with a recipe file. A better process would have been to involve Mrs. Stove in discussion of steps which might be taken to enable her to improve her cooking skills. Perhaps she knows of friends, relatives, or neighbors from whom she could request recipes. Perhaps she could make use of the public library. Perhaps there is a county extension agency or some other organization to provide the services of a home economist to Mrs. Stover.

Offering an intervention plan too quickly creates two problems. First, this action may deny clients' opportunities to work toward solutions to their own problems thus denying clients' involvement in their own problem-solving effort. Second, premature assumption of responsibility for an intervention plan may blind us to client strengths which may be brought to bear on the problem and toward accomplishing the goal. With our orientation toward problems, we may at times fail to identify and mobilize the many strengths of our clients. To compensate for this danger, we suggest that development of an intervention plan include a systematic review of client strengths. You may find it useful to develop a list of client strengths and then to carefully consider with your client how these might be used to accomplish each goal. Strengths, of course, include the personal resources of the client as well as the resources of family, friends, neighbors, and ethnic groups to which the client is attached. Possible strengths for Mrs. Stover might have included statements like, "talks at least once a week with her mother," "occasionally has coffee with the neighbor," and "has visited the local public library."

The service contract, including the intervention plan, may be oral or in written form. Reducing agreements to written form may appear a bit cumbersome but we think it has some clear advantages. A written contract will help us identify ambiguities and improve the specificity of the plan. It will reduce the likelihood of misunderstanding and aid evaluation. Putting plans in written form will also be an aid to learning, especially in your early work at developing contracting skills. Figure 10–1 provides an illustration of what a written plan might have looked like for the Stover case. Note that this example also contains time limits for completion of the various tasks. Setting time limits helps maintain progress toward completion of goals and provides a basis for client-worker evaluation of their own progress.

Date: February 3 (Monday)
Problem: Mrs. Stover is unable to prepare an attractive variety of meals for her family.
Goal: Mrs. Stover will develop ability to prepare additional dishes. *Specific goal:* By February 10, Mrs. Stover will be able to prepare and serve her family a dish she has not previously prepared.

Available
resources:

Mrs. Stover	*Agency and worker*
1. Has weekly contacts with mother.	1. Has recipe file available.
2. Shares coffee with neighbor.	2. May request services from a home economist.
3. Has been to public library.	

Plan:
1. On February 4, Mrs. Stover will invite her neighbor to coffee and make inquiries about recipes for preparation of low-cost main dishes.
2. By February 5, Mrs. Stover will call at the public library and check cookbooks for two or three new recipes.
3. Worker will contact the county extension agency to determine if: (1) the service of a home economist consultant is available; and, (2) if the agency has recipes available for low-cost main dishes.
4. Friday, February 7, worker will telephone Mrs. Stover to review progress on securing recipes. We expect that Mrs. Stover will be able to select a recipe to try over the weekend.
5. February 8 or 9, Mrs. Stover will prepare a new dish for her family.
6. February 10, Mrs. Stover and worker will meet at 10 A.M. to evaluate the plan and to decide about next steps.

FIGURE 10–1: Example of service contract for Stover case

Think back now to the Troy case mentioned in the last section. Mrs. Troy and the worker had reached agreement on the goal of getting John out of the house but no intervention plan had been developed. Clearly there are several ways by which the worker and Mrs. Troy might proceed to accomplish this goal. Put yourself in the place of a worker and think a bit about possible intervention plans. What are the possible strengths that you might explore with Mrs. Troy? What are alternative ways to accomplish the goal? To help sharpen your thinking, we encourage you to draft out a possible service contract. To keep this from becoming a one-sided effort, which of course is quite inconsistent with thrust of social work practice we have been presenting, you might team up with a classmate with one of you playing the role of Mrs. Stover and the other, the social worker. If you do this, and we hope you will, pay particular attention to your ability to identify and focus the client's strengths in relation to the goal (remember all people have strengths) and your ability to explore with your client alternative courses of action that might be used to reach the goal. Also recall the material we presented in Chapter 7 on communication; first, you secure your client's views and then you may share from your experience when this is related to the problem at hand.

When negotiating interventive means, you are responsible for considering four important limitations on worker activity. These limitations are time, skill, ethics, and agency function. No worker can make unlimited time available to a specific client. Time constraints on you must always be considered in entering into a service contract. You cannot responsibly commit yourself to activities which extend beyond the time they have available; conversely, a client can reasonably expect you to do what you say you will do. Consider this incident. A skilled, generally capable worker recently placed a 14-year-old boy in a foster home. The worker was cognizant of the fact that the youth might have some initial adjustment problems and indicated that they would be visiting together on a weekly basis to talk about any placement problems. This worker, however, was employed in a large agency with a heavy case load and, because of the pressure of time, was unable to visit with the boy until four weeks after the placement was made. By this time, the boy had justifiably become disillusioned and angry with the worker and rejected efforts by the worker to become jointly involved in problems that were occurring in the placement. The youth ran away and eventually became institutionalized. Had this worker made a realistic contract—to see the boy once a month instead of once a week—the client and worker might have been able to maintain their communication and to engage in more effective problem solving. A common misconception held by many new workers is to confuse the intensity of service with the quality of service. Poor quality service is provided when workers make commitments that they cannot meet, and, conversely, frequent contacts between worker and client do not necessarily imply high-quality service. The Stover case reprinted in the next chapter is a good example of quality, but largely nonintensive, service. What is required is the ability to plan your time so you will not make commitments beyond the time available.

Second, you should not enter into service contracts that call for activity on your part which exceeds your skills. It is a professional's responsibility to be aware of strengths and weaknesses and not to enter into agreements that exceed one's ability. When a client requires a specialized skill which you do not possess, such as marriage counseling or bargaining with a large bureaucracy, then the negotiated intervention plan will include involvement of an expert or specialist to assist with this aspect of the intervention. In our discussion of a service plan for the Stover case, the worker was checking about the service of a home economist. We do not expect most social workers to be experts in cooking or nutrition. Should Mrs. Stover and this worker decide these skills and knowledge are necessary, then the worker would assist Mrs. Stover by arranging for a specialist to assist with this aspect of the work. Recall, also, that in "The House on Sixth Street" which you read in Chapter 1, the worker and clients made use of specialists in city planning and law.

Third, you will avoid involvement in intervention plans that commit you to unethical behavior. An obvious example would be the securing of economic resources through illegal means. An economic crisis might be alleviated by a burglary, but it would obviously not be appropriate for you to participate in planning or executing such an action. You will also be unlikely to agree to participate in a plan which involves exploitation of others or furthers patterns of racial or ethnic discrimination.

Murdach notes in the article included with Chapter 8 (Reading 8–3) that the organizational context provides a limitation on problem solving. We have discussed this issue in Chapter 5 but we note here again that agency function provides a further limitation for worker-client contracts. This unfortunate limitation derives from the tendency to organize social services in this country around functional specializations rather than to provide generic services (Wilensky & Lebeaux, 1965, pp. 233–282). You can, however, seek to define agency functions broadly, consider the possibility of requesting exceptions to agency limitations, and work within your agency to secure a broader definition of its functions. Some ways to accomplish such changes are discussed further in Chapter 5. But as long as agencies have community sanctioned functions you must be cognizant of this source of limitation on the commitments you make to clients.

In the next chapter, worker activity to move from problem to solution will be discussed in terms of interventive roles. Before these roles are utilized, however, a service contract must be developed to specify the nature of both worker and client activity. As in the definition of the problem and of goals, any differences between worker and client in these areas are to be resolved prior to implementing any intervention plan.

WORKER/CLIENT DIFFERENCES OF VIEW

Murdach, in the article included with Chapter 8 (Reading 8–3), and Seabury, in the article included with this chapter (Reading 10–2), both note the likelihood of worker/client conflict in the problem-solving model. We expect this will be a regular occurrence and is likely to be quite desirable. When human beings come together, we expect that perceptions, thinking, and world views may be quite different. We also expect, however, that in the process of work and sharing together both growth and change will occur.

You should not expect to find your relationship with clients free from differences and conflict. Rather, hope for commitment and expect to work hard to find a common ground from which you and the client can move. Murdach offers some helpful suggestions in this regard; you may find it helpful to go back and review this material (Reading 8–3).

We agree with Seabury's view that efforts to avoid conflict are counterproductive and result in corrupt contracts in which the worker and client are working toward different goals:

> Corrupt contracting will not take place if, during the early stages of contract negotiation, all parties conscientiously and explicitly state their thoughts, desires, and expectations. In many cases, however, corrupt contracting does occur because one or several parties fear that being explicit may cause conflict; this conflict will not be resolvable and therefore service will terminate even before it has begun. This logic is faulty, of course. Deceit serves no purpose, and honesty is always the appropriate strategy. There is nothing inherently bad about conflict, and attempts to avoid it during contracting are naive. Working out differences early in the contract process means that each party has a better chance to do some true negotiating of contract terms. In fact, when contracting goes too smoothly, it is often a sign that one side is selling out to the other.
>
> An important principle in contracting is that conflict should not be avoided, differences must be teased out and negotiated, and the sooner differences are revealed the better it is for the service process. Even if the conflict cannot be resolved and no contract is agreed upon at the beginning, at least no time or energy will have been wasted on the corrupt contract. An agreement between worker and client not to pursue service because of recognized differences or conflict is, in fact, a good contract.

We think that much of your work with clients will involve negotiation and efforts to find a common ground regarding the problem definition, goals, and intervention plan. Often you will need to persevere in the effort. The worker who comes back to a supervisor after a single contact with the client and announces that he or she is closing the case because an agreement could not be reached, does not understand the nature of negotiation. Contrast this with the efforts of the worker in the Stover case (Reading 11–1) who spent several weeks and much effort to maintain contact with Mrs. Stover before a common goal could be developed.

RECAPITULATION

The service contract is a plan jointly negotiated by the worker and client which defines the problem-for-work, specifies the goals, and provides an intervention plan designed to move from the problem to the goals. The process of negotiating the service contract culminates in a commitment on the part of both worker and client to implement the plan. Once negotiated, the service contract is binding on both the worker and the client and is not subject to unilateral changes—changes can, of course, be jointly negotiated.

Four principles have been implied in this chapter which can be stated explicitly.

1.   Joint negotiation of the service contract connotes precisely what the words imply. The contract involves input from both worker and client. We indicated disagreement with the concept of diagnosis because of a lack of client input in the decision making that leads to a diagnosis. But frequently workers also err in the other direction—in failing to provide their own input for fear that it might hamper the client's right to self-determination. A worker's professional judgment, experience, and background are all sources of knowledge and information that should be available to the client in joint decision making. The key is to arrive at a service contract which is truly joint—one representing the best merged collective judgment of both you and client.

2.   The worker is expected to bring a broad knowledge base to the process of arriving at a service contract. This base will include knowledge of human functioning, of the social environment, and of the interaction of the two. The worker will be expected to draw on the sources of knowledge identified in Chapters 2 and 4 and to apply those sources to the specific client situation under consideration.

3.   The focus of the service contract and the intervention plan will be consistent with the concept of social functioning. This means that the worker and the client must be alert to the widest possible range of goals and interventive approaches. The target of change may be the client, forces in the environment, or the interaction of the two. Although no worker can be expected to master all change strategies, you can be expected to be aware of the broad repertoire of change strategies available to the profession and to be able to select jointly with the client the strategy most appropriate for the client and, if you cannot provide that service, to be able to locate it elsewhere in the community. Methodological specialties may be necessary, but they cannot be justified as blinders.

4.   The development of a service contract is a cognitive process involving thinking, reasoning, and decision making. Feelings are important, but planning should be done on a rational basis. The planning may, of course, involve plans to deal with feelings. Further, rational planning precedes interventive activities. This does not deny the spiral concept of practice which has been identified in earlier chapters and which will be made more explicit in Chapter 15 on evaluation. But whenever you are engaged in interventive efforts, those efforts should be based on a deliberate, rational service contract negotiated with the client.

A LOOK FORWARD

This chapter has described a crucial component of social work processes. The joint client-worker development of a rational plan that defines the problem-to-be-worked, establishes objectives, and specifies an interventive plan is a prerequisite to intervention. In Chapters 11 and 12 the discussion centers on worker intervention activities. Evaluation is discussed in Chapter 15; evaluation is an essential part of work with clients which shows social work processes to be more dynamic and continuous than has been implied in the linear description of the problem-solving process.

The two articles included with this chapter develop additional ideas regarding contracting. The article by Anthony Maluccio and Wilma Marlow offers a useful discussion of contracting which provides for explicit client involvement and can be used with client systems of various sizes. Brett Seabury offers some very helpful comments about avoiding corrupt contracts but also offers notes of caution. He warns of situations in which contracting may be impossible, problematic, or even counterindicated. His examples of impossible situations—when clients desire goals which are impossible to achieve or seek goals or desire means which are inconsistent with the values of the social worker—seem to us to illustrate situations in which a common ground has not been found. We find both articles stimulating and hope they contribute to your thinking about this central, we would say essential, element of social work practice.

Reading 10-1

*The Case for the Contract**

Anthony N. Maluccio and Wilma D. Marlow

The contract is among the basic concepts utilized in social work that are inadequately formulated and incompletely incorporated into practice. There has been little effort to clarify its theoretical foundations, delineate its uses, and test its validity. It has been mentioned frequently in the literature as a pact, working agreement, or therapeutic alliance. Referring to clients' and workers' hidden or double agendas, writers have spoken of covert, implicit, and "corrupt" contracts. However, a review of the literature reveals no comprehensive discussion or formulation of a conceptual framework.

Lack of clarity about the contract, its limited development, and its restricted application to social work practice may be factors that contribute to the clash of worker-client perspectives, client discontinuance, and the frustrations that clients and practitioners encounter when they try to work together meaningfully and productively.

This article attempts to stimulate interest in examining, conceptualizing, and using the contract. To do so seems timely in light of the current critical reassessment of roles and methods of social work, changing attitudes toward consumers of services, and new ideas about the helping process.

A pertinent aspect of changing theory and practice is the growing conviction that the client or consumer has an important role in formulating policy and planning program. One model of service delivery proposes that the consumer have a choice in what services are provided, some control over how and by whom services are delivered, and a real opportunity to participate (Meenaghan & Mascari, 1971). It is logical to extend the concept of "maximum feasible participation" in policy-making and planning to direct and personal interaction between social workers and clients, whether the latter are individuals, families, groups, or communities. Clearly conceived and properly used, the contract can serve as an important tool in helping consumers achieve such participation. It might also become an integral feature of the emerging "life model" of practice, which stresses optimum utilization of the client's own life processes and resources.

THE CONTRACT IN THEORY

The origins of the term *contract* as applied to social work are not clear. Writings on group work in the 1940s and 1950s include implicit references to the contract, as seen in Coyle's discussion (1948, pp. 88–90) of the "grouping process" in group formation and Trecker's formulation (1955, pp. 23–35) of the group worker's role as "agent of the agency." In 1951, Hamilton (pp. 148–180) alluded to the contract, without naming it, in discussing the application process. She saw as fundamental the worker's responsibility to make explicit the conditions and the term of help available from the agency. In 1957, Perlman (p. 149) made one of the earliest references to the contract as a pact.

Major social work scholars gave the contract some attention at a 1969 symposium on comparative theoretical approaches to case-work. In formulating the problem-solving model, Perlman (1970, p. 155) indicated that people establish a contract when they decide to use the agency and the worker for help in coping with their problem, thus moving from the role of applicant to that of client. Rapoport (1970, p. 291) identified the contract as a significant step in crisis intervention, noting that by the end of the initial interview goals should be agreed upon and mutual expectations spelled out between client and worker (1970, p. 291). Scherz (1970, p. 237) defined the contract in family therapy as a "conscious agreement between family and worker to work in certain ways toward certain goals." In the behavior modification approach to casework, Thomas (1970, p. 196), saw validity in an explicit contract and spoke of written as well as verbal agreements. In Smalley's discussion (1970, pp. 98–121) of the functional orientation, the concept of the contract is implicit in her use of time phases related to beginnings and endings of treatment; according to her, a time-limited contract may be fulfilled, renewed, or renegotiated. In the psychosocial approach, Hollis (1970, p. 45) acknowledged that the term was widely used and that practitioners increasingly preferred to state explicitly the end results of the initial phase of casework before engaging in treatment.

Although these scholars represent differing philosophical and theoretical orientations to casework, the concept of the contract appears compatible to practice within the separate frameworks. In particular, they convey a sense that clients are emerging from their traditional roles as passive recipients of service to active self-determining people who cooperate with the worker more and more consciously and deliberately in the helping process.

The literature on community organization has given limited consideration to using the contract for reaching a working agreement between the worker and the

client. On the contrary, goals and roles have usually been analyzed from the perspective of the worker (Rothman, 1964).

In group work, Schwartz has stressed that the establishment of a "working agreement" is a fundamental task of the worker. According to his formulation, the rules and boundaries within which worker and group members operate determine their working contract and influence their functions. The contract essentially corroborates the convergence of the worker's and the client's tasks and "provides the framework for the work that follows, and for understanding when the work is in process, when it is being evaded, and when it is finished" (Schwartz, 1971, p. 8). Other writers on group work concur with Klein (1970, p. 51) that the contract is "an agreement about expectations of the reciprocal roles of the worker, the members, and the sanctioning agency."

Thus the contract has received some attention in social work, but its elaboration has remained at a limited and simplistic level. In general, theorists have tended to equate it with the working agreement that concludes the initial, exploratory phase of social work intervention. Similarly, writing from a psychoanalytic perspective, Menninger (1964, pp. 15–42) has argued that the contract can be used to clarify the mutual expectations of patient and therapist, reach agreement about appropriate expectations, and spell out the conditions of their cooperation.

The underlying thesis of this article is that the contract has potential value as an ongoing, integral part of the total process of intervention. Further elaborated in theory and deliberately applied to practice, the contract can crystallize and exploit to the maximum degree the process and substance of the work in which practitioner and client engage. The use of a contract can help facilitate worker-client interaction, establish mutual concerns, clarify the purposes and conditions of giving and receiving service, delineate roles and tasks, order priorities, allocate time and plan constructively for attaining goals, and assess progress on an ongoing basis.

THE CONTRACT DEFINED

Although it is a much talked about term among practitioners, the contract has not been clearly defined in social work. The legal profession has attempted to define it since the contract constitutes the basic framework for a substantial portion of legal practice. Although the diversity of elements and perspectives inherent in the concept has prevented the devising of an entirely satisfactory or universally accepted legal definition, one that is widely quoted is the following: "A contract is a promise, or set of promises, for breach of which the law gives a remedy, or the performance of which the law in some way recognizes as a duty" (Williston, 1957, sec. 1). Except for the idea that the contract is a legally enforceable agreement, the elements in this definition are pertinent to social work, especially the notions of mutual promise and duty between the contracting parties.

Webster's *Third New International Dictionary* defines contract as a "covenant," a "compact," or "an agreement between two or more persons to do or forbear something." These words suggest mutuality, participation, and action.

For the purposes of social work, the contract may be defined as *the explicit agreement between the worker and the client concerning the target problems, the goals, and the strategies of social work intervention, and the roles and tasks of the participants.* Its major features are mutual agreement, differential participation in the intervention process, reciprocal accountability, and explicitness. In practice these features are closely interrelated.

MUTUAL AGREEMENT

Mutual agreement between worker and client concerning the nature and course of interaction is an essential component of practice. Many writers agree that mutuality must be established at the outset and maintained throughout contact (Gottlieb & Stanley, 1967). Agreed upon goals, roles, and tasks are fundamental in determining the direction, quality, and content of intervention.

Research studies and clinical reports substantiate the fact that difficulties and frustrations result from a lack of agreement between client and worker or from a clash in their perspectives (Mayer & Timms, 1969; Silverman, 1970). Worker and client may be operating under different assumptions—especially if varying expectations were not adequately discussed—and thus may not always have the same perceptions of what constitutes help or treatment.

Practitioners often find it difficult to establish mutuality in the crucial areas of goals and methods. Some resort to a double agenda, in which workers formulate for themselves a set of goals that are different from the ones they share with the client. Greenhill (1972, p. 509) reports that he used to set up therapeutic contracts with families that included agreement to work together in relation to a child's problems. Covertly, however, he would intend to work with the entire family's problems, a plan he divulged to family members only after they became involved in treatment. Greenhill was referring to experiences of his early years in family therapy, but seasoned practitioners sometimes superimpose their own goals on those of clients. Beall (1972) warns of the dangers of a "corrupt contract," when the client's stated goals conceal implicit and opposing ones. Operating with such a contract in a clinical setting can reinforce neurotic aims rather than promote therapeutic change.

Deliberately considering the contract in each situation can help reduce clashes in perspectives, clarify vague or confusing expectations, and enhance the possibility of meaningful cooperation in working toward realistic, mutually agreed upon goals. Client and worker must share their understanding of assistance sought and to be given. Without this, the concept of mutuality is hollow. Furthermore, exploring and spelling out mutual expectations can help client and worker stay attuned to the reality of the current situation and can reduce the tendency toward regressive transference and countertransference (Rapoport, 1970, p. 291).

As Schubert (1971, p. 7) notes, the contract is useful at an early stage for formulating certain basic understandings in order to determine whether the client has come to the appropriate agency, whether the service needed can be offered, who is going to give it, what if any are the conditions for providing the service, whether any eligibility requirements are to be met, what fees if any will be charged, and what other persons may be involved. Client-worker agreement about these important aspects can be a powerful force in mobilizing energies for a common cause.

In group work, Garvin (1969) describes research showing that agreement between the worker and the group member on their expectations of each other is positively correlated with the worker's performance and with progress in group problem-solving. Similarly, Brown's intensive investigation (1971, pp. 99–115) of early group sessions reveals that developing mutual expectations as early as possible is significantly related to later group functioning and member satisfaction. The findings of studies of small groups support these results. They indicate that members' agreement about a group's goals and means of achieving goals leads to improved motiva-

tion and functioning (Raven, 1960 & Rietsema).

In community organization, the contract might be applied, for example, when worker and clients are preparing to negotiate and bargain with their change target. It is essential that group and worker agree on proposed demands, lines of attack and defense, potential concessions, allocation of roles, and choice of strategies. Discussing and adopting an explicit contract that establishes consensus on these points could clarify planning and give the participants a sense of solidarity.

DIFFERENTIAL PARTICIPATION

Practice theory has focused primarily on the worker's functions and responsibilities, devoting limited attention to the client's role and tasks. The respective contributions of client and worker to social work intervention have not been clear, especially with regard to the client's perception of the worker's role.

The concept of the contract not only emphasizes the importance of *joint* participation in the common enterprise of intervention but also highlights the *differential* participation of client and worker. As Grosser (1969, p. 19) points out: "A view of worker and client as having different but equal roles is not simply a theoretical concept; it is a practical prerequisite to operationalizing such innovations as worker partisanship and client participation."

The worker has a major responsibility to delineate with the clients the unique aspects of their participation at each phase of the process. The contract is a tool for such delineation, and for both client and worker it is an ongoing reminder of their collaborative relationship and different responsibilities.

Efforts have been made recently to differentiate between tasks and roles of clients and workers. Reid (1972, p. 67) formulates the worker's primary roles as follows: to define with the client the most effective course of action in resolving the problem and to direct intervention toward helping the client achieve the necessary tasks.

Vattano (1972) speaks of the "power-to-the-people movement" as a challenge to traditional practice through its emphasis on self-help groups. Members of the groups provide direct services to each other, while social workers function as peers, catalysts, researchers, or theory builders.

Zweig (1969, pp. 26–27) depicts the role of the legislative ombudsman, in which the worker is a bridge between the client and the elected representative. The worker may motivate applicants initially seeking help with their own needs to deal with policies affecting them. The client then becomes an activist rather than a target for intervention. As an administrative ombudsman, the worker expedites the bureaucratic processes involved in service delivery and guides the client or consumer through them.

Studt (1968, pp. 42–46) proposes a basic framework for social work practice that incorporates the following features: (1) The client is the "primary worker in task accomplishment" and carries the major responsibility. (2) The social worker has a secondary responsibility "to provide the conditions necessary for the client's work on a task." (3) No one but clients can perform the tasks that their own life-stage and specific situation require.

Implementation of the contract is founded on the belief that clients ultimately must exercise their rights to self-determination. When clients assume the responsibility for choosing among alternatives and use their own skills and resources to deal with their agreed upon tasks, this enhances their motivation, investment, and self-esteem. The client's meaningful participation in making decisions and formulating the contract is based on the recognition that people are spontaneously active, seeking, and striving beings. The insights of ego psychology highlight the fact that the active, seeking person who carries out personal commitments and who takes responsibility for one's actions experiences a sense of achievement and competence in performing this role. In the process of developing the contract, the worker can discover ways to enhance the client's sense of identity and independence by offering opportunities for choice, self-determination, and self-mastery.

The possibilities inherent in this approach are increasingly evident as social workers move away from the traditional view of service planned for and provided to the client by a worker who is more knowledgeable, objective, or expert. For example, involuntary clients in a correctional setting were able to engage in meaningful decision-making once the opportunity was offered and stimulated (Studt, 1968, pp. 42–46). In a child-care agency an innovative focus on decision-making was constructive, time saving, and advantageous to adoptive applicants and children awaiting placement. Applicants were given the responsibility for deciding, on the basis of photographs shown them early in the adoption process, which child they wished to adopt—a decision traditionally made by the worker at the end of the evaluation process (Shireman & Watson, 1972).

RECIPROCAL ACCOUNTABILITY

The client and the worker are accountable to each other in various ways, each having an ongoing responsibility to fulfill agreed upon tasks and work toward agreed upon goals. The contract can help make both parties as aware as possible of their reciprocal obligations.

The client's responsibility must be emphasized. Insufficient attention to it may partially account for the limited involvement of some clients in the helping process or their withdrawal from it. In child welfare settings, this lack may help explain parents' psychological abandonment of placed children. A contractual alliance with parents of emotionally disturbed children in residential treatment would clarify their accountability, bring into sharp focus their role in treatment, and make the concept of a family-centered program more dynamic.

Beck (1969) points out that "professionals tend to be accountable to other professionals rather than to the consumers of their services." In social work, accountability has typically been related to the worker's role as agency representative and to the agency's mandate from the community. It has been stressed that being within an agency complicates the worker's efforts to be accountable to the client. But this view is changing. Patti and Resnick (1972, p. 57) argue that, although organizational expectations realistically constrain workers, "professionals can work within an agency and retain their primary commitment to client welfare."

The increased responsiveness to clients that is inherent in the use of a contract helps shift the worker's sanction away from the community toward the client. This is especially evident in situations of advocacy, in which a worker's engagement by the client system is established through a contractual alliance featuring mutual accountability.

EXPLICITNESS

Explicitness is the quality of being specific, clear, and open. Although its importance is obvious, the degree to which it is implemented in practice is debatable.

Frequent double agendas, implicit or covert contracts, and discrepant client-worker expectations have been mentioned. Often in casework practice the client sees one problem or target of intervention, while the worker sees another—usually related to a subtle or underlying difficulty. The client is interested in obtaining tangible help with an immediate need but "the caseworker doggedly pursues a different agenda, namely, one of trying to get the client to see the 'real' problem underneath it all" (Reid, 1972, p. 61).

The contract offers an opportunity to spell out as openly as possible the conditions, expectations, and responsibilities inherent in the planned interaction. Therefore a fundamental task of the worker is to clarify contractual expectations and obligations. Research on brief treatment has corroborated the value of formulating explicit and specific goals (Reid & Shyne, 1969). To the traditional exhortation to "start where the client is" might be added: "and let the client know where you are, and where you are going." An explicit contract can help give the client more ethical protection than is possible through unspoken or covert contracts.

The client must be explicit as well as the worker. Emphasis on explicitness in contract formulation would actively engage the client's cognitive functions and resources—and such engagement has proved valuable in crisis intervention. In addition, the worker would be more likely to be continually "tuned in" to the needs that the client feels. In his formulation of task-centered casework, Reid (Reid & Shyne, 1969, p. 61) suggests requiring "that clients themselves explicitly acknowledge the problem and express a willingness to work on it." The rationale is derived from evidence that in social work practice the client's perception of the situation is more important than the worker's view of the problem.

APPLICATION TO PRACTICE

Little experimentation with the contract has been reported in social work practice. At present, its formal use appears to be atypical or innovative rather than regularly incorporated in practice.

Child welfare workers have used a written contract to delineate mutual responsibilities between agency and foster or adoptive parents. However, no published account of their experiences is available.

In a mental health setting oriented toward transactional analysis, the concept has been used with patients briefly hospitalized following a crisis. The initial interview was focused on establishing "a clear verbal contract" that outlined specific problem areas, appropriate goals, and methods of treatment. The contract alleviated "many of the fears of the patient concerning "strange" things that might happen on a mental health unit. The patient knows exactly the nature of the therapeutic contract and realizes that the patient will have an important role to play in determining the course of treatment" (Brechenser, 1972).

A family agency serving an upper-middle-class community reports successful experiences with the written contract as an integral tool in treatment. Goals and tasks of participants, schedules for contacts, fees and methods of payment, options for renegotiation, and other pertinent factors are spelled out. The agency has noted a clearer understanding of treatment goals by client and worker, wiser use of time, and greater awareness of time limits. There was also a growing realization that the contract could be used in setting boundaries for the treatment relationship (Lessor & Lutkus, 1971).

The written contract has considerable merit with clients requesting help with interpersonal problems. Whether it can be validly adapted to others needs further testing.

FLEXIBILITY

To be a truly dynamic tool, the contract should be used flexibly. If either the worker or the client rigidly adheres to its conditions—which they may tend to do with a written contract—this limits its usefulness, especially when the client's or the worker's perception of the situation changes. The binding restrictions and penalties of legal contracts would be inapplicable to social work and would constrain the creativity and spontaneity of both client and worker.

To guard against rigidity, there should be provisions for reformulation or renegotiation by mutual consent as circumstances change, problems are resolved, or the focus of intervention alters. Changes in the contract should be based on open discussion by all parties and should not be subverted by client, worker or agency. Emphasis should remain on the client's perceived need rather than on the worker's interpretation. When a short-term contract expires, a client wishing further help over a protracted period could ask to negotiate a new one.

Questions may be raised in connection with flexibility. how meaningful is a contract if its breach does not incur some form of punishment, loss, or suffering? Will contract modifications be discussed so frequently that the real issue of working on the problem is delayed or avoided? Will the contract become the goal of client-worker interaction rather than the means of attaining the client's goals? These are potential problems to explore.

As social workers formulate contracts more actively and deliberately, they should also consider the legal ramifications. In our society a contractual agreement may be legally binding even when it is not written. Will partial or total failure to fulfill its terms therefore render the practitioner or agency subject to law suits or malpractice claims?

It is evident that much more must be done in exploring the use of the contract, putting it into operation, and developing principles of action applicable to different client populations in diverse settings. Implementation must take into account the client's characteristics, capacities, and motivation. For example, using the contract with children or with involuntary clients may require special modifications of techniques and procedures.

In effect, the contract can be more or less complex, depending on how ready and able the client is to engage in formulating and utilizing it. In many situations, the client's social, physical, or psychological characteristics limit the ability to formulate an explicit contractual agreement. It is important to experiment with use of the contract to test its validity, identify its limitations, and derive specific operational guidelines.

POTENTIAL OF THE CONTRACT

The contract can contribute significantly to the positive outcome of social work services. In particular, it can bring focus and meaning to inherent values and principles implicit in social work practice and make the contracting parties more aware of them. If workers have a conviction about the contract and implement it fully, they can help the client participate more actively in dealing with the client's own situation. In so doing, they can affirm the client's preeminent role in social work intervention.

The contract has the potential to serve as an active instrument for engaging worker and client in meaningful and productive interaction for the following reasons:

It is derived from their shared experience in exploring a situation and reaching agreement on goals and tasks.

It gives both practitioner and client a sense of immediate involvement and meaningful participation and signifies their mutual commitment and readiness to assume responsibility.

It provides a base line for periodically reviewing accomplishments, assessing progress, and examining the conditions of agreement.

At its present stage, the contract does not offer specific propositions and principles of action for use with different types of consumers of social services. But there is sufficient evidence from clinical practice and from research on crisis intervention, brief treatment, and client discontinuance to suggest that the use of some form of contract in social work merits systematic experiment and research in various settings, with varying periods of service, and with clients having different characteristics and problems.

This article aims to contribute to developing cumulative theory for practice in this important area. Analysis of practice experiences and research findings could refine the concept further, formulate its specific components and operational guidelines, validate its incorporation into the helping process, and explore its efficacy in enhancing the client's perception and use of social services.

Reading 10-2

Negotiating Sound Contracts with Clients*

Brett A. Seabury

Contracting is gaining acceptance as a basic procedure in social work practice (Collins, 1977, pp. 13–15; Croxton, 1974, pp. 169–185; Estes & Henry, 1976, pp. 611–622; Maluccio & Marlow, 1974, pp. 28–35; Seabury, 1976, pp. 16–21; Stein, Gambril Wiltse, 1974, pp. 20–25). Research on contract approaches to service is appearing in the literature which seems to consider contracting from a favorable perspective (Hosch, 1973; Perlman, 1968, pp. 172–176; Reid, 1975; pp. 3–9; Rhodes, 1977, pp. 125–140; Seabury, 1976; Stein & Gambril, 1977, pp. 502–513). There is a great need in the practice and educational communities, however, to analyze contract procedures critically in order to improve existing formulations. The purpose of this article is to define contracting more precisely by identifying those circumstances in which contracting fails. The article is not intended to disparage contracting. On the contrary, it proposes to identify weaknesses and to present alternate or refined procedures that will prevent contract failures and therefore strengthen contracting.

There are four practice situations in which contract procedures may be employed (Maluccio & Marlow, 1974, pp. 28–37). (1) There is the *ideal* condition in which client and worker establish an explicit, mutual, flexible, and realistic working agreement on all the major treatment terms. Client and worker have much in common such as values and perception of service processes, the agency resources match the client's need, and both the client and worker are able to articulate, understand, and pursue the work in the service process. (2) In an *impossible* situation contracting cannot be employed because there is little or no chance that any significant agreement between worker and client can be achieved, as with an acutely psychotic patient. Examples of such situations will be discussed briefly in this article. (3) Contracting is *problematic* if a marginal working agreement is reached after much difficulty, following which client and worker often fail to achieve positive results in the service process. The article will focus on this type situation. (4) Finally there are those circumstances in which contracting is *contraindicated* and engaging in contract procedures would be detrimental to clients. In a severe crisis that requires the worker to act quickly based on professional expertise, for example, it would be detrimental to take the time to involve the client in a mutual decision making process. Contraindicated circumstances are not discussed in the social work literature and will not be the focus of this article, but they should be considered in future discussion and research on contract procedures.

IDENTIFYING IMPOSSIBLE CONTRACTING SITUATIONS

Contracting in social work is a mutual decision-making process. It is primarily a verbal enterprise, whether spoken or written, and requires that all parties to the agreement be rational and competent at

* This is a slightly adapted version of a paper presented at the National Association of Social Workers' Fifth Biennial Professional Symposium in San Diego, California, in November 1977. Reprinted with the permission of the American Public Welfare Association from *Public Welfare* 37:2. Copyright 1979 by the American Public Welfare Association.

the time of negotiation. Extremely disturbed, retarded, brain damaged, intoxicated, or emotionally excited persons as well as young children are not able to engage in a shared decision-making process. Verbal information is distorted by such clients and a worker would find it extremely frustrating and ultimately impossible to reach agreement on contract terms in a normal face-to-face interview.

In trying to contract with difficult clients, it is usually necessary to expand the client system to include other family members or significant others. Through this expansion of the unit of attention, it is possible for the worker to develop a viable contract with other more receptive or responsible persons. In some cases it is also possible to contract directly with these clients through the use of nonverbal communication techniques and procedures such as play, fantasy, art, visual aids, and projective exercises.[1] Because social workers, for the most part, have not been educated and trained in these techniques, it is not possible at present for them to contract with severely disturbed clients.

The client sometimes seeks goals that are beyond the resources of the agency or service network, beyond the expertise or power of the worker, or beyond her or his capability to achieve. When clients suggest desirable goals that are impossible to achieve, the social worker is placed in a contractual dilemma. It may be possible to help a client trim down (i.e., do some reality testing on) and unrealistic goal that involves the client's capabilities. The worker, for example, can help a physically handicapped client recognize the limitations that a handicap might impose in various occupations. It is impossible, however, for the worker to enter an agreement with a client to provide a resource that does

not exist. Even an agreement that just "seeks" such resources is very frustrating for both worker and client. Unless both client and worker have the time, energy, and commitment to pursue resource development on the community level, goals that require an unavailable resource are unattainable.

Contracting also is impossible when a client is seeking an objective or is willing to employ a means or procedure that violates the values of the social worker. It is impossible, for instance, for a Catholic caseworker in a Catholic agency to provide abortion counseling to a client who wishes to terminate a pregnancy. It would even be impossible for this same caseworker to refer this client to an agency that does provide abortion counseling. Though it may be desirable to remain nonjudgmental in a social work relationship, there are limits to how objective a worker can remain.

When there is a fundamental clash in values, the worker must acknowledge this conflict and responsibly inform the client. But even informing the client of one's values is insufficient because there is no room for negotiation as discussion continues. There is no opportunity for the client to shape the worker's values—nor would it be expected that the client could or should do this. Instead, the worker's values are imposed on the contract terms. Unless the client clearly understands and agrees to this imposition, there is no way for worker and client to work together toward mutual decisions. The most equitable resolution would be to terminate the arrangement so that the client can seek a more flexible service arrangement with another worker.

The reason for discussing *impossible* situations is not to suggest that service is in fact impossible in these instances, but instead to indicate that a contract form of service is not viable. Workers who try to contract under such conditions are

---

[1] Discussion of these procedures is beyond the scope of this paper.

wasting effort and time that might be better spent on other approaches. As contract procedures are refined and newer techniques are developed, it may well be that some of these impossible situations will lend themselves to contracting.

PROBLEMATIC SITUATIONS LIMIT POSSIBILITIES OF SUCCESS

This section will not attempt an exhaustive discussion of problematic contract situations, but instead will focus on three common occurrences in contracting. These particular instances are also being presented in order to point up alternatives that can be employed to prevent contract failure.

A common problem in contracting is the "corrupt" contract of which there are several kinds and in which both worker and client may engage (Beall, 1972, pp. 77–81). Either worker or client—or both—may enter into a contract agreement with hidden agendas (Rhodes, 1977, p. 131). This means that a party proceeds with contracting without explicitly stating an objective or negotiating that objective. For example, a worker may agree to work on a particular problem identified by a client, all the time hoping that at some point the service process will move to some underlying problem that the worker perceives. Because of their different perceptions, each party may experience some confusion. Frustration may result when an unspoken objective is not met. In fact, parties may work at cross purposes and the contract is bound to fail.

Another kind of corrupt contract occurs when there are several persons in the client system and/or several persons in the worker system. A corrupt contract results when agreements are kept from some parties and when agreements with one party may in fact conflict with hidden agreements with another party. For example, a corrupt contract that is employed by workers to get a reluctant married couple to seek service is to negotiate individually with each spouse, claiming that the reason for seeing them together is to help the other spouse with his or her problem. Each spouse proceeds believing the problem belongs to the other, when in fact the worker sees that both have the problem. This type of corrupt contract can also occur between professionals working as a team when they make agreements that are in conflict with each other.

The problem with a corrupt contract is that sooner or later the hidden agenda or contradictions in agreements are discovered, and the service process is ruined when the parties realize they have been deceived. At the point of discovery, service is usually terminated and what little progress may have been made is destroyed.

Corrupt contracting will not take place if during the early stages of contract negotiation all parties conscientiously and explicitly state their thoughts, desires, and expectations. In many cases, however, corrupt contracting does occur because one or several parties fear that being explicit may cause conflict; this conflict will not be resolvable and therefore service will terminate even before it has begun. This logic is faulty, of course. Deceit serves no purpose, and honesty always is the appropriate strategy (Chaiklin, 1974, pp. 266–274). There is nothing inherently bad about conflict, and attempts to avoid it during contracting are naive. Working out differences early in the contract process means that each party has a better chance to do some true negotiating of contract terms. In fact, when contracting goes too smoothly, it is often a sign that one side is selling out to the other.

An important principle in contracting is that conflict should not be avoided, differences must be teased out and negotiated, and the sooner differences are revealed the better it is for the service process. Even if a conflict cannot be resolved and no contract is agreed upon in the beginning, at least no time and energy will have been wasted on a corrupt contract. An agreement between worker and client not to pursue service because of recognized differences or conflict is, in fact, a good contract.

The involuntary client. Another difficult contracting problem results when service is imposed on an involuntary client. Clients bring with them varying degrees of reluctance when entering the service network. In fact all clients, even those seeking help, enter the role of being helped with some reluctance because of the way that role is structured in our society. (Ask any client whether it is more blessed to give than to receive.) Some involuntary clients are reluctant to engage in the helping process because they resent being coerced by an outside authority (courts, parents, school principals), and some clients refuse to acknowledge the problems that others (authorities) claim they have. Some clients do not view the service they are being pushed into as a way of getting help nor the worker as a legitimate helper even though they do acknowledge problems; others are simply terrified of an unknown process that is being thrust upon them. These are some of the basic types of resistance that involuntary clients may bring, and some clients possess all of them (e.g., a juvenile offender referred for a court-ordered service).

Contracting with clients who have been "captured" is difficult because the essence of contracting is client self-determination. Contracting involves full client participation and true mutuality in negotiating, yet involuntary clients want no part of the process. They simply want out: how then can a worker establish some parity and mutuality in a process that involves clients against their will?

The fact is that contracting with captured clients—such as prisoners and abusive parents—is different from contracting with clients who voluntarily seek services for problems that they acknowledge. Many captured clients are not only involved in negotiating a contract with their workers, but they are also ensnared in legal arrangements such as court orders. It is crucial that the terms of the legal arrangements be distinguished from the stipulations of the social work contract. The worker must distinguish between the conditions of service imposed by the courts and those conditions that can be negotiated with the worker. The client must understand that court-ordered stipulations are not negotiable with the worker while other areas of the service process are open to negotiation. For example, an abusive parent must know what it means when the court orders removal of a child and must understand the conditions under which a child may be returned by the court. The parent must also know which areas of the services—target problems, goals, procedures—can be negotiated with the worker so that progress can be demonstrated and a favorable report returned to the court. As the client distinguishes between court-ordered provisions and those that can be decided mutually with the worker, she or he will begin to discern those areas of the service process in which he or she can again claim self-determination.

Another procedure that can be used with involuntary clients is to help them to recognize areas of disagreement. This technique is useful in helping clients reach an agreement with the worker when there appears to be little common ground between worker and client. Basically the procedure can be employed to clarify any treatment term such as target problem, goal, or procedure. The client and worker make a list of their individual perspectives on a given term. In a court-ordered procedure, the worker would also list the court's perspective on a given term. When these lists are compared, it is possible to identify the disagreements about particular terms. It is also possible that some areas of agreement might emerge and that this consensus would form the initial basis of a contract. Even if there are no areas of agreement between the client and worker, the client can be encouraged to see that there is no agreement and that this disparity in perspectives might be a place to start.

Parents	Social worker	Court
Biased judge	Child abuse	Child abuse
Loss of child	Poor impulse control	Alcoholism
Nosy neighbors	Marital problems	
Debts	Financial problems	

TABLE 1: Differing perspectives on target problems in a child abuse case

Table 1 demonstrates how abusive parents who have lost custody of their child might be engaged in searching for a target problem. It shows that there are many areas of disagreement on this one term, and that by making these various perspectives explicit and discussing the disparities among client, worker, and court, the negotiation process is begun. It is clear in this example that "child abuse" is a court term and that, whether parents admit abuse or not, the term will remain a problem area. The table also shows that there is potential common ground between worker and parents in the area of financial problems. But even if this commonality does not exist, the very process of pointing out discrepancies will have some impact on the parents as they come to see that others perceive them differently. It will also give them a chance to react to these perceptions. This very process, though it may be charged with emotion and conflict, is a negotiation process and is vital to effective contracting.

In contracting with captive or coerced clients, it must be emphasized that explicitness and honesty are very important. It is also crucial that the worker engage continuously in the clarification of perspectives, positions, and the differences between terms mandated by a higher authority and those open to negotiation between worker and client.

Secondary contracting presents its own set of problems. A secondary contract is an ancillary agreement that supports or facilitates the primary contract between worker and client. Such agreements may be negotiated with significant others in the client's life (friends, relatives), with significant others in the service network (other professional helpers), or between individuals in a multiperson client system (family or formed group). Social work is boundary work, and there are probably few situations in which a client and worker are autonomously engaged in a single contract (Hearn, 1974, pp. 364–366). In fact, a social worker sometimes will expend more energy in secondary contracting, that is, making arrangements with others in behalf of the client, than in direct contact with the client (Bush, 1977, pp. 48–50, 84–88). In such cases, it will be obvious to skilled practitioners that a primary contract with a client depends on a good, collaborative network of secondary contracts.

Three basic problems can arise in secondary contracting. A difficulty often occurs with beginning practitioners who are unfamiliar with the service network and how many significant others are involved in the client's life. Ignorance of the connections that a client has with significant others may jeopardize the primary contract that a worker negotiates with a client. It also may produce a situation in which significant sources of influence or help are ignored, and in some cases it may lead to contradictory contracting between the client and various service providers (Hoffman & Long, 1969, pp. 211–234).

Corrupt contracts can be a problem in secondary contracting. Secondary as well as primary contracts are corruptible. Hidden agendas and contracting in secret with one person at cross purposes to an agreement with another can take place in secondary contracting. For example, workers may not collaborate openly or honestly with other service providers, or a worker may try to deceive another service provider in order to get a client accepted for service. As in primary contracts, corrupt contracting may work to get arrangements started, but when the corruption emerges and the discrepancies are recognized, the entire network of agreements can collapse.

A common consequence of this kind of failure is that these other service providers may later engage in sabotage behavior in retaliation for having been deceived. Sabotage is a major problem in secondary contracting, and it is the most harmful to clients. When relationships between service providers or relationships between client and significant others is so poor that sabotage occurs, it is practically impossible for the primary contract between client and worker to succeed.

The worker must be able to recognize a lack of information about significant others, corruption, and sabotage in secondary contracting because all three problems can result in the destruction of the primary contract or can prevent the goals of the primary contract from being achieved. In order to avoid or minimize these problems, a worker must gain a fairly comprehensive knowledge of significant others in the client's life as well as significant other service providers who might be engaged or who already are in contact with the client. Both worker and client must discuss these various significant others and assess their potential value or detriment to the terms of the primary contract.

Secondary contracts should be purposefully planned with the client's knowledge and negotiated with the client's participation whenever possible. It may sometimes be necessary to collaborate and involve others, while in other circumstances it might be necessary to deliberately bypass or find ways to neutralize the influence of significant others. Whatever decisions are made and carried out, the client should participate in the planning and negotiating of secondary contracts. The unfortunate reality of secondary contracting is that it is often time consuming, is more difficult to arrange than primary contracts with clients, and is not nearly as rewarding as direct work with the client. For these reasons secondary contracting is often avoided, and an important aspect of social work practice is not adequately addressed.

THE USE OF PROFESSIONAL EXPERTISE IN CONTRACTING

This article has presented some major reasons for the failure of contracts and has also proposed some procedures and strategies to solve these problems. It has not attempted a comprehensive treatment of all situations in which contracts fail, and for the most part has not analyzed those circumstances in which contract failure is mainly attributable to worker behavior and skill.

In closing, it should be pointed out that the worker sometimes is solely responsible for contract failure. Some workers are unable to contract successfully with clients because of their own perceptions of "competent" practice. They may perceive themselves as having a special, professional expertise; they do not see any merit in "bargaining" with a client (after all, the client may be the one who caused all the trouble in the first place); and they are unable to establish any parity in the decision-making process. These workers are confused about how to use their expertise and tend to impose their "professional judgment" on the client. These workers believe that the right contract term is the one that their professional judgment dictates and that, until the client "sees the light" and stops resisting the worker's suggestions, service will not proceed productively.

On the contrary, a worker who adopts a contract approach does not use professional expertise in this manner. Instead, the worker who contracts successfully uses his or her professional skill to facilitate the client's participation in the contract process. The worker's professional judgment is shared, but the content of a decision is not as important as the client's participation in that decision. A worker who contracts successfully worries less about exactly which problem is identified or which procedure is adopted, and is concerned more about who initiates an idea or suggestion, what responsiilities are shared or divided in carrying out a decision, and how involved the client is in the whole process.

Client self-determination is a critical practice ethic, and contract procedures are designed to embody this important principle.

References

Bartlett, Harriet M. *The common base of social work practice.* New York: National Association of Social Workers, 1970.

Beall, Lynette. The corrupt contract: Problems in conjoint therapy with parents and children. *American Journal of Orthopsychiatry* January 1972, *42*, 77–81.

Brechenser, Bertram M. Community control: A distraction, not an answer. *Social Work,* October 1969, *14*, 14–20.

Brechenser, Donn M. Brief psychotherapy using transactional analysis. *Social Casework,* March 1972, *53*, 173–176.

Brown, Leonard N. Social worker's verbal acts and the development of mutual expectations with beginning client groups. Ph.D. dissertation, Columbia University School of Social Work, 1971.

Bush, Sherida. A family-help program that really works. *Psychology Today.* May 1977, 48–50; 84–88.

Chaiklin, Harris. Honesty in casework treatment. *Social Welfare Forum* 1973, New York: Columbia University Press, 1974.

Collins, John. The contractual approach to social work intervention. *Social Work Today,* February 1977, *8*, 13–15.

Coyle, Grace L. *Group work with American youth.* New York: Harper & Row, 1948.

Croxton, Tom A. The therapeutic contract in social treatment. In Paul Glasser et al. (Eds.), *Individual change through small groups.* New York: Free Press, 1974.

Estes, Richard, & Henry, Sue. The therapeutic contract in work with groups: A formal analysis. *Social Service Review,* December 1976, *50*, 611–622.

Garvin, Charles. Complementarity of role expectations in groups: The member-worker contract. In *Social Work Practice:* Proceedings (Ninety-Sixth Annual Meeting). New York: Columbia University Press, 1969.

Gottlieb, Werner, & Stanley, Joe H. Mutual goals and goal-setting in casework. *Social Casework,* October 1967, *48*, 471–477.

Greenhill, Laurence.   Making it. In Andrew Ferber, Marilyn Mendolsohn, & Augustus Napier (Eds.), *The book of family therapy*. New York: Science House, 1972.

Grosser, Charles F.   Changing theory and changing practice. *Social Casework*, January 1969, *50*, 16–21.

Hamilton, Gordon.   *Theory and practice of social casework* (2d ed.). New York: Columbia University Press, 1951.

Hearn, Gordon.   General systems theory and social work. In Francis Turner (Ed.), *Social work treatment*. New York: Free Press, 1974.

Hoffman, Lynn, & Long, Lawrence.   A systems dilemma. *Family Process*, September 1969, 211–234.

Hollis, Florence.   The psycho-social approach to the practice of casework. In Robert W. Roberts & Robert H. Nee (Eds.), *Theories of social casework*. Chicago: University of Chicago Press, 1970.

Hosch, Dorothea.   *Use of the contract approach in public social services*. Los Angeles: Regional Research Institute in Social Welfare, University of Southern California, 1973.

Klein, Alan F.   *Social work through group process*. Albany: State University of New York at Albany, 1970.

Lerner, Barbara.   *Therapy in the ghetto*. Baltimore: Johns Hopkins Press, 1972.

Lessor, Richard, & Lutkus, Anita.   Two techniques for the social work practitioner. *Social Work*, January 1971, *16*, 5–6.

Maluccio, Anthony N., & Marlow, Wilma D.   The case for the contract. *Social Work*, January 1974, *19*, 28–37.

Mayer, John E., & Timms, Noel.   Clash in perspective between worker and client. *Social Casework*, January 1969, *50*, 32–40.

Mayer, John E., & Timms, Noel.   *The client speaks: Working class impressions of casework*. New York: Atherton Press, 1972.

Meenaghan, Thomas M., & Mascari, Michael.   Consumer choice consumer control in service delivery. *Social Work*, October 1971, *16*, 50–57.

Menninger, Karl.   *Theory of psychoanalytic treatment*. New York: Harper & Row, 1964.

Patti, Rino J., & Resnick, Herman.   Changing the agency from within. *Social Work*, July 1972, *17*, 48–57.

Perlman, Helen Harris.   *Social casework: A problem-solving process*. Chicago: University of Chicago Press, 1957.

Perlman, Helen Harris.   Persona: Social role and personality. Chicago: University of Chicago Press, 1968, pp. 172–176.

Perlman, Helen Harris.   The problem-solving model in social casework. In Robert W. Roberts, & Robert H. Nee (Eds.), *Theories of social casework*. Chicago: University of Chicago Press, 1970, pp. 129–181.

Polansky, Norman A., Borgman, Robert D., & de Saix, Christine.   *Roots of futility*. San Francisco: Jossey-Bass, 1972.

Rapoport, Lydia.   Crisis intervention as a mode of brief treatment. In Robert W. Roberts, & Robert Nee (Eds.), *Theories of social casework*. Chicago: University of Chicago Press, 1970.

Raven, Bertram H., & Rietsema, Jan.   The effects of varied clarity of group goal and group path upon the individual and his relationship to his group. In Dorwin

Cartwright, & Alvin Zander (Eds.), *Group dynamics: Research and theory.* Evanston, Ill.: Row, Peterson & Co., 1960.

Reid, William J.   Target problems, time limits, task structure. *Journal of Education for Social Work,* Spring 1972, *8,* 58–68.

Reid, William J.   A test of a task-centered approach. *Social Work,* January 1975, *20,* 3–9.

Reid, William J., & Shyne, Ann W.   *Brief and extended casework.* New York: Columbia University Press, 1969.

Rhodes, Sonya.   Contract negotiation in the initial stage of casework service. *Social Service Review,* March 1977, *57,* 125–140.

Ripple, Lillian, & Alexander, Ernestina.   Motivation, capacity and opportunity as related to casework service: Nature of the client's problem. *Social Service Review,* March 1956, *30,* 38–54.

Rothman, Jack.   An analysis of goals and roles in community organization practice. *Social Work,* April 1964, *9,* 24–31.

Scherz, Frances H.   Theory and practice of family therapy. In Robert W. Roberts, & Robert Nee (Eds.), *Theories of social casework.* Chicago: University of Chicago Press, 1970.

Schubert, Margret.   *Interviewing in social work practice.* New York: Council on Social Work Education, 1971.

Schwartz, William.   On the case of groups in social work practice. In William Schwartz & Serapio R. Zalba (Eds.), *The practice of group work.* New York: Columbia University Press, 1971.

Seabury, Brett.   The contract: Uses, abuses, and limitations. *Social Work,* January 1976, *21,* 16–21.

Seabury, Brett.   The poor need services, too. Paper delivered at the 103rd Annual Forum of the National Conference on Social Welfare, Washington, D.C., June 16, 1976.

Shireman, Joan, & Watson, Kenneth W.   Adoption of real children. *Social Work,* July 1972, *17,* 29–39.

Silverman, Phyllis R.   A re-examination of the intake procedure. *Social Casework,* December 1970, 625–634.

Smalley, Ruth E.   General characteristics of the functional approach: A brief statement of the origins of this approach. In Robert W. Roberts, & Robert H. Nee (Eds.), *Theories of social casework.* Chicago: University of Chicago Press, 1970.

Stein, Theodore, & Gambrill, Eileen.   Facilitating decision making in foster care: The Alameda project. *Social Service Review,* September 1977, *51,* 502–513.

Stein, Theodore, Gambrill, Eileen, & Wiltse, Kermit.   Foster care: Use of contracts. *Public Welfare,* Fall 1974, *32,* 20–25.

Studt, Elliot.   Social work therapy and implications for the practice of methods. *Social Work Education Reporter,* June 1968, *16,* 22–24.

Thomas, Edwin J.   Behavioral modification and casework. In Robert W. Roberts & Robert Nee (Eds.), *Theories of social casework.* Chicago: University of Chicago Press, 1970.

Trecker, Harleigh B.   *Social group work—Principles and practices* (rev. ed.). New York: Whiteside, 1955.

Vattano, Anthony.   Power to the people: Self-help groups. *Social Work,* July 1972, *17,* 7–15.

Wilensky, Harold L., & Lebeaux, Charles N.   *Industrial society and social welfare.* New York: Russell Sage Foundation, 1958.

Williston, Samuel.   *A treatise on the law of contract* (3d ed.). Mt. Kisco, N.Y.: Baker, Voorhis, 1957.

Zweig, Franklin.   The social worker as legislative ombudsman. *Social Work,* January 1969, *14,* 25–33.

Part Three

Tools for Doing
the Decided

Chapter 11
Interventive Roles:
Implementation of the Plan

Chapter 12
Interventive Methods:
Implementation of Roles

Chapter 13
Teamwork for
Social Work Practice

Chapter 14
Endings in Social Work

Chapter 15
Evaluation

Chapter 16
Conclusions

Chapter 11

Interventive Roles:

Implementation of the Plan

The service contract has been negotiated and agreement achieved, and client and you are now prepared for the hard business of intervention. You are confronted with the challenge of actually using abilities, skills, knowledge, and contacts to assist the client in reaching mutually defined goals. Your activity in this area will be discussed in terms of interventive roles. The concept of interventive roles will be defined, and five such roles—broker, enabler, teacher, mediator, and advocate—will be discussed. Some general considerations about conceptualizing intervention in terms of roles will be noted, and finally a configuration of interventive roles appropriate for the generalist worker will be set forth.

THE CONCEPT OF INTERVENTIVE ROLES

A more explicit statement of the concept of interventive roles can be developed by examining meanings for the terms *intervention* and *roles*. Throughout this book we have been using the term *intervention* in a more restricted and narrower sense than do many of our social work colleagues. This usage of the term refers to activities undertaken subsequent to the development of a service contract and directed toward the achievement of goals specified in the service contract. Some social work scholars and practitioners use the term in a more global way to refer to all social work activities, including data collection and contracting (or assessment) functions as well as change efforts. This concept is often expressed by the statement that "treatment begins at the opening of the first contact between worker and client."

We do agree with the notion that patterns of relationship and communication begin to develop when the client and the practitioner first meet, but we wish to differentiate the exploration of problem and goals and data collection on the part of both worker and client from goal-directed, jointly planned change efforts. We prefer a more limited use of the concept of intervention: (1) to maintain the focus on activities directed toward goal attainment and (2) to minimize the danger of making the concept of contracting secondary, or perhaps losing it, in efforts to produce change. We see danger in the desire of workers, and sometimes clients, to produce change quickly and move ahead with change activities without first developing a contract which clearly specifies the problem, objectives, and interventive activities to be utilized in accomplishing the objectives. Maintaining a narrower definition of intervention and also stressing the functions of data collection and contracting will tend to keep these three aspects of social work processes in a more balanced perspective. Intervention in our usage therefore refers to social work processes which occur after a service contract has been developed and are directed specifically to the achievement of goals specified in that contract.

Role is a global concept with wide usage in the sociological, social-psychological, and psychological literature; but the term is not always used consistently (Biddle & Thomas, 1966, pp. 1–50; Gross, Masson, & McEachern, 1958, pp. 21–47; Neiman & Hughes, 1959). For our purposes, role refers to the behaviors expected of a person. Role enactment will refer to the actual translation of these expectations into behavior. In a global sense people's roles, can be conceived as comprising the total universe of expectations which they hold for their own behaviors as well as the expectations of their behaviors which are held by others. But our focus is much narrower; interventive roles will refer to the behavior by means of which both client— an individual, a family, a group, or a community—and the worker expect the worker to help accomplish goals specified in the service contract. One of the central points stressed in Chapter 10 was that intervention, along with all other social work processes, is undertaken jointly by the worker and the client. This chapter, however, focuses specifically on the worker's interventive activity.

Discussion will center on five interventive roles—those of social broker, enabler, teacher, mediator, and advocate. This is not an exhaustive listing. Some authors conceptualize the social worker's roles differently or add other roles. Charles Grosser's article discusses four roles in relation to community development programs (see Reading 11–2). The literature also includes references to such additional roles as therapist (Briar, 1967, pp. 19–33), encourager (Biddle & Biddle, 1965, p. 82), ombudsman (Payne, 1972), bargainer (Brager & Jorcin, 1969), and lobbyist (Mahaffey, 1972). Bisno's conceptualization (1969) of nine social work methods appears very similar to our concept of role. The interventive roles of broker, enabler, teacher, mediator, and advocate, however, provide a useful framework for the beginning social work practitioner to utilize in conceptualizing interventive activity. The value of the framework is further enhanced because, as is true of the concept of contract, it is not limited by the size of the relational system; workers can use it to conceptualize their interventive roles whether they are working with individuals, small groups, or larger systems.

Our limiting the definition of intervention and our organization of this chapter around the concept of interventive roles is not meant to deny or ignore the importance of specific change modalities.[1] Rather than attempt to catalog change modalities (many of which wax and wane as the culture and the profession emphasize different approaches), we chose to conceptualize intervention in a way which transcends specific modalities. The concept of interventive roles provides a framework for the analysis of interventive activity that is indepenent of the change modalities currently in vogue. Chapter 12 will discuss some change methods and processes which are generic to social work, useful for the beginning practitioner, and have withstood the test of time for social work.

THE ROLE OF SOCIAL BROKER

How will you enact the role of social broker? Analogies from other fields may be useful. How is the role of stockbroker enacted? Presumably a stockbroker assists clients in defining their resources and developing investment objectives; once this has been accomplished, brokers utilize their contacts and knowledge of the market to select stocks that will assist clients in reaching the defined investment objectives. How about the real estate broker? Again, Realtors®[2] assist clients in analyzing their resources and needs to define objectives in terms of the type of home the client wishes to buy. Then, using their knowledge of the available resources, Realtors will assist in matching the client's needs to the available housing. And so it is in the enactment of the social broker role. The worker serves as a linkage between the client and other community resources. Harold McPheeters and Robert Ryan (1971, p. 18), writing for the Southern Regional Education Board, note that the primary function of the broker is linkage, which they describe as follows:

> The primary objective is to steer people toward the existing services that can be of benefit to them. Its focus is on enabling or helping people to use the system and to negotiate its pathways. A further objective is to link elements of the service system with one another. The essential benefit of this objective is the physical hookup of the person with the source of help and the physical connection of elements of the service system with one another.

The activities of the worker are directed toward making connections between the client and the community in order to accomplish the objectives specified in the service contract. Serving as a social broker requires a broad knowledge of community resources as well as a knowledge of the operating procedures of agencies so that effective connections can be made.

What are some examples of social brokering? The worker who arranges

---

[1] For one such list of modalities with additional references, see Whittaker (1974, pp. 200–248). Other works which may be of use include Roberts and Nee (1970); Rothman (1968, pp. 16–47); Tropp (1968); and Whittaker (1970), pp. 308–322. See also articles under "Social Casework," "Social Group Work," "Social Planning and Community Organization" in the *Encyclopedia of Social Work* (New York: National Association of Social Workers, 1977.).

[2] The term Realtor® refers to a member of the National Association of Realtors who subscribe to the Code of Ethics.

for a client to receive marital counseling, for job placement of an unemployed person, or for improved housing functions as a social broker if these activities involve connecting the client to other resources. The worker who brings specialized resources to groups—outside experts who may provide valuable information to the groups—is functioning as a social broker in that the worker provides linkages between the client and additional community resources. Or, when working with a community group, the worker can assist the group by identifying sources of funding for programs or additional outside expertise that can assist the organization in moving toward defined goals. A common element in all these examples is making a referral in order to connect the client to another resource. Referral is a basic part of the enactment of the social broker role; and assisting a client to find and use a needed resource is frequently the most important service a worker can provide. The process of making a referral will be reintroduced in the concluding portions of this section as we discuss the integration of the roles of brokers, enabler, teacher, mediator, and advocate and will be further developed in Chapter 14.

THE ROLE OF ENABLER

You take an enabler role when intervention activities are directed toward assisting clients to find the coping strengths and resources within themselves to produce changes necessary for accomplishing objectives of the service contract. The major distinguishing element of the enabler role is that change occurs because of client efforts; the responsibility of the worker is to facilitate or enable the client's accomplishment of a defined change. A common misconception in discussing the enabler role is to see it only as a change that occurs within the client or in the client's pattern of relating to others or the environment. However, the enabler role can also be used to help the client find ways of altering the environment. The distinguishing feature of the enabler role is that the client effects the change with the worker performing a supporting or enabling function for the client.

The worker who assists a group of neighborhood residents in thinking through the need for a new day-care center, in identifying factors that must be considered in establishing the center, and in planning the steps that might be taken to provide day care will be serving as an enabler to a community group. The worker who helps a group to identify sources of internal conflict as well as influences that are blocking the group from moving toward its defined goals and then to discover ways of dealing with these difficulties is serving as an enabler in relation to the group. Likewise, the worker who assists a mother in identifying problems in her relationship with her child and in identifying and selecting alternative courses of action to improve that relationship is also serving as an enabler.

Encouraging verbalization, providing for ventilation of feelings, examining the pattern of relationships, offering encouragement and reassurance, and engaging in logical discussion and rational decision making are also avenues by which the enabler role might be enacted. Utilizing enabling as the interventive role will, of course, involve the worker primarily in contacts with the client system rather than with external systems. But, as noted, the client system can be an individual, a group, or a community.

THE ROLE OF TEACHER

Teaching is another interventive role available to you and your client. You may provide clients with new information necessary for coping with problem situations; assist clients in practicing new behaviors or skills, and may teach through modeling alternative behavior patterns. The worker who supplies low-income parents with shopping and nutritional information or who provides parents with information regarding child development for coping with difficult problems of children is performing a teacher role. The worker who uses role playing to transmit different ways of responding to the authority of teachers and principals to an adolescent may be performing a teaching role. Or a neighborhood group desiring to influence a city council to secure more frequent refuse services may need to be taught through role playing or other approaches how to make the request to the city council. And the worker who carefully checks out the meaning of words and phrases may, through modeling, teach clients how to communicate. The teaching role has many similarities to the enabling role inasmuch as it is directed primarily to strengthening clients' abilities to cope and change the problems in the situation they are experiencing. The role is sufficiently important and useful in social work, however, that it warrants separation from enabling. Although the two roles may tend to overlap we perceive the enabling role as involving the worker's effort to help clients mobilize existing resources within the client systems whereas the teaching role involves introducing additional resources into client systems.

Teaching is an important aspect of social work practice. Frequently you will provide clients with information necessary for decision making; in some situations information may be all that a client needs to accomplish the defined goals. Giving information must be clearly distinguished, however, from giving advice. "Giving information" implies supplying clients with data, input, or knowledge which clients are free to use or not to use on their own behalf; "giving advice" implies that the worker knows what is best for the client. Workers rarely give advice, but providing information is an important service they render to clients.

One of the five tasks of the social work function as identified by Schwartz is the contribution of data which may help the client cope with social reality and the problem which is being worked. Schwartz (1961, pp. 146–171) also, however, offers three important warnings: (1) workers must recognize that the information they offer is only a small part of the avilable social experience; (2) the information should be related to the problem that brings the client and worker together; and (3) opinions should be clearly labeled as opinions and not represented as facts. Virginia Satir (1964, pp. 97–100) clearly identifies workers' responsibilities to contribute from their own experiences in working with troubled families. She also notes a second major function of the educational component of counseling—modeling communication. In their approach to clients and to problem solving, workers provide a model of behavior which clients may emulate. Albert Bandura (1967), a behavioral psychotherapist, further describes the use of modeling as a device for teaching clients new behavior patterns. In the sense of providing information and of providing modeling behavior, teaching is an important interventive role.

THE ROLE OF MEDIATOR

Mediation involves efforts to resolve disputes that may exist between the client system and other persons or organizations. When resolving disputes is an important step in accomplishing the service goals, you will use the role of mediator. If a young person has been expelled from school and the service contract has the goal of getting the student back into school, then the social worker may need to serve as a mediator between the young person and the school authorities. Or, perhaps a neighborhood group wishes to secure a playground but is unable to mount sufficient political clout to do so because of rivalries with another neighborhood organization; such a situation may call for you to serve as a mediator between the two organizations. A worker serving in a battered women's shelter will undoubtedly find themselves mediating disputes between clients and the husbands. Likewise, in many child welfare settings, workers will find themselves mediating conflicts for the child between the parents regarding custody.

The mediator role will involve the social worker in efforts to assist their client and the other party to the dispute to find a common ground on which they might reach a resolution to the conflict. The worker will be called upon to engage in a series of actions directed toward constructive conflict resolution. There is burgeoning literature regarding conflict resolution (Deutsch, 1973; Jandt, 1973; Miller & Simons, 1974; Smith, 1971; Tedeschi et al., 1973; Walton, 1969).

The social worker in the role of mediator will use techniques to try to bring about a convergence of the perceived values of both parties to the conflict, help each party recognize the legitimacy of the others' interests, assist the parties in identifying their common interests in a successful outcome, avoid a situation in which issues of winning and losing are paramount, attempt to localize the conflict to specific issues, times, and places, break the conflict down to separate issues, and help parties identify that they have more at stake in continuing a relationship than the issue of the specific conflict. Persuasion and conciliation procedures will be used by the social work mediator.

We have identified the use of the mediator role in resolving disputes between the client system and external systems. Some of the same procedures may also be used to resolve disputes within the client system as may occur when a social worker is working with groups or families. While in one sense this is mediation, intraclient system dispute settlement can also be considered use of the enabling role inasmuch as resolving these intrasystem disputes is essential in enabling the client system to mobilize resources to move toward the accomplishment of the goals in the service contract. A debate as to when is mediation mediation and when is it enabling is not particularly useful although this issue illustrates that the boundaries separating the various interventive roles may not be fixed.

THE ROLE OF ADVOCATE

Advocacy is a concept which social work has borrowed from the legal profession. As advocate, the social worker becomes the speaker for the client by presenting and arguing the client's cause when this is necessary to accomplish the objectives of the contract. As Charles Grosser notes, the advocate in social work is not neutral but, like the advocate in law, is a partisan representative for the client (see Reading 11–2). The advocate will argue, debate, bargain, negotiate, and manipulate the environment on behalf of the client. Advocacy differs from mediation; in mediation the effort is to secure resolution to a dispute through give and take on both sides. In advocacy the effort is to win for the client; advocacy efforts are frequently directed toward securing benefits to which the client is legally entitled. Advocacy, like the other roles, can be used with client systems of various sizes.

Advocacy is becoming an increasingly popular role of social workers. Unlike the broker, enabler, teacher, and mediator roles, however, advocacy can be used without the direct involvement of the client. This creates a danger of falling to the temptation of serving as a client's representative without having a clear contract with the client to do so. Lawyers do not become the representatives for clients until clients have retained them and authorized them to extend this service; likewise, social workers should be sure they have an explicit contract with the client prior to engaging in advocacy activities.

ROLES ARE NOT FUNCTIONAL SPECIALIZATIONS

The discussion of social work intervention roles as discrete entities can lead to misconceptions. We do not recommend this conceptualization of interventive roles as a basis for functional specializations; we think it would be inappropriate for you to consider specializing as broker, enabler, teacher, mediator, or advocate. Any such specialization would limit your ability to be of service to a client. Rather than specializations, you will require abilities in all roles so that you and the client can select the most appropriate interventive role for each client situation. Each of the roles may be used in some client situations; this provides you and the client with alternative approaches to use in achieving goals. Consider, for example, the following excerpt from a report made by a social worker in a Head Start program. At the request of Mrs. B, the worker had come to her home to take an application to enroll the child in the program; the discussion described here occurred right after the application was completed.

The last question was "Why do you want your child in Head Start?" Mrs. B answered by saying that he had to learn to behave better and he needed to be around other children more than he was. Putting the form aside, I asked her what sort of problems she was having with Jimmy. He had been sitting at her side, surprisingly quiet for a three-year-old. In response to my question Mr. B told me about taking Jimmy to the child guidance center and what the doctor had told her. Apparently the doctor had tested Jimmy and then talked to Mrs. B. She had complained of his bad behavior and that she didn't know how to discipline him. Apparently the doctor told her that the problem might be hers and not Jimmy's. He said that she was lonely and insecure and maybe needed some guidance in handling her children. She discussed this freely and admitted that this might be true. I asked her whether she would like to have me come over to talk to her about ways to handle Jimmy. She said definitely yes, that she couldn't do a thing with him.

In this excerpt we note the development of a preliminary service contract. There appears to be agreement that Mrs. B is having difficulty in the way she is handling Jimmy, and the goal is for her to learn new ways of handling him. The interventive role by means of which the worker proposes to accomplish this is to talk with Mrs. B about her parenting of Jimmy. The worker is proposing the enabler and possibly the teacher role, but this is a situation where the roles of broker, mediator, and perhaps advocate might have been used. Had this worker explored the situation more completely with Mrs. B, the intervention plan might have been different. For example, further exploration with Mrs. B about what happened at the child guidance center, about her perceptions of what the doctor said, about her thinking and feelings concerning the experience, and about her willingness to return to the clinic might have led to an intervention plan involving the worker's serving as the linkage between Mrs. B and the clinic. Or, possibly, if there appeared to be a problem with the manner in which the clinic related to Mrs. B, the worker might have used a mediator role to solve these disputes or advocate role to serve as Mrs. B's representative at the clinic. Note that the objective remains the same—to help alter Mrs. B's way of relating to her son—but that the intervention plan to accomplish it may involve counseling with Mrs. B, serving as the linkage between Mrs. B and the clinic, or acting as Mrs. B's representative to the clinic. Consideration of all three alternatives is not likely to occur, however, unless the worker is both willing and able to use all three roles and is prepared to explore the client situation adequately before arriving at an intervention plan.

A second misconception that can grow out of a discussion of roles is that a worker will use only one role with each client. To the contrary, an intervention plan may combine elements of various roles. This can be illustrated by discussing the referral process—a major part of the social broker role. If a contract has been negotiated which calls for referral in order to achieve its objectives, three distinct subsequent steps are involved. These are preparation of the client, preparation of the referral organization, and follow-up. Preparation of the client includes discussion of what the referral will involve and what the referral agency expects and requires enabling and teaching roles. At this stage the worker is attempting to enable the client to make effective use of the referral agency. Ethel Panter (1966) offers a useful discussion of client preparation in terms of its ego-building impact on clients. Referral also generates feelings and reactions to loss on the part of both client and worker; this aspect of referral will be discussed further in Chapter 14. Enabling skills are used to help clients deal with their reactions to new agencies or workers and are necessary to successful completion of a referral.

Preparation of the referral agency involves the sharing of information about the client (with the client's full knowledge and usually with the client's consent). In some situations an agency may be reluctant to accept a referral and to provide a service which it is mandated to provide. When this happens, the worker may need to use either mediation or advocacy. After the actual referral has been made (that is after the client makes initial contact with the referral organization), the worker will follow up with both the client and the organization. Ideally, follow-up should be a part of the initial planning. As a result of follow-up, the worker may learn about client resistances to continuing the service or the referral organization's resistance to continuing with the client which may require use of enabling, teaching, mediation, and/or advocacy.

This model of social brokerage supplemented by the other roles to help a client secure services required is one which will frequently be used by the generalist social worker. A worker skilled at involving the client in developing a service contract and skilled at helping the client to find and utilize the resources necessary to meet the objectives of the contract will provide an extremely useful, largely unavailable, service to clients. Such an approach, however, requires the ability to use skills to humanize the ways in which services are delivered and to assist agencies in meeting their responsibilities to clients.

RECAPITULATION

Intervention has been defined as the social worker's activity directed toward achieving the objectives of a service contract. Five interventive roles have been discussed—social broker, enabler, teacher, mediator, and advocate. Any of these roles may be used to reach the same contract objectives: this provides client and worker with alternative approaches to intervention. In addition, the roles may be used in conjunction with one another to reach the same objectives. A focus on social brokerage in which enabling and teaching are used to assist the client in utilizing community resources, and mediation and advocacy are used to influence the way the resources are delivered to the client may be a major part of the services provided by the generalist social worker.

A LOOK FORWARD

The Stover case (Reading 11–1) illustrates use of all the interventive roles we discussed in work with a family. As you read this case, try to identify where the worker is a broker, enabler, teacher, mediator, and advocate. Also note the persistence and patience with which the worker engages Mrs. Stover. Many workers would have closed this case as one in which a problem could not be identified and a contract developed. This worker's willingness to remain available and to extend herself set the stage for a very helpful series of interventions. Although the contracts in this case are not as explicit as we recommend, clearly the worker has not moved ahead with interventive efforts until there is an agreement between worker and client. In the second reading (Reading 11–2) Charles Grosser discusses the application of interventive roles in community development programs.

In the next chapter we further develop some of these ideas in terms of helping clients maintain and develop confidence. Subsequent chapters discuss the issues of teamwork, termination, and evaluation.

Reading 11–1

Stover Family*

This family was referred to Family Service Agency from the child protection unit of the County Department of Public Welfare. The family at time of referral included Earl (husband and father) age 43, June (wife and mother) age 39, and three children. The two oldest children (George, age 12 and Larie, age 5) are June Stover's children by a previous marriage; Eileen, age 4, is of this marriage.

Mr. and Mrs. Stover had been active with 22 social agencies during the past 15 years. Mrs. Stover has had three marriages, the first after she became pregnant while in high school. She never lived with her first husband. Her second husband was a seriously developmentally disabled ward of the state. She had four children by him, three of whom were placed for adoption. She became involved with Mr. Stover while still married to her second husband, her first child by Mr. Stover arriving four months after their marriage. Mrs. Stover has shown other signs of instability and attempted suicide eight years ago.

Mr. Stover has been known to the Veterans Administration since his army discharge 10 years ago as a psychoneurotic. He is reportedly alcoholic. During contacts with Family Service three years ago, Mrs. Stover reported a number of episodes of physical abuse of herself and the children by Mr. Stover.

Since the present marriage there have been six complaints of neglect of the children. These have originated from Mrs. Stover's relatives, her former husband and his relatives, the school nurse, and the minister. The Child Protection Unit has

found insufficient evidence to proceed on these charges. Workers have found it difficult to work with Mrs. Stover; when contacted by a worker, she has been superficially cooperative but then avoids workers whenever possible. If an appointment is made in advance, she is never home. Family Service was reluctant to reopen the case as indications were that this woman can't use help. However, on plea from the Public Welfare Department, we decided to make another attempt to provide service.

Eileen Stover, the four-year-old, has had a condition believed to be muscular dystrophy. Previous workers have found Mrs. Stover "unrealistic" in her attitude toward this.

MARCH 20 TO APRIL 15

I have tried to contact the Stover family since Family Services accepted the case without any success. The Public Welfare worker says it is impossible to find Mrs. Stover at home if she knows who is coming and that Mrs. Stover is not to be trusted at all. She agrees to everything and does nothing. On April 13, I sent a note saying I would call on April 15; this time Mrs. Stover was home.

The Stovers have two rooms on the second floor of a large house the ground floor of which is in the process of being remodeled. Though I had previously sent a note advising of my plan to call, Mrs. Stover indicated that she couldn't talk to me since her husband was sleeping. Mrs. Stover is a woman of medium height, quite dirty in appearance with old slacks, a man's shirt hanging out, and bare feet. She is in her seventh month of pregnancy. I referred to

---

* A case study prepared for this text.

the previous contacts of Family Services and other agencies and explained we had decided to come to see Mrs. Stover as we knew about a number of problems which she might be continuing to have. I indicated that I was aware of her previous marital difficulties and the fact that she had temporarily left her husband last March, we knew that this resulted in difficulties for the family as a whole. Mrs. Stover's immediate reaction to this was to say that the situation has cleared up and she feels that the marital relationship is now OK. She did, however, appear responsive to interest in her problems and accepted an office interview for April 23. She intends to go to General Hospital in the morning of that date in connection with Eileen's muscular dystrophy, mentioning that she finds these trips to the hospital clinic very wearisome and dislikes the long waiting period. She thinks that Eileen is improving, however.

APRIL 23

Mrs. Stover did not keep appointment. On repeated calls in person I did not find her home. I made two appointments by telephone, neither of which she kept.

JUNE 24

Worker finally located Stover family when welfare called to say they had moved to Jonesville. On this date I found them both home. The present housing of the Stover family is a four-room shack raised about five feet from the ground on stilts beside the river. The home was flooded out in the floods two years ago. There is no foundation. The beams and supporting joists in the house were seriously weakened by the flood. The sides and interior partitions are still caked with dirt from the flood.

There is no sign of paint on the interior or exterior of the house and all in all the house is barely habitable. The front door has a drop of about four feet to the ground with only a crude ladder. The home has two bedrooms, a living room, and kitchen. These are adequate in size. Toilet facilities are of the outdoor variety. The shack was previously owned by an elderly bachelor who died. The house was in estate when the Stovers moved in, and they are paying $125 a month which may be applied toward a purchase price if the Stovers decide to stay.

Mr. and Mrs. Stover were both present. Mr. Stover is a small-built man neatly dressed, unshaven, and quiet. Mrs. Stover had made him aware of the fact that I had seen her earlier. He indicated in reply to my inquiry that he knew what it was about. He said that they were getting on well now outside of the fact that he is unemployed at the present. He said that the previous difficulties between himself and Mrs. Stover had been due largely to his alcoholic problem. Quarrels occurred usually when he was drinking. He would get angry and has a strong temper. He indicated that he thought welfare workers knew about these episodes in the past. He said that there have been no such happenings now for the last 10 months. I asked him to what did he attribute the change. He feels that difficulties arose because of his nervousness and unemployment. When he is nervous he starts drinking and they go round and round again. He said that he had been employed pretty steady during the last summer and fall, mostly on temporary labor jobs. The reason he can't get employment now as a carpenter is that the employer must insure him and in order to do this he must pass a physical examination. Thus, he finds himself confined largely to odd jobs and casual labor jobs. Another thing which bothers him about employment is the fact that he gets nervous working too close to too many people and that he dislikes working for other people. Small things bother him, he is easily irritated and has a quick temper. He would prefer to work for himself. He prefers country life to the city life. His ambition would be to get a small farm of his own where he could grow vegetables and so on for the market. The problem here is lack of capital and he doubts if he will get a chance to do this. Mr. Stover seemed to be feeling that they are getting on well at this time. They appear to present a united front to the world. Mrs. Stover neither nodded nor spoke in support of much of what her husband said. She also made a point of saying in his presence that she felt his drinking had improved.

JULY 17

Again, I failed to find the Stovers at home on visits I made by appointment. On a visit, July 15, it appeared as though they had moved again. Public Welfare Department had no new address. But, on this date, to my surprise Mrs. Stover came into the office. She was neatly dressed in a clean dress and had her hair done up; this was the first time I have seen her where she had obviously given some attention to her appearance. She seemed uneasy about the story she had to tell, and was trying to be placating. She said she had decided to leave her husband, because he has been drinking heavily, mostly wine, and has been beating her and the kids. She is afraid of what will happen. She can't talk to him because he is sensitive and trying to find out what is wrong merely antagonizes him more. He was on the wagon up to June but started drinking again. Mrs. Stover felt this had something to do with the troubles with housing and also that Mr. Stover had picked up with a neighbor man who drinks and they have been going out together. Mr. Stover she said "gets nervous and edgy." He orders the kids and Mrs. Stover around. Nothing she does pleases him. She is called all sorts of names by him when he gets drunk.

Mr. Stover pushed Eileen down in the yard because she got in his way.

Mrs. Stover hasn't notified Public Welfare of the change in circumstances. She is out of money and the baby is due shortly. I gave her a check for immediate needs and advised her to go immediately to the Welfare Board and get things straightened out with them. She was obviously attempting to charm me into helping her with this as she says the Welfare Board won't do anything for her. I agreed to talk to AFDC about her application there.

JULY 18 TO SEPTEMBER 1

Together Mrs. Stover and I made application for AFDC and arranged for care of the children during her confinement. I visited with her twice in the hospital. After the baby's birth Mrs. Stover moved in with her sister without notifying Public Welfare. I pointed out to her that this was why she had trouble with AFDC. She complained they couldn't trust her but this behavior certainly seemed to prove their point. Mrs. Stover said she was planning on moving again. She promised to notify AFDC and workers of her new address; this time she did.

SEPTEMBER 15. AFDC VISIT TO MRS. STOVER

Mrs. Stover, Eileen, and Peter, the baby, were at home; the two children played happily in the apartment. Eileen has come to know me. The apartment consists of three good-sized rooms in a row in an old apartment building. Mrs. Stover has the apartment neat and clean. She was dressed in slacks and noticeably cleaner and paying more attention to her appearance herself. Mrs. Stover mentioned she has bought winter clothes for the children. But, not all she needs yet. She showed me her AFDC budget with totals $345 per

month, of which $180 has to be signed over
by Mr. Stover from his disability pension.
Mr. Stover held up signing the documents
which would permit this to be done, but
instead gave Mrs. Stover some money
himself in September, and is offering to
do this every month. Mrs. Stover refused
this offer and reported the whole matter
to the VA office and they will contact him.
By law she feels he will be required to
sign the document since part of his disability pension is for his wife and children.
She feels Mr. Stover is still trying to spoil
her plans or to get back and live with her.
I raised the question of Mrs. Stover's plans
regarding the marriage. Mrs. Stover seems
quite sure at this point that she wants a
permanent separation. She would want a
rule that Mr. Stover would visit the children, but only when sober and could only
visit his two children; that is, Peter and
Eileen. Mrs. Stover again admitted ambivalent feelings about Mr. Stover. She has
always felt she needed him, couldn't get
along without him. She was ready to put
up with his drinking to some extent. She
was always afraid of being alone in the
world. On the other hand she regards him
as an intelligent man, who is not at all
hard to get along with when not drinking.
However, she now feels his drinking has
got to the point where he can't control it
and he won't admit it. She is risking her
own safety and realizes now that staying
with Mr. Stover may cost her the family.
The children could be harmed or it might
be necessary for an agency to place them.
At the present time Mrs. Stover doesn't
know where Mr. Stover is.

SEPTEMBER 22

I suggested that Mrs. Stover make her
need for a stove known to her AFDC
worker. She doesn't wish to tell them. I
pointed out that she could be cheating herself since it is my understanding that
AFDC can assist with a need of this kind.

I indicated that her reluctance to approach
them regarding this matter seemed to indicate that all was not yet well in her relationship to AFDC or her feeling about the
agency and asked what did she feel was
the trouble. Mrs. Stover again said she
doesn't trust them. You never know what
they'll do behind your back. Checks have
been held up when she didn't fully appreciate the reason. She has been given to
understand that she is a baby-sitter for
her own children. AFDC, she feels, are
paying her in that capacity and have given
her to understand that they may fire her
at any time. I brought up incidents indicating that there had been reasons for concern about the children in the past. I interpreted that is seemed to me that dangers
seemed to lie more in Mrs. Stover's disturbed marriages. That I have observed
that she has feeling for the children, she
has indicated clearly to me that she wants
to keep them, and it appears to me that
she is capable of caring for the children
as well. On the other hand, we had to consider the emotional effect on the children
as well as possible physical dangers in
the violence that had occurred in her marriages. Mrs. Stover again said she knows
I'm there because of the children. She indicated that she doesn't resent this from me
because she knows I'm out to support her
effort to get out of the tangled marital situation. She does resent this from AFDC
workers; however, on the other hand, she
recognizes that she has given AFDC workers reason for concern because of her
avoidance of them. I pointed out that Mrs.
Stover can improve and is improving her
relationship with AFDC by going out of
the way to inform them of changes and
needs. Mrs. Stover pointed out that lately
she has been phoning her AFDC worker
about every change and circumstance. We
decided that Mrs. Stover would explore
the possibility of getting the stove from
her landlord and failing this will think further about approaching AFDC. The diffi-

culty as she sees it, is that she doesn't want to ask for extra things for fear that she will be thought too demanding. She has considerable doubt about explanation that a request of this kind might even help to convince AFDC that she wants to meet the needs of her family.

Mrs. Stover says that she thinks perhaps they regard her as lacking in intelligence. I challenged this by pointing out that AFDC records actually show her to be of very superior intelligence (reported IQ is 142). Mrs. Stover indicated in response to this that she knows about her own high intelligence, recalls going with a sister to have IQ test. Mrs. Stover went with the sister mainly to reassure her, since the sister was unwilling to go on her own. Mrs. Stover knows that her IQ is 142 though she doesn't recall who told her this. I explained this placed her within the upper 1 percent of the population in intelligence whereupon Mrs. Stover demanded "Where has it got me?" She went on to say, "My life is a complete mess," pointing out her three unhappy marriages at 39, the fact that she has been all confused, recognizes she has brains but has never been able to use them properly. Here she mentions that she didn't do as well in school as she should have, always had her nose in a book, has always had a liking for books but cannot use this information in her own life. Her dream of what a proper job for her would be is that of a librarian. At times, she thinks that after five years or so when Peter is older and in school, she would like to have some kind of training for work, and her first choice would be library work. Her future plans she thinks are in terms of working and supporting her children and she stressed that she wants *no more men.*

Mrs. Stover further raised the question of how could she have made such a mess of her life. I then discussed the importance of feelings, that these are often as important as brains in determining what we do

and suggested that she has to work on the problem of how her experiences and life and her feelings have landed her where she is. She can still use books to acquire knowledge and training, but this is not enough by itself. Mrs. Stover seemed very taken by this and said she should think more about how she gets her life in such a mess. I agreed that this was a good time to do it while immediate pressures are less.

OCTOBER 13

Mrs. Stover volunteered that she is not feeling well, has been cranky lately. This she attributes to her current concern about her husband. At times she feels lonely and that she needs him. Most of the time, however, she is contented to stay apart from him, but gets restless and starts to move things around in the apartment. I commented that the children are cleaner and better clothed, that I had noticed her in several situations giving instructions to the children and that they seemed to obey her well and willingly. Mrs. Stover feels this is a gain she has made (particularly with regard to housework) since the change in her marital situation. Her housing is much improved over what she has had in the past, she also feels that here she has less on her mind, is less confused and knows what she is after, and there is more satisfaction for her in doing housework. She used to depend largely on her family for this sort of thing and there is a certain satisfaction for her in being able to make some decisions on her own or with the support of the agency without having to turn to her mother.

OCTOBER 20

Discussed with Mrs. Stover that Public Welfare had requested a conference so that we might work together better. I told her what material I would be sharing with them. I invited her comments but she was upset and angry as she was sure they wanted to discontinue AFDC.

OCTOBER 26. CONFERENCE WITH PUBLIC WELFARE

Public Welfare is concerned about Mrs. Stover's record of unstable marriages, the fact that they have often been unable to keep in touch with her or to keep up with her changes of address, is prepared to keep AFDC in cash, but is concerned about a possibility of repetition of her unsatisfactory mental experience and can she really keep Mr. Stover at arm's length? A review of developments in the case by Family Service indicates that Mrs. Stover is presently trying to free herself of concern regarding the situation she has got herself into. A decision was made because Mrs. Stover shows good feeling for the children and capacity to meet their needs, that AFDC will be continued in cash subject to further period of time which will be spent on working out Mrs. Stover's problems in relation to men and her marriages. Question of Mrs. Stover's distrust of AFDC was discussed in some detail, and it was felt that AFDC worker will try to create an opportunity to discuss this at some length with Mrs. Stover and thus reassure her of their interest and frankness with her.

NOVEMBER 3. VISIT TO MRS. STOVER BY APPOINTMENT

At this time Eileen and Peter were taking their regular afternoon sleep and the other children were in school. Mrs. Stover now seems to have the household well organized, and the children are regular in sleeping habits, and there is a marked improvement in the appearance of the apartment, with all floors swept and the dust off the furniture and the kitchen in good order. Mrs. Stover was dressed in blue denims for housework, but was neat and clean apparently paying more attention to her personal appearance. The interview began with a discussion of the meeting with Public Welfare. Much of this was a review of the reasons for concern of both our agency and AFDC about the children and Mrs. Stover's marital relationships. Mrs. Stover brought up that she had had considerable apprehension about the meeting, being concerned that there might be plans on the way to cancel her allowance again. Since the last interview, her AFDC worker visited and spent an hour with her. Mrs. Stover felt this interview helped a great deal, she is now more satisfied that AFDC is on her side and anxious to support her efforts to do better. She was greatly relieved, she indicated, by assurance that her allowance would not be arbitrarily cut off unless the AFDC worker was unaware of her whereabouts. Mrs. Stover brought up a further problem in connection with running the household. She is now getting more interested in housework and cooking. She is realizing how little she knows about cooking. She attempted to cook a goose for the family, but due to improper cleaning of the goose beforehand, spoiled it. She claims the food that she knows how to prepare is plain and unattractive and she feels she is lacking in knowledge of skill in cooking. The children do some complaining about the food. George recently pointing out that other children he knows get more variety than he does. It was arranged that I will bring a recipe file for Mrs. Stover containing a large variety of recipes and some instructions on food preparation and menus. Mrs. Stover is also interested in tackling her budget problems in a more organized fashion, and felt she would use budget envelopes from the agency in which she would keep track of her expenses for two months, to gain a more accurate idea of where her money is going.

NOVEMBER 10. VISIT TO MRS. STOVER BY APPOINTMENT

She indicated that since starting divorce action she has been feeling edgy and had trouble sleeping last night. Mrs. Stover feels she has a need to get married. After divorce it is "open season" and there is some danger that she would make another mistake, although she reiterates that she is through with men. Mrs. Stover feels that the first step is one of getting used to living without a man in the household. She feels that possibly she picks husbands of the kind she does because she feels sorry for them. Her father was a man who needed reforming. At this point I relayed information that I had from her family's record regarding her father, to the effect that he was a smooth dapper man, who was openly unfaithful to his wife, and had an alcoholic problem. Then Mrs. Stover said this described him to a T. She realizes also that her mother was trying to reform her father and perhaps Mrs. Stover is doing the same thing. She expressed considerable hostility toward her father, pointing out that it was all take on his part and no give. Her mother played right into this attitude since she rushed around doing everything for him without too much protest and never drew the line. Mrs. Stover has had the attitude too, that a man is someone who bosses you around and she feels she expects this from men and obeys them. She feels that she catered to her husband, did everything possible to pacify, didn't complain about his drinking, didn't draw the line for him beyond which he couldn't go or she would terminate the marriage. Instead of this she let the abuse go on without really facing him with it until she finally ran out on the situation. She related this again to her mother, pointing out that her mother was just as much at fault as her father. She indicated she realized this as an adolescent. She became aware that her mother needn't take everything she

took from the father, but in fact was encouraging him in his behavior by being too forgiving. Mrs. Stover is sure that this has been her pattern in relation to men also.

She brought up that realizing all these things about herself makes her feel guilty, edgy, and anxious. This morning she feels better, but didn't sleep very well last night. At least she is now not as doubtful as before about what she wants to do. I pointed out that her anxiety is a natural part of finding out things about herself. Mrs. Stover then brought up that she still has ambivalent periods about her husband being away. She describes this as a feeling of loneliness and realization that by just saying the words she could have him back, and at times she is tempted to do this. However, she has held the line firmly, and as she accomplished a little more on her own and the care of the children, she has less of this feeling of wanting him back. At the moment she realizes the need for larger housing since there is no privacy for George. She handles periods of anxiety by getting busy in the apartment, housecleaning, preparing meals, or sewing. Time doesn't hang heavily on her hands especially with her young children. She feels that she is now giving them more attention than ever and maybe giving Peter too much attention. During the period at his grandmother's he got used to having somebody playing frequently and interrupts her housework to do this. Mrs. Stover's own tendency with the children has been to do too much for them. Larie hasn't yet fully learned how to dress herself and Mrs. Stover recognizes this is because Mrs. Stover has taken too much responsibility for this herself.

I posed for Mrs. Stover the question of what she has been looking for in the husband, what does she feel she wants. Mrs. Stover feels she has been wanting someone to look after her, who would in a sense be a good father for her. She laughed about this, recognizing how far she had deviated from that in her actual choice of husbands.

NOVEMBER 25. HOME VISIT TO MRS. STOVER BY APPOINTMENT

Mrs. Stover was in the middle of moving, was up high on a ladder installing curtains and so I did not prolong the interview. Mrs. Stover, however, wanted to tell me about a new angle that has occurred to her. She pointed out that this is the first time that she has lived alone with her children following disruptions of her marriages. Before that she always went home to mother and from mother's home she picked up with another man. When Mrs. Stover came to the present building where she was living, her mother told her that she would be lonely living by herself, that she would never make a go of it, that she ought to stay in the mother's home. Mrs. Stover realized that this was typical of her mother's attitude. There is some tendency here for her mother to keep her tied to her, and Mrs. Stover recognized that she was a willing participant in this. She has never felt capable of managing her own life or making decisions on her own and has had to turn to her mother all through her life for even small decisions. She made moving to her present apartment a sort of test case, since she took the decision herself and made a point of not telling anybody about it until after she had rented the larger apartment. After doing this she acted as if she had really taken a step on her own and accomplished something. She then described how she was "the good little girl" at the home all her life. From an early age her mother seemed to expect her to take a lot of responsibility for caring for her younger brother and later her sister. She changed, dressed, and bathed them when they were toddlers though at the time she was only 9 or 10 herself. Part of this was due to the fact that her mother

was frequently sick. When Mrs. Stover was in grade 10, her mother was ill in the hospital for a considerable time, during which she left Mrs. Stover who was then 15, with the total responsibility for the household. The father also expected her to function as the mistress of the home. As this situation was intolerable for her and it was at this time that she got involved with her first husband and became pregnant by him. He was an older man who offered her companionship. He seemed to take it for granted that she would sleep with him and she did. At the time, she felt she acted largely on impulse, meeting her needs or the man's needs without much thought given to it. Her first marriage was a runaway marriage and only lasted for a few days. The mother had been in bed around this time for one year with "bad legs." Mrs. Stover recalls at this time trying to cook the meals and run the house and hating to come home from school every day. Whenever she got a chance she stuck her nose in a book. She recognizes that reading has always been an escape to her. Now she doesn't read for this purpose as much, however. Her first husband seemed at first to offer her affection and wouldn't endlessly criticize her as the father did.

DECEMBER 8. VISIT WITH MRS. STOVER BY APPOINTMENT

I suggested during a telephone conversation that we review where we had got to date; Mrs. Stover had accepted this.

On my arrival for the interview she started by pointing out her new apartment which has a large living room, kitchen, and two bedrooms, and will permit George to have his own room where he can be and later on joined by Peter. Mrs. Stover deliberately made the decision without advance consultation with her mother, which she used to always do, or with myself. She felt this was something of a gain in itself since she used to have so much trouble making decisions.

Mrs. Stover also mentioned that the children are getting more attention than they used to. In fact she feels they may be getting too much attention, particularly Peter who she probably spoils. I didn't at this point pick up on this, but inquired in what other ways did Mrs. Stover feel that changes had occurred.

Mrs. Stover said that she feels more secure with herself. This is the first time she has ever had her own place. When her marriages failed in the past, she always went back to mother.

I raised the question with Mrs. Stover of how she felt she had been able to change this. Mrs. Stover mentioned first the fact that she has nice neighbors. They are friendly, cooperate with her, and she gets a real feeling of support from them. For example, the family across the hall, who have a car, take her shopping in order to permit her to buy her things at a supermarket, since there is no supermarket in the immediate area.

Along this same line Mrs. Stover brought up the fact that she had some activity with the school. Mrs. Stover laughingly commented "I'm all tangled up with the school around planning parties." The school had asked the assistance of some parents to act as "party room mothers" to help look after the children. Mrs. Stover and a neighbor, Mrs. Kirby had gone to the school to do this and have been asked by the school to recruit 11 more mothers to act in this capacity. Mrs. Stover has been on the phone a lot about this. While it is a chore and a nuisance, she enjoys it, and she has a lot of respect for the school principal. It makes her feel good to know the school trusts her with such a job.

In response to my further questions as to why Mrs. Stover feels she is functioning differently, Mrs. Stover mentioned her increased self-confidence. She related this to her contact with Family Service and

AFDC branch, since the two agencies have demonstrated a lot of confidence with her. She said, "You must have this confidence in me or you wouldn't have spent as much time helping me as you did." This, Mrs. Stover states, has raised her own self-confidence and her feeling of being able to do things. She also used to lie awake at night worrying about whether her AFDC check was going to come. Now she doesn't do this. She described also, in relation to Family Service, as feeling of having someone available to her if things did go wrong or get difficult.

Mrs. Stover also brought up some negatives. She said for one thing thinking about herself makes her feel like "she is peeking inside other people." At times it makes her edgy and nervous. She sees other people making the same mistakes and having the same problems she did. This sometimes makes her uncomfortable. Then she either wants to leave such people or doesn't feel relaxed with them.

Mrs. Stover went on to discuss her concern about Eileen who next fall will be old enough to start school. Mrs. Stover doubts if this will be possible, however, because of Eileen's clinging to her mother. Mrs. Stover said that Eileen simply can't keep up with the other children nor can she follow their games.

In response to my question, Mrs. Stover clarified that her concern at this point is not with Eileen's present behavior so much as the fact that it may be difficult to get her started in any kind of educational program next fall. She hopes to use the time between now and next fall to foster a little independence in Eileen. I supported this idea pointing out several ways in which Mrs. Stover could achieve this; through encouraging Eileen in outdoor play, deliberately conditioning her to stay with the neighbor for short periods of time at first which could be lengthened later, provided the neighbor was willing to help with this plan. I also suggested giving Eileen a good deal of encouragement for anything she can accomplish since she is aware of her inability to keep up with the other children.

I suggested that over the next few months that plans be worked out to have Eileen get an aptitude test at the school's Guidance Office, and if necessary, disclose the possibility of Eileen's enrolling in the nursery school for retarded children. Mrs. Stover was skeptical about this plan. She wasn't sure she wanted to ask the school about this. Worker pointed out that this was the way she felt about AFDC too, and things worked out better when she bared her problems with them.

JANUARY 16

Telephone call from Mrs. Stover inquiring whether I thought she should move. She has been offered an apartment in the same building a floor above her existing apartment, that is cleaner, with more closet space and would have more privacy for George and more living space in general. Mrs. Stover wound up by wondering if I ought to look at it and approve the new apartment that she was considering. I indicated willingness to do this, but said that I was quite willing to trust her own decision on the matter.

JANUARY 19

Mrs. Stover announced that she had thought over the decision about moving and decided against it. The thing that had decided her against it had been the fact that as soon as she talked it over with the children she noticed that they became very anxious and edgy. She noticed this in all of the children except Peter. This made her realize the extent to which the children had been upset by the moves she had in the past, together with her other troubles, and she said, "I figured I'd be losing more than I gained by moving now."

Mrs. Stover had also been concerned about the fire hazard about living on the third floor, had recently heard an opinion quoted by the fire marshal to the effect that the old building is a big firetrap and would burn rapidly. This is a special problem for Mrs. Stover since she has not only Peter, but Eileen to be treated like a baby in a situation of this kind.

JANUARY 25. HOME VISIT BY APPOINTMENT

Mrs. Stover at this point was involved in washing, explaining that she has been borrowing the neighbor's washing machine and taking it whenever she can get it.

I explained to Mrs. Stover her eligibility for supplementary assistance from AFDC for a washing machine and outlined the procedure. Mrs. Stover was initially lukewarm to this idea. I raised the question with her as to why she was reluctant. Mrs. Stover expressed ideas which she had also expressed at an earlier time, that is, that it wasn't smart to ask AFDC worker for too much, the less you ask them for the better off you are and so on. I took issue with this pointing out that this seems to be part of a larger problem; AFDC is aimed at enabling her to bring up children and its purpose can be frustrated unless she takes responsibility for letting AFDC worker know of needs. The latter is not and cannot anticipate everybody's needs in advance. Mrs. Stover accepted this, brought up that she is expecting a visit from the AFDC worker and will let me know result of this.

Mrs. Stover brought out that she enjoys the job of calling the parents for the school party. This makes her feel that she is helping the school out.

I mentioned PTA as an aid to any feelings of isolation which Mrs. Stover might have as a result of being tied down, new in the district, and so forth. Mrs. Stover said she liked the idea of PTA or something which will "Broaden my life out a little bit," but at the same time her family keeps her busy, time if anything goes too fast. She does have considerable association with adults through the immediate neighbors. She didn't really know about PTA.

FEBRUARY 8

Mrs. Stover had had a visit from AFDC worker, who according to Mrs. Stover didn't like the apartment because of the lack of play space for the children. Mrs. Stover had raised problem of washing machine and bedding with the AFDC worker who said to make arrangements to get the bedding on time payments if necessary, paying for it out of her household allowance included in the AFDC budget. Mrs. Stover has gone ahead and done this. She is awaiting a chance to get the three estimates on the washing machine which I had discussed with her and which had been confirmed by AFDC worker.

Mr. Stover had sent toys for the children in a surprise move. He had sent them through his mother who had delivered them. Mrs. Stover had accepted them without question because she thought the mother-in-law possibly didn't know from Mr. Stover that Mrs. Stover was averse to taking anything from him. Mrs. Stover was very angry that Mr. Stover had used deception in this manner. I wondered if Mrs. Stover could explain her attitude in this matter of fact manner as soon as possible to the mother-in-law to prevent the latter from being used as a go-between in the future. Mrs. Stover accepted this idea. She is on good terms with the mother-in-law and feels she could explain the whole situation to her quite readily.

MARCH 15

Mrs. Stover says she has again been troubled by Mr. Stover phoning the lady upstairs. I made a suggestion to Mrs. Stover for handling these calls as follows: Ask the person calling to leave his name and number. If he calls again, that she encourage the neighbor to tell him that she is not taking any more calls for Mrs. Stover. Mrs. Stover seemed pleased at this plan.

MARCH 22

Mrs. Stover said that Eileen is starting to go outside on her own without being urged by Mrs. Stover. Mrs. Stover since our recent clarification had felt more relaxed about this and is letting Eileen also go out on the back porch. She formerly had done this, but kept running out every few minutes. I brought out again that I thought there was an intermediate stage between school and home; that is, a stage in which Eileen would have a place to go to develop a range of activity beyond the home and be able to play with the other children.

Mrs. Stover said she feels more confident that this sort of thing can be done now and that much of the problem was probably her own attitude toward Eileen. She brought up the possibility of East School summer program for pre-kindergarten children which she had heard about last year. The idea of this program as Mrs. Stover understands it is to give the children some experience of being away from their parents and getting used to the school building. This has been discussed at the last PTA meeting that Mrs. Stover had attended. These meetings take place in the afternoons at the school. At the next meeting Mrs. Stover is planning to go 15 minutes early to see the teacher about Larie's progress in kindergarten. The plan is that she will take Eileen with her, and during the interview with the teacher, Eileen will play with the group of other children at the school.

George is continuing to get good school reports, but does not like school work in some of its aspects. He doesn't like writing stuff down.

I asked how she handles this and she said she tries to encourage George to recognize that school can't be all pleasurable activities, nor will he necessarily like all of his teachers. The thing for him to do is to try to cultivate an attitude of putting up with these unpleasant aspects, because there are so many things about school he likes. I supported Mrs. Stover in this, pointing out the desirability of consistently encouraging George in responsible attitudes.

APRIL 12

Mrs. Stover discussed the Easter party at school and her taking Eileen. The teacher had noticed that Eileen was attached to her mother. Eileen nonetheless went cheerfully to play with the other children and allowed Mrs. Stover to go in and see the teacher by herself. The teacher had said also that from talking to Eileen she feels that Eileen should be able to start with the others in kindergarten. The teacher had apparently liked Eileen and felt she would be very glad to have her in the class. She had indicated to Mrs. Stover that at the end of the kindergarten year a decision could be made regarding a special class for Eileen.

Mrs. Stover wanted to tell me also that there has been some good development regarding her AFDC. Her AFDC worker had said that "the welfare had found Mrs. Stover could be relied on." Mrs. Stover was very pleased about this. The welfare also got her a washing machine, Mrs. Stover having finally got the three estimates.

APRIL 15

Psychological report received regarding Eileen. Eileen scored at the borderline defective intelligence level in this examination, with an IQ of 74.

APRIL 18. VISIT TO MRS. STOVER BY APPOINTMENT

This interview was taken up with a discussion of a report from the psychologist which I had brought with me. In going over the report it became evident that Mrs. Stover was having a good deal of difficulty accepting the report that Eileen is developmentally disabled.

In relation to planning a school program based on the report, Mrs. Stover felt that she would like to take the teacher up on her statement that she felt Eileen could do well and the teacher could do well with Eileen in the kindergarten group the first year, followed by an evaluation of progress and the probability of a special class or school after that. Mrs. Stover prefers this class to possible use of the nursery for developmentally disabled children.

MAY 3. HOME VISIT BY APPOINTMENT

Mrs. Stover began the interview by some further remarks regarding Eileen. She felt the last two discussions had helped clarify her own thinking regarding this problem. She said she feels more relaxed with Eileen and Eileen is continuing to play outside a good deal with other children.

I raised the problem of her plans about the divorce. How does she feel about this at this point? Mrs. Stover said that she still feels that it may as well sit. She had not had much recent trouble with Mr. Stover and is hoping that he had decided not to bother her. She would take divorce action only if she had more trouble with Mr. Stover at least for the present. In the meantime, she is keeping her mind closed on the whole subject.

Mrs. Stover went on to say that she would like some further help in future interviews with the problem of raising her kids. At the moment she is concerned about George who is having problems in school. He comes home at noon hour crying. She and one of George's teachers don't get along either. Mrs. Stover feels that this teacher is extremely punitive in her attitude toward George. She is rapping George over the knuckles with a ruler. On Monday of this week George had been ill and Mrs. Stover phoned the school explaining this, leaving word in the office. It had been arranged that Mrs. Stover would phone back when George was ready to return. She did this Tuesday morning as George returned to school. Later in the morning Mrs. Stover received a call from the teacher claiming that George was playing hookey, though it was subsequently verified that George was in school. George didn't even have a class with the teacher that morning. Mrs. Stover argued that it was none of her business. George had recently made a mistake on his arithmetic calculations and the teacher made him stay after school and do them over 200 times each. Shortly after this she had sent home a paper to Mrs. Stover which she had refused to mark because the writing was too faint. Mrs. Stover showed the paper to me and the writing was quite legible and clear. As a result of this George had had to do these calculations a total of 600 times. George says that when he gets out of school "he feels like killing somebody." As a result of what Mrs. Stover believes is the punitive treatment of George by the teacher, George is now taking the attitude "to heck with school." Mrs. Stover says that George really knows he has no choice in the matter of attending school, nor is he at all likely to truant.

I picked up on this offering to visit the school and to review the problem with the principal and the school social worker with Mrs. Stover present or not as she desired. In advance of this we could work how best to present the problem to the school in such a way as not to make it strictly as a complaint against the teacher, but put it on the basis of concern about George and his discouragement about the school situation. Mrs. Stover said she liked this idea except that she felt she wanted to try this out on her own; she felt she could use the approach which I had suggested and do it herself.

This led to a discussion of how she should handle this with George. To this point Mrs. Stover had been very careful not to side completely with George and point the teacher up as the villian. When he comes home crying she puts her arm around him and comforts him. On the other hand she has tried to help him see that he is likely to meet other teachers like this one, that this is part of going to school. George has wanted a transfer to another school but at this point she thinks it is too late in the year. I supported Mrs. Stover in her stand with George and her plan to go to the school to discuss it.

MAY 10

Mrs. Stover was quite angry at Public Welfare bringing out that her budget has been reduced by $15 a month. She talked in terms of going off AFDC and going to work. I asked her to examine this carefully in terms of what it would mean to her to try to manage the children and work at the same time, and what it would mean also of her relationship with the children, how much she could give them, and so on. I concurred in the idea of her working as a long-term goal but suggested very careful consideration of this as something she could do soon. After this Mrs. Stover calmed down and said she realized this was not a constructive thing to do. I thereupon brought up the possibility of using a home economist as a consultant to help Mrs. Stover get the most out of her present budget. Mrs. Stover said, "I'm all for that," but added that she felt she is managing pretty economically at present. She doesn't see where she is going to manage with a $15 decrease.

I later saw the home economist briefly and a joint visit with home economist was planned for May 24.

MAY 25

Brief home visit taking clothing supplied by home economist, including a dress for Mrs. Stover, three small comforters for the younger children, a jacket for Eileen.

JUNE 6. VISIT TO MRS. STOVER BY APPOINTMENT

We initially discussed Mrs. Stover's arrangements with the home economist regarding the budget. Mrs. Stover said, "She showed me how I could cover all my expenses and a little extra." She added that she hoped this could be done, but she remained somewhat skeptical. She currently planned however to "give this a try" and to confer further with the home economist on any difficulties that come up.

She has recently heard indirectly that Mr. Stover is planning to get married. His son by an earlier marriage lives just a short distance down the street from Mrs. Stover's present location. I inquired what Mrs. Stover's reaction to this information was and she said she feels greatly relieved. It had made her feel that she was free of him, and had also made her realize the extent to which she still had a feeling of protectiveness toward him, and a feeling of responsibility of him. She felt she had come to realize that it was this more than anything else that had been a barrier to her taking divorce action. This latest news takes the decision out of her hands and she agreed with my comment that she feels that it gets her off the hook. She had always had some sort of feeling that it was her duty to stay with Mr. Stover no

matter what he did, since he needed to be looked after.

I asked where does Mrs. Stover feel she is at with this problem at the moment. Mrs. Stover went on to talk in terms of her former pattern of running away from one situation into a worse one. She wouldn't allow anybody to help her, or to get close enough to her to help her. She feels now she understands more why she got into this series of messes and is less apt to jump before she looks. She cites her impulse to throw over AFDC as an example of how she used to operate, but now she stops and thinks before she makes a decision of this kind.

Mrs. Stover went on to talk about her present feeling of having something of her own and the fact that she is not afraid any more of losing it. She feels comfortable also in her attitude toward men of not having anything to do with them. She said, "My way of looking at a man now is in terms of what can he give me as a husband that is better than what I've got now. So far I haven't met anybody who I thought could measure up to this." She is not going to feel any responsibility to save a man.

Here she went on to add that she continues in her former attitude that she and men just don't mix, that basically she has no use for men and this would prevent her ever having a productive relationship with a man. On the other hand, she does worry about the effects of her extreme dislike of men and her frank prejudices toward men on the children; she doesn't want the girls to be prejudiced against men and she has an adolescent boy.

I introduced the idea of discussing in the future interviews the specific methods she may use in teaching the children about such matters and in cultivating attitudes toward men.

JUNE 14

I further raised with Mrs. Stover the question of her instruction of the children.

I went over some material abstracted from a recent book dealing with attitudes of adolescents toward the opposite sex. This was done by way of introducing Mrs. Stover to the book and the possibility of her using it with George. Mrs. Stover said that she felt the book would be useful to her. The children do not volunteer much in this area nor do they ask many questions. She tried to deal with these on a factual basis as they come up.

Mrs. Stover indicated that she feels it is her own attitudes that are important. Nonetheless, she can perhaps avoid giving the children a biased attitude toward men. I suggested presenting Mr. Stover and his problems in as favorable a light as possible to the children, attempting to avoid running him down. Mrs. Stover thought this would be quite possible for her. The children speak little of Mr. Stover, but seem settled in the attitude that he doesn't want to be with the family. George shows some resentment, occasionally commenting that they are better off now than they were when Mr. Stover was in the family. Mrs. Stover felt she could make use of my suggestion of using occasions when George makes remarks of this kind to point out that Mr. Stover has his problems too, but also has his good points, and it was more a matter of can't rather than didn't want to be a father to the family.

JUNE 28. VISIT TO MRS. STOVER BY APPOINTMENT

Mrs. Stover was flying around in a complete dither and made the remark, "I ain't going to talk to you long." To my inquiry as to what had happened Mrs. Stover said that the other day her AFDC worker had informed Mrs. Stover that her apartment is not a fit place for the children to live. She had told Mrs. Stover to go to the housing project and to apply for an apartment. Mrs. Stover had done this and had been told that there was an apartment avail-

able and that she should be prepared to move in three days. Mrs. Stover talked at first as though she hadn't been given any choice in the matter. When I inquired about this, however, she agreed that it is her decision as to whether or not she goes to the housing project. She clarified that she feels that it is circumstances that are forcing her into moving so quickly. By this she means that she has to take an apartment while it can be got.

Later Mrs. Stover phoned again, wanting to know if I had any information as to why the county might have held up her check since she did not receive it. Later Mrs. Stover found out that the check had been sent to her new address by the county, but since Mrs. Stover's name was not on the mailbox, the check had been returned. It will now be sent back to her again and it will likely be two or three days before Mrs. Stover receives it. Mrs. Stover is angry at AFDC again as she says the workers told her that she couldn't say when this would be since it takes a variable amount of time, and had advised Mrs. Stover not to get too excited about it, that to make such a big fuss over a check being late was neurotic.

JULY 6. HOME VISIT TO MRS. STOVER'S NEW APARTMENT IN THE HOUSING PROJECTS

The family has a two-bedroom unit, Mrs. Stover and the girls having one room and the boys having the other.

The interview consisted of a review of Mrs. Stover's current difficulties with AFDC and a discussion of future plans around vacation and possible termination.

The most recent incident has aroused considerable fresh hostility in Mrs. Stover toward the AFDC since she stoutly maintains that she told the worker that the check should be mailed to her new address. Mrs. Stover said, "I can't do anything with the Welfare." Whatever they try to plan together, hitches develop. At this point she was making a joke about having been called neurotic, explaining that the previous day she and her mother and sisters and the children had gone on an outing, and the joke of the day amongst her mother and sisters had been don't go near June, she's neurotic. A further difficulty that developed was the fact that when the family got to the apartment the electricity was not connected. Two days later the company had come out and connected it on the date of deposit.

We then tried to analyze the difficulties with AFDC from the point of view of Mrs. Stover's part in them. I pointed out that with her dealings with our agency she showed good capacity to plan, and why was there this difference? Mrs. Stover, in thinking about it felt that it might be a matter that she has greater feeling about the AFDC and that in her doings with AFDC she is tense and more apt to fly off the handle, partly from past conflict with the welfare and partly from the fact that the AFDC is in a sense a more authoritative position with her than is Family Service since they have what she feels is absolute control over the purse strings. Mrs. Stover agrees that being in this frame of mind, she is especially likely to have misunderstanding or antagonism with the AFDC. On the other hand, she feels that the agency contributes to this itself by the hurried manner in which everything is handled, the fact that AFDC workers come to her place unexpectedly to see her, often catching her off guard, and come up with things such as the order to move to the new apartment, which seemed to come out of the blue. On top of this, Mrs. Stover feels pushed around by AFDC, maintaining she was told that she would have to move to public housing development. Mrs. Stover sees no solution at present, of feeling that she never hit it off with welfare and finds it difficult to visualize the time when she ever will. Her current attitude

is that the best thing is to do what they tell her, try to avoid breaking any regulations, and keep out of trouble.

Mrs. Stover said she guessed the main thing in her dealings with AFDC would be to try to keep from getting excited and losing her head, realizing that she is more prone to do this by virtue of the past relationship with AFDC. The remainder of the interview consisted of a discussion of future plans and goals. Mrs. Stover was aware of coming vacation plan and the possibility of termination we had discussed several times earlier. Mrs. Stover gave some evaluation at this point of what she thought the relationship with Family Service means to her. She sees it largely as a control on impulsive behavior. Before acting she phones me and I help her think the thing through so that she acts in a more planned way and not on the spur of the moment. Despite her recent difficulties with the AFDC, she feels there has been real improvement to the point where they at least have greater trust in her and she some greater trust in them. Then, too, she has had less difficulty with her husband for a long time, and has a feeling of having made some progress in getting Eileen ready for a more wholesome school experience when the time comes. In the light of all this she feels that objectively considered, her situation is better and she can probably handle it more easily than she could before. The vacation could be a kind of planned period to see how she manages, and tentative appointment was set for follow-up visit in August.

AUGUST 30

The interview consisted of a review of the earlier plan of termination. Mrs. Stover obviously had mixed feelings about it. On the one hand she reiterates her former sentiments about having fewer problems, being better able to manage with them at this point. She is now meeting things that she had difficulty in handling or that threw her. On the other hand, her tie to the agency implies some security for her, inasmuch as she knows that if things do take a downturn, she can always turn to the agency. I explained that she could do this in any case, but she is wanting us to hold it open, and it was agreed that this would be done at least for the present.

SEPTEMBER 18

The school social worker telephoned regarding Eileen, Mrs. Stover started Eileen in kindergarten at the beginning of this month. It was noted that the school's health records shows that Eileen has muscular dystrophy, and the teacher had spoken to the social worker about this, wanting further clarification of it. It was also the teacher's observation that Eileen showed no ability to relate to other children in her group. Eileen is, after all, only four to begin with and won't be five until October but Mrs. Stover had, during her visits to the school last May and June, talked the problem over with the school staff, and they had agreed to start Eileen.

I clarified the medical diagnosis with the social worker. The school social worker felt that continuing Eileen in kindergarten might also be good in view of the problem of the mother's overprotection of Eileen and the fact that the mother is trying to overcome this and has been working on it for some months. If Eileen's limitations are accepted in the group and not much is expected of her in way of either skills or sociability for the present, it is quite likely that she will be able to make some kind of an adjustment to the kindergarten situation. Failing this, the possibility of Eileen's admission to a school for retarded children should be considered. Matters were left that the school social worker will call us further in about six weeks, and that period will be used to see how Eileen gets along.

Later in the day I dropped in on Mrs. Stover to discuss the school's report. Mrs. Stover said that she recognized Eileen is behind the group in sociability, and we briefly reviewed the report which we had obtained in April regarding her intellectual state.

At the same time, Mrs. Stover was pleased Eileen had been able to separate herself from the mother and also from Larie without apparent difficulty. Her immediate reaction is that she wants to visit the school soon and see the teacher and get more information on it for herself.

A further visit will be planned for a month's time after Mrs. Stover has had a chance to visit the school. Despite the previous plan to terminate, both Mrs. Stover and the school are at this time wanting the agency to stay at least until the matter of Eileen's problem has been worked out.

SUMMARY. OCTOBER 18 THROUGH DECEMBER 1

Mrs. Stover had visited the school in October and got a very favorable report on Eileen. Mrs. Stover said the teacher told her that Eileen cannot comprehend things with the rest of the children, but her behavior is not abnormal nor does it an any way hamper the class or harm the other children. Eileen plays very little with the other children though she is beginning to make some tentative overtures to them according to Mrs. Stover. On the other hand the teacher was reassuring and talked to Mrs. Stover about this, pointing out that lots of children play by themselves in the classroom situation. On November 16 a further brief report was received from the school social worker which confirmed the information that came from Mrs. Stover.

SUMMARY. DECEMBER 1 THROUGH JANUARY 8

The two interviews during this period with Mrs. Stover were concerned largely with working through her feelings about the agency closing its case.

In the midst of her conflict about worker's leaving, another incident reactivated Mrs. Stover's hostilities toward the AFDC. This led to a lengthy discussion of how Mrs. Stover has been in a family which has been on welfare as far back as she can remember and had built up certain more or less fixed attitudes toward the welfare agency. These included a feeling of being pushed around, worthless, and not treated as an individual. She heartily agreed with my point that partly this stemmed from being chronically on the receiving end and never having a feeling of being able to give to others. In addition Mrs. Stover's belief in the welfare agency as an almost all powerful agency, which is apt to do anything without any explanation, seems unshakable at this point.

FEBRUARY 15. LAST VISIT

In this termination interview Mrs. Stover summed up her feelings as follows: "We've changed in the fact that we are more settled, more of a family instead of five people. Each is different that is to be expected, but we are more united, kind of. That's the biggest change, more secure in ourselves as a family. Larie and George and I each worried about ourselves instead of all of us. Now it isn't so much a personal worry as how is this family going to get along. We think of the good of the family rather than for each one. It's not so much what you've said and done as what you've listened to. I could talk things over and sort them out, kind of. I could bring up things that I wouldn't ordinarily be able to tell people. If I told these things to others, they would get all mixed up in my problem, but you don't.

I think too, I've found out there is always a reason for the way welfare acts. And, if I try I can usually find out what it is. And the school is so much help to me with Eileen. They trust me."

ENTRY FOR RECORD

April 23. Call received from Mrs. Stover and telephone referral done to Miss Bithy, social worker at the school for retarded regarding Eileen.

ENTRY FOR RECORD

June 17. Call from school social worker to report on the family. The school has been asking "What kind of casework did Mrs. Stover receive?" There has been remarkable change in the children. Physical care greatly improved. Larie is described as "top girl in her class." Eileen has made a great deal of progress in relating to other children. School wondering what has happened to account for the change. The social worker and I agreed that it is a cumulation of things over two years rather than anything recent and dramatic. She will talk further to the teachers. Later telephoned Mrs. Stover and relayed the school's message. She was very pleased and said that she herself notices a big change in Eileen. Application is pending for Eileen's admission to the School for Retarded Children.

ENTRY FOR RECORD

September 11. Mrs. Stover called to say Eileen enrolled at the School for Retarded Children and enjoying the experience. She is very tired when she gets home. She leaves the home readily, however, in the morning, much to the surprise of Mrs. Stover.

Reading 11-2

*Community Development Programs Serving the Urban Poor**

Charles F. Grosser

A discontinuity exists between the theory and the methodology of community organization. Recognition of this is evidenced in the recent literature. Kahn (1964, pp. 9, 19) notes:

One cannot plan for the education, job training, placement, or counseling of deprived inner-city youth without new concentration on the public sector generally. What was often tokenism in welfare council participation would not do for these endeavors. . . . One must learn to deal with, involve, plan with, bring pressure upon, or even to cause changes in, local and state governmental bodies. . . .

. . . until recently, the community organization method was conceptualized entirely in relation to the enabling role. . . . The enabling took the form of facilitating leadership development of consensus about direction to be taken or winning local assent to leadership-sanctioned direction and plans—not of shaping planning out of true communitywide involvement in goal setting.

Morris and Rein (1963) similarly indicate that

the requirements of the new community demand skill in invocating special points of view and in living with other professionals who advocate competing points of view.

One major factor impelling new developments in community organization practice is the increased attention by the field to the client group with which it is engaged: specifically, beginning to work directly with the recipients—rather than exclusively with the providers—of social welfare service. As the term is used in this paper, *neighborhood community development* means community organization efforts being made with lower-class, minority group, urban slum residents. The goals of these efforts are to engage the poor in the decision-making process of the community, both to overcome apathy and estrangement and to realign the power resources of the community by creating channels through which the consumers of social welfare services can define their problems and goals and negotiate on their own behalf. Much of the experience gained from these efforts can be generalized for application to most groups of deprived persons.

The purpose of this paper is to explore some of the consequences emerging from community organization's growing engagement with the poor person. Briefly discussed are (1) the substantive areas and issues with which community organization practice will have to deal, (2) a consideration of the role of the community worker, and (3) a brief review of the issue of the organizational forms that practice will take.

SUBSTANTIVE AREAS AND ISSUES

Community organization in neighborhood development programs signifies direct engagement with the problems of the poor person. More than any other group in our society, the poor expend a major portion of their efforts to achieve the "good life" through interaction with agencies of

---

* Copyright 1965, National Association of Social Workers, Inc. Reprinted by permission of the author and publisher from *Social Work* 10:3 (July 1965), pp. 15–21.

city government. It is with the local
branches of the department of welfare, the
police, the housing authority, the board of
education, and similar agencies that the
poor person negotiates for a share of the
community's resources. Striving toward
the equitable distribution of these resources is the programmatic strategy that
must accompany any bona fide effort to
encourage the residents of the inner-city
slum to help themselves. If neighborhood
development denies or ignores this fact,
in the eyes of the local residents it is at
best sham and window-dressing, at worst,
deceit. Lower-class, minority group individuals cannot be expected to feel that
they have a part in the determination of
their own destinies in the face of such
grievances as denial of welfare to nonresi-
dents, forcing parents to take legal action
against their child under the relatives' responsibility laws, categorization as an
"undesirable tenant" with no right to face
one's accusers and no recourse to appeal,
arrest and interrogation characterized by
prejudice and brutality, and an inferior,
segregated school system. To attempt to
facilitate clients' adjustment to such a social system is to betray their interests.
Therefore, if local community development programs are to be successful, it
must be recognized that local efforts at
self-expression will be directed at the
agents of government in an attempt to
bring about solutions to such injustices as
these.

Further, in order to arouse people who
have been systematically socialized into
apathy and inaction—in some cases, over
several generations—it may be necessary
to teach them that the solutions to their
problems lie in the hands of certain governmental agencies, and that these agencies are sensitive to well-publicized mass
efforts, particularly in election years.
Lower-class, alienated non-participating
people will not be induced to organize by
appeals to their sense of civic duty, patrio-

tism, or morality, or other exhortations to
exercise their obligations of citizenship.
Such individuals will organize only if they
perceive organization as a means to an
immediate end. It should be pointed out—
without becoming involved in a means-
ends, process-content discussion—that
these programs require a great deal more
attention to material objectives than has
been true in the past. Community development in slum neighborhoods is, after all,
essentially a process for the redress of
grievances that are the cumulative result
of the differential distribution of community resources. To avoid partisanship in
the name of objectivity and service to the
"total community" is, in effect, to take a
position justifying the pittance that has
been allotted from the health, educational,
and social welfare coffers to the residents
of the inner-city slum.

An applied example of the foregoing
was a voter-registration campaign conducted in New York City by Mobilization
for Youth last summer and fall (Bailey &
Pinsky, 1965). Geared to the registration
of eligible minority group nonvoters, the
campaign was not run on the model of
the League of Women Voters, which
presses voters to fulfill their civic duty.
Instead, it was focused on the ballot's
Proposition 1, which provided for additional low-income housing, and on the recently enacted "stop-and-frisk" and "no-
knock" laws. Because these issues have
great pertinence for the Lower East Side
slum community, they were used to encourage voter registration. MFY was careful to avoid creating unrealistic expectations of immediate success regarding these
issues; rather, it argued that Proposition
1 was sure to be defeated unless the people of New York City carried it by a large
enough plurality to overcome the upstate
opposition, and that the "stop-and-frisk"
and "no-knock" laws violate the rights and
dignity of the suspect and are a reflection
of a general lack of political accountability

and of abstinence from voting by the poor person, who is more often arrested and interrogated than any other citizen.

THE ENABLER ROLE

The traditional stance of the community organizer as enabler is based on two assumptions, one valid, the other invalid. The valid assumption is that self-imposed actions growing out of a community's assessment of its own needs have a value and permanence that do not inhere in actions imposed from the outside. The invalid assumption is that the enabling role is the only one by which this desirable end may be brought about. In this section several alternatives are suggested that are believed to be viable.

It should be noted, first, that the role of enabler, geared to process, may itself be limited as a strategy for facilitating community self-help. For example, one text on community organization method draws on the experience of a special governor's committee set up in Colorado to deal with pervasive problems in the state's mental institutions as illustrative of proper work by a community organizer. Conditions within the institutions were unsatisfactory, and individuals were being improperly and illegally committed:

the legislation [directed at the problems] recommended by the governor's committee did not get very far in the ensuing session of the state assembly, although a more substantial program might have resulted if the committee, or even a considerable bloc within the committee, had been willing to manipulate or use undemocratic methods. It was rightly felt, however, that this might jeopardize future working relationships—in short, that process or means was as important as the immediate goal (Murphy, 1954, p. 22).

Although such judgments may be possible in statewide interdisciplinary committees, direct contact with those immediately affected by such decisions in a neighborhood community development

program precludes any such cavalier determination of the client's fate.

THE "BROKER" ROLE

Familiar in such nonsocial work contexts as real estate and the stock market, the role of "broker" was instituted in the Mobilization for Youth program in 1962. It appears to have been first suggested for social work practice by Wilensky and Lebeaux (1958, p. 286). These writers postulated a need for "guides, so to speak, through a new kind of civilized jungle" and spoke of social work as "an example par excellence of the liaison function, a large part of its total activity being devoted to putting people in touch with community resources they need but can hardly name, let alone locate."

The community organization worker brings the component of collective action to the broker role, adding a potent factor to the process. Through collective "brokerage activity," the notion of collective solutions is introduced; that is, administrative and policy changes are undertaken to affect whole classes of persons rather than a single individual. The following comment, taken from a report of a Mobilization for Youth community organizer, illustrates the point:

Residents of the Lower East Side have brought their welfare problems . . . such as late checks, insufficient funds to pay large utility bills, no winter clothing, dispossess notices, and a host of others . . . to Casa de la Communidad, since it first opened in February 1963. These problems were handled by the caseworkers . . . who shared the facilities with the C.O. worker. . . . All too often, no real change seemed to result either in the lives of the clients or in the procedures of welfare. The same clients tended to come over and over again from emergency to emergency (Kronenfeld, 1965).

It was as a result of this experience that two community organization efforts in the welfare area were launched: a welfare information center and an organization of welfare clients holding court support orders. The latter group sought a collective resolution to the problems created by the determination of budgets on the basis of income ordered by a court but rarely received by the family.

THE ADVOCATE ROLE

It has been the experience of workers in neighborhood community development programs that the broker role is frequently insufficiently directive. Therefore, the role of advocate has been co-opted from the field of law. Often the institutions with which local residents must deal are not even neutral, much less positively motivated, toward handling the issues brought to them by community groups. In fact, they are frequently overtly negative and hostile, often concealing or distorting information about rules, procedures, and office hours. By their own partisanship on behalf of instrumental organizational goals, they create an atmosphere that demands advocacy on behalf of the poor person. If the community worker is to facilitate productive interaction between residents and institutions, it is necessary to provide leadership and resources directed toward eliciting information, arguing the correctness of a position, and challenging the stance of the institution.

In short, the worker's posture, both to the community residents and to the institutional representatives with whom the worker is engaged, is that of advocate for the client group's point of view. While employing these techniques, the worker is not enabler, broker, expert, consultant, guide, or social therapist (Ross, 1955, pp. 220–228). The worker is, in fact, a partisan in a social conflict, and the worker's expertise is available exclusively to serve client interests. The impartiality of the enabler and the functionalism of the broker are absent here. Other actors in this social conflict may be using their expertise and resources against the client. Thus the community organizer may need to argue the appropriateness of issuing a permit while the police argue its inappropriateness, or the worker and tenant may take the position that building-code violations warrant the withholding of rent while the landlord argues their nonexistence. There may even be differences among social workers. For example, a community organization worker may claim certain welfare benefits for a group of clients over the opposition of a social investigator, or a community worker and a city housing authority worker may take opposite sides over the criteria the housing authority uses to evict tenants in city projects as undesirable.

In jurisdictional disputes or if organizational prerogatives are at issue, it is not uncommon to find social workers at odds with each other. When issues of professional ideology or politics are involved, vigorous advocacy is the rule rather than the exception, as a casual glance through the professional journals shows. Why is it not possible for such advocates to be recruited for the poor from the ranks of social workers? This is one of the orders of today's business.

Outside the courtroom, attorneys for defendants and plaintiffs often mingle in an atmosphere of congeniality. Social workers do not enjoy this kind of professional relationship. It is likely that the partisan advocacy postulated will evoke virulence from the public agency that is directed against the worker. The following charges were made by school principals of a local district ("Report of Twenty-Six Principals of Districts 1–4," 1964) as a result of the actions of a group of parents who were part of the MFY community organization program:

> We find that a group of its staff is fomenting suspicion and enmity toward the schools . . . this group is largely in the CO program. . . .
>
> Mobilization workers have been engaged in a war on the schools. . . .

Parents and children are encouraged to make such complaints. This means the MFY is accumulating a secret dossier on the teachers in the area. . . .

The social worker from MFY began to assume the mantle of "guardian.". . .

It should be noted . . . how a controversy between MFY and the principals is transformed into a conflict between the community and the schools.

Such a response is not surprising since advocacy, if effective, will cause public agencies to spend more money, create more work for their already harassed staff, and focus the community's attention on the agencies' shortcomings.

THE ACTIVIST ROLE

Once the fact is recognized that community development efforts on behalf of the poor will produce partisan situations, it must be conceded further that the community organizer—or, for that matter, any other service worker in the urban slum— must choose which side to be on. The same logic that legitimates the roles of broker and advocate leads inevitably to another role that of activist. Morris and Rein (1963, p. 174) have pointed out:

Political knowledge and skill to achieve one's ends have often been considered by social workers to be unprofessional. We have somehow believed that strong advocacy of a particular point of view and the development of techniques to achieve those ends violate our professional commitment to the democratic process. The question for us is whether our commitment to professional neutrality and noninvolvement is to continue to sustain our professional practice.

The traditional neutrality of the social work profession has much to recommend it, but it has been exercised to the detriment of certain client groups. Morris and Rein suggest that if this policy of noninvolvement persists, the function of community organization practice will be limited to coordination. If community organization is to find a role in community development, it cannot be exclusively neu-

tral, hence the role of activist must also be embraced.

Except for the heroes of the American Revolution, this nation has had a culturally estranged view of the political and social activist. Despite their ultimate vindication, the abolitionist, suffragette, and labor organizer are still viewed as historical mutants by the community at large. Activists are characterized as "outsiders" and "agitators" to this very day, whether they play their roles in Selma, Alabama, or between Houston and Delancey Streets in New York City.

However, the activist role is and has been a legitimate stance for the social worker, especially the community organizer, and it must be available to be chosen from among other strategies when community needs require such activity. The passivity and objectivity of the service professions is after all something of a myth: people are urged to action of all sorts— to visit a dentist, sit up straight, curb their dogs, contribute to the Red Cross, and, in some communities, to register and vote and to support the PTA. In neighborhood community development, students are urged to stay in school, tenants to keep off project lawns, dropouts to join the Job Corps, and mothers to use well-baby clinics. Why should not tenants who are without heat also be urged to withhold rents, parents with grievances to boycott the schools, or citizens without franchise to take to the streets in legal public demonstration as a means to redress their grievances?

The answer to this point has been a matter of contingency, not reason. Some members of the profession have expressed concern that recourse to roles other than that of enabler—particularly that of activist—entails manipulation of the client group or community. The writer is convinced that the choice of role bears no relevance whatsoever to the issue of manipulation. As an attempt to achieve goals determined by the worker rather than the clients, manipulation can be accomplished by many techniques. Activists and advocates, no less than enablers and brokers, must make judgments on the basis of their professional appraisal of the client's needs, without regard to political expedience, personal ideology, or the vested interests of the agency.

Although techniques of activism are being sought, they are, in the main, unformulated. A body of literature is beginning to evolve, however, based on the philosophy and tactics of nonviolent direct action. For example, Oppenheimer and Lakey (1965) describe such techniques as haunting, renouncing honors, hartal,[1] boycott, demonstrations, leafleting, picketing, vigils, and role playing. They also suggest forms for record-keeping and typical budgets for voter registration projects, provide notes on security in the Deep South and offer advice on how to conduct oneself if arrested (including such specific suggestions as wearing two sets of underwear to absorb the shock of being dragged and using a bucket of water to remove traces of tear gas). Social workers should not be intimidated by the notion of incorporating some of these suggestions into their method: their strangeness stems largely from unfamiliarity. It might be noted that the many civil rights workers who have sought counsel and technique from social workers have frequently found social work methods somewhat strange also and have wondered how they might be incorporated into the methodology of nonviolence.

ORGANIZATIONAL FORMS OF NEIGHBORHOOD DEVELOPMENT

Those in community organization practice who have wrestled with the problems

---

[1] "Hartal" is defined by *Webster's Third New International Dictionary* as "concerted cessation of work and business especially as a protest against a political situation. . . ."

of neighborhood development in urban slums have found the issue of the organizational forms that their efforts should take a troublesome one. In what form should slum residents organize to mount efforts toward self-help? When the forms that voluntary associations take in the middle-class community are examined, a proliferation of styles, purposes, and patterns of participation, as varied as the personalities and social circumstances of those who participate in them, is discovered. Social workers do not have the temerity to suggest that there is a single optimal form that middle-class voluntarism should take. The assumption that such a form exists for collective action in the slum community is equally untenable.

Rather than debate on the relative merits of various alternatives, what is needed is to determine the strategies that will be most effective.

Forms of organization, their structure, and their affiliations if any will depend on the job decided on and the personnel available. The worker may want to join an existing group in order to influence it; the worker may want to set up an ad hoc or temporary group composed either of individuals or of representatives of other groups; or the worker may want to create a new group (Oppenheimer & Lakey, 1965, p. 43).

Neighborhood work has been conducted with groups on the basis of common cultural patterns (hometown clubs), common social problems (welfare or housing organizations), physical proximity (building or block organizations), social movements (civil rights groups), specific task orientation (voter-registration campaigns), and the operation of a resource center (storefronts). If it has not yet created the technology or method of neighborhood community development work, social work efforts at community organization in urban slums have at least established the legitimacy of such efforts.

Commenting editorially on this issue as

reflected in the MFY experience, the *New York Times* (1964) stated:

If Mobilization for Youth is to do more than merely ameliorate the lot of the poorest elements of the community, it must teach them to help themselves by concerted efforts. . . . Any form of social protest is bound to generate controversy, and some forms clearly raise serious questions of propriety for an agency that draws so much of its support from government funds. . . . But the poor must be encouraged to believe that there are ways to express their views on the need for social betterment. . . . The right to fight City Hall is as much a prerogative of the poor as of any other group of citizens; it is only when those who dwell in the slums and have too little to keep themselves and their families in dignity surrender to a supine sense of total futility and helplessness that the community has real cause to worry.

References

Bailey, Betty Jo, Pinsky, Sidney.   1964 voter registration drive. Unpublished report. New York, Mobilization for Youth, 1965.

Bandura, Albert.   Behavioral psychology. *Scientific American*, March 1967, *216*, 78–86.

Biddle, Bruce J., & Thomas Edwin J.   *Role Theory: Concepts and research*. New York: Wiley, 1966.

Biddle, William W., & Biddle, L. J.   *The community development process: The rediscovery of local initiative*. New York: Holt, Rinehart & Winston, 1965.

Bisno, Herbert.   A theoretical framework for teaching social work methods and skills with particular reference to undergraduate social welfare education. *Journal of Education for Social Work*, Fall 1969, *5*, 5–17.

Brager, George A., & Jorcin, Valerie.   Bargaining: A method in community change. *Social Work*, October 1969, *14*, 73–83.

Briar, Scott.   The current crisis in social casework. In *Social Work Practice, 1967*. New York: Columbia University Press, 1967.

Deutsch, Morton.   *The resolution of conflict*. New Haven, Conn.: Yale University Press, 1973.

Gross, Neal, Masson, Ward, & McEachern, Alexander W.   *Explorations in role analysis*. New York: Wiley, 1958.

Jandt, Fred.   *Conflict resolution through communication*. New York: Harper & Row, 1973.

Kahn, Alfred J.   Trends and problems in community organization. In *Social Work Practice 1964*. New York: Columbia University Press, 1964.

Kronenfeld, Daniel.   Community organization and welfare. Unpublished report, New York, *Mobilization for Youth*, 1965.

Mahaffey, Maryann.   Lobbying and Social Work, *Social Work*, January 1972, *17*, 3–11.

McPheeters, Harold L., & Ryan, Robert M.   *A core of competence for baccalaureate social welfare and curricular implications*. Atlanta, Ga.: Southern Regional Education Board, 1971.

Miller, Gerald, & Simons, Herbert (Eds.).   *Perspectives on communication in social conflict*. Englewood Cliffs, N.J.: Prentice-Hall, 1974.

Morris, Robert, & Rein, Martin.   Emerging patterns in community planning. In *Social Work Practice, 1963*. New York: Columbia University Press, 1963.

Murphy, Campbell.   *Community organization practice*. Boston: Houghton Mifflin, 1954.

Neiman, Lionel J., & Hughes, James W.   The problem of the concept of role—A re-survey of the literature. In Herman D. Stein & Richard A. Cloward (Eds.), *Social perspectives on behavior*. New York: Free press, 1959.

Oppenheimer, Martin, & Lakey, George.   *A manual for direct action*. Chicago: Quadrangle Books, 1965.

Panter, Ethel.   Ego building procedures that foster social functioning. *Social Casework*, March 1966, *47*, 142–143.

Payne, James E.   Ombudsman roles for social workers. *Social Work*, January 1972, *17*, 94–100.

Report of twenty-six principals of district 1–4. New York: City of New York, 1964. Mimeographed.

Roberts, Robert W., & Nee, Robert H. (Eds.).   *Theories of social casework*. Chicago: University of Chicago Press, 1970.

Ross, Murray G.   *Community organization*. New York: Harper & Row, 1955.

Rothman, Jack.   Three models of community organization practice. In *Social Work Practice, 1968*. New York: Columbia University Press, 1968.

Satir, Virginia.   *Conjoint family therapy: A guide to therapy and technique*. Palo Alto, Calif.: Science and Behavior Books, 1964.

Schwartz, William.   The social worker in the group. In *Social welfare forum, 1961*. New York: Columbia University Press, 1961.

Smith, Clagett.   *Conflict resolution: Contributions of the behavior sciences*. Notre Dame, Ind.: University of Notre Dame Press, 1971.

Tedeschi, James, et al.   *Conflict, power and games*. Hawthorne, N.Y.: Aldine Publishing, 1973.

Tropp, Emanuel.   The group: In life and in social work. *Social Casework*, May 1968, *49*, 267–274.

Walton, Richard.   *Interpersonal peace making*. Reading, Mass.: Addison-Wesley Publishing, 1969.

Whittaker, James K.   Models of group development: Implications for group work practice. *Social Service Review*, September 1970, *44*, 308–322.

Whittaker, James K.   *Social treatment: An approach to interpersonal helping*. Hawthorne, N.Y.: Aldine Publishing, 1974.

Wilensky, Harold L., & Lebeaux, Charles N.   *Industrial society and social welfare*. New York: Russell Sage Foundation, 1958.

Chapter 12

Interventive Methods:
Implementation of Roles

This chapter continues the discussion of the action phase of the problem-solving process and focuses on the carrying out of the varying roles that the social worker may find useful. To carry out a plan requires the same knowledge and skills discussed previously: (1) use of communication; (2) development and use of the relationship; (3) development and use of resources; and (4) the social worker's use of self. However, the action phase often requires that these skills be differently organized and utilized in that the purpose of their use has changed. Rather than trying to define the problem, or set the goals, or analyze and integrate as in the assessment stage, the worker and client are now involved in a focused effort to bring about some action toward the goals that have been set by the methods agreed upon and guided by the plan.

In all social work activities with all sizes of systems and types of systems (client, target, action, change agent, professional and problem recognition system), the practitioner uses these skills, although their organization and focus will be different depending upon purpose, plan, and type of action. For example, in carrying through on acting as an advocate for the client system, the worker may be engaging in the negotiation of conflict. This will require the use of self in setting a particular climate (relationship), great self-awareness and self-discipline, and excellent skills in use of certain types of communication. In attempting to carry out the role of helper for an individual client, workers will also be interested in setting and maintaining a particular climate, will use certain types of communication, will need to be aware of their own needs and impulses, and will discipline their use of self. However, the *particular* type of relationship, the *particular* things communicated, the *particular* use of self will be different because the purpose, role, and type of system are different. Thus all social work activities require the four primary abilities in some combination.

There are four tests that all change processes need to meet if they are to be helpful to others. First is the rule of *parsimony*—all actions taken should be as simple and economic as possible in the ways they intervene in the life space of any living system. Work with the client systems is very seldom focused on total change of a total system. Actually, the social work process becomes more individualized and differentiated the more it is shaped by the goal, the problem, and the individual plan. All action should follow the salient features of the plan. By this we mean that careful consideration should be taken of the major thrust of the plan. Above all both action and plan should be relevant to the goals. We need to view ourselves as agents of the clients in attempting the changes. We need to be guided by the climate goals and we need to have considerable humility as to our ability to contribute effectively.

Another important principle of working toward change is that efforts to bring about change in either the client system, or other systems, may be addressed to the feeling, the thinking, or the acting of the individuals that compose the target system or toward their transactions as guided by them. These three capacities of the human ego are, as we have said before, so interrelated that change in any one characteristic may result in change in all, and change in any one capacity of one person in a group may change all aspects of the system. It is important to address the element or elements that seem most salient to resolving the problem.

For example: a mother, with a seriously retarded child, is having great difficulty developing skills to care for it properly. She does not understand retardation and feels that it must all be her fault. She has overwhelming feelings of guilt, of loss and grief, of shame, of helplessness. It is best to start with her feelings and hope that as one helps her through acceptance and reassurance, she will feel better and thus act better in the ways she approaches her child? Or is it better to see that she has some help with the child and is taught some needed skills and hope that in caring for the child and hope that as she is able to successfully cope with her baby, her self-esteem, and enhanced sense of competence will change her feelings. Or do you rely on knowledge and hope that if she understands mental illness better, her feelings will change and her actions improve? In this situation, the best action will undoubtedly combine some judicious use of all three.

This principle is equally true (as a further example) in an advocacy situation in which the worker has demanded and received the opportunity to meet with the board of directors of an agency about certain policies that exclude many clients who need the service. One may approach the board by trying to assess whether it is the board members' feeling about these clients and such service, or their belief about the problems that might lie in such an expansion or their lack of the resources needed for expansion that keeps them from offering service and to attempt to focus change efforts on that element. Or is it one board member's feeling, thinking, and so on that is causing the problem; or is it a battle for control between two groups on the board that is holding up action?

In considering the selection of approaches to the client or target system, the worker will also need to consider the focus of the work. In other words is the primary focus to produce some effect on an individual or is it to change the interaction of individuals within a family system, or is it to change the community target system?

A simple scheme for categorizing the focus of the work follows:

1. *Primarily focused on some change in the individual client as target system either through one-to-one work with the individual or through work with the individuals' experience as a member of their family or a group.*
2. *Primarily focused on change in the interactions of the members of a client group or family as a social system.* Here the interaction between and among members is the target system.
3. *Primarily focused on helping the client system to carry through on plans to change a target system.* One of the primary examples of this is the task-oriented group called a committee. There are also tenants' groups, welfare rights' groups, and so on. Although many times this may be the focus of one-to-one work, as well.
4. *Primarily focused on helping the client system to change the transactions between itself and another system.* In this instance the target system is the transactions between the two systems. Often this may be transactions between a family and another social system, but it may also be between an individual and another social system such as the school, or even the extended family.

In working with human systems for whatever purpose and toward whatever change, there are two factors to take into consideration in everything one does. One factor is the climate that the worker offers the system (relationship) within which the work is done, and the other is the work itself. In other words, the how and the what is a part of every action. We are going to develop some suggested classifications of the what and how in the following discussion. These suggestions are not related to size of system but rather to the purpose of the process and may be used with any size system. We are going to discuss these techniques as they apply to the target system as they are aimed at bringing change. In many instances the target system will be the client system, but it may be other systems with which the practitioner is involved. These techniques are not exhaustive, as they do not cover everything a social worker does, however, they do represent the approaches most commonly used by social work practitioners. They are grouped in clusters because that is the way they are usually used. However, one may borrow from different clusters in order to more effectively carry out purpose.

ENCOURAGEMENT

Encouragement, by itself, is used as a cluster with a system that has the capacity, ability, and knowledge to work at the problem on its own, provided it has a little approval, acceptance, and support. It will often be used with other types of client systems in combination with other techniques. In fact, it is one of the most used clusters of techniques. The techniques used for this purpose are listening, reflection back to the system of what it has been communicating, giving an opportunity for ventilation, occasionally giving reassurance, or expressing confidence in the system's work. In

using these techniques, the worker is responding to the actions and communication of the system but is not adding new things to what is already being
produced by the system.

The climate that the worker offers to accompany these techniques involves
freedom and independence for the client system to pursue its own course
and acceptance and expectance that the system can and will pursue the
work. The worker is emotionally responsive to the system's feeling, thinking,
and doing but always in such a way as to convey respect for the system's
own ability to act.

ENHANCING AWARENESS OF OWN BEHAVIOR

Enhancing awareness of the system's own behavior is used primarily
with a system that needs to understand just what it may be contributing
to the problem. Behavior as used here includes both feelings and thinking.
The useful techniques are outlined in the following discussion. The system
may be helped to see itself more clearly if the worker paraphrases what
the system has said.

Paraphrasing.   This means that the worker restates the basic message
in similar, but usually fewer, words—both as a test of the worker's understanding but also in order that the system might hear its own productions.
In order to do this, the worker must listen very carefully for the basic message. Then, the worker, in what is communicated to the client, must remain
very close to what is being expressed, simplifying to make clear, and synthe-
sizing what the content, feelings, thinkings, or behavior mean to the worker.
Workers are always tentative in their synthesis submitting it for the system's
approval, amendment, or rejection. While sharing how they heard the system's message, the worker watches carefully for clues that either confirm
or deny the accuracy and helpfulness of the rephrasing.

Clarifying and reflecting.   Clarifying and reflecting are other techniques
that are helpful in improving awareness of behavior. These go beyond paraphrasing, which expresses only what is implied by the system. Clarifying
and reflecting both connect islands of feelings, experiences, and thinking
that the system left unconnected or may not see as connected. Thus, the
workers' communication will be seen by the client system as something
very different from paraphrasing. Reflecting carries the feeling of trying to
understand the world as the target system does. It is a sharing of the way
the worker reads the total message. The worker selects and pulls together
the best mix of context, feelings, and action from the productions of the
target system in order to advance the understanding of the system and
thus bring change from new understanding. Clarifying summarizes core material and brings vague material into sharper focus. It identifies themes that
seem to run throughout the behavior of the client system, drawing conclusions from the material presented. In clarifying, the worker makes a guess
regarding the system's basic meaning and offers it, along with an admission
of the worker's confusion, for consideration, or the worker may admit confu-

sion as to meaning and try to restate what the client has said. The worker may also ask for clarification, repetition, or illustration from the client system if it appears that the clients might understand the situation better if they tried to clarify it for the worker.

Checking perception and focusing. Perception checking is a way of helping the system realize what it has just produced. The worker paraphrases what the worker believes was said and asks for confirmation or further clarification. Focusing is helpful in that it can be used to emphasize a feeling or idea from a vast array of verbalization and to reduce confusions, diffusion, and vagueness. Thus the worker assists the system in focusing on assumptions, ways of thinking, notions, or feelings which may be hidden in the discussion. Workers should use their own feelings of confusion and sense of the system's direction as a guide to decide when to focus. *Appropriate questioning* is also helpful in clarifying for a system the effect of its behavior. Questions can be used to lead the system to further clarify information, feelings, experiences, and can serve to encourage the system to explore feelings and thinking or to elaborate on those already discussed.

Summarizing and interpreting. As with questioning, summarizing can be used for many purposes, but in this cluster, it is used to check the worker's understanding and to encourage the clients to explore the material more completely. Interpreting is an active process of explaining the meaning of events to clients so that they are able to see their problems in a new way. The worker may interpret events presented from three perspectives: the client's own frame of reference, the worker's frame of reference, and from the frame of reference of another system. This latter is often done in the brokering or mediating role when the worker may present the target system with the frame of reference of the client system for the target systems' consideration, and hopefully for its understanding. Or the process may be reversed, and the client system may be presented with the target system's frame of reference. The worker also may offer alternative frames of reference by relabeling the material presented. An example of relabeling is found in the old story of the pessimist as one who sees the glass of water as half empty in which case the worker then pointed out that it was half full. Another example is found in the behavior of Tom Sawyer who labeled the work of whitewashing the fence for his Aunt Polly as a privilege rather than drudgery. As a result, he was promoted from worker to supervisor and collected considerable treasure as his friends bid for the privilege of becoming his workers.

In interpreting, practitioners introduce their understanding of *what they think the message or behavior means* from their theory of human growth and behavior. This requires considerable skill and the following rules must be observed. Keep the language simple and close to the system's message. Offer notions in a very, very tentative way as a possible contribution. Always solicit the client system's evaluation of just what the contribution is. In face of the client's denial that the contribution is pertinent, do not hold to it as correct, but also do not negate it entirely, for example. "It may not be a helpful idea, but I would like to do some more thinking about it . . ."

Informing.   Another technique useful in increasing one's awareness of one's own behavior is informing which involves giving information, suggestions, or advice. Informing is probably underused by many workers in that they assume that the system has certain knowledge and skills that they may not possess. If, in informing, the system indicates that it already has such information, the worker can apologize for the repetition. Generally workers give information, suggestions, or advice about four aspects of the situation. The worker may use informing and checking to establish a common understanding about the situation between worker and other system. Informing is also used to share with the system the worker's view of the situation—how the worker adds it up. Informing may involve the sharing by the worker of some suggestions as to actions the system might want to try or it may involve the straight communication of new knowledge about the situation.

Actions.   Clients may be encouraged to try a new way of responding to others or of handling their transactions with others followed by evaluation of the results of the changed action. In this way, clients gain an understanding that their behavior influences the behavior of others as well as learning new social skills.

Confrontation.   This technique is discussed last because it is probably the most difficult to use correctly. Confrontation is always hard for the system to accept or consider because it always involves some unmasking of distortions in the system's feelings, experiences, or behavior. The worker identifies certain patterns that lie buried, hidden, or beyond the immediate knowledge of the system. It is something the system never either thought about and/ or was willing to accept before. Acceptance of confrontation is also difficult because it carries some challenge to do something about these things that have not yet even been acknowledged by the system. It must be used as a mode of caring and involvement and not as punishment or discipline. Possibly no other technique offers such a tempting avenue for the worker to act out unacknowledged feelings about either self or the other system than the use of this technique. It is so easy to say that the system needs to face honestly what it is doing, that it needs to be shocked out of an unwillingness to work, and so on. These comments may cover the worker's anger or frustration with the client system, may cover the worker's punitiveness toward the client, or may reveal the worker's own hidden need to appear powerful or all knowing in interaction with the client.

To be used effectively, the confrontation must be based on a deep understanding of the implication for the system in being presented with this material by the worker. The worker needs always to keep in mind the question of how this action helps the client to move toward desired change or cope with the situation's demands. Confrontation is always given tentatively with a motivation to help and as a part of the involvement with the client. Done poorly with a vulnerable system, it can result in a quick accommodation to the worker's views or in the system's withdrawal from contact with perhaps considerable anger, either of which are ineffective ways of trying to solve problems. A problem of using confrontation with a system, other than the client system, is that the target system may take out its anger and hurt at the worker's activity on the client system and punish that system since the worker is not so vulnerable. Finally, confrontation should be used only after a careful evaluation of the relationship and what such information will mean to the system within the already established climate of working together.

Relationship.   In using this group of techniques to enhance the system's awareness of its own behavior, the primary stance of the worker is that of a concerned collateral resource. The worker uses such techniques when there is considerable expectation that the system is capable of taking the lead in problem solving with a little help. The relationship while warm and supporting is also strongly task oriented and leaves the control for the action in the hands of the client involved. The worker stands beside, supports, and comments on the action toward problem-solution but does not become actively involved in the "doing." This stance on the part of the worker is also important for the next group of techniques. The worker may be more active in contributing information and perspective in the type of work discussed in the next section.

ENHANCING THE CLIENT'S AWARENESS OF OTHERS' BEHAVIOR

In working to enhance the system's awareness of the meaning of other ways of behaving, the worker may use all the techniques described earlier but will be much more active in informing the client about the perspective of other systems. The worker may be much more active in simply giving knowledge about the expected norms of behavior. As an example of this, it is often found that parents who are experiencing trouble in their interaction with their children may have no notions of what kind of behavior to expect from their children. Or the school system may be very punitive toward a child for certain behavior that is a part of the culture from which he child comes. Or a group of male professors may be totally unaware of why the group's climate changed after they referred to the middle-aged woman professor, who was chairing the group, and two other women members as "the girls." In these situations when client systems are ignorant of the values or needs of the other systems, new information alone may be extremely helpful.

However, to accept and use new information often requires that the client change cherished ways of viewing human relationships and transactions. This may result in resistances that need to be worked through.

Allowing the client to ventilate feelings and to think about expectations and norms of others is helpful and may prepare the way for some reframing of what is expressed. If a client can express anger or frustration with the other system, it will then be better able to either listen to new information or engage in logical discussions, which may be helpful. Perhaps two of the most helpful techniques in this area are the prediction of events and the discussion as to how they may be handled differently than the client's usual way of responding. Thus the client system may consider alternate ways of behaving in order to achieve a difficult relationship with others. Or the client system may be supported in discussing the problem with the other system or systems. In either of these approaches the client system may be encouraged to rehearse how these new actions will be carried out and ways of evaluating the results.

Relationship.   The feeling tone of the relationship will vary in this situation largely in relation to the client's investment in the meaning they attach to the behavior of others. It may vary all the way from that of a concerned collateral resource to a strong supportive relationship. (See Reading 12–1.)

SOCIALIZATION INTO EFFECTIVE ROLE PERFORMANCE

These techniques are usually used with a client system (individual, family, or group), although they could be adapted to any other system that is having significant difficulty fulfilling its role. Usually the client systems, for which this is a problem, are identified by another system, and the worker enters the potential client system uninvited. There will be a range of clients within this group—many of which may respond to techniques discussed earlier—but here relationship to the worker is central to the process.

Relationship.   In discussing this type of intervention, we are going to begin with a discussion on the stance of the worker because, in no other situation are the worker's feelings about the client and the worker's ability to trust and to give without expecting back more important.

In this type of situation, workers must exercise exceeding care as to how they cross the boundaries of the potential client system as uninvited intruders. They must demonstrate complete respect and complete concern for the system, but paradoxically, they also may need to take a firm, positive stance within most of these situations. They need to be strong and active in their involvement with the system. They are not standing by as a collateral resource, but rather they must be part of the action. In such situations the worker usually needs to come across as a knowing authority with considerable power, but this must be connected with the communication of a commitment to using it in behalf of the client and the communication of the belief that the client is someone special. Needless to say—the worker must deeply feel this as the client will quickly sense a fraud. Initially these clients usually do not trust, and there is no reason why they should. The workers must understand and accept that they do not have the right to demand liking or trust from either the client or target system if they are to work in these types of situations. They must not only deeply respect this stance on the part of the client, but they must prove their trustworthiness by pointing out to the client that there are realistic limits to their trustworthiness. Since they initially entered the system as the agent of a community problem-identifier, there are usually requirements that the worker must report certain things back to the community or take certain actions on behalf of the community. Thus there are realistic limits to workers' ability to act totally as agents of the client system. This must be acknowledged from the beginning of contract. The worker needs to allow and encourage such clients to be as dependent as necessary in the interests of protecting them from further damage and in the interests of building the kind of relationship necessary for the problem solving that has to go on. This is critical. Workers who are fearful of dependency are seldom helpful in these situations. Workers must have frequent contacts with the client. One can never socialize certain client systems into a role with once a month visits. These types of situations call for a very special kind of person. The worker who would do this kind of work needs to be a strong, courageous person willing to risk a great deal without expecting a return and yet able to accept the dependency of others freely. It requires the greatest of caring, because it requires uncondi-tioned giving while leaving the system free to fail without recriminations.

The worker needs to start work in these situations by attempting to estab-lish some mutual goals. But again we would caution that these goals are something the client wants—often involving the worker in some concrete giving of agency resources or of finding other resources to give aid. In order to help clarify what is meant, we wish to quote the following:

> The idea of setting goals by mutual agreement may be a good, professional one in most instances. But [with this type of client] it is an empty exercise. Any objectives involving a generally better life must be the worker's . . . [the clients] will believe them only after they have been demonstrated. More to the point are the basic survival needs . . . which [the clients] may expect the worker to supply (Polansky, Borgman & De Saix, 1972, p. 26).

This quote is an excellent demonstration of a misunderstanding of goal setting, at least in the problem-solving model. The author of this quote makes the automatic assumption that the only meaningful goals are those the work-ers might wish for. It highlights the importance of the position of differentiat-ing between the worker's view and the client's view. The client's wish for some basic survival needs is the clients' goal, a very important goal, and the very best goal to start with. The point is that the practitioner does not decide what the client needs and automatically go about securing resources to meet client need. To decide what the client needs without participation of the client only contributes further to the client's inability to cope with life. Instead the worker involves the clients in a discussion of what they see as their needs and what they want to meet these needs. The client is involved in articulating and prioritizing their wants, considering alternatives to the resources they may see as desirable, setting goals and considering the preferred way they see for fulfilling these wants. As an example of the involvement of the client in this process, let us consider the example of Mrs. James.

> Mrs. James, an AFDC mother with three small children, living in a state with a very minimal grant, had not been able to stretch her grant to cover clothing for the children or herself. All four were badly in need of clothes. The worker was aware of a church that had collected used clothing for such persons. On her way to visit the James family she stopped by the church office and selected some of the better clothes and gave them to Mrs. James. Mrs. James expressed gratitude, but the next time the worker came to the home she saw the clothing, dirty and

torn piled in a corner and the family still seemed poorly dressed. The worker was angry and upset at what she saw as the lack of appreciation for the clothing and her effort to secure resources to meet the needs of the clients.

The worker talked with her supervisor who suggested that perhaps Mrs. James should be involved in considering the clothing she needed and the problems of adequate care of various types of clothes. Then perhaps the worker could make arrangements to take Mrs. James to the church to select the particular garments that she wanted to meet her need. In the process of discussing the types of clothes that Mrs. James wanted, the worker could also consider with her the care of the articles if they were to serve the family well over time. While concerned with the amount of time such effort took and secretly considering it very inefficient, the worker followed through on the plan. Three months later, Mrs. James was still carefully laundering and mending the clothes that she had selected, and was proudly talking of "her new clothes." By making decisions and taking action in her own behalf, around her own wants, Mrs. James's family was better clothed and she had developed some coping skills that were valuable in managing her family.

The exercise of setting such a goal should not only give the worker a place to start, but it should remind all workers of the differences between their perspective and that of the client. There can be no more important goals than those that involve the worker in securing concrete needs for decent living on the part of the client.

Active supplying of resources.   Since in many of these situations, the goals that are important to the client involve concrete survival needs, the activities of the worker in supplying such concrete resources are extremely important in solving some very critical problems of the client system. In the securing of such resources, the worker is usually actively involved in the work of physically getting the things. The worker does not act as broker or mediator for the client, expecting the client to carry through on most of the action alone. In attempting to help an individual to cope with role demands that have not been met previously, the worker also will need to be skilled in the use of advice, guidance, and encouragement. In addition they will need to use the skills of helping the client in gradually being able to understand the others' position.

How active and firm the worker is in the use of these techniques will be based on the clients' motivation, ability, resources within their own control, and how they see the problem and goal. One of the important techniques is that of the worker's active securing of resources for the client. The worker does the work of securing the material things rather than acting as a broker or mediator for the clients' activities.

Direct intervention.   The worker also intervenes directly into the living situation of the client and acts for the client in the transactions with many systems. The worker usually imposes minimal demands on the client. However, in all of this, the goal is to help the client toward better role performance. Therefore, the worker needs to be scrupulous about reporting back what is being done and using this as teaching-learning material. The worker also uses modeling and identification, sets appropriate limits for client behavior, and requires clients to be as active in their own behalf as they can be with success. The worker uses all the minute particular details of life as material for teaching appropriate role behavior.

Action. Perhaps one of the most effective ways to socialize a client system into effective role performance is through involving the client in planning necessary actions to reach desired goals and in taking responsibility for carrying out such necessary tasks within their ability to do so. One must be cautious with such clients that one does not involve them in planning actions beyond their ability to satisfactorily complete. In the case of client systems just beginning to take tentative steps to act in their own behalf, failure at planned tasks can further discourage them from any future attempt and may further convince them of their inability to cope. However, involving the client in careful consideration of tasks they seem able to perform can serve to enhance their self-image and further their sense of growth and competence. To participate with the client in planning and engaging in successful task completion requires that the worker identify, mobilize, and ally with the client's potential abilities and ways of coping. It further demands that the worker be able to engage in consideration of the minute particulars in planning and rehearsing actions. The worker must be available to support and encourage. (For further discussion of use of action, see Reading 12–2.)

DEALING WITH ROLE TRANSITIONS OR ROLE LOSSES

In this situation, the client system usually has functioned satisfactorily within a certain role but now faces the certain transitions within that role (switching from being the mother of a teenager to the mother of a married woman) or certain losses of that role function (the loss of the role of wife with the death of the husband all that means in both feeling and finding new behavior patterns or, similarly, the loss of the role of worker with retirement).

Given this purpose, the worker needs to use a good many of the techniques described earlier, with special emphasis on ventilation, educating, informing about the resources and pitfalls in the new role, reassurance, listening, and conveying acceptance. In addition, temporarily the worker may need to act for clients and may need to intervene in the in-life situation. Once again action plays a central part in taking on new and different roles. Clients try on new roles by acting within those parameters.

Relationship. The relationship that the worker offers is one of warmth and caring. The worker must appear strong and yet compassionate. The worker must allow the client to be dependent for a period of time and must have frequent contacts. The worker is active and central in the process of working together.

SUPPORTING ROLE PERFORMANCE

Both institutional systems and client systems often have trouble with adequately fulfilling their role performance. This classification overlaps with other classifications. However, it is very important and in many ways represents the heart of social work practice: for many people the purpose of requesting help is to find a concrete resource that is needed to support them in adequately fulfilling their notion of their accepted performance of a valued role. Many of these clients need little but information as to the appropriate resources, how to find them, and how to gain access to them.

In such situations the work with the client is usually reality oriented, and the stance of the worker is such as to leave the client in full control of feeling, thinking, and acting. The only change effort is to supply information about resources, or perhaps to act as broker. To engage in this type of work, the worker needs to have a good, sound knowledge of the community and its resources. The worker needs to be as skilled as possible in the requirements of eligibility and routes of access to such services. The worker also needs to know who to approach in the other system if some brokering is needed.

Although with many clients the worker may be involved only with supplying necessary information about resources, there are other clients that fall into this classification that need much more help. They need much encouragement and support. They may need help in understanding their own behavior and that of others. As an example: Mr. Keene (the client whom we met earlier, whose wife had been hospitalized and whose children needed care) is a good example of a client that needed tremendous help and support in performing an effective role as a father once he had lost the support of his wife for his role performance. However, he was also suffering from problems in role transition in that he was having to take over some of the activities that, in his culture, are ordinarily found within the mother's role. In addition, his role as a husband was suddenly significantly altered, and the transactions between the husband and wife in the family system were shattered. Thus, he needed help both with certain aspects of role transition and with most aspects of role support. The worker's efforts to supply resources to shore up the parent role were not enough. He needed help with self-awareness and with understanding others' behavior. He needed to understand ways to relate to and to utilize the new systems in his life, such as the doctors and the hospital personnel. He needed to understand how alteration in the capacity of his wife to perform both the role of wife and of mother affected his role performance of husband and father. And, remember, effective role performance involves feeling, thinking, and acting. Mr. Keene needed to be approached on all three levels.

USE OF NETWORKS AS RESOURCES

Included in this chapter are some articles that emphasize particular types of worker action. One very important paper is a description of the use of the clients systems' social networks as resources for help (see Reading 12–3). While this article discusses working with Indian tribes as social networks, the principles of the article are true for any social network.

The author identifies five distinctive functions of social networks that need to be considered. (1) Social networks provide an identity for their members and meet other religious, social, or financial needs (this is particularly true with oppressed groups in which the social network offers much social and financial protection). (2) Networks usually include the extended family as a central part and may use kinship terms. (3) There is an organized hierarchy present in each network, and it is important for the worker to know and respect this organization. (4) Rapid informal communication is a characteristic of social networks, and workers need to understand, respect, and know how to use this to the advantage of the client system. (5) The network has much unconscious meaning to the members. Networks, as a social system, have boundaries and accepted ways of being admitted to the system. The worker needs to know something of the accepted pattern for crossing these boundaries as well as how one shows respect for these. Once across the boundaries, and accepted as a helper, the worker will often find that techniques listed under the two increasing awareness categories will be of help in working with network systems. In this type of work, the worker's stance is that of a collateral resource to the network in its effort to deal with its members.

SUPPORT AND ACTION

There are two other papers reproduced in this chapter. One is a paper that one of the authors wrote as a way of questioning the notion that certain techniques do not result in personality change and growth (see Reading 12–1). This paper has somewhat more elaborate discussions of some of the techniques mentioned in the earlier material, and it looks at what techniques are supportive of ego-growth and functioning of the individual. The paper is not developed to apply to other than the client system—group or individual. The same is true of the paper on action (see Reading 12–2). Both papers are significant in considering the change process of client systems.

THE RELATIONSHIP OF ROLES AND TECHNIQUES

Depending upon the fit between the purpose for which the clusters of techniques may be used and the purpose of the use of the role, the various clusters of techniques fit within certain roles. We have attempted to organize them as follows:

1. In the enabler role the worker operates to help clients find resources within themselves and will find the techniques listed under *encouragement, awareness of self,* and perhaps *awareness of others* to be useful.

2. In the roles of broker, mediator, or teacher, the worker will find the techniques listed under *awareness of others* and *awareness of self* useful with the client system, the action system, and the target system. The techniques under supporting role functioning, or working with role transitions will be useful with client systems. And certainly the use of social resources and use of social networks are basic to these roles.

3. This brings us to the role of advocate and to the fact that in attempting to socialize a client system into certain role expectations, one is acting as an advocate of either society or other systems. For example, in an abuse situation, one is acting as the advocate of the child although one may see

the parents as both the target system and the client system. In addition, many of the suggestions about relationship, use of power and authority, and active intervention are applicable to advocacy work with action or target systems as well as with client systems.

RECAPITULATION

In this chapter, we have discussed certain techniques that may be used in carrying out the action plan that has been made. These techniques fit within the roles discussed in Chapter 11. We would urge that all readers read the selections that follow this chapter for a richer development of certain critical aspects of helping techniques.

A LOOK FORWARD

In the next chapter we will focus on another important helping process— the use of teamwork. One of the most central of social work activities is the mobilization of resources that are needed to solve the client's problems. This is often done through collaborative work with colleagues from other disciplines or collaborative work with social workers in other agencies. Collaborative efforts and teamwork date back to the earliest days of social work practice, yet we have not developed a very extensive literature detailing the methods by which such work can be successfully carried out. You will find that much of your time as a social worker is taken up with collaborative planning and action. We hope that this next chapter is of help to you as you engage in such tasks.

Reading 12-1

*An Attempt to Examine the Use of Support in Social Work Practice**

Beulah Roberts Compton

The concept of support in human interaction is much older than social work practice. Social work as a profession grew out of the concern of individuals in an urban society of ever-growing complexity to find a way of assisting their fellow men and women in distress. Early social workers were "friendly visitors" attempting to sustain and encourage those who had fallen on evil days by environmental manipulation, direct advice and guidance, and expressions of concern and encouragement. These early visitors became the forerunners of a profession, and the techniques they used became, along with other techniques, a part of the methods of support and environmental manipulation.

PRACTICE WITH THE INDIVIDUAL

In the early 1940s with the appearance in casework of attempts to define and describe the major treatment methods and to organize and structure these methods into a system of practice theory, supportive treatment was first given recognition as a major helping approach, although it was still considered a simple one (Selby, 1956, pp. 400–414). All attempts to develop concepts of differential treatment methods that have appeared in the literature of the profession from 1940 until the present have included a group of techniques that have been called "supportive" or "sustaining." Just as the method has constantly appeared in the classification system, the techniques grouped together to make up

---

* An original article prepared for this text.

the method have also been consistent. The commonly mentioned techniques are (1) direct guidance and advice in practical matters, (2) environmental modification with the provision of specific and tangible services as needed, (3) the provision of opportunity for clients to discuss freely their troubling problems and their feelings about them, (4) expressions of understanding by the helper, along with assurance of interest in and concern for the client, (5) encouragement and praise implying confidence in the client's worth and abilities, and (6) protective action and exercise of professional authority when needed. The commonly listed supportive techniques suggest that the worker provide a therapeutic environment, based on understanding, concern, and acceptance in which clients can feel free to talk about their worries and concerns. The helper must take an active rather than a passive role in helping the individual to focus on the problem, in giving pertinent advice and suggestion, in reassuring, encouraging, and helping with specific practical planning. The worker should also be willing and able to enter into planning for everyday problems.

With the exception of Hollis's work (1964, pp. 52–63), the classification systems in casework have tried to label the therapeutic methods according to "level" or "depth" of help given. Support has been considered a "simple" method on the lower end of the scale of casework treatment; the aim or goal of this method was seen as helping the clients to feel more comfortable and to assist them in calling on existing strengths and resources. Support was thought to bring about relief of symptoms and better adaptive functioning through making the client feel more secure, reassured, accepted, protected, safe, and less anxious and less alone. This method was considered appropriate for (1) the person who was too weak to tolerate work toward change and (2) the well-integrated person who was temporarily threatened by an overwhelming external crisis (Selby, 1956, pp. 400–414). It was assumed that the help offered by this method would not lead to personality change. Through environmental change and increased internal comfort, the individual might be enabled to maintain present functioning or to function at a somewhat improved level, but this was not assumed to represent basic change.

It might be well to consider that the early attempts to identify treatment methods and goals in casework practice came only a few years after the theory of the unconscious and the theory of psychic determinism as developed by Freud and other psychoanalytic writers and teachers had become widely available to social workers. These insights into human motivation and the increased understanding of human behavior that they offered were eagerly sought by caseworkers as such knowledge offered a new understanding of and seemed to hold the answers to questions that previously seemed unanswerable. In the light of the impact of this new knowledge on social casework practice and of the limits of the knowledge available (at this time only Freud's early writings about the ego were available in America), it is perhaps understandable that caseworkers tended to see internal structural conflict as the primary factor that brought people to grief in the business of living. In the excitement at the promise of this new understanding, it is perhaps also understandable that early caseworkers did not differentiate between using psychoanalytic theory to advance the aims and understanding of their own professional practice and the taking over of aims of psychoanalytic practice for themselves. Thus there grew within the profession a tendency to allot the highest status and value to those activities that seemed aimed at the resolution of internal conflict by helping the clients to develop "insight" into their conflicts whose genesis was to be found in early life experience (Simon, 1964).

In recent years social work has perhaps become more sophisticated about the use of borrowed concepts and certainly psychoanalytic researches into the development and functioning of the ego have extended knowledge about personality structure and its interrelationship with social reality. However, these developments do not seem to have had the same impact upon social casework practice theory as did the earlier materials. Casework has used the knowledge of defense mechanisms provided by ego psychology, but it has not been as active in attempting to extend other concepts from ego psychology (except in certain fragmented instances, such as the development of crisis theory or in certain family counseling practices) to the reciprocal relationships between individuals and their situation.

PRACTICE WITH THE GROUP

Group work practice grew from different roots and at a different time. At the time when social caseworkers were struggling with the new knowledge of intrapersonal structure and functioning, group work was only beginning to be conscious of itself as a movement. Group work did not begin as a method of helping people in trouble to solve their problems but as a way of organizing individuals into groups for purposes of self-help toward a better way of life. The insights and concepts used by the early group workers did not come from the psychoanalytic theory with which caseworkers were struggling. Rather they came from education, especially from John Dewey, and from sociologists who were active in the self-help movements. As the years passed and group work became a part of the social work profession, its practitioners still were primarily engaged in helping groups of essentially normal individuals toward an increased self-development.

At the present time, however, the utilization of group work as a way of dealing with the individual's problems of social functioning is growing at a fast pace, and group work practitioners are becoming increasingly involved in attempts to use the insights from psychoanalysis and from group dynamics in developing practice theory for use with "treatment groups." There is also evidence of borrowing from casework practice theory; for example, Louise Frey (1962, pp. 35–42) took the list of treatment techniques considered "supportive" in casework literature and attempted to apply them to group work practice. She accepted the casework theory that support is "generally regarded as beneficial to people with weak egos and to the usually well-functioning person who is in a crisis that has impaired integrative capacity to some extent." This makes support seem safe enough, yet it does leave a question about the people served in groups who do not belong in these categories and who may actually be harmed in such a group and kept from treatment (more intensive?) sorely needed.

Frey's effort is the only example we could find in group work literature of a consideration of the interrelationship of certain group work techniques and the concept of support. In her consideration she seems to have borrowed the concept whole from casework including the dictum regarding the limits of its usefulness. Yet, the group worker's experience in work with developmental groups should be able to make a very large contribution to the concept of the ways in which the client system is supported in its efforts toward growth. At the other end of the continuum, Fritz Redl's efforts (1957) with the aggressive and disturbed child in a group or lifespace situation offers much material that workers need to consider in building a common theory of supportive practice with client systems for the totality of social work practice.

It would be hoped that in borrowing personality theory as a basis for a further development of work with groups, group work would not attempt to apply the older theory that casework borrowed at a particular point in time in its development of practice theory to group work practice in the present. Rather the two methods should join in attempting to see what both the older and the more recent theories of the nature of human beings mean for the totality of social work practice theory with any size of client system and for the specifics of method and technique.

There is a growing literature of ego psychology and of the nature of human learning that challenges the earlier Freudian psychoanalytic view of human beings as primarily seeking homeostasis as the most desirable state of human life. Rather the human need for goal-directed growth is seen as being a basic need. The ego analysts give increased importance to situational events and to the learning of adaptive behaviors for reasons other than to discharge or control instinctual psychological energies. They emphasize that people select and control their own behaviors to achieve particular consequences which have meaning to them quite apart from innate psychological energies. People give evidence of response patterns learned independently from the reduction of instinctive drives. There is a growing push to integrate knowledge of the cognitive and affective aspects of the individual; a growing recognition that one cannot separate the need to learn and grow from the need to understand and control feelings so that an individual can grow. Social rules and individual behavior are seen as reciprocal influences, with society making possible the existence of the person and the full expression of innate characteristics other than the instinctive psychological energies (Erickson, 1950, 1959; White, 1963).

The implicit model, at least for many psychiatrists, if not for social workers, is psychoanalysis. The ideal model, I believe, is life itself, the natural processes of growth and development and the rich trajectory of the life span. . . .

The more we learn about the optimal conditions for human growth—the psychophysiology of health, the normal methods of satisfying needs, ways of learning to achieve sublimations and problems—and conflict solving—the more we shall be able to utilize the knowledge as a model for our psychotherapy. . . .

There are two assumptions underlying my argument which should be made explicitly. The first is that there are two major tendencies in all people from birth to death which are ceaselessly in opposition. These might be termed the progressive trends . . . in human nature. Our lives are circumscribed by these polarities. The second assumption is that, other things being equal, progressive forces are the stronger. Growing up, all education and that special form of education known as psychotherapy are based on such forces. Viewed in this framework, mental illness would then be an expression of blocks, obstructions, interferences, arrests and fixations of the progressive forces, which leads to and results in a strengthening and reinforcement of the regressive trends. Our therapeutic task, then, is twofold. First we must identify and help remove the blocks and obstacles; with our typical orientation to pathology this is often the major focus of many psychotherapists. Second, we must identify the progressive forces with which we can ally ourselves and which at the appropriate time, we can help mobilize. This as-

pect of our therapeutic task tends to be relatively neglected. Yet it may be the most effective instrument for the removal of obstacles. Of all these forces, love is the most effective antidote to anxiety (Bandler, 1963).

SUPPORTIVE PRACTICE WITH DIFFERENT-SIZE CLIENT SYSTEMS

If we as social workers may borrow Dr. Bandler's suggestion that we model our helping processes on life itself and the natural processes of growth and development, we essentially have two tasks in helping people: (1) to identify obstacles and blocks to the system's growth and to become a partner with the strength of the client to remove or ameliorate them and (2) to identify the progressive forces of the client system with which we can ally ourselves at the appropriate time. Given this position, all our efforts with client systems in social work practice are supportive as the focus in on development and is aimed in increasing ability to cope with life pressures.

Given this way of regarding social work practice, we have moved beyond the earlier concept of support as a way of maintaining the status quo to the concept of support as growth-producing. We could perhaps borrow further from the Bandler article and identify two large classifications of direct treatment methods: (1) those methods aimed at sustaining or restoring previous capacities now buried under crisis and stress and (2) those aimed at progressive growth, at developing new and different capacities and strengths.

Louis Towley (1957, p. 422) is quoted by Frank Bruno as saying "Social work's secret tool is the infinite untapped, unused, unsuspected capacity for growth in the sovereign individual personality . . . of all types and breeds of social worker, the group worker most consciously accepts this democratic premise in his work." We do not want to do violence to Towley, but in the light of the greater understanding of the ego that is available to us today, it seems that it might be possible to rephrase the statement somewhat, for example, in the attempt to help people with problems of social functioning, social work must be primarily concerned with the infinite untapped, unused, unsuspected capacity for growth in the sovereign individual personality . . . all social workers should be most concerned with this principle of ego psychology.

If one is to operationalize the concept of ego-support, it is perhaps necessary that one state the functions of the ego, the techniques that support each function, and the way that such techniques are held to be useful. This task needs to be done but is beyond the scope of this paper. However, perhaps we can examine it in light of how we might move from the broad idea that all social work techniques may be considered to have this broad purpose to the examination of the specifics of treatment.

The provision of needed concrete resources, the therapeutic relationship, and the problem-solving process (in other words, the work on the task) are the elements of social work and must be worked within any size client system. Perhaps these elements might be examined in relation to the concept of the two classifications of social practice. The provision of resources to clients in need is as old as social work itself. Early social workers often felt that they could help people solve their problems by doing things to them— by rearranging their life situations for them. This often proved totally ineffective and, with the advance of the Freudian view that people come to grief because of internal conflict, often came to be viewed as a lesser part of the social work process. There were times when it appeared as though environmental manipulation was something done for the client quite apart from the rest of the "treatment"

effort, and the client could be made to feel as though the need of concrete aid was an obstacle in the path of more elegant treatment.

USE OF RESOURCES

In supportive practice the worker is active in securing necessary concrete aids for the clients so that their energies may be saved for the problem-solving work and life made more comfortable—a human value of some worth in itself. It is recognized that the workers' willingness to involve themselves freely in the active seeking out and utilizing of concrete aids may not only help the client deal with obstacles and so preserve or restore system functioning, but it may also serve to build a sense of worth that is important in system growth. It is recognized that doing things for the clients even when they could possibly do them for themselves is not necessarily dependency producing but rather may be strengthening when the client is fully engaged in the decision-making process and allocation of problem-solving tasks that should precede any action of a professional person on behalf of the client system. The considerations of concrete resources and their selection for use, the considerations of how one uses such resources and to what end, the growth of a feeling of responsibility as one participates in decisions about one's life—all serve to support the progressive forces of the client system. If clients are able then to actively seek out and utilize resources on their own, so much the better, but to require them to do this at the expense of greatly heightened anxiety or possible failure feeds the regressive forces of the personality.

USE OF RELATIONSHIP

In supportive social work, the quality of the relationship that the worker seeks to create, regardless of system size, is that of a partnership for work. It is based in current reality as a good working relationship needs to be. The relationship has both a nurturing quality and an expectation that the client or group will participate appropriately in the problem-solving process. However, the expectation is paced to the client's capacity, and the acceptance will continue even if clients find it difficult to work on their part(s) of the task. Within the relationship, there is a lending of the worker's strength to supplement areas where the client is weak. To be effective this must be a loan freely given, but it is a loan, not a gift, for while the loan need not be repaid and carries no interest payments, there is the implication that this loan is made for the purposes of the system's development of its own strength. Elements of concern and respect have a major place in such a relationship. There is a recognition that both the client and the worker bring something of value to the working together. We believe that there is a common quality in the development and use of the relationship in supportive work whatever the size of client system that lies in the climate for work and in the attitude of the worker toward the clients—attitudes of attentiveness, receptivity, acceptance, and expectation.

USE OF SUPPORTIVE METHODS

The problem-solving methods themselves do not lend themselves as well to the global approach as does the discussion of the relationship and the provision of resources. Whatever may be said about the commonness of methods of offering service to different-sized client systems, when things get to the point of the worker across the desk from an individual or a worker in a circle with a group we see that they are doing different things, and workers need to develop somewhat different skills for different-sized client systems. However, it would seem possible to con-

sider some common techniques of support and examine what these mean for what one does with any system. In the first place, we suspect that no one technique of problem-solving can be considered supportive in and of itself. It is supportive within the context of the relationship and within a pattern of techniques. In other words, we do not use any one technique in grand isolation but rather techniques are used in patterns and within a relationship. Let us attempt to examine some common techniques to see how these are used differentially in the one-to-one and in the one-to-group situation.

Reassurance. Reassurance, the expression of recognition and approval of the client's capacities, achievements, feelings, and needs, is a common procedure of supportive treatment. It is usually seen as a passive technique in which the worker approves an expression of the client. It could well be broadened into an active search for the strengths of the client—for the areas in which the system is able to cope successfully. When these areas are identified, the worker needs to take an active part in identifying them with the client. It might be well to keep reassurance as it is now understood and add "active recognition of the coping strengths of the client" to the list. The active component of the search for strengths seems to convey the worker's active concern and partnership to the client. Reassurance is primarily used as a technique of sustaining or restoring system capacity, but when used in conjunction with other techniques, it can be a part of help aimed at growth. In the one-to-one situation workers carry the burden of doing the reassuring. However, this depends upon a positive, warm relationship and the client's acceptance of the worker's authority to make the technique a helpful one. In the group situation group members may carry the burden of this with any particular member. The group members' discussion of their common problems and the member's growing awareness that feelings and needs are shared by others is reassuring.

Educational methods.   It is important in this consideration of the techniques of support that thought be given to the position of the worker as a teacher. One of the contributions of ego-psychology has been the recognition that the ego operates by means of its cognitive processes as well as its affective energies. Problem-solving in our complicated society requires not only that feelings and impulses be controlled but that the ego have at its disposal the knowledges and skills necessary to problem-solving. We often made the tragic mistake of confusing lack of cognitive and/or social skills for resistance or low motivation. We must remember that the client without cognitive or social skills in our society is as vulnerable as the emotionally ill. This technique demands that the worker give careful, painstaking consideration to the small details of daily living. It requires a careful examination of reality with the worker actively supplying the knowledge the client does not possess. In work with groups, the group members may supply much of this direct teaching. The use of program media to provide opportunities for mastery and achievement and the development of structure and democratic organizational procedures are important ways that the group work may implement this technique. Workers may also use the members' involvement in decision making and conflict resolution as education in social skills as well as finding this technique useful for developing the ability to control feelings and to express oneself in a disciplined way that is an important part of personality growth. In the one-to-one situation the worker teaches decision making by carefully helping the client to collect the facts, to weigh them,

to make considered judgments, to consider consequences of choices made, and to plan to implement the choice. The technique of education in cognitive and social skills is primarily one directed at growth rather than ego-sustaining. It is time-consuming and demands patience on the part of the worker. It has been used more extensively in work with client groups rather than in one-to-one work and has been used most extensively in work with groups of children, but it needs to become a better-understood part of practice with any size client system.

Rehearsal.   In working with groups the worker may use the group interaction so that the individual has a specifically structured experience in a protected social environment in which social learning may take place and within which the client may practice carrying out a task. There is a somewhat similar technique called "rehearsal" that may be used in work with individuals. This is a detailed consideration in the interview situation of the exact details of how the client will carry out a specific task. In either situation the clients may be encouraged to "role play" the way they intend to carry out the action later in the real situation. They can be encouraged to think of any obstacles that may appear in actually attempting the task and to consider why they may come up and how they can meet them. This technique is used as either a sustaining or a growth technique. Its purpose is determined by whether it is used to help the clients accomplish tasks that they have previously been able to handle but are now unable to cope with or whether it is used to help clients carry out new methods of coping with problems.

Advice and guidance.   Advice and guidance are appropriate parts of the supportive treatment method. Here the worker uses professional knowledge and authority to express to the client, individual group member, or group an opinion about a course of action. As a rule this procedure is only used at a time when the clients are unable to find their own solution or when they need permissive authority to pursue a course of action. In the group the members often offer each other this type of support or they may become auxiliary helpers of the worker in this regard. This technique is usually considered a sustaining technique—a way of rescuing a faltering system in an emergency—with the hope of helping the client through a crisis situation. However, one of the most remarkable facts of the helping process is that a gain in one area of functioning can release the progressive forces of the system and effect a redistribution of energies which is reflected in an improvement of functioning in many areas not directly touched on. Thus advice and guidance, if it helps a client deal successfully with an overwhelming situation, may be a growth-producing technique.

Modeling and identification. Closely related to advice and guidance is the worker's presentation of self as an ego-ideal for the client's consideration. In using this procedure the workers do not, as in advice and guidance, present themselves as authorities. Rather they present themselves as active partners who might act this particular way if confronted with this problem. They attempt to leave the client free to adopt or reject this particular pattern, but they present it as a possible model that might be examined if the client were interested. In work with the group, one or several, group members may assume this role with any other member. This fact allows greater use of this technique in work with groups, where other members may support or reject any model offered, than in individual work where, unless the client recognizes the need of help, is ready to use it, and is secure in the work-

er's concern, it may be impossible to resist the inherent authority of the worker and reject the model that does not fit. This technique is used primarily in situations where one is hoping for ego-growth through identification with the strength of another.

Logical discussion. The system's capacity for rational behavior is used in the technique of logical discussion. If the client or the group has certain strengths in the methods of problem-solving, if there are skills and knowledge to make appraisals of reality, if there is the ability to see alternatives and consequences, then logical discussion can serve to both sustain the system and to support its growth as it appeals to the capacity for rational behavior. However, if the client system had no opportunity in the life situation to approach the problem-solving process in this manner, this technique may be totally beyond it and may lead to further frustration and the destruction of motivation. Again, this is a technique that can be used with a client group with less concern as the group members can support each other in expressing openly the group frustration with such expectations. In the individual situation the client, alone with the worker, often does not have this strength and so must internalize frustration as a discouragement with self and functioning that cannot meet the expectations of the worker.

Ventilation. The worker often needs to elicit the client systems' expression of feelings about what may be happening to them. This technique releases energy that was bound up in the management and repression of the feeling and so acts to increase the capacity of the client system. It also serves to increase the client's sense of worth and thus the sense of hope. In the group the program activities may be used to increase the individual's acting out of feelings in an appropriate way and may thus increase the individual's capacity to handle emotions appropriately without excessive denial or repression.

Use of limits. The use of limits appropriately is often another neglected technique of the supportive method. Workers so often think of treatment in terms of the liberation of the ego of the client from maladaptive restrictions that we do not consider carefully enough that limits set within a nurturing relationship may also be a need and may contribute to the support and growth of the client system. The appropriate use of limits may serve to help the client gain control of the impulses, but in addition it may build a sense of worth within the client system in that we care enough to risk hostility by such action, and that we believe the client is strong enough to accept the limits set. In work with groups the worker does not have to carry the entire burden of this technique. Group members will often set limits for each other either by a direct limit-setting in relationship to the behavior of one or a number of members, or by setting rules for the entire group. In fact, the preoccupation of certain groups with rules is indicative of the importance of such limits for the growth of the system.

Confrontation. Confrontation may be used two ways in supportive help. It is used to identify stereotyped or patterned behavior or ways of feeling and thinking in order that the clients' or system members' capacity to see themselves more accurately is increased. It may also be used with certain clients in order that they may better see and understand the way they are seen by others. This is the first step in helping the clients or members consider whether in light of new awareness they want to change their behavior or learn ways of accepting the judgment of others if they do not change. In working with a group the worker may do this with the entire group or in relation to a particular member. However, members often engage in this kind of activity in relation to each other. As the member's relationship to other members does not carry the authority aspects of the worker's relationship, this can be used with a greater freedom and less precaution in the group than in the worker-to-client relationship. This technique is used primarily when the goal is the growth of the client system.

SUMMARY

There are other techniques that need examination in light of their use to support the functioning of the client system. It is hoped that this brief list will serve as only a beginning. Certainly the use of ego-supportive techniques differentially with proper attention to the diagnosis of the clients or members with their problems in their situations is a challenge worthy of the highest knowledge and skill of the worker. It demands a unique combination of mind and heart and hand from the worker who would practice it in the interest of the client.

Reading 12-2

Action as a Tool in Casework Practice *

Anthony N. Maluccio

In casework practice there is extensive use of action—active doing, performing, or experiencing. Yet, action as a concept has received very little attention in the literature. There are various reasons for this omission. An important one is the emphasis on the person as a sentient being and on the primacy of clinical dialogue. Perhaps a more crucial reason is the lack of a theoretical framework capable of providing an adequate rationale for the use of action and stimulating the emergence of pertinent practice principles.

Theorists have long recognized the significance of action and have alluded to its theoretical underpinnings,[1] but the conceptual development of action has been so limited and fragmented that it appears to be a tool in search of a theory. An appropriate framework is necessary to give meaning and substance to action as a tool and to further its integration into the processes of casework.

This article examines the use of action in casework largely within the context of ego psychology. The central aim here is to clarify the purposes of action, its rationale, and the conditions necessary for its effective use in practice. The reason for choosing the context of ego psychology is that it offers a promising approach, especially through its recent emphasis on the autonomous development and functioning of the ego, the dynamic transaction between the person and the environment, and the crucial role played by a person's activities in adapting and coping efforts and in the ongoing struggle to achieve autonomy, competence, and identity. The formulations of such theorists as Erik H. Erikson (1959), Heinz Hartmann (1958), and Robert W. White (1963) counteract the classical Freudian emphasis on instinctual forces and tension reduction as the determinants of behavior. At the same time, they underline the notion of the human organism as an active rather than merely reactive participant in life.

POSITIVE PURPOSES OF ACTION

Action has been viewed as appropriate in social work primarily with such clients as hard-to-reach or nonverbal persons, severely deprived or disorganized families, and psychiatric patients in resocialization programs. Increasingly, however, empirical evidence supports the validity of the use of action as an integral feature of casework with a wider range of clients. Crisis intervention, behavior modification, Gestalt therapy, family treatment, and milieu therapy emphasize experiential learning and the use of activities in the here-and-now situation of the person.

In family therapy, practitioners introduce role-playing and other activities in order to develop the client's capacity to cope with life challenges through involvement in concrete experiences. In residential treatment of disturbed children, work-

---

* Reprinted by permission of Family Service Association of America, publisher, from *Social Casework* 55:1 (January 1974), pp. 30–35.

[1] See Austin (1948); Hamilton (1951, pp. 246–249); and Oxley (1971). Austin and Hamilton point to the use of action in restructuring the environment and providing the client with positive reality experiences and opportunities for growth. Oxley highlights action as a major feature of a proposed life-model approach to casework treatment and suggests its significance in varied social work contexts.

ers arrange for children and parents to participate in social and cultural activities as a means of enhancing their competence and promoting a positive sense of self. In crisis intervention, quick involvement in life activities by the client is viewed as an essential step in resolution of the problem. In play therapy with children, activities constitute a basic medium of communication and interaction.

Ego psychology highlights the value of using action for such broad purposes as enhancement of the client's self-image, development of autonomy and competence, flowering of latent potentialities and innate creativity, and provision of opportunities for growth and mastery. Action can also serve as a means of facilitating and making alive in practice the expression of such basic elusive professional tenets as client participation and self-determination.

The utilization of action for these purposes is especially pertinent within the context of an expanded conception of casework, one encompassing not only clinical treatment but help through a variety of resources, services, and practice modalities. Such a conception underscores the worker's responsibility to identify, mobilize, and ally with the client's potentialities, natural life processes, and adaptive patterns. The purposes of action thus are consonant with a revitalized casework method patterned after life itself. In her formulation of a life model of practice, Carel B. Germain (1973) stresses the use of purposive activity as a major means of stimulating the client's growth, adaptation, and progressive forces.

Many case situations typically encountered by social workers may be imaginatively redefined to generate opportunities for the productive use of coping, striving, and goal-directed action. For example, activities may help a young unmarried mother to gain competence as a new parent, when her situation is defined as one involving a problem in role transition rather than an underlying personality conflict. A crisis such as the death of a father in a young family may be approached as a challenge to the mother, suggesting multiple action strategies for helping her to call on her own resources and to enhance her skills in bringing up the children. A disorganized, multiproblem family may be helped to engage in an active struggle toward fulfillment, as well as survival, through involvement in meaningful activities and growth-producing experiences.

Action may be employed differentially in casework practice: as a diagnostic tool, to assess a person's special areas of aptitude and competence, quality of interaction with others, and so on; as an instrument of treatment, to provide a client with an opportunity to test him or herself or to develop social skills; as the culmination of treatment, by facilitating a course of action, such as obtaining a job; as a measurement of the outcome of casework, by evaluating the results of particular client and worker activities; and as a means of mobilizing other people, instrumentalities, and resources in the client's ecological context.

ARTIFICIAL AND NATURAL ACTIVITIES

A distinction should be made between artificial activities that are provided for a client and natural activity or action that arises out of the life situation.

Artificial activities include role-playing, play therapy, and participation in activity groups. These activities are appropriately used as vehicles for learning, as media of communication, or as opportunities to practice desired behaviors. Often, the client's participation in one or more of them is necessary as preparation for engagement in life itself. Thus, there can be a complementary use of artificial and natural activities. For example, a school social worker found that, following participation in a discussion group of mothers with similar needs, an inner-city mother was able to go successfully through the experience of conferring with school personnel on behalf of her underachieving child. She then felt a real sense of satisfaction as she shared her experience with other mothers in the group.

In contrast to activities that are artificially introduced into the helping situation, action involves real experiences (such as work, or play, or social interaction) emerging from life. Natural activities can be more meaningful and potentially more effective, since they are more closely related to the person's natural life processes of growth and adaptation.

A family service agency worker had tried to involve Mr. A, an isolated elderly man, in social activities at a neighborhood center. These efforts were unsuccessful, as Mr. A seemed disinterested in contact with his peers or in leaving his home. Eventually, he was faced with the need to relocate owing to redevelopment. As the worker accompanied him on various apartment-hunting trips in different parts of the city, Mr. A began to reminisce about his life experiences, showed much interest in the ways the city had changed, and expressed his desire to move into a setting with opportunity for companionship.

RATIONALE FOR THE USE OF ACTION

In an earlier era of casework, insight or self-understanding was idealized as the preferred goal of treatment. More recently has come the realization that insight is not enough and may not even be necessary. It has been recognized that, with or without self-understanding, a person's activities play a critical role in personality growth, adaptation, and social functioning.

An individual's active participation in successful transactions with the environment appears to be a prerequisite for growth, mastery, and identity. White (1963, p. 150) postulates that human behav-

ior is motivated by an innate, autonomous drive to deal with the environment, which he terms *effectance* or *competence motivation*. He also stresses that the ego is strengthened through the person's successful action upon the environment, resulting feelings of efficacy, and the cumulative development of a sense of competence. The individual changes and grows through involvement in activities providing opportunities for need satisfaction, task fulfillment, crisis resolution, and learning of social skills (Cumming & Cumming, 1962, pp. 213–218).

Engagement in purposive, goal-directed activities can stimulate the persons coping efforts and strengthen the adaptive capacities. The experience of success in meaningful life activities can serve to improve coping skills, enhance personal well-being, and encourage new attempts. In his discussion of extratherapeutic experiences in psychoanalysis, Franz Alexander (1946, p. 40) notes that

successful attempts at productive work, love, self-assertion, or competition will change the vicious cycle to a benign one; as they are repeated, they become habitual and thus eventually bring about complete change in the personality.[2]

In her extensive research on child development, Lois B. Murphy (1962, pp. 354–355) observes that there is a significant correlation between a child's activity and the capacity to cope with the environment; although excessive degrees of activity can lead to destructive consequences, in general it seems that active children are more successful in achieving mastery partly because they come in contact with more aspects of the environment, are confronted with more choices, and have more opportunities to practice and develop different skills. A child's successful completion of activities is closely related to the sense

_____
[2] For an extensive analysis of the role of action from a psychoanalytic perspective, see Wheelis (1950).

of adequacy and self-worth and the capacity to gain respect from others.

With adults as with children, doing can lead to feelings of worth and satisfaction, to fuller awareness of one's self and one's impact upon the world, and to greater understanding of one's environment. In many important ways, action constitutes an essential instrument for learning, for development of one's reality-testing, and for self-actualization.

Many of the people who come to the attention of social workers reveal a limited capacity for reality-testing, a seemingly inability to learn, a sense of helplessness and frustration in their efforts to act upon their environment, and a low degree of self-esteem. Often, their life situations and environmental pressures have launched them onto a path of despair and frustration leading to cumulative failures and the dulling of their innate potentialities and creative strivings. In Bruno Bettelheim's terms (1971, pp. 68–78), they are human beings whose autonomy or ability to govern themselves has withered away through excessive external management of their affairs in a mass age.

In casework practice, it is with these persons in particular that action can be utilized as a means of providing opportunities for developing their identity, for exercising their often atrophied drive toward competence, and for turning the trajectory of their ego development toward a positive direction. In an increasingly mass-oriented society, human beings increasingly need to be meaningfully involved in purposeful activities in their own behalf.

Every social worker encounters cases in which opportunities for constructive action evolve naturally out of the client's situation.

An institutionalized man in a psychiatric hospital finds that he can perform well in a work experience. An adolescent in a correctional setting is given the opportunity to channel leadership qualities into organizing leisure activities with peers.

A troubled child in a public school experiences delight in completing a difficult assignment. An unwed pregnant woman plans temporary living and working experiences which keep her in the mainstream of active life rather than passively awaiting confinement.

CONDITIONS NECESSARY FOR EFFECTIVE ACTION

Action does not necessarily lead to constructive change; there is no simple, linear connection between engagement in action and achievement of desired results. The eventual outcome is dependent upon a variety of interacting variables or conditions.

Client's readiness to change. The worker needs to consider the client's readiness to undertake certain activities. Beyond the capacity to perform a given action, there must be some tension needing release and some motivation toward an objective of importance to the person. The tension and motivation can be expressed in different forms, such as anxiety, dissatisfaction with life, guilt, or even a hopeless dream or a fanciful ambition.

The quantity and quality of the client's tension influence the timing of the activity. In some situations, an impulse-ridden person may need help in delaying action. In general, however, the timing of the activity should be geared to the person's spontaneity. Henry A. Murray and Clyde Kluckhohn (1953, p. 19) point out that human beings in our society are typically required by social commitments and role responsibilities to act, even when they are not truly ready, in order to integrate their actions with those of others. Although this pattern is functional in terms of survival and role relationships, it results in a loss or reduction of spontaneity.

Choice of alternatives. Another necessary condition in the effective use of action is the opportunity for client consideration of alternative courses. This opportunity

can help people to evaluate various possibilities, to test their readiness, and to
choose the most appropriate alternative.
Furthermore, the deliberative process can
stimulate people's cognitive growth and
mastery, mobilize their decision-making
functions, and reinforce the sense of autonomy that comes from involvement in
purposive activities consonant with their
needs as well as societal requirements.
The worker plays an important role
through provision of information concerning the potential effects of the action, of
feedback heightening the client's awareness of reality, and of support in taking
a risk. Client-worker interaction becomes
more meaningful and productive as both
parties go through the process of reaching
agreement on specific goals, tasks, and
procedures.[3]

In considering alternative courses of action, it is useful to keep in mind the principle of equifinality derived from systems
theory or the notion that the same result
can be achieved through following diverse
pathways. The provision of diverse opportunities for action may tap the individuals'
potential to look at the world in novel
ways and facilitate the selection of the
activity most suited to their personal
method of coping and their particular
drive for competence. People cope differently with similar life crises, and if workers understand the person's unique ways
of coping and adapting, they will be better
able to perceive prospective opportunities
for action that may maximize the effective
outcome of the client's struggle toward
mastery.

A child welfare practitioner described a pertinent
experience with Jean, a blind 12-year-old girl
placed in foster care following the death of her
parents. When Jean was confronted with the impending demolition of her natural family's home

owing to urban renewal, she urged the worker
to take her on a final tour of the house. During
this visit, Jean methodically touched everything in
each room, climbed into the attic, played the pi-
ano, and ran repeatedly around the backyard.
While alternately crying, laughing, talking, and
pausing in silence, Jean recalled innumerable family experiences and vividly traced her family's history and her own development. In reliving the past
in a spontaneous and active manner at a crucial
point in her life, Jean was courageously bracing
herself for the future.

Relevance.   The relevance of the proposed activity to the client's life situation
is a further determinant of its effectiveness. The action should be meaningfully
related to the person's goal or problem as
defined. In addition, it should be consonant with natural growth processes, lifestyle, significant life events, and developmental stage in the life cycle. Good
opportunities for action are often missed
because of excessive reliance on artificial
or formal procedures such as the office interview. Practice could become more
meaningful and rewarding if social workers would function more spontaneously in
the natural surroundings of clients and
thus discover and encourage their often
dormant potentialities.

In this regard, Esther E. Twente (1965)
poignantly describes the strengths and
creativity shown by older clients in their
own home or group activities: the retired
farmer who gains pride and pleasure in
seeing others enjoy his singing; the elderly
woman who takes music lessons by correspondence and derives satisfaction from
entertaining her fellow residents of a nursing home; the 90-year-old widow who
seeks fulfillment in her embroidery, gardening, and vase collection; and the many
others in whom the creative urge finds rich
expression as life draws to a close.

In a life-oriented model of practice, the
worker need not carry the entire or even
major responsibility in direct work with
the client. A fundamental function of the

---

[3] The client-worker contract can serve as a dynamic tool in the process of considering and selecting
appropriate courses of action. See Maluccio and Marlow (1974).

worker is to identify and mobilize the energies of people and systems that are more directly and significantly involved in the client's own life space, such as resources in the immediate family, in the social network, or in the school or work settings. In some situations, the client-worker relationship will appropriately be the primary vehicle of help. In others, however, the effective use of action will occur through other people, with the worker playing indirect roles. The emphasis will be on utilizing the environment itself as a basic means of helping (Germain, 1973, p. 326).

Client's participation. Another important condition for effective use of action is maximum participation by the client in the activity. Through its focus on the role of one's own action in personality development, ego psychology underscores the primacy of client tasks and reinforces the hierarchy of interventive strategies, which has served as a guiding principle in casework practice: Doing *for* the client ⟶ Doing *with* the client ⟶ Doing *by* the client.

Availability of support systems. Finally, a prerequisite for action is the availability of appropriate social systems and supports, of an environmental climate with varied opportunities for success and achievement. Following an extensive review of clinical and experimental findings in situations of social isolation and extreme stress, Stuart C. Miller (1962, p. 8) concluded that the maintenance of ego autonomy is strongly dependent on appropriate inputs or "stimulus nutriments" from the environment. In social work there is an increasing awareness of the validity of this conclusion and of the urgent need to develop social institutions and systems more conducive to human growth. There is emphasis on the importance of the worker's (and the profession's) participation in action designed to "socialize" services, to restructure inadequate or detrimental societal systems, and to contribute to the development of environmental conditions providing maximum opportunity for each person to grow, to establish identity, and to achieve an increasingly satisfying level of competence (Meyer, 1970). Action is one of the basic tools through which the client and worker can seek to modify and humanize the environment.

CONCLUSION

Action, informed by the insights of ego psychology, can become one of the more promising and fundamental features of a life-oriented casework practice. However, to exploit the potential inherent in its use, social workers need to devote more deliberate attention to action. Their rich experiences should be gathered and examined, so that more specific guidelines and principles can be derived and action can be moved closer to becoming an explicit component of practice theory.

Action should not be viewed as an exclusive or separate mode of treatment. In life there is normally no rigid dichotomy between action and thought or feeling and talking. Action is an integral part of the complex whole representing human behavior and social interaction. To be effectively used in casework practice, it must be creatively integrated with the emotional, cognitive, and perceptual components in each client's experiences.

Reading 12-3

Therapy in Tribal Settings and Urban Network Intervention*

Carolyn L. Attneave

Most professionals in therapy are aware of the importance of extended family and friends in the lives of their patients. In a growing wave of experimentation and innovation, the walls of the one-to-one therapeutic model have been breached or rebuilt around new groupings. A variety of group process models, ranging from group therapy sessions, through sensitivity training and marathon weekends, attempt to supply social settings artificially created. Family therapy has become established as one mode of incorporating an intimate social context into the consulting room. One of the newest groupings to be presented to the professional mental health community is *network therapy*.

Network therapy seems to be based upon the concept of mobilizing the family, relatives, and friends into a social force that counteracts the depersonalizing trend in contemporary life patterns. The concept appears particularly attractive to those attempting to counteract the isolation experienced by urban residents. Ross Speck (1967a) refers to the networks as creating a "clan" or "tribal unit" which can then support, oppose, expose, and protect its members in effective ways (Speck 1967b, 1967c, 1967d, 1967e). Such networks have been potent forces in breaking through the isolation of schizophrenic patients, and network therapy in various forms could also be used in community psychiatry with other types of patients.

In reading or listening to presentations of this type of therapy, one notices that the professional therapeutic role is often obscured by the novel elements associated with conducting therapy in homes, sometimes with groups 40 to 70 people. The dramatic results from the mobilized resources of the simulated clan seem to follow without the processes involved being seen clearly. Because the facets of network therapy activity most frequently given attention by the reader or listener are those new to psychotherapists, the network therapist is often seen as a catalyst—or perhaps deprecated as a social director. In actuality, the network therapist's role is probably more nearly analogous to that of the orchestral conductor. Good conductors do more than beat out the time and set limits for individual solos or subgroup harmonies, but specifying what they do in objective terms is difficult. Comparing therapy as it is applied to an already existing clan structure with what is done in a created network may clarify some of the essential elements of the network therapist's role.

It is tempting to assume that if there were enough networks to replace lost ties with clans and tribes, therapists would become unnecessary or perhaps would automatically be able to increase effectiveness many fold. However, this halo hung over from the dream of the noble savage can be partially challenged by the presentation of two cases from a natural tribal setting where the professional role can be seen from a slightly different perspective.

* Reprinted by permission of the publisher from *Family Processes* 8 (1979) pp. 192–210.

Natural clans and networks, like other human institutions, can focus energies in healthy or pathological directions.

The interventions to be described took place during a period when several American Indian tribes composed 30 to 40 percent of the population being served by a community guidance service. A real effort to develop methods of providing services to this population, previously nonconsumers of psychiatric assistance, was enhanced by the fact that the therapist was of American Indian descent, belonging to a closely related tribe. This is mentioned in passing since some of the opportunities for participatory intervention might not have been accessible to other therapists. The aim of the current discussion is not to write a prescription for how to do therapy with Indian families. Rather it is hoped that by describing and reflecting on this experience, basic understandings of the processes of network therapy will be clarified.

CHARACTERISTICS OF THE TRIBAL NETWORK-CLAN

Before presenting case material, a description of the social organization as it has evolved in these tribes may be helpful. While close-knit extended family ties are not unique to American Indians, or even universal among them, extended families are often seen as viable social units. Predictable meetings of the extended family and a focus of concern for its members can be found in many tribes. In spite of the kinship of members, its composition is not technically an exact replica of the "clans" described by anthropologists. The term *network-clan* seems to describe its combination of contemporary social organization and its links with a more classically described past.

There are five distinctive features characterizing a social unit that combines the traditions of an older clan structure and the features of urban networks as described by Speck (1967b) and by Bott (1957).

1. Each network-clan has a constellation of reasons for existence. Various foci provide not only an identity but also activities that satisfy religious, social, or financial needs in varying combinations. Religious elements are broadly defined to include the use of ritual related to, and derived from, older tribal customs and ceremonies. Social elements include family reunions, festival elements, vacations, and status recognition of individuals and groups in a formal manner. Financial factors include charging tourists and non-Indians admission to public pow wow's, barter sale of crafts and costume materials, and the yearlong money raising projects that support group activities. Many of these are familiar activities of any similar group, such as box suppers and bingo games. Others events such as wild onion dinners and hand games have an Indian flavor, as do the organizing work of a pow wow club and its committees, the practicing of dancing and singing, and the making of costumes.

2. Although the network-clan may or may not use kinship and adopted kinship terms among all members of the network, an extended family always seems to be a nuclear part of a network-clan unit. Originally anthropologists derived the idea of clans from inherited and automatically assigned family roles. These strictly hereditary clan structures are often no longer viable units of contemporary Indian life, although aspects remain observable in some tribes. (All cultures have such remnants, although we often do not recognize our own—for example, the survival of the social register as a vestige of the feudal aristocratic system.)

At this point in social evolution, each individual, upon reaching maturity or thereafter, has the choice of continuing in the family's network of Indian relationships, changing networks, or disengaging from all close-knit tribal participation.

Where a role is passed from father to son, this process is not automatic but done by group consensus. The son or daughter can also decline, a modern option not free of stress but sometimes exercised consciously as well as by default. Much of the confusion about inherited clan membership may be due to the Indian use of kinship titles "in the Indian way." "Uncle," "grandfather" and the like are not easily translatable, falling between functional realities and geneological abstractions.

3.   Some organizational hierarchy is present in each network-clan. The power structure is usually organized as simply as possible while still permitting the attainment of goals. This hierarchical characteristic permits rapid mobilization and provides elements of continuity and stability over time, which therapist created urban networks often lack. The persistence of newsletters and meetings of urban networks beyond termination by the participating therapist points toward a feeling of need for continuity by the substitute clan. However, the urban therapeutic network is mobilized out of a crisis of social and individual pathology and focuses on a self-limiting purpose, while the Indian network-clans have a life pattern independent of a single personal crisis.

4.   Informal rapid communication among members is characteristic of network-clans. The "Moccasin Grapevine" is often astounding in the efficiency with which information is transmitted within and between networks. One dramatic historical example is the arrival of an Indian leader in El Paso, Texas, to pay respects at the time of President Harding's death before most of the white community had received the news. In the urban network setting, the therapist tends to encourage

or organize telephone committees and newsletters in an attempt to supply this characteristic formally. Within the observed tribal networks no addition of formal authority and structure seems to be necessary, although occasionally the white man's techniques of assigned responsibility are used by the tribal business committee or in activities involving non-Indians.

5.   An important characteristic of network relationships, either clan or created, is the presence of significant unconscious components. Many observations provide evidence of this, such as the speed of informal communication and the tremendous amount of energy that can be mobilized to accomplish a common goal. Often therapeutic gains from participation which remain otherwise unexplained can be understood by analyzing the unconscious transactions.

However, in a created network therapists are much freer to interpret to the assembled group. While it may seem that therapists often call attention to those unconscious elements as part of their role, they also must at times resist pressures by parts of the network to bring out material ahead of another segment's readiness.

In a clan or tribal setting one is somewhat protected by the need to fill a role and to use the language understood by the people in a literal and symbolic sense as well as a verbal one. Its members would be unable to discuss their own activities in language other than their own. For example: Even if the identity of the tribes in these examples were divulged, no would-be researcher could go there and ask to be taken to a meeting of the network or the "clan." The demands of courtesy would forbid the Indian to lose all ability to speak English. Since the researcher wanted something, (goodness knows what), he/she would be sent or taken to someone. The results might well resemble

Coronado's search for the Seven Cities of Cibola—with less serendipity of discovery.

This therapist became a participant in the network-class, and while retaining a professional role, used the Indian modes of relationship and communication rather than clinical techniques alone. Although this was facilitated by a heritage of Indian descent, these skills can be acquired by non-Indians who are genuinely interested and concerned. In urban networks the same factors operate but are often masked by the assumption of a common culture.

The existence of viable network-clans with these characteristics is probably to be found in many American Indian tribes which have survived with identity and integrity. In these healthy tribal cultures some variety of network-clans permits individuals to deal with the tensions of living in two worlds: a non-Indian world of occupational, technological, and educational elements and a social-religious-cultural world organized around "the Indian way." In socially deteriorating and disorganized tribes, a few very rigid structures may exist, and their heirarchical control of social relationships may operate to perpetuate the pathology.

A more descriptive analysis of the Indian way of life belongs elsewhere. To examine the processes of therapy involving the network-clan, two examples are appropriate. In the first case discussed, the chronology will be detailed to show the evolution of therapeutic modes of intervention from a referral for individual therapy to the involvement of a network-clan of about 40 or 50 persons.

TRADITIONAL APPROACHES PRIOR TO NETWORK-CLAN THERAPY

The case of Maria was a direct referral after the Court's Child Protective Agencies had intervened. An Indian mother was charged with child abuse and a six-year-old girl had been placed in a foster home before the therapist was peremptorily summoned to the task of making clinical evaluations and "doing therapy."

Several options were open in fulfilling this role of therapist. A traditionally oriented therapist could have found grist for years of 50 minute hours by focusing on the life history of the mother and daughter: The mother, who was from a deprived nonnurturing family of another tribe in another state, had borne this girl before her present marriage and had left her at age three months to be raised by the maternal grandmother. After acquiring sufficient education to become both socially and geographically mobile, this woman had entered into a marriage with a man from a different tribe and was raising four more children successfully. Into this household was thrust a previously rejected child symbolizing a repressed and rejected past. This situation could have been seen as a classic case for prescribing classic therapy.

A social reformer could have attacked the white man's officialdom for demanding parental acceptance of responsibility without an investigation, planning or providing social service support. Added steam could accrue from observing that when the girl apparently acted out her mother's frustrations, one could have easily established that the local officials reacted punitively toward the family. Careful investigation revealed a superficial scalp cut which bled profusely as the only evidence of a "battered child." The need for reform and improvement was obvious, and making a test case of this situation could have been justified by a good many professionals and politicians. However, it did not appear that "justice" was desired by the Indian family. Nor could this clinician see any therapeutic gain for the child and mother in the court hearings that would have been involved.

A family therapist might have worked with the household around the problems of introducing an older sibling into a home with four younger children and would have recognized the presence of the husband's 80-year-old father in the home. These several subsystems within the household would be included.

In fact, this was the initial level of interventive contact. During a series of home visits to the parental household, the brief history sketched earlier was amplified. The stepfather related his willingness to assume parental responsibility but expressed his confusion about the realities involved. Maria was very different from the couple's own children, for her early childhood had little in common with theirs.

During the intervening six years, the maternal grandmother had become an alcoholic and Maria had survived by wandering about the village snatching or begging food, lucky to get an occasional bath, sleeping, playing, watching as the life of the streets ebbed and flowed about her. The authorities were forced to take notice as she reached school age and, as is often the case, summarily notified the mother that she should assume her forgotten responsibilities.

A drive of over 1,000 miles each way during a single weekend left little time for orientation and preparation of either family or child, even if anyone had tried to do so. A confused child and willing but exhausted family had trouble understanding one another from the start. Induction into household and school patterns hit many snags. Some routines were explicitly explained or easily absorbed. Others were not, often because no one realized the need for it.

For instance, Maria was said to be unwilling to share with the other children. It was a family custom that about once

a week one of the adults brought home a bag of candy. One of the children was selected to have the privilege of passing it around the family circle. The child then could have those few pieces of candy left over as a special treat. When it was Maria's turn to do this, she grabbed the sack of candy, ran off, and ate it all herself. The hue and cry of righteous indignation left the parents exhausted, all of the younger ones in tears, and the paternal grandfather silent, brooding, and withdrawn.

There had been many such incidents, which became explicable only in terms of Maria's past. She had never lived with an intact family. How could she know that there would be a bag of candy *every* week? She didn't know from experience that if you had a morning meal, you were going to have a second meal during the day. She didn't know how to set a table, she didn't know how to wash a dish. She didn't know much about washing clothes, or even that somebody would wash them for you if you put them in the right places. She had the idea that you wore clothes until they were worn out, and then if you threw them away, somebody might give you something new. She didn't know anything about the domestic organization of the home, and she didn't know the local Indian language.

Another factor emerged in these family sessions, Mrs. T., the mother, was probably not reacting solely in terms of classical theories of her own childhood neglect and of repression. This child was also playing out some of the mother's own present frustration in relating to her husband's family and tribe. Mrs. T. hadn't been fully inducted into it, and she felt isolated socially. She particularly didn't know how to get along with her sisters-in-law. In the course of a family session, this feeling was clarified together with the therapist's query about how they might become better understood.

Up to this point therapy had proceeded

along familiar family therapy dimensions. The case could be abstracted to fit almost any intercultural family pattern. However, Maria's mother had married into a network-clan organized around her husband's parents, his sisters' families, and their close friends.

This network clan had been concerned about the problem of Maria and was scheduled to convene that weekend to consider it. A non-Indian therapist might not have been invited to attend, or might even have attempted to convene a similar meeting elsewhere. In this instance, a recognition of intertribal kinship as well as professional concern about Maria and her family brought about the invitation for the therapist to attend the meeting, and the therapeutic arena shifted.

INTRODUCTION INTO THE NETWORK-CLAN

The first meeting was almost like moving into a marathon session since it lasted from sundown to sundown and involved, all told, about 50 people. After a hearty and fortifying supper, the key family members, about 20 adults, sat in a ceremonial meeting all night. Others cared for children, visited, and prepared a regular and a ritual breakfast as well as the midday feast.

During this first meeting there were three types of change accomplished. (1) The therapist was inducted into the network-clan. It was now possible to define the professional role as that of helping them solve problems in their own context, not of imposing outside solutions. Being a participant gave the therapist maneuvering power as a part of the network as well as providing a link to the outside world. (2) There was a better definition of the problem as details were shared. (3) The helplessness which everyone in the network felt was nondestructively expressed.

At this stage, it was possible to shift the attitudinal balance from one that piled on shame and guilt, with ostracizing behavior, to one of shared problem-solving. But goodwill alone is not enough, and much work continued in the related areas.

Maria herself was permitted by the court to revisit her home only in the therapist's company for the 24 hours of the "meeting." Meanwhile in the foster home, she was being taught how to live in an organized household—washing, dressing, daily chores, routines of meals, and weekly shopping from a secure income. These lessons, in addition to individual therapy sessions, over a period of three months, were undoubtedly preparing her for reentry into her own mother's home as a more competent part of a family.

NETWORK INTERVENTION—"INDIAN STYLE" THERAPY

Another absent ghost haunted the parental household, that of the grandmother who raised Maria and her mother. Following the generally expected principle that talking about her might lead to insight and reintegration, the topic was introduced during the continued family sessions.

It is tempting to describe the frustrations experienced by a traditionally trained psychotherapist interacting with the Indian culture. When one's whole learning is oriented around discursive discussion, insight development, and verbal tools, it is disconcerting, to say the least, to seek for toe holds in a situation where they are not the modal avenues of communication. Perhaps this exchange about the grandmother will give a sample:

Therapist: "It might help us understand if we knew more about your mother—." Mrs. T. reacts with a startled glance, immediately her eyes lowered to her lap, and a faint blush . . . Grandfather directs a piercing look at therapist and then stares out the window—. Mr. T. sugars his coffee and shifts in his chair, checking visually the group around the table. . . . Therapist sits like a bump on a log . . . as do all the others. Mr. T. picks up his cup, sighs and says, "Well it might—." More silence, but it feels less tense.

At this point, a 4- and 3-year-old tumble into the room excited and everyone's attention is shifted to their immediate needs.

As this confusion simmers down, the family turns their attention to practical immediate problems. School is to begin shortly, and they feel Maria should be at home to begin locally. A weekend before school opens is also time for another meeting and they wish to use it to celebrate Maria's birthday along with that of one of the younger siblings, according to their custom. Permission for the visit as well as the therapist's participation is arranged. An hour or so later, as time to leave arrived, one of the older men asked the therapist abruptly, "You think it might help if we knew more about the grandmother?" The only possible response is to count silently to 10, echo aloud the father's earlier, "Yes, I think it might," and finish putting on one's coat while listening to the familiar "um-gh" in response.

Maria and the therapist arrived on a sunny afternoon a couple of weeks later, carefully prepared for Maria's reentry into the network. She had purchased a bag of candy and gum with the pennies she had "earned" in the foster home, and during the 40-mile drive she counted over and over one piece of candy and one piece of gum for each half sib and adult she knew, and a reassuring surplus for any others who might come. This time Maria was bringing the bag of sweets, and her anxiety was as high as if someone had explained that by doing so she could make amends for her past behavior and henceforth participate in the family ritual of sharing. Symbolically it was her bid for induction into the family.

This was indeed accomplished, but in even more dramatic and comprehensive fashion than the therapist had foreseen. As the car pulled up under a tree and the family came out to greet Maria, she suddenly gave a cry of recognition and thrust one of her offerings into the hands of a strange woman standing on the porch. The network, mulling over the therapist's remark, had stretched its links across two states and brought the absent grandmother to spend two weeks!

During the next 24 hours the bestowing of a tribal name at dawn and the eating of a very American birthday cake at the noon feast completed Maria's restoration to the family and network. During the ceremonial meeting of adults, the grandmother and her new husband sat as honored guests and had many things explained to them. Included were elements that had not been explicitly comprehended by Maria's mother, but which she now learned without embarrassment or loss of status. She was also able to fulfill an important ceremonial role, with her mother present, and thus symbolize the new integration of self and identity she had acquired without having to deny or bury her past. The husband also gained some sense of unsuspected dimensions of her as a person. Mr. T. was able to express his appreciation of his wife publicly as well as to secure the network's expressions of supportive interest and pleasure in her and in Maria.

The next afternoon sitting on the hillside the therapist observed Maria and her half siblings and cousins playing around a tire swing. Around an outdoor fire, Mrs. T. and some of the other women were showing the grandmother how to make "fry bread" and over further under the trees a group of men, including step-grandfather, were drumming softly, practicing songs, and shaving kindling.

Grandfather T., the eldest member of the network-clan, stopped beside the therapist and watched the same scene. After a few minutes he observed "Hum—a good idea to know that grandmother. . . ." Then with a piercing glance and the suspicion of a twinkle he gathered himself up to walk off. Turning, he raised an arm that embraced the group below in a majestic sweeping gesture—"*That* is much better than a lot of noisy talk."

FOLLOW-UP IMPLEMENTATION

The network had delegated to the therapist the role of negotiating with the court and child welfare system for Maria's return. There was ample clinical evidence that the emotional climate in the household had changed, and that both parents and daughter had experienced growth that foreshadowed good prognosis. This professional opinion enabled the court to return custody, providing the therapist maintained contact and assumed responsibility for "supervising" the family during a probationary period.

During subsequent network meetings, the therapist shifted the arena of interaction from the ceremonial fire to the women's and children's activities behind the scenes. It was possible then to handle in context a series of minor misunderstandings by helping the sisters-in-law make explicit many things which neither they nor Mrs. T. realized were not being communicated.

Hatty's tea is an example. Hatty, 60 years old plus, arrived at each meeting for the final midday outdoor feast in a clattering wheel chair with several devoted assistants. She was old, cranky, and imperious—a chronic diabetic who had lost a leg and most of her eyesight. To an outsider it appeared that her every whim brought scurrying subservient people to bring her what she wanted. But, whenever Mrs. T. tried to follow suit, she was brushed aside, often abruptly. The ice tea she prepared especially was poured out. If she passed the bowl of canned peaches, it was devoured by someone else, while another woman or teenager ran up the house to open a new can for Hatty.

The therapist could ask the "dumb questions" Mrs. T. had not and uncovered the fact that Hatty's tea must be made with dietetic sweetner, so the whole group drank that type rather than risk a mix-up. Mrs. T.'s pitcherful had been dumped

quickly so that this secret would not be divulged to Hatty. However, only Hatty was given nonsugar packed peaches, or other special foods. Everyone else had lived with the collusion to protect Hatty from her own appetites so long that no one realized they needed to explain it ahead of time. Then when Mrs. T. had tried to fit into what she understood only partially as deference to the matriarch, she had kept creating minor emergencies. No space or time was left at the moment of crisis for explanations, and her hurt pride and withdrawal had not helped find them later.

It was also possible to utilize the informal group situations to deal with the toilet training lapses of the oldest sibling who had been displaced by Maria, and with a number of other situations which could have erupted again into a cycle of frustration and anger. The dual roles of supporting appropriate role behavior and catalyzing and clarifying interactions in the various subsystems were interspersed with periods that permitted ventilation of feelings and instruction in child care and normal development. Holding all this together in context was the sharing with the network-clan joys, sorrows, tasks and satisfactions. In this setting, network therapy becomes a variant of participant observation that might be termed "participant intervention."

At the end of 15 months, this family had survived several other crisis without disintegration. Both mother and daughter were functioning well socially and intrapsychically. The network-clan remained intact and consisted chiefly of the grandfather, wife, husband of this family, 5 paternal aunts and their families, together with about 8 or 10 other families of men designated as uncles or nephews in the Indian way.

At the latest word, this network-clan had ·coped with arrangements for the guardianship and protection of another patient—a handicapped youth whose parents had died. Their plan and efficiency have saved the white community the cost of institutional care, and the youth from developing a full blown psychosis. In between such meetings for therapeutic purposes, the network-clan has celebrated birthdays, coped with the disruptions of death, the drafting of young men, and welcomed home Viet Nam veterans. Continuity into the future seems assured for a healthy social unit which already has a history of more than 50 years.

DEATH AND DESPAIR IN A SICK NETWORK-CLAN

The second example also involves a network-clan with a single extended family at its core. At the time the therapist entered the picture, it was composed of a grandmother, several adult sons' and daughters' families, and their close or significant friends. This network was deteriorating rapidly. There had been two murders, a suicide, a crippling assault, and the death from a heart attack of the grandfather who had headed the group.

The man upon whom the network then depended for survival was acutely and suicidally depressed. He was ambivalent about assuming the leadership role. He was not only concerned about his ability to cope with the task, but he was overwhelmed with a feeling of guilt and loss of face about a dishonorable Army discharge, after 15 years of honorable military service. This element assumed real importance because of the cultural importance of honor in battle as an Indian tradition, which might not have parallel importance in another culture. In additon to suicidal ruminations, his symptoms included an inflammation of shrapnel induced arthritis sufficient to render him unemployable, at a time when many of his kin were also facing financial crisis.

Clinical judgment indicated that this man required inpatient hospitalization. Rather than arrange a quick admission to the United States Public Health Service Indian Hospital, the network-clan and the patient were invited to participate in finding a solution. This seemed imperative since it had appeared to the therapist even before this man presented himself as a patient, that the network-clan itself was sick.

The first stage was a rapid gathering of the network-clan at the grandmother's home. This permitted introducing two elements that had been lost: First, an element of hope in getting treatment for the potential leader and second, some success experiences in reaching short-term reachable goals. These quick success experiences actually consisted of raising $20.00 via a bingo game and finding temporary employment for one son. It was also possible for the clan to offer support and help for the therapist in treating the depressed patient, which could be received gratefully.

The network-clan, reeling from a series of disasters, had been unable to exchange positive experiences in this fashion between its members for some time and consequently had been resonating and amplifying pathology. Once this pathology was dampened, it was possible to discover that admission to a VA Hospital would symbolically expunge the dishonorable discharge. This was arranged through the therapist's liaison with the professional agencies and was ceremonially validated in a formal meeting.

As a result of the opportunities for interaction with individual network members during these activities, the therapist was able to share the grief with the grandmother and other individuals in such a way that they found a release in tears and could get about the work of mourning, which eliminated another source of pathology within the network.

Supportive contacts between the network-clan and the depressed man began within hours of his brief hospitalization.

Although the VA psychiatry department found him "unsuitable" for psychotherapy, his somatic and suicidal symptoms disappeared and his arthritis was brought under medical control. The network worked through the patient's practical problems by helping him find a job, transportation, and so on, as well as providing the therapeutic relationships needed. He was able to show his own resilience three months later when he handled the details of a terminal illness and funeral of another of the network members. That event would probably have triggered another wave of suicide-murder catastrophies had not pathology been halted within the group.

Within 12 months the destructive processes had been reversed and the reciprocal healing strengths of network and ex-patient network-clan leader were such that he and one or two others were visibly assuming interlocking leadership roles as tribal representatives at pow wows and in the elected tribal business organization.

Evidence that real changes in network pathology had occurred is deduced from the fate of one family unit which for a variety of reasons (mainly job opportunities) moved several hundred miles away at the height of pathological period. This family was not present during the period of therapeutic intervention and was out of touch with the network in an unusual fashion. Before contact was reestablished, the state newspapers headlined that this family had another "unexplained" murder and suicide incident which left only one surviving child. In an institution for delinquents at the time of the parents' deaths, the child continues to be both "incorrigible" and "isolated."

This continued antisocial experience of that one surviving delinquent is in contrast to the other children of the network-clan who survived similar family destruction during the pathological period. They have now faded into public anonymity. Local authorities ignore them since they are in school, not delinquent, and not in need of "public assistance" as they have been scattered among network-clan families. While clinicians might predict some psychic scar tissue, they probably could not write a better therapeutic prescription than the network's cooperative distribution of nurturing responsibilities. It is probable that a professional clinic or agency could not deliver these services as efficiently as the restored network-clan.

ESSENTIAL ELEMENTS OF THE THERAPEUTIC ROLE IN NETWORK INTERVENTION

The purposes of these brief descriptions of therapeutic intervention within existing rather than newly constituted networks has not been to write a prescription for delivery of psychotherapy to American Indians, although it was proven to be one effective way to provide clinical service to a previously unreachable population. One hopes that by examining the experience one may be better able, in various settings, to isolate the essential features of network therapy as a process of intervention.

That a clan type of social organization can be either healthy or pathological is one concept that needs overstatement because it may get lost in a discussion of urban network therapy where emphasis is on creating a new social institution. Where therapists can utilize an existing clan-network, they may have to spend as much time on repair as innovators do in creating a healthy social system for urbanites who have become isolated.

A requisite then for network therapy is to have leverage to promote social health and to limit, control, or reverse the sickness of the network itself, as well as that of some of its individual members. Simply to assemble or create a network unleashes a great deal of psychic energy and the odds are generally in favor of this having a positive balance. However, the therapist needs the same skills and insights obscurely understood as operative in group processes in order to reinforce positive vectors and permit network organization to align itself in such a way as to heal rather than hurt its members.

An advantage of working with existing clan-networks is that they already have established channels of communication, mechanics of assembly, and a simple power structure. The urban network therapist often uses up a good deal of time creating the minimal social organization. This makes it difficult at times for therapists to disengage themselves from responsibility for administrative tasks in order to retain a set of therapeutic roles. They also need some disengagement in order to retain some disengagement in order to retain some efficiency, because they serve a total client population of which any single network is only preconsciously aware.

The energy required to organize a network and be clinically effective as well may dampen the ardor of many therapists initially attracted by the powerful tool of network therapy. It also probably accounts for the comparatively short life of most urban therapy networks. The novelty of the organizing role and the sense of power derived from successful network intervention are both certainly attractive to therapists. However, one must be wary lest one become preoccupied with being a "chief" when one wants and needs to be a "medicine man."

The "medicine man" role of offering therapy cannot be lost if network intervention of any type is to be successful. Networks and clans are made up of individuals, some of whom from time to time need to be seen and treated as individuals. These may require only on the spot, in context, opportunities to ventilate, express grief, or grasp an insight firmly. Such brief interventions are often handled peripherally in a clan network, but they may

and sometimes should be accompanied by interpretations to part or all the group. There is no substitute for clinical judgment about this and there is a real need for freedom of action to follow up insights and play out subliminal clinical hunches.

In addition, other individuals within networks may need one of the more traditional therapies, either medical or psychiatric. These services may be supplied by therapists in their own practice or by the referral and follow-up route depending on the combination of particular circumstances, therapists' ability and time, and the availability of other resources. There seems to be no evidence to substantiate a preference for either referral or do-it-yourself individual therapy as part of network activity. There does seem to be evidence that if network intervention is to be effective the members should validate and support the referral. The therapist must also have the type of clinical judgment that can recognize the need for intensive individual therapy and the sense of responsibility that will see that it is provided.

The question of referral brings up a third probable role of a network therapist: that of linking or coordinating between the network and the institutionalized resources of the external community at large. This really is not a new concept of a therapeutic role. Community mental health professionals have become aware of the need to provide support to clients in order to utilize a host of already established insitutions and services. In fact, such coordination is one of the basic services required for federal funding and for professional interest in the techniques of "consultation" and "coordination" of ecological systems in relation to treatment.

This linking role is very clear-cut when a therapist enters the network-clan of a tribal minority culture. As was indicated in these two examples, effective liaison with the Veteran's Administration, courts, child protective agencies, and so on, were essential facets of the solution of referred problems. In the Indian network-clan setting, it becomes obvious that the therapist is often the only person present who can translate clan needs into terms acceptable to majority culture's institutions. However, in urban middle-class situations, a therapist should be wary of assuming that the network members have knowledge and skills to communicate with the existing resources and to handle problems in the supra-network power structure. When a lack of these techniques is recognized, therapists must thread their way between the Scylla of doing the coordination themselves and the Charybdis of teaching the network members social-political skills.

Probably the only safe guideline to offer therapists is a warning not to choose either route at the expense of their other therapeutic roles. Separating this role from that of treating social and individual pathology may make such decisions easier and may elicit some additional impetus to develop techniques that will accomplish several tasks at once.

A final comment may be made in comparing the processes of network therapy in urban settings and in clan-oriented social settings. Where network clans do not exist, they can be created effectively for critical cases. However, it often is difficult to justify the effort and expense of this activity for situations in which the supportive interaction might be seen as optimal therapy, but the symptoms are not dramatic enough to assemble family, friends, and neighbors. A network-clan such as the one described here exists independently of the crisis of a member and can be mobilized to deal with many situations before they require drastic last ditch measures.

It is probable that even in the socially isolating environment of our present megalopolitan centers the vestiges of old networks and the seedlings of new ones can be found. Some pioneers in preventive mental health practice are already turning attention to nurturing these potentials (Taber, 1969). Others have less consciously developed a "sense of community" or of "family" in their research interventions. Mental health consultants may find that time invested in creating new social institutions or in "revitalizing" old ones may be an excellent investment of resources. Creative social engineering may seem far afield from therapy, yet the processes of pathology and health in any personality cannot be separated from the network of social relationships in which the individual is enmeshed.

In comparing network therapy as intervention in a setting where a clan-like social structure already exists and in settings where it must be created, it has been possible to focus on several facets of the therapeutic role: first, the need to treat social pathology by an application of skills and insights derived from family and group therapy; second, the need for individual therapeutic skills, both in crisis interaction and on a long-term basis; and, third, the need for providing linkages with the institutions and external community as is seen in community psychiatry.

Areas for further study are sketched in relation to the functioning of healthy and pathological networks in other contexts, both urban and tribal. In passing, questions are raised of theoretical and practical importance concerning the extent to which the network therapist can or should become a "social engineer."

Reading 12-4

Rural Social Work Practice: Clinical Quality *

M. Ellen Walsh

The literature on rural mental health practice is replete with descriptions of community values, techniques for community outreach and program development, and delineations of barriers to effective service delivery. According to a recent literature review done for the National Institute of Mental Health, however, "There is little especially pertinent to rural settings on the specifics of treatment apart from total program description" (Flax et al., 1979, p. 50).

This article will describe several characteristics of a model for delivery of clinical service to rural clientele. The effectiveness of these qualities of clinical practice is based upon the author's personal experience as a therapist in several rural communities, discussions with other rural-based clinical practitioners in the area, and the literature. By and large, generalizations drawn relate to a rural clientele at local mental health center outstations in five rural communities in Washington. Requests for service were self-initiated, frequently following a word-of-mouth referral from a former mental health center client. Local employment in these communities is primarily in the logging industry or in agriculture, although in other respects (size, availability of services, remoteness) the communities varied widely. There were slightly more female than male clients. Extensive prior footwork, including public relations work and relationship building, had been undertaken by the mental health center for the past five years.

There are many difficulties inherent in initiating mental health services in a rural area; however, they will not be addressed at length in this article (Cedar & Salasin, 1979). A successful program development strategy is a necessary prelude to the kind of clinical intervention delineated here. This article does not intend to propose specific techniques or modalities, but will characterize a practice stance or clinical style that can be adapted to fit a broad range of intervention modalities. A style that reflects authenticity, attention to the subtleties of hierarchy in the treatment relationship, and frank respect for the client is particularly well-suited to a rural population.

ELEMENTS OF CLINICAL STYLE

There is no question that an attempt to apply certain treatment modalities to a rural population will involve stretching the classical models to some extent. Successful social work practitioners in rural areas are both versatile and flexible in clinical treatment and do not tend to be rigid adherents of any specific treatment modality. Rural clinical treatment requires a clinician whose practice stance does not rule out transparency as a concept (Rogers, 1961, p. 67). Lack of anonymity for the professional in a rural area has been documented repeatedly (Bischoff, 1976, p. 8; Solomon, 1980), and clients who encounter their therapist at the cafe, the post office, and community gatherings of various sorts are apt to be acutely sensitive to differences in personal style between these gatherings and the treatment session. A clinician's willingness to behave in an au-

---

* Reprinted with permission of author and Family Service Association, publisher, from *Social Casework*, October, 1981.

thentically personal way with clients during the treatment session is an especially useful quality of practice in communities that place a high value on integrity and self-sufficiency. The clinician whose personal maturity and self-understanding does not lead him or her to have any large investment in identifying with the "mystique" of the "therapist" will, therefore, fare better in rural practice. The flavor of some of the literature on community organization for social workers in rural areas is reflected in this statement by Jim Morrison: "Other characteristics that rural community organizers would do well to possess are the ability to reject ideology, a sense of humor . . . and the capacity to work authentically" (Morrison, 1976, p. 60).

The oft-described emphasis on self-sufficiency, personal responsibility, and self-determination in the rural community value system lends a certain bonus to the work of the clinical practitioner in these areas (Cedar & Salasin, 1979). That is, unlike many of their urban counterparts who are looking for a wizard/witch doctor in their therapist, rural clients are more likely to accept the concept of personal responsibility for change, and are more prepared for that inevitable moment in treatment when a client is faced with the realization that there is no magic dust at the therapist's fingertips. Although these are generalizations about client value systems and sensitivity to particular qualities of treatment, it is important to keep in mind that these are modal characteristics. As in any large population, there is great variation in individual makeup and flavor, and every rural client will not embody the self-reliance and sensitivity to inauthenticity reported here.

DANGERS OF CLASSISM

There are dangers of classism, real or perceived, on the part of the therapist in rural settings; and it is helpful to develop a perspective for understanding class sensitivity. Richard Sennett and Jonathan Cobb refer to class prejudice as "inferring a man's dignity from his social standing," and propose that "lower" or "working" class persons experience a "subordination in social position . . . as the result of circumstances of birth and class" (Sennett & Cobb, 1972, pp. 251, 119). Milton Mazer differentiates between values of middle-class American life and rural values, which tend to be more traditional (Mazer, 1976, p. 25). Mazer describes a dilemma faced by rural populations which he dubs "value-inconsistency." That is, a population with a deeply-felt traditional value system is confronted daily with an alternate (often oppositional) set of assumed values via the media. Most television, radio, and advertising reflect an urban value stance that is a far cry from the principles rural communities hold dear (Mazer, 1976, p. 25). Hence, there is a preestablished "we versus them" (Reul, 1974) notion in the minds of rural dwellers. Sennett and Cobb perceive this dynamic as a byproduct of a "contest for dignity." "If you are a working class person, if you have had to spend year after year being treated by people of a higher class as though there probably is little unusual or special about you to catch their attention . . . then to try to impugn the dignity of persons in a higher class becomes . . . an affirmation of your own claims for respect." (Sennett & Cobb, 1972, p. 148).

These reflections on urban class conflict shed some light on rural dwellers' perceptions of formally educated "city slickers," a stereotype that all too frequently includes mental health professionals. Perhaps in view of this backdrop, the rural clientele's acute sensitivity to classism will begin to make sense.

A therapist in a rural area will be more quickly effective, and will be more apt to reduce the likelihood of perceived classism, if he or she is particularly careful to use the client's own clichés and stock phrases in treatment, with perhaps a parenthetical "as you call it," or "as you say." Using even minimal professional jargon may ruin an otherwise potentially significant educational intervention technique. Translating sophisticated models into rural idiom requires a sound conceptual familiarity with the material being presented. Also, rural people are by and large people of few words. Their use of language is sparse, and frequently short phrases or single words suffice to communicate. In the interests of presenting the client with a style of communication that is familiar, rural clinicians should follow suit.

PACING

Pacing is another interesting variable of rural clinical work. Rural clients are apt to offer highly-charged new information almost in passing, as though there is nothing special about this material. It is particularly important that the therapist not "jump" on these new hints, but rather to note the revelations and allow several minutes to pass before alluding to them. In so doing the therapist may gather more peripheral information than would have been revealed had he or she explored it immediately. It is difficult to analyze the rural client's apparent preference for a moderate pace to explore sensitive data, but it may correspond to the slower pace of rural life. The therapist should allow several minutes to pass before responding to this new information. The rural client places a high value on the time the therapist spent in reflection on the new information and is more convinced of acceptance than if he or she had hurried.

AUTHENTIC PRESENTATION

A willingness to present oneself authentically has many implications for rural treatment. Most rural clients have a fine-tuned sensitivity to dishonesty and incongruency. New rural practitioners should ask themselves throughout the treatment session, "Do I really mean it? Am I telling the truth?" For example, when presented with a complex monologue by a client, a rural practitioner needs to be especially careful not to feign understanding to "facilitate the flow." Even a less-simulated assumed "understanding" has its dangers. Rural clients are, at some level, acutely aware of the particularly unique, rich, and complex nature of their personal experience. Making evident the struggle to comprehend posture and facial expression is frequently a potent intervention. This obvious attention bespeaks a basic awareness of the uniqueness of the client and mitigates against a self-perception (by the therapist) of professional omnipotence (which a rural client is apt to regard as one-upmanship in any event).

ATTENTION TO PARAPHRASING

Rural clients are likely to react to a perceived conventionalization of emotions in paraphrasing and attempted normalization of client behavior and experience. For example, in the following situation: Maggie, the client, says "We've been through this kind of thing before, Jim and I, three or four times. The other women are always much younger, and I imagine they're very beautiful. I'm working all day harvesting and canning—putting up the apricots this week—and he's being seduced by these women who actually have time to file their nails and wear shiny polish! He mentioned that last week, that she'd been wearing polish. How can I compete with that? Yeah, he's always sorry, and he always tells me about it, and it's always a one-shot deal, but I'm beginning to feel like a tired old rag."

The therapist would be ill-advised to respond with such a phrase as: "It sounds like you're experiencing some jealousy, Maggie." Special attention needs to be paid to avoid use of jargon and the subsuming of reported emotion into a stock word or phrase (other than that of the client). There is a price to be paid for such "tidying up" of material presented by the rural client.

POINTING OUT AMBIVALENCE

Another general characteristic of the rural client is that he or she is more apt than the generally better-educated, more well-read urban client to present to the therapist with a one-dimensional picture of him- or herself. That is, this kind of client is more apt to disown the alternate side of the ambivalence when experiencing conflicting feelings in a given area. Therefore, with rural clients therapists must be particularly careful to avoid referring to or presenting the missing side of the ambivalence. For example, if a rural client is currently denying his concerns about the effect his aging will have on continued employment in the logging industry, it may be better for the therapist to lean *with* him toward his described *lack* of concern, adding a millimeter of emphasis in that direction, and wait for the client to balance the scales for himself. Thus, the therapist, rather than parading his or her intuitive prowess and mobilizing an already cautious defense system, gives the client an opportunity to portray the other side of the ambivalence himself. For example:

Client: I've always been a good breadwinner. Colleen and the kids have never wanted for anything important.

Therapsist: Your family sounds like it's always been able to count on you, George.

Client: And it has. It has counted on me. Been dependable that way. [Silence.] And the company's been a good place to work. Boss knows what I'm worth to 'im. Paycheck's always on time. I work as fast as I ever did. Be hard for 'em to replace some-

body who knows as much about the business as I do. Good company it is.

Therapist: Your family relies on you and you rely on the company. Sounds like the company is an excellent place to be working, George. Sounds like they always stick by their workers, never let you down. You know that's unusual these days, workin' a place that holds to its own every time like that. Must make you real comfortable being there.

Client: Yeah. Good job. [Silence.] I've always said.

Therapist: Good to hear about, George. A place everybody can feel fine about.

Client: Well now, it's not perfect, though. Tom Rutger got the ax a couple years back.

Although not always effective, this technique frequently hits paydirt with rural clients. They do not want to leave the therapist with *too* much of a misimpression.

CAREFUL INTEPRETATION

Another helpful attitude in rural practice is tentativeness in material presented to the client relating to assessment. Rural clients will more likely than not regard interpretation as infringement. As previously stated, they are very alert to issues of classism and one-upmanship on the part of the therapist, and, correspondingly, are very responsive to perceived respect and genuine appreciation of them by the therapist. When it is impossible to resist sharing a potentially accurate assessment or explanation of behavior with a rural client, the therapist can state it with hesitant carefulness. For example, "Hey, you know, this notion just flew across the back of my mind, and I guess I may as well check it out with you . . ." or "I'm just fishing here, and I know it, but . . . Do you suppose that's a possibility?"

A variation on this sensitivity to disrespect is many rural client's quick reaction to overnurturance by a therapist. They will not comment on this, but at some level aware of the ultimately patronizing quality of overinvolvement by a professional, they simply will not return for treatment. To harbor vestiges of an "under-my-wing" attitude toward a client is a message that the therapist does not view the client as a whole, complete person with adequate resources and capabilities to deal with the struggles at hand. To comment on such a basic tenet of social work practice may appear superfluous, yet clinical work in rural areas can lead one to an awareness of more and more subtle indices of underlying attitudes on the part of therapists. Absolute separateness on the part of the therapist portrays a respect for the client's aloneness which is invaluable in work with a rural population.

Therapists must take special care to avoid the temptation to steer the interview with rural clients, unless the therapist has elicited a clear indication from the clients that they are indeed willing to explore a given area in greater depth. This permission can be in the form of an informal contract, and may be a simple "Would it be all right with you, Louise, if we talked a little further about your mom's illness?" or, "Can we slow down and look at that a moment, Ralph?" Rural clients will usually tell the therapist if they do not care to do so, and should this be the case, the therapist has at least indicated a willingness to tackle a sensitive area at such time as the client is prepared to do so. Steering without contracting, then, becomes an acceptance issue in work with rural clients.

OWNING

As an overall stylistic emphasis in rural work, there is perhaps nothing as powerful as authenticity, as previously mentioned. "Owning" is magic with most of these clients, and a therapist who easily acknowledges his or her momentary confusion, ambivalence, or lack of familiarity

with the subject at hand quickly wins the respect of a client population which places a high value on individual rights and self-assuredness. Nondefensive "owning," besides being an accurate representation of oneself at a given moment, is good modeling. This style is especially helpful to the professional new to a particular rural community, who will be encountering many references to a community history with which he or she is as yet unfamiliar.

Leon Ginsberg (1976) states, "Many of the things that happen may be based upon little remembered but enduringly important family conflicts, church schisms, and crimes. It may require months of investigation before a newcomer in a rural area fully understands" (p. 6).

"Owning" extends as well to the area of clinical faux pas. Should a client's storytelling send a therapist into a couple of minutes of personal reflection, it is recommended that he or she admit this interruption to the client. For example, "Excuse me, Frank. What you were saying made me think of something else that's going on, and I haven't been paying close attention for a minute, here. Can you go over that again? I was with you up to the point where you said Jan had no business interferring with the kids."

Despite most therapists' fears of revealing such incidents, rural clients are probably aware of these lapses anyhow, and the admission wins respect for its honesty and may relieve the client to some degree ("Hmm. Everyone's attention flags from time to time. But *this* person is actually going to let me know when that happens! They don't want to miss anything. They are genuinely interested in me.")

Comfort with self-revelation of this type can be acquired, and a willingness to expose oneself personally can have far-reaching effects on the treatment process with rural clients. One of the more obvious indicators of its efficacy is the apparent influence it has on duration of treatment;

perhaps as a result of the increased trust that such styles of "leveling" can elicit. Attention to this point has led to a practice stance with rural clients which involves the therapist divulging personal internalized processes at selected moments during the session, either to check out an intuitive perception, or to highlight a treatment issue. For example, "Carol, there's something I want to tell you. I notice that whenever you talk about your huge fights with Marv—the big ones, where you're afraid he might fire you, when you're telling me what you say to him, I get this uneasy feeling inside. Like part of me just finds itself wondering if you're really telling me the whole story, or something. Not that I believe you're lying, I just get a strange feeling in the back of my mind, so I guess I should ask you if you know what I might be reacting to."

If a client in this type of interaction does not acknowledge awareness of peripheral issues influencing such an experience, the therapist can say something like, "Well, perhaps it's got more to do with me than it does with you. I just wanted to let you know about it. I don't like having things like that going across my mind without checking them out."

TRADITIONAL VALUES AND ROLES

Expressing emotions

A final area of comment on rural clinical practice is related to traditional family values and role orientations. The rural male client, for example, will tend to have a negative self-outlook on crying, while other means of discharging strongly felt emotions (that is, chopping wood, shouting) are seen as both allowable and occasionally necessary. Male clients is used here with the awareness that tears are not thought to be "manly," however, this flavor of tears fiercely held in (and self-respect linked somehow to this restraint)

can be found in rural females as well. Perhaps it bespeaks a "strong people don't cry," or a "grownups don't cry" value that overlays the more obvious sex-role identification.

Therapists in rural areas must develop some style of practice to use during those moments when a rural male client is close to tears. It may be preferable to discuss this issue at some time early in treatment when tears are not close to the surface. The subject of crying can be framed as a natural healing process which discharges distress. This reframing can be done in a casual manner with few words. For instance, if a rural client is feeling the therapist out with a teaser on the subject while recounting history: ". . . and Ted shed a tear over that incident, I can tell you." The therapist can reply, "Well, you know, they say you *see* things more clearly after a good cry." If a man is close to tears the therapist can give him concerned attention, and occasionally hand him a tissue by way of encouragement. Tears are a delicate matter with the rural man because too *much* focus will tend to close him up in the interest of self-protection. It is necessary for the therapist to maintain a clear and well-conveyed respect for the client throughout the period of strong emotion, and to avoid anything that looks like overnurturance. A simple "Go ahead, Frank, it's a good idea," or "Go on, Frank, it's good for you," is all the therapist need say. After a crying incident there are generally opportunities to address the subject further:

Client: I'm sorry. I'm sorry. Hate to cry. Damn kid.

Therapist: Ah, Frank. Way I look at it, we need a good cry, time to time. Keeps us from exploding.

Client: Makes me feel so goddamn weak.

Therapist: Makes all of us feel kind of tired and open, after a cry. But you know, Frank, they say it's a good idea to let it out, now and then. And they say when you're all through crying, if you go back and look at what started you off to begin with, you'll see it clearer, somehow. Look at it a little different, more accurately.

Exaggerated verbal anger

The verbal expression of anger by rural male clients will also fit the classic sex-role stereotype of the aggressive male. A combative, aggressive, intimidating verbal expression ("I'm going to shoot that so and so if he comes into the store again!" or "I'll burn the place down before I let him get it!") is the norm, and is usually merely a style of communication. Generally speaking, it is not to be taken literally. It is a means of communicating how upset the client is. It is not, however, out of line for a therapist to check on the matter. There is usually no need for subjective alarm on the part of the therapist; the appropriate move is toward the feeling content of the expression rather than to literal interpretation of it.

Using familiar terms

One clinical advantage of traditional family role orientation is illustrated by the female client who takes care of a husband and family wholeheartedly while ignoring many of her own personal needs and refusing to look at her own vulnerability. Whatever the presenting problem, should this kind of picture appear, the therapist need not go into any sophisticated, intellectualized rationales for self-care. The pre-existing role orientation gives the therapist a whole language with which to access the resources and capabilities within the client. For example:

Therapist: Ah, Marilyn, sounds to me like you're being an excellent mother to everyone but Marilyn.

Client: What do you mean?

Therapist: I mean it seems like everyone around you except you has someone being

a real good mother to them. You could use a little of that yourself, Marilyn.

Client: Think I need someone like a mother to take care of me?

Therapist: Marilyn, what if you were your own mother right now? Not your real mom. I mean, the part of *you* that is a mom. The mother inside of you. And this other part of you, the part that's been hurting so much lately, needed some comfort and some words of wisdom. What would you tell yourself?

Client: I don't usually think of it that way.

Therapist: You mean, think of being your own kid, like that?

This approach can work very effectively with rural clients. Although usually taken aback by the notion of being a "good mother" to themselves (that is, initiating self-care behaviors), they are familiar with the concept through *family* terminology, and they know where to look for those resources and skills. Therapists should try to use family terminology to get their point across, whenever it fits, with rural clientele.

EXCELLENCE THE KEYSTONE

Clinical work is an aspect of rural social work practice that is inextricably linked to other areas of practice such as community development, program planning, outreach, and consultation. It is the keystone of rural practice. One's professional reputation, referrals, and perceived dependability and expertise flow from high-quality clinical work. When a practitioner is making a fund raising plea to a town council, and is linked clinically in various ways with several members of the council (for example, the wife of one an exclient, an adolescent son of another a current client), clinical excellence will come into play in fund raising. If the town is very small, a clinician will find that reputable citizens discuss the quality of their clinical interventions and listen closely to friends who have had reason to develop an opinion about them.

The flavor of rural America is distinctive enough to point toward some uniquely applicable qualities of clinical work. Clinical models derived from rural practice transfer well into urban work, although, the converse generally is not true. Rural practice grooms a therapist for increased authenticity, attention to subtleties of hierarchy in the treatment relationship, and genuine respect for the client. These qualities fare well in any area of clinical practice. Although he was not referring to it, Sheldon Kopp captured the crux of rural clinical work very well: "The humanistic therapist meets the man he tries to help as one risking human being to another" (Kopp, 1971, p. 15).

Rural clients expect that kind of bareness between themselves and anyone to whom they reveal themselves intimately, including a therapist. They are not overly fond of affection, even if it be in the interests of maintaining a "professional" facade. One's professionalism becomes evident in the integrity with which one behaves, rather than in any more classic role enactment.

References

Alexander, Franz. Extratherapeutic experiences. In Franz Alexander & Thomas M. French (Eds.), *Psychoanalytic therapy: Principles and applications*. New York: Ronald Press, 1946.

Austin, Lucille N. Trends in differential treatment in social casework. *Social Casework*, June 1948, *29*, 203–211.

Bandler, Bernard. The concept of ego-supportive psychotherapy. In Howard J. Parad & Roger R. Miller (Eds.), *Ego-oriental casework: Problems and perspectives*. New York: Family Service Association of America, 1963.

Bettelheim, Bruno. *The informed heart*. New York: Avon, 1971.

Bischoff, Herbert G. W. Rural settings: A new frontier in mental health. Paper presented at Summer Study Program on Rural Mental Health Services, University of Wisconsin, Madison, Wisconsin, June 1976, p. 8.

Bott, E. *Family and social network*. London: Tavistock Publications, 1957.

Bruno, Frank J. *Trends in social work, 1874–1956*. New York: Columbia University Press, 1957.

Cedar, Toby, & Salasin, John. *Research directions for rural mental health*. McClean: MITRE Corporation, July 1979.

Cumming, John & Cumming, Elaine. *Ego and milieu: Theory and practice of environmental therapy*. New York: Atherton Press, 1962.

Erikson, Erik H. *Childhood and society*. New York: Norton, 1950.

Erikson, Erik H. *Identity and the life cycle: Psychological issues*. (Monograph no. 1.) New York: International Universities Press, 1959.

Flax, James W., et al. *Mental health and rural america: An overview and annotated bibliography*. Washington, D.C.: U.S. Department of Health, Education, and Welfare, 1979.

Frey, Louise. Support and the group. *Social Work*, October 1962, *7*, 35–42.

Germain, Carel B.   The ecological perspective in casework practice. *Social Case-work,* July 1973, *54,* 223–230.

Ginsberg, Leon.   An overview of social work education for rural areas. In Leon Ginsberg (Ed.), *Social Work in Rural Communities.* New York: Council on Social Work Education, 1976.

Hamilton, Gordon.   *Theory and practice of social casework* (2d ed.). New York: Columbia University Press, 1951.

Hartmann, Heinz.   *Ego psychology and the problem of adaptation.* New York: International Universities Press, 1958.

Hollis, Florence.   *Casework: A psychosocial therapy.* New York: Random House, 1964.

Kopp, Sheldon.   *Guru-metaphors from a psychotherapist.* Palo Alto, Calif: Science and Behavior Books, 1971.

Maluccio, Anthony N., & Marlow, Wilma D.   The case for the contract. *Social Work,* January 1974, *8,* 28–37.

Mazer, Milton.   *People and predicaments.* Cambridge, Mass.: Harvard University Press, 1976.

Meyer, Carol H.   *Social work practice: A response to the urban crisis.* New York: Free Press, 1970.

Miller, Stuart C.   Ego autonomy in sensory deprivation, isolation, and stress. *The International Journal of Psychoanalysis,* January–February 1962, *43,* 1–20.

Morrison, Jim.   Community organization in rural areas. In Leon Ginsberg (Ed.), *Social work in rural communities.* New York: Council on Social Work Education, 1976.

Murphy, Lois B.   *The widening world of childhood.* New York: Basic Books, 1962.

Murray, Henry A., & Kluckhohn, Clyde.   Outline of a conception of personality. In C. Kluckhohn & H. A. Murray (Eds.), *Personality in nature, society and culture* (2d ed.). New York: Alfred A. Knopf, 1953.

Oxley, Genevieve B.   A life-model approach to change. *Social Casework,* December 1971, *52,* 627–633.

Polansky, Norman A., Borgman, Robert D., & de Saix, Christine. *Child Neglect: Understanding and Reading the Parent.* New York: Child Welfare League, 1973.

Reul, M. R.   *Territorial boundaries of rural poverty: Profiles of exploitation.* Lansing, Mich.: Michigan State University Cooperative Extension Service, 1974.

Rogers, Carl.   *On becoming a person.* Boston: Houghton Mifflin, 1961.

Selby, Lola G.   Supportive treatment: The development of a concept and a helping method. *Social Service Review,* December 1956, *30,* 400–414.

Sennett, Richard, & Cobb, Jonathan.   *The hidden injuries of class.* New York: Random House, 1972.

Simon, Bernece.   Borrowed concepts: *Problems and issues for curriculum planning. Health and disability concepts in social work education.* Proceedings of a Workshop Conference, School of Social Work, University of Minnesota, Minneapolis, Minnesota, April 1964, 31–42.

Solomon, Gary.   Problems and issues in rural community mental health—A review. Lubbock: Texas Technical University, Department of Psychology, 1980.

Speck, Ross V.   Psychotherapy of family social networks. Paper presented at the Family Therapy Symposium, Medical College of Virginia, Richmond, 1967(a).

Speck, Ross V.   The politics and psychotherapy of mini- and micro-groups. Paper presented at Congress on Dialectics of Liberation, London, 1967(b).

Speck, R. V., "Psychotherapy of the Social Network of a Schizophrenic Family," *Fam. Proc.,* 6, 208–14, 1967(c).

Speck, R. V. and Olans, J., "The Social Network of the Family of a Schizophrenic: Implications for Social and Preventive Psychiatry," paper presented at the Annual Meeting of the American Ortho. Assoc., March, 1967(d).

Speck, R. V. and Morong, E., "Home-Centered Treatment of the Social Network of Schizophrenic Families: Two Approaches," paper presented at Annual Meeting of the American Psychiatric Assoc., May, 1967(e).

Taber, Richard H. Providing mental health services to a low socio-economic black community without requiring that people perceive themselves as patients: An ecological system approach to a community group. Paper presented at 46th Annual Meeting of the American Orthopsychiatric Association, New York, 1969.

Twente, Esther S. Aging, strength, and creativity. *Social Work,* July 1965, *10,* 105–110.

Wheelis, Allen. The place of action in personality change. *Psychiatry,* May 1950, *13,* 135–148.

White, Robert W. *Ego and reality in psychoanalytic theory.* New York: International Universities Press, 1963.

Chapter 13

Teamwork for
Social Work Practice

This chapter moves from a primary focus on the client system and the change agent system that has been the center of the discussion throughout most of this book to consider other systems that involve the social worker. The focus is now on the principles of constructing and working within a particular type of action system—the professional team. Social workers may, of course, be involved in other types of action systems, but teams are such an important part of their work that the authors feel that a chapter should be devoted to the principles of building and using them.

In working with the client system, a practitioner often becomes aware that members of that system are also being served by other helping institutions of the community. Or it may be that in the role of broker (see Chapter 11) workers become aware of the need to link clients with various services they may require but cannot supply. Or it may be that a service that workers are able to offer, such as the care of children away from their homes, require them to become part of a team in order to supply that service effectively. (In the care of children away from their homes, the social worker will of necessity be involved either with foster parents or with the child-care personnel of an institution.)

In any case, *one* important skill of social work practice is the capacity to operate as a productive member of a "service team." The following concepts and methods, which the authors believe are important to the notion of teamwork, will be discussed in this chapter: the problem of competition, the problem of professional and agency culture, and the problem-solving approach to teamwork and methods of planning and sharing.

In addition to the material in the chapter itself two other articles have been included that should be read as an integral part of this chapter. The two readings deal with teamwork within an agency, an institution, or some rather structured system in which certain assignments can be made to certain staff members on the part of an administrator or director and in which there are certain sanctions that can be applied by this same authority as to assigned task performance (see Reading 13–1). In this type of situation, it is possible for the team members to be selected for their expertise, for them to be bound by the common goals of the setting even if they come from different professions, and for them to develop working relationships over a period of time. This is a difficult assignment, and one about which little has been written in the literature.

However, there is another aspect of teamwork that may be even more difficult to understand and about which equally little is written. This involves teams composed of individual social workers representing a wide variety of agencies, who are brought together on an hoc basis to operate cooperatively in the interests of a particular client system. The members of this type of team could be considered as making up the action system discussed in Chapter 4. Chapter 13 focuses on the dynamics of the interactions of such teams. These teams differ from those discussed in the readings in that there is no one sanctioning authority to make assignments or evaluate performance. Instead each member represents and is responsible to a different authority. Time allocated for defining the problem, establishing working relationships, and performing the tasks may be extremely brief and pressures to come up with a quick and simple answer are often great. It is the hope of the authors that the readers can draw an understanding of the team process from both the chapter and the two readings that will be useful as they attempt to construct, or participate in constructing, action systems.

OBSERVATIONS ON TEAMWORK

For much of its history social work has been concerned with the fragmentation of helping services, although this concern has often focused upon the costliness of such fragmentation to the community rather than upon the problems such service might create for the client. Through much of the 1800s there were periodic efforts to establish methods of collaboration between the various social agencies of the community. In the early 1900s with Dr. Cabot's employment of social workers in the hospital setting, the problem of collaboration across professional lines was introduced. In the 1950s one of the authors was a part of a community effort to examine the impact upon clients of the fragmentation of social work services. She well remembers one client to whom she posed the question of whether or not it would be easier for her if she had to deal with only one practitioner rather than several. She thought a moment and then said, "I don't know. I think maybe I can use more than one because they are there for different purposes: for example, the county welfare worker is there to tell you how to spend your money, and the Catholic Social Services to console me." This client had reconciled a certain difference between services into a consistent pattern of living which we, as professionals, have not been able or willing to attain.

It is strange that, in spite of periodic efforts to establish better collaboration, relatively little progress has been made in understanding the way in which professionals do or do not work together. I would guess that many of you, when you become social workers, will spend perhaps as much as 25 or 30 percent of your time in dealing with other professions, and if you throw in lunch and coffee breaks, the figure may be even higher. Without effective teamwork and collaboration, clients and families in the social service system are caught in a nightmarish fragmentation of care. When families and clients are left alone to resolve professional conflicts, to reconcile these incongruities, and deal with often contradictory advice, multiple talents and inputs, no matter how skillful from the view of the professional, becomes burdensome rather than helpful.

It is essential, therefore, that we get involved in learning the skills of effective teamwork. Yet we are reluctant. It reminds me of one story told by Dr. Weiner about the man who was crossing the street and was hit by a truck, and some people passing by rushed over to see if they could help. Lo and behold, they saw the man crawling away as fast as he could on hands and one knee, dragging one leg helplessly. They said, "Where are you going? Don't you realize that you have just been hit by a truck. You need help." The man replied, "Please leave me alone. I don't want to get involved." Like the man, social workers are involved in teamwork and/or interdisciplinary collaboration. Social workers are active players. The sense of satisfaction with what they do as well as their frustrations will be affected by how well they are able to participate. Our participation in helping each other to deliver services is as important as direct contact with our clients. In fact, our direct contact with our clients will only be helpful as we can effectively use teamwork. If all these things are true, why is it that we have such trouble in working across professional lines. What are some obstacles to effective collaboration?

The first obstacle is the myth that all that is required is a spirit of cooperation. There isn't one person I know that would define himself or herself as uncooperative. If we are the kind of people who are friendly, outgoing, thoughtful of others—who possess all these good things that all of us who read this text do—good interdisciplinary collaboration will follow us all the rest of the days of our lives and will dwell in peaceful work situations the rest of our professional lives. There are two notions that feed into this. One notion is that anyone can get along with others; that this is not a professional skill. The other notion is that teamwork rests totally on personality variables and thus, see no need to pay attention to specific knowledge or skills. While personality dimensions are important, we are lost if we reduce the collaborative processes to psychological dimensions alone. We must resist the tendency, only too prevalent among the psychologically sophisticated, to handle our frustrations in dealing with others by assigning unconscious, malevolent motivations to those others. That is too easy and leaves us too pure. However, there is one psychological factor that we may need to take into consideration. That factor is the tendency to resist difference; to see and evaluate difference in terms of right and wrong. If something is different from something else then one must be preferable to the other. And if this is so, then the "right" must be of more value than the "wrong." There is a further tendency, when the difference is among individuals, to assign less valuable qualities to the "different one," such as: "impulsive, soft, etc." rather than "objective, scientific, etc." And if the difference is between professions, one primarily composed of men and one of women, I will leave the results to the reader's imagination.

A second obstacle to effective collaboration is the feeling of helplessness in the face of the power of authority of another profession. Social workers complain of this in almost all secondary settings in which they work. We need to remember that the central message in such complaints is "there is nothing we can do to influence the course of things when we have such limited power." We must come to grips with our conception of power and authority if we are to work collaboratively. First, we need to remember that if we see ourselves as powerless, then we are truly without power. If we say we can't do something, then we can't. We can only effectively carry out something that we believe possible. We also need to remember that there are two types of authority—the authority of position and the authority of competence. The authority of competence is granted us by our colleagues, by those with whom we interact each day. Thus, when we see a colleague as having more authority than we do, we need to remember that we have given them a part of this authority. And we need to allot ourselves a certain authority. All professionals need power and authority—the power and authority to help—for effective helping requires these qualities. We must be willing to allocate to the other professionals the authority that is necessary to effectively carry out the responsibilities that are allocated to them, but we need to retain the authority and power we need to carry out our job. I believe that in general social workers tend to underestimate their power vis-à-vis other professions. One reason we may see ourselves as so powerless may be, paradoxically, because we feel, or want to be so omnipotent. If we cannot solve a problem that has plagued people for a generation we feel that we are failures. Our expectations need to be more realistic.

The third obstacle has to do with the definition of the parameters of the profession. It is inevitable that professionals charged with working with individuals and their relationships will have areas of overlap, certain tasks that either professional could do. These areas may need to be negotiated around individual's situations, and can be effectively handled in this way. However, conflict over who does what often causes bitter feelings and raises barriers to collaboration. There is a tendency for the representatives of each profession to see their turf as being the "village green" and other professions as occupying only individual plots of ground attached to the central green. This has been a problem for social work in that, having poorly defined parameters, social workers often tend to see their function as too all-encompassing. And there are some professionals that deny difference all together in saying that "any member of the staff can deal effectively with any problems." This reminds me of Lidtz's notion of the "enmeshed family" that must deny difference, and that way lies an inevitable deterioration of service. We need to work on defining areas of overlap as well as areas of special competence.

Another dimension of collaborative skill for social workers as well as for members of other professions is the ability to engage in role negotiation: to be able to identify what it has sanction for and what it does not have sanction for, to develop ways to appropriately broaden its sanction and to bargain for turf, especially when other professionals may have some claim to some of the same territory.

The last obstacle to working in a focused way on collaboration has to do with the nature of a profession. Knowledge of human beings, of the nature of growth and development, of the genesis of human problems, of the forces that keep problems in place is overwhelming and sometimes contradictory. Most of it is not generated by professionals but is borrowed from the more basic disciplines. Each profession borrows the knowledge most related to its function and that best supports the methods of practice that it has developed. Such knowledge is then integrated into a usable whole. The result of such a process is that each professional is educated to operate from a different conception of human nature, of human conduct, with different beliefs, assumptions, and expectations about people, what and how they act and carry their human relationships. Each profession develops different styles of communication and methods of problem solving, especially data collection. Each profession has a different notion of what is "effective outcome." Thus, the rivalry and conflicts that arise between professionals are not totally a struggle for power or control or the desire to be acknowledged as right. Much of the problem comes from these very different beliefs and expectations, these specialized conceptions of how people act, or should act, how people change, and how they should be treated, guided, and helped when in need. I do not think that professions should see things from the same perspective. In difference, there is strength. I do not want a physician at the scene of my accident putting his primary effort into trying to help me understand my pain. I want him or her to act as necessary to deal with the physical damage first and foremost. However, if my injuries are extensive and handicapping, I would hope he or she would explore the possibility of social work help. Professionals, because they are called upon to act, have to believe that their approach is "right." If we are to be helpful, we have to believe in what we are doing and our way of doing it. The ability to endure the ambiguity of acting on knowledge as though it were certainty, while recognizing that there is no certainty, is a difficult strain for all professionals. Physicians seek cure. Social workers seek more social competence and expanded ways of coping with social life. These goals are not incongruent, but they often generate conflict over which is of more value. Thus, we need to recognize the inevitability of conflict and difference and learn to negotiate it in the interests of effective help to patients and their families, and we need to abandon the notion that difference is wrong, that absolute agreement is possible, and that if we cannot agree then something is wrong with one of us—usually you.

THE PROBLEM OF COMPETITION

When helping persons, groups, or organizations attempt to work together on a common problem shared by a common client system, there are both cooperative and competitive elements in the relationship between the helpers. Cooperative work requires that we disclose our relationship with the client to other helping authorities who are valuable because they bring different knowledge, roles, and functions to the helping process. This means we must be willing to cross barriers of difference. This is not easy. One is constantly amazed at the subtle, and sometimes not so subtle, ways practitioners compete in professional interaction whose stated purpose is coopera-tion. In most agencies and professional associations, there are infinite possi-bilities of competitive behavior: "I understand the needs of those children better than the foster mother or the teacher"; "My work is more central to the client's welfare than yours"; "My supervisor knows more than your supervisor"; "My agency or my job is where the action really is."

The prevalence of competition in areas in which it is inappropriate, and even destructive to the rational interests of the competing individuals, has been highlighted by experiments in game theory. Game theory is a discipline that seeks to obtain understanding of the problems of human interaction and decision making by studying human exchange from the perspective of strategic games. One game that game theorists use in many different forms is the "non-zero-sum game." Its purpose is to determine under what condi-tions players will cooperate. In contrast to win-lose games, where there is a winner and a loser, these games are so structured as to make it absurd to play uncooperatively. A player who fails to cooperate has no chance of winning and considerable chance of losing. Nevertheless, researchers in the area of human cooperation are always struck by the frequency with which uncooperative play predominates and, even more surprising, by the frequency with which they play becomes even more competitive as the games go on, and players experience the full negative effects of competition. It is almost as though, once caught in a win-lose situation, the players cannot extricate themselves even though it is demonstrated that it is a destructive situation. And, in social work practice, the most unfortunate aspect of com-petitive interrelationships of practitioners is that it is the client who is dam-aged by them. Perhaps social workers are especially vulnerable to competi-tiveness because it is their status and authority that are involved and the client's welfare that is at stake.

Game theorists have sought to explain this behavior and to isolate varia-bles that will determine how a player will behave. As a result of their efforts, players have been classified into these categories: (1) maximizers, who are interested only in their own payoffs; (2) the rivalists, who are inter-ested only in defeating their partners and are not concerned with the result of the game itself; and (3) the cooperators who are interested in helping both themselves and their partners. These have been studies of non-zero-sum games under conditions in which communication between players was impossible and under conditions in which it was encouraged. Improved com-munication seemed to increase cooperation only in the case of the coopera-tors, who were already interested in bettering the results for both sides. It failed to change the behavior of the maximizers or the rivalists (David, 1970).

It is possible for practitioners to work toward changing a "maximizer" (one interested only in one's own gain) or a "rivalist" (one only interested in "being one up" or in "putting others down") into a "cooperator" (one interested in helping both oneself and one's colleagues to aid the client) by the kind of climates they establish in their professional conferences and associations. For example, the practitioner can actively recognize the impor-tance of each team member in the execution of a task. Child-care staff, who often carry the heaviest burden of the daily stress of living with and loving disturbed and deviant children, often find that their efforts go unrewarded by the professional staff, who may assume that they are the only ones who *really know* what the child is like or what the child needs. In a conference where helping people risk proposing a change in a particular way of working, it becomes critical whether they are rewarded for having attempted something worthwhile or whether their suggestions are seen as something for someone else to "top" or "negate." Rivalists often spend a great deal of time developing verbal ability and skill in the use of professional language. They often use this ability and skill to make the point that anyone who risks a new suggestion really does not understand the underlying dynamics or the person would not be so naive as to make the proposal. This is a cheap way to be "one-up," if that is what is sought. It demonstrates superior knowledge and sophistication at absolutely no cost as the one who is "put down" seldom challenges the negative predictions for fear that they might prove true, thus further revealing ignorance. Such challenges are especially difficult to contend with when they are presented in elegant professional language and with a knowing air. In such a situation the cost is borne by the person who risks making a proposal and by the client system involved.

THE PROBLEM OF PROFESSIONAL AND AGENCY CULTURE

Effective collaboration requires that helping persons demonstrate respect and trust, expectation, and acceptance, in their interactions. The discussion of how respect and trust are demonstrated in the helping relationships also has relevance to professional working relationships. We are all taught the importance of accepting and respecting clients, but we seldom examine what this means when applied to colleagues.

To work effectively together, to have meaningful exchange, one somehow has to respect the position from which the other acts. The worker who is involved in work across professional agency lines must be perceptive and understanding about the point of view of the other organizations and their professional staff. One mark of a profession is its value system. An important part of all professional education and staff development is the attempt to socialize workers to their agency and their profession (see Chapter 3). By this we generally mean working toward the internalization of the values and culture of the profession so that the professional person in whom this process has taken place is constrained to work in certain ways and to take certain positions. This is critically important as protection to the client system, since in the helping process workers must use themselves and their judgment. There is no way another can dictate to the worker exactly how to use oneself to carry out any specific action in any specific situation. Therefore, the only assurance we have that a professional person really can be trusted with professional tasks is that action is on the basis of deeply internalized feelings and judgments that stem from professional values and knowledge. This is the only meaningful protection we have in using a professional's services. However, internalization of professional values and culture as the "right" way is usually an unconscious process. Internalization can cause tremendous problems in interagency collaboration unless we become aware of our values and culture as our beliefs and our climate and learn to recognize that others have their values and their culture.

In addition to undergoing a process of professional socialization and identification, professional social workers (and members of other professions as well) as a rule work within established institutional settings. The machinery through which they do their work sets boundaries to the ways in which, for practical purposes, they define the problems with which they work. Also, within these institutional settings a professional subculture grows up which, like all cultures, has its own value system and accepted ways of operating. Workers who are engaged in collaborative work with persons outside their own agency need to care about their agency and be a part of it and yet to have the capacity to step out of this culture in order to be analytical about it. They need to be understanding of what is going on in their own agency and yet not be trapped within a particular way of approaching problems. They need to be able to recognize that other workers have an equal identification with their agencies and an equal need to protect the functioning of those agencies. The social and helping services in the community, their organization, and ways of working must be understood if we are to utilize their services effectively in the service of our clients. Specialized conceptions of how people in need act, or should act, and how they should be helped, guided, or treated can result in bitter rivalry and conflict.

In speaking of fragmentation in the helping professions, Lawrence Frank (1954, p. 89) writes:

> For example, a family may in its varied contacts receive professional care, advice, and services from a physician, a nurse, a social worker, a nutritionist, a home economist, a probation officer, a lawyer, or judge, a minister, a psychologist, a teacher, a guidance counselor, an industrial relations advisor, a banker, a group worker, and so on, each of whom may give that family irreconcilable advice and treatment, guidance in how to live, keep health, maintain a home and family, care for and rear children, resolve family discord, and all other aspects of living, especially human relations. The family is expected to resolve these professional conflicts, to reconcile these incongruities, and often mutually contradictory advices into a coherent, consistent pattern of living, a reconciliation which the professionals will not or cannot attain.

In that same article Frank (p. 90) writes:

> Thus students in medical school, nursing, social work, law, engineering, business, architecture, public administration and the graduate departments of the social sciences and humanities are being inculcated each with a different conception of human nature, of human conduct, with different beliefs, assumptions, expectations about people, what and how they act and carry on their human relations. All of these students are going out to practice in our communities, with what Veblen once called the "trained incapacity of specialists" unable to communicate or collaborate in their practice or even to recognize what other specialists see and do. Indeed, we often find bitter rivalry and open conflcts arising not entirely from professional competition but from these very different beliefs and expectations, these specialized conceptions

of how people act, or should act and how they should be treated, guided and helped when in need.

THE PROBLEM-SOLVING APPROACH TO TEAMWORK

How does one define the concept of teamwork? The *American Heritage Dictionary* defines it as the "cooperative effort of an organized group to achieve a common goal." The definition seems to refer workers to some of the concepts of problem solving. It seems to require that team members see the payoff in the honest attempt to identify the most appropriate actions and resources which they can supply to help the client. Thus the purpose of coming together as a team is not to "win" one's way or prove one's "rightness" but to utilize the different capacities brought by the different members of the team in order to expand our knowledge and our range of skills so that we can offer the client the best service in the direction that the client wishes to go. Teamwork requires that we keep this direction clearly before us as the reason we are together. In teamwork it is essential to recognize that we are trying to build interagency organizations and/or professional teams that function effectively in the interest of the client and the desired goals. We need to function in the interests of the job to be done. They need to keep a problem-solving focus so that we can communicate around a defined task. Our own problems of communication and relationship must be worked out so that they can offer the client the most effective help possible.

METHODS OF PLANNING AND SHARING

In working with the client system, workers have come to the conclusion that they cannot offer all the service clients need or that clients may need some help in thinking through what is seen as important factors in service. What do the workers do? The first thing they may want to do is to discuss this with their supervisors in order to check out their thinking, and their knowledge of where they might turn for help. The second important step is to talk with the client about how the client sees this notion. Workers may present this to the client as something that must be done in light of the nature of the problem, the goals sought, and the limits of service (for example, they may tell parents who need to place a child about foster home services and the necessary work with the foster mother), or they may present it as something on which they and the client can come to a decision (for example, workers may say that their understanding and assessment of the situation might be helped if they could discuss the problem with the psychiatrist on the agency staff).

In beginning a working relationship with other helping persons toward offering their clients better service, workers have the choice of asking clients whether they want to join workers in their conferences and planning or whether they assume that workers should carry this role alone. Practitioners working jointly with a client seem to have developed a pattern of meeting together privately in order to pool their observations and knowledge of the problem and to come to some understanding of how to proceed. Sometimes clients are told about this meeting, and sometimes they are not. Sometimes the possibility of such a meeting is used as a threat to clients. It is our position that clients should be actively involved in consideration of the way different professionals can be used to help with their problems and that clients must be told about all professional consultations involving them. We would much prefer to offer our clients the opportunity to come with us to meetings with other professionals and to participate in the deliberations so that they may understand what is involved and that they may speak for themselves.

In any case, before approaching another resource, the worker should talk with the client about that resource, about how it may be used, about what it can offer, about why it is suggested at this point, and about what is involved in getting in touch with it and utilizing it. The client should understand what will need to be shared with the other agency. The street gang that the practitioner has been working with as an unattached worker may be very anxious and concerned when the practitioner suggests that an organized agency could offer them a meeting place and opportunities for recreation. What is the worker going to have to tell the agency about them? Will the agency invite them in if it knows about their behavioral history? Is the agency going to try to run them? The parents of an angry, acting-out daughter will have similar questions if foster home placement is suggested as a temporary measure to help both child and parents think things out. Will the foster parents need to be told that the girl steals? What will the foster parents expect of them? Under what conditions will they be able to see their daughter? To take her home? How can foster parents help when they, her own parents, have failed?

The client and the worker will need to discuss how the new service will be contacted and involved in their affairs. The expectations and requirements of the new service via-à-vis the client will need to be carefully gone into and understood. What will be shared about the client will need to be considered. It is usually helpful to ask clients what they think the agency will need to know or should be told about them?

What does one share with another agency about one's client? One shares with team members what they need to know in order to work with the client toward solution of the problem in the way the client and you have decided it will need to be worked out. The problem of sharing information with others is not a simple one. When we do this type of sharing, we are inevitably confronted with the question of how the other person will use the information in the interests of the client? Social workers who place children in foster homes often face conflicts about what to tell foster parents about the children placed with them. And what information about the natural parents do they share? We have a need to present our clients (parents and children) in a positive light—yet how much information can be kept secret when foster parents and children live intimately as a family? There is no ideal answer to this question. However, one principle that is essential in approaching it is to keep the client system aware of what is being shared and why.

When more than one worker is involved with the same client system, the best device we have for joint planning and joint monitoring of our work is the case conference. The client should be told about these conferences and their outcomes. As stated earlier, it is very productive to give some thought to the client's involvement in such conferences. The questions one must ask in deciding this are "Will attending the conference help clients in their analysis of the problem?" "Will it help give clients a sense of being in control of their own destiny?" "Or is the conference likely to make them feel overwhelmed by professionals and by the problems they see in the situation?" "Will the decisions being made demand specific behavior of the client, or are they primarily decisions related to agency policies and parameters of service?" "Is it possible for the client to provide meaningful input into the conference?"

In order to work together successfully with a client, the practitioners involved usually need to meet together at least once. There is no substitute for this meeting, and lack of time is not an adequate excuse. Having served as practitioners in large public agencies and carried large case loads, the authors must admit to violations of this principle. However, the fact that something is not done does not negate its importance. We hope that workers will adopt this as a desirable way of working even if they cannot follow through in all cases. Letters and telephone calls are an unsatisfactory substitute for at least one face-to-face planning session around a particular case. In each case conference someone must take the position of leader. The leader takes the responsibility for seeing that all agencies and persons involved in the case are included in the conference, for defining the purpose and focus of the conference, for seeing that everyone present is heard, for clarifying the plans of action and who is to do what and when, and for helping to resolve any conflicts. The conference should result in group acceptance of the part each agency is to play. This agreement is facilitated by recording the conclusions of the conference before its termination. Thus everyone has a chance to correct the common plan, and later everyone receives a copy of it. Each agency then carries the responsibility for following through on the plan (which can be seen as a design for coordination) or for pointing out the necessity of changing it. The leader should also have the responsibility of seeing that the plan is implemented by each agency involved. The leader, in effect, becomes the "captain of the treatment team." Who is to serve in this role and how one is to be selected should be decided before the team actually begins the action phase of the work with the client. The assignment of this responsibility is an allotment of power and authority. The problems involved in accepting such a position must be considered in this light. There should be a clear focus on the purpose of the conference, and drifting away from that focus should be limited. If there are problems of working relationships between the members of the team, these should be approached as problems-to-be-solved and worked through to some acceptable conclusion or they will distort the team's relationship to the client.

RECAPITULATION

In this chapter we have discussed the problems of teamwork in the interests of offering the client system more adequate help in their problem solving. The aspects of competition that may be involved have been discussed as well as the problem of professional and agency culture. Some of the things that go into establishing a team have also been suggested.

A LOOK FORWARD

We want to emphasize once again the importance of using the two articles at the end of this chapter as a part of any consideration of teamwork. In the next chapter we will be considering the importance to the practitioners of endings in social work practice. There are three types of endings: referral to another helping service, transfers to another worker, and termination of contract.

Reading 13-1

*Team Building in the Human Services**

Eugene Hooyman

Everyone has a different definition of a team. Some think of teams in very general terms (for example, football team, family, or symphony orchestra), while others have a very specific image (for example, social work professionals working together 40 hours per week planning for their clients' needs). While football teams, families, and symphony orchestras all involve some critical aspects of team functioning, they are obviously not this paper's focus. Nor is the focus so narrow that it excludes paraprofessionals, clients, and/or professionals other than social workers or limits the purpose to planning for clients' needs.

A variety of views have been expressed regarding the nature of teams including teams as "action systems" (Pincus & Minahan, 1973, p. 194), "a group of people interacting together" to accomplish the work of the organization (Leuenberger, 1973, p. 26), "relatively permanent work groups" (Reilly & Jones, 1974, p. 227), "workers who are functionally interdependent" (Solomon, 1977, p. 181), and a "group of people who possess individual expertise," make individual decisions, and have a common purpose (Brill, 1976, p. xvi). Views expressed regarding the composition of teams include "the social workers and the

people they work with" (Pincus & Minahan, 1973, p. 194), "any grouping of social welfare personnel" (Briggs, 1973, p. 4), and "peers and their immediate supervisor" (Reilly & Jones, 1974, p. 227). Regarding the purpose of team building, views include "improving the problem-solving ability" (Reilly & Jones, 1974, p. 227) and "improvement of interpersonal relationships among those workers who are functionally interdependent" (Solomon, 1977, p. 181).

Each of these views emphasizes a different aspect of teamwork or team building. Reilly and Jones (1974) and Solomon (1977) focus on the process of developing teams as a strategy in organizational development which is applied to business and industry as well as the human services. Brill (1976) defines a team as a group of human service professionals, that is, an interdisciplinary or interprofessional team. Pincus and Minahan (1973) view the team from the perspective of social workers and who can best assist them in influencing some change. Leuenberger (1973) and Briggs (1973) perceive the team as composed of only social workers. All these views share the perception that the team is an ongoing, interdependent group with a common task. While the task focus distinguishes the team from other growth groups or social groups, effective interpersonal functioning is recognized as essential to teamwork.

In this article, teamwork or team building will be discussed as it relates to the human services, excluding business or industry but including the social worker and other human service professionals. In this

* An original article prepared for this book. The materials included in this article are based to a large extent on materials used in a two semester 12-credit course sequence entitled "Team Building in the Health Services" offered from 1976 to 1978 by the School of Public Health, University of Minnesota. The author acknowledges the contributions of the following faculty team members who helped team-teach this course: Robert Schwanke (public health interdisciplinary studies.), Miriam Cohn (social work), Eleanor Anderson (public health nursing), and Barbara Reynolds (public health nursing).

discussion, teams may include paraprofessionals and clients as well as professionals, depending upon the team's purpose. Although the team's composition may include clients, the work of the team has a focus different than providing therapy.

BENEFITS UNDERLYING TEAM BUILDING

What are the values implicit in team building? When is teamwork most appropriate? What are the strengths and limitations of the team approach? These questions are important considerations for anyone expecting to be a team member in the human services.

The team idea began to emerge as early as 1928 when the famous Hawthorne Experiment revealed that the most significant factor in increasing productivity among workers was the "building of a sense of group identity, a feeling of social support and cohesion that came from increased worker interaction" (Dyer, 1977, p. 8). Other studies revealed that trainees who developed into cohesive team units during training programs demonstrated the largest increase in community service activity after the workshop (Lippitt, 1949), and that the efficiency and effectiveness in services to clients improved more with the team approach than with the case method of service (Briggs, 1973).

The decision to assign a task to an individual or to a team is often a difficult one. There are five factors to consider: (1) nature of the task; (2) characteristics of individual team members (that is, expertise, commitment to the outcome, and dependence on each others' support of the outcome); (3) importance of producing a high quality product; (4) importance of a high degree of commitment to the solution—the importance of accepting the product or decision; and (5) operating effectiveness of the team. Individuals are generally better than teams with respect to creative tasks

and independent tasks while teams are generally better than individuals with respect to convergent or integrative tasks and goal-setting tasks (Sherwood & Hoylman, 1978).

Figure 1 summarizes the strengths and limitations of the team approach (Brieland, Briggs, & Leuenberger, 1973; Brill, 1976; Dyer, 1977; Sherwood & Hoylman, 1977). This summary clearly illustrates most teamwork values. Although the list of limitations is as long as the list of strengths, many limitations are examples of poorly functioning teams (for example, poor leadership, dominating individuals, unresolved conflict, poorly defined outcomes, and so on). Thus these limitations are not rooted in the nature of teamwork but rather in the inadequacies of skills in leadership, conflict resolution, good formulation, and so on.

FORMING A NEW TEAM

Four major factors need to be considered in forming a new team: (1) the size of the team; (2) the composition of the team; (3) the structure under which the team will begin functioning (for example, basic norms); (4) the procedures by which the team will begin functioning (for example, time and place of meetings). Although the structure and procedures develop primarily throughout the team's growth, it is highly desirable to identify beforehand or early in the team's life the basic structure and procedures by which the team can begin to function. The team's size and composition also may change as the team develops, but there must be some clear definition of these from the very beginning.

Size. A team's size depends primarily upon the desired outcomes and the best ways of achieving these. The team should be large enough to include all the skills and perspectives important to task achievement. The type and degree of inter-

Strengths

Pools more knowledge and information

Facilitates communication between professionals, paraprofessionals, agencies, and clients

Breaks down stereotypes members might have of other professionals, paraprofessionals, agencies, and clients

Encourages the development of individual areas of expertise

Provides opportunities for personal and professional development

Provides for examination and evaluation of ideas and issues with differing perspectives represented

Increases the variety of potential solutions to a problem

Focuses on total problems rather than segments

Reduces overlapping functions

Provides a more comprehensive range of services

Creates an opportunity for wider and more effective use of relevant experts/specialists and paraprofessionals

Provides for an effective way of introducing paraprofessionals into an agency

Provides for support among members

Generates enthusiasm and motivation among members

Produces work more meaningful and personally satisfying to members

Increases the influence upon the target of change

Produces a higher quality product

Increases the acceptance of the outcome

Limitations

Pressures members toward conformity

Primative discussion of solutions leads to hasty decisions

Lack of members' commitment to the team approach and/or outcome blocks progress

Causes greater fragmentation of services

May be less contact with clients

Takes more time than consultation or referral

Communication processes become complex and difficult to control

Complex processes make teams cumbersome and slow moving

Poorly defined outcomes create confusion, tension, and conflict

Lack of role definition and overlap in functions create confusion, tension and conflict

Status differences produce tension and conflict

Poor leadership causes leadership struggles and wastes time

Unresolved conflicts block progress

Hidden agendas detract from team purpose

Dominating individuals stifle other potentially productive members

Difficulties in scheduling meetings

Difficulties in including the right mix of people while maintaining a workable size

Difficulties in justifying to administrators cost in time and money

FIGURE 1:   Strengths and limitations of the team approach

action needed to achieve the desired outcome should also be a consideration in determining the size (Brill, 1976). Five to six members is a desirable size for teams in the human services (Kane, 1975).

Small teams may not provide sufficient opportunities for members to develop their individual areas of expertise, and team members may become overworked because they do not have sufficient resources for achieving the purpose. Also small teams may provide too limited a range of learning opportunities, if that is a desired outcome of the team (for example, training of paraprofessionals) (Brieland, 1973). However, in teams of three, there is a tendency for two-one splits.

If the team is too large, on the other hand, communication can become unwieldy. Great demands are placed on the leader of large groups because the pro-

cesses become more complex. Active members tend to dominate more as the team size increases, while passive members tend to withdraw more. Actions become more anonymous, and the feeling of closeness among members diminishes. Rules and procedures tend to become more formalized in larger teams (Kane, 1975). Formation of subgroups or subteams which would work on specific tasks is frequently used effectively to counteract some of the difficulties caused by teams being too large.

Composition. Determination of the team's composition refers to putting together the best mix of people who will contribute to and gain from the team's internal functioning as well as the achievement of the team's external purpose. There must be a workable balance of certain heterogeneous and homogeneous characteristics. The type of characteristics to be considered are (1) descriptive—the position an individual occupies—profession, age, race, sex, and so on; and (2) behavioral—the way in which a person functions in a position (Pincus & Minahan, 1973).

Descriptive characteristics may be either heterogeneous or homogeneous, depending upon the team's purpose. For example, if the team's purpose requires input from numerous disciplines, the team should be composed of members heterogeneous with respect to their profession (that is, an interdisciplinary or interprofessional team). If the purpose of the team is to provide services to a minority population, it may be essential for the team to be homogeneous with respect to race.

Behavioral characteristics refer to the following three functions that may be used by team members: task function, maintenance functions, and self-oriented functions. Task functions are those functions most directly related to performing the task of the team. Their purpose is to facilitate the team in the problem-solving process. Maintenance functions are related to team-centered activities and behavior. Their purpose is to maintain productive interpersonal working relationships and provide a cohesive team climate in which all members' resources are used effectively as the team is working on its task. Self-oriented functions are either irrelevant to the task or are disruptive to the team's problem-solving process and interpersonal working relationships (Morris & Sashkin, 1976).

Some of the task functions which are needed in the team are:

- *Initiating.* Giving ideas and directions; proposing objectives or tasks, defining a team problem; suggesting a problem-solving procedure.
- *Elaborating and clarifying.* Exploring and expanding ideas; interpreting ideas and suggestions; defining and proposing alternatives; clarifying confusions.
- *Coordinating.* Putting together and integrating ideas and concepts.
- *Summarizing.* Focusing the work flow on the task; drawing the work together; proposing to the team a decision or conclusion which they can accept or reject.
- *Technical and recording.* Arranging the physical setting, recording the work of the team.
- *Giving and seeking information.* Offering facts and asking for clarification; requesting more facts relating one's own experience to the problem.
- *Giving and receiving opinions.* Stating an opinion or belief; looking for expressions of feeling from members.

Some of the maintenance functions which are needed in the team are:

- *Encouraging and supporting.* Praising members for their relevant contributions.
- *Harmonizing.* Mediating and working through differences; relieving tensions.
- *Gatekeeping.* Providing opportunities for others to share ideas and participate in discussions; keeping communication channels open.
- *Process observing.* Giving feedback to the team on how the team is working together.
- *Following.* Giving acceptance to the ideas of others; showing acceptance with nonverbal behavior.
- *Standard setting.* Helping to set standards or norms for the team.
- *Compromising.* Problem-solving one's own conflicts with others.

Some of the self-oriented functions which are visible in teams are

- *Aggression.* Attacking others.
- *Blocking.* Resisting without cause; opposing most of time.
- *Attention seeking.* Calling attention to oneself; boasting; pleading a special interest.
- *Dominating.* Taking over and leading the team in an inappropriate direction.
- *Diverting.* Joking inappropriately; indulging in horse play inappropriately.

An effective team must have an appropriate balance of task and maintenance functions and a minimum of self-oriented functions. Too many maintenance functions and too few task functions may result in more of a social club than a work group. Too many task functions and too few maintenance functions may result in an unproductive work group which is frustrated with its inability to resolve critical interpersonal barriers (for example, unresolved conflict). Although most team members with training in teamwork are able to perform several of these task and maintenance functions, it is rare for anyone to be skilled in all functions. Team members tend to be skillful in either the maintenance functions or the task functions, but not both. Thus it is extremely important for a team to be composed of members who collectively will fulfill all of the task and maintenance functions necessary for effective teamwork.

Although there are numerous other considerations for the composition of the team, such as personal compatibility and complementary needs, the most important considerations are the descriptive and behavioral characteristics mentioned earlier.

Structure. The basic structure of a team is oftentimes set up before the team first meets. Structure refers to the basic norms or standards of behavior and belief that are imposed on a team from the out-side (that is, by the organization, group, and/or individual to which the team has some accountability) or within (that is, by other group members) (Kane, 1975).

Norms around leadership and decision-making, that is, how leadership is defined and how decisions are made, are two types of norms which determine to a large extent how the team will function. For example, the choice for an agency director to appoint an authoritarian leader to a team or allow a team to choose its own leadership will have far-reaching consequences in that team's life. The societal norm of democracy that the majority rules, often imposed implicitly on organizations and teams, limits the team in creatively considering other decision-making procedures which may be more effective for it.

Procedure. There are a number of administrative or operating procedures which need to be established before a team is able to begin functioning. Setting the time and the place for the first meeting is an obvious administrative procedure, but it is frequently done without adequate consideration. A meeting time must be found which is most convenient for everyone's schedule. Setting the time without consultation from all team members may result in major problems at a later stage. The length of time devoted to each meeting, the frequency of meeting, the length of time between meetings, and the time of the day when the team meets are also important considerations about the use of time (Pincus & Minihan, 1973).

The determination of the place to meet, and the physical or structural arrangement of chairs, tables, and so on can have a great impact on team functioning. For example, a carpeted room of an appropriate size for the team with pleasant colors, adequate lighting and ventilation, and appealing pictures significantly influences the creation of a supportive and trusting climate, whereas the absence of these physical qualities makes it difficult to achieve such a climate.

DYNAMICS AND STAGES OF TEAM FUNCTIONING

Earlier reference was made to the behavioral characteristics necessary in the composition of the team, that is, task functions and maintenance functions. Self-oriented functions, although present in teams, hinder overall effectiveness and should be eliminated to whatever extent possible. The appropriate mix and balance of task and maintenance functions are without a doubt the most critical determinants of effective team functioning. The lack of appropriate mix and balance of these functions are the most frequent cause of serious problems in team functioning.

The necessary mix and balance of task and maintenance functions will vary, depending upon the team's needs at any given point in its life. For example, at one point in time it may be necessary to spend a considerable amount of time focusing on the resolution of interpersonal conflict (that is, a maintenance function) and temporarily set aside working directly on the external task (that is, all task functions). By focusing all energies on the resolution of the conflict, the team is more likely to resolve the conflict and therefore be able to move on to accomplishing the team's purpose. By ignoring the conflict, or by suppressing it, the conflict is likely to become more explosive and more difficult or impossible to resolve. Consequently the team will neither resolve the conflict nor accomplish the team's purpose. The team members are likely to become frustrated and react to the critical internal issue (that is, the conflict) in counterproductive ways, such as not coming to meetings, nervous laughing which further suppresses the conflict, isolating the members involved in the conflict, expressing frustration through hurtful and indirect comments, and so on.

Considerable skill is needed by team members to first diagnose team needs in relation to the mix and balance of task and maintenance functions at any given point in time and then to perform the needed task and maintenance functions in an effective manner. These diagnostic and intervention skills need to be developed through skill building experiences and cannot be developed through reading alone. However, it is also necessary to have conceptual frameworks upon which diagnostic and intervention decisions are based.

At least two important dimensions need to be included in team skill building and knowledge acquisition: (1) dynamics in team functioning and (2) developmental stages of teams. Just as theorists have conceptualized stages of individual development (Erikson, 1950), they have also conceptualized stages of team development (Brill, 1976; Jones, 1975; Schutz, 1966). Within each stage of team development, as well as across stages, certain predominant team dynamics can also be identified.

Dynamics in team functioning. The dynamics in the team's life are innumerable and often-times interdependent and occur simultaneously. The task and maintenance functions already discussed are thought to be the primary influence on these dynamics.

Five important team processes or team dynamics are problem-solving, communication and feedback, leadership, decision-making, and conflict resolution. These areas are not mutually exclusive but overlap a great deal. Dynamics in team functioning have been identified in the literature on group dynamics (Cartwright & Zander, 1968; Johnson & Johnson, 1975; Pfeiffer & Jones, 1971).

Problem-solving. Problem-solving is a systematic approach the team may use to accomplish its task. It is a process that involves changing the present state of affairs to a desired state of affairs. The sequential steps are identifying the problem, diagnosing the problem, establishing goals, considering alternative ways of resolving the problem, choosing one of the alternatives, implementing the selected alternative, and evaluating its effectiveness.

It is essential for the team to proceed on the accomplishment of its task systematically. Therefore, it is helpful if all team members are aware of the general problem-solving process and the particular step which the team is focusing on at any point in time. Problems arise when steps are passed over, when some team members are focusing on one step and others are focusing on a different step, or when the team becomes "stuck" on one step. Four elements are considered basic to small group problem-solving: (1) agreement on the desired state of affairs; (2) structures and procedures for collecting, understanding, and utilizing relevant information about the present state of affairs; (3) structures and procedures for generating potential solutions, for deciding upon and implementing the best solution, and for evaluating its effectiveness; and (4) accomplishing the above three activities while at the same time increasing the effectiveness of the group's problem-solving capabilities. While the first three elements are critical to resolving the immediate problem or task in any team, the last element is especially critical to team building when the work group will continue functioning beyond the resolution of the immediate problem or accomplishment of the task (Johnson & Johnson, 1975).

Communication and feedback. Interpersonal communication is a process through which one person sends a message to a receiver with a conscious intent of affecting the receiver's behavior. Communication is basic to all small group functioning, and includes receiving, sending,

interpreting, and inferring verbal messages (words) and nonverbal messages (expressions, gestures, and environmental arrangements) all at the same time. The communication process is strongly influenced by the sender "encoding" or putting part of "self" in the message being sent and the receiver "decoding" or putting part of "self" in the message being received (Johnson & Johnson, 1975).

Several skills are important to effective small group communication. Specific skills of sending messages involve the following:

1. Clearly "own" your messages by personal pronouns, such as *I* and *my*.
2. Make your messages complete and specific.
3. Make your verbal and nonverbal messages congruent with each other.
4. Be redundant.
5. Ask for feedback concerning the way your messages are being received.
6. Make the message appropriate to the receiver's frame of reference.
7. Describe your feelings by name, action, or figure of speech.
8. Describe other member's behavior without evaluating or interpreting.

Some specific skills of receiving messages involve the following:

1. Paraphrase the content of the message and the feelings of the sender accurately and in a nonevaluative way.
2. Describe what you perceive to be the sender's feelings.
3. State your interpretation of the sender's message and negotiate with the sender until there is agreement as to the message's meaning (Johnson & Johnson, 1975).

Feedback refers to verbal and nonverbal responses which express the effects one's behavior has upon others (Bormann & Bormann, 1976). Giving and receiving feedback is a use of the communication process which is most important to team building because it is the mechanism through which effective behavioral change does occur. Giving and receiving feedback may take on a number of dimensions: (1) verbal, such as "no"; or nonverbal, such as leaving the room; (2) conscious, such as nodding assent; or unconscious, such as falling asleep; (3) spontaneous, such as "thanks a lot" or solicited, such as "yes, it did help"; and (4) formal, such as completing a post meeting reaction form; or informal, such as a slap on the back or a hug for a job well done.

Feedback can be helpful or destructive depending on several variables. The rules or guidelines for giving and receiving effective and helpful feedback are similar to the skills needed for effective communications. They are

1. Helpful feedback is descriptive, not evaluative, and "owned" by the sender.
2. Helpful feedback is specific, not general.
3. Helpful feedback is relevant to the self-perceived needs of the receiver.
4. Helpful feedback is desired by the receiver, not imposed on him or her.
5. Helpful feedback is timely and in context.
6. Helpful feedback is useable, concerned with behavior over which the receiver has some control (Lippitt, Watson, & Westley, 1958).

While feedback can be considered the basis for any effective team skill building effort, communication can be considered the basis for all human interaction and for all group functioning.

Leadership. Leadership can be broadly defined as the process of influence occurring among mutually dependent team members. Leadership implies influence from one member upon other members and can be designated from an outside authority, chosen by other team members, or assumed by an individual ex-

erting some type of influence on other members. Although there is oftentimes one recognized leader in a team, any member is involved in leadership behavior when that member influences others to help the team accomplish its purposes (Johnson & Johnson, 1975).

Leadership can be looked at in terms of the source of the power or influence being exerted on other members. There are six sources of power which a leader might possess: reward, coercive, legitimate, referent, expert, and informational. Reward power refers to the ability to deliver positive consequences or remove negative consequences as a response to other members' behaviors. Coercive power refers to the ability to inflict negative consequences or remove positive consequences in response to other members' behaviors. Legitimate power refers to that influence resulting from a person's position in the team or organization or larger group, and/or from special responsibilities a person has as a result of that position. Referent power is that influence a person has because of being respected and/or well liked. Expert power is that influence a person has as a result of team members' perceptions that the member has some special knowledge or skill and is trustworthy. Informational power is that influence a person has as a result of resources or information which will be useful in accomplishing the team's purpose (French & Raven, 1959).

Leadership can also be defined in terms of behavioral functions. These task and maintenance functions—the primary leadership functions essential to a team—have already been identified and discussed earlier in relation to the team composition.

Leadership is situational with respect to the team's maturity level. The level of maturity refers to the team's ability to set high but attainable goals, the willingness and ability to take responsibility, and the education and/or experiences of the team.

In a newly formed team, the effective leader is one who focuses primarily on task functions. As the team members' maturity increases in terms of accomplishing a specific task, the effective leader begins to diminish task functions and increase maintenance functions. Finally, when the group is fully matured, the effective leader becomes one of the members where task and maintenance functions are shared by all members. This final state of maturity is the ideal state most frequently desired by teams, but seldom achieved (Hersey & Blanchard, 1976).

Leadership can also be viewed in terms of the degree of direction given to a team. An autocratic leadership style refers to strong, directive behavior toward the team by the leader. While a democratic style encourages group decision-making and member choice, a laissez-faire style allows complete freedom to the team. Stronger work motivation and more cohesion develops with a democratic style; more dependence, discontent, and hostility develops with an autocratic style; and less work, poorer quality work, and more play occurs with a laissez-faire style (Lippitt & White, 1972).

How one chooses to provide leadership in a team depends primarily upon an analysis of what the team needs and the level and range of leadership skills. However, one's perception of need is strongly influenced by values about teamwork and about the nature of human interaction. One who perceives human beings as basically fallible and needing to be controlled will tend to choose a more directive or autocratic style, while one who perceives human beings as full of creative potential waiting to be released will tend to choose a less directive or democratic style.

Decision-making. Decision-making refers to one step in the problem-solving process whereby the team uses some method of agreeing on which alternative is the best solution for the problem or task facing the team. In a broader context, decision-making refers to any team situation which demands agreement by all members before it can move ahead. Because this step is so critical to the problem-solving process and to effective team functioning, it deserves special consideration.

An effective decision is one which maximizes the use of time and resources and is fully implemented by team members. An effective decision also enhances the problem-solving abilities of the team. There are several methods by which decisions can be made in teams: (1) agreement of the entire team whereby all members understand the decision and support it (consensus); (2) majority vote; (3) minority of team members imposing their agreement on the team; (4) averaging individual opinions of team members; (5) member with the most authority makes decision after group discussion of the issues; and (6) member with the most authority makes decision without a group discussion.

As mentioned earlier, the norm for decision-making frequently is imposed on the team explicitly by the person or organization to which the team is accountable or implicitly through the unspoken norms of organizations, the society, or other powerful groups to which team members are individually or collectively accountable. Ideally, the team should set its own norm for decision-making before engaging in the problem-solving process. The team should choose the method that is best for (1) the type of decision that has to be made; (2) the time and resources available; (3) the history of the team; (4) the nature of the task; (5) the type of climate the team wants; and (6) the type of setting in which the group works.

Consensus is the decision-making procedure most preferred by teams when the decision is an important one and the consequences of the decision affect all team members. It is also the most time-consuming process because all members need to understand the issues and the decision, must have opportunities to tell how they feel about the decision, and must support the decision as an experimental effort even if they have reservations about it. This method tends to produce an innovative, creative, and high quality decision with high commitment from team members to implement the decision. It also enhances the team's decision-making and problem-solving capacities and builds cohesion. However, it would be a serious mistake to use this method inappropriately, that is, when these criteria do not warrant its use (Johnson & Johnson, 1975).

Conflict resolution. Conflict exists when incompatible activities occur. One activity is incompatible with another activity when it prevents, blocks, interferes with, or makes the other activity less effective or less likely (Deutsch, 1969). Several characteristics define a conflict situation: (1) at least two parties are involved in the interaction; (2) perceived or real mutually exclusive goals and/or mutually exclusive values exist; (3) interaction is characterized by behavior intended to defeat the opponent or to gain a mutual victory; (4) parties face each other using opposing actions and counteractions; and (5) each party attempts to gain a power advantage over the other party (Filley, 1975).

Several generalizations can be formulated relating to characteristics of social relationships which increase the likelihood of conflict. The likelihood or opportunity for conflict is greater when (1) the limits of each party's jurisdiction are ambiguous; (2) conflicts of interest exist between the parties; (3) communication barriers exist; (4) one party is dependent upon another; (5) there are a large number of organizational levels, specialties represented, and differentiated jobs in the organization; (6) there is informal interaction among the parties, and they all participate in decision-making; (7) consensus is necessary; (8) standardized procedures, rules, and regulations are imposed; and (9) unre-

solved prior conflicts exist (Filley, 1975).

Conflict can exist between a team and another individual or group external to the team or between team members within the same team. Conflict within a team is the most frequently suppressed type of conflict and the most difficult to manage. Team members with a strong value of cooperative involvement with one another often perceive conflict as a threat and inherently negative to effective team functioning. Furthermore, team workers frequently approach all conflict situations with one predominant style, and they lack the skill and adaptability to use the most appropriate approach for each conflict situation which arises.

Conflict, per se, is neutral. It is a reality that exists and must be recognized and managed. The individual, team, organization, and/or society involved in conflict situations give conflict its negative or positive value.

A practical model for dealing with conflict is one which takes the dimensions of personal goals and the concern for relationship into account. The degree of importance or concern for each of these dimensions then determines the conflict style. If one party in a conflict situation seeks to meet individual goals at all costs, without concern for a relationship with or the needs of the opponent, that party is using a "win-lose" conflict style. The party using this style defines the situation so that there will be a winner and a loser and will try to win at all costs. A second style is a "yield-lose" style where one party views the relationship with the second party as the most important consideration, much more important than the achievement of individual goals. The party using this style yields position in the conflict situation and loses, hoping that this will allow the relationship to survive. A third style is a "lose-leave" style where the party has low concern for both the goals and the relationship with the opponent. This party loses by default through withdrawing from the situation. A fourth style is a "compromise" style where the party has a moderate degree of concern for both the goals and the relationship with the opponent. The party using this style will attempt to reach compromises whereby everyone wins some and loses some. The fifth style is an "integrative" style where the party has a high concern for both the goals and the relationship with the opponent. The party using this style defines the conflict in terms of a problem situation to be worked out collaboratively by all concerned parties in order that everyone will end up a winner. This is the problem-solving style that is generally preferred. However, each style may be effectively used in different situations, depending upon the issue's nature and importance and how the opponent views and approaches the conflict situation.

The parties to a conflict situation must hold several beliefs if the problem-solving style of conflict resolution is to be used effectively. Parties must believe in the availability and desirability of a mutually acceptable solution. They must believe in cooperation rather than conflict and that everyone is of equal value. They must believe that others' views are legitimate statements of their positions and that differences of opinion are helpful. They must believe in the members' trustworthiness and that other members will choose to cooperate rather than compete (Hall, 1969). Teams must work towards developing a problem-solving approach to conflict resolution. Team members must openly explore their beliefs and orientations with respect to conflict. Conflicts within teams must be viewed as problem situations in which mutually acceptable solutions are not only possible, but desirable.

Stages of team functioning. Individuals, small groups, communities, organizations, and societies each have a life span, a beginning to an ending. Analysis of the life processes that occur within the life span indicates similarities in the way in which they develop. These similarities are frequently formulated into models depicting the phases or stages of development. The team also has a life span, with numerous life processes occurring at different times in its development.

A variety of views have been expressed regarding the phases or stages of team development. One view which focuses on the dimension of the team's interpersonal relations, is that there are three basic phases: *inclusion,* or finding one's place in the team; *control,* or determining one's influence in the team; and *affection,* or determining one's closeness with other team members (Schutz, 1966). Another view, which focuses on the two dimensions of the team's primary maintenance functions and its primary task functions, is that there are four developmental stages related to each dimension: dependency, conflict, cohesion, and interdependency for the maintenance dimension; and work orientation, organization, information sharing, and problem-solving for the task function dimensions (Jones, 1975).

A third view, which also focuses on the two dimensions of the team's maintenance functions and its task functions, is that both of these dimensions are related to five developmental stages: orientation, accommodation, negotiation, operation, and dissolution (Brill, 1976). Figure 2 summarizes the relationship of the two dimensions to each of the five stages. The frequency of waves with respect to each of the task and maintenance functions represent the importance and intensity of a particular function to each of the five stages.

The first stage, orientation, refers to the determination of each member's position in the team. Members define boundaries and learn what is expected of them. They become acquainted with one another and provide support to each other in dealing with common anxieties about both the task and their relationships with one an-

A.   Task achievement skills: Task functions related to productivity

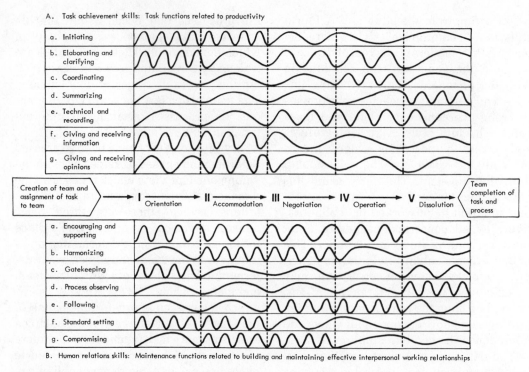

B.   Human relations skills: Maintenance functions related to building and maintaining effective interpersonal working relationships

FIGURE 2:   Task and maintenance skill development in the life stages of the team

other. The primary task functions related to this stage are initiating and giving and receiving information. The primary maintenance functions are encouraging and supporting, gate-keeping, and standard setting.

The second stage, accommodation, refers to the adaption of team members to each other and to the team model. Members find their place in the team in terms of how their expertise relates to the task and how they relate to one another. Communication processes become developed, values and norms become set, and the structure and climate of the team become established. This stage is characterized by conflict. The primary task functions are giving and receiving information, giving and receiving opinions, and initiating. The primary maintenance functions are harmonizing, standard setting, and compromising.

The third stage, negotiation, refers to those transactions related to both positions and tasks carried out. Members bargain with one another about who is going to do what and who will be dependent upon whom. The primary task functions are elaborating, clarifying, technical, and recording. The primary maintenance functions are harmonizing, standard setting, and compromising.

The fourth stage, operation, refers to purposeful action resulting in change. Team members actually carry out the responsibilities agreed to in the previous stage. The primary task functions remain the same as above. The primary maintenance functions are encouraging, supporting, and following.

The final stage, dissolution, refers to the completion of the task and the separation of team members' from one another. The primary task function is summarizing, and the primary maintenance function is process observing.

While Figure 2 summarizes the necessary integration of task and maintenance functions with the team's dynamic life stages, it is important to emphasize that neither the functions nor the stages are as distinct and separate as they may appear. For example, although summarizing and process observing are functions most predominant in the final stage of a team's life, these functions must also occur at other stages of development. The team is a complex and dynamic functioning system which integrates task and maintenance dimensions throughout its life.

COMMON PROBLEMS AND ISSUES IN TEAM BUILDING

A list of ten of the most common problems and issues which someone working on a human services team is likely to confront is presented as follows, and some brief suggestions are made for dealing with each of the problem areas.

Bringing and keeping all team members on board. New members frequently join a team after it has been functioning effectively for some time, while other members leave the team before it has accomplished its task. Still other team members fail to be involved in all meetings, come late, and/or leave early. The process of integrating new members into the team, catching up members who have missed one or two meetings or come late, and adjusting to members who temporarily or permanently leave before the job is done is an important process frequently neglected in teamwork.

It is essential to take the necessary time to quickly bring the new or late members up to date with the team's accomplishments. The time spent doing this can also serve to summarize events for the rest of the team. If a new member joins a team, it is important to make introductions to

the rest of the team and help that person feel welcome and needed. Clarifying role and responsibilities in relation to the task and in relation to other team members' roles and responsibilities also can be helpful in this respect. Team members who leave temporarily or permanently often create gaps with respect to both the task and the team process. It is quite appropriate, and important, to spend some time in team meetings to express group feelings of loss and to reintegrate their functioning.

Maintaining a clear focus and strong team commitment to purpose. Team members frequently lose sight of goals and/or lose their commitment to the goals, particularly when an unresolved team process (for example, unresolved conflict) misdirects or suppresses team energy and prevents the team from moving ahead. Periodically, it is necessary to restate for everyone what may seem to be explicit team goals and to test each member's commitment to accomplishing those goals. Doing this is especially important immediately after the team has struggled with a major process issue (for example, an unresolved conflict).

Dealing with appropriate interpersonal needs. As mentioned earlier in this article, work groups tend to ignore interpersonal processes important to task accomplishment. The skills of diagnosis and intervention with respect to maintenance functions in teams are basic to team building.

Struggles over leadership. The most frequent conflicts in teams arise around the issue of how much influence one member has in relation to other members. One effective way to deal with leadership struggles is recognize and legitimize that all members have valuable contributions and maximize each member's opportunities to make their contributions to the group. Clarifying and defining individual areas of expertise helps to create an atmosphere of mutual influence and shared leadership. In situations where a strong leadership style exists but is not accepted, it may be necessary for someone in the team to raise the issue of leadership with the team and openly discuss and decide upon what leadership style would be preferred.

Physical and time arrangements.   Problems are often related to making arrangements for meetings which take into account everyone's time schedule and are reasonably convenient for all concerned. The physical setting for meetings is much more important to effective team functioning than most people realize. Taking time for making necessary arrangements can save time in the long run.

Communication.   Communication processes become tremendously complex in teams, particularly as the team size increases. The failure to send clear messages and to listen actively can cause anger and resentment among members. Effective team communication skills are an absolute necessity to the smooth functioning of a team.

Conflict.   Intense, unresolved conflicts, whatever their causes, are probably the most frequent reasons for team members losing commitment and leaving the team before the job is done. People who have experienced more negative than positive consequences from conflicts are understandably afraid of conflict and avoid it or withdraw from it whenever possible. Most people are without the necessary skills to deal with conflict resolution effectively.

Coping with self-oriented behavior.   In most teams, at least one individual engages in destructive self-oriented behavior. If this behavior is allowed to continue unchecked, the team will undergo severe difficulties and may discontinue functioning altogether. Self-oriented behavior needs to be redirected in order that the needs expressed can be met outside the team situation.

Unrealistic work expectations.   Teams are occasionally assigned unreasonable tasks or are requested to complete tasks by unreasonable deadlines. If the team accepts this responsibility without confronting the realities of the situation which make the task completion impossible, the team is setting itself up for a failure experience.

Acceptance and respect among team members.   Team members frequently fail to recognize, accept, and respect other members' values and expertise. This occurs most frequently with respect to members' value orientations and expertise in performing task or maintenance functions in the team. Members with a strong value on the importance of task functions in team building tend not to see the value of maintenance functions, and vice versa. Thus members who have the real potential of complementing one another in two very important dimensions of team building perceive themselves in conflict.

Maintenance functions are especially important, not because they are more important considerations than task functions, but because they are so frequently overlooked or ignored in teams. Societal and organizational norms generally stress the importance of task accomplishment (for example, the Protestant work ethic) much more than the achievement of strong interpersonal relationships. A team that is influenced by the norms of the larger units to which it is accountable most frequently overemphasizes task accomplishment and underemphasizes interpersonal working relationships. Therefore, to achieve the best task-interpersonal balance in teams, it is especially important to emphasize maintenance functions.

SUMMARY AND CONCLUSION

Team building is a dynamic process of developing effective interpersonal working relationships and problem-solving abilities among several individuals who are mutually dependent upon each other for achieving a task objective. An ideal team is one which is continually in the process of evaluating and improving its task and maintenance functions throughout every stage of its life.

The team approach is not appropriate for every situation. In choosing whether or not to use the team approach, strengths and limitations of teams must be carefully reviewed in light of the desired outcomes and the characteristics of potential team members. Size, composition, structure, and operating procedures are important considerations in forming a new team.

Achieving an appropriate balance of task and maintenance functions is the most critical aspect of effective team functioning. Considerable diagnostic and intervention knowledge and skills are needed with respect to achieving the most appropriate balance of these functions throughout all stages in the life of a team.

The need for team training in the human services often becomes most apparent after the human service professional has had a number of negative team experiences on the job. Unfortunately, a negative attitude toward the team approach is also frequently developed with avoidance becoming the response. Individuals who expect to work in the human services should recognize that a large part of their work will involve ongoing collaborative relationships with other professionals, paraprofessionals, and clients. The people who ultimately have the most to lose by a lack of professional expertise in teamwork are the poor, the disadvantaged, and the oppressed people whom workers are trying hardest to serve.

Reading 13–2

Politics of Interprofessional Collaboration: Challenge to Advocacy*

Mildred D. Mailick and Ardythe A. Ashley

Social workers are increasingly being called on to translate strongly held professional values into ethical actions. They are faced with dilemmas posed by conflicting claims and must choose actions involving competing commitments. The complex settings in which they practice generate a series of problems for professional behavior, and there are few guidelines available to help social workers in responding to them.

* From *Social Casework: The Journal of Contemporary Social Work* published by Family Service Association of America (March 1978).

This article will explore the political dilemmas inherent in the application of two practice activities strongly supported by the social work profession. The first of these is that social workers practicing in complex interdisciplinary settings should participate in and promote collaboration with other professionals in providing integrated and comprehensive service in the interest of the client. The second is that social workers have a responsibility, enunciated in the Code of Ethics, to act as advocates for their clients (National Association of Social Workers, 1980). The major questions are how advocacy and collaboration interact and whether they pose conflicts to the worker when they are pursued jointly.

COLLABORATION

Collaboration is a complex activity taking a variety of forms and changing over time. Its purposes are twofold: (1) to provide more effective service to the client-consumer, and (2) to manage staff tensions (Weiner, 1979). It has as its goal the achievement of some degree of consensus by a group of individuals about a plan of action and its execution. It usually includes an interpersonal process in which members of a working group contribute, each from his or her knowledge and skill, to the accomplishment of a task and are responsible, as a group, for the outcome. The rationale for social work participation in collaborative activities is based on the recognition of the complexity of human problems, the high degree of knowledge, technology, and skill needed to meet them, the specialization of function, and the resulting requirements of coordination and integration of the work of the providers on behalf of the clients.

Collaborative activity is also valued because it is assumed to be synergistic, that is, the services offered by the group are of greater scope and value than individual contributions separately applied would be. A process of cross-fertilization of ideas is presumed to occur that encourages new perspectives and reformulations of difficult problems and solutions that exceed the boundaries of separate disciplines. This proposed synergistic quality has not been adequately tested or empirically documented.

Collaborative activities have the potential for both lessening or heightening staff tensions. For some, the need to work in concert with others creates added strains. The more specialized and technical the task, the more difficult it is for the individual to accommodate to the time orientation, work routines, and value systems of other professions. The more generalized the task and the more the individual professional is dependent on the cooperation of others in its accomplishment, the greater the motivation for collaborative activity.

The process of working together creates the need for a method of tension reduction, a medium for resolving the problems that develp when those of diverse education, frames of reference, socialization, value systems, and work styles are required to coordinate their efforts. The nature of the client's problem is an added source of tension. A well-functioning collaborative group can provide for the resolution of group tension whether generated by staff interaction or by the emotional drain of work with the clients. The ventilation of feelings and the validation of emotional responses serve to lessen the need for those to be irrationally displaced to the work situation and the clients.

The term collaboration usually evokes an image of a team meeting. This is unfortunate because collaboration is a process and the team meeting is only one of a range of techniques or mechanisms by which this process can take place (Weiner, 1979). More broadly construed, interprofessional collaboration includes communication and coordination by means of consultation, unified record keeping, written data feedback, informal sharing of information and ideas, formal staffings, grand rounds, and other group or team meetings. This broadened concept of collaboration more truly mirrors the reality of the ways in which professional groups interact on a day-to-day basis.

THE CULTURE OF THE INTERPROFESSIONAL COLLABORATIVE GROUP

Small-group theory suggests that those engaged in collaborative activities are likely to develop a group culture, ideology, authority system, division of labor, and set of norms. Although these groups may vary depending on purpose, size, auspice, and participants, the *sine qua non* of all of them is the development of the value of cooperation and the push toward consensus. Consensus allows for a unified plan to be agreed on and for each participant to carry out his or her own specific function within that plan.

Collaborative groups have been criticized as being vulnerable to intellectual inbreeding (Eiduson, 1964, pp. 714–721). The need for consensus and the wish to avoid extending long and burdensome controversies may lead to compromise and decision making based on insufficient information. Collaborative groups sometimes develop stereotyped methods of responding to problems. One theoretical formulation may gain ascendancy and be applied to problems for which it is not particularly appropriate. If one member of the group rises to challenge or to express a difference of opinion about the theory, the inquiry sometimes is interpreted as an indication of disloyalty, contentiousness, or an inability to get along. The questioner may be ignored, responded to in a condescending manner, or subtly punished by exclusion from the elite circle. Cohesion as a primary goal displaces service in the best interest of the client. The pressure of the individual worker to fit in and to maintain the goodwill of the collaborative group is very strong.

The pressure for consensus does not fall equally on all of the participants. The relative autonomy of members of the collaborative group are related to their status and power and are usually heavily dependent on the prestige of the profession and its perceived centrality to the goals of the group. Some group members have legally sanctioned functions that increase their power and authority. Others are more peripheral or are dependent on their colleagues' goodwill to perform their tasks.

Personality traits as well as age, sex, socioeconomic status, and racial or ethnic factors also contribute to the member's position within the group. The resultant status differentials add complexity to the group structure and culture and create a situation in which low-status or aspiring members are likely to adhere more strongly to the group values, while high-status individuals are relatively independent of them.

The participants' adherence to the norms of the interprofessional culture are also affected by their ties to their own professional associations. When these associations are strong and have the sanction to monitor their members' professional behavior and control their rights to practice, they exert considerable power. Members are likely to develop strong professional group identifications that take precedence over loyalty to the norms of the institution or the collaborative culture. The American Medical Association and the American Bar Association are examples of this type of professional organization. Physicians and lawyers are more likely to invoke their professional code of ethics as justification for not acceding to institutional group pressure. However, when the professional association is weaker, it is less likely to influence its members' behavior, primary identification, and loyalty. Its members, having a weaker external professional anchoring, are more vulnerable to the pressure of the collaborative culture and less able to take an independent stance.

Because it does not control access to practice, the National Association of Social Workers can monitor the behavior only of those social workers who voluntarily submit to its sanctions. Its Code of Ethics is general and could possibly be construed to support either conformity to institutional norms or pursuit of a more radical course. One study of its members suggests that a high professional role identification is not a good predictor of orientation to client needs, but rather appears to indicate either that the social worker will hold conservative conformist attitudes or take an independent client-oriented stance (Epstein, 1970, pp. 87–92).

SOCIAL WORKERS IN AN INTERPROFESSIONAL COLLABORATIVE CULTURE

Social workers participate in interprofessional collaborative activities in a wide variety of settings. These include public health programs, child guidance clinics, mental health agencies, schools, courts, and inpatient and ambulatory care programs in hospitals. In addition to these direct service activities, the social worker also collaborates with other professionals in policy and program planning, administration, and research (Kane, 1975, pp. 1–2).

In many settings, the collaborative process is useful to social workers because it encourages a structure for cooperation, a culture for consultation, and development of consensus among professionals. It promotes the inclusion of social workers in planning and execution of services. Collaboration regularizes and institutionalizes social workers' contacts with other professionals and secures their inclusion in the interprofessional group. This is important to social workers because in many settings it provides them with independent access to clients appropriate to their service. In this way, social workers can exercise a greater amount of control over the quality and the quantity of their work, rather than be dependent on others for referrals. Because of these benefits, as well as because of the belief that it provides better service to the client, social workers are often the initiators of collaborative efforts. Other professionals, who are less dependent on their colleagues to perform their work, are likely to be more resistant. Social workers are quite often in a position of pressuring or trying to influence col-

leagues to meet with them and plan collaboratively. They respond with frustration and disappointment when they are rejected or not afforded appropriate respect and cooperation. Much like the outsider or the younger child who wants to become part of the in-group, the wish to be considered a part of the central group is very strong. Once social workers do gain entry into the group, they are likely to be eager to consolidate their position within it.

Robert K. Merton, in his discussion of reference group behavior, points out that: "Insofar as subordinate or prospective group members are motivated to affiliate themselves with a group, they will tend to assimilate the sentiments and conform with the values of the authoritative and prestigeful stratum in that group" (Merton 1968, p. 308).

Thus, in order to gain acceptance by the higher status or more powerful segment of the collaborative group, social workers may tend to adopt its values and assimilate and conform to its sentiments and norms. Ties to their own professional (social work) reference group are attenuated, and, when there are conflicts in values between them, the social worker may be pulled toward an identification with the collaborative group. One source of conflict for the social worker may be in relation to the practice of advocacy.

ADVOCACY

Primacy of the client's interest as an ethical precept is part of the heritage of the social work profession. The term "advocacy" gained currency during the 1960s, emerging as a "new component" of practice evolved by the community organizers, who were grappling with the problem of helping powerless clients to deal with complex welfare institutions. At first concerned with class action, they soon expanded to working with individual clients as well. Advocacy, as practiced by the individual social worker, is a concept borrowed from the legal profession. Just as a lawyer is bound to do everything legally possible to further his or her client's interest, the social work advocate is intended to be an unequivocal partisan serving the interests of the client, even, in the extreme, in opposition to the policies of his or her own agency.

The use of the term "advocacy" has always created ferment, discord, and discomfort among social workers. Many have come to associate it with the move toward deprofessionalization that occurred during the late 1960s. Others reject it because they cannot support some of the Machiavellian tactics that are attributed to it. Yet, the NASW Code of Ethics has been interpreted to make advocacy for clients obligatory for all social workers.

The ambiguity of the concept of advocacy creates problems in its application to practice and, thereby, discourages its use. Sometimes it is difficult for the social worker to define who the client is. Conflicting claims may place the social worker in the uncomfortable position of determining the priority of need between the individual, the family, the institution, the community, the general public, or even future generations. Closely allied to this problem is the difficulty of defining what the client's best interests are. Is the social worker to leave this determination entirely to the client and act as his or her agent? Or, should the social worker negotiate with the client about both goals and methods of attaining these interests? The social worker's definition of need will always be affected by his or her personal, professional, and bureaucratic perspectives. Considering the usual power differential between worker and client, can a true consensus be arrived at?

Further problems arise in considering the boundaries and limits of advocacy. In its broadest definition, most social work practice could be conceptualized as advocacy in the client's interest. When it is so defined, advocacy loses its identity as a unique aspect of practice. Can advocacy be restricted only to those instances in which the social worker and client or client group reach an explicit contract to intervene in whatever systems are necessary in order to attain a specific service, benefit, or right?

The practice of advocacy sometimes creates problems of personal jeopardy for the worker. The status of the social worker as an advocate has never been well accepted by the profession or legitimized by the institutions for which he or she works. There are limitations on the practice of advocacy within one's own organization. Beyond these limits, the social worker usually finds little support from his or her own colleagues or from the institution as a whole. The difficulty is in establishing what the limits are, and when it is incumbent on the worker to supervene them, even if it might lead to dismissal or loss of a chance for advancement.

Advocacy and collaboration considered together

Advocacy and collaboration share in common many methods of achieving their goals. The provision of information, education, clarification, problem solving, the suggestion of alternatives, and persuasion are all techniques that apply to both activities. Advocacy does, however, imply additional tactics, such as the mobilization of organizational pressure, the development of coalitions, and mild coercion. Most important, advocacy requires placing the interest of the client above other considerations, even though this sometimes results in an increased level of discord with colleagues. The culture of many collaborative groups emphasizes cooperation. It should, but often does not, allow for a process to occur in which conflicts, differences of opinion, and approaches to problems are thoroughly aired and resolved. Compliance is achieved at the expense of individual contributions and creativity.

THE PRACTICE OF ADVOCACY IN THE COLLABORATIVE GROUP

Social workers in collaborative groups are often in a quandary about if, when, and how they should challenge the norm of cooperation and consensus and take an independent position in advocacy for their client. Of utmost importance in working with a collaborative group is the capacity to listen, to be respectful, to understand the implications of other professional opinions, to be willing to recognize and accept areas in which the expertise of colleagues is unique, and to defer to special knowledge when appropriate. However, the process of deferring should be based on professional judgment and on an active evaluation of what is best for the client, not on acquiescence to group pressure. Social workers must respect their own values, knowledge, and frame of reference when they have an honest difference of opinion or conflicting perceptions of problems.

When the social worker differs from his or her colleagues, natural questions follow: Who is right? Is there, in fact, a right or wrong position in the situation being considered? Or, are the differences related to divergent professional perceptions and value systems? How much of the difference can be attributed to a worker's style? Can the social worker set his or her own style, frame of reference, and value system above those held by others in the collaborative group (Connaway, 1975, pp. 381–388)?

In a mental health setting with a treatment program for drug offenders, for example, a social worker was seen as constantly giving the clients special privileges and undermining the team's efforts to "socialize" the clients. What the social worker was doing was allowing the clients time off from the program's meetings and activities in order to pursue welfare monies and various other concrete social services. The worker felt a responsibility to advocate for the clients' right to these services, although, for the team, the work of the therapeutic program was paramount.

In the absence of unequivocal answers to these vexing questions, will the social worker respond, as Merton suggests, to the pressure of the opinion of the dominant profession in the reference group, redefining or reinterpreting the client's need to coincide with it?

Social workers cannot lay special claim to having a higher level of knowledge or devotion to the welfare of the client than other professions. Each professional group has a formal or informal code of ethics that espouses the primacy of client need. Each has a defensible knowledge base and theoretical framework that directs the selection of relevant data in defining the problems of the client and developing appropriate solutions. However, the interpretation of what is good for the client may differ markedly. The psychosocial orientation and the holistic approach of the social worker often points to different solutions than those of other professionals. It is difficult for the social worker to "go against the crowd." Yet, they are bound by their Code of Ethics not to remain silent.

In a day-treatment facility for chronic alcoholics, for example, a social worker presented the case of an elderly eccentric artist to the team, which included vocational counselors, a nutritionist, psychiatrists, and paraprofessionals. On the basis of the presentation, a psychiatrist diagnosed the man as being a chronic, undifferentiated schizophrenic, and prescribed prolixin for him. The client experienced the medication as punitive, and complained that it made him sleepy and unable to paint. The social worker advocated for the client's right to remain drug free, particularly as he was not currently abusing alcohol. This created extreme tension within the team and, eventually, the worker acquiesced.

Perhaps part of the discomfort or burnout experienced by social workers working in collaborative groups is that they must either bear the disapproval of their collaborative peers and take an independent stance or they must suffer ethical dissonance and loss of identity with their own profession by not adhering to their Code of Ethics.

When to advocate

A second set of questions facing the social worker is *when* to advocate for the client. Should the social worker take a stand in opposition each time he or she is in disagreement with the collaborative group, or is it better to develop a political approach, choosing only the most important occasions to do so? The worker in the collaborative group runs the risk of losing the respect of colleagues by invoking the right to dissent too often and then may be excluded from the group, circumvented, or ignored, thus losing the capacity for any influence at all. However, when the worker begins to make selections about which client to advocate for, it reduces the sense of consistency and security in decision making. Under the pressure of need for acceptance by the group, the worker may select only the most flagrant cases for advocacy, abandoning those whose situations are less pressing or more ambiguous.

Political acumen is an important component of the practice of advocacy. The worker needs to develop a series of principles to draw on in the selection of situations on which he or she will take a stand. These may include setting priorities for those cases in which advocacy would support the client's right to exercise choice or preference, encourage the establishment of a precedent of importance or value to the total client group, point up a gap in service, or call into question a strongly held theory, value, or stereotype of the collaborative group.

In an outpatient clinic for pregnant women in a highly pressured, research-oriented teaching hospital, for example, the basic nutritional education of the clients was being neglected, in spite of the presence of nutritionists on the staff. However, several research studies on the nutritional patterns in poverty populations were in full swing. The social workers could continue to do the basic education case by case or advocate for a shift in emphasis involving another department's activities. This posed many dilemmas at the individual, team, and departmental levels.

The principles guiding the selection of priorities might vary depending on the institution or field of practice, but, if made explicit, should serve to strengthen the decision making of the worker.

How to advocate

The question of *how* to advocate requires the development of a broader theoretical knowledge base and a wider range of skills. These need to be explicitly included in both class and fieldwork education. Many schools of social work, like the profession as a whole, have been ambivalent about teaching advocacy as a component of practice. They neither disavow it nor adequately support it. Although the educational process encourages the development of diagnostic and treatment sophistication and enhances communication skills, it provides few opportunities to learn the dynamics of organizational behavior or to gain experience and expertise in political intervention in the organization and the community. Simon Slavin has pointed out that a lacuna exists in professional education, in that the positive functions of conflict and methods of analyzing different status positions, role sets, power dimensions, constituencies, and coalitions have lagged behind other areas of knowledge in the curriculum (Slavin, 1969, pp. 47–60).

In a newborn nursery of an inner-city hospital, for example, many of the young admissions were infants withdrawing from methodone or heroin because of their mothers' dependency. These babies were referred to by the medical staff as "D.A.'s" (drug addicts). The parents were treated with such disrespect that they often reduced their visits to the nursery or refused to come at all. They would then be persecuted by the staff for being inattentive to their infants. Social work students on the interprofessional team attempted to break this cycle through formal or informal confrontations and failed.

CONCLUSION

In addition to better educational preparation, the social work profession as a whole has to offer much stronger support for advocacy. The new Code of Ethics adopted by the National Association of Social Workers in 1979 may facilitate this because it is more specific and detailed in its enunciation of the obligations of social workers toward clients. The professional organization must strengthen its power as a reference group, so that social workers can draw on their identification with it in their interactions with the collaborative group. It should provide forums for social workers to share concern for clients, represent those collective concerns in the political arena, and encourage the development of more effective advocacy approaches in each of the fields of practice.

Social workers might also be supported in their capacity to advocate if their administrators provide appropriate leadership and modeling of advocacy in their own sphere of influence. The social work department should recognize the strains in working in collaborative groups and provide opportunities for the workers to discuss their problems and develop principles for the practice of advocacy.

Finally, social workers must consider their position within the collaborative group. A full appreciation of the complexity of the collaborative culture and a recognition of the role relationships with each member of the group is necessary. The social worker must come close enough to the collaborative group to promote cooperation and mutual support, but maintain sufficient distance so that the group's norms will not be overwhelming. In the absence of a powerful position within the group, the social worker can build coalitions with others who have similar orientations. A careful exploration of the group's activities may reveal areas of autonomy that are available either because no one else is in contention for them or because conflicting powers neutralize each other and allow for freedom for the social worker to be independent. Above all, the social worker must understand that he or she is not dealing with a private trouble that needs to be handled in a personal way, but a professional problem for which principles of practice can be developed that will help to guide effective professional behavior.

References

Bormann, E., & Bormann, N. *Effective small group communication.* Minneapolis: Burgess Publishing, 1976.

Brieland, D., Briggs, T., & Leuenberger, P. *The team model of social work practice.* Syracuse, N.Y.: Syracuse University Press, 1973.

Briggs, T. An overview of social work teams. In D. Brieland et al. (Eds.), *The team model of social work practice.* Syracuse, N.Y.: Syracuse University Press, 1973.

Brill, N. Teamwork: *Working together in the human services.* Philadelphia: J. B. Lippincott, 1976.

Cartwright D., & Zander A. *Group dynamics: Research and theory.* New York: Harper & Row, 1968.

Connaway, Ronda S. Teamwork and social worker advocacy: Conflicts and possibilities. *Community Mental Health Journal,* Winter 1975, *11,* 381–388.

David, Morton D. *Game theory.* New York: Basic Books, 1970.

Deutsch, M. Conflicts: Productive and destructive. *Journal of Social Issues,* 1969, *24,* 7–43.

Dyer, W. *Team building: Issues and alternatives.* Reading, Mass.: Addison-Wesley, 1977.

Eiduson, Bernice T. Intellectual inbreeding in the clinic? *American Journal of Orthopsychiatry,* July 1964, *34,* 714–721.

Epstein, Irwin. Professional role orientations and conflict strategies. *Social Work,* October 1970, *15,* 87–92.

Erikson, Erik H. *Childhood and society.* New York: Norton, 1950.

Filley, Alan. *Interpersonal conflict resolution.* Glenview, Ill.: Scott, Foresman, 1975.

Frank, Lawrence K. The Interdisciplinary frontiers in human relations studies. *Journal of Human Relations,* Fall 1954, *2,* 89–92.

French, J., & Raven, M. The basis of social power. In D. Cartwright (Ed.), *Studies in social power.* Ann Arbor: University of Michigan, 1959.

Hall, J. *Conflict management survey.* Kansas City: Telemetrics, 1969.

Hersey, P., & Blanchard, K. Leader effectiveness and adaptability description (LEAD). In W. Pfeiffer & J. Jones (Eds.); *The 1976 annual handbook for group facilitators.* Ann Arbor, Mich.: University Associates, 1976.

Johnson, D., & Johnson F. *Joining together: Group theory and group skills.* Englewood Cliffs, N.J.: Prentice-Hall, 1975.

Jones, Howard (Ed.). *Towards a new social work.* Boston: Routledge & Kegan, Paul, 1975.

Kane, R. The interprofessional team as a small group. *Social Work in Health Care,* Fall 1975, *1,* 19–32.

Kane, Rosalie A. *Interprofessional teamwork.* Manpower Monograph no. 8. Syracuse, N.Y.: Syracuse University School of Social Work, 1975.

Leuenberger, P. Team dynamics and decision making. In D. Brieland et al. (Eds.), *The model of social work practice.* Syracuse, N.Y.: Syracuse University Press, 1973.

Lippitt, R. *Training in community relations: A research exploration.* New York: Harper & Brothers, 1949.

Lippitt, Ronald, Watson, Jeanne, & Westley, Bruce. *The dynamics of planned change.* New York: Harcourt Brace Jovanovich, 1958.

Lippitt, Ronald, & White, Ralph K. *Autocracy and democracy: An experimental inquiry.* Westport, Conn.: Greenwood Press. 1972.

Merton, Robert K. *Social theory and social structure.* New York: Free Press, 1968.

Morris, W., & Sashkin, M. *Organizational behavior in action: Skill building experiences.* St. Paul: West Publishing, 1976.

National Association of Social Workers. Policy Statement Number 1, as adopted by the 1979 NASW Delegate Assembly, effective July 1980.

Pfeiffer, W., & Jones, J. *The 1971 annual handbook for group facilitators.* Ann Arbor, Mich.: University Associates, 1971.

Pincus, Allen, & Minahan, Anne. *Social work practice: Model and method.* Itasca, Ill.: F. E. Peacock Publishers, 1973.

Reilly, A., & Jones, J. Team building. In W. Pfeiffer & J. Jones (Eds.), *The 1974 annual handbook for group facilitators.* Ann Arbor, Mich.: University Associates, 1974.

Schutz, W. *The interpersonal underworld.* Palo Alto, Calif.: Science and Behavior Books, 1966.

Sherwood, John J., & Hoylman, Florence M. *Utilizing human resources: Individual versus group approaches to problem-solving and decision-making.* Lafayette, Ind.: Purdue University Press, 1977.

Slavin, Simon. Concepts of social conflict: Use in social work curriculum. *Journal of Social Work Education,* Fall 1969, *5,* 47–60.

Solomon, L. Team development: A training approach. In W. Pfeiffer & J. Jones (Eds.), *The 1977 annual handbook for group facilitators.* Ann Arbor, Mich.: University Associates, 1977.

Weiner, Hyman. Knowledge and skills for collaborative care. Paper presented at the Institute on Collaborative Practice in Health Care, Long Island Jewish-Hillside Medical Center, New Hyde Park, New York, February 8, 1979.

Chapter 14

Endings in Social Work Practice

This chapter will deal with three endings of the client-worker relationship: referral, transfer, and termination. So often, we are deeply concerned about clients only as long as we are involved in the interaction, but when we are no longer the primary professional(s) we may leave the clients to find their own way(s). It should be recognized that how a client-worker relationship ends may be crucial to what clients take with them in terms of gains. In situations involving nonvoluntary adolescent clients, one cannot help but be struck at the way, in which we make ourselves indispensable at the beginning of our contacts with clients; and when clients feel they need workers most, which is always at the time of termination or transfer, we are often so preoccupied with our own new beginnings either with other clients or with a new setting that we are unavailable to the client. Referral, transfer, and termination have three factors in common: (1) some kind of problem identification has brought the worker and the client together for a greater or a lesser period of time; (2) the client is being sent on to a new phase, a new experience, another source of help, leaving the worker behind or being left behind by the worker; and (3) more is involved than simply saying good-bye and wishing everyone well. However, as each of the three tasks is different, they will be discussed separately in this chapter. We will begin with referral.

REFERRAL

Referral is a process that comes into play whenever a client or a service instigator requests our involvement in a situation that falls outside the parameters of the agency's defined services or whenever workers define a problem as beyond their expertise or their agency's parameters of service. In its simplest terms, referral means that, rather than explore the situation themselves, they suggest that someone who has come to them for help should go to another source. Since the request for help has been defined as falling outside the agency's service responsibilities, it is often tempting to see their responsibility as ending when we state this fact to the person who requested our involvement. This is perhaps the end of their responsibility as an agent of a particular bureaucracy. But it is not the end of the professional responsibility. Professional commitment requires workers to assume responsibility not only for judgments and actions but for the results of judgments and actions. If workers hold themselves out as persons concerned with the struggles of others, with problems of coping, then they must be concerned not only with offering adequate service in connection with those problems that fall within the defined "turf," but also with offering the same skilled help to enable persons to reach the proper source of help. The first step in developing skills in referral is to know what it means to an individual to ask for help either for oneself or for others. (The subject of asking for help was discussed in Chapter 9.) That knowledge is crucial in considering referral.

As a way of considering referrals, let's examine the case example discussed in Chapter 1 of "The House on Sixth Street." The reader will remember that Mrs. Smith came to the neighborhood center to request help with her housing situation. Fortunately, she came to an agency which could offer help not only to her but to all the tenants who shared her problem. Thus, Mrs. Smith's original request came within the agency's parameters of service, and in the process of exploring her request the practitioner was able to redefine the problem so that it became a community organization problem. This resulted in more effective action than would have been taken if the worker had defined the problem as only Mrs. Smith's. But suppose that Mrs. Smith had turned to her Aid to Families with Dependent Children (AFDC) worker (as the only worker she knew) to talk about her problem, and suppose that the worker had pointed out to her that the welfare board already had knowledge of the situation and had reduced the rent it was paying the landlord and that that was all it could do. What would have happened? Or suppose that Mrs. Smith had felt that her AFDC worker really cared very little about her troubles and that she had then gone to a family agency she had heard about, and that the worker there had pointed out that the agency could not offer help in a situation that was primarily between her, the welfare board, and the landlord. Is it not conceivable that Mrs. Smith would decide that there was no help for a person in her situation and that all the tenants would have gone on living in the same situation?

Now suppose instead that the female worker at the private agency had told Mrs. Smith that she could not help with the problem but that she would help find someone who could. Three days later the private agency worker reaches the welfare worker who says she has done all she can and she does not know what else can be done. Two days later the worker at the private agency finds out about the service center. The first of the next week, she calls Mrs. Smith and tells her about the center, urging her to go there. By now Mrs. Smith and her children have endured another uncomfortable week, two social workers have said they cannot help, but she has been told that another worker might. How likely is it that Mrs. Smith will again bundle her four children up and trudge out to seek help at this new place?

But suppose that the female family worker tells Mrs. Smith that she cannot help directly, but that this does seem to be a very difficult situation for her and her children so she would like to find out who could help. The family worker calls the welfare worker while Mrs. Smith is in the office and learns that the welfare worker cannot help. She asks the welfare worker whether she knows where such help can be sought. She looks up the agencies listed in the agency directory that most communities publish. While Mrs. Smith is still in her office, she finds out about the service center and calls to see whether it can help and what Mrs. Smith needs to do to get its help. She asks Mrs. Smith whether and when she wants to go there and arranges an interview time with a worker whose name she gives Mrs. Smith. She shares this information with Mrs. Smith (often writing down names and addresses is helpful), being sure Mrs. Smith understands how to get in touch with the center worker and what the center worker will need to know about her situation. She expresses her interest in seeing that Mrs. Smith gets some help and her understanding that it is hard to be shuffled around from agency to agency before finding anyone who will really listen. She expresses concern that Mrs. Smith get help and urges Mrs. Smith to get in touch with her again if this particular plan does not work out. In this case Mrs. Smith will probably get to the service center. She will also approach the new worker and the demand that she repeat her story once again with some confidence in herself and her judgment in seeking help. Because of the experience she had with the family worker she will expect to be met by a center worker who is concerned. Her quest for help has been met in a way that has furthered her confidence in her capacity to manage her life in a manner more satisfying for her.

Suppose you are driving in a strange city, thoroughly lost, but hoping to work the problem out rather than stop and ask someone for directions is a common experience. What happens if you stop and ask someone who reels off complicated, generalized and vague directions? When you ask for an estimate on how far away the destination is, the person says "quite a ways" and looks "put off" by the question. How do you feel? Do you decide that you were better off trying it on your own? You have taken the trouble to ask, but are no further ahead now than before. In fact, you may be worse off because you have now wasted another half hour and feel more confused and less adequate than before.

This example illustrates the problems and principles in referrals. First, it is necessary to recognize that asking for help for yourself or others is not a simple process. Second, it is necessary to understand that when you decide to talk the situation over with someone else, the time of that decision and the move to implement it is a vulnerable period. It has taken something to get to this point. This short, vulnerable period, in which the client is open to consideration of the work to be done, is all too often followed by despair if something positive and forward moving is not offered.[1] Most people wait until long after they have become aware of a problem before they seek help. They try to solve the problem alone until they become convinced of their inability to do so, so that their sense of capacity to cope has already had enough blows without the worker's telling them that they have again made a mistake by approaching the wrong resource.

The more threatening a problem is to the people asking help, and the

---

[1] This principle is the basis of crisis theory and other emergency services which the reader may want to explore but which cannot be developed here.

more disorganized and confused they are, the less able they are to follow through on complicated directions or to gather up the strength to retell their problem. Anyone who has experienced certain difficulties and been sent to several places before they reached the person who could help (even if the problem was only getting approval to drop one course and add another) can well understand the feelings of frustration or discouragement or anger that come with the demand that one explain the situation over and over again only to be referred somewhere else each time. Maybe the problem was finally straightened out to one's satisfaction, but at the cost of considerable time and effort. What would it have meant to have had someone pick up the telephone and find out the right place to go and what to do?

Social agencies and the help they offer are complex businesses. It is a testimony to most people's competence that they are able to approach the appropriate agency most of the time. Rather than expect all clients to be able to handle the original request appropriately, workers should be surprised that any do so. The worker should treat client confusion and uncertainty as a natural effect of the confusing pattern in which we seem to work.

A generalized goal for practice should be that, if workers cannot offer active help toward solving a problem, they at least leave clients as well prepared to deal with it as they were when workers met them. Workers should recognize that by holding themselves out as helping persons and by being in a position that invites or allows the client to approach the worker, they have engaged in an interaction with them that places a responsibility upon the worker that is not to be discharged by a simple statement that they have come to the wrong place.

TRANSFER

Transfer is the process by which the client is referred to another worker, usually in the same agency, after the initial worker has been working with the client on the problem. Although the transfer is sometimes made because workers find that they have difficulty in working with the problem or the client, usually it occurs because the initial worker is leaving the agency to take a job elsewhere.

In transfer three entities are involved: the present worker, the client, and the new worker. When clients learn that practitioners are soon to leave the agency, or that for any other reason the workers cannot continue with them, they may feel deserted and resent an ending that is imposed prematurely on them. They may feel that, in leaving, the worker is breaking the contract in which they were offered service and may resent what appears to be the worker's irresponsibility and lack of concern. Many factors may interact to determine the client's reaction. The most important will be the type of client system, the problem, and the type of relationship developed between the worker and the client. For the client whose problem involves internal system changes and who has had life experiences involving painful separations, the worker's departure may evoke all the accumulated pain of the other separations. A task-centered adult group working toward change in the community may also feel a sense of betrayal and desertion but may be more actively concerned about the competence of the new worker who will be involved with them in their work. Unexpected endings are a part of life, and workers who have made a decision that forces an ending to their association with clients must be aware of their own feelings, workers who will replace them, and the possible reactions of clients if the experience is to be as positive as possible for the clients.

Workers may have difficulty with their own feelings. They may feel that they are indeed betraying the client and violating the contract. They may feel that no other workers can really take their place with their clients and may subtly impart this judgment to the clients in ways that increase the clients' feelings of uncertainty. Leaving the agency can evoke painful feelings of separation in the worker. Workers may also be anxious about the demands of their new jobs, or so deeply absorbed in these new demands that they do not give the problems of transfer their full attention. Or all these feelings may churn within them in some complex, interrelated struggle.

The transfer may also pose some problems for new workers. They may wonder whether they can offer as effective help as did the first worker and may meet clients with a kind of defensiveness and a determination to prove themselves rather than continue the work together. They may, therefore, move out too rapidly with new ideas that clients are not ready for. Clients may be angry and hurt about the transfer and because of this, as well as their feelings of loyalty and trust for the first worker, it is often necessary for them to mark some time and do some testing before they are willing to move on. It is to be expected that certain clients will lose much of their trust in the worker and be afraid to risk establishing a new relationship with another person who may also leave. The new worker needs to recognize all these things, especially the right of the clients to have their feelings and take the time they need to deal with them.

A transfer is less hurtful and destructive to the work being done when there is time for both client and worker to deal with it, and for the new worker to get involved in an orderly manner. When a transfer is necessitated by the first worker's leaving the agency, clients often regard it as a desertion. They may feel that if they were important to the worker or, worse yet, if they were a good and safisfying client, the worker would stay with them. Clients need to be told as soon as possible about the worker's leaving, and they need to participate with the worker in the planning for transfer to another worker or, possibly, to terminate their contact with the agency. The clients' feelings about the change should be recognized by the worker. The worker can invite the client to discuss these feelings. At times, and particularly in group situations, clients can be encouraged to role play the transfer, from their concern about the first worker's departure through their beginning with a new worker. They can discuss or role play their fantasies about the new worker.

Clients need opportunities to meet with the new worker. The first time the new worker may just stop in for a minute to be introduced by the old worker and say hello. After the new worker leaves, the old worker may discuss with clients what their feelings and thoughts are about the new worker from just this introduction.

The second time, if the client system is a group, the new worker may attend a meeting as an observer, or, if the client system is an individual or a family, may sit in on an interview. The old worker remains "in charge," so to speak, and the new worker is just there to get acquainted. At the third encounter the two workers operate as a team, with the new worker gradually assuming the primary professional role. At this encounter the two workers can talk together, trying to assess where they are and how the new worker understands and evaluates the contract, with the client as observer. This helps the client to understand very clearly what the new worker is told and what the new worker's commitment is. There might be a fourth, formal session at which the new worker is in charge, but there should be a time at the end of the session for the client and the old worker to meet together (in the absence of the new worker) for good-byes and for assessment—both of what has been accomplished by the first worker and of the client's expectations of the second.

If the transfer is being brought about because the client feels that there is a problem between the client and the first worker, the situation is different in that it is the client that is leaving the worker. In this situation, the worker needs to carefully examine the worker's own feelings and to be sure that the client is left totally free to move on to another relationship.

TERMINATION

Social work intervention is always time-centered. At its best, it is directed toward the realization of goals that are specific enough for progress to be measured in relation to them. In *Social Work with Groups*, Helen Northen (1969, p. 222) makes a statement about termination with groups that is applicable to all sizes and types of systems:

> The purposeful nature of social work implies that from time to time it is necessary to assess the desirability of continuing service to the members. The judgment may be that there has been progress toward the achievement of goals and there is potential for further improvement, in which case the service should be continued. Another decision may be that little, if any, progress has been made; if this is combined with little potential for changing the situation, the service should be discontinued. Still another evaluation may be that progress toward the achievement of goals has been sufficient, and the service should be terminated. Social workers have undoubtedly anticipated termination from the beginning of their work with the group and have clarified with the members its possible duration, so that the goals and means toward their achievement have been related to the plans for both individuals and the group. Nevertheless there comes a time when the worker and the members must face the fact of separation from each other and often, also, the end of the group itself.

Evaluation, the appraisal of the progress that worker and client system as a working partnership have achieved, is an ongoing process. The ultimate test of the effectiveness of social work practice is the extent to which positive movement toward the goals set has been accomplished. Thus the goals as initially developed between client and worker, as periodically evaluated, and as modified periodically by joint agreement become the criteria for evaluating progress. Whenever termination is being considered, a thorough review and evaluation of what has or has not been accomplished and of the processes by which these gains were made or failed to be made, is imperative. In their own, unilateral evaluation, workers may begin to wonder whether the goals are in sight, and they may be the ones to introduce the matter of termination. Or, clients may indicate that they are beginning to believe that they are ready to move on to a new experience and leave the worker behind. This is often communicated to the worker by the client's behavior rather than by verbal discussion. Clients begin to miss appointments or indicate with pride that they took some unilateral action toward the goal. These are ways of saying that they can "go it alone."

In talking about the indications for termination in the group, Helen Northen (1969, p. 225) says much the same thing:

> As the group moves toward readiness for termination, there are clues to guide practitioners in their activities with the group. The goals that members have for themselves and each other have been partially achieved, at least, although movement in the group may have been faster for some than for others. Members come to talk about some of the changes that have taken place in them and in the group. Attendance becomes irregular unless the worker makes special efforts to motivate members to continue until the final meeting. . . . The structure tends to become more flexible; for example, by giving up official roles within the membership or by changes in time, place, and frequency of meetings. . . . Cohesiveness weakens as the members find satisfactions and new relationships outside the group.

The need for termination, whether introduced by the client or the worker, should be discussed well in advance of the termination date to allow sufficient time for this aspect of worker and client experience with each other to be as productive as other parts of work together. To quote Helen Northen (1969, p. 228) once again:

> The time span between the initial information about termination and the final meeting of the group will vary with many factors, including the group's purpose, the length of time the group has been together, the problems and progress of the members, their anticipated reactions to termination, and the press of the environment on them.

These elements should be considered in working with individuals or families. In general the tasks of termination are (1) working out the conflict for both worker and client between the acknowledgment of improvement and goal achievement and the movement away from help; (2) working out the fear of loss of the relationship and of the support of a concerned person; (3) examining the experience and recognizing the progress made; (4) considering how this experience can be transferred to other problems as they come along; (5) examining what is involved in stabilizing the gains made; and (6) clarifying the worker's continuing position.

Termination of a relationship has great meaning, and a great investment of emotions and feelings of one person with another entails grief at such a loss. This grief may involve the following typical reactions: (1) the denial of termination (clients refuse to accept the notion of termination and behave as though it were not going to happen); (2) a return to patterns of earlier behavior or a reintroduction as problems of situations and tasks that have been taken care of long ago; (3) explosive behavior in which the client says that the worker was wrong when the worker thought that the client could go it alone; or (4) a precipitate break in the relationship by the client as though to say that the client will leave the worker before the worker leaves the client.

For social workers, termination stirs up emotions about both their professional activities and their feeling for their clients. They will undoubtedly feel pleased about the progress which has been made, but, like the client, will feel a sense of loss and grief in the parting. They may find that termination stirs up mixed feelings about the quality of their work: guilt about not having been able to do better; fear of the client's efforts to go ahead independently.

In the final disengagement, workers make it clear that the door is open, that they will be available for future problem solving if this falls within their agency's services, and if it does not, that they will help find an agency that is appropriate. They assure their clients of their continued interest in them and of their belief in their ability to move on to other goals and other efforts. It is often well to mark the last contact by some symbol. With a family, group, or organization a party can be helpful. In some instances, a formal letter of accomplishment of goals may be very meaningful.

RECAPITULATION

This chapter's discussion has focused on three special tasks in social work—referral, transfer, and termination. These are situations in which workers terminate their relationship with clients. In referral the client's request is considered to be beyond the parameters of the agency's services and the client is referred to others before any significant work on the problem is done. In transfer and termination, the client and the worker have established a relationship over a period of time. The authors have urged that these three special tasks are important aspects of the social work process and that workers should see them as involving significant skills.

Reading 14-1

*Termination in Context**

Howard Hess and Peg McCartt Hess

One of the distinctive characteristics of social work process is its temporary nature. Thus, termination is a natural conclusion, whether worker-client interaction has entailed a single interview for the purpose of assessment and referral or a series of interviews over time in the context of the therapeutic relationship. Once termination has begun, issues of separation and self-sufficiency are central. Interaction is dominated by recognition that at a point in time the process will cease and both client and social worker will make a determination about the value of their work together. Due to the potency of the issues of separation and evaluation, the ending is broadly recognized as a difficult phase for both client and practitioner (Fox, Nelson, & Bolman, 1969, p. 63; Shulman, 1979, p. 92; Siporin, 1975, p. 337). In many instances ambivalence about the ending causes both to vacillate in their judgments about the appropriate conclusion to their work. The capacity to bring resolution to this ambivalence determines the quality of the termination experience.

In mastering termination, clients must accomplish two general tasks: first, they must confront and begin to accept the impending separation from their helpers; and second, they must come to terms with the outcome of the helping process. Client awareness of both loss and outcome is stimulated by the encroaching time limit of termination. At no other phase in the process is time such a powerful influence. The press of time requires client and practitioner to confront both the limits of their

relationship and the importance of client self-responsibility and autonomy.

Because clients and practitioners often form close attachments, termination typically requires working through of the grief resulting from a break in these ties. Movement through the grief process involves a giving up or decathexis of and substitution for the lost object. This process is supported by the clear evaluation or review of accomplishments. The termination phase thus demands an intricate management of both loss and evaluation of gain. The presence of one theme provokes the other, ultimately allowing termination to occur. If the goals of working together have been accomplished, clients can be helped to acknowledge the appropriateness of ending. Conversely, if the goals have not been accomplished, the client can be helped to determine whether the goals were realistic and how problem solving can continue after the end point with the practitioner. When the helping process is disrupted, the termination work should clarify the nature of the necessary referral or transfer. As the work is reviewed, clients often experience a blend of pride in accomplished change, hope for the future, and sorrow about the loss of a valued resource. As the themes of loss and evaluation resonate against one another, the client moves toward a resumption of living exclusive of the helping process or toward continuation of the process with another helping person.

The following vignette taken from student process recording of a final interview captures the interrelationship between loss and evaluation during the ending phase. The social work student and client

---

* An original paper written especially for this text.

both struggle with bringing closure to an experience which is somewhat new for both of them:

Student: I was wondering if we could talk a little bit about . . . We haven't talked very much about the fact that this is my last visit to you. I just wanted to hear how you're feeling about that.

Client: I'd rather you'd stay on . . . and still come . . . In a way I hated for you even to come today because I said I won't see her from now on . . . I said, well maybe I'll just leave the house and that way she might have to come back . . . I said no, I'll just wait.

Student: Endings are hard, C., and it's hard for me, too, because you've been a very important person to me these last months.

Client: You've helped me a lot. When nobody else could. Just sitting down and talking. Other people say you're wrong, you're wrong. You're crazy. You think you are crazy. What's wrong with you? That's all I ever hear from B. I can't talk to B about nothing.

Student: It feels good to be able to talk and to say what's on your mind and not be judged. I'm glad that it has been helpful to you to have someone to talk to. I think you've done some things for yourself, too, C. That's kind of what I'd like to pay attention to just now.

Client: What?

Student: I'd like to talk about what you've been doing for yourself that has been helping.

Client: Yeah, but you know I just started almost not wanting to go back to the doctor's and the only thing that made me really want to go back was that I started bleeding yesterday.

Student: Uh huh.

Client: Cause I really started feeling again like I just didn't care no more.

Student: I wonder . . .

Client: Easy let down . . . It's easy for me to feel let down like that. *Very* easy.

Student: I wondered . . . I was thinking about what you had said last time. That you didn't want to be dependent on anybody

and so forth. If that might have something to do with the fact that you had grown dependent on me over these past few months and that I was going to let you down just like everybody else has.

Client: I was thinking about how I'll feel about that other social worker. I don't know if I'll be able to talk to her like I've been able to talk to you . . . I might feel angry toward her. I've been thinking about that and feeling if maybe I'd feel angry because she's trying to take S's place. [Note: This is the first time C. has referred to me in an interview by name. It impressed me as a way to touch as closely as it is possible for her to.] And it won't be the same.

In this instance, client and social work student have worked together to resolve problems of a life-threatening nature. Although both agree that the treatment should continue with another social worker, the exploration of the client's ambivalence, of feelings of loss and anger, as well as of evaluation of gains made thus far facilitate closure and an effective transfer.

THE CONTEXT OF TERMINATION

Although the termination phase is unique it cannot be accurately understood outside of the context of an entire course of treatment. Decisions made early about focus and goals directly determine the potential for review during termination. One of the major integrative dimensions that can be traced throughout the entire treatment process is the attachment that develops during early and middle phases between client and helper. Consequently, awareness of differential relationship patterns becomes crucial in the planning and management of termination. In addition, termination always occurs within a specified social context, including the organization which both sponsors and shapes the helping process. The practitioner must be able to relate the ending of treatment to each of these factors conceptually.

PROBLEM DEFINITION

Clarity about the focus of the helping process is a necessary prerequisite to successful termination. Specification of client problems and agreement about goals leads naturally to determination of how long the treatment will continue and how activities will be structured. Goals are established which then are reworked throughout the helping process and reflected in the specific termination plan. In this respect the quality of termination review can be directly correlated with the clarity of formulated treatment goals. Lack of precision in the early and middle phase of the work creates difficulty in measuring the extent to which the goals have been achieved. The point of termination then becomes more difficult to fix and relationship may become the focus of the work together, rather than a vehicle.

If client problems are developmental or life transitional in nature, the termination might well be designed to allow periodic return of "checking-in" with the practitioner as the developmental progression continues (Golan, 1981, p. 269). On the other hand, if the client problems are related to specific material or physical difficulties a fixed end point might be appropriate. When the expectations of the outcome of the helping process are shared and based upon a skillful assessment, the format of termination will have already been suggested.

It must be remembered that clients' expectations concerning what will be derived from the helping process are maintained both by hopes for specific change as well as the subjective meaning or value of the helping relationship. As the work progresses, the practitioner must monitor and maintain the appropriate balance between goal achievement and relationship gratification. Termination decisions

should reflect awareness of client uniqueness in this regard.

THE HELPING RELATIONSHIP

The attachment between client and social worker is the source of both the pain experienced in termination and the support helpful in the ending period. The impending separation is a violation of the wish intrinsic in most meaningful attachments that the relationship would remain permanently active. For this reason, termination may be approached with ambivalence by both client and practitioner. This ambivalence in a sense recapitulates the ambivalence initially experienced about the beginning of the work together. Our knowledge about the separation/individuation process verifies the presence of strongly felt, often contradictory, feelings and ideas about leaving valued others (Kauff, 1977, pp. 3–18). Mastery of termination necessarily includes the capacity for both client and practitioner to experience and share a variety of reactions to the ending.

One way that social workers can guide termination is to both teach clients about the predictable reactions to loss and to aid them in identifying those reactions when either directly or indirectly expressed. Various authors have written about the predictable stages of the grief process: denial, anger, sadness, acceptance, and disengagement (Germain & Gitterman, 1980; Kubler-Ross, 1969; Lindemann, 1956, pp. 7–21). Caution must be exercised so as not to assume that all clients uniformly transverse these stages in lockstep fashion or that all clients react to termination with the same intensity. However, it is generally recognized that both clients and practitioners are prone to deal with termination initially with denial. The expression of this denial may take many forms, varying from general detachment to premature discontinuation of sessions. Initially, denial may provide the client with space for adaptation. Appropriate focus by the practitioner often aids in surmounting the denial and allows open exchange about the pain and confusion associated with loss. Practitioners may experience uncertainty about their own capacity to deal with the ending and encourage clients to remain in a state of denial as a form of self-protection. As noted earlier, separation and ending inevitably evoke self-examination regarding competence and accomplishment. Social workers and clients alike are forced to confront their own limitations. Denial may become a protection from self-doubt.

It is the responsibility of the practitioner to guide the ending process through appropriate timing of interventions and use of self-disclosure. The honest expression of practitioners' own reactions during the termination phase facilitates the client's experience and expression of feelings and ideas stimulated by termination. Through this mutual exchange or sharing of responses, the reality of the ending is verified.

One of the major tasks of termination is to construct a bridge between treatment and clients' subsequent problem-solving efforts. In part this may be accomplished through a synthesis of termination evaluation and future planning. Clients should be empowered through the termination process to embark upon a self-directed course of action based upon realistic assessment of their problem-solving strengths. Mastery of termination issues supports client self-esteem and reinforces the client's hope that ongoing progress can be achieved. The work of the ending also frees the client to reinvest energy in appropriate life tasks and ongoing relationships which support problem solving.

Differential patterns of attachment

In the foregoing discussion, the open-end helping relationship between an individual client and practitioner was utilized

as the vehicle for discussing feelings related to loss in termination. However, individual counseling is but one variation of the social work helping process. Many clients present problems related to either inadequate resources or information and have limited interest in or need for counseling. In addition, certain clients are best helped within their families or in small groups.

Variations both in client problems/ goals and modality used are associated with important qualitative differences in the nature of the ending or termination of the helping process. In different types of work together the nature of the client-practitioner attachment varies as does the kind of focus and length of time required for successful mastery of the termination phase. The following two-dimensional typology in Figure 1 represents variations in termination related to the social worker's primary treatment activities and system size. Variations considered relate to the attachment typically developed and resultant implications for the termination process.

Counseling

Individual counseling often allows for the development of a high degree of mutual attachment. The longer the duration of the process the more pronounced the intimate tie may become. Termination of individual counseling is quite likely to

Primary Activities	System Size		
	Individual	Group	Family
Counseling			
Education			
Resource Mobilization (Referral, mediation, advocacy, brokerage)			

FIGURE 1

prompt elements of the grieving process for client and practitioner in response to loss. The termination of a predominantly counseling individual relationship may be time consuming and is typically discussed in the literature as requiring focused attention throughout the last sixth of the helping process. For example, in treatment of a year's duration the last eight weeks would be utilized for ending as would two of the last 8–12 interviews in short-term treatment (Reid & Epstein, 1972, pp. 22–23; Shulman, 1979, p. 95). Inattention to termination or prolonged use of denial may provoke regression and circumvent solidification of gains. The practitioner's role is to monitor and persistently call attention to the dynamics inherent in the ending phase.

Counseling with families and small groups can also entail a high degree of relationship intensity between client and practitioner. The major distinction between family or group and individual treatment is that any single client's attachment is to multiple others. In fact, one of the practitioner's major goals in work with families and small groups is to facilitate individuals' communication with others as well as to solidify members' attachments with one another. The attachment between individual client and practitioner is diffused throughout the client system. Although a family's termination with the practitioner may be painful to individual family members, the experience of loss is often modified by the reality that the family is likely to remain intact and members can resort to one another for support. The practitioner's role during termination is to underscore the family's interpersonal resources. Loss of the practitioner is moderated by the attachments shared by family members and by review of the system's shared treatment accomplishments.

In the group, several phenomena may be present (Shulman, 1979, p. 92). If the group is ongoing, or naturally formed such as neighborhood group, a classroom, or cottage unit, individual group members may turn to one another for assistance during and following termination. Therefore, loss of the practitioner may stimulate a different reaction than that which occurs in a formed group which disbands at termination. Such a termination can be quite emotionally charged due to the members' loss of multiple objects, including the group as a whole, other group members and the group worker. The group practitioner must facilitate the members' ability to detach from and dissolve the group. The loss theme resonates throughout the small group and is reworked in relationships not necessarily directly involving the group worker. In this instance, the practitioner places major emphasis upon the group members' efforts to deal with the loss of one another and acts as a catalyst, encouraging member interactions.

Educational interventions

Educational interventions tend to maintain a focus upon cognitive processes with new learning the major goal rather than emotional change or stabilization. Although intimate relationships certainly can develop when the helping goals and supporting interventions are educational, the attachment between client and practitioner may be less intense affectively than described above. The point of termination is often preset by the specific nature and amount of material to be learned. There is typically less client concern that termination will endanger the maintenance of that which has been learned and more of an emphasis upon continued practice and utilization of new skills beyond the context of treatment. The practitioner's educational interventions encourage generalization of learning through rehearsal and practice in the client's natural environment. A clear focus upon evidence of the client's learning and self-sufficiency is the most effective method of reinforcing gains during the ending period. Educational interventions with families (family life education) or groups (parent education groups) are not likely to result in intense attachments between clients and practitioners. Feelings of loss are limited by the lesser degree of dependency encouraged by the educational focus.

RESOURCE MOBILIZATION

Interventions focused upon resource mobilization may include referral, mediation, brokerage, and/or advocacy. The relationship in these instances is often experienced intensely with a rapidly developing attachment occurring between client and practitioner. This is likely either because of the urgency of the identified problem or the closely shared mobilization effort directed toward an outside source. However, in spite of the intensity of the effort, the worker's position is transitional: a way station to an additional helping resource somewhere else. Consequently, termination is focused heavily upon the success of resource mobilization and less upon the attendant interaction between client and practitioner. Resource mobilization with families, such as foster families, and groups, such as community or neighborhood groups, is also highly task focused. Termination is expected when the resource is activated but might include a provision for additional contact should resource problems reappear. Although attachments may be strong throughout a specific period, the relationship expectations are clearly delimited. Therefore termination may be less affectively charged and may require differential emphasis upon evaluation of outcomes rather than issues of loss or grief.

Certain general statements can be made about the presence of differential helping relationships based both upon the primary activities and the system size with which interventions occur:

1. The more exclusive the relationship between client and practitioner the more intense will be the attachment between them. Greater intensity of attachments is likely to necessitate greater attention to the grieving process. Generally family and group system sizes allow multiple resources for resolution of grief. Feelings of loss are diffused and shared with other clients.

2. The greater or more pervasive the dependency and/or attachment developed between client and practitioner, the more emotionally charged the termination is likely to be. The ending phase of such relationships will require sensitive support and encouragement toward self-sufficiency. Certain interventions as discussed above more typically result in client dependency upon the practitioner than do others.

3. The greater the extent to which clients can continue in relationships which were a part of the helping process, the more limited will be their reactions to the loss of the practitioner. Clients in families and ongoing groups are more likely to be able to substitute one another for the lost practitioner and thereby more readily resolve the grieving process.

4. Both themes of loss and evaluation can be expected to be present in the termination of each helping relationship, and therefore client ideas and feelings with regard to each theme should be recognized and explored.

In summary, the differential character of relationship patterns contributes to the balance of these themes. For example, counseling relationships must include a period of time for grief work in order to progress through termination. Educational interventions, focused upon the efficacy of the learned content and rehearsal for its use suggest an ending phase linked to learning transfer and opportunity for clients to participate in problem-solving efforts beyond the treatment situation. Successful treatment will therefore be less exclusively shared by client and worker and require considerably less focus upon their relationship. In the area of resource mobilization attachment may be temporarily strong, but soon offset by the fulfillment of a need or linkage to another helping resource. The theme of termination might be expected to be upon the success of resource linkage rather than the dimension of losing the helper.

The typology in Figure 2 is presented (p. 566) to illustrate the central points in the above discussion.

While the above guidelines provide a framework for anticipating the balance of loss and evaluation themes in termination, it is recognized that each case is unique. Practitioners often engage in multiple intervention activities throughout the helping process; thus termination might be a blend of the characteristics described. In addition, individual clients' sensitivity to loss will further influence the balance of these themes in the ending process.

Organizational influences upon the ending phase

Even as termination is defined by the client's problem and the nature of the helping relationship, it is shaped by the organizational context within which social work intervention occurs. The organizational mission delineates boundaries both for the nature of the client problems addressed and the typical or preferred treatment modalities utilized. Intra- and interorganizational factors may also affect the timing and process of termination.

The impact of organizational mission upon the process of termination is most evident in settings which provide social work services as a "secondary service," such as hospitals, schools, emergency shelters, and the workplace. In such set-

tings clients are typically eligible for the practitioner's assistance only for the duration of their involvement with the primary service. Thus, when patients are discharged from the hospital, children reach the end of the school year, clients leave an emergency shelter, or employees experience a change in employment, their relationship with a social worker employed by the organization is most likely terminated. While such setting-specific endings are planned for and anticipated openly by client and practitioner together, the ending itself may be experienced as an unnatural or premature closure. A social worker in a children's hospital noted: "Each morning when I come in to work, the first thing I do is check the census to see who's missing." Such abrupt endings may be accompanied by a brief follow-up period for attention to termination issues or referral of the client for continuing services. However, provision of time to accomplish the tasks of termination is crucial both for clients, whether or not they seek services elsewhere, and for the practitioners, who must begin with other clients necessarily anticipating the likelihood of premature closure.

Settings in which social services are the primary organizational mission also structure beginnings and endings of client-practitioner relationships through available program options and preferred treatment modalities. For example, clients may be referred within the agency following problem definition and assessment to a six- or eight-week divorce adjustment group. Public agencies mandated to serve all persons requesting services in a geographic area, such as a community mental health center, may develop guidelines limiting the length of time client services are available or the modalities to be utilized, such as crisis intervention, planned short-term treatment, or group treatment. In the process of contracting with clients, such agency guidelines should be openly

Primary activities	System size		
	Individual	*Group*	*Family*
Counseling	Attachment may be intense. Loss in termination may include considerable grief, must be openly managed, and processed in mutual interaction.	Attachment may be intense but shared with group worker, group as a whole and other members. Grief may be considerable; when formed groups terminate focus must be maintained upon ending and multiple separations. In natural groups loss moderated by ongoing ties between members. Termination should include support of groups' ongoing motivation to support members.	Attachment may be intense, but is shared with other family members. Loss moderated by family's continuation. Termination focus upon improved attachments and communication within family system.
Education	Attachment may be of moderate intensity. Ending often preset in original plan and focuses upon success in learning and generalization beyond treatment setting.	Attachment usually more moderate in intensity.	Attachment often more moderate in intensity.
		Differences persist between formed and natural groups, but have less impact upon the nature of termination. Emphasis in both groups upon evaluation of learning. Some formed groups may continue after treatment ends.	As family is usually ongoing, termination includes focus upon members' mutual support and application of learning that has occurred.
Resource Mobilization (referral, brokerage, mediation, advocacy)	Attachment may be intense, but transitional and/or intermittent. Loss moderated by attachment to new resource and/or need satisfaction. Focus is upon evaluation of mobilization with door open for return. Loss not usually theme in termination discussion.	Attachment may be intense but present between multiple group members.	Attachment may be intense and may have resulted in strengthening family relationships.
		Termination should enhance groups' capacity to locate and utilize resources independently. During this phase some formed groups will develop into natural groups maintaining their ties.	Termination should enhance the family's capacity to locate and utilize resources independently. Specific skills regarding use of resources learned by family members may be consolidated during termination.

FIGURE 2

shared, both to minimize the client's personal rejection at the time of ending and to maximize the realistic definition of treatment goals.

Other organizational factors also impact upon the progression of the helping process. For example, requirements for practitioner productivity or third-party reimbursement for agency services may contribute to subtle or explicit pressures upon practitioners. Expectations that social workers continue with clients beyond contracted services to maintain a percentage of direct service time or to terminate prematurely due to the exhaustion of reimbursement benefits by the client may be conveyed. Practitioners may be asked to terminate with clients prematurely in order to serve growing numbers of persons on the waiting list. Such pressure regarding the treatment process present ethical dilemmas for the individual social worker as well as for the organization and inevitably impact upon the practitioners's feelings about the employing agency and about beginnings and endings with clients.

Interorganizational pressures may also occur when clients have been referred involuntarily by the courts or other systems, such as the workplace and schools. Potential difficulties in the ending phase are presented for client and practitioner alike when the problem definition and/or length of treatment are determined externally and as a condition for a child's return home from foster care, an employee's return to work, or a continuation of probation.

Organizational commitments to professional training shape the termination process. An exploratory study of students' termination of individual clinical work at the end of an academic year found that students in the sample appeared to learn about termination primarily from their agency supervisors (Gould, 1978, pp. 235–69). Students' first-year field agency supervisors as well as several of the second-

year supervisors had encouraged students not to discuss the predictable training-related ending of treatment with their clients until the latter part of treatment (Gould, 1978, pp. 235–251, 260–261).

The approach encouraged with these students places both student practitioner and client in a compromising position. While the organization's desire to present students as employees may be benign in intent, the potential destructive impact of this misrepresentation upon the helping process, particularly in the termination phase, is a matter of concern. "Where agencies are open and direct about their training function, and present their students as supervised learners, termination is less complicated by guilt and resentment. Clients expect the student's departure at the end of the academic year and termination and transfer are most likely to be viewed as legitimate" (Germain & Gitterman, 1980, p. 257).

Thus the organizational context, even as the clients' problems and the differential nature of the client-practitioner relationship, influences the nature of the help offered and received. Therefore it is crucial that inter- and intraorganizational factors be fully and openly weighed early in the process as client and practitioner explore goals, options, and tasks together, and in the ending phase as feelings and content regarding loss and evaluation emerge. Any other stance jeopardizes the productive completion of the ending phase and the positive evaluation of work together.

THE ROLE OF SELF-AWARENESS IN TERMINATION

The nature of the tasks presented during the ending phase demands openness on the part of the worker to intense feelings and reactions from the client, including sadness, anger, and negative evaluation of their work together. The predictable themes of the ending phase frame important areas for social worker's introspection and action.

Competent use of the professional self relies upon continuing self-examination and self-awareness. Social workers necessarily explore their own attitudes, values, experiences, and feelings in order that the interaction between worker and client be guided by the client's rather than the worker's needs and concerns. In the termination phase, these include experiences with and feelings about separations generally; feelings and concerns about the worker's competence as a helping person; and feelings about a specific client system and the ending of work together.

The predictable stirring of memories and feelings associated with separation for both client and worker is the major consistent theme in the description of the process of termination: "The ending process in a helping relationship can trigger feelings of the deepest kind in both worker and client. This is the reason why there is potential for powerful work during this phase as well as ineffective work if the feelings are not dealt with" (Shulman, 1979, p. 93). The social worker's ability to deal with these feelings in the helping interaction builds upon awareness of the personal meaning of separation. Therefore, the practitioner's own experiences with separation and assumptions about clients' feelings emerge as areas for reflection. The practitioner's experiences, whether with death, divorce, geographic moves, or other losses or transitions may affect the ability to individualize the meaning of the ending to a specific client. Painful or recent separation experiences may prompt the practitioner to deny the importance of the ending to the client in order to avoid remembering or re-experiencing painful feelings.

When the termination is based upon the practitioner's own timetable and needs rather than that of the clients, self-aware-ness of own feelings is particularly important. For example, practitioners leaving an agency or students completing a semester of agency-based practicum training (Gould, 1978, pp. 235–269; Moss & Moss, 1967, pp. 433–437) may experience conflict due to acting in their own self-interest rather than concern for the client. A second-year social work student described her reactions to termination: "I haven't yet had any real terminations with clients— all my cases have ended when the placement is over—I feel so guilty to quit working with my clients because my time is over, not because we're through. I have offered to volunteer here at the agency when the placement is over." Persons completing professional training are also typically in the process of separating from the university, from the student role, from practicum agency and field instructor, and from classmates. Therefore, client terminations become part of a broader current separation experience. It is important that the multifaceted nature of this transition period be explored and understood by the student practitioner (Husband & Scheunemann, 1972, pp. 505–513).

A second area in which the practitioner must be self-aware is that of confidence in own competence. Inevitably, the evaluative component of ending raises the questions, "Have I done well by this client? Could I have done more to be helpful?" It is not possible to evaluate and review client goal accomplishment without scrutiny of the practitioner's sensitive and skilled use of self in the process. While it has been concluded that the major reason for professional inattention to termination as a phase of treatment "seems to be the general sensitivity to loss and separation" (Fox et al., 1969, p. 62), another contributing factor may be the profession's general sensitivity to accountability and evaluation. Germain and Gitterman emphasize, however, that "Endings can be particularly valuable to workers' efforts to build professional knowledge and to refine their skills. Careful assessment of outcomes with clients, identifying what was helpful and what was not helpful, and why, can gradually be generalized to the level of practice principles" (Germain & Gitterman, 1980, p. 278). Objective evaluation and conceptualization of one's practice is preceded by self-examination and acknowledgement of the practitioner's level of training and experience and the professional expectation of continued growth. Each termination provides further information regarding the practitioner's strengths and professional learning needs.

Feelings of inadequacy or guilt about failure to help a particular client, however, should be shared and examined with supervisor, consultant, or colleagues to determine the reality of this assessment and to prevent transmission of the message that the client should either reassure the practitioner of her worth or confirm lack of worth.

The specific meaning for the practitioner of a particular client and of that client's termination also merits self-examination. For example, has this client been particularly gratifying? Or ungratifying? Is this client terminating with little accomplished? Has the client's success or lack of success taken on a special meaning for the practitioner personally or within the organization? Does the practitioner have fantasies of a continuing relationship with the client? Is there relief at the idea of terminating with this client? Have organizational pressures become an issue in the treatment and termination? Levinson writes that "during treatment the therapist has an opportunity to participate in a creative process in which a new or modified self emerges . . . Saying good-bye to the patient by the therapist can be akin to saying good-bye to a part of himself" (Levinson, 1977, p. 483). The meanings of termination are uniquely personal to the practitioner as well as to the client. Anticipating these meanings is an important aspect of preparation for the disciplined and conscious use of self in attending to the meaning of the ending for the client.

Practitioners anticipate the ending in part through exploring their personal reactions to separation, feelings of professional worth and adequacy, and reactions to each unique ending. Self-awareness in these areas enables the worker to help the client express feelings and to skillfully assist the client throughout the ending phase.

SUMMARY

Whether brief or long term, the intent of the helping process is to make a difference in the life of the client. It is through the process of termination that this difference can be understood, evaluated, and maintained. The major task of the practitioner during the ending phase is to help the client move from denial of the inevitable ending point to exploration of ideas and feelings related both to outcome of the helping process and the termination of the helping relationship. The practitioner's ability to accomplish this task will depend upon his/her own self-awareness and skills as well as his/her own conceptual grasp of the multifaceted context within which termination occurs: the client's problems and goals, the differential nature of the helping relationship, and the sponsoring organization. Thus, each termination can be uniquely anticipated and sensitively completed.

References

Fox, Evelyn, Nelson, Marian, & Bolman, William.   The termination process: A neglected dimension in social work. *Social Work,* October 1969, *14,* 63.

Germain, Carel, & Gitterman, Alex.   *The life model of social work practice.* New York: Columbia University Press, 1980.

Golan, Naomi.   *Passing through transitions.* New York: The Free Press, 1981.

Gould, Robert.   Students' experience with the termination phase of individual treatment. *Smith College Studies in Social Work,* June 1978, *48,* 235–269.

Husband, Diane, & Scheunemann, Henry.   The use of group process in teaching termination. *Child Welfare,* October 1972, *51,* 505–513.

Kauff, Priscilla.   The termination process: Its relationship to the separation individuation phase of development. *International Journal of Group Psychotherapy,* 1977, *27,* 3–18.

Kubler-Ross, Elisabeth.   *On death and dying.* New York: Macmillan, 1969.

Levinson, Hilliard.   Termination of psychotherapy: Some salient issues. *Social Casework,* October 1977, *58,* 483.

Lindemann, Erich.   Symptomatology and management of acute grief. In Howard Parad (Ed.), *Crisis intervention: Selected readings.* New York: Family Service Association, 1956.

Moss, Sidney, & Moss, Miriam.   When a caseworker leaves an agency: The impact on worker and client. *Social Casework,* July 1967, *48,* 433–437.

Northen, Helen.   *Social work with groups.* New York: Columbia University Press, 1969.

Reid, William, & Epstein, Laura.   *Task centered casework.* New York: Columbia University Press, 1972.

Shulman, Lawrence.   *The skills of helping.* Itasca, Ill.: F. E. Peacock Publishers, 1979.

Siporin, Max.   *Introduction to social work practice.* New York: Macmillan, 1975.

Chapter 15

Evaluation

Social workers, along with other human service professionals, are increasingly being called upon to justify the effectiveness of their services. The last decade might be considered the age of accountability for human services—a decade in which evaluation has taken on serious proportions with both clients and other persons in the communities being served requiring evidence of the worthwhileness of social service programs. With taxpayer reluctance to fund unproven programs and reduced resources available for human services, the demand for hardheaded evaluation will continue.

We consider evaluation to be the application of scientifically sound research methodology to measure both change processes and the results or outcomes of change efforts. As in any good research, the evaluation is directed toward measuring the outcomes of interventions (the dependent variables), to measure the change processes or the nature of the interventions themselves (the independent variables), and to do so with a research design which permits workers to attribute the outcome to the change processes. The terms *sumative* and *formative* are frequently used to refer to the two types of evaluations. Sumative refers to the study of program outcomes or effectiveness; formative evaluations refer to the study of program processes.

Both types of evaluation will also occur on two levels. At the program level, social workers are asked to measure the impact of and the nature of programs such as child protection, family counseling, community development, and so on. This might be referred to as program evaluation research. But evaluation research will also occur at the level of individual worker and client relationships. Just as we can ask what is the nature of human service programs, what are their outcomes, and what leads us to believe that the programs lead to the outcomes so too can we ask what is the nature of individual intervention made by social workers and clients, what are their presumed outcomes, and what leads us to believe that the interventions led to the outcomes? As part of the services provided to each client, each individual social worker is called upon to be a researcher, to apply sound scientific methodology to an understanding of the nature of interventions and measurement of impacts. Each worker and client might ask what are our activities (independent variables)? What are our goals (dependent variables)? And how can we relate activities to the goals? In Chapter 2 we talked about testing our assumptive knowledge and the commitment to the scientific method as a response to the discomfort which occurs in the light of incomplete knowledge. As we carry out this commitment in our cooperation with program evaluation efforts and our own obligations to be competent researchers with our clients, we test our assumptive knowledge and contribute to knowledge development in the profession.

BALANCING SUMATIVE AND FORMATIVE EVALUATIONS

For many of us the term *program evaluation* carries the connotation of a sumative program evaluation; that is, an attempt to assess the extent to which a program is reaching its objectives. While sumative evaluations are useful in making judgments about the worth of a program, they have very little usefulness unless the program or interventions used are well conceptualized and understood. Knowing that goals are being accomplished is of little use unless we also know how they are being accomplished; likewise, knowing that goals are not being accomplished is not useful unless we are clear as to what interventions were used and failed to accomplish the desired goals. For example, if one finds a reduction in child abuse after a parent skills training program, a laudable goal might well have been accomplished. But unless we understand clearly the nature of the parent training program that presumably led to the reduction in child abuse, the finding is of little practical value because, not knowing the nature of the program, we would not be in a position to replicate it in the future. Or, assume that a social worker is working with a senior citizens group toward a goal of securing more adequate police protection in their neighborhood. Even if the goal is accomplished, say more foot patrols are assigned to the neighborhood at hours when senior citizens would like to be on the streets, unless the worker can document how this goal was accomplished, the finding is of limited value and will not contribute to the developing knowledge base of the profession.

Unfortunately, in much of social work, as well as other human service professions, our independent variables (the program or intervention methods used) are poorly conceptualized. Thus efforts to measure outcomes may be very premature unless workers are also simultaneously engaging in formative evaluations directed toward conceptualizing and measuring the nature of the intervention used. Studies of program and interventive processes are essential to the development of the knowledge base of the profession and, as Rutman and Hudson suggest, are an essential prerequisite to sumative evaluations (see Reading 15–1). Before talking about program or intervention effectiveness (that is, sumative evaluations) we first need to be able to answer a series of questions about the program itself:

1. What am I attempting to accomplish? What are the goals which have been set for the program or the service contract for the individual worker and client? Clarity about goals is essential for either type of evaluation.

2. What is the population for which these goals are to be accomplished? In some cases this may be an individual, a group of clients, a neighborhood, or an even larger population.

3. What are the components or parts of the program or intervention plan which are necessary to accomplish the goals for the defined population or client? One should be able to specify all of the program components or interventions which will be occurring in an effort to accomplish the goals.

4. How do these components or parts fit together? Do some need to precede others? Do some occur concurrently? How do the parts of the program fit together into an integrated intervention plan to accomplish the desired goals? At this point flowcharts might be drawn to illustrate relationships among the various intervention strategies and how they relate to accomplishing the final goals.

5. What are the reasons for believing that, if the intervention strategies are carried out, the goals will be accomplished? This, of course, moves into the area of intervention theory; workers must have some ideas, some hypotheses that will lead them to predict that goals will be accomplished if they complete the prescribed intervention plan. Part of evaluation is to test these hypotheses—to test assumptive knowledge and expand the knowledge base of the profession.

Perhaps an illustration of this process would be helpful. Let's go back to the senior citizens group who are working with a social worker to increase public safety in their neighborhood. These seniors like to be out visiting during the late afternoon and early evening hours; however, they feel very insecure in their immediate neighborhood because of concern about muggings, purse snatchings, and so on. If it is assumed that they have decided on an immediate goal of attempting to have a pair of police officers assigned to patrol the neighborhood on foot during the 3:00 to 11:00 P.M. shift to supplement the regular squad car patrols, the goal is rather clear. The immediate plan is to develop an intervention plan which will presumably lead to that goal. In thinking through ways of accomplishing the goal, the seniors and their social worker decided that they first needed to influence the chief of police to secure the chief's support for the notion of a foot patrol for their neighborhood and then second to influence the city council to secure some additional resources for the neighborhood. They decide that in the process of implementing this plan, they will need to bring two kinds of pressure to bear—knowledge and political. They will need to assemble facts concerning the number of crimes against the elderly that are occurring in the neighborhood as well as the extent to which activities of the seniors may be limited by fear of being out at night. Second, even with the knowledge, they will need to in some way mobilize a show of political support to convince the city council members that this is an important issue for their attention. After considerable brainstorming and planning, the social worker and clients may well have developed an intervention plan similar to that represented in Figure 15–1.

Figure 15–1 is a simplified flowchart of an intervention plan which indicates the various components to the effort to produce change and shows their relationship. Formative evaluation would then be directed at monitoring the extent to which each of these activities occurs. If the persons responsible for gathering the evidence failed to do so and failed to have an impact on the police chief, then the worker and clients have a clearer understanding

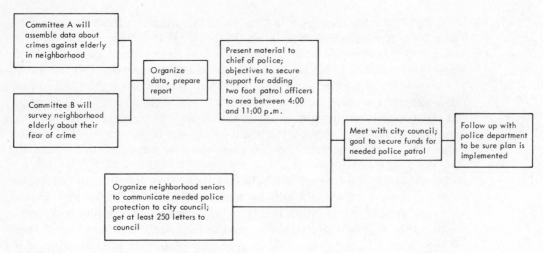

FIGURE 15–1:   Flowchart of intervention plan

of what went wrong in accomplishing their goals. Or, conceivably, the plan may be perfectly implemented but still the goals are not accomplished; if this should happen we may well have done a sumative evaluation and are able to make a judgment that the plan itself was not appropriate. Client and worker in this situation would then consider alternative plans and strategies for accomplishing their goals—perhaps they are going to need to work to unseat some city council members or perhaps form coalitions with other organizations in order to bring additional political pressure to bear to secure the desired goal.

This illustration also points out another distinction which is sometimes useful in regard to sumative evaluation—the distinction between outputs and outcomes. We have generally been referring globally to outcomes as the program results. But one might note from this illustration that the output of the intervention was the assignment of a team of foot patrol officers to the neighborhood whereas the desired outcome was the reduction in crime against senior citizens. The question of whether the output, that is, the two patrol officers, will actually lead to the outcome is, of course, a separate research question which will be of critical interest to this social worker and the group of clients. Thus one can ask, do the program activities lead to the outputs and do the outputs lead to the outcomes? In this connection outputs are referred to as the immediate desired accomplishments of the program and the outcomes as the more long-term gains which the outputs are presumed to accomplish.

All social workers have a responsibility to be researchers with their clients. An appropriate beginning place for our research efforts will be in conceptualizing and measuring the nature and extent of our intervention activities. Before we do this, we need to have a clear picture of how we are going to go about intervening and why we believe that the interventions, if accomplished, lead to the immediate goals we and our client(s) have established. If this is done, we can then begin thinking about sumative evaluation or measuring the extent of goal attainment. Research and evaluation is a continuous process providing a flow of data in which we can continually reassess goals, intervention plan, and even the problem definition.

CONTINUOUS CLIENT EVALUATION

Figure 15–2 offers a schematic representation of the problem-solving process showing evaluation as providing feedback loops permitting client and worker to assess continuously the problem they have defined for work, the objectives they have selected, and the interventive plan they have formulated. Client and worker are continuously involved in an ongoing evaluation of their experiences in trying to produce change. Their evaluation may indicate a need to redefine the problem (or define an entirely new problem), to reassess objectives (or develop new objectives), or to alter the intervention plan. The impact of evaluation and feedback loops is to reduce the linearity of the problem-solving model and to permit the model to take on a dynamic, systematic, constantly changing quality. The opportunity to change problem definition, goals, and intervention plan does not, however, remove from you the responsibilities of being sure that any changes are negotiated with the client and that any intervention activities are undertaken on the basis of a clearly specified service contract. Experience with interventive activities may indicate a need for a change in the contract, but changes in contracts cannot be made unilaterally.

In Chapter 10 we stressed the importance of clearly specifying goals. This is an essential prerequisite to evaluation. Without client and worker clarity as to goals, the evaluation of progress toward the accomplishment of goals is impossible. Likewise, a clear specification of the intervention plan is necessary to assess whether client-worker activities are appropriate for reaching the desired goals. Without a clear specification of the intervention plan, client and worker cannot evaluate whether what is happening leads or fails to lead to goal accomplishment.

The specification of measurable, concrete goals is one of the more difficult

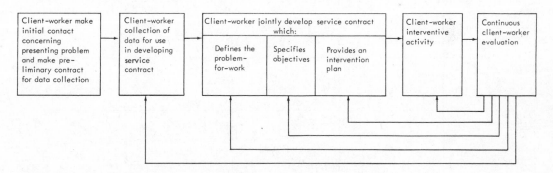

FIGURE 15–2: The problem-solving model

Evaluation provides feedback loops enabling client and worker to continuously reevaluate the adequacy of the data base and/or renegotiate the service contract by changing the problem definition, the objectives, or the intervention plan.

tasks of the social work practitioner. Goal Attainment Scaling, first proposed in 1968 (Kiresuk & Sherman, 1968), as a useful evaluation tool to evaluate patient progress in mental health programs but which can be utilized in any program where goal-setting is a part of the process. Goal Attainment Scaling procedures have been used to measure client progress toward service goals, student social workers' progress toward the accomplishment of learning goals, and agency progress toward the accomplishment of organizational goals. Goal Attainment Scaling is particularly useful to the social work practitioner, because it permits the individualization of goals; there is no effort to impose predetermined, standardized goals. Rather, client and worker work toward the accomplishment of goals individually tailored to a particular situation. The procedures, however, only measure the extent of goal attainment; they do not in anyway measure the importance or significance of the goals themselves, nor do they determine the intervention methods. How goals are achieved is not a part of Goal Attainment Scaling.

The grid used in Goal Attainment Scaling is reproduced in Figure 15–3. It provides for the development of scales—one for each goal—with five levels of predicted attainment for a specified period of time; the levels range from the most unfavorable to the most favorable outcome thought likely,

FIGURE 15–3:   Goal Attainment Follow-Up Grid

Program using GAS_____	Date of scale construction _____ Follow-up date _____		
LEVELS OF PREDICTED ATTAINMENTS	SCALE HEADINGS AND SCALE WEIGHTS		
	SCALE: 1 $(w_1 = \ )$	SCALE 2: $(w_2 = \ )$	SCALE 3: $(w_3 = \ )$	SCALE 4: $(w_4 = \ )$
Most unfavorable outcome thought likely			
Less than expected success			
Expected level of success			
More than expected success			
Most favorable outcome thought likely			

with the expected level of outcome at the midpoint on each scale. At least one scale should be developed for each problem area, and a heading should be provided for each scale. As many scales as are necessary may be developed. Once the scale headings have been provided, a follow-up date should be set, and the predicted level of outcome for each scale as of the follow-up date should be indicated.

Where do client and worker expect to be at the specified follow-up date? The entire goal may not be attained by that time; the task, therefore, is to indicate the expected level of accomplishment by the follow-up date. The next steps are to indicate the most unfavorable outcome and the most favorable outcome thought likely by the follow-up date; then the intermediate levels—less than expected success, expected level of success, and more than expected success—can be completed. The levels of predicted attainment should be specified objectively enough to be reliably scored on the follow-up date. Whenever possible, quantification is desirable, but it is not absolutely essential in establishing the scale levels.

A second concern is to be sure that each scale is both exhaustive and mutually exclusive. None of the five levels of success should overlap (each should be mutually exclusive), and the scale levels should account for all outcome possibilities thought likely (be exhaustive). After the scales have been developed, they can be set aside until the designated follow-up date. Scoring consists of checking what has been accomplished on each scale at the designated follow-up date. Kiresuk and Garwick (1974) present a formula for calculating an overall Goal Attainment Scale and also discuss the procedures for weighting scales if some are thought to be more important than others.

Figure 15–4 on page 578 illustrates a completed set of Goal Attainment Scales which might have been developed with Mrs. B in the situation described in Chapter 11. After study of this example you might begin experimenting with Goal Attainment Scaling. The procedures can be used in any situation where goals are set, so Goal Attainment Scaling can be learned without actually working with clients. Personal learning goals can be set. How many books will be read next month? How many articles? What are your goals in terms of grades this term? What percent of written assignments will be completed on time? Your own learning plans will provide ample opportunity to begin work with Goal Attainment Scaling.

ASSISTING WITH PROGRAM EVALUATION

Increasingly social agencies are being called upon to establish the effectiveness of their services. Accountability extends beyond the evaluation by worker and client of the extent to which they are achieving service contract goals. It also utilizes the principles of scientific research to measure the extent to which agency program goals are being attained and at what cost. The article by Leonard Rutman and Joe Hudson identifies phases in program evaluation and discusses issues and problems of each phase (see Reading 15–1). Studies can be made of outcomes (the extent to which programs are achieving defined goals) or of efforts (the processes agencies

Program using GAS Head Start Intercity Client Mrs. B		Date of scale construction 8-1-73 Follow-up date 9-1-73		

LEVELS OF PREDICTED ATTAINMENTS	SCALE HEADINGS AND SCALE WEIGHTS			
	SCALE 1: (w_1 =)	SCALE 2: (w_2 =)	SCALE 3: (w_3 =)	SCALE 4: (w_4 =)
Most unfavorable outcome thought likely	Mrs. B reports angrily yelling at Jimmy daily or oftener during last week in August.	No action on or discussion of Mrs. B's loneliness.	No discussion or action about returning to clinic.	
Less than expected success	Mrs. B reports angrily yelling at Jimmy more than 3 times but less than daily during last week in August.	Mrs B discusses her loneliness but can not make plans to deal with it.	Mrs. B is discussing her reaction to the clinic but has not formulated plans to return.	
Expected level of success	Mrs. B reports angrily yelling at Jimmy no more than three times during last week in August.	Mrs. B is discussing her loneliness and making plans to join a group.	Mrs. B has discussed her reaction to the clinic and plans to secure a return appointment.	
More than expected success	Mrs. B has discontinued angrily yelling at Jimmy but has not discovered another way to discipline him.	Mrs. B has initiated contacts with a group.	Mrs. B has telephoned the clinic for a return appointment.	
Most favorable outcome thought likely	Above, and Mrs. B is using another form of discipline before becoming angry with Jimmy.	Mrs. B has attended one group meeting.	Mrs. B has been into the clinic for a return appointment.	

FIGURE 15–4:   Goal Attainment Follow-Up Grid (examples of scales which might have been developed with Mrs. B)

utilize to reach goals). Process studies are particularly necessary to enable social agencies to more adequately conceptualize and identify the program inputs they utilize to reach goals. Just as interventive means must be conceptualized and related to objectives defined in the service contract, so at the level of program evaluation, inputs must be conceptualized and related to program goals or outputs. The need to adequately conceptualize inputs and goals is the same whether the effort is to evaluate a client's progress or a program's accomplishment.

A recurring theme noted by Rutman and Hudson is the conflict between practitioner and researcher. They think both must make compromises if program evaluation is to be conducted, and they regard program evaluation as essential to the establishment of accountability. Practitioners may be asked to more completely conceptualize their activity and goals. However, practitioners utilizing the service contract should find this a comparatively easy process. In addition, the practitioner may be asked to fill out forms and maintain records which are essential for the evaluation function. Just as the evaluation of client progress provides feedback from which the worker and client can renegotiate their service contract, so formal program evaluation should provide feedback to the worker concerning the effectiveness of particular interventive means. While cooperating with researchers may involve additional effort on the part of the practitioner, the payoff in knowledge and better service should justify the effort.

RECAPITULATION

Your involvement with evaluative effort will occur at two levels. You and your client will be involved in a continuous process of evaluating the extent to which the goals of the service contract are being accomplished. This evaluation provides feedback loops and an opportunity to continuously renegotiate the problem for work, objectives, and interventive means in relation to the problem. You will also be called upon to cooperate and assist with broader agency program evaluation. Such efforts will provide feedback concerning the interventive approaches which appear to be most effective in given circumstances. Evaluation at both levels requires an explicit statement of goals and conceptualization of interventive means or program inputs. One model for measuring goal attainment—Goal Attainment Scaling—was discussed in relation to the measurement of client progress.

Reading 15-1

Evaluation Research in Human Services*

Leonard Rutman and Joe Hudson

In the past several years there has been a growing demand for the formal evaluation of human service programs. This increased interest has been reflected most dramatically in the amount of funds being allocated for program evaluations and this work is becoming increasingly accepted as an integral part of program planning and policy-making in the human services. It is expected that evaluation research can meet two major goals: (1) identify the manner in which programs are carried out, particularly to determine whether they are actually implemented in the way intended; and (2) assess the impact of programs on the target group of consumers. In other words, the expectation is for evaluation research to provide a basis for both monitoring programs and holding them accountable. Ultimately, soundly conducted evaluative research aims at contributing to the more effective and efficient delivery of human service programs.

The increased demand for evaluation research stems from several sources. Funding organizations are exerting greater demands for rigorous research on the programs they support. In part due to the relative scarcity of funds available for human service programs, funding bodies are searching for relatively objective measures on program effectiveness as a condition for the provision of ongoing financial support. No longer are funding bodies satisfied with testimonials from program personnel about the value of their service. Assessments of program effectiveness provided by practitioners and administra-

tors are likely to be viewed with some skepticism inasmuch as any criticism of the worth of these programs poses a threat to professional practice, status, and, ultimately, job security.

In addition to the increased skepticism of funding organizations to potentially self-serving statements by program managers regarding the worth of the services being provided, descriptive reports which provide little more than bookkeeping information on the numbers, characteristics, and per unit cost of clients served by the agency are being viewed as insufficient to warrant the allocation of scarce funds. Instead, human service programs are being asked to provide evidence derived from outcome studies to demonstrate the extent to which programs are meeting stated goals.

Concern about the effectiveness of human service programs has been accelerated with the appearance of research reports showing that many programs have not achieved significant positive effects for the clients served (Bailey, 1966; Eysenck, 1961; Fisher, 1973; Robison & Smith, 1971). In fact, it has become almost axiomatic that the more rigorous the research conducted, the less significant the demonstrated outcomes of a variety of programs. A consequence of such research findings is a growing disenchantment with human service programs by the public as well as by various funding organizations.

Aside from the general concern of determining the effectiveness of programs, human service professionals have become interested and involved in evaluative research for the purpose of testing theory

---

* An original article prepared for this text.

and improving practice. This trend is particularly evident in the considerable amount of research conducted on various learning theories and the "behavior modification" approaches developed from them.

The increasing demand for rigorous evaluative research has also been influenced by the growing popularity of the demonstration project as a strategy for program development and policy-making. Many federal departments have taken the initiative in stimulating the growth of demonstration projects through legislation providing for the funding of "innovative" programs. The usual pattern in funding demonstrations has been to support the development of small-scale pilot programs which include an extensive research component. It is expected that information provided through rigorous study of pilot programs will have relevance for more general program development and policy formulations.

Despite the optimism about the possibilities of evaluation research in monitoring and measuring the impact of human service programs, there are formidable obstacles to pursuing these aims. Several factors contaminate efforts to implement adequate research procedures: (1) the existence of latent purposes for conducting the evaluation study, which can result in the distortion of research to justify decisions about the possible termination, continuation, or expansion of programs; (2) ethical issues, especially in regard to denying service to a control group; (3) administrative constraints; (4) legal requirements; and (5) professionals' prerogatives. The prevalence of these factors in evaluation research efforts underscores the need for an understanding of the sociopolitical process of planning and implementing evaluative research. Such an endeavor would place particular emphasis on adjustments in the stages of planning and conducting the research with particular at-

tention paid to the potential consequences of choosing various alternatives in the development of the final research design and the way in which it is implemented. Also required is an understanding of the factors related to the use of research findings for program changes or policy-making. In this context, a sociology of evaluative research would help to explicate the numerous issues relevant to evaluative studies of human service programs.

PERSPECTIVES FOR EVALUATING HUMAN SERVICE PROGRAMS

Judgments regarding the relative worth of human service programs are common. The general public have varying opinions regarding the success of programs such as Aid to Families with Dependent Children (AFDC) in meeting the problem of low income among these families, of health insurance programs in meeting the medical problems of the aged and/or indigent, and of such child welfare services as foster care in meeting the needs of children requiring substitute care. In the absence of a factual basis for making such decisions, judgments are largely based on values. programs are viewed as being "good" or "bad" in relation to the characteristics of people availing themselves of the service, attitudes toward work and independence, and differing views about the appropriate role of the state in attempting to ameliorate social problems and personal difficulties.

In addition to the common process in which the public formulates opinions about various programs, assessments about the relative worth of human services are also continually made by practitioners and administrators who are responsible for implementing the services as well as by the funding organizations supporting these programs. Having a deep investment in the services being provided, practitioners and administrators quite naturally extoll the virtues of their program. And it is such subjective testimonials which all too commonly are presented to funding organizations in an effort to gain continued support. Not having access to more rigorous types of information for assessing the value of particular programs, funding organizations are frequently placed in the position of relying upon the subjective information provided by the program personnel.

While evaluation research also entails making judgments of worth about particular programs, it differs from the relatively simple and common process of informal evaluation based largely upon opinion. In evaluation research, emphasis is placed on the application of commonly accepted research procedures to collect data which provides the basis for judgments of worth. Evaluation research is, first and foremost, a process of applying scientific procedures to accumulate reliable and valid evidence on the manner and extent to which specified activities produce particular effects or outcomes. The focus is on the end product—the effects of programs and policies—as well as on the efficiency and effort involved in achieving these outcomes. In addition to providing a basis for determining the relative success or failure of human service programs, the evidence derived from evaluation research can be used to suggest needed modifications in the current operation of the target programs.

THE EVALUATION RESEARCH PROCESS

As indicated previously, a crucial feature of the planning and conduct of evaluation research is the sociopolitical process in which the researcher and the relevant program participants (clients, practitioners, and administrators) develop the focus of the evaluative task, engage in working through the design, specify the procedures for implementing the research, cooperate in the research undertaking, and consider the implications of the research findings for program planning. There are numerous reasons for engaging in such a collaborative process. Through this involvement, the researcher can become more familiar with the organizational context within which the program operates, the explicit purposes of the research, the goals which the service presumably attempts to accomplish, and the attributes of the program being evaluated. As a consequence there is a greater likelihood that the evaluation will deal with the concerns considered most important by those intimately involved with the program as opposed, for example, to those which are of interest only to the researcher. Involvement in this process is also likely to increase the probability of obtaining the cooperation of practitioners who are often anxious about having their work evaluated. Finally, the likelihood of implementing changes suggested by the study is increased when program personnel have been involved in the entire planning process.

The formal collaboration of program administrators and staff with the evaluation team should focus initially on completing what Wholey (1977) and his colleagues have called an "evaluability assessment." The aim of such an assessment is to help clarify the decision-making system to be served by the evaluation and the questions to be answered. A number of sequential tasks are involved. First, identifying the primary intended users of the evaluation and determining from their perspective what activities and objectives go to make up the program under study. A second task then becomes the collection of information on the program activities, goals, objectives, and underlying causal assumptions. Such information can usually be found in program documents or obtained by interviewing program staff. A third task is to synthesize the information that has been collected in a "rhetorical program model." This is a flow model or series of models that depict the program resource inputs, intended program activities, intended impacts, as well as the assumed causal links between the program inputs and the expected impacts. A fourth task is determining the extent to which such a program model is sufficiently clear so that evaluation is likely to be both feasible and potentially useful to the intended users. Two criteria are applied in arriving at such judgments: (1) The extent to which the intended users of the evaluation agree on a set of measures for program activities and program objectives and, (2) the extent to which the intended users of the evaluation agree on a set of plausible, testable assumptions that link program activities to program outcomes and impacts. An "evaluable program model" is the expected product of this task and will include only those program activities and objectives for which there exist agreed-upon measures of success and testable causal relationships. The fifth and final step in the evaluability assessment then involves presenting the results of the analysis to the program managers and intended users and reaching agreement on an evaluation plan.

The sociopolitical context in which the evaluation task is formulated and conducted having been mentioned, and the importance of assessing the evaluability of the program having been underscored, it is now possible to identify the various stages of the evaluation process. (1) The purposes or motives for undertaking the evaluation research must be made explicit. (2) The program must be clearly defined. (3) Program goals need to be stated in clear and relatively simple language which is free of jargon and ambiguous terminology. (4) Measures must be developed which can provide information on the relative progress that the program has made toward the attainment of the stated goals. (5) A research design must be developed which incorporates the purpose of the investigation as well as peculiarities of the program and its goals. (6) The implementation of the research requires continuous monitoring to facilitate reliable data collection as well as to determine whether the program is actually carried out in accordance with the originally agreed-upon procedures. (7) The findings are interpreted and the implications of the results for program changes and policy formulations are drawn.

It should not be assumed that an evaluation effort entails a linear progression from one discrete research stage to the next. Rather, the identified stage should most accurately be seen as dynamically interrelated. The resolution of critical issues at any one stage will often have implications for others. For example, an original purpose of conducting evaluative research may have been a desire to test program effects. This purpose is likely to be modified if there is no clearly defined program with specific goals to be evaluated. The revised purpose may then be one of conducting research aimed at "discovering" the specific nature of the program and eliciting the relevant goals. In turn, this revised purpose will have direct implications for the research design since the focus is on exploration and discovery as opposed to verification.

Unlike research conducted in laboratories, the stages of evaluation research are usually exposed to a variety of constraints in the "real world" and, as a consequence, are subject to a number of contaminating and confounding factors. These factors pose major problems to the evaluation effort. Such annoying realities dictate that the planning and conduct of evaluation research as well as the implementation of the research findings be viewed as a sociopolitical process involving the joint efforts of the researcher, administrator, and practitioners.

Aside from their service orientation

which usually involves relatively little appreciation of the benefits and requirements of research, practitioners are generally anxious about having their practice scrutinized under the microscope of the researcher because of the possibility of having practice weaknesses revealed. In addition to fears about pointing out the shortcomings of their program, agency administrators are naturally concerned about the extent to which the introduction of research procedures will disrupt the provision of service to clients. The researcher, on the other hand, is mainly concerned with applying rigorous research procedures to the agency setting in spite of administrative or programmatic constraints. By being sensitive to these differing orientations and commitments to the human service program, the program evaluator can anticipate potential conflicts which often emerge in evaluative research and, hopefully, deal with the conflicts to the benefit of the evaluation and program tasks. Consequently, there is a great need in the field of evaluation research to explicate such research/program conflicts and work toward providing alternative and mutually satisfying resolutions. This kind of perspective on the part of both the researcher and agency representatives can help develop potentially fruitful negotiations to the mutual benefit of the research and, ultimately, the program.

Purpose. Evaluation research efforts are generally justified on the basis that they contribute to the assessment and modification of human service programs through a rigorous investigation of the relationship of particular interventions to the outcomes produced. Viewed in this light, evaluation research is a feedback mechanism providing the necessary information for adapting programs to more effectively meet client needs. For the funding organization, evaluation research can provide the necessary justification to ter-

minate, continue, or expand human service programs. In addition to these explicit or overt rationales for conducting evaluation research, there may be latent or covert reasons for conducting such studies which may be at variance with the explicit or overt purpose (that is, better understanding the nature of human service programs and the assessment of their impact). Suchman (1972) has termed studies guided by such covert purposes as "pseudo-evaluations." Included in this list of such misuses of evaluation are (1) *eye-wash*—a deliberate focus on the surface appearance of a program to make it look good, (2) *white-wash*—an attempt to cover up program failures during the investigation, (3) *submarine*—the political use of research to destroy a program, (4) *posture*—evaluation research as a ritual that has little substance, and (5) *postponement*—using evaluation to postpone needed action.

For the specification and clarification of research purposes, it is necessary to clearly identify the type of information which the research is expected to produce. This entails a process involving the researcher and the program representatives jointly clarifying the explicit purposes of the evaluation prior to the formal initiation of the project.

Three major purposes of an evaluative project can be identified—assessing program effort (inputs), program effects (outcomes), and program efficiency (economy). The evaluation of program effort is typically geared toward an assessment of the amount and kind of inputs used in pursuing program goals. These inputs may take the form of money, equipment, personnel, work activities, and so on. In the human services, program inputs typically constitute the experimental or treatment variable. That is, assessments of program effort involve descriptive accounts of the program "means" assumed to be causally linked to the program "ends" or goals. However, the mere assessment of program effort does not provide a test of such an assumption. While a necessary condition, effort is not in itself sufficient for the achievement of program goals. Suchman (1967), for example, has compared studies of effort to assessments of the number of times a bird flaps its wings without any attempt being made to determine the distance flown.

Evaluations of effort in human service programs are common. Most agencies are expected to provide yearly reports on the number of clients served by the program, the number of client contact hours, number of staff, and the allocation of staff to various duties. These "service bookkeeping" reports are roughly analogous to stockholder reports with the major difference that statements of profit and loss— the effects of the effort—are excluded.

Two assumptions about the program effort are crucial. First, it is assumed that there is a logical and empirical relationship between the goals which have been specified for the program and the procedures to be used in their achievement. Second, it is usually assumed that the program is implemented in the originally specified manner. Both assumptions point to the need for outcome studies to provide descriptive accounts of the effort expended. In short, evaluations designed to measure the effects of programs should also include a relatively clear specification of the amount and type of effort expended toward the accomplishment of the desired outcomes.

The evaluation of program effects or outcomes has to do with the extent to which the program achieves its stated goals. Questions of effect deal with the ends or goals of the program and in this way provide a yardstick to be used in assessing the central concern of an evaluation project: Does the program accomplish what it is designed to do? To use Suchman's analogy (1967) again, the assessment of program effectiveness attempts to

determine how far the bird has flown and only secondarily, as in the case of effort studies, how many times it flapped its wings.

Efficiency in achieving specified program goals is another explicit purpose for conducting evaluative studies. Essentially, this means testing the relationship between the amount and type of effort expended and the effects accomplished. In other words, efficiency is a function of the relationship of inputs to outcomes. In assessing program efficiency, one is concerned with obtaining information on the extent to which alternative and less costly means could have been used to achieve comparable results.

All too often people involved in human service practice react to questions of program efficiency as somehow below their professional dignity. This reaction seems to be based on the assumption that where humans are involved in receiving service, questions relating to the efficiency of these services are callous or are irrelevant to professional practice. However, the concern with efficiency merely acknowledges an obligation to provide such services in the least costly form compatible with considerations of the dignity and respect which is due to program recipients.

Each of these three explicit purposes of evaluation research warrants serious consideration. Ideally, provision should be made in the research design to collect information pertinent to each purpose. The extent to which it is possible to include measures for each of these purposes, however, is related to the nature of the program being evaluated (that is, its stage of development, the specificity of the program and its goals, and so on) and the reasons established for undertaking the research.

Articulation of the program's components. As noted earlier in the discussion of the evaluability assessment, prior to the implementation of an evaluative study, a program's components must be identified, conceptualized, and standardized. This should result in a clear explication of the "experimental" or independent variable. Rather than referring to programs by such a vague term as *counseling* it becomes necessary to clearly conceptualize and operationalize this term into such varied activities as budgeting, job finding and placement, and particular types of treatment procedures. Unless program components are clearly specified, questions regarding which particular program ingredients have a major effect on the accomplishment of specific as well as on overall goals cannot be adequately answered.

The specification and measurement of the impact of a program's components are important since experts in the field of evaluative research generally agree that the evaluation of entire programs is often beyond the capabilities of existing methodology (Suchman, 1967; Wholey, Scanlon, Duffy, Fukumoto, & Vogt, 1971). Since evaluations of total programs are so complex and have such limited generalizability, a more common strategy is variable testing—singling out specific components of the program and testing their effectiveness in meeting limited goals. Despite the obstacles involved in conducting global program evaluations, they are commonly undertaken because such information is used as a basis for decision-making about continuation, expansion, or termination of programs. On the other hand, variable testing is commonly viewed as a means of improving specific interventions without, in the process, posing a threat to the entire program.

Specification of goals. Since evaluation research attempts to determine the manner and extent to which a program achieves particular effects, a basic precondition of conducting such research is the clear articulation of program goals. In many respects, clearly stating the goals of human service programs is one of the most difficult and vexing problems of the evaluative process. A major reason for this is that programs commonly set lofty and vague goals. Such goal statements as "the improvement of social functioning," "increasing mental health," "prevention of criminality," and "strengthening family ties" are so vague as to make it difficult, if not impossible, to develop empirical referents or measures.

The formulation of operationalized program goals requires a joint effort between agency personnel and the researcher (Mager, 1972). In this collaboration both the agency representatives and the researcher can make major contributions by bringing their respective expertise to the process. The agency representatives should have a clearer understanding of what the program entails in its day-to-day work and what they consider program priorities, particularly as these relate to possible indicators of "success" or "failure." On the other hand, the researcher—especially in the case of an external evaluator—presumably brings a more objective perception to the program and should therefore be able to view it in a relatively detached manner which can be of assistance to program personnel in ferreting out and articulating simply stated and relevant goals.

Besides helping to facilitate the articulation of specific and discrete program goals, the researcher must constantly emphasize the necessity of formulating goals which have direct relevance to the program being evaluated. Goals stated in specific and practical terms are useless as focal points for evaluating a program unless they clearly relate to the program services being provided. Otherwise, program failure can be attributed to the existence of irrelevant goals and not to the weakness of the program itself.

A problem to bear in mind constantly

in the goal specification stage is the possible existence of conflicting goals. When viewed independently, each goal statement may appear to be appropriate, but when goals are appraised in conjunction with each other, potential conflicts may then become apparent. An example of conflicting program goals would be the case of increasing the number of police walking beats in a part of a city and, along with this, the goal of reducing "juvenile delinquency" as measured by police apprehensions. The very fact of increasing the number of police walking beats within the area may well have the effect of increasing the number of young people apprehended and brought to court.

Deciding whose goals should be used as the basis for evaluation is another thorny problem. The program may not be pursuing the goals which have been listed in organizational manuals or conveyed to the general public. On the other hand, a potential danger of having the researcher identify goals for the program is that program personnel can disclaim such goals as their priorities in the provision of services. A similar danger exists if the funding organization specifies the goals of the program to be evaluated. The funding body should, however, examine the goals which program personnel have identified and make decisions regarding the allocation of funds on that basis. This provides further justification for relying on a joint process in which researcher and program personnel articulate relevant goals.

A further task of the goal specification stage is the careful consideration of goal levels. For most human service programs a number of different goal levels can be specified—from the most ideal or ultimate level down through the intermediate level to more immediate and practical goals. An assumption is made that there is a logical connection between the most immediate through the ultimate goals. That is, the achievement of the immediate goals should have relevance for goal achievement at more remote levels.

In evaluation research, theory should be an important consideration in goal-setting and particularly in terms of the generalizability of results, the replication of the test in different situations and in suggesting further related studies. Goals can be specified on the basis of some *a priori* theoretical rationale underpinning the program. Conversely, it is possible to proceed in reverse order and generate theoretical propositions from the test of efforts in accomplishing program goals (Glaser & Strauss, 1967).

Specification of measures. Once the human services program and its goals are identified, a major task is the development of measures or indicators which provide a basis for determining whether or not the services were successfully implemented and whether or not they succeeded in achieving the stated goals. A number of considerations are crucial at this stage. First, in addition to developing measures on the overall goals of the program (for example, reducing poverty), there is also the need to specify measures aimed at the outcome of discrete program goals (for example, increased employment, improved education and health, and so on). Measures for the program's components (that is, its methods and procedures) must also be developed. In evaluating group treatment, for example, it would be possible to develop measures which would yield data on the frequency of meetings, attendance at meetings, the focus of group sessions, the nature of the members' participation, the particular approaches used by the group leader, and the quality of the worker's intervention.

A second consideration is the criteria used to reflect the accomplishment of program goals. On this question the use of "soft" versus "hard" data is relevant and basic to the question of the reliability and validity of the measures used. Such tangible measures as age, sex, time, grades in school, as well as relatively objective data on standardized personality and attitudinal tests can be assumed to have a known degree of reliability and validity. There are also relatively "soft" criteria which are commonly used in less rigorous evaluation studies—personal opinions, subjective estimates, ratings obtained from participant observations, case illustrations, and so on. While these types of information can be used to reflect the flavor of a program and to document typical or extreme situations which may occur in the life of a program, their use as indicators of program success are limited. Such measures are commonly biased both by the interests of the evaluator as well as by the unrepresentative character of the events or cases to which the evaluation is applied.

A third major issue centers on data collection procedures. Evaluation research studies vary in the extent to which practitioners are relied upon for the accumulation of data. Although relying on information collected by practitioners may be less expensive and threatening to these workers, the possibility of bias is great.

Developing the design.   The design for evaluative studies must take into consideration the purpose of the investigation as well as the nature and goals of the program to be evaluated. Once these considerations have been taken into account in developing an "ideal" design, modifications are often called for because of ethical issues and a host of administrative and political constraints pertinent to the implementation of the design.

In those situations where it is both administratively feasible and relevant to the type of information desired, the model of a controlled experiment represents the ideal design for evaluative studies. It is depicted in the accompanying diagram (Stouffer, 1950).

	Before	After	After—before
Experimental group	X_1	X_2	$d = X_2 - X_1$
Control group	X'_1	X'_2	$d' = X'_2 - X'_1$

To implement this design, two equivalent groups are developed. Equivalence is best obtained through random assignment to experimental and control groups. The "before" measure provides the base line from which change is determined. The experimental group is exposed to the program being evaluated while the control group is not. At a determined follow-up period, "after" measures are made. By comparing the "before" measures with the "after" measures, it is possible to indicate the changes logically assumed to have been produced by the experimental program.

This controlled experimental design can provide information on (1) effectiveness—by comparing the difference in outcome between the experimental and control groups; (2) the nature of the program—by monitoring the program and documenting how it is actually implemented in practice, particularly in regard to desired outcomes; and (3) efficiency—by purposefully manipulating program components to determine comparative expenditures in time, staff, money, and other resources.

Although the experimental design can yield various types of fruitful information, it is extremely demanding in regard to the preconditions which must be met for its proper implementation. The use of this design assumes that the experimental variable (that is, the program or treatment) is clearly articulated and operationalized, stable over time, accessible to manipulation, and amenable to being monitored. It also assumes the existence of clearly defined goals and/or effects with a rationale linking the program to the goals and/or effects. These preconditions should be met through program planning and management and involve a collaborative effort between researchers and program staff. Unless these preconditions have been met, the evaluation of program effectiveness and efficiency is not warranted.

Even if the purpose of the investigation and the preconditions for conducting an experimental design exist, there are formidable obstacles in implementing such an approach for the evaluation of human service programs. Ethical arguments concerning the denial of service have been advanced in opposition to the development of experimental and control groups. Such arguments assume that the service being evaluated is highly beneficial to potential clients and that to deny it to some people would be cruel. However, considering the evidence on the outcomes of human service programs, this argument is not terribly convincing. Rigorously conducted evaluation studies have revealed that many programs do not produce major changes. In this light, there would seem to be some merit in denying or delaying the provision to some people of a service which is of questionable value in order to ultimately improve the program. This issue can also be dealt with in another manner. Rather than to deny service entirely, the experimental program can be compared with an alternative approach administered to a control group.

In addition to difficulties posed by ethical arguments, administrative contraints may prevent the establishment of control groups, by the use of random assignment procedures. Such constraints include geographical considerations, the nature of the service, or the characteristics of the client. Instituting random assignment procedures often necessitates major changes in the delegation of cases to practitioners. Such changes can create havoc in implementing the program (for example, by having probation officers cover a very wide geographical area). Alternative methods of developing control groups are available. The most common alternative is to establish a control group through matching procedures as this involves the selection of cases which are comparable on variables which seem to have some relationship to the outcome.

Monitoring the program and the research. Once the research design has been developed and plans for implementing the research as part of the everyday routine of the agency have been arranged, the task of monitoring the project becomes a primary concern. It is not sufficient to initiate a research project and assume that the agreed upon program procedures and data collection arrangements will be closely followed throughout the life of the project. Rather, carefully conducted evaluation research demands that close attention be devoted to determining the extent to which the program as well as the research procedures are in fact carried out in accordance with the originally stated plans.

A major reason for monitoring the evaluation project is the common conflict which often develops between the service goals of the program, which requires relative freedom to operate, and the demands of research for control. The crucial question here is whether research can be done in settings where a prime concern is the care and treatment of people and where the control of all factors influencing the results may be impractical. In a controlled experimental design, for example, it is usually necessary for the researcher to act like a snarling watch-dog ready to oppose any alteration in program and procedure for fear that it might contaminate the agreed upon procedures and render the evaluation useless. On the other hand, some writers view the relationship between research and program development as dynamic and reciprocal (Suchman, 1967). In this view, feeding back information from the evaluation to the program in order to affect both the objectives and procedures is held to be paramount. The extent to which there are controls on the program's operation and feedback of research findings are largely dependent on the purpose of the evaluative study. If information is needed on the ultimate worth of program ideas as a basis for continuation or termination of a particular program, then a controlled situation would be insisted upon. And there would only be deliberate manipulation of program variables which have been predetermined for their contribution to the overall experiment. On the other hand, if evaluative research is viewed primarily as an ongoing means for modifying programs, then feedback of information can be provided to change the program.

Utilization of findings. The ultimate payoff of conducting evaluation research is the extent to which the research findings are incorporated into program policies and procedures for the more effective and efficient delivery of services. The degree to which such an aim is accomplished will be largely a function of the extent to which relevant program staff are aware of, involved in, and committed to the research. This leads to the major thesis: Evaluation research should be viewed as a sociopolitical process which involves applying research methods to an organizational context. It requires a partnership between research specialists and those directly involved in the delivery of program services.

Such a partnership should, ideally, be initiated and formalized during the initial planning and negotiating stages and maintained through the conduct of the research to the assessment of the information obtained and the discussion of the implications of the findings for needed modifications in the program. This is not meant to underemphasize the policital and social factors extraneous to the research which will exert a major influence on the manner and the extent to which the findings will be used. Nevertheless, a high degree of involvement by the administrative decision-makers in the evaluation process should at least minimally help to ensure the relevance and use of the information obtained for the central issues confronting the organization.

CONCLUSION

This paper has identified and discussed the major components of the evaluation research process. Particular emphasis has been placed on the linkages between each of the stages in the research and the sociopolitical aspects of planning and conducting evaluation research of human service programs. The manner and extent to which relevant parties—practitioners, administrators, and representatives of funding organizations—are actively involved in the research process will, in large part, determine the quality of the information obtained as well as its relevance and utility for improving the human services.

References

Bailey, Walter C.   Correctional outcome: An evaluation of 100 reports. *Journal of Criminal Law, Criminology and Police Science,* June 1966, *57,* 153–160.

Eysenck, Hans.   The effects of psychotherapy. In Hans Eyseneck (Ed.), *Handbook of abnormal psychology.* New York: Basic Books, 1961.

Fisher, Joel. "Is casework effective? A review. *Social Work,* January 1973, *18,* 5–20.

Glaser, Barney A., & Strauss, Anselm L. *The discovery of grounded theory: Strategies for qualitative research.* Hawthorne, N.Y.: Aldine Publishing, 1967.

Kiresuk, Thomas J., & Garwick, Geoffrey. Basic goal attainment scaling procedures. In *Project evaluation report, 1969–1973,* ch. 1, of the Program Evaluation Project. Minneapolis, 1974.

Kiresuk, Thomas J., & Sherman, Robert E. Goal Attainment Scaling: A general method for evaluating comprehensive community mental health programs. *Community Mental Health Journal,* 1968, *4,* 443–453.

Mager, Robert F. *Goal analysis.* Belmont, Calif.: Fearon, 1972.

Robison, James, & Smith, Gerald. The effectiveness of correctional programs. *Crime and Delinquency,* January 1971, *17,* 67–80.

Stouffer, Samuel A. Some observations on study design. *American Journal of Sociology,* January 1950, 356–359.

Suchman, Edward A. *Evaluative research.* New York: Russell Sage Foundation, 1967.

Suchman, Edward A. Action for what? A critique of evaluative research. In Carole H. Weiss (Ed.), *Evaluating action programs.* Boston: Allyn & Bacon, 1972.

Wholey, Joseph S. Evaluability assessment. In L. Rutman (Ed.) *Evaluation research methods: A basic guide.* Beverly Hills, Calif.: Sage Publications, 1977.

Wholey, Joseph S., Scanlon, John W., Duffy, Hugh G., Fukumoto, James S., & Vogt, Leona M. *Federal evaluation policy: Analyzing the effects of public programs.* Washington, D.C.: Urban Institute, 1971.

Chapter 16

Conclusions

Through these chapters and the selection of readings, we have attempted to share our perspective on social work practice. That perspective can be developed and adapted by you regardless of the setting or relational system in which you choose to practice. In this brief conclusion we reemphasize three recurring themes of the book. These themes are central to this model of practice.

SOCIAL WORK AS A PROBLEM-SOLVING PROCESS

The focus of social work practice is on the relationship between individuals and their environment. A social worker's activities are directed first toward defining and then toward resolving problems that develop in this interaction. We emphasize a distinction between the processes of problem definition and intervention with the latter occurring on the basis of a client-worker contract which specifies the problem-for-work. This formulation does not specify or limit the social problems which may be subject to social work attention. The problem may be within the individual or the environment, or, as is frequently the case, it may stem from the nature of the person-situation interaction. Also inherent in the problem-solving theme is the notion that the problem has been felt or experienced by some person or group who wish to have it resolved. The experiencing of stress from a problem (either internal or external to the individual) provides the impetus or motivation for the client to become involved with the social worker in a problem-solving endeavor.

SOCIAL WORK AS A CLIENT-WORKER RELATIONSHIP

All aspects of problem solving are undertaken by the worker and client in partnership developed within and affected by the emotional climate of the relationship. The partnership nature of the process extends to decision making as to the nature of the problem and the desired objectives as well as the actual change efforts. This partnership aspect of the work permits operationalization of the concepts of individualization and client self-determination but also demands accurate understanding of the irrational elements of the feeling developed on part of both worker and client. The worker is not perceived as an expert in what is best for the client but rather as an expert in facilitating a problem-solving process and in mobilizing resources to assist this process. Partnership implies joint input from worker and client—joint decision making and joint intervention. Participation on the part of the worker is as essential as participation on the part of the client.

SOCIAL WORK AS A RATIONAL PROCESS

Problem solving is a rational process in which worker and client jointly define the problem, specify objectives, and work toward the accomplishment of the objectives. Evaluation is the component of this process that provides feedback loops enabling the client-worker partnership to redefine the problem, goals, or intervention plan. The evaluation feedback loops provide a dynamic, systemic quality to the process. The worker, throughout the process, has the responsibility of maintaining a rational stance toward problem solving involving explicit problem definition, specific goals, and a rational plan to accomplish the goals. While all of these components may be changed on the basis of experience and evaluation, whenever activity is being undertaken with a client, the worker is responsible for the clarity of the joint agreement concerning specific problems, goals, and means.

THE BEGINNING

Through this book we have set forth principles in the areas of problem solving, partnership, and rational process which may serve as useful guides to you. These principles, however, will be applied in unique, ever-changing client situations. Their application requires the exercise of professional judgment. Such judgment involves the ability to make decisions and engage in actions guided by a set of principles. It is developed from continuous experience and learning.

We hope that your beginning practice will be more exciting, less frustrating, and more positive than the experiences of this worker, who, after two social work jobs, decided to seek other employment:

> I asked when she first became interested in social work. She said that in her senior year in college she decided she would like to be a social worker. She felt she wanted to go into social work so she could help people help themselves and that helping people was her main reason for wanting to be a social worker.
>
> I asked whether she had expectations about the duties of the social worker. She said that she felt she could remake people's lives. I asked her to elaborate a little more on this and she said that she felt she could help people adjust to their problems in order to have healthy personalities. I asked her what she found when she started work, and she said that when she got her position she found she couldn't remake people's lives because she had a lot of paperwork and reports dealing with her clients. She said she could not change people's patterns of behavior as easily as she thought she could. These behavior patterns are so incorporated into their lives that it is difficult to change their set behaviors. She didn't have enough time to do all that she wanted to help the clients and had to limit her time so that she could interview all her clients, which was a difficult job. Usually AFDC mothers

were especially hard to interview because they would change residence about four times a year. She said that only later at the private agency (her second job) was she able to give more time to her clients.

I asked her what kind of people she dealt with at the private agency. She said she took care of adoptions and unwed mothers and that she really liked it better than the public welfare because she had more time with her clients. But she said that this was where she realized something would have to change. I asked her to elaborate, and she said that many times she just didn't have answers for all the problems of her clients. When a client was really open with her, she felt that many times she didn't know quite how to handle the situation. She said she could not go running to a supervisor in the middle of an interview asking what to do now. She said that these certain moments could not be recaptured at any time. She decided that she needed more education, but she didn't know whether she wanted to take two more years of school.

This worker had little concept of partnership and perceived herself as being responsible for finding the solution to the client's problems (remaking their lives) and for being the sole change agent. Perceiving herself as the sole expert, she became anxious when she did not have immediate answers to client's questions. While it is probably fortunate that this particular person chose to leave social work, we may at times experience similar dilemmas.

As our experience and professional maturity increases, we will find less need to define ourselves as the expert holder-of-solutions-to-the-client-problems and will be increasingly able to acknowledge gaps in knowledge (knowledge on the part of both client and worker) and to engage the client in a joint quest for the necessary information. No worker is expected to know everything; disillusionment and disaster await those who think they do. What is required is the ability to involve clients, professional colleagues, supervisors and others in comfortably and jointly seeking out the information required for rational problem solving.

If you are seriously pursuing social work, you are about to embark on a journey requiring outstanding self-discipline. Earlier we used the analogy of the figure skater and noted that the truly creative use of self in a spontaneous way occurs only after hours and hours of discipline and practice. The ability to engage spontaneously and comfortably in a partnership for problem solving with clients does not come naturally, but it develops with self-discipline, with learning, with experience, and with practice. We have found the challenge exciting and rewarding and we hope that you will enter the profession with both a sureness of what you are doing and a tentativeness which permits change as new information comes to light.

In the final reprinted article, Jay Haley offers some serious advice on how to be a failure. We hope you find the ideas useful and will avoid the pitfalls he identifies.

Reading 16–1

*The Art of Being a Failure as a Therapist**

Jay Haley

What has been lacking in the field of therapy is a theory of failure. Many clinicians have merely assumed that any psychotherapist could fail if he wished. Recent studies of the outcome of therapy, however, indicate that spontaneous improvement of patients is far more extensive than was previously realized. There is a consistent finding that between 50 and 70 percent of patients on waiting list control groups not only do not wish treatment after the waiting list period but have really recovered from their emotional problems—despite the previous theories which did not consider this possible. Assuming that these findings hold up in further studies, a therapist who is incompetent and does no more than sit in silence and scratch himself will have at least a 50 percent success rate with his patients. How then can a therapist be a failure?

The problem is not a hopeless one. We might merely accept the fact that a therapist will succeed with half his patients and do what we can to provide a theory which will help him fail consistently with the other half. However, we could also risk being more adventurous. Trends in the field suggest the problem can be approached in a deeper way by devising procedures for keeping those patients from improving who would ordinarily spontaneously do so. Obviously, merely doing nothing will not achieve this end. We must create a program with the proper ideological framework and provide systematic

training over a period of years if we expect a therapist to fail consistently.

An outline will be offered here of a series of steps to increase the chance of failure of any therapist. This presentation is not meant to be comprehensive, but it includes the major factors which experience in the field has shown to be essential and which can be put into practice even by therapists who are not specially talented.

1. The central pathway to failure is based upon a nucleus of ideas which, if used in combination, make success as a failure almost inevitable.

Step A: Insist that the problem which brings the patient into therapy is not important. Dismiss it as merely a "symptom" and shift the conversation elsewhere. In this way a therapist never learns to examine what is really distressing a patient.

Step B: Refuse to directly treat the presenting problem. Offer some rationale, such as the idea that symptoms have "roots," to avoid treating the problem the patient is paying his money to recover from. In this way the odds increase that the patient will not recover, and future generations of therapists can remain ignorant of the specific skills needed to get people over their problems.

Step C: Insist that if a presenting problem is relieved, something worse will develop. This myth makes it proper not to know what to do about symptoms and will even encourage patients to cooperate by developing a fear of recovery.

Given these three steps, it seems obvious that any psychotherapist will be incapacitated, whatever his natural talent. He will not take seriously the problem the patient brings, he will not try to change that, and he will fear that successful relief of the problem is disastrous.

One might think that this nucleus of ideas alone would make any therapist a failure, but the wiser heads in the field have recognized that other steps are necessary.

2. It is particularly important to confuse diagnosis and therapy. A therapist can sound expert and be scientific without ever risking a success with treatment if he uses a diagnostic language which makes it impossible for him to think of therapeutic operations. For example, one can say that a patient is passive-aggressive, or that he has deep-seated dependency needs, or that he has a weak ego, or that he is impulse-ridden. No therapeutic interventions can be formulated with this kind of language. For more examples of how to phrase a diagnosis so that a therapist is incapacitated, the reader is referred to *The American Psychiatric Association Diagnostic Manual*.

3. Put the emphasis upon a single method of treatment no matter how diverse the problems which enter the office. Patients who won't behave properly according to the method should be defined as untreatable and abandoned. Once a single method has proven consistently ineffective, it should never be given up. Those people who attempt variations must be sharply condemned as improperly trained and ignorant of the true nature of the human personality and its disorders. If necessary, a person who attempts variations can be called a latent layman.

4. Have no theory, or an ambiguous and untestable one, of what a therapist should do to bring about therapeutic change. However, make it clear that it is untherapeutic to give a patient directives for changing—he might follow them and change. Just imply that change happens spontaneously when therapists and patients behave according to the proper forms. As part of the general confusion

that is necessary, it is helpful to define therapy as a procedure for finding out what is wrong with a person and how he got that way. With that emphasis, ideas about what to do to bring about change will not develop in an unpredictable manner. One should also insist that change be defined as a shift of something in the interior of a patient so that it remains outside the range of observation and is uninvestigable. With the focus upon the "underlying disorder" (which should be sharply distinguished from the "overlying disorder"), questions about the unsavory aspects of the relationship between therapist and patient need not arise, nor is it necessary to include unimportant people, such as the patient's intimates, in the question of change.

Should student therapists who are not yet properly trained insist upon some instruction about how to cause change, and if a frown about their unresolved problems does not quiet them, it might be necessary to offer some sort of ambiguous and general idea which is untestable. One can say, for example, that the therapeutic job is to bring the unconscious into consciousness. In this way the therapy task is defined as transforming a hypothetical entity into another hypothetical entity and so there is no possibility that precision in the therapeutic technique might develop. Part of this approach requires helping the patient "see" things about himself, particularly in relation to past traumas, and this involves no risk of change. The fundamental aim is to emphasize "insight" and "affect expression" to student therapists as causes of change so they can feel something is happening in the session without hazarding success. If some of the advanced students insist on more high-class technical knowledge about therapy, a cloudy discussion of "working through the transference" is useful. This not only provides young therapists with an intellectual catharsis but it gives them a chance to make transference interpretations and so have something to do.

5. Insist that only years of therapy will really change a patient.

This step brings us to more specific things to do about those patients who might spontaneously recover without treatment. If they can be persuaded that they have not really recovered but have merely fled into health, it is possible to help them back to ill health by holding them in long-term treatment. (One can always claim that only long-term treatment can really cure a patient so that he will never ever have a problem the remainder of his life.) Fortunately the field of therapy has no theory of overdosage, and so a skillful therapist can keep a patient from improving for as long as ten years without protest from his colleagues, no matter how jealous. Those therapists who try for twenty years should be congratulated on their courage but thought of as foolhardy unless they live in New York.

6. As a further step to restrain patients who might spontaneously improve, it is important to offer warnings about the fragile nature of people and insist they might suffer psychotic breaks or turn to drink if they improve. When "underlying pathology" becomes the most common term in every clinic and consulting room, everyone will avoid taking action to help patients recover and patients will even restrain themselves if they begin to make it on their own. Long-term treatment can then crystallize them into therapeutic failures. If patients seem to improve even in long-term therapy, they can be distracted by being put into group therapy.

7. As a further step to restrain patients who might spontaneously improve, the therapist should focus upon the patient's past.

8. As yet another step with that aim, the therapist should interpret what is most unsavory about the patient to arouse his guilt so that he will remain in treatment to resolve the guilt.

9. Perhaps the most important rule is to ignore the real world that patients live in and publicize the vital importance of their infancy, inner dynamics, and fantasy life. This will effectively prevent either therapists or patients from attempting to make changes in their families, friends, schools, neighborhoods, or treatment milieus. Naturally they cannot recover if their situation does not change, and so one guarantees failure while being paid to listen to interesting fantasies. Talking about dreams is a good way to pass the time, and so is experimenting with responses to different kinds of pills.

10. Avoid the poor because they will insist upon results and cannot be distracted with insightful conversations. Also avoid the schizophrenic unless he is well drugged and securely locked up in a psychiatric penitentiary. If a therapist deals with a schizophrenic at the interface of family and society, both therapist and patient risk recovery.

11. A continuing refusal to define the goals of therapy is essential. If a therapist sets goals, someone is likely to raise a question whether they have been achieved. At that point the idea of evaluating results arises in its most virulent form. If it becomes necessary to define a goal, the phrasing should be unclear, ambiguous, and so esoteric that anyone who thinks about determining if the goal has been achieved will lose heart and turn to a less confused field of endeavor, like existentialism.

12. Finally, it cannot be emphasized enough that it is absolutely necessary to avoid evaluating the results of therapy. If outcome is examined, there is a natural tendency for people not fully trained to discard approaches which are not effective and to elaborate those which are. Only by keeping results a mystery and

avoiding any systematic followup of patients can one ensure that therapeutic technique will not improve and the writings of the past will not be questioned. To be human is to err, and inevitably a few deviant individuals in the profession will attempt evaluation studies. They should be promptly condemned and their character questioned. Such people should be called superficial in their understanding of what therapy really is, oversimple in their emphasis upon symptoms rather than depth personality problems, and artificial in their approach to human life. Routinely they should be eliminated from respectable institutions and cut off from research funds. As a last resort they can be put in psychoanalytic treatment or shot.

This program of twelve steps to failure—sometimes called the daily dozen of the clinical field—is obviously not beyond the skill of the average well-trained psychotherapist. Nor would putting this program more fully into action require any major changes in the clinical ideology or practice taught in our better universities. The program would be helped if there was a positive term to describe it, and the word "dynamic" is recommended because it has a swinging sound which should appeal to the younger generation. The program could be called the therapy which expresses the basic principles of dynamic psychiatry, dynamic psychology, and dynamic social work. On the wall of every institute training therapists there can be a motto known as *The Five B's Which Guarantee Dynamic Failure:*

Be Passive

Be Inactive

Be Reflective

Be Silent

Beware

Index

A

Acceptance, 232–39
Action, 468, 473
  artificial activities, 487
  conditions for effective use, 489
  differential use, 487
  natural activities, 487
  positive purposes, 486
  rationale for use of, 488
Active supplying of resources, 472
Activist role, 459
Adaptation, 109
Advice giving, 78
Advice and guidance, 483
Advocacy, 544–46
  in collaborative groups, 546–48
  in community organization, 458–59
Advocate, role of, 433
Agency policy, worker's relation to, 189–91
Agency structure, 187
Aguilar, Ignacio, 288, 292
Aguilera, Donna C., 55
Akers, Ronald L., 100
Alberti, Robert E., 55
Alexander, Ernestina, 234, 399
Alexander, Franz, 488
Allport, Gordon W., 112, 292
Ambivalence, 507
American Association of Social Workers, 39

Anthony, William A., 296–97
Antonovsky, Aaron, 139
Articulation, problems of, 292
Assessment, 396–98
  process of, 398
  summary of activity, 373
Attachment, differential patterns of, 562
Auerswald, Edgar H., 158, 331
Austin, George, 375
Authentic presentation, 506
Authority, legal use of, 80–82
  and power, 239–40
Averchenko, A., 302
Awareness of own behavior, 466–67
Awareness of other's behavior, 469

B

Baer, Betty L., 39–40
Bailey, Betty Jo, 456
Bailey, Walter C., 580
Balint, Michael, 342
Bandler, Bernard, 480
Barber, Bernard, 97
Barghi, John H., 337
Barriers, attitudes as, 293
Bartlett, Harriett M., 5, 35, 397
Basave-Fernandez, Agustin, 329
Bask, Charles L., 337
Bateson, Gregory, 273
Beall, Lignette, 417
Beck, Aaron T., 52, 55
Beck, Bertram, 412

Behavior, adult anger with, 257
Behavior patterns, variety of, 146–47
Bell, N., 28
Benavides, Eustolio, 260
Benfield, Edward, 328
Bennis, Warren, 24, 199
Berelson, Bernard, 99
Berkowitz, Sidney, 38
Berger, P., 149
Bertcher, Harvey J., 298, 299, 301
Bettelheim, Bruno, 489
Bibring, E., 52
Biddle, Bruce, 128, 428
Biddle, William W., 428
Biestek, Felix, 220
Bischoff, Herbert G. W., 504
Black community life, 169
Blacks, relationship to society, 168
Blackwell, Kate, 200
Blair, Glean M., 95
Blanchard, K., 535
Blau, Peter M., 169
Blauner, Robert, 168
Bloom, Allen, 273
Bloom, Samuel W., 342
Boehm, Werner, 4, 39, 132
Bolman, William, 559
Borgman, Robert D., 396
Bormann, E., 533
Bormann, N., 533
Boundaries, crossing of, 350
  in systems theory, 147
Bowlby, John, 256

Brager, George, 97, 199, 428
Brechenser, Bertram M., 413
Brenner, C., 133
Briar, Scott, 43, 45, 67, 199, 428
Briggs, T., 527
Brill, Naomi, 527
Broker, role of, 429
Brokering, examples of, 430
Brown, Leonard, 410
Brown, Robert, 271
Bruner, Jerome S., 375
Bruno, Frank, 480
Buckley, Walter, 112, 118, 122, 148, 149, 150
Bureaucracy, 180
  changing the, 191–93
  criteria of, 180
  conflicts with professional, 182
  indirect influence on, 202–3
  limitations of, 180–81
Bureaucrat
  strategic concerns, 193
  tactics of, 193
  types of, 184
Bureaucratic rules, 200
Bureaucratic succession, 200
Bush, Sherida, 419
Bypassing, 203

C

"C" Street Network, 332
Cameron, Roy, 55
Caplan, Gerald, 53
Carkhuff, Robert R., 241, 296–97
Carmichael, Stokely, 168
Case Conference, 525
Categorization, in learning, 140
Cedar, Toby, 505
Chaiklin, Harris, 417
Change, 123–24
  goal-directed, 136
  nature of, 110
  processes, 462–64
  radical tactics of, 204–5
  social structure, 168–69
Chase, Stuart, 291
Checking perception, 467

Checkout, 272
  in interviewing, 285
  phase, 271
Children, coercion of, 80
Chin, Robert, 112
Choice, concept of, 147–48
  in individual lives, 109
  nature of, 74
Cicourel, Aaron V., 337
Clapp, Raymond F., 96
Clarifying, 466
Clark, Kenneth, 168, 331
Classification of individuals, 71
Classism in rural work, 505
Client, non-English speaking, 288
Cobb, Jonathan, 505
Coercion, use of, 79
Collaboration, 542, 545–46
Collaborative groups, culture of, 540–42
Collins, John, 415
Colonization, internal, 168
Commitment and obligation, 231–32
Communication
  barriers to, 275–81
  clarification, 298
  combined reflections, 297
  defined, 271
  empathic, 294–95
  exploration, 298
  expressive, 294
  levels of, 273
  reflection
    of content, 296
    of feeling, 296
    of meaning, 297
  seeking expression, 299
  sharing
    feeling, 300
    information, 301
    knowledge, 301
    opinion, 301
  in small groups, 533
  two forms of, 534
  written, 285
  problems, 272
  process, 272
  skills, 273

Community
  assessment, 169
  development
    neighborhood, 455
    defined, 455
    process for redress, 456
Community management, 171
Community mental health, assumptions of, 167
Community organization
  activist role in, 459–60
  advocate role, 458–59
  issues, 455–56
  methology, 455
  with the poor, 455
  substantive areas, 455
Competence, 111, 134–35, 488
Competition, 519–521
Compton, Beulah R., 262
Concern for other, 228–30
Confidentiality, lie of, 255
Conflict resolution, 536
Conformity, lie of rewards of, 255
Confrontation, 301, 468, 485
Congruence, 241–43
Connell, Charles, 274
Contract, 157
  application to practice, 413
  defined, 409
  definition of, 395
  example of, 401
  flexibility in, 413–14
  as mutual agreement, 409–10
  participation in, 410–11
  potential of, 414
  preliminary, 360
  theory of, 407–9
  worker-client differences, 403–4
Contracting, reciprocal
  accountability in, 411
  explicitness in, 412
  four principles of, 405
  expertise in, 420
  problems in, 417–18
  when contraindicated, 415–16
  when useful, 415
Contract phase, skills in, 365

Control, loss of, 52
Cooley, C. H., 329
Cooper, Shirley, 249–50, 292
Coping, 138–39
  mechanisms, 53–54
  resources of, 139
Cormican, Elin J., 289
Cormican, John D., 272, 289–90
Coser, Lewis A., 169
Council on Social Work Education, 40
Courage, 248
Cournoyer, Barry R., 273, 284, 294
Coyle, Grace, 221
Creativity, 246–247
Crisis, 53–55, 138–39
Crisis intervention, 55
Cronback, Lee, 95
Croxton, Tom A., 337–415
Culture, professional, 197, 521
  agency, 527
Cumming, Elaine, 488
Cumming, John, 488
Curriculum Study, 39
Curry, Andrew W., 292

D

Dalton, Gene W., 26
Data, sources of, 362–65
Data collection
  areas of, 361–62
  methods of, 362–65
  principles of, 349
Davenport, Judith, 245
Davis, John D., 337
Davison, Gerald C., 52
Decision-making, 396–98, 535
DeLo, James S., 292
Depression, 52
  reactive, 52
De Saix, Christine, 376
DeSchweinitz, Elizabeth, 27
DeSchweinitz, Karl, 27
Desire to help, 247–48
Deutsch, Karl W., 122
Deutsch, Morton, 432
Dewey, John, 311
Deykin, Eva Y., 291

Diagnosis, 397–98
Diagnostic orientations, 156
Dialects, 289, 290
Difference, 109, 139–42
Differences, subcultural, 293
Direct intervention, 472
Discomfort, 136
Dishonesty, of professionals, 252
Diversity, 109–10, 139–42
Donovan, John B., 325
Duffy, Hugh G., 586
Dumont, Matthew, 73
Durkheim, Emile, 168
Dyal, William M. J., 325
Dyer, W., 527
Dysfunctioning, 111

E

Ecological metaphor, 376
Ecological models, 7
Ecological pheomenology, 158–60
Eco-map, 377–79, 381–82
Educational methods, 483
Effectance, 134, 488
Ego
  functions of, 133
  psychology, 479–80, 487, 132–38
  support, 481
Emmons, Michael L., 55
Empathy, 235–39
Empey, Lamar, 100
Enabler, role of, 430–31
Encoding, 272
Encouragement, as interventive method, 465
Engel, G., 256
Entropy, 120, 146
Entropy, negative, 120–46
Environment, 107–9
Epstein, Irwin, 200
Epstein, Laura, 80, 544
Equal, concept of, 139–40
Equifinality, 123–24, 146
Equilibrium, 111, 148
Erikson, Erik, 24, 134–35, 480, 486
Erickson, Maynard L., 100
Estes, Richard, 415

Ethics
  Code of, 78, 84, 541, 543
  professional, 196
Evaluation, 556–57
  defined, 571
  formative, 571
  program, 572
  sumative, 571
Evaluative research, design, 588
  goals of, 580
  process, 582–84
  purpose, 556
  stages of, 583
Exchange theory, 148–49
Expectation, 232–33
  and acceptance, 232–33
External intervention, 172
Eysenck, Hans, 147, 580

F

Falk, Julia S., 290
Fantl, Berta, 288, 289, 293
Federico, Ronald C., 39–40
Feedback, 122–23, 272, 533–34
Fibush, Esther, 292
Fisher, Joel, 580
Flax, James W., 504
Focusing, 301, 476
Fordor, Anthony, 144
Fox, Evelyn, 559, 568
Fraley, Yvonne L., 224
Francis, W. Nelson, 290
Franck, Thomas M., 200, 204, 205
Frank, Jerome D., 233–34, 235
Freidson, Elliot, 337
French, J., 534
French, Thomas M., 136
Freud, Sigmund, 52, 132–33, 337
Freudian theory, 147
Frey, Louise, 479
Friedson, Elliot, 197
Fromm, Erich, 229
Frustration, 137
Fukumoto, James S., 586

G

Galaway, Burt, 262
Gambril, Eileen, 415
Garcio, Alejandra, 288

Garland, James A., 24
Garvin, Charles, 45–47, 410
Gatchel, Robert I., 52
Gaylin, Willard, 75
Genuineness and congru-
    ence, 241–43
Genogram, 382–86
Germain, Carel B., 6, 7, 10, 22,
    108, 375, 376, 399, 487, 561
Gitterman, Alex, 5, 7, 22, 23,
    249, 250, 399, 561, 569
Glasser, Barney A., 587
Goal setting, 358–60, 373, 398–
    400, 471–72
Goal-attainment scaling,
    576–78
Goal-directed behavior, 146
Goals, characteristics of,
    399–400
Goff, Regina, 95
Goffman, Irving, 337
Golan, Naomi, 53, 342, 561
Goldberg, Gale, 22
Goldstein, Howard, 28, 112,
    144, 149–50, 156–57, 228,
    232, 240
Goldstein, N., 96
Goode, W. J., 96
Goodman, James A., 250
Goodnow, Jacqueline, 375
Gordon, William, 5, 23, 34, 68,
    69
Gottlieb, Naomi, 199
Gottlieb, Werner, 409
Gottschalk, Leonard, 235
Gould, Robert, 567, 568
Gouldner, Alvin, 26, 200
Green, A. D., 200
Green, William A., 292
Greer, James H., 51, 52
Gross, Neal, 428
Groups, practice with, 478–79
Growth, push toward, 109–10
Guttentag, Marcia, 97

H

Haley, Jay, 28, 240, 273, 341
Halleck, Seymour L., 252, 255
Halmos, Paul, 68
Hamilton, Charles, 168
Hammond, Corydon D., 295,
    300, 301

Hanlan, Archie, 199
Hardman, Dale G., 77, 81, 91
Harlow, H., 256
Hartman, Ann, 122, 134, 141,
    365, 375
Hartman, Heinz, 486
Hatcher, Hayes A., 81
Hawthorne Experiment, 528
Health, definitions of, 141–42
Hearn, Gordon, 375, 419
Help
    elements of, 347
    giving and taking, 346
    requirements of taking,
        347–48
Helping person, characteris-
    tics, 245–47
Henry, Sue, 415
Hepworth, Dean H., 295, 300,
    301
Hersey, P., 535
Hiroto, Donald S., 52
Ho, Man Keung, 387
Hoffman, Lynn, 419
Hollingshead, August M., 94
Hollis, Florence, 144, 292, 477
Homeostasis, 145
Honesty, prerequisite to, 257
Hope, 135–36
Hosch, Dorothea, 415
Hudson, Joe, 572
Hughes, James W., 428
Husband, Diane, 568
Hyman, Herbert H., 99
Hyman, Irwin, 199

I

Id, 133
Identification, 484
Iflund, B., 96
Individualization, 71
    guidelines to, 70
Information
    as element of goal-directed
        behavior, 146–47
    problems in giving, 431
Informing, 468
Institutional arrangements as
    social problems, 21
Interdisciplinary approach,
    158–60
Interpretation, 467, 507

Intervenor, role of, 335
Intervention
    limits on, 402–3
    planning for, 400–403
        problems in, 400–401
Interventive methods
    focus, 465
    models of, 11
    roles
        discussion of, 427–28,
            433–35
        examples of, 433–34
Interview
    characteristics of, 274
    neutrality in, 284–85
    reliability of, 274
    responsibilities, 281–83
    techniques of, 283
    validity of, 274
Interviewing responses, 284

J

Jackel, Merl M., 291
Jackson, Don D., 273
Jacobs, Paul, 51
Jakubowski-Spector, Patri-
    cia, 55
Janchill, Sister Mary Paul,
    112, 116, 144
Jandt, Fred, 432
Johnson, D., 534
Johnson, F., 534
Johnson, Wendell, 233, 235,
    316
Jones, J., 527
Jones, Hubert, E., 24
Jones, R. Stewart, 95
Jorcin, Valerie, 428

K

Kace, Morris, 337
Kadushin, Alfred, 23, 34, 39,
    271, 286, 289, 290
Kahn, Alfred J., 39, 455
Kahn, Robert, 274
Kane, Rosalie, 342
Kaplan, Abraham, 38
Keith-Lucas, Alan, 222, 226,
    227, 229, 230, 246, 342
Keller, Suzanne, 95
Kim, Bok-Lim C., 293
Kinsey, Alfred C., 100

Klein, Melanie, 52
Klenk, Robert, 121
Klerman, Gerald L., 291
Klockars, Carl B., 81
Klugman, David J., 293
Knowledge, 10
 classes of, 105
 dealing with incomplete, 47–48
 function of, 41–43
 necessity of, 43
 in a profession, 34
 sharing of, 301
Koestler, Arthur, 112
Kolodny, Ralph L., 24
Konopka, Gisela, 6, 221
Kubler-Ross, Elisabeth, 561
Kuhn, Alfred, 42
Keene case, 370

L

Language differences, 288
Laxarus, Arnold A., 52, 337, 342
Labeling, 71
Labels
 as barriers, 272
 diagnostic, 291
 use of, 290
Lakey, George, 460
Leader, Arthur, 293
Leadership, 534–535
League of Women Voters, 456
Learned helplessness, 50–53
Lee, Porter, 6
Lefcourt, H. M., 135
Leopold, Edward, 330–32
Lerner, Barbara, 181–83, 320–96
Lessor, Richard, 413
Leuenberger, P., 527
Levenson, Bernard, 200
Levinson, Daniel, 107
Levy, Charles, 67, 74
Lewinsohn, Pete M., 52
Lewis, Harold, 9
Lewis, Oscar, 96, 97, 98
Lewis, Ronald, 387
Liberman, Bernard, 135, 136
Libet, Julian, 52
Licensing, 195–96

Life-model, 6
 defined, 22
 problem classification, 23
Limitations, 255–56
Limits, use of, 485
Lindblom, Charles E., 202
Lindeman, Erich, 561
Linguistic problem areas, 288
Linton, Ralph, 169
Lippit, Ronald, 527, 534, 535
Lipton, Douglas, 82
Litman, Robert Z., 293
Logical discussion, 484
Long, Lawrence, 419
Loss, 52
Lutkus, Anita, 413
Lutz, Werner A., 375

M

Maas, Henry S., 95
Mager, Robert F., 586
Mahaffey, Maryann, 428
Maher, Thomas F., 199
Mahoney, Michael J., 55
Maier, Steven F., 51
Maintenance in community, 172
Malone, Charles, 331
Maluccio, Anthony N., 23, 72, 337, 395, 396, 407, 415
Marchwardt, Albert H., 290
Maria, discussion of, 113–14
Marlow, Wilma, 23, 395, 396, 407, 415
Martin, Carl, 199
Martinson, Robert, 82
Mascari, Michael, 407
Maslow, A. H., 147
Masson, Ward, 428
Mastery, importance of, 134–35
Maturing people, 246
Mayer, John, 360, 396, 409
Mazer, Milton, 505
McClelland, David C., 97, 325
McClure, Marilyn E., Vigil, 260
McEachern, Alexander, 428
McPheeters, Harold, 429
Mediator, role of, 432
Meenaghan, Thomas M., 407
Meichenbaum, Donald, 55

Menninger, Karl, 71
Merton, Robert K., 21, 71, 129, 169
Messick, Janice M., 55
Meyer, Carol H., 7, 22, 41, 292
Meyerhoff, Barbara, 100
Middleman, Ruth, 22
Milford Conference, 39
Miller, D. R., 98, 329
Miller, Gerald, 432
Miller, Henry, 43, 45, 67, 82
Miller, Ronald, 199
Miller, Walter B., 94, 97
Miller, William R., 53
Minahan, Anne, 7, 22, 108, 112, 127, 144, 149, 150, 222, 527
Minuchin, Salvador, 331, 332
Mitchell, Kevin, 228, 241
Mobilization for Youth, 456
Modeling, 484
Monitoring, 589
Morality, the lie of, 253
Morgan, Betty, 205
Morgan, Ralph, 184–85
Morris, Robert, 455, 459
Morrison, James, 505
Moss, Miriam, 586
Moss, Sydney, 586
Motivation, 135, 137
 concepts of, 111
Miranda, Manuel R., 260
Multifinality, 123–24
Murdach, Allison D., 336, 403
Murphy, Lois B., 488

N

Nader, Ralph, 200, 204, 205
Nagel, Ernest, 169
National Advisory Commission on Civil Disorders, 170
National Association of Social Workers, 40, 196, 541, 543
Native Americans, 387
 community work with, 391
 family counseling with, 390
 group work with, 390–91
 handicaps in treating, 387–88

Native Americans—*Cont.*
  relationships with, 389
  traits of, 388
Nee, Robert N., 157
Needleman, Carolyn Emerson, 205
Needleman, Martin L., 204, 205
needs
  in community, 172
  differentiated from wants, 74
Neighborhood development, organizational forms of, 460–61
Neighborhood work, types of, 460–61
Neiman, Lionel J., 428
Nelson, Miriam, 559
Nisbet, Robert A., 21
Network
  characteristics of, 493–94
  intervention, 501–3
  as resources, 474
  therapy, 492
Nobelteens, 333
Noise, 272
Nonviolent action, tactics of, 460
Northern, Helen, 222, 556, 558
Nye, Ivan, 100

O

Objectivity, 242, 243
Obligation, 231, 232
Observation of self, 247
O'Connell, Patricia, 24
O'Connor, Gerald, 81
Olson, D. H. L., 169, 170, 171
Oppenheimer, Martin, 460
Organization, the bureaucratic, 180
Organizational hierarchy, 200
Overmier, Bruce, 51
Overton, Alice, 81
Owning, 508
Oxley, Genevieve B., 72, 73

P

Pacing, in rural work, 506
Parad, Howard J., 53

Paraphrasing, 466, 506
Parloff, Morris B., 96
Parsonian Theory, 148
Parsons, Talcott, 169
Participation, expectation of, 73
Partnership, 396
Pathology, definitions of, 141–142
Patti, Rino J., 199, 200
Pawlak, Edward J., 199
Payne, Stanley, 283, 428
Perlman, Helen Harris, 45, 130, 131, 132, 135, 219, 221, 312, 337, 415
Perrow, Charles, 201
Personal deficit model, 111
Personality, elements of, 133
Petkas, Peter J., 200
Piliavin, Irving, 199
Pincus, Allen, 7, 22, 108, 112, 125, 127, 222, 144, 149, 150
Pinsky, Sidney, 456
Podell, Lawrence, 199
Polansky, Norman A., 396
Polemis, Bernice, 234
Polya, George, 312
Power, 239–40
Powers, Edwin, 96
Practice, division of labor in, 23
Principle, defined, 37
Problem, defined, 351–58
Problem identification, summary of activity, 372–73
Problem recognition system, 345–46
Problem solving as life process, 308–9
  basic assumptions, 319
  blocks in, 367–68
  building support, 340
  demands of client system, 319
  discovering a common interest, 339
  elements of, 309
  essential tasks of, 369
  foundations of, 311
  getting started, 348
  knowing the context, 338
  negotiating solutions, 340

Problem solving as life process—*Cont.*
  outline, 323
  political framework for, 338
  practitioner's responsibility for, 313
  skills of, 320, 338
  steps in, 309, 319
  value of, 314, 318
Problems
  environmental, 25
  maladaptive interpersonal, 27
  transitional, 24
Process
  defined, 308
  described, 308–9
  requirements of, 308
Profession
  attributes of, 33
  community sanctions of, 195
  differentiated from discipline, 34
  as a system, 194
Professional organizations, purpose of, 195
Professionalism, 242–43
Professionals, autonomy of, 196
Progressive forces, 111, 480
Pruger, Robert, 182, 193
Psychoanalytic constructs, 123
Pumphrey, Muriel, 220
Pumphrey, Ralph, 220
Purcell, Francis, 6
Purposive systems, 122–23
Puzzle, 367
  solution to, 374

R

Race and relationship, 248–49
Rainwater, Tee, 94
Rank, Otta, 147
Rapoport, Anatol, 118
Rapoport, Lydia, 53, 54, 198, 410
Raven, M., 534
Reassurance, 482
Redl, Fritz, 479

Referral, 551–52
Reflecting, 466
Regressive forces, 480
Rehearsal, 483
Reichsman, F., 256
Reid, William J., 74, 80, 308, 412, 415
Reilly, A., 527
Reims, Nancy, 245
Rein, Martin, 4, 6, 7, 455, 459
Reissman, Frank, 94, 97, 100
Relationships
  definition of, 220
  development of, 226
  differential use of, 224, 564
  common elements, 223
  elements of, 228–43
  emotional quality of, 228
  individual purpose, 225–26
  irrational elements in, 228, 243–44
  source of, 228
  nonrational, 228
  normative purpose, 225
  operational purpose, 225
  purpose of, 224
  rational elements in, 243–44
  for social work, 10
  source of irrational elements, 228
  use of, 227
Reliability, defined, 274
Rescue fantasy, 73
Research, contamination of, 581
Resistance, sources of, 280
Resnick, Herman, 199
Reul, M. R., 505
Reynolds, Bertha C., 220
Rhodes, Sonya, 415, 417
Rich, John, 271
Richmond, Mary Z., 39, 220
Ripple, Lillian, 136–37, 234, 399
Robison, James, 580
Roberts, Robert W., 157
Rogers, Carl, 147, 504
Role assignments in, family system, 141
Role, 128–30
  achieved, 128–30

Role—*Cont.*
  ascribed, 128–30
  complementary, 128–32
  conflict, 128–32
  incongruity, 130–31
  losses, 473
  patterns, 129
  set, 128–32
  skills in carrying out, 463
  and techniques, 475
  theory, 128–32, 148–49
    useful concepts of, 131–32
  traditional in rural groups, 509
  transition, 473
Rosenthal, David, 96
Ross, Murray G., 458
Rothman, Jack, 408
Ruddock, Ralph, 149
Rules, tinkering with, 200
Rutman, Leonard, 572
Ryan, Robert M., 121, 429

S

Salomon, Elizabeth, 67
Sanction, 11
Satir, Virginia, 271, 431
Scanlon, John W., 586
Schaeffer, Alice, 28, 249–50
Scheunemann, Henry, 568
Schneiber, Karen, 199
Schubert, Margaret, 271, 410
Schulman, Lawrence, 28
Schumacher, Edward, 325
Schwartz, William, 3, 6, 7, 11, 23, 68, 74, 78, 80, 281, 294, 403, 431
Schwartz mediating model, 3
Seabury, Brett, 23, 27, 403, 415
Segal, H., 256
Selby, Loea, 477–78
Self
  awareness, 244–45, 366
  determination, 67, 75
    and legal authority, 79
    of worker, 78
  esteem, 135–36 worker's presentation of, 369
Self awareness, role in termination, 567–68

Seligman, Martin, F. P., 50–53
Senna, Joseph J., 199
Sennett, Richard, 505
Sharing, feeling, 300
Shaw, David A., 52
Sheppard, H., 24
Shireman, Joan, 411
Short, James S., 100
Shulman, Lawrence, 294, 298, 299, 300, 301, 599
Shyne, Ann W., 412
Silverman, Marvin, 80
Silverman, Phyllis, 409
Simon, Herbert, 121, 202, 432
Simpson, Ray H., 95
Sensitivity, 248
Siporin, Max, 22, 108, 336, 559
Smalley, Ruth E., 147, 156
Smith, Clagett, 432
Smith, Gerald, 580
Smith, Kevin, 337
Smith, Veon G., 295, 300, 301
Social diagnosis, 39
Social functioning, 5
  problems of, 21
Social problems, social work's relation to, 21
Social work
  definition of, 4, 5
  focus of, 4, 5
  as interstitial profession organization of, 21
  process of, 156–58
  purpose of, 3, 4
  strain in, 198
Social work practice
  defined, 4
  levels of, 10
Social work roles and relationships, 222
Social worker
  as advocate, 458–60
  certified, 195
Socialization, 470–471
Solasin, John, 505
Solomon, Gary, 504
Solomon, L., 527
Solomon, Richard L., 51
Specht, Harry, 6, 199, 120
Speck, Ross, 492
St. Pierre, C. Andre, 293

Stability, 123–24
  functions of, 140–41
  need for, 111
Stanley, Joe H., 409
Steady state, 145–46
Stein, Irma D., 112
Stein, Theodore, 415
Steiner, Gary A., 99
Strauss, Anslem L., 337, 338, 587
Strean, Herbert, 112
Strength, using client, 72
Stress, 138–39
Studt, Elliot, 23, 411
Suchman, Edward A., 584, 586
Sullivan, Harry Stack, 341
Summarization, 298
Summarizing, 467
Superego, 133
Supervisor, function of, 187–89
Support
  appropriate use of, 478
  goal of, 477–78
  social structure, 170
  as social work method, 477
  techniques of, 477
Supporting role performance, 473
Supporting practice, use of relationship, 481
Supportive practice
  with different size systems, 480
  use of resources in, 481
Symbols, 272
System
  action, 127
    output, 150–52
  areas of intervention, 152
  boundaries, 113, 120–21
  change agent, 126
  client, 126–27
  control center, 150–51
  defined, 112–13
  elements, differentiation of, 146
  problem identification, 128
  professional, 127–28
  target, 127

Systems
  appraisal of, 150–56
  conceptual, 125–28
  goal-directed, 145–46
  open, 119–20
Systems theory, 112–28
  as conceptual framework, 112–19
  empirical aspects of, 119–25
  functions of in social work, 157–58
  philosophical implications, 147–49
  use of, 114–17
  value of, 124–25, 375
    for social work, 144–45
Szaz, Thomas, 252

T

Taber, Merlin A., 6
Taber, Richard H., 330
Tasks in supportive practice, 480
Teacher, role of, 431
Team approach, 529
  assignment, 528
  building, issues in, 539–40
  composition, 529
  functioning
    dynamics in, 532–33
    stages in, 532–33, 537–39
  maintenance functions, 530
  procedure, 531–32
  self-oriented functions, 530–31
  size, 528–29
  structure, 531
  task functions, 530
Teamwork
  defined, 523
  obstacles to, 517–19
Tedeschi, James, 432
Tension in systems theory, 121
Termination, 556–58
  client tasks, 559
  context of, 560
  organizational influence, 565

Theory
  criteria for selection of, 45, 105–12
  levels of, 38
Thomas, Edwin J., 128, 428
Thomas, Gloria, 381
Thompson, James D., 201
Thompson, Sophie, D., 289
Thornton, Jerry W., 51
Tillich, Paul, 69
Timms, Noel, 360, 396, 409
Toch, Hans, 72
Todd, Frederick, 55
Tolman, Edward, 375
Towle, Charlotte, 78, 136
Towley, Louis, 480, 481
Trader, Harriet, 46, 134
Transfer, 554–56
Transmitting, 272
Trapp, Emanuel, 368
Treatment
  elements of rural, 504
  methods, classification of, 480
Truax, Charles B., 241, 228
Trust, lie about, 256–57
Tucker, Samuel, 167
Turnqest, BeAlva, 292
Tyler, Inez M., 289

U

Udry, J. Richard, 94
Uncontrollability
  objection, 51
  perceived, 51
Undergraduate Social Work Curriculum Development Project, 39

V

Validity, defined, 271
Value orientation, diversity of, 76
Values, 9
  client consideration of, 77
  defined, 68
  essential, 68
  professional, 197–98
  traditional in rural groups, 509
Vattano, Anthony J., 6, 411
Velasquez, Joan, 260

Ventilation, 484
Vickery, Anne, 144, 149–50
Vogel, E., 28
Vogt, Leona M., 586
Von Bertalanffy, Ludwig, 112, 147–48
Voss, Harwin L., 100

W

Want, as problem, 308
Wants
  defined, 74
  differentiated from needs, 74
  as focus for social work, 75

Wasserman, Henry, 187
Watson, Jeanne, 534
Watson, Kenneth W., 411
Weakland, John N., 273
Weinberg, Jon, 293
Weiner, Hyman, 542
Weinstein, Malcolm S., 52
Weisband, Edward, 200, 204–5
Weissman, Harold H., 182, 200
Weissman, Myrna M., 291
Wesley, Bruce, 534
Whaley, Joseph S., 586
White, Alfred, 261

White, Ralph K., 535
White, Robert, 134, 480, 486, 488
Wilber, Max, 180–83
Wilensky, Harold L., 180, 403
Wilks, Judith, 82
Williston, Samuel, 409
Wilson, Robert W., 342
Wiltse, Kermit, 415
Witmer, Helen, 96
Wold, Carl L., 293

Z

Zuft, Lorrain, 337
Zweig, Franklin, 411

This book has been set Computer Assisted Photo-comp in 10 point Melior and 9 point Optima, leaded 2 points. Part numbers and titles are 27 point Optima. Chapter numbers and titles are 20 point Optima. The size of the type page is 33½ by 50½ picas.